Financial Analysis with Microsoft® Excel®

SEVENTH EDITION

Timothy R. Mayes

Metropolitan State College of Denver

Todd M. Shank

University of South Florida – St. Petersburg

CENGAGE
Learning·

Australia • Brazil • Mexico • Singapore • United Kingdom • United States

CENGAGE
Learning®

Financial Analysis with Microsoft® Excel®,
Seventh Edition
Timothy R. Mayes

VP, GM Science, Math & Quantitative Business:
Balraj S. Kalsi

Product Director: Joe Sabatino

Sr. Product Manager: Mike Reynolds

Content Developer: Adele Tait Scholtz

Marketing Director: Natalie King

Marketing Manager: Heather Mooney

Content Project Manager: Jennifer Ziegler

Associate Media Developer: Mark Hopkinson

Manufacturing Planner: Kevin Kluck

Art and Cover Direction, Production Management, and
Composition: Lumina Datamatics Inc.

Cover Image: Cover Screenshots are used with permission
from Microsoft Corporation, Microsoft Excel® is a
registered trademark of Microsoft Corporation.
© 2014 Microsoft.

Intellectual Property

    Analyst: Christina Ciaramella

    Project Manager: Betsy Hathaway

Library of Congress Control Number: 2014945654
ISBN: 978-1-285-43227-4

Cengage Learning
20 Channel Center Street
Boston, MA 02210
USA

Cengage Learning is a leading provider of customized learning solutions with
office locations around the globe, including Singapore, the United Kingdom,
Australia, Mexico, Brazil, and Japan. Locate your local office at:
www.cengage.com/global

Cengage Learning products are represented in Canada by
Nelson Education, Ltd.

To learn more about Cengage Learning Solutions, visit **www.cengage.com**

Purchase any of our products at your local college store or at our
preferred online store **www.cengagebrain.com**

Printed in the United States of America
Print Number: 01   Print Year: 2014

Dedicated to Wassana Pengsiri, the kindest and most patient person that I know.

ทุ่มเทให้กับวาสนาเพ็งศิริคนใจดีและอ่อนโยนมากที่สุดที่ผมรู้จัก

Contents

Contents

CHAPTER 3   *The Cash Budget   71*

CHAPTER 4   *Financial Statement Analysis Tools   107*

Preface

Electronic spreadsheets have been available for microcomputers since the introduction of VisiCalc® for the Apple I in June 1979. The first version of Lotus 1-2-3® in January 1983 convinced businesses that the IBM PC was a truly useful productivity-enhancing tool. Today, any student who leaves business school without at least basic spreadsheet skills is truly at a disadvantage. Much as earlier generations had to be adept at using a slide rule or financial calculator, today's manager needs to be proficient in the use of a spreadsheet. International competition means that companies must be as efficient as possible. No longer can managers count on having a large staff of "number crunchers" at their disposal.

Microsoft first introduced Excel in 1985 for the Apple Macintosh and showed the world that spreadsheets could be both powerful and easy to use, not to mention fun. Excel 2.0 was introduced to the PC world in 1987 for Microsoft Windows version 1.0, where it enjoyed something of a cult following. With the introduction of version 3.0 of Windows, sales of Excel exploded so that today it is the leading spreadsheet on the market.

As of this writing, Excel 2013 (also known as Excel version 15) is the current version. Unlike Excel 2007, which introduced the Ribbon interface, Excel 2013 is more evolutionary than revolutionary. The changes are mostly cosmetic, though changes to the way that charts are created and edited are truly useful. While the book has been written with the current version in mind, it can be used with older versions, if allowances are made for the interface differences. The user interface is even more different on the Apple Mac, but Excel for Mac 2011 supports virtually all of the features discussed in this book. The only missing feature of which I am aware is pivot charts.

Purpose of the Book

Financial Analysis with Microsoft Excel, 7th ed., was written to demonstrate useful spreadsheet techniques and tools in a financial context. This allows readers to see the material in a way with which they are familiar. For students just beginning their education in finance, the book provides a thorough explanation of all of the concepts and equations that are usually covered. In other words, it is a corporate finance textbook, but it uses Excel instead of financial calculators.

Students with no prior experience with spreadsheets will find that using Excel is very intuitive, especially if they have used other Windows applications. For these students, *Financial Analysis with Microsoft Excel*, 7th ed., will provide a thorough introduction to the use of spreadsheets from basic screen navigation skills to building fairly complex financial models. I have found that even students with good spreadsheet skills have learned a great deal more about using Excel than they expected.

Finally, I feel strongly that providing pre-built spreadsheet templates for students to use is disservice. For this reason, this book concentrates on spreadsheet building skills. I beli that students can gain valuable insights and a deeper understanding of financial analys actually building their own spreadsheets. By creating their own spreadsheets, studen have to confront many issues that might otherwise be swept under the carpet. It con amazes me how thankful students are when they are actually forced to think rather to "plug and go." For this reason, the book concentrates on spreadsheet build (though all of the templates are included for instructors) so that students will be to think and truly understand the problems on which they are working.

Target Audience

Financial Analysis with Microsoft Excel is aimed at a wide variety of students and practitioners of finance. The topics covered generally follow those in an introductory financial management course for undergraduates or first-year MBA students. Because of the emphasis on spreadsheet building skills, the book is also appropriate as a reference for case-oriented courses in which the spreadsheet is used extensively. I have been using the book in my Financial Modeling course since 1995, and students consistently say that it is the most useful course they have taken. A sizable number of my former students have landed jobs in large part due to their superior spreadsheet skills.

I have tried to make the book complete enough that it may also be used for self-paced learning, and, if my e-mail is any guide, many have successfully taken this route. I assume, however, that the reader has some familiarity with the basic concepts of accounting and statistics. Instructors will find that their students can use this book on their own time to learn Excel, thereby minimizing the amount of class time required for teaching the rudiments of spreadsheets. Practitioners will find that the book will help them transfer skills from other spreadsheets to Excel and, at the same time, refresh their knowledge of corporate finance.

A Note to Students

As I have noted, this book is designed to help you learn finance and understand spreadsheets at the same time. Learning finance alone can be a daunting task, but I hope that learning to use Excel at the same time will make your job easier and more fun. Be sure to experiment with the examples by changing numbers and creating charts.

You will likely find that learning the material and skills presented is more difficult if you do not work the examples presented in each chapter. While this will be somewhat time consuming, I encourage you to work along with, rather than just read, the book as each example is discussed. Further, I suggest that you try to avoid the trap of memorizing Excel formulas. Instead, try to understand the logic of the formula so that you can more easily apply it in other, slightly different, situations in the future.

Make sure that you save your work often and keep a current backup.

Organization of the Book

Financial Analysis with Microsoft Excel, 7th ed., is organized along the lines of an introductory financial management textbook. The book can stand alone or be used as an adjunct to a regular text, but it is not "just a spreadsheet book," and shouldn't be treated as a cookbook with recipes. In most cases, topics are covered at the same depth as the material in conventional textbooks; in many cases, the topics are covered in greater depth. For this reason, I believe that *Financial Analysis with Microsoft Excel*, 7th ed., can be used as a comprehensive primary text. The book is organized as follows:

- Chapter 1: Introduction to Excel 2013
- Chapter 2: The Basic Financial Statements
- Chapter 3: The Cash Budget
- Chapter 4: Financial Statement Analysis Tools
- Chapter 5: Financial Forecasting
- Chapter 6: Break-Even and Leverage Analysis
- Chapter 7: The Time Value of Money
- Chapter 8: Common Stock Valuation
- Chapter 9: Bond Valuation
- Chapter 10: The Cost of Capital
- Chapter 11: Capital Budgeting
- Chapter 12: Risk and Capital Budgeting
- Chapter 13: Portfolio Statistics and Diversification
- Chapter 14: Writing User-Defined Functions with VBA
- Chapter 15: Analyzing Datasets with Tables and Pivot Tables
- Appendix: Directory of User-Defined Functions in Famefncs.xlam

Extensive use of built-in functions, charts, and other tools (e.g., Scenario Manager and Solver) throughout the book encourages a much deeper exploration of the models presented than do more traditional methods. Questions such as "What would happen if..." are easily answered with the tools and techniques taught in this book.

Outstanding Features

The most outstanding feature of *Financial Analysis with Microsoft Excel*, 7th ed., is its use of Excel as a learning tool rather than just a fancy calculator. Students using the book will be able to demonstrate to themselves how and why things are the way they are. Once students create a worksheet, they understand how it works and the assumptions behind the calculations. Thus, unlike the traditional "template" approach, students gain a deeper understanding of the material. In addition, the book greatly facilitates the professors' use of spreadsheets in their courses.

The text takes a self-teaching approach used by many other "how-to" spreadsheet books, but it provides opportunities for much more in-depth experimentation than the competition. For example, scenario analysis is an often recommended technique, but it is rarely demonstrated in any depth. This book uses the tools that are built into Excel to greatly simplify computation-intensive techniques, eliminating the boredom of tedious calculation. Other examples include regression analysis, linear and nonlinear programming, and Monte Carlo simulation. The book encourages students to actually use the tools that they have learned about in their statistics and management science classes.

Pedagogical Features

Financial Analysis with Microsoft Excel, 7th ed., begins by teaching the basics of Excel. Then, the text uses Excel to build the basic financial statements that students encounter in all levels of financial management courses. This coverage then acts as a "springboard" into more advanced material such as performance evaluation, forecasting, valuation, capital budgeting, and modern portfolio theory. Each chapter builds upon the techniques learned in prior chapters so that the student becomes familiar with Excel and finance at the same time. This type of approach facilitates the professor's incorporation of Excel into a financial management course since it reduces, or eliminates, the necessity of teaching spreadsheet usage in class. It also helps students see how this vital "tool" is used to solve the financial problems faced by practitioners.

The chapters are organized so that a problem is introduced, solved by traditional methods, and then solved using Excel. I believe that this approach relieves much of the quantitative complexity while enhancing student understanding through repetition and experimentation. This approach also generates interest in the subject matter that a traditional lecture cannot (especially for nonfinance business majors who are required to take a course in financial management). Once they are familiar with Excel, my students typically enjoy using it and spend more time with the subject than they otherwise would. In addition, since charts are used extensively (and are created by the student), the material may be better retained.

A list of learning objectives precedes each chapter, and a summary of the major Excel functions discussed in the chapter is included at the end. In addition, each chapter contains homework problems, and many include Internet Exercises that introduce students to sources of information on the Internet.

Supplements

The Instructor's Manual and other resources, available online, contain the following:

(These materials are available to registered instructors at the product support Web site, http://www.cengagebrain.com/).

- The completed worksheets with solutions to all problems covered in the text. Having this material on the product Web site allows the instructor to easily create transparencies or give live demonstrations via computer projections in class without having to build the spreadsheets from scratch.

- Additional Excel spreadsheet problems for each chapter that relate directly to the concepts covered in that chapter. Each problem requires the student to build a worksheet to solve a common financial management problem. Often the problems require solutions in a graphical format.

- Complete solutions to the in-text homework problems and those in the Instructor's Manual and on the product Web site, along with clarifying notes on techniques used.

- An Excel add-in program that contains some functions that simplify complex calculations such as the two-stage common stock valuation model and the payback period, among many others (see the Appendix for a complete listing of the functions). Also included is an add-in program for performing Monte-Carlo simulations discussed extensively in Chapter 12, and an add-in to create "live" variance/covariance matrices. These add-ins are available on the Web site.

Typography Conventions

The main text of this book is set in the 10-point Times New Roman True Type font. Text or numbers that readers are expected to enter are set in the 10 point `Courier New` True Type font.

The names of built-in functions are set in small caps and boldface. Function arguments can be either required or optional. Required inputs are set in small caps and are italicized and boldface. Optional inputs are set in small caps and italicized. As an example, consider the **Pv** function (introduced in Chapter 7):

$$\textbf{Pv}(\textbf{\textit{RATE, NPER, PMT}}, \textit{FV, TYPE})$$

In this example, **Pv** is the name of the function, and **RATE**, **NPER**, and **PMT** are the required arguments, while *FV* and *TYPE* are optional.

In equations and the text, equation variables (which are distinct from function arguments) are italicized. As an example, consider the *PV* equation:

$$PV = \frac{FV_N}{(1 + i)^N}$$

I hope that these conventions will help avoid confusion due to similar terms being used in different contexts.

Changes from the 6th Edition

The overall organization of the book remains similar, but there have been many changes throughout the book. All of the chapters have been updated, but the more important changes include:

Chapter 1—Updated for Excel 2013, including coverage of the new charting interface that uses buttons for chart elements and panels for formatting.

Chapter 2—Added contribution analysis to the common-size statements, and new coverage of the common-size statement of cash flows. The latter motivates a new discussion of the **CHOOSE** function as well as the Data Validation tool.

Chapter 4—Added the *extended* DuPont method for decomposing the ROE into its more basic components.

Chapter 5—Added the **SLN** function for calculating straight-line depreciation, as well as a section on using the **SLOPE** and **INTERCEPT** functions to get regression parameters without running a full regression analysis.

Chapter 6—Added a new section that explicitly shows the linkage between the break-even point and the various measures of leverage.

Chapter 7—New coverage of the **EFFECT** and **NOMINAL** functions for converting interest rates.

Chapter 8—Added two additional multi-stage dividend growth common stock valuation models (the traditional three-stage model, and a three-step model).

Chapter 11—Added the new Arnold and Nixon method of calculating the MIRR based on the profitability index. This more clearly shows the linkage between NPV and MIRR.

Chapter 13—Extensive changes were made to the methodology for calculating the efficient frontier. Instead of using the Solver to calculate each portfolio, I am now using it to calculate just two portfolios. The remaining portfolios are calculated as a weighted average of those two portfolios. This significantly speeds up the process of charting the efficient frontier. Additionally, I have added a utility function and used it to chart an indifference map and show how to find the optimal portfolio for an investor by maximizing utility in the Solver. Finally, I changed all of the calculations to use sample statistics, instead of population parameters, because Excel now has a sample covariance function.

Chapter 14—Added coverage of Do...Loops (Do...While and Do...Until), as well as new coverage of optional arguments and ParamArray, which allows for an unlimited number of function arguments. I also added a section with some best practices for VBA programming.

Chapter 15—Added coverage of the new TimeLine feature for filtering pivot tables by date and time. In addition, all of the data used in the examples has been updated, and new problems added.

A Note on the Internet

I have tried to incorporate Internet Exercises into those chapters where the use of the Internet is applicable. In many cases, the necessary data simply is not available to the public or very difficult to obtain online (e.g., cash budgeting), so some chapters do not have Internet Exercises. For those chapters that do, I have tried to describe the steps necessary to obtain the data—primarily from either MSN Money or Yahoo! Finance. It should be noted that Web sites change frequently and these instructions and URLs may change in the future. I chose MSN Money and Yahoo! Finance because I believe that these sites are the least likely to undergo severe changes and/or disappear completely. In many cases, there are alternative sites from which the data can be obtained if it is no longer available from the given site. All Excel spreadsheets for students' and instructors' use (as referenced in the book) are available at the product support Web site http://www.cengagebrain.com.

Acknowledgments

All books are collaborative projects, with input from more than just the listed authors. This is true in this case as well. I wish to thank those colleagues and students who have reviewed and tested the book to this point. Any remaining errors are my sole responsibility, and they may be reported to me by e-mail.

For this edition, I would like to thank two of my colleagues at Metro State: Juan Dempere and Su-Jane Chen were very kind to review chapters or sections of chapters. The input of the anonymous reviewers who responded to surveys is also greatly appreciated. I would also like to thank Debra Dalgleish, an author of several books on pivot tables, Microsoft Excel MVP, and a blogger at http://blog.contextures.com/, for answering some technical questions about pivot tables.

I would also like to thank the several reviewers who spent a great deal of time and effort reading over the previous editions. These reviewers are Tom Arnold of the University of Richmond, Denise Bloom of Viterbo University, David Suk of Rider College, Mark Holder of Kent State University, Scott Ballantyne of Alvernia College, John Stephens of Tri State University, Jong Yi of California State University Los Angeles, and Saiyid Islam of Virginia Tech. I sincerely appreciate their efforts. In particular, I would like to thank Nancy Jay of Mercer University–Atlanta for her scrupulous editing of the chapters and homework problems in the first three editions.

Many people long ago provided invaluable help on the first and second editions of this text, and their assistance is still appreciated. Professional colleagues include Ezra Byler, Anthony Crawford, Charles Haley, David Hua, Stuart Michelson, Mohammad Robbani, Gary McClure, and John Settle. In addition, several of my now former students at Metropolitan State University of Denver were helpful, most especially, Peter Ormsbee, Marjo Turkki, Kevin Hatch, Ron LeClere, Christine Schouten, Edson Holland, Mitch Cohen, and Theresa Lewingdon.

Finally, I wish to express my gratitude to Mike Reynolds (Senior Product Manager), Adele Scholtz (Content Developer), and Heather Mooney (Marketing Manager) of the Cengage Learning team. Without their help, confidence, and support, this book would never have been written. To anybody I have forgotten, I heartily apologize.

I encourage you to send your comments and suggestions, however minor they may seem to you, to mayest@msudenver.edu.

Timothy R. Mayes
June 2014

CHAPTER 1

Introduction to Excel 2013

After studying this chapter, you should be able to:

1. *Explain the basic purpose of a spreadsheet program.*

2. *Identify the various components of the Excel screen.*

3. *Navigate the Excel worksheet (entering, correcting, and moving data within the worksheet).*

4. *Explain the purpose and usage of Excel's built-in functions and user-defined functions.*

5. *Create graphics and know how to print and save files in Excel.*

The term "spreadsheet" covers a wide variety of elements useful for quantitative analysis of all kinds. Essentially, a spreadsheet is a simple tool consisting of a matrix of cells that can store numbers, text, or formulas. The spreadsheet's power comes from its ability to recalculate results as you change the contents of other cells. No longer does the user need to do these calculations by hand or on a calculator. Instead, with a properly constructed spreadsheet, changing a single number (say, a sales forecast) can result in literally thousands of automatic changes in the model. The freedom and productivity enhancement provided by modern spreadsheets presents an unparalleled opportunity for learning financial analysis.

Spreadsheet Uses

Spreadsheets today contain built-in analytical capabilities previously unavailable in a single package. Years ago, users often had to learn a variety of specialized software packages to do any relatively complex analysis. With the newest versions of Microsoft Excel, users can perform tasks ranging from the routine maintenance of financial statements to multivariate regression analysis to Monte Carlo simulations of various hedging strategies.

It is literally impossible to enumerate all of the possible applications for spreadsheets. You should keep in mind that spreadsheets are useful not only for financial analysis, but also for any type of quantitative analysis whether your specialty is in marketing, management, engineering, statistics, or economics. For that matter, a spreadsheet can also prove valuable for personal uses. With Excel, it is a fairly simple matter to build a spreadsheet to monitor your investment portfolio, plan for retirement, experiment with various mortgage options when buying a house, create and maintain a mailing list, and so on. The possibilities are quite literally endless. The more comfortable you become with the spreadsheet, the more uses you will find. Using a spreadsheet can help you find solutions that you never would have imagined on your own. Above all, feel free to experiment and try new things as you gain more experience working with spreadsheet programs, particularly Excel.

The above is not meant to suggest that Excel is the only analytical tool you'll ever need. For example, Excel is not meant to be a relational database, though it has some tools that allow it to work well for small databases (see Chapter 15). For bigger projects, however, Excel can serve as a very effective "front-end" interface to a database. It also isn't a complete replacement for a dedicated statistics program, though it can work well for many statistical problems. Although Excel can be made to do just about anything, it isn't always the best tool for the job. Still, it may very well be the best tool that you or your colleagues know how to use.

Starting Microsoft Excel

Excel 2013 Icon

In Windows, you start programs like Excel by double-clicking on the program's icon. The location of the Excel icon will depend on the organization of your system. You may have the Excel icon (at left) on the desktop or in the taskbar. Otherwise, you can start Excel by clicking the Windows Start button and then choosing Microsoft Office from the All Programs menu and then Excel 2013. In Windows Vista or 7, you can also type Excel into the search box at the bottom of the Start menu.

For easier access, you may wish to create a Desktop or Taskbar shortcut. To do this, right-click on the Excel icon in the All Programs menu and either choose Create Shortcut or drag the icon to the Desktop or Taskbar. Remember that a shortcut is not the program itself, so you can safely delete the shortcut if you later decide you don't need it.

Parts of the Excel Screen

If you have used Excel 2007 or 2010, then you will be familiar with most of the user interface in Excel 2013. Compared to Excel 2003 or earlier version, it is dramatically different. In particular, all of the old and familiar menus are gone, having been replaced by the new Ribbon interface. However, aside from the user interface, Excel 2013 still works very much like previous versions.

FIGURE 1-1
MICROSOFT EXCEL 2013

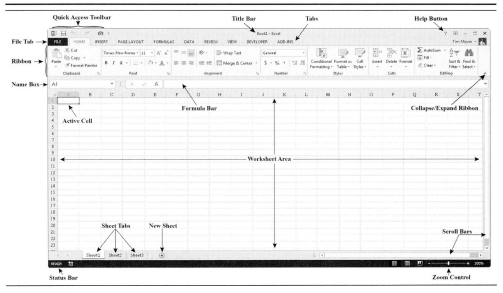

In Figure 1-1, note the labeled parts of the Excel screen. We will examine most of these parts separately. Please refer to Figure 1-1 as you read through each of the sections that follow.

The File Tab and Quick Access Toolbar

The File tab in Excel 2013 is similar to the File menu in most other Windows programs. It can be opened either by clicking the tab or by pressing Alt-F (most of the keyboard shortcuts from previous versions will still work). Click the File tab when you need to open, save, print, or create a new file.

The File tab also contains additional functionality. It opens in what is known as *Backstage View*, which takes over the entire window. This additional space, compared to a menu, allows for much more information to be displayed. For example, if you click the Print tab on the left side you get access not only to all of the print settings, but also to print preview on the same page. The Info tab is where you can set the document properties (author, keywords, etc.), inspect the document for hidden data that may reveal private details, encrypt the spreadsheet, and so on.

Finally, the File tab is the pathway to setting the program options. At the bottom of the tabs on the left you will find a link to Options. This launches the Excel Options dialog box where you can set all of the available options. It is advisable to go through the Excel Options to familiarize yourself with some of the things that you can control. While you may not understand all of the choices, at least you will know where to go when you need to change something (e.g., the user name, macro security level, or the default file locations).

You also have the ability to customize the Ribbon interface. Click the File tab, choose Options, and then select Customize Ribbon in the dialog box. Here you can create new tabs, move buttons from one tab to another, remove them completely, and even export your customizations so that others can use them.

The Quick Access toolbar (typically abbreviated as QAT) is located above the File tab and, by default, provides a button to save the current file as well as the Undo and Redo buttons. If you regularly use commands that aren't located on the Home tab, you can easily customize the Quick Access toolbar to add those commands by right-clicking the QAT and choosing "Customize Quick Access Toolbar..." The dialog box is self-explanatory. You can also add or remove commands, such as Print Preview, by clicking the arrow to the right of the QAT.

The Home Tab

FIGURE 1-2
EXCEL 2013 HOME TAB

Immediately below the title bar, Excel displays the various tabs in what is known as the *Ribbon*. Tabs are the toolbars that replaced the menus of pre-2007 versions. The Home tab contains the most commonly used commands, including the Cut, Copy, and Paste buttons, and the various cell formatting buttons. You can learn what function each button performs by placing the mouse pointer over a button. After a few seconds, a message will appear that informs you of the button's function. This message is known as a *ToolTip*. ToolTips are used frequently by Excel to help you identify the function of various items on the screen.

Note that several of the buttons (e.g., the Copy and Paste buttons) on the Ribbon have a downward-pointing arrow. This is a signal that the button has options besides the default

Paste

behavior. For example, by clicking the arrow on the Paste button you will find that there are several choices regarding what to paste (e.g., just the formula, or the value without the formula, etc.). Clicking the upper half of a split button invokes the default purpose.

The other tabs are named according to their functionality, and you will quickly learn which one to choose in order to carry out a command. Table 1-1 shows the other tabs and a short description of what they do.

TABLE 1-1
OTHER TABS IN THE EXCEL 2013 RIBBON

Tab	What It Does
File	File management features (open, save, close, print, etc.)
Insert	Contains buttons for inserting pivot tables, charts, pictures, shapes, text boxes, equations, and other objects.
Page Layout	Has choices that control the look of the worksheet on the screen and when printed. You can change the document theme, the page margins and orientation, and so on.
Formulas	This is where to go when you want to insert a formula, create a defined name for a cell or range, or use the formula-auditing features to find errors.
Data	Contains buttons to guide you through getting data from other sources (such as an Access database, a Web site, or a text file). Launch tools such as the Scenario Manager, Goal Seek, Solver, and the Analysis Toolpak.
Review	Here you will find spell check, the thesaurus, and also commands for working with cell comments and worksheet protection.
View	Contains commands that control the worksheet views, zoom controls, and the visibility of various objects on the screen (such as gridlines and the formula bar).
Developer	Has tools that allow you to access the VBA editor, insert controls (e.g., dropdown lists), and work with XML. This tab is not visible by default, but can be enabled in Options.
Add-Ins	This is where older Excel add-ins that create custom tool bars and menus will be located. Not visible unless older add-ins are installed.

Note that another set of tabs will appear when you are working on charts. The Design and Format tabs contain all of the options that you will need for working with charts (see "Creating Graphics" on page 26). Furthermore, add-in programs may create additional tabs.

The Formula Bar

As you work more in Excel to create financial models, you will find that the formula bar is one of its most useful features. The formula bar displays information about the currently selected cell, which is referred to as the active cell. The left part of the formula bar indicates the name or address of the selected cell (H9 in Figure 1-3). The right part of the formula bar displays the contents of the selected cell. If the cell contains a formula, the formula bar displays the formula while the cell displays the result of the formula. If text or numbers have been entered, then the text or numbers are displayed.

FIGURE 1-3
THE EXCEL 2013 FORMULA BAR

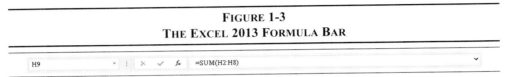

The f_x button on the formula bar is used to show the Insert Function dialog box. This dialog box helps you to find and enter functions without having to memorize them. It works the same as the Insert Function button on the Formulas tab. See page 22 for more information.

The chevron at the right of the formula bar is used to expand the formula bar. This is useful if you have long formulas that occupy more than one line. You can expand the formula bar even further by dragging its lower edge.

The Worksheet Area

The worksheet area is where the real work of the spreadsheet is done. The worksheet is a matrix of cells (1,048,576 rows by 16,384 columns),[1] each of which can contain text, numbers, or formulas. Each cell is referred to by a column letter and a row number. Column letters (A, B, C, ..., XFD) are listed at the top of each column, and row numbers (1, 2, 3, ..., 1048576) are listed to the left of each row. The cell in the upper left corner of the worksheet is therefore referred to as cell A1, the cell immediately below A1 is referred to as cell A2, the cell to the right of A1 is cell B1, and so on. This naming convention is common to all spreadsheet programs. If not already, you will become comfortable with it once you have gained some experience working in Excel.

The active cell can be identified by a solid black border around the cell. Note that the active cell is not always visible on the screen, but its address is always named in the leftmost portion of the formula bar.

---

1. This is known as the "big grid" because it is much larger than in pre-2007 versions of Excel, which only supported up to 65,536 rows and 256 columns.

Sheet Tabs

FIGURE 1-4
THE SHEET TABS

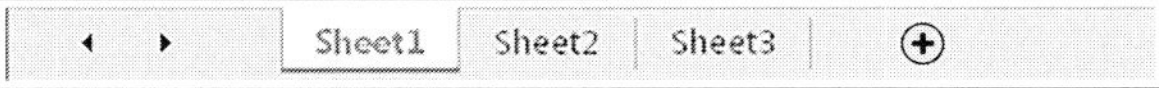

| ◄ | ► | Sheet1 | Sheet2 | Sheet3 | ⊕ |

Excel worksheets are stored in a format that allows you to combine multiple worksheets into one file known as a *workbook*. This allows several related worksheets to be contained in one file for easy access. The sheet tabs, near the bottom of the screen, enable you to move easily from one sheet to another in a workbook. You may rename, copy, or delete any existing sheet or insert a new sheet by right-clicking a sheet tab with the mouse and making a choice from the resulting menu. You can easily change the order of the sheet tabs by left-clicking a tab and dragging it to a new position. To insert a new worksheet, click the New Sheet button to the right of the last worksheet.

It is easy to do any of these operations on multiple worksheets at once, except for renaming. Simply click the first sheet and then Ctrl+click each of the others. (You can select a contiguous group of sheets by selecting the first and then Shift+click the last.) Now, right-click one of the selected sheets and select the appropriate option from the pop-up menu. When sheets are grouped, anything you do to one sheet gets done to all. This feature is useful if, for example, you need to enter identical data into multiple sheets or need to perform identical formatting on several sheets. To ungroup the sheets, either click on any nongrouped sheet or right-click a sheet tab and choose Ungroup Sheets from the pop-up menu. Another feature in Excel 2013 allows you to choose a color for each sheet tab by right-clicking the tab and choosing a Tab Color from the pop-up menu.

The transport buttons to the left of the sheet tabs are the sheet tab control buttons; they allow you to scroll through the list of sheet tabs. Right-clicking either of these buttons will display a pop-up menu that allows you to quickly jump to any sheet tab in the workbook. This is an especially helpful tool when you have too many tabs for them all to be shown.

Status Bar

The status bar, located below the sheet tabs, contains information regarding the current state of Excel, as well as certain messages. For example, most of the time the only message is "Ready" indicating that Excel is waiting for input. At other times, Excel may add "Calculate" to the status bar to indicate that it needs to recalculate the worksheet because of changes. You can also direct Excel to do certain calculations on the status bar. For example, in Figure 1-5, Excel is showing the average, count, and sum of the highlighted cells in the worksheet.

FIGURE 1-5
THE STATUS BAR

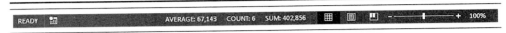

By right-clicking on this area of the status bar, you can also get Excel to calculate the count of numbers only, minimum, or maximum of any highlighted cells. This is useful if you need a quick calculation that doesn't need to be in the worksheet.

The right side of the status bar contains buttons to change the view of the worksheet (normal, page layout, and page break preview) as well as the zoom level.

Navigating the Worksheet

There are two principal ways for moving around within the worksheet area: the arrow keys and the mouse. Generally speaking, for small distances the arrow keys provide an easy method of changing the active cell, but moving to more distant cells is usually easier with the mouse.

Most keyboards have a separate keypad containing arrows pointing up, down, left, and right. If your keyboard does not, then the numeric keypad can be used if the Num Lock function is off. To use the arrow keys, simply press the appropriate key once for each cell that you wish to move across. For example, assuming that the current cell is A1 and you wish to move to cell D1, press the Right arrow key three times. To move from D1 to D5 press the Down arrow key four times. You can use the Tab key to move one cell to the right. The Page Up and Page Down keys also work as you would expect.

The mouse is even easier to use. While the mouse pointer is over the worksheet area it will be in the shape of a fat cross. To change the active cell move the mouse pointer over the destination cell and click the left button. To move to a cell that is not currently displayed on the screen, click on the scroll bars until the cell is visible and then click on it. For example, if the active cell is A1 and you wish to make A100 the active cell, click on the arrow at the bottom of the scroll bar on the right hand part of the screen until A100 is visible. Move the mouse pointer over cell A100 and click with the left button. Each click on the scroll bar moves the worksheet up or down one page. If you wish to move up, click above the thumb. If down, click beneath the thumb. The thumb (or slider) is the button that moves up and down the scroll bar to indicate your position in the worksheet. To move more quickly, you can drag the thumb to the desired position.

If you know the name or address of the cell to which you wish to move (for large worksheets remembering the cell address isn't easy, but you can use named ranges) use the Go To

Find &
Select ▾

command. The Go To command will change the active cell to whatever cell you indicate. The Go To dialog box can be used by clicking the Find & Select button on the Home tab and then choosing the **G**o To… command, by pressing the F5 function key, or by pressing the Ctrl+G key combination. To move to cell A50, simply press F5, type: A50 in the Reference box, and then press Enter. You will notice that cell A50 is now highlighted and visible on the screen. You can also use Go To to find certain special cells (e.g., the last cell that has data in it) by pressing the **S**pecial… button in the Go To dialog box.

Selecting a Range of Cells

Many times you will need to select more than one cell at a time. For example, you may wish to apply a particular number format to a whole range of cells, or you might want to clear a whole range. Because it would be cumbersome to do this one cell at a time, especially for a large range, Excel allows you to simultaneously select a whole range and perform various functions on all of the cells at once. The easiest way to select a contiguous range of cells is to use the mouse. Simply point to the cell in the upper left corner of the range, click and hold down the left button, and drag the mouse until the entire range is highlighted. As you drag the mouse, watch the left side of the formula bar. Excel will inform you of the number of selected rows and columns. In addition, the row and column headers will be highlighted for the selected cells.

You can also use the keyboard to select a range. First change the active cell to the upper left corner of the range to be selected, press and hold down the Shift key, and use the arrow keys to highlight the entire range. Note that if you release the Shift key while pressing an arrow key you will lose the selection. A very useful keyboard shortcut is the Shift+Ctrl+Arrow (any arrow key will work) combination. This is used to select all of the cells from the active cell up to, but not including, the first blank cell. For example, if you have 100 numbers in a column and need to apply a format, just select the first cell and then press Shift+Ctrl+Down arrow to select them all. This is faster and more accurate than using the mouse.

Many times it is also useful to select a discontiguous range (i.e., two or more unconnected ranges) of cells. To do this, simply select the first range as usual and then hold down the Ctrl key as you select the other ranges.

Using Defined Names

A named range is a cell, or group of cells, for which you have supplied a name. Named ranges can be useful in a number of different ways, but locating a range on a big worksheet is probably the most common use. To name a range of cells, start by selecting the range. For ▤ Define Name ▾ example, select A1:C5 and then choose Define Name from the Formulas tab. In the edit box at the top of the New Name dialog box, enter a name, say MyRange (note that a range name cannot contain spaces or most special characters). Now, click the OK button and the range is named. Figure 1-6 shows how the dialog box should look. Note that at the bottom the **R**efers to edit box shows the address to which the name refers.[2]

FIGURE 1-6
THE DEFINE NAME DIALOG BOX

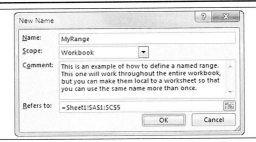

You can also enter a comment that provides more detail about the range and control the scope of the name. Scope refers to location within which the name doesn't need to be qualified by a sheet name. For example, MyRange was defined to have Workbook scope. Therefore, we can refer to that range from any cell of the entire workbook by just using its name (=MyRange). However, if the scope had been restricted to Sheet1, then from Sheet2 we would refer to the name with =Sheet1!MyRange. Note that defined names must be unique within their scope. So you can only have one workbook-scoped range named MyRange, but you could have one MyRange per worksheet if it is scoped to the sheet level.

Once the range is named, you can select it using the Go To command (Find & Select then **G**o To…, or press F5). The name will appear in the list on the Go To dialog box. An even faster method is to use the Name Box on the left side of the formula bar. Simply drop the list and choose the named range that you wish to select.

Named ranges can be used in formulas in place of cell addresses and can be used in the **SERIES** function for charts. Defined names don't have to refer to a cell or range. They can be used to define a constant or formula instead. For example, you might create the name Pi and in the **R**efers to box enter: =3.14159 instead of a cell or range address. You can use that name in formulas whenever you need the value of Pi, though Excel already has a **PI** function. As useful as they can be, there is no requirement for you to ever use defined names.

---

2. Notice that the name is actually defined as a formula. This is important for some of the more advanced uses of named ranges. For example, we can use a name to define constants, do calculations, or to create a reference to a range that grows as data is added.

Entering Text and Numbers

Each cell in an Excel worksheet can be thought of as a miniature word processor. Text can be entered directly into the cell and then formatted in a variety of ways. To enter a text string, first select the cell where you want the text to appear and then begin typing. It is that simple.

Excel is smart enough to know the difference between numbers and text, so there are no extra steps for entering numbers. Let's try the following example of entering numbers and text into the worksheet.

AutoFill Handle

Select cell A1 and type: `Microsoft Corporation Sales`. In cell A2 enter: `(Millions of Dollars)`. Select A3 and type: `2008 to 2013`. Note that the entry in cell A3 will be treated as text by Excel because of the spaces and letters included. In cells A4 to F4 we now want to enter the years. In A4 type: `2013`, in B4 type: `2012`, select A4:B4, and move the mouse pointer over the lower right corner of the selection. The mouse pointer will now change to a skinny cross indicating that you can use the AutoFill feature.[3] Click and drag the mouse to the right to fill in the remaining years. Notice that the most recent data is typically entered at the left and the most distant data at the right. This convention allows us to easily recognize and concentrate on what is usually the most important data.

We have set up the headings for our first worksheet. Now let's add Microsoft's sales (in millions of dollars) for the years 2008 to 2013 into cells A5 to F5 as shown in Exhibit 1-1.

EXHIBIT 1-1
THE FIRST WORKSHEET

	A	B	C	D	E	F
1	Microsoft Corporation Sales					
2	(Millions of Dollars)					
3	2008 to 2013					
4	2013	2012	2011	2010	2009	2008
5	77849	73723	69943	62484	58437	60420

Source: Microsoft Corporation, Microsoft® Investor Relations, http://www.microsoft.com Retrieved: Nov 2013.

Formatting and Alignment Options

The worksheet in Exhibit 1-1 isn't very attractive. Notice that the text is displayed at the left side of the cells, while the numbers are at the right. By default, this is the way that Excel aligns text and numbers. However, we can easily change the way that these entries are displayed through the use of the formatting and alignment options.

---

3. The AutoFill feature can be used to fill in any series that Excel can recognize. For example, type `January` in a cell and drag the AutoFill handle to automatically fill in a series of month names. You can also define your own series by clicking the Edit Custom Lists button under General in the Advanced category of Excel Options.

Before continuing, we should define a few typographical terms. A "typeface" is a particular style of drawing letters and numbers. For example, the main text of this book is set in the Times New Roman typeface. However, the text that you are expected to enter into a worksheet is displayed in the `Courier New` typeface. Typeface also refers to whether the text is drawn in **bold**, *italics*, or perhaps ***bold italics***.

The term "type size" refers to the size of the typeface. We normally refer to the type size in "points." Each point represents an increment of 1/72nd of an inch, so there are 72 points to the inch. A typeface printed at a 12-point size is larger than the same typeface printed at a size of 10 points.

Informally, we refer to the typeface and type size combination as a font. So when we say "change the font to 12-point bold Times New Roman," it is understood that we are referring to a particular typeface (Times New Roman, bolded) and type size (12 points).

For text entries, the term "format" refers to the typeface, size, text color, and cell alignment used to display the text. Let's change the font of the text that was entered to Times New Roman, 12 points, bold. First, select the range A1:A3. Now, on the Home tab, click on the Font list so that the font choices are displayed and then select Times New Roman from the list.

Next, click the Bold button and then choose 12 from the font size list. Notice that as you scroll through the Font and Size lists, the selected text is displayed as will look on the worksheet. This is known as *Live Preview*, and it works for many, but not all, of the formatting features in Excel 2013. Because none of these changes actually take effect until you validate them by clicking, you can scroll through the choices until the text looks exactly right. You can also make these changes by right-clicking the selected cells and choosing Format Cells… from the menu. The choices that we made can be found on the Font tab.

We can just as easily change the font for numbers. Suppose that we want to change the years in cells A4:F4 to 12-point italic Times New Roman. First select the range A4:F4. Select the proper attributes from the Home tab, or right-click and choose Format Cells. Note that this change could also have been made at the same time as the text was changed, or you could now press Ctrl+Y to repeat the last action. You could also add the Repeat button to the Quick Access toolbar. Just click arrow at the right of the Quick Access toolbar and choose More Commands…. Now select the Repeat button and then click the Add button in the dialog box.

Our worksheet is now beginning to take on a nicer look, but it still isn't quite right. We are used to seeing the titles of tables nicely centered over the table, but our title is way over at the left. We can remedy this by using Excel's alignment options. Excel provides for seven different horizontal alignments within a cell. We can have the text (or numbers) aligned with the left or right sides of the cell or centered within the cell boundaries. Excel also allows centering text across a range of cells.

Let's change the alignment of our year numbers first. Highlight cells A4:F4 and then click the Center button in the Alignment section of the Home tab. Notice that the numbers are all centered within their respective cells.

Next, we will center our table title across the whole range of numbers that we have entered. To do this, select the entire range across which we want to center our titles. Highlight cells A1:F3 and select <u>F</u>ormat Cells from the right-click menu. Click on the Alignment tab and then select "Center across selection" from the Horizontal alignment list. Click on the OK button and notice that the titles are indeed centered across columns A to F.

Be aware that there is also a button on the Home tab that will "Merge and Center" the selected cells. This button will have the appearance of doing the same thing as "Center across selection," but it doesn't. In addition to centering the text, it also merges all of the selected cells into one big cell that spans multiple columns and/or rows. Using this button may create alignment and many other problems if you later decide to insert additional columns into the worksheet. At some point, you will probably find that you need to unmerge the cells in order to, say, sort a range. Generally speaking, it is better not to use the Merge and Center button. If necessary, there is an <u>U</u>nmerge Cells command in the same button.

Formatting Numbers

Aside from changing the typeface and type size, when dealing with numbers we can also change their appearance by adding commas and dollar signs and by altering the number of decimal places displayed. Furthermore, we can make the numbers appear differently depending on whether they are positive or negative. For example, we might want negative numbers to be red in color and displayed in parentheses rather than using the negative sign. You can also experiment with designing custom number formats, but for now we will stick to the more common predefined formats.

Microsoft is a large company, and its sales have ranged from $60 billion to over $77 billion during 2008 to 2013. Numbers this large, even when expressed in millions of dollars, become difficult to read unless they are written with commas separating every third digit. Let's format our sales numbers so that they are easier to read.

Select the range of sales numbers (A5:F5) and choose <u>F</u>ormat Cells from the right-click menu and then click on the Number tab. You are presented with the Number Format dialog box which contains a list of formatting categories. For now, select Number from the <u>C</u>ategory list. This will give you the option to choose the number of decimal places displayed, choose whether or not to use a 1000 separator, and select the format of negative numbers. We want to display the sales numbers with commas separating every third digit and two decimal places, so change the decimal places to 2 and check the box to add a 1000 separator.[4] Click on the OK button and notice that the numbers are now displayed in a more readable format. You could accomplish almost exactly the same format by clicking the

---

4. Note that in the United States we use a comma as the 1000 separator. In many other countries a decimal point is used instead. Excel determines which to use based on the settings in the Windows Control Panel's Region and Language settings utility.

Comma Style button on the Ribbon (there is a slight alignment difference between the two methods—you cannot center numbers formatted with the comma style).

At this point, we have made several formatting changes to the Microsoft Sales worksheet. Your worksheet should look like the one in Exhibit 1-2. All of this formatting may seem tedious at the moment, but it will quickly become easy as you become more familiar with the choices. Furthermore, the payoff in readability will be worth far more than the few seconds spent formatting the worksheet.

EXHIBIT 1-2
ORIGINAL WORKSHEET REFORMATTED

	A	B	C	D	E	F
1			Microsoft Corporation Sales			
2			(Millions of Dollars)			
3			2008 to 2013			
4	2013	2012	2011	2010	2009	2008
5	77,849.00	73,723.00	69,943.00	62,484.00	58,437.00	60,420.00

Source: Microsoft Corporation, Microsoft® Investor Relations, http://www.microsoft.com Retrieved: Nov 2013.

Adding Borders and Shading

Text formatting is not the only design element available in Excel. We can also liven up worksheets by placing borders around cells and shading them. In your worksheet, select A4:F4 (the years). Right-click the selection and choose **F**ormat Cells and then select the Border tab from the dialog box. There are 13 different line styles that can be applied, and you can change the color of the lines. Click on the thick solid line (fifth down on the right side) and then click on both of the top and bottom lines in the sample view. Click the OK button to see the change.

Next, with A4:F4 still selected, we will add shading. As before, choose **F**ormat Cells from the menu but this time select the Fill tab. This tab allows you to set the background color and pattern of the cells. Click on a light gray color and then press the OK button. Now, to make the numbers more readable make them bold. Your worksheet should now look like the one in Exhibit 1-3.

EXHIBIT 1-3
THE WORKSHEET WITH BORDERS AND SHADING

	A	B	C	D	E	F
1			Microsoft Corporation Sales			
2			(Millions of Dollars)			
3			2008 to 2013			
4	2013	2012	2011	2010	2009	2008
5	77,849.00	73,723.00	69,943.00	62,484.00	58,437.00	60,420.00

Source: Microsoft Corporation, Microsoft® Investor Relations, http://www.microsoft.com Retrieved: Nov 2013.

Entering Formulas

So far, we haven't done anything that couldn't just as easily be done in a table in Microsoft Word. The real power of spreadsheets becomes obvious when formulas are used. Formulas will enable us to convert the data that we have entered into useful information.

At the moment, our sample worksheet contains only sales data for Microsoft. Suppose, however, that we are interested in performing a simple analysis of the profitability of Microsoft over the 2008 to 2013 time period. In this case, we would also need to see the net income for each of the years under study. Let's make some modifications to the worksheet to make it more useful.

TABLE 1-2
MICROSOFT NET INCOME 2008 TO 2013

Year	Net Income
2013	21,863.00
2012	16,978.00
2011	23,150.00
2010	18,760.00
2009	14,569.00
2008	17,681.00

Source: Microsoft Corporation, Microsoft® Investor Relations, http://www.microsoft.com Retrieved: Nov 2013.

Add the data from Table 1-2 to the sample worksheet in cells A6:F6, immediately below the sales data, and apply the same format. Now, we have a couple of problems. The title of our worksheet, in cell A1, is no longer accurate. We are now putting together a profitability analysis, so we should change the title to reflect this change of focus. Select cell A1 (even though the title is centered across A1:F1, Excel still keeps the data in A1) by clicking on it. Notice that the text appears in the right hand side of the formula bar. To edit the title, click on the formula bar just to the right of the word "Sales." Backspace over the word "Sales" and then type: Profitability Analysis, and press Enter to accept the change.

Our only remaining problem is that the data in the worksheet are not clearly identified. Ideally, we would like to have the data labeled in the column just to the left of the first data point. But, there is no column to the left of the data! There are several ways to overcome this problem. The easiest is to simply insert a column to the left of column A. To accomplish this, select column A entirely by clicking on the column header where it has an "A." Notice that the whole column is highlighted (we can do this with rows as well). Now, click the Insert button on the Home tab and choose Insert Sheet **C**olumns. The new column is magically

Insert

inserted, and all of our data have been moved one column to the right. In cell A5 type: Sales and in A6 type: Net Income.

If you are following the examples exactly, the words Net Income probably do not fit exactly into A6. Instead, part of the text is cut off so as not to overflow onto the data in B6. We can easily remedy this by changing the width of column A. Click the Format button on the Home tab and choose Column **W**idth. In the edit box type: 20 and press the Enter key. Column A should now be wide enough to hold the text that we have added and will add later.

Format

We can now proceed with our profitability analysis. Because of the dramatic growth in sales over the years, it isn't immediately clear from the data whether Microsoft's profitability has improved or not, even though net income has increased over this time. In this type of situation, it is generally preferable to look at net income as a percentage of sales (the net profit margin) instead of dollar net income. Thankfully, we don't have to type in more data to do this. Instead, we can let Excel calculate these percentages for us. All we need to do is to enter the formulas.

Formulas in Excel are based upon cell addresses. To add two cells together, we simply tell Excel to take the contents of the first cell and add it to the contents of the second. The result of the formula will be placed in the cell in which the formula is entered. In our problem, we need to find net income as a percentage of sales. We will do this first for 2013.

Before entering our first formula, we should insert a label identifying the data. In cell A7 type: Net Profit Margin. Change the active cell to B7 where we want to place the result of the calculation. The problem that we want to solve is to take the number in cell B6 (net income) and divide it by the number in B5 (sales). In Excel, division is represented by the forward slash (/), so in B7 type: =B6/B5. *The equals sign must precede all formulas in Excel*, otherwise it will treat the formula as text and will not calculate the result. Press the Enter key to calculate the result of the formula. You should get 0.2808 as the result.

In this example, we typed the formula directly into the cell because the small size of our worksheet made it easy to know what cells we wanted to use in the formula. In many instances, this is not the case. In more complicated worksheets, it is usually easier to use *pointer mode* to enter formulas. In pointer mode, we use the mouse to point to the cells that we want to be included, and Excel inserts them into the formula. Move to C7 and we will enter the formula using pointer mode. First, type = to place Excel in edit mode. Now, instead of typing C6, click on C6 with the mouse. Notice that C6 appears in the formula bar to the right of the equals sign. Press the forward slash key to indicate division and then click on C5. In the formula bar you should see the formula "=C6/C5." Press the Enter key to calculate the result of the formula. The result should be 0.2303.

Let's change the format of these cells so that they are easier to read. In this case, it would be nice to see them in percentage format with two decimal places. First, highlight cells B7:C7. Right-click and choose **F**ormat Cells, and click on the Number tab. From the Category list, click on Percentage and then set the Decimal places to 2. Press the Enter key or click the OK button. You could also apply this format by using the Percent Style button on the Ribbon. To get two decimal places, you would then need to click the Increase Decimal button in the same group. Figure 1-7 shows these and other formatting icons.

FIGURE 1-7
NUMBER FORMATTING ICONS

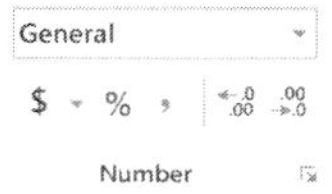

Copying and Moving Formulas

We have now calculated the net profit margin for 2013 and 2012, but that still leaves four years for which we need to enter formulas. Repeatedly typing essentially the same formula can get tedious. Fortunately, we can simply copy the formula, and Excel will update the cell addresses to maintain the same relative relationships. For example, we know that for 2011 the formula should read "=D6/D5." If we copy the formula from C7 to D7, Excel will change the formula from "=C6/C5" to "=D6/D5" automatically.

This works because Excel treats all cell references as relative. When you typed the formula in cell B7 (=B6/B5) Excel read that as "take the contents of the cell that is one row above the current cell and divide that by the contents of the cell that is two rows above the current cell." When copying formulas, Excel maintains the same relative cell relationships so that the formulas are updated. When we copy to the left or right, Excel updates the columns in the formulas. When we copy up or down, Excel changes the rows.

To change this behavior, we could use *absolute references* instead. An absolute reference always refers to the same cell, no matter where you copy it. To create an absolute reference, type dollar signs before the column letter and row number. For example, $B$6 will always refer to cell B6. The "$" tells Excel to not change the reference. We can also create *mixed references*. In a mixed reference only the column or row remains constant, not both. For example, $B6 is a mixed reference (column absolute, row relative). If the formula is copied down, it will change to $B7, but if it is copied across it will still be $B6. On the other hand, B$6 (column relative, row absolute) will still be B$6 if copied down, but will change to C$6 if copied across. We will make heavy use of absolute and mixed references in later chapters. Note that you can use the F4 key to cycle through every possible reference type. Simply enter a cell address and repeatedly press F4 until you get the type of reference you need (e.g., $B$6, B$6, $B6, B6).

EXHIBIT 1-4
A PROFITABILITY ANALYSIS FOR MICROSOFT

	A	B	C	D	E	F	G
1		Microsoft Corporation Profitability Analysis					
2		(Millions of Dollars)					
3		2008 to 2013					
4		2013	2012	2011	2010	2009	2008
5	Sales	77,849.00	73,723.00	69,943.00	62,484.00	58,437.00	60,420.00
6	Net Income	21,863.00	16,978.00	23,150.00	18,760.00	14,569.00	17,681.00
7	Net Profit Margin	28.08%	23.03%	33.10%	30.02%	24.93%	29.26%

Source: Microsoft Corporation, Microsoft® Investor Relations, http://www.microsoft.com Retrieved: Nov 2013.

Rather than retyping the formula for our other cells, let's simply copy from C7. First, select C7 and then click the Copy button on the Ribbon. Now highlight cells D7:G7 and click the Paste button. At this point, your worksheet should closely resemble the one in Exhibit 1-4.

We can see from Exhibit 1-4 that Microsoft's net profit margin has varied somewhat over this period, but despite the ups and downs, the margins are quite high compared to those of most other companies.

In addition to copying formulas (which maintains the relative cell references), they can also be moved. Moving a formula to a different cell has no effect on the cell references. For example, we could move the formula in B7 (=B6/B5) to B8. To do this, select B7 and then click the Cut button (scissors icon). Next, select B8 and then click Paste. Notice that the result in B8 is exactly the same as B7 because the formula is unchanged. Now click the Undo button on the Quick Access toolbar to return the formula to B7.

Formulas (or anything else) may also be moved with the mouse. Simply select the cells containing the data that you want to move, position the mouse pointer at the edge of the cell so that it changes to an arrow, and then click the left mouse button and drag the cell to its new location. Now move the formula back to B7. The worksheet should again resemble the one pictured in Exhibit 1-4.

Mathematical Operators

Aside from division, which we have already seen, there are four additional primary mathematical operations: addition, subtraction, multiplication, and exponentiation. Table 1-3 summarizes the five basic operations and the result that you should get from entering the example formula into cell B8.

TABLE 1-3
MATHEMATICAL OPERATIONS

Operation	Key	Formula	Result in B8
Addition	+	=B5+B6	99,712
Subtraction	–	=B5–B6	55,986
Multiplication	*	=B5*B7	21,863
Division	/	=B6/B7	77,849
Exponentiation	^	=15^2	225

Parentheses and the Order of Operations

Using the mathematical operators provided by Excel is straightforward in most instances. However, there are times when it gets a bit complicated. For example, let's calculate the rates of growth of Microsoft's sales and net income. To calculate the growth rates we usually want the compound annual growth rate ($CAGR$, which is the geometric mean growth rate) rather than the arithmetic average growth rate. The general equation for the geometric mean growth rate is:

$$\overline{G} = \sqrt[(N-1)]{\frac{X_N}{X_0}} - 1 = \left(\frac{X_N}{X_0}\right)^{\frac{1}{(N-1)}} - 1 \tag{1-1}$$

where $\overline{G}$ is the geometric mean, N is the count of the numbers in the series, X_0 is the first number in the series (2008 sales in our example), and X_N is the last number in the series (2013 sales).

Translating this equation into Excel is not as simple as it may at first appear. Doing this correctly requires knowledge of operator precedence. In other words, Excel doesn't necessarily evaluate formulas from left to right. Instead, some operations are performed before others. Exponentiation is usually performed first. Multiplication and division are usually performed next, but they are considered equal in precedence so any multiplication and division are evaluated from left to right. Finally, addition and subtraction are evaluated and they are also considered equal in precedence to each other.

We can modify the order of operations by using parentheses. Operations enclosed in parentheses are always evaluated first. As a simple example, how would you evaluate the following expression?

$$X = 2 + 4/3$$

Is X equal to 2 or 3.33? Algebraically, X is equal to 3.33 because the division should be performed before the addition as Excel would do. If the answer we were seeking was 2, we could rewrite the expression using parentheses to clarify:

$$X = (2+4)/3$$

The parentheses clearly indicate that the addition should be performed first, so the answer is 2. When in doubt, always use parentheses because using them unnecessarily will not cause any problems.

To calculate the compound annual growth rate of sales, move to cell A8 and type: `Sales Growth`. Now, enter the following into B8 using equation (1-1): `=(B5/G5)^(1/5)-1`. Pressing the Enter key will reveal that the growth rate of sales for the five-year period was 5.20% per year (you may have to reformat the cell to display as a percentage with two decimal places). To determine the average growth rate of net income, type: `Net Income Growth` into A9 and then copy the formula from B8 to B9. You should find that the compound annual rate of growth of net income has been 4.34% per year and that the formula in B9 is: `=(B6/G6)^(1/5)-1`. Notice how the row references were updated when you copied the formula down.

Using Excel's Built-In Functions

We could build some pretty impressive worksheets with the techniques that we have examined so far. But why should we have to build all of our formulas from scratch, especially when some of them can be quite complex and therefore error-prone? Excel comes with hundreds of built-in functions, and more than 50 of them are financial functions. These functions are ready to go; all they need is for you to supply cell references as inputs. We will be demonstrating the use of many of these functions throughout the book, but for now let's redo our growth rate calculations using the built-in functions.

Because we want to know the compound annual *rate of growth*, we can use Excel's built-in **GEOMEAN** function.[5] To use this function the syntax is:

$$\text{=GEOMEAN}(\textit{NUMBER1}, \textit{NUMBER2}, \ldots)$$

The **GEOMEAN** function takes up to 255 cell addresses (or ranges) separated by commas. As is usual in Excel, we can also supply a range of cells rather than specifying the cells individually. Remember, we want to find the geometric mean *rate of growth* of sales, not the

---

5. We could calculate the arithmetic mean using the **AVERAGE** function, but this would ignore the compounding and overstate the true average growth rate. This function is defined as =**AVERAGE**(*NUMBER1*, *NUMBER2*, ...).

geometric mean of the dollar amount of sales. Because the **GEOMEAN** function simply calculates the Nth root of the product of the inputs, we need to redefine our inputs (we used the dollar amount of sales in our custom-built formula). Let's add a row of percentage changes in sales to our worksheet.

Move to A10 and enter the label: % Change in Sales, then select B10 and enter the formula: =B5/C5-1. The result in B10 should be 0.0560, indicating that sales grew by 5.60% from 2012 to 2013. Now copy the formula from B10 to each cell in the C10:F10 range. Note that we don't copy the formula into G10 because that would cause an error since H10 doesn't contain any data (try it, and you will see #DIV/0! in G10, meaning that your formula tried to divide by zero).

Now, to calculate the compound average annual rate of sales growth we need to enter the **GEOMEAN** function into B11: =GEOMEAN(B10:F10). Because our data points are in one contiguous range, we chose to specify the range rather than each individual cell. Let's also supply a label so that when we come back later we can recall what this cell represents. Move to A11 and enter: Sales Growth.

Have you noticed any problems with the result of the **GEOMEAN** function? The result was a #NUM! error, rather than the 5.20% that we got when using our custom formula. Either our custom formula is incorrect or we have misused the **GEOMEAN** function. Actually, this type of error is common and easily overlooked. What has happened is that when using the **GEOMEAN** function, we didn't fully understand what goes on behind the scenes. Remember that **GEOMEAN** simply takes the Nth root of the product of the numbers. When multiplying numbers that are less than 1, the result is even smaller, not larger as is the case with numbers greater than 1. What we should have done is calculated the geometric mean of the price relative changes (i.e., one plus the percentage change).

To correct the error, replace the formula in B10 with: =B5/C5 and copy it to the other cells. Now replace the formula in B11 with: =GEOMEAN(B10:F10)-1. The result is 5.20%, exactly the same as our previous result. To avoid errors like this one, you must absolutely understand what the built-in formula is doing. *Never blindly accept results just because Excel has calculated them for you.* There is an old saying in computer science: "garbage in, garbage out."

At this point, your worksheet should closely resemble the one pictured in Exhibit 1-5.

EXHIBIT 1-5
ANALYSIS OF MICROSOFT'S GROWTH RATES

◢	A	B	C	D	E	F	G
1		Microsoft Corporation Profitability Analysis					
2		(Millions of Dollars)					
3		2008 to 2013					
4		*2013*	*2012*	*2011*	*2010*	*2009*	*2008*
5	Sales	77,849.00	73,723.00	69,943.00	62,484.00	58,437.00	60,420.00
6	Net Income	21,863.00	16,978.00	23,150.00	18,760.00	14,569.00	17,681.00
7	Net Profit Margin	28.08%	23.03%	33.10%	30.02%	24.93%	29.26%
8	Sales Growth	5.20%					
9	Net Income Growth	4.34%					
10	% Change in Sales	1.0560	1.0540	1.1194	1.0693	0.9672	
11	Sales Growth	5.20%					

Source: Microsoft Corporation, Microsoft® Investor Relations, http://www.microsoft.com Retrieved: Nov 2013.

Using the Insert Function Dialog Box

With the hundreds of built-in functions available in Excel, it can be difficult to remember the name of the one that you want to use or the order of the arguments. To help you with this problem, Excel provides the Insert Function dialog box, a series of dialog boxes that guide you through the process of selecting and entering a built-in formula.

Clear▾

fx
Insert
Function

Let's use Insert Function to insert the GEOMEAN function into B11. First, select cell B11 and then clear the current formula by clicking the Clear button on the Home tab and then choosing Clear Contents (or, press the Delete key on the keyboard). Find the Insert Function button (pictured at left) on the Formulas tab and click it to bring up the first Insert Function dialog box.

In the first dialog box click on Statistical in the "Or select a category" list. The "Select a function" list will now contain all of the built-in statistical functions. Scroll down this list and click on GEOMEAN. Notice that there is a definition of the function at the bottom of the dialog box. Click on the OK button to change to the next dialog box, which is pictured in Figure 1-8.[6]

6. Note that this dialog box is frequently in the way of your work. You may click and drag any part of the dialog box to move it out of the way.

FIGURE 1-8
THE EXCEL 2013 FUNCTION ARGUMENTS DIALOG BOX

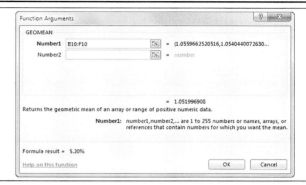

In the Function Arguments dialog box, you will see prompts and definitions for each of the inputs to the selected function. In this case, we want to click and drag the mouse over the B10:F10 range. This range will appear in the "Number 1" edit box. Click on the OK button to have the function entered. Notice that the result is 105.20%, not the 5.20% that we expected. We need to subtract 1 from the result of the function, so click in the Formula bar and type -1 after the **GEOMEAN** function and then press Enter. The formula in B11 should be: =GEOMEAN(B10:F10)-1. Note that the 1 that we are subtracting represents 100% of the starting value.

Insert Function is an easy way to discover new functions and to use familiar ones. You can also find functions by using the function category buttons on the Formulas tab. Choosing a function from one of those lists will lead to the same Function Arguments dialog box. However you get there, using it will make Excel much easier for you to learn and use.

If you already know the name of the function that you need, you can skip the Insert Function dialog box. Just type = and then start typing the function name. Excel will automatically create a Formula AutoComplete menu listing functions that match what you have typed. When you see the function name, you can use the arrow keys to select it and then press the Tab key to begin entering the arguments. As you enter the function arguments, you will see a ToolTip that reminds you of their order.

FIGURE 1-9
FORMULA AUTOCOMPLETE

"Dot Functions" in Excel 2013

In Excel 2010, Microsoft introduced a new naming convention for some functions. The new functions contain a "dot" in their names. For example, the STDEV.S function calculates a sample standard deviation and is identical to the STDEV function that has been in all earlier versions of Excel. In this case, the new naming convention is meant to more clearly convey the purpose of the function. In other cases, a dot function uses a new algorithm to calculate more precise results.

In all cases, the older versions of the functions are available for compatibility with older versions of Excel. If a file is created using the dot functions in Excel 2013 and then opened in Excel 2007 or earlier, the result will be a #NAME! error. That happens because older versions aren't aware of the existence of new functions. In this book, we will use the compatibility functions unless otherwise noted.

If a worksheet that you create may be used on older versions of Excel, you should run the Compatibility Checker before saving the file. This will warn of compatibility problems, including the use of the new dot functions. To use the Compatibility Checker, click the File tab and then Info. Click the Check for Issues button and then choose Check Compatibility. This will launch a dialog box like that shown in Figure 1-10, which is showing that there is a potential problem in Sheet1 of the workbook due to the use of functions that are incompatible with versions from Excel 97 to Excel 2007. Note that the dialog box shows the number of occurrences of each problem and the sheet on which they are located. If there is only one problem then clicking the Find link will take you to that cell. If there is more than one problem, then the easiest way to find them is by clicking the Copy to New Sheet button. This will create a new worksheet with a report that identifies each cell with a problem, including a hyperlink that will take you straight to that cell.

FIGURE 1-10
THE COMPATIBILITY CHECKER

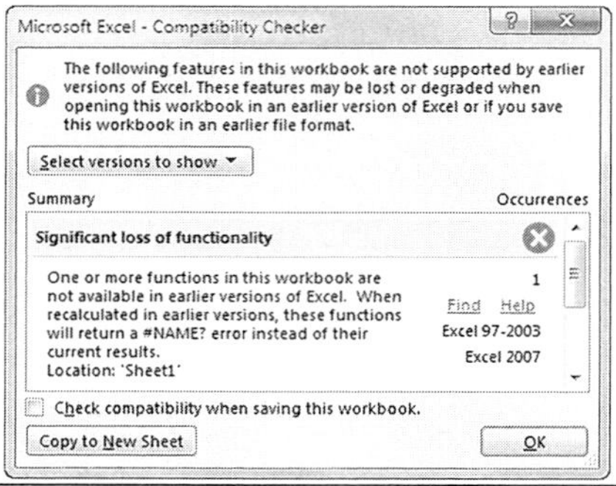

Using User-Defined Functions

There are times when you need to calculate a complex formula and Excel doesn't have a built-in function that will do the job. In this case, you can either type the formula into a cell (which can be very tedious) or use a user-defined function. A *user-defined function* is similar to a built-in function, except that it was created by somebody other than the Excel development team at Microsoft. User-defined functions can be purchased, downloaded from the Internet, or you can create your own. Writing them in Excel's macro language (Visual Basic for Applications, see Chapter 14) is beyond the scope of this chapter, but I have included several functions in the Famefncs.xlam file, which can be found on the official Web site for this book.[7] Download the file and save it to your hard drive in an easy-to-remember location. These functions will be used occasionally throughout the book, especially in later chapters.

Before using a function you must open Famefncs.xlam. This file is a special type of Excel file known as an *add-in*. An add-in can be opened just like any other Excel file, or it can be set to open automatically every time you start Excel. To make the functions in this file available at all times, click the File tab and then Options. Click Add-Ins and then choose Excel Add-ins from the Manage list and click the **G**o button. This will open the Add-Ins dialog box as pictured in Figure 1-11.

FIGURE 1-11
THE ADD-INS DIALOG BOX

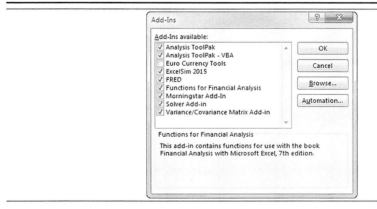

---

7. In Excel 2007 and later, file names with extensions that are .xlsm or .xlam contain macros. These files may require special security settings before Excel will allow the macros to run. Go to the File tab, then Options, and set up your Trusted Locations in the Trust Center. You may still receive warnings for some files, but if you are sure that they are safe then allow the macros to run.

Click the Browse button, navigate to the directory where you saved the file, and choose Famefncs.xlam. It will be added to the Add-Ins dialog box as shown above, and the functions in the file will now be available to use in all of your workbooks. If you can't access the functions, make sure that you save the file in one of your trusted locations as mentioned in footnote 7.

Using a user-defined function is almost exactly the same as using a built-in function. The only difference is that the file containing the functions must be opened in order for the functions to be known to Excel. You can even use the Insert Function dialog box (select the User Defined function category, which is only available when user-defined functions are installed).

As an example of the use of user-defined functions, I have created one to calculate the geometric mean rate of growth of sales from the dollar amounts instead of the price relatives that we used earlier. The function is defined as[8]:

FAME_GEOMEAN(*SALES*)

FAME_GEOMEAN is the name of the function, and **SALES** is the required range of cells that contain the sales figures. The function automatically calculates the formula given in equation (1-1) on page 19.

Now, in your original worksheet, select cell B12 and then bring up the Insert Function dialog box. Choose the User Defined category to display the list of functions that were supplied with this book. In the "Select a functio**n**" list, select the macro named **FAME_GEOMEAN** and then click the OK button. In the edit box for Dollar Values enter B5:G5, which is the range that contains Microsoft's sales. Click on the OK button and see that the answer is exactly the same as before. The function in B12 is: =FAME_GEOMEAN(B5:G5).

We will use more of the user-defined functions from this add-in in later chapters.

Creating Graphics

In our simple profitability analysis, it is obvious that Microsoft's profit margins have been somewhat volatile over the last six years. Many times, you will build much more complicated worksheets where the key trends are not so easy to spot, especially by others who didn't build the worksheet. You may also find that you need to give a presentation, perhaps to a group of investors to convince them to invest in your firm. In cases such as

---

8. This function was written specifically to calculate a compound average growth rate from dollar values. It does not duplicate Excel's **GEOMEAN** function, so do not use it as a substitute for that function.

these, tables full of numbers may actually obscure your point. People (and students too!) tend to get a glazed look in their eyes when examining tables of numbers. The solution to this problem is to present a chart of the numbers to illustrate your point. Fortunately, high-quality graphics are a snap with Excel.

There are three ways that charts can be created in Excel: in separate chart sheets, embedded in the worksheet, or as in-cell charts known as *Sparklines*. We will cover each of these methods in turn.

Creating Charts in a Chart Sheet

When you want to focus only on a chart, then it is best to create it in its own chart sheet. We can create a chart separate from the worksheet by selecting the data and inserting a new chart sheet. Let's try creating a graph of Sales versus Net Income for Microsoft.

First select the data in the A4:G6 range and then right-click the tab for the current worksheet (which is probably labeled "Sheet 1"). From the menu that appears, choose Insert. You will now be presented with a list of different file types from which to select. Because we want to create a chart, select Chart from the list and press Enter or click OK.

A chart sheet will open with your data displayed automatically in a Column chart. It won't have a chart title or axis titles and will require a few other enhancements. Note that you now have two additional tabs in the Ribbon (Design and Format) that are specific to working with charts. These are known as *contextual tabs* because they only appear in the context of editing a chart. If you want another type of chart, you can click the Change Chart Type button on the Design tab.

Let's begin to fix our chart by adding a title. Select the chart and then click the Chart Elements button that appears in the upper-right corner. Click the Chart Title item and choose the Centered Overlay option. In the text box that appears, type: Microsoft Sales vs. Net Income and then click outside the box to lock in the title.

You will follow a similar procedure for the axis titles. Click the Axis Titles item in the Chart Elements button and then choose Primary Horizontal Axis Title to insert both the x and y axis titles. For the x-axis double click the "Axis Text" label and then type: Years, and for the y-axis type: Millions of Dollars for the title.

Your chart should now resemble the one in Exhibit 1-6. We will see how to fix the reversed x-axis after the next section.

EXHIBIT 1-6
A STAND-ALONE CHART

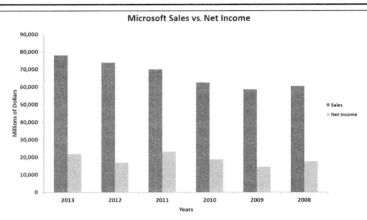

Source: Microsoft Corporation, Microsoft® Investor Relations, http://www.microsoft.com Retrieved: Nov 2013.

Creating Embedded Charts

You may want to create a chart that will be saved and displayed within the worksheet itself. Such a chart is referred to as an "embedded chart" because it appears within the worksheet. Unlike a separate chart sheet, embedded charts can be displayed and printed on the same page as the worksheet data. If necessary, embedded charts can be printed separately from the worksheet.

To create an embedded chart, first switch to your worksheet. Now select A4:G6 as before and then click the Insert tab. Click the Column button in the Charts group and then choose the first type listed under 2-D Column. The chart will appear in the middle of your worksheet. To resize the chart, click and drag any of the selection boxes on its perimeter. To move the chart, click on a blank area inside the chart and drag it to wherever you want it to be. Your worksheet should now resemble the one in Exhibit 1-7, except for some minor formatting changes. You can enter the chart and axis titles exactly as before.

Move
Chart

Note that you can move your embedded chart into a separate chart sheet and vice versa. Just right-click in the chart and choose Move Chart from the shortcut menu. There is also a Move Chart button on the Design tab. You can even move your chart to a different worksheet in this way.

EXHIBIT 1-7
A WORKSHEET WITH AN EMBEDDED CHART

	A	B	C	D	E	F	G
1		Microsoft Corporation Profitability Analysis					
2		(Millions of Dollars)					
3		2008 to 2013					
4		*2013*	*2012*	*2011*	*2010*	*2009*	*2008*
5	Sales	77,849.00	73,723.00	69,943.00	62,484.00	58,437.00	60,420.00
6	Net Income	21,863.00	16,978.00	23,150.00	18,760.00	14,569.00	17,681.00
7	Net Profit Margin	28.08%	23.03%	33.10%	30.02%	24.93%	29.26%
8	Sales Growth	5.20%					
9	Net Income Growth	4.34%					
10	% Change in Sales	1.0560	1.0540	1.1194	1.0693	0.9672	
11	Sales Growth	5.20%					
12		**Microsoft Sales vs. Net Income**					
13–21							

Microsoft Sales vs. Net Income — bar chart, Millions of Dollars (0.00 to 100,000.00) by Years (2013, 2012, 2011, 2010, 2009, 2008), series Sales and Net Income.

Source: Microsoft Corporation, Microsoft® Investor Relations, http://www.microsoft.com Retrieved: Nov 2013.

Formatting Charts

We have now created a basic chart of Sales versus Net Income, but it probably isn't quite what you expected. First of all, we normally expect that the most recent data in a chart is on the right side and the oldest on the left. Because we have created our worksheet data in the opposite direction (a common convention), our chart is backward and a quick glance might suggest that sales and profits have been declining.

In Excel, every element of a chart is treated as a separate "object." This means that each element can be selected and edited separately from the other elements. In addition, these chart objects are somewhat intelligent. They "know" what actions can be performed on them and will present a menu of these actions if you right-click on them. The major objects in any chart include each data series, the plot area, the gridlines, the axes, the axis titles, the chart title, and any text boxes entered into the chart. To select an object, all that you need to do is to click on it. Once the object is selected, it will have small squares (selection handles) surrounding it. In some cases this will result in the selection of multiple items (e.g., the entire data series, or the entire legend), but you can often narrow the selection with a second click (not a double-click). With this knowledge, let's edit our chart.

First, we want to turn the x-axis around so that the data are presented in the order that we normally expect. Right-click on the x-axis (or the axis labels) to show the shortcut menu. Once the menu appears, choose **F**ormat Axis. This will launch the Format Axis panel on the right side of the window. Under Axis Options, choose the Date A**x**is type so that Excel understands that our year numbers are dates. It will flip the axis so that it reads left to right as we would expect. If we had entered full dates in the heading (e.g., 6/30/2014), then Excel would have recognized the dates and created a date axis that we wouldn't need to flip.

We could also flip the axis by selecting "**C**ategories in reverse order" from the same panel. This will reverse the x-axis, but also move the y-axis to the right side of the chart. If that isn't what you want, click on "At maximum cate**g**ory" in the same dialog box to move the y-axis back to the left side. This method is best used when your x-axis labels are text. If they are dates, then the previous method is better.

Now suppose that we wanted to change the chart title so that it shows the years that are covered by the data. Simply click on the chart title to select it, then click at the end of the title. You could begin typing immediately, but we want to put the new text on a second line. Press Enter to begin a new line and then type: 2008 to 2013 and press the Esc key or click anywhere else on the chart. You may need to resize the font to make the title fit.

Next, let's move the legend to the bottom of the chart to see if it looks better there. Right-click on the legend and choose **F**ormat Legend from the shortcut menu. Select **B**ottom from the choices presented. Click the X in the upper-right of the Format Legend panel to close it and return to the chart. Now the plot area of the chart looks squashed. To fix this, click in the plot area to select it and drag the selection handles until the plot area is the proper size. Your worksheet should now resemble the one in Exhibit 1-8.

Changing the Chart Type

Excel offers many different types of charts: everything from the column chart that we have created to 3-D bar charts and radar plots. Some of these chart types are very sophisticated, even allowing you to rotate them to see a different view of the data. Despite these potential complexities, changing the chart type is very straightforward.

Change
Chart Type

Let's assume that we would prefer to see the data in our chart presented as two lines, rather than as columns. To make this change, right-click anywhere inside the chart and choose Change Chart Type from the menu (or the button on the Design tab). Select a type of Line chart and click OK. The chart is now displayed as a line chart. You can even change the type of an individual data series. For example, you might want to see Sales as a Column chart and

Net Income as a Line on the same chart. Give it a try. Right-click on the Sales data series, choose "Change Series Chart Type…" and change the chart type to Clustered Column.

EXHIBIT 1-8
WORKSHEET WITH REFORMATTED CHART

	A	B	C	D	E	F	G
1				Microsoft Corporation Profitability Analysis			
2				(Millions of Dollars)			
3				2008 to 2013			
4		*2013*	*2012*	*2011*	*2010*	*2009*	*2008*
5	Sales	77,849.00	73,723.00	69,943.00	62,484.00	58,437.00	60,420.00
6	Net Income	21,863.00	16,978.00	23,150.00	18,760.00	14,569.00	17,681.00
7	Net Profit Margin	28.08%	23.03%	33.10%	30.02%	24.93%	29.26%
8	Sales Growth	5.20%					
9	Net Income Growth	4.34%					
10	% Change in Sales	1.0560	1.0540	1.1194	1.0693	0.9672	
11	Sales Growth	5.20%					
12							
13							
14							
15							
16							
17							
18							
19							
20							
21							

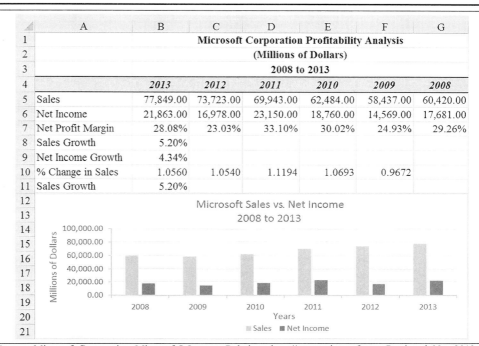

Source: Microsoft Corporation, Microsoft® Investor Relations, http://www.microsoft.com Retrieved: Nov 2013.

Another option would be to create an XY Scatter chart, where each point represents an (X,Y) coordinate. This type of chart would be more appropriate for our data because the x-axis data (the years) is numerical. This type of chart also eliminates the need to flip the x-axis. Column and Line charts are best suited to categorical data, and Scatter charts are best for numerical data. One exception is when you have dates as the x-axis data. Line and Column charts allow for a date axis that gives great flexibility. Figure 1-12 shows the Scatter chart.

You can also change other formatting in the chart very easily. Excel has many built-in chart styles, and you can choose one from the Chart Styles button next to the chart (or on the Design tab). These styles were created with complimentary colors so that they look nice, even if you don't have any design skills.

FIGURE 1-12
SALES VS. NET INCOME AS A SCATTER CHART

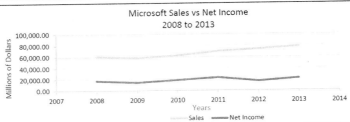

Source: Microsoft Corporation, Microsoft® Investor Relations, http://www.microsoft.com Retrieved: Nov 2013.

If you want to change just the color of the columns (or line) for Sales, simply right-click on one of the data points and choose Format Data Series. Select Fill and then Solid Fill. You can now choose the exact color that you want to apply to the data series. You can also change the border around the bars and add a shadow for a three-dimensional effect.

Be careful about applying too much "eye candy." Excel 2013's charting ability makes it easy to fill the chart with effects that add nothing to the viewer's understanding of the data. Typically, excessive formatting distracts from the message of the chart (e.g., see just about any so-called info-graphic on the Internet). Excel charting and data visualization experts[9] generally recommend that you use the correct type of chart and keep the formatting as simple as possible. After all, the purpose of a chart is to make data easier to understand; it isn't supposed to be a work of art.

Creating Sparkline Charts

Sparklines are a type of "word" chart created by Edward Tufte, a statistician and data visualization expert. They are tiny charts that are intended to be presented as a "word" in a line of text or next to data in a table. Their chief purpose is to display trends and variability in a very compact space.

Line

Let's add a few sparklines to our worksheet to show the trend in sales, net income, and net profit margin over time. Select cell C5 and then click the Insert tab and choose the Line button in the Sparklines group. In the dialog box choose B5:G5 as the **D**ata Range and then click OK.

---

9. For example, see Jon Peltier, an Excel charting expert who maintains the PTS blog at http://peltiertech.com/WordPress. Stephen Few is a data visualization expert and author who maintains the Visual Business Intelligence blog at http://www.perceptualedge.com/blog/.

You will now have the sparkline chart in H5, but notice that it seems to indicate that sales have been declining. As before, this is because our data is listed from newest to oldest so we need to flip the x-axis. On the Design tab for the sparkline, click the Axis button and choose **P**lot Data Right-to-left. Now we can easily see, in a very compact space, that sales have been trending upward for the last six years.

Axis

You can follow the same steps to create sparklines for net income and the net profit margin, or you can simply use the AutoFill handle to copy the sparkline from H5. We can now apply additional formatting, such as adding markers to each data point by making use of the options available on the Design tab.

EXHIBIT 1-9
PROFITABILITY ANALYSIS WITH SPARKLINES

	A	B	C	D	E	F	G	H
1		Microsoft Corporation Profitability Analysis						
2		(Millions of Dollars)						
3		2008 to 2013						
4		2013	2012	2011	2010	2009	2008	Trend
5	Sales	77,849.00	73,723.00	69,943.00	62,484.00	58,437.00	60,420.00	
6	Net Income	21,863.00	16,978.00	23,150.00	18,760.00	14,569.00	17,681.00	
7	Net Profit Margin	28.08%	23.03%	33.10%	30.02%	24.93%	29.26%	
8	Sales Growth	5.20%						
9	Net Income Growth	4.34%						
10	% Change in Sales	1.0560	1.0540	1.1194	1.0693	0.9672		
11	Sales Growth	5.20%						

Source: Microsoft Corporation, Microsoft® Investor Relations, http://www.microsoft.com Retrieved: Nov 2013.

If you want to change the type of Sparkline chart, simply select the Sparklines and then click the type of chart that you want in the Design tab. Note that you cannot delete Sparklines by pressing the Delete key. Instead, click the Clear button in the Design tab, or right-click them and delete them using the shortcut menu.

Printing

There are many times when a worksheet displayed on screen accomplishes all that you need. Other times there is no escaping the need for a hard copy. Excel makes printing a worksheet both easy and flexible. For small worksheets all that needs to be done is to click the File tab, and then on the Print tab click the Print button. This will print the worksheet immediately, using the default printer and settings. Note that the preview of the printout is shown in this tab instead of a separate window as in older versions of Excel.

Larger printing tasks are only slightly more complex. Suppose that our profitability analysis of Microsoft needs to be printed so that it can be distributed at a meeting. As a first step, we need to decide if we want to print the entire worksheet or only a portion of it. In this case, let's assume that we wish to print the whole worksheet, except that we want to print the graph on a separate page so that it can more easily be converted to an overhead transparency.

Print
Area

Because we wish to print the numbers and chart separately, we need to tell Excel the range of cells that we want printed. Select the range A1:G11, choose Print Area on the Page Layout tab, and then Set Print Area. Notice that a light gray line now surrounds the range that we have selected for printing. Before actually printing a worksheet, it is good practice to preview the output to make sure that it looks exactly as we want. This will save both time and paper. From the File tab choose the Print tab. Excel will now display a likeness of the actual printed page. If it doesn't look exactly the way that you want, you can change some options. For example, if the gridlines appear on the print preview, you can turn them off on the Page Layout tab by unchecking the Print option under Gridlines.

If you have followed the examples to this point, you might, depending on the type of printer you are using and the font size, notice that our worksheet is too wide to fit on one page. Because we would ideally like to fit the whole worksheet on one page, we have some adjustments to make. Essentially we have two options: either change the page orientation to print sideways (i.e., landscape mode) or have Excel reduce the printout to fit on one page. Each of these methods is equally viable, but let's go for the reduction to one page.

From the Print tab, we can click the button that shows the current scaling choice (probably No Scaling) and choose an option from the list. You can also set custom scaling options by clicking the Page Setup link, which will launch the Page Setup dialog box. In the Fit to: pages wide by __ tall and enter a 1 in both boxes. We also don't want the gridlines to print. Click on the Sheet tab and make sure that the Gridlines option is deselected (no check mark in the box). Click OK to return to Print Preview.

At this point, everything should be ready for printing, so click on the Print button. Excel now returns to the normal view and presents you with the print dialog box. Because we want to print the whole range that we have selected, make sure your printer is ready (turned on, has paper, etc.) and click OK. Your page should look nearly identical to the on-screen version.

To print the chart on a separate page, we first need to click on it so that it is selected. Now, to print the chart simply select Print from the File tab. Presto! The chart prints out on its own page. Of course, you will still see the Print Preview and be able to use the page setup options for charts just as we did for the worksheet.

What if you wanted to print the chart on the same page as the worksheet? Simple, just select the entire range that you want to print, including the chart. Now repeat the steps from above (resetting the print area), and the worksheet and chart will print on the same page. An easier alternative is to select the range to print, choose Print from the File tab, and make sure that Print Selection is selected in the Settings section.

Using Excel with Other Applications

Suppose that you are writing a report on the profitability of Microsoft for the past six years. Chances are good that you are writing the report in one of the major word processing programs. Your word processor probably allows for the creation of tables that can display all of the information that you have created in Excel, but it lacks the computational sophistication and graphics power of Excel. Similarly, Excel lacks the text processing power that you need to write the report. Fortunately, it is very easy to harness the strengths of both programs and combine the results.

While some word processors will read Excel files directly from your disk, this is not usually the easiest way to incorporate spreadsheets into your word processing files. Instead, it is usually easiest to use some variant of copy and paste, just like we've used within Excel itself. Every time you copy data from Excel, it goes to the clipboard. The contents of the clipboard are available to any other application that cares to access them. All you need to do is copy the data from within Excel, switch to the other application, and then paste from its menus.

Simply pasting the Excel data into a word processor usually results in the word processor reading the data and creating a table. While this may be all that you need, many times it would be more convenient if you could still edit the data in its native environment. In other words, it would be nice if you could still take advantage of Excel's built-in functions and recalculation ability. You can. Instead of using the paste command, use Paste Special.

The Paste Special command allows much more freedom in how the data is stored inside the word processor. For example, if you choose to paste the data as a "Microsoft Excel Worksheet Object" you will be able to edit the data from within the word processor by simply double-clicking on it. If you are using Microsoft Word 2013, the Ribbon will change to that of Excel, and you can edit the data exactly as if you were in Excel.

Alternatively, you can link the data to your worksheet so that when you make changes in Excel, they are automatically reflected in your word processor. Finally, you can paste a noneditable picture of your data into your document. Either of these last two methods will consume less memory than embedding the worksheet.

Quitting Excel

In previous versions, you could exit from Excel by selecting Exit from the File tab. However, due to user confusion between closing files and exiting, this option was eliminated in Excel 2013. Now to close the workbook and exit you must repeatedly click the Exit button in the upper right corner of the Excel window to close each open workbook and eventually the program itself. Note that if you attempt to close a file without saving your work, Excel will warn you and ask if you would like to save the file.

Best Practices for Spreadsheet Models

A spreadsheet model (specifically a financial model in this book) is simply a spreadsheet designed to solve a particular problem. A properly designed model requires a good deal of thought before the first formula is written. It should be functional, flexible, well-organized, easy to use, and nice looking. While we cannot tell you what font you should use, we can provide several rules that are common to good spreadsheet design.

1. Create an area specifically for the variables (inputs) in the model. The input area should be separate from the calculation area whenever possible. If there are a lot of variables, then the input area should be on a separate worksheet (usually the first worksheet in the workbook). This will make it easy to change the assumptions behind the model. Further, cells containing formulas that should not be modified by end users should be protected (Review tab, Protect Sheet).

2. Do not enter a number directly into a formula, unless it will never change. Numbers that may be changed should be entered into the input area, or calculated if possible. This will help to minimize errors in the model and greatly simplify the changing of assumptions. It is much better to change a number in one cell than to have to remember to change it in five formulas.

3. Your model should be well-organized and nicely formatted. This will not only help you to minimize errors, but will also make it easier for others to understand. A haphazardly created model may return the correct answers, but it will be difficult to understand. Even if nobody else will ever see your spreadsheet, you will probably have to look it over in the future. The effort that you expend in designing the model will be paid back many times over in future time savings.

4. If your formulas are long or use complex logic, make sure to document them. A simple explanatory cell comment (choose New Comment from the Review tab) or a textbox describing the logic of the model can save

enormous effort when debugging formulas. Writing your own user-defined functions in Visual Basic for Applications (VBA, see Chapter 14) can help to simplify your model, particularly if the formula is needed in several places.

5. Always test your model thoroughly before declaring it finished. While your model may produce correct answers for your expected input values, it may not work properly in every conceivable case. It is important to change your inputs several times, and verify the output. Make sure to use some numbers that don't seem realistic to see what happens. This will often uncover errors in formula logic. Your formulas should be written so that they can handle anything that you may throw at them. **IF** statements, Data Validation, and Conditional Formatting are quite useful in this regard.

Keep these five rules in mind when building your models, and you will be much more productive and less likely to create flawed models.[10]

Summary

In this chapter, we have discussed the basics of Microsoft Excel 2013. You should have gained a basic understanding of such topics as entering text and numbers, entering formulas, formatting, graphics, and printing. We have also discussed some important considerations for designing spreadsheet models.

In the chapters ahead, we will cover many of these topics in more depth. We will, at the same time, introduce you to financial analysis and describe how Excel can make this analysis easier and more productive. Along the way, we hope to help you develop the reasoning, critical thinking, and quantitative skills that are so necessary in the field of finance today.

---

10. The IT Faculty of The Institute of Chartered Accountants in England and Wales (ICAEW) has published "Twenty Principles for Good Spreadsheet Practice" that is worth reading. It is available at: http://www.ion.icaew.com/itcounts/post/twenty-principles-for-good-spreadsheet-practice.

TABLE 1-4
FUNCTIONS INTRODUCED IN THIS CHAPTER

Purpose	Function	Page
Calculate the geometric mean	GEOMEAN(*NUMBER1*, *NUMBER2*,...)	20
Calculate the arithmetic mean	AVERAGE(*NUMBER1*, *NUMBER2*,...)	20
An alternate way to calculate the geometric mean using dollar values	FAME_GEOMEAN(*SALES*)	26

Problems

1. Suppose that at the end of December 2008 you purchased shares in Apple, Inc. (Nasdaq: AAPL). It is now five years later and you decide to evaluate your holdings to see if you have done well with this investment. The table below shows the end-of-year market prices of AAPL.

AAPL Stock Prices	
Date	**Price**
2008	82.53
2009	203.76
2010	311.89
2011	391.60
2012	519.13
2013	561.02

a. Enter the data, as shown, into a worksheet and format the table as shown.

b. Create a formula to calculate your rate of return for each year. Format the results as percentages with two decimal places.

c. Calculate the total return for the entire five-year holding period. What is the compound average annual rate of return?

    d.   Create a Line chart showing the stock price from December 2008 to December 2013. Make sure to title the chart and label the axes. Now, create an XY Scatter chart of the same data. What are the differences between these types of charts? Which type of chart is more appropriate for this data?

    e.   Experiment with the formatting possibilities of the chart. For example, you might try changing it to a 3-D Line chart and fill the plot area with a marble background. Is there any reason to use this type of chart to display this data? Do the "enhancements" help you to understand the data?

2.   In your position as research assistant to a portfolio manager, you need to analyze the profitability of the companies in the portfolio. Using the data for 3M Co. below:

Fiscal Year	2013	2012	2011	2010	2009
Total Revenue	30,871	29,904	29,611	26,662	23,123
Net Income	4,659	4,444	4,283	4,085	3,193

    a.   Calculate the net profit margin for each year.

    b.   Calculate the average annual growth rates for revenue and net income using the GEOMEAN function. Is net income growing more slowly or faster than total revenue? Is this a positive for your investment in the company?

    c.   Calculate the average annual growth rate of total revenue using the AVERAGE function. Is this result more or less accurate than your result in the previous question? Why?

    d.   Create a Column chart of total revenue and net income. Be sure to change the chart so that the x-axis labels contain the year numbers, and format the axis so that 2013 is on the far right side of the axis.

3. Repeat Problem 2 using the data below for Yahoo! Inc. However, this time you should create a copy of your worksheet to use as a template. Replace the data for 3M with that of Yahoo.

Fiscal Year	2013	2012	2011	2010	2009
Total Revenue	4,680	4,987	4,984	6,325	6,460
Net Income	1,366	3,945	1,049	1,232	598

a. Do you notice anything unusual about Yahoo's growth rates? Do the growth rates that you calculated seem reasonable going forward?

b. Which company was more profitable in 2013? Which was more profitable if you take a longer view? Would this affect your desire to invest in one company over the other?

4. Using the data for Adobe Systems Inc. (Nasdaq: ADBE), presented below:

Fiscal Year	2013	2012	2011	2010	2009
Sales	$4,055	$4,404	$4,216	$3,800	$2,946
EBIT	423	1,180	1,099	993	691
Interest Expense	68	67	67	57	3
Total Net Income	290	833	833	775	387
Basic EPS from Total Operations	0.58	1.68	1.67	1.49	0.74
Total Assets	10,380	9,975	8,991	8,141	7,282
Accounts Payable	62	50	87	52	59
Total Liabilities	3,656	3,309	3,208	2,949	2,392
Retained Earnings	6,929	7,003	6,529	5,981	5,300
Net Cash from Operating Activities	1,152	1,500	1,543	1,113	1,118
Free Cash Flow	963	1,229	1,333	943	998

a. Calculate the ratio of each years' data to the previous year for each of the above items for Adobe. For example, for the year 2013, the ratio for sales is $4,055/$4,404 = 0.92075.

b. From your calculations in part a, calculate each year's rate of growth. Using the example in part a, the ratio is 0.92075, so the percentage growth in sales for 2013 is $0.92075 - 1$ or -7.925%.

c. Calculate the average growth rate (using the **AVERAGE** function) of each of the above items using the results you calculated in part b. These averages are arithmetic averages.

d. Use the **GEOMEAN** function to estimate the compound annual average growth rate (CAGR) for each of the above items using the results that you calculated in part a. Be sure to subtract 1 from the result to arrive at a percent change. These are geometric averages.

e. Compare the results from part c to those for part d for each item. Is it true that the arithmetic average growth rate is always greater than or equal to the geometric average (CAGR)?

f. Contrast the results for the geometric averages to those for the arithmetic average for the variables listed below. What do you observe about the differences in the two growth estimates for Interest Expense and Net Income? What do you observe about the differences in the two estimates for Total Liabilities and Retained Earnings? Hint: Look at the results from part b (the individual yearly growth rates) for each variable to draw some conclusions about the variation between the arithmetic and geometric averages.

   1. Sales
   2. EBIT
   3. Total Assets
   4. Accounts Payable
   5. Retained Earnings

Internet Exercise

1. Choose your own company and repeat the analysis from Problem 3. You can get the data from MSN Money at http://money.msn.com/investing. To retrieve the data for your company, enter the ticker symbol. Now choose Financials and then Income Statement from the menu. Display the annual income statement and copy the sales and net income data. Now enter the data into your template.

CHAPTER 2

The Basic Financial Statements

After studying this chapter, you should be able to:

1. *Explain the purpose and format of the firm's three basic financial statements: the income statement, the balance sheet, and the statement of cash flows.*

2. *Build these statements in Excel with data for any company, and create common-size versions of them.*

3. *Link worksheets together so that formulas in one worksheet can reference data in another and update automatically when changes are made.*

4. *Use Excel's Outline tool to selectively display or hide parts of a financial statement.*

5. *Use Data Validation to prevent data entry errors.*

Much of financial analysis takes as its starting point the basic financial statements of the firm. It is therefore crucial that the analyst have a strong fundamental understanding of these statements. There are three basic financial statements:

1. The *income statement* summarizes the results of the firm's operations over a period of time. The income statement tells us the total revenues and expenses for the time period and also contains several different measures of the accounting profits earned by the firm. Typically, income statements are prepared for different time periods, usually monthly, quarterly, and annually.

2. The *balance sheet* describes the assets, liabilities, and equity of the firm at a specific point in time. Assets are the (tangible or intangible) things that a firm owns. Liabilities are the firm's debts. Equity is the difference between what the firm owns and what it owes to others. Because the balance sheet is specific to a point in time, it is much like a photograph. What it shows was true when the snapshot was taken, but is not necessarily true when it is viewed.

3. The *statement of cash flows* outlines the sources of the firm's cash inflows and shows where the cash outflows went. Activities that bring cash into the firm are referred to as *sources* of cash, while those that take cash out of the firm are referred to as *uses* of cash.

In this chapter, we will build each of these three statements for Elvis Products International, a small producer of Elvis memorabilia. Each financial statement will be created in its own worksheet in the workbook, and we will create links between the sheets as necessary. Before beginning, open a new workbook.

The Income Statement

The income statement is a fairly simple document that begins by listing a firm's revenues (perhaps by sources or in total) followed by all of the firm's expenses. The result of the income statement is the net income for the period. Net income represents the accounting profit left over after all expenses and taxes have been paid from the revenue for the period.

Principle 1:
Make Excel do as much of the work as possible. Whenever possible, a formula should be used rather than entering numbers. In the long run this will minimize errors.

Building an Income Statement in Excel

Exhibit 2-1 presents the income statement for Elvis Products International (EPI) for the year ending December 31, 2014. We will build this income statement first and then use it as a base for creating the 2013 income statement.

Principle 2:
Format the worksheet so that it is easy to understand. Borders, shading, and font choices are more than just decorations. Properly chosen, they can make important numbers stand out and get the attention they deserve.

While we are building the income statement, we want to keep a couple of general principles in mind. Principle 1 says that we want to make Excel do as much of the work as possible. Any time a value can be calculated, we should use Excel to do so. The reasoning behind this principle is that we want to avoid mistakes and increase productivity. A little thought before beginning the design of a worksheet can help minimize data entry errors and increase productivity by reducing the amount of data that needs to be entered.

Principle 2 says that we should format the worksheet in such a way as to make it easy to comprehend. There are many times that you will create a worksheet for others to use or for your own use at a later date.

EXHIBIT 2-1
EPI'S INCOME STATEMENT FOR 2014 AND 2013

	A	B	C
1	Elvis Products International		
2	Income Statement		
3	For the Year Ended Dec. 31, 2014		
4		*2014*	*2013*
5	Sales	3,850,000	3,432,000
6	Cost of Goods Sold	3,250,000	2,864,000
7	*Gross Profit*	*600,000*	*568,000*
8	Selling and G&A Expenses	330,300	240,000
9	Fixed Expenses	100,000	100,000
10	Depreciation Expense	20,000	18,900
11	*EBIT*	*149,700*	*209,100*
12	Interest Expense	76,000	62,500
13	*Earnings Before Taxes*	*73,700*	*146,600*
14	Taxes	29,480	58,640
15	*Net Income*	*44,220*	*87,960*
16			
17	Notes:		
18	Tax Rate	40%	

Properly organizing the data and the judicious use of color and fonts can make the worksheet easier to use and modify.[1] Worksheets that are disorganized and sloppily formatted waste the time of the audience and do not engender faith in their results.

Format

It is usually helpful when working with multiple worksheets in a workbook for each sheet to be given a name other than the default. Worksheets can be renamed using the Format button on the Home tab or by right-clicking the sheet tab. Right-click "Sheet1," choose **R**ename, and then type Income Statement over the existing name. This step is important because when we later begin referencing data on this sheet, the references will require the name of the sheet in addition to the cell reference. Note, however, that you can always rename the sheet later and any formulas referencing it will automatically be updated.[2]

---

1. We would like to emphasize the word "judicious." Some people overuse fonts and end up producing documents with a definite ransom note appearance. Do yourself, and others, a favor by limiting your use of fonts to one or two per document.

2. This is always true for references within the same workbook. However, suppose that we have two workbooks called X and Y. If X contains a reference to a cell in Y, it will be updated automatically as long as both workbooks are open. If X is closed when the sheet name is changed in Y, then you will see a #REF! error the next time you open X and will have to manually change the reference.

We will begin building the income statement with the titles in A1:A3. Remember, if the need arises, we can always insert new rows or columns into the worksheet at a later time. In A1 type: Elvis Products International; in A2: Income Statement; in A3: For the Year Ended Dec. 31, 2014. The first line of the title identifies the company, the second identifies the type of statement, and the third identifies the time period that the statement covers. Now center the titles by selecting A1:C3. Choose Format Cells, select the Alignment tab, and then select "Center Across Selection" under Horizontal. Note that Excel provides an icon in the Alignment group of the Home tab that is titled "Merge and Center" and accomplishes a similar alignment. However, in addition to centering the titles over the selected columns it also merges the cells into one. This can create problems if we later decide to insert a new column or change formatting. In general, you should never use the Merge and Center icon.

How to proceed from this point is largely a matter of preference. We could move line by line through the income statement, entering a label followed by the value. An alternative is to enter all of the labels and then all of the numbers. The second method seems preferable at this point so that we may concentrate on the numbers. The labels are going to be in column A and the numbers in column B. It is good practice to enter a label indicating the end of the period above the data, so move to B4 and type: 2014.

Beginning in A5, enter the labels exactly as they appear in Exhibit 2-1. It is likely that you will find that some of these labels are too long to fit in only one cell. To fix this problem, we need to change the width of column A. There are several ways to accomplish this in Excel. The slowest method is to select a cell in column A and then click the Format button on the Home tab. Next, choose Column Width and enter: 30 in the edit box. If you are using some font other than 12-point Times New Roman, you will have to experiment with different numbers to find the appropriate width for the column. Alternatively, we could let Excel determine the appropriate width. Select column A, and click the Format button. Now choose Autofit Column Width and Excel will automatically make the column wide enough to accommodate the longest text in the column.

 As usual, there is a shortcut available. Move the mouse pointer over the column headers, and you will notice that the pointer changes its shape (to that pictured at left) as it passes over the boundary between columns. Click while the pointer is over this boundary and drag until the column is wide enough to accommodate the text. You can also double-click on the column boundary, and Excel will set the column width to the best fit for the data. Each of these techniques can also be used to change the height of a row.

When entering large numbers, it is often preferable to display them in thousands or millions of dollars, instead of the full amount. For EPI, we will enter the numbers in full precision and later apply a custom number format. Move to B5 and enter: 3,850,000.[3]

---

3. There is no need for you to type the commas. However, Excel will accept numbers with commas if you type them in. If you don't type them, you will need to apply a format that includes commas.

Keeping principle 2 in mind, we would like the numbers to display with commas and no decimal places. Because each cell can maintain a number format, regardless of whether it contains any numbers, we will pre-format the cells that we are going to use. Select cells B5:C15 and click the Comma Style button in Home tab. Now click the Decrease Decimal button twice so that no decimal places are displayed. When we enter numbers into these cells, they will automatically take on the format that we want.

Move to B6 and type: 3,250,000 for cost of goods sold. This is the total cost of the products sold to customers, including inventory shrinkage and write-downs for damaged or outdated products. Notice that, as promised, the number in B6 appears with commas.

Gross profit is the amount left over after paying for the goods that were sold. To calculate gross profit, we subtract cost of goods sold from sales. Again, we want Excel to make all of the calculations, so in B7 type: =B5-B6. Selling, general and administrative (SG&A) expense is an input, so enter: 330,300 in B8. Fixed expenses (rent, salaries, etc.) for the period are an input, so enter: 100,000 in B9. Depreciation is also an input in this case, so in B10 enter: 20,000.

Earnings before interest and taxes (EBIT) is gross profit less all remaining expenses other than interest and taxes. Any of several formulas could be used for this calculation, for example, the obvious formula for EBIT in B11 is: =B7-B8-B9-B10. However, obvious formulas aren't always the best. We could simplify this equation somewhat by making use of the **SUM** function. The new formula would be: =B7-SUM(B8:B10). **SUM** is a built-in Excel function that returns the summation of the arguments. **SUM** is defined as:

$$\text{SUM}(\textit{NUMBER1}, \textit{NUMBER2}, \ldots)$$

where ***NUMBER1*** is the first number (or cell address), *NUMBER2* is the second, and so on. Excel will also accept ranges in place of any individual cell reference. There are two advantages of using the **SUM** function in this case: (1) It is faster and more compact and (2) the range will automatically expand if we insert a new row. The second advantage is the most important. If we add another category of expense by adding another row above row 9, for example, our formula would automatically incorporate the new row by changing to: B7 – Sum (B8:B11). If we used the original formula, we would have to remember to change it after adding the new row.

Σ AutoSum ▾   **SUM** is one of the more commonly used built-in functions, so common that Microsoft has included the AutoSum button (pictured at left) in the Editing group on the Home tab to automate the summation of rows or columns of numbers. To use the AutoSum button, simply select the cell where you want the formula to be placed and then click the button. Or, you can use the Alt+= keyboard shortcut. Excel will make an intelligent guess about which cells you want included, and it is usually correct. If it guesses wrongly, simply select the range that you wish to include and Excel will make the change. Note that the AutoSum button doesn't work when you are editing a formula in the formula bar.

The AutoSum button has proved so popular that its functionality has been improved. If you click the little arrow to the right of the AutoSum button, it will drop down a list of alternative functions. Now you can more quickly use the **AVERAGE, COUNT, MAX,** or **MIN** functions just by choosing a function from the menu.

In B12 enter 76,000 for the interest expense. Next, we will calculate earnings before taxes with the formula: =B11-B12 in cell B13. EPI pays taxes at the rate of 40% on taxable income, so in B18 type 40%. We will calculate the dollar amount of taxes in B14 with: =B13*$B18. Note that this lets us easily change the tax rate without having to edit formulas. Finally, *net income* is the profit earned by the firm after all revenues and expenses have been taken into account. To calculate net income, enter =B13-B14 in cell B15.

As you can see, EPI's net income for the fiscal year 2014 was $44,220. However, for analysis purposes, we normally are not overly concerned with net income. Net income does not accurately represent the funds that a firm has available to spend. In the calculation of net income, we include depreciation expense (and/or other noncash expenses such as depletion or amortization), which ostensibly accounts for the decline in the value of the long-term assets of the firm. Because nobody actually wrote a check for the depreciation expense, it should be added back to the net income number to give a better, though not complete, picture of the cash flow for the period. Cash flow is the number one concern for financial analysts.

Creating EPI's income statement for 2013 doesn't take nearly as much work. First, select B4:B15 and copy the cells using the Copy button on the Home tab. Select C4 and click the Paste button. Don't forget to change C4 to: 2013. Now you have an exact copy of the 2014 income statement. Enter the numbers from Table 2-1 into the appropriate cells.

TABLE 2-1
EPI'S 2013 INCOME AND EXPENSES

Category	Value
Sales	3,432,000
Cost of Goods Sold	2,864,000
SG&A Expenses	240,000
Depreciation Expense	18,900
Interest Expense	62,500

Notice that you only had to enter the new numbers. The formulas are updated and recalculated automatically. So instead of entering 11 cells of formulas or numbers, you only had to enter six numbers and no formulas at all. Your worksheet should now resemble the one in Exhibit 2-1, page 45.

The layout of the income statement that we have seen is the one normally used by analysts outside the firm. Those inside the firm will have more information and may find that Excel's Outline display will make the worksheet easier to understand and maintain. To learn about outlining, see page 62.

The Balance Sheet

The balance sheet is usually depicted in two sections: the assets section at the top or left side, and the liabilities and owner's equity section at the bottom or right side. It is important to realize that the balance sheet must balance (thus the name). That is, total assets must equal the sum of total liabilities and total owner's equity. Each of these sections is usually further divided into subsections.

On the asset side, there are two subsections. The *current assets* section describes the value of the firm's short-term assets. Short-term, in this case, is defined as one year or the time it takes for the asset to go through one operating cycle (i.e., from purchase of raw materials to sale to collection of cash). Typical current assets are cash, accounts receivable, and inventories. *Fixed assets* are those assets with lives longer than one year. Examples of fixed assets include vehicles, property, and buildings.

Like assets, liabilities can be subdivided into two sections. *Current liabilities* are those liabilities that are expected to be retired within one year. Examples are items such as accounts payable and wages payable. *Long-term liabilities* are those that will not be paid off within the current year. Generally, long-term liabilities are made up of various types of bonds, bank loans, and so on.

Owner's equity represents the difference between the value of the total assets and liabilities of the firm. This part of the balance sheet is subdivided into contributed capital and retained earnings. *Contributed capital* is the investment made by the common and preferred stockholders of the firm. *Retained earnings* is the accumulation of the undistributed profits of the firm.

Building a Balance Sheet in Excel

The process of building a balance sheet in Excel is very similar to building the income statement. EPI's 2014 and 2013 balance sheets, as shown in Exhibit 2-2, will serve as an example.

EXHIBIT 2-2
EPI'S BALANCE SHEET

	A	B	C
1	Elvis Products International		
2	Balance Sheet		
3	As of Dec. 31, 2014		
4	*Assets*	*2014*	*2013*
5	Cash and Equivalents	52,000	57,600
6	Accounts Receivable	402,000	351,200
7	Inventory	836,000	715,200
8	*Total Current Assets*	*1,290,000*	*1,124,000*
9	Plant & Equipment	527,000	491,000
10	Accumulated Depreciation	166,200	146,200
11	*Net Fixed Assets*	*360,800*	*344,800*
12	*Total Assets*	*1,650,800*	*1,468,800*
13	*Liabilities and Owner's Equity*		
14	Accounts Payable	175,200	145,600
15	Short-term Notes Payable	225,000	200,000
16	Other Current Liabilities	140,000	136,000
17	*Total Current Liabilities*	*540,200*	*481,600*
18	Long-term Debt	424,612	323,432
19	*Total Liabilities*	*964,812*	*805,032*
20	Common Stock	460,000	460,000
21	Retained Earnings	225,988	203,768
22	*Total Shareholder's Equity*	*685,988*	*663,768*
23	*Total Liabilities and Owner's Equity*	*1,650,800*	*1,468,800*

We will keep EPI's balance sheets in the same workbook, but on a different worksheet, as the income statement. Keeping related data in the same workbook allows for easy referencing. Using separate worksheets allows us to keep the worksheets uncluttered and makes it easier to design the worksheets. Right-click on the Sheet2 tab and select **R**ename from the menu. Type Balance Sheet as the new name for this worksheet.

Enter the labels from Exhibit 2-2 into the blank worksheet. Notice that many of the labels in the balance sheet are indented. There are two ways to accomplish this effect. The method that we usually use, and are using here, is to first type the text into the cell and then click the "Increase Indent" button (pictured at left) in the Alignment group of the Home tab.

An alternative method would be to insert the indented labels into column B instead of column A. This way, by controlling the width of column A, we could control the depth of the indentation. The labels in column A will simply overlap into column B as long as there is no text in the cell to the right. However, this method can cause problems if a new column is inserted between A and B, so the increase indent button method is a better choice.

In EPI's balance sheet, nearly everything is a direct input so we won't discuss every cell. The italicized entries are formulas that we will discuss for 2014. The formulas for the 2013 balance sheet can be copied from the 2014 balance sheet. As with the income statement, you should enter the numbers as shown and apply the same number format.

In the asset section, the first formula is for total current assets in B8. This is simply the sum of all of the current asset accounts, so the formula is: =SUM(B5:B7). Next, we calculate EPI's net fixed assets. This is equal to plant and equipment less accumulated depreciation, so in B11 enter: =B9-B10. Finally, calculate total assets by adding the current assets and net fixed assets with the formula: =B8+B11.

The liabilities and owner's equity section is similar. We will calculate several subtotals and then a grand total in B23. Total current liabilities in B17 is calculated with: =SUM(B14:B16). Total liabilities is calculated with the formula: =B17+B18 in B19. Total shareholder's equity is calculated in B22 with: =B20+B21. And, finally, we calculate the total liabilities and owner's equity in B23 with: =B19+B22. Copy these formulas into the appropriate cells in column C and enter the numbers from Exhibit 2-2 to create the 2013 balance sheet.

To achieve the underlining and shading effects pictured in the exhibits, select the cells and then choose **F**ormat Cells from the shortcut menu and click on the Border tab. To set the type of border, first click on the line style on the left side of the dialog, and then click on the location of the line in the Border area of the dialog. If you want to shade the selection, click on the Fill tab and then select the color and pattern for the shading. It is usually best to make the text in a shaded cell bold so that it can be clearly seen. Before continuing, make sure that your worksheet looks like the one in Exhibit 2-2.

Improving Readability: Custom Number Formats

When the dollar amounts on a financial statement are very large they can be a little confusing and hard to read. To make the numbers easier to read, we can display them in thousands (or millions) of dollars using a custom number format. For example, EPI's sales for 2014 were 3,850,000. We can apply a custom number format that will display this amount as 3,850.00. This is commonly done in annual reports or any other report that lists large dollar amounts.

Return to the Income Statement worksheet and select B5:C15. To create the custom number format, choose **F**ormat Cells from the shortcut menu. On the Number tab choose the Custom category, which is where we will define our own number format. We can begin by choosing a predefined number format. Here we will choose the "#,##0.00" format from the list. If we add a comma after the format then Excel will display the numbers as if they have

---

EXHIBIT 2-3
THE INCOME STATEMENT WITH A CUSTOM NUMBER FORMAT

	A	B	C
1	Elvis Products International		
2	Income Statement		
3	For the Year Ended Dec. 31, 2014 ($ in 000's)		
4		*2014*	*2013*
5	Sales	3,850.00	3,432.00
6	Cost of Goods Sold	3,250.00	2,864.00
7	*Gross Profit*	*600.00*	*568.00*
8	Selling and G&A Expenses	330.30	240.00
9	Fixed Expenses	100.00	100.00
10	Depreciation Expense	20.00	18.90
11	*EBIT*	*149.70*	*209.10*
12	Interest Expense	76.00	62.50
13	*Earnings Before Taxes*	*73.70*	*146.60*
14	Taxes	29.48	58.64
15	*Net Income*	*44.22*	*87.96*

been divided by 1,000. Two commas would display the numbers as if they had been divided by 1,000,000 and so on. In the **T**ype edit box add a single comma after the chosen format so that it looks like "#,##0.00,". You will see an example of what your formatted numbers will look like in the Sample area of the dialog box. The numbers that you have entered will appear to have been divided by 1,000, but this affects only the appearance of the numbers. You should always enter the full number and then format it to look the way that you wish. The manner in which Excel displays numbers will not affect any calculations. Regardless of the format, numbers are always saved with full precision. The format only changes what we see on the screen, not what is kept in memory. To see the full number, select the cell and look in the formula bar.

Before continuing, edit cell A3 so that it says: For the Year Ended Dec. 31, 2014 ($ in 000's). This will allow anyone looking at your worksheet to instantly understand that the numbers are displayed in thousands of dollars. Your income statement should now look like the one above in Exhibit 2-3.

Because the income statement has been reformatted, it makes sense to use the same number format on the balance sheet for consistency. Switch to the Balance Sheet worksheet and select cells B5:C23 (see Exhibit 2-2, page 50). Now, choose **F**ormat Cells and go to the Custom category. Select the format that you just created from the list (it should be at the bottom of the list). Finally, change the title in A3 so that it indicates that the dollar amounts are shown in thousands. Your balance sheet should now look like the one in Exhibit 2-4.

EXHIBIT 2-4
THE BALANCE SHEET WITH A CUSTOM NUMBER FORMAT

	A	B	C
1	Elvis Products International		
2	Balance Sheet		
3	As of Dec. 31, 2014 (S in 000's)		
4	*Assets*	*2014*	*2013*
5	Cash and Equivalents	52.00	57.60
6	Accounts Receivable	402.00	351.20
7	Inventory	836.00	715.20
8	*Total Current Assets*	*1,290.00*	*1,124.00*
9	Plant & Equipment	527.00	491.00
10	Accumulated Depreciation	166.20	146.20
11	*Net Fixed Assets*	*360.80*	*344.80*
12	*Total Assets*	*1,650.80*	*1,468.80*
13	*Liabilities and Owner's Equity*		
14	Accounts Payable	175.20	145.60
15	Short-term Notes Payable	225.00	200.00
16	Other Current Liabilities	140.00	136.00
17	*Total Current Liabilities*	*540.20*	*481.60*
18	Long-term Debt	424.61	323.43
19	*Total Liabilities*	*964.81*	*805.03*
20	Common Stock	460.00	460.00
21	Retained Earnings	225.99	203.77
22	*Total Shareholder's Equity*	*685.99*	*663.77*
23	*Total Liabilities and Owner's Equity*	*1,650.80*	*1,468.80*

Creating your own number formats in Excel is easy, if you understand a few key points. The number format code is a series of wildcard characters. Both the # sign and 0 work as a stand-in for any digit. The difference between them is how leading and trailing zeros around the decimal point are handled. The # sign will not display leading or trailing zeros, while 0 will. Generally, use # signs to the left of the decimal point and 0 to the right. For example, to display 1542.2 with a thousand separator and two decimal places, we might use a format code of "#,###.00" and see 1,542.20. If we left off the last 0 in the code, the result would be 1,542.2 (notice that the trailing zero is missing). If some of your numbers will be less than one, then using "#,##0.00" would be better because that will preserve the zero to the left of the decimal point.

Custom formats can do many other tricks. You can add color that varies based on the sign of the number, have different formats for positive and negative numbers, add text, and make numbers align on the decimal point. Note that custom formats are saved with the workbook, so you will have to recreate them in any future workbooks. To learn more about creating custom formats search for "create or delete a custom number format" in the online help.

Common-Size Financial Statements

A technique widely used by financial analysts is to examine *common-size financial statements*, which display the data not as dollar amounts, but as percentages. These statements provide the analyst with two key benefits:

1. They allow for easy comparisons between firms of different sizes.

2. They can aid in spotting important trends, which otherwise might not be obvious when looking at dollar amounts.

As we'll see, common-size financial statements are easy to create and make it simple to glean important insights that are not immediately obvious when looking at dollar amounts.

Creating Common-Size Income Statements

A common-size income statement is one that shows all of the data as a percentage of the firm's total revenues. Before beginning, remember that we want to make full use of Excel's capabilities to be as productive as possible. Instead of creating a new, blank worksheet and re-typing all of the labels, we will make a copy of the Income Statement worksheet. Right-click on the sheet tab and choose **M**ove or Copy… from the shortcut menu. To create a copy, be sure to click on "**C**reate a copy" at the bottom of the dialog box. Note that the copy can be placed anywhere in the current workbook, in a new workbook, or any other open workbook. Place it before the Balance Sheet workbook. Right-click on the sheet tab and rename the worksheet to Common-Size Income Statement.

We now have a perfect copy of the income statement that we can convert into a common-size income statement. The formulas that we use will reference data from the Income Statement worksheet; so it is helpful to understand how these references are created. In order for Excel to know where to get the data it has to be told the location and name of the file, the name of the worksheet, and the cell address. For example, a reference to a cell in another workbook would look something like the following:

=C:\'[File Name.xlsx]Sheet1'!A1

Notice that the path to the file is listed first, then the name of the file is in brackets. This allows Excel to find the file on your computer. The file name is followed by the name of the worksheet, then an exclamation point, and then the cell address. If the path, file name, or worksheet name contains spaces, then everything after the equals sign and before the exclamation point will be enclosed in single quotes. Fortunately, you won't have to type all of this. Instead, just type an equals sign and then switch to the appropriate worksheet and click on the cell you want to reference. Excel will fill in all of the details. If the data in the original worksheet changes, then the data will be updated automatically in the worksheet with the reference.

We can now create the common-size income statement with only two simple changes. First, in B5 type = and then switch to the Income Statement worksheet. Now click on B5 and type / and then click on B5 again. Finally, press the Enter key and your formula will be: ='Income Statement'!B5/'Income Statement'!B5. Now, change the number format to a Percentage format with 2 decimal places. You should now see that the result is 100.00%.

We are going to copy that formula to every cell in the income statement, so we need to use a mixed reference (see page 17) in the denominator so that it will update appropriately. Therefore, you will need to edit the reference in the denominator so that it will always reference row 5. Change the formula by adding a $ before the 5, so that it becomes: ='Income Statement'!B5/'Income Statement'!B$5.

Paste

At this point, we want to copy this formula to every other cell in the worksheet. However, if we do a normal copy and paste, our underline formatting will be destroyed. To get around this problem, copy the cell and then select all of the other cells (B6:C15 and C5). Now, instead of pasting, choose Paste Special from bottom of the Paste menu on the Home tab. As shown in Figure 2-1, this allows us to choose exactly what and how to paste the data. In the list of options, choose Formulas and number formats.

FIGURE 2-1
THE PASTE SPECIAL DIALOG BOX

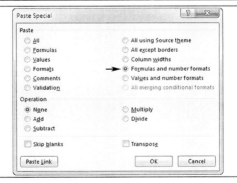

You have now created a common-size income statement with a minimum number of steps. It should resemble the one shown in Exhibit 2-5. You can easily see why this is a useful tool for analysts. At a glance, you can see that Cost of Goods Sold has risen by about 1% and that SG&A expense has risen by about 1.5% in 2014 relative to sales. Also, looking at row 15 instantly shows that the firm's net profit margin (see page 121) has decreased by more than half.

We can see how the changes in each of the items contributed to the decline in net income by doing a *contribution analysis*. Simply calculate the change in each item and sum them to get

Format Painter the change in net income. In E4 type: Contribution and then select C4 and click the Format Painter on the Home tab to copy the format. Now click E4 to paste that format. In E6 enter the formula: =C6-B6 and then copy it to the other cells shown in Exhibit 2-5. From this we can easily see that the change in Cost of Goods and SG&A were the largest contributor to the decline in net income.

EXHIBIT 2-5
EPI'S COMMON-SIZE INCOME STATEMENTS

	A	B	C	D	E
1	Elvis Products International				
2	Common-size Income Statement				
3	For the Year Ended Dec. 31, 2014				
4		*2014*	*2013*		*Contribution*
5	Sales	100.00%	100.00%		
6	Cost of Goods Sold	84.42%	83.45%		-0.97%
7	*Gross Profit*	*15.58%*	*16.55%*		
8	Selling and G&A Expenses	8.58%	6.99%		-1.59%
9	Fixed Expenses	2.60%	2.91%		0.32%
10	Depreciation Expense	0.52%	0.55%		0.03%
11	*EBIT*	*3.89%*	*6.09%*		
12	Interest Expense	1.97%	1.82%		-0.15%
13	*Earnings Before Taxes*	*1.91%*	*4.27%*		
14	Taxes	0.77%	1.71%		0.94%
15	*Net Income*	*1.15%*	*2.56%*		*-1.41%*

Creating a Common-Size Balance Sheet

The common-size balance sheet can be created just as we did for the income statement. The only difference is that the balance sheet entries are displayed as a percentage of the firm's total assets instead of total revenues.

To make the common-size balance sheets for EPI, proceed in the same manner as for the common-size income statements. Create a copy of the existing Balance Sheet worksheet and rename the sheet to Common-Size Balance Sheet. In cell B5 enter: ='Balance Sheet'!B5/'Balance Sheet'!B$12. That formula will calculate the cash balance as a percentage of total assets. We want to do the same for every item, so copy the formula and then select all of the cells on the balance sheet. Use Paste Special to paste only the Formulas and number formats. Your common-size balance sheet should look like the one in Exhibit 2-6.

EXHIBIT 2-6
EPI'S COMMON-SIZE BALANCE SHEET

	A	B	C
1	Elvis Products International		
2	Common-size Balance Sheet		
3	As of Dec. 31, 2014		
4	*Assets*	*2014*	*2013*
5	Cash and Equivalents	3.15%	3.92%
6	Accounts Receivable	24.35%	23.91%
7	Inventory	50.64%	48.69%
8	*Total Current Assets*	*78.14%*	*76.53%*
9	Plant & Equipment	31.92%	33.43%
10	Accumulated Depreciation	10.07%	9.95%
11	*Net Fixed Assets*	*21.86%*	*23.47%*
12	*Total Assets*	100.00%	100.00%
13	*Liabilities and Owner's Equity*		
14	Accounts Payable	10.61%	9.91%
15	Short-term Notes Payable	13.63%	13.62%
16	Other Current Liabilities	8.48%	9.26%
17	*Total Current Liabilities*	*32.72%*	*32.79%*
18	Long-term Debt	25.72%	22.02%
19	*Total Liabilities*	*58.45%*	*54.81%*
20	Common Stock	27.87%	31.32%
21	Retained Earnings	13.69%	13.87%
22	*Total Shareholder's Equity*	*41.55%*	*45.19%*
23	*Total Liabilities and Owner's Equity*	100.00%	100.00%

Building a Statement of Cash Flows[4]

Boiled down to its essence, a firm participates in two kinds of financial transactions: those that increase the cash balance (cash inflows, or *sources* of funds) and those that decrease the cash balance (cash outflows, or *uses* of funds).

One way that a financial analyst can determine how well a firm's management is performing is to examine how they are managing the shareholder's money. The accounting profession has developed the *Statement of Cash Flows*, which is useful for this type of analysis. The statement of cash flows summarizes the causes of changes in the firm's cash balance. Essentially, it converts the accrual-based net income into cash flow.

---

4. We present the *indirect method* of constructing the statement of cash flows because this method is used by most companies. The alternative is known as the *direct method*, but it is rarely used.

Changes in the cash balance can be determined as shown in Table 2-2:

TABLE 2-2
DETERMINING THE CHANGE IN THE CASH BALANCE

	Beginning Cash Balance
+	Cash inflows (sources)
−	Cash outflows (uses)
=	Ending Cash Balance

The statement of cash flows is organized into three sections according to how the cash flows were generated:

1. *Cash Flows from Operations* – cash flows that are generated by the firm in the ordinary course of conducting its business.

2. *Cash Flows from Investing* – cash flows that result from buying and/or selling long-term assets such as land, buildings, machinery, and long-term securities.

3. *Cash Flows from Financing* – cash flows resulting from obtaining or repaying long-term capital. This includes changes in long-term debt, common equity (but not retained earnings), and the payment of dividends.

The most obvious source of operating cash flow is sales and other revenues. Similarly, the most obvious uses of cash are the firm's expenses. However, we already have this information on the income statement and don't need to repeat it in the statement of cash flows. Therefore, instead of putting nearly the entire income statement into the Cash Flows from Operations section, we will only enter net income, which is a summary of the entire income statement. In addition, we will add back the depreciation expense (and other noncash charges) because, in reality, there was no cash outflow associated with depreciation. The rest of the entries on the statement of cash flows will be *changes* in balance sheet items, though a few will be left out for reasons that we will discuss later.

Unlike the income statement and balance sheet, which are mostly exercises in data entry, the statement of cash flows is primarily made up of formulas. Because these formulas reference many different cells in the workbook it is generally easiest to use Excel's pointer mode when entering them. To begin, insert a new worksheet and rename it to Statement of Cash Flows. Enter the labels as shown in Exhibit 2-7 and then apply our custom number format to the cells in B5:C21.

EXHIBIT 2-7
STATEMENT OF CASH FLOWS FOR EPI

	A	B	C
1	Elvis Products International		
2	Statement of Cash Flows		
3	For the Year Ended Dec. 31, 2014 ($ in 000's)		
4	**Cash Flows from Operations**		
5	Net Income	44.22	
6	Depreciation Expense	20.00	
7	Change in Accounts Receivable	-50.80	
8	Change in Inventories	-120.80	
9	Change in Accounts Payable	29.60	
10	Change in Other Current Liabilities	4.00	
11	**Total Cash Flows from Operations**		-73.78
12	**Cash Flows from Investing**		
13	Change in Plant & Equipment	-36.00	
14	**Total Cash Flows from Investing**		-36.00
15	**Cash Flows from Financing**		
16	Change in Short-term Notes Payable	25.00	
17	Change in Long-term Debt	101.18	
18	Change in Common Stock	0.00	
19	Cash Dividends Paid to Shareholders	-22.00	
20	**Total Cash Flows from Financing**		104.18
21	**Net Change in Cash Balance**		-5.60

The first two items under Cash Flows from Operations are Net Income and Depreciation Expense. As previously mentioned, these are unique items because they are the only ones on the statement of cash flows that come from the income statement and are also the only items that are not represented as changes from a previous period.[5] Also realize that Net Income summarizes every other item on the income statement. Therefore, if we were to include Sales, for example, we would be double counting. To enter the net income first type an = in B5 and then (before pressing the Enter key) click on the sheet tab for the Income Statement. Excel will change to the worksheet containing the income statement. Now click on B15 and press Enter. At this point, Excel will switch back to the Statement of Cash Flows worksheet and your formula in B5 should read: =`'Income Statement'!B15`. This formula directs Excel to pull the value from cell B15 on the Income Statement worksheet into B5. If we change some values in the income statement, any change in net income will automatically be reflected in the statement of cash flows.

We can make referencing other sheets slightly easier if we display two or more sheets on the screen at once. We will use this technique to complete the statement of cash flows.

---

5. Actually, we could calculate depreciation expense as the change in accumulated depreciation.

New Window   Arrange All

First, switch to the Income Statement sheet and then click the New Window button on the View tab. This will open a second copy of the workbook. Click the Arrange All button and then choose **V**ertical from the dialog box. You should now see two identical copies of the workbook. In one of the copies, click on the sheet tab for the Statement of Cash Flows. In B6, type = and then click anywhere on the income statement. Now scroll down so that cell B10 is visible and click on it and press the Enter key. The formula in B6 of the Statement of Cash Flows should read: `='Income Statement'!B10`, and the value should be 20,000. If you didn't already apply the custom number format that we used on the income statement, then you will need to apply it now. Select B5:C21 and then select **F**ormat Cells from the right-click menu and apply the same custom format. Alternatively, you can click on any cell in the Income Statement worksheet and then click the Format Painter icon on the Home tab to copy the format. Now, select B5:C21 on the Statement of Cash Flows worksheet to paste the format. Regardless of the method you use, the value in B6 will be displayed as 20.00, although the actual value in the cell is 20,000.

The rest of the statement of cash flows can be completed in a similar manner, except that we will be calculating *changes* in balance sheet items. Because we are done with the income statement, we now want to display the balance sheet in that copy of the workbook. Click on the sheet tab labeled Balance Sheet. You should now have both the Statement of Cash Flows sheet and the Balance Sheet displayed.

At this point, we must be careful with respect to the signs of the numbers entered into the statement of cash flows. In general, when an asset increases that represents a cash outflow (i.e., a *use* of funds). An asset that decreases represents a cash inflow (i.e., a *source* of funds). Liability and equity items are exactly the opposite. We represent uses of funds as negative numbers and sources of funds as positive numbers on the statement of cash flows.

TABLE 2-3
SIGNS OF CASH FLOWS FOR THE STATEMENT OF CASH FLOWS

Type of Item	Direction of Change		Order of Subtraction
	Increase	Decrease	
Asset	–	+	Older – Newer
Liability or Equity	+	–	Newer – Older

Table 2-3 shows how to always get the sign correct. As an example, EPI's accounts receivable balance increased from $351,200 in 2013 to $402,000 in 2014. Because the firm invested in accounts receivable by making more loans to customers, it represents a use of funds and should be indicated with a negative sign on the statement of cash flows. On the other hand, the accounts payable balance increased and, because it is a liability, represents a source of funds. It will have a positive sign on the statement of cash flows.

The formula for the change in accounts receivable in B7 should be: =`'Balance Sheet'!C6-'Balance Sheet'!B6`. Because it is an asset, we are subtracting the newer value from the older value as shown in Table 2-3. The change in inventories can be found by simply copying this formula down to B8. For liability and equity items the direction of the subtraction will be reversed. This will ensure that the sign is always correct no matter how the numbers change.

The formula to calculate the change in accounts payable in B9 is: =`'Balance Sheet'!B14-'Balance Sheet'!C14`. In B10, to get the change in other current liabilities, we use the formula: =`'Balance Sheet'!B16-'Balance Sheet'!C16`. Now we calculate the total cash flows from operations in C11 with: =`SUM(B5:B10)`. Note that we have skipped over the short-term notes payable. That is because notes payable is not an operating current liability. Generally, any interest-bearing liability is included in the Cash Flows from Financing section.

If you are paying close attention, then you probably noticed that we haven't included the change in the cash balance in this section. The reason is that the change in the cash balance is the final result of the statement of cash flows. We will calculate that by summing the subtotals from each of the three sections (see C21 in Exhibit 2-7). Remember, the purpose of the statement of cash flows is to explain the actions that resulted in the new cash balance, so including the change in cash would be double counting.

Cash flows from investing are those cash flows generated from investments (or dis-investments) in long-term assets. In the case of EPI, that means plant and equipment.[6] This change can be calculated in B13 by the formula: =`'Balance Sheet'!C9-'Balance Sheet'!B9`. Even though we only have one number in this section, for consistency we will calculate the total cash flows from investing in C14 with: =`B13`.

For the final section, our first item is the change in notes payable. This item increased from $200,000 in 2013 to $225,000 in 2014, representing a cash inflow of $25,000. In B16 enter the formula: =`'Balance Sheet'!B15-'Balance Sheet'!C15`. Next, we can calculate the change in long-term debt with the formula: =`'Balance Sheet'!B18-'Balance Sheet'!C18`. Even though common stock didn't change during the year, it should still be included. In B18, enter: =`'Balance Sheet'!B20-'Balance Sheet'!C20`.

Cash dividends paid to shareholders in 2014 were $22,000. This is calculated with the formula:

$$\text{Dividends Paid} = \text{Net Income} - \text{Change in Retained Earnings}$$

---

6. We do not use Net Fixed Assets, as that would result in double-counting depreciation expense.

Dividends paid are always a use of funds, so in B19 enter the formula: =-('Income Statement'!B15-('Balance Sheet'!B21-'Balance Sheet'!C21)). Note that the parentheses are important in this case and that the result should be –22,000. Again, we can total the cash flows from financing in C20 with: =SUM(B16:B19).

Finally, in C21 we calculate the net change in the cash balance by adding up the subtotals, so the formula is: =SUM(C11:C20). Note that this should exactly equal the actual change in the cash balance from 2013 to 2014, otherwise you have made an error. The most common errors are likely to be either a wrong sign or an omitted item.

Because you no longer need the second copy of the worksheet, you may close either copy by clicking the Close button in the upper right corner of the window. Note that if you save the workbook with more than one view, it will retain that setting and both views will be visible when you reopen the workbook.

Before continuing, make sure that your worksheet resembles that pictured in Exhibit 2-7 on page 59.

Using Excel's Outliner

Most people were first introduced to outlining as a tool to help organize a paper by considering the major ideas first and progressively moving to the details. Excel's outliner works similarly, except that it is not really a tool for organizing ideas, but a tool to show or hide whatever level of detail is appropriate in a spreadsheet. It is reminiscent of the "directory tree" that is used in Windows Explorer for browsing through directories.

Excel can automatically build an outline based on the formulas that you have entered. It looks for cells that summarize information in other cells and considers those to be top level. For example, consider the statement of cash flows that we created in Exhibit 2-7. Once an outline is applied to this sheet, we can collapse it so that it appears like the screen fragment in Exhibit 2-8.

Excel is sometimes smart enough to apply an outline automatically, but we will do it manually to get exactly the result that we want. Select A4:C10 on the Statement of Cash Flows worksheet and then press Shift+Alt+Right arrow (or click the top half of the Group button on the Data tab). In this case we want to group by rows, so just press Enter when the

Group   Ungroup

dialog box appears. You will see an outline symbol appear at the left of the selected cells. If you click on the symbol, the outline will collapse so that it shows only the summary cell. Clicking the outline symbol again will restore the display. To create the other parts of the outline, select A12:C13 and A15:C19 and repeat the above steps for each range.

EXHIBIT 2-8
STATEMENT OF CASH FLOWS WITH ONLY LEVEL 1 DISPLAYED

	A	B	C
1	Elvis Products International		
2	Statement of Cash Flows		
3	For the Year Ended Dec. 31, 2014 ($ in 000's)		
11	Total Cash Flows from Operations		-73.78
14	Total Cash Flows from Investing		-36.00
20	Total Cash Flows from Financing		104.18
21	Net Change in Cash Balance		-5.60

Click here to show level 1 only →

Click here to show both levels

Click these buttons to expand any section

If you make a mistake or decide that you don't like the outline feature, you can clear the outline by clicking the lower half of the Ungroup button and choosing **C**lear Outline from the menu.

Outlining is especially useful for presentations to people who don't need to see all of the details. It frees you from creating a separate summary worksheet. For example, we could create an outline of an income statement. Suppose that the income statement worksheet that we use inside the firm contains a breakdown of sales by product, several categories of cost of goods sold, and so on. When we need to provide the income statement to those outside the firm we may not wish to provide all of that detail. Instead, simply print a copy from the outline with the appropriate level of detail. Note that if you print an outlined worksheet, only the levels displayed on-screen will print. However, if you copy an outlined worksheet, all of the details will be copied and will be visible to anybody who has the copy.

Distributing workbooks with "hidden" data has been the source of many embarrassing, and potentially costly, stories. For example, a lawyer working for Barclays Capital on its agreement to purchase some of the assets of Lehman Brothers reformatted a worksheet and accidentally exposed 179 hidden rows before creating a PDF file for submission to the bankruptcy court. Those previously hidden rows contained information regarding contracts that Barclays did not want to purchase but that were inadvertently included in the offer.[7]

Excel 2013 has a feature designed to avoid this and similar errors. Before distributing a workbook use the **I**nspect Document feature to search for and remove, if necessary, hidden data. This feature can be found in the Info tab under the File tab. Click the Check for Issues button and choose **I**nspect Document.

---

7. See http://abovethelaw.com/2008/10/the-case-for-sleep-what-happens-in-excel-after-dark/.

Common-Size Statement of Cash Flows

Earlier we saw that the common-size income statement and balance sheet were useful analysis tools. We can also create a common-size statement of cash flows though they are less commonly used.

Unlike the income statement and balance sheet, there are at least two different numbers that are used as denominators: sales or the beginning cash balance. We will start by using sales in the denominator and then see how we can create a worksheet that can be toggled between the two different versions.

As before, create an exact copy of your statement of cash flows worksheet. In B4 enter: % of Sales so that it is clear that we are using sales in the denominator. Now for each item, except the subtotals, divide the original formula by the 2014 sales from the income statement. For example, in B5 our original formula was ='Income Statement'!B15. We want to change this to be a percentage of sales, so edit the formula to: ='Income Statement'!B15/'Income Statement'!$B$5. When you have changed each formula in this way, your worksheet should look like the one in Exhibit 2-9.

EXHIBIT 2-9
COMMON-SIZE STATEMENT OF CASH FLOWS USING SALES

	A	B	C
1	Elvis Products International		
2	Common-size Statement of Cash Flows		
3	For the Year Ended Dec. 31, 2014		
4	**Cash Flows from Operations**	**% of Sales**	
5	Net Income	1.15%	
6	Depreciation Expense	0.52%	
7	Change in Accounts Receivable	-1.32%	
8	Change in Inventories	-3.14%	
9	Change in Accounts Payable	0.77%	
10	Change in Other Current Liabilities	0.10%	
11	**Total Cash Flows from Operations**		-1.92%
12	**Cash Flows from Investing**		
13	Change in Plant & Equipment	-0.94%	
14	**Total Cash Flows from Investing**		-0.94%
15	**Cash Flows from Financing**		
16	Change in Short-term Notes Payable	0.65%	
17	Change in Long-term Debt	2.63%	
18	Change in Common Stock	0.00%	
19	Cash Dividends Paid to Shareholders	-0.57%	
20	**Total Cash Flows from Financing**		2.71%
21	**Net Change in Cash Balance**		-0.15%

It can also be useful for the beginning cash balance to be the denominator. We can create another copy of the statement of cash flows and proceed as before, or we can change this one so that it can toggle between the two versions. This is what we will do.

We need to be able to switch the denominator in our formulas, depending on which version the user wants to view. The **CHOOSE** function picks a value based on an index number, and is defined as:

$$\text{CHOOSE}(\textbf{\textit{INDEX}}, \textbf{\textit{VALUE1}}, \textit{VALUE2},\dots)$$

where **INDEX** is a number between 1 and 254, and the **VALUE** arguments are the items from which to choose. The **VALUE** arguments can be numbers, text, cell references, defined names, and so on. We will use **CHOOSE** to select the cell to use in the denominator based on an index number entered by the user in cell F1. Enter: Denominator as a label into E1, and 2 into cell F1 before proceeding.

Change the denominator in cell B5 so that the formula is: ='Income Statement'!B15/ CHOOSE($F$1,'Income Statement'!$B$5,'Balance Sheet'!$C$5). Now, copy the **CHOOSE** function from the denominator and then paste it into the denominator of each of the other items. Your worksheet should now resemble Exhibit 2-10.

EXHIBIT 2-10
COMMON-SIZE STATEMENT OF CASH FLOWS USING BEGINNING CASH

	A	B	C	D	E	F
1	Elvis Products International				Denominator	2
2	Common-size Statement of Cash Flows					
3	For the Year Ended Dec. 31, 2014					
4	**Cash Flows from Operations**	**% of Beginning Cash**				
5	Net Income	76.77%				
6	Depreciation Expense	34.72%				
7	Change in Accounts Receivable	-88.19%				
8	Change in Inventories	-209.72%				
9	Change in Accounts Payable	51.39%				
10	Change in Other Current Liabilities	6.94%				
11	**Total Cash Flows from Operations**		-128.09%			
12	**Cash Flows from Investing**					
13	Change in Plant & Equipment	-62.50%				
14	**Total Cash Flows from Investing**		-62.50%			
15	**Cash Flows from Financing**					
16	Change in Short-term Notes Payable	43.40%				
17	Change in Long-term Debt	175.66%				
18	Change in Common Stock	0.00%				
19	Cash Dividends Paid to Shareholders	-38.19%				
20	**Total Cash Flows from Financing**		180.87%			
21	**Net Change in Cash Balance**		-9.72%			

Finally, we need to change the label in B4 so that it shows the correct denominator. We can use the same idea, so in B4 enter: `="% of "&CHOOSE($F$1,"Sales","Beginning Cash")`. Note that we are using a text formula here to build a text string. This concept is fully explained in "Calculating Text Strings" on page 74.

One other number could be used as the basis of the common-size statement of cash flows: the net change in the cash balance (cell C21). We leave this as an exercise for the reader.

Using Data Validation to Prevent Input Errors

A user of your common-size statement of cash flows could enter anything into cell F1, but we would like to restrict them to entering only a 1 or 2 (or 3, if you completed the exercise above). This can be done by applying a *Data Validation* rule to the cell.

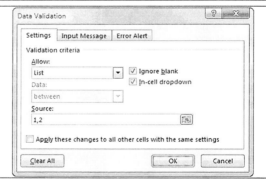

Excel allows for seven different types of validation rules, or you can write a formula to test for valid entries. Select cell F1 and then go to the Data tab and click the Data Validation button. This will launch a dialog box where you can set the rule for the cell (Figure 2-2).

FIGURE 2-2
THE DATA VALIDATION DIALOG BOX

We want to restrict the user's choices to a list of numbers, so from the **A**llow dropdown choose List, and enter 1, 2 in **S**ource. This will create a dropdown list when the cell is selected so that the user can make a valid choice. Because the user can still type in the cell, we will also show a prompt and, if necessary, an error message.

Set a prompt for the user by going to the Input Message tab and typing Enter 1 for a Sales-based statement, or 2 for a beginning cash balance-based statement in the Input message box. This message will appear whenever cell F1 is selected. Finally, go to the Error Alert tab and type Only 1 or 2 are allowed in the **E**rror message box. If the user enters anything else in the cell then a message box will appear alerting them to the error.

Summary

In this chapter, we have discussed the three primary financial statements: the income statement, the balance sheet, the statement of cash flows, and common-size versions of each. You should have a basic understanding of the purpose of each of these statements and know how to build them in Excel.

We have demonstrated how worksheets can be linked so that formulas in one worksheet can reference data on another sheet. Custom number formatting was introduced, and we saw how outliner can be a useful tool for selectively displaying or hiding data. Finally, we have showed how Data Validation can be used to prevent users from making data entry errors.

Make sure that you have saved a copy of the EPI workbook because we will be making use of this data in future chapters.

TABLE 2-4
FUNCTIONS INTRODUCED IN THIS CHAPTER

Purpose	Function	Page
Total numbers or a range of cells	SUM(*NUMBER1*,*NUMBER2*, ...)	47
Average numbers or a range of cells	AVERAGE(*NUMBER1*,*NUMBER2*,...)	48
Count the numbers in a range	COUNT(*VALUE1*, *VALUE2*, ...)	48
Find the maximum of numbers in a range	MAX(*NUMBER1*,*NUMBER2*, ...)	48
Find the minimum of numbers in a range	MIN(*NUMBER1*,*NUMBER2*, ...)	48
Select a value based on an index number	CHOOSE(*INDEX*, *VALUE1*, *VALUE2*,...)	65

COMMON SIZE

- INCOME STATEMENT => BASED ON SALES (so when Common size is complete sales will equal 100%
, Balance Sheet => Based on Total Assets
. SOCF => Sales on Income Statement.
✗ For every Denominator will be an absolute reference $
— Use F4

Problems

1. Using the data presented below:

Mike Owjai Manufacturing
Income Statements
For the Years 2013 and 2014

	2014	2013
Sales	$2,625,000	$2,422,500
Cost of Goods	1,704,975	1,621,875
Gross Profit	**920,025**	**800,625**
Depreciation	63,000	53,250
Selling & Admin. Expense	652,350	626,250
Lease Expense	48,750	48,750
Net Operating Income	**155,925**	**72,375**
Interest Expense	84,000	51,000
Earnings Before Taxes	**71,925**	**21,375**
Taxes	25,174	7,481
Net Income	**$46,751**	**$13,894**

Notes:

Tax Rate	35.00%	35.00%
Shares	75,000	60,000
Earnings per Share	$0.62	$0.23

Mike Owjai Manufacturing
Balance Sheet
For the Year Ended December 31, 2014

	2014	2013
Assets		
Cash	$39,000	$30,750
Marketable Securities	1,826	15,750
Accounts Receivable	315,000	279,000
Inventory	386,250	315,000
Total Current Assets	742,076	640,500
Gross Fixed Assets	2,010,000	1,627,500
Accumulated Depreciation	426,750	363,750
Net Plant & Equipment	1,583,250	1,263,750
Total Assets	**$2,325,326**	**$1,904,250**
Liabilities & Owner's Equity		
Accounts Payable	378,750	217,500
Accrued Expenses	26,250	22,500
Total Current Liabilities	405,000	240,000
Long-term Debt	878,325	795,750
Total Liabilities	1,283,325	1,035,750
Common Stock ($1.00 par)	75,000	60,000
Additional Paid-in-Capital	518,250	406,500
Retained Earnings	448,751	402,000
Total Owner's Equity	1,042,001	868,500
Total Liab. & Owner's Equity	**$2,325,326**	**$1,904,250**

a. Recreate the income statement and balance sheet using formulas wherever possible. Each statement should be on a separate worksheet. Try to duplicate the formatting exactly.

b. On another worksheet, create a statement of cash flows for 2014. Do not enter any numbers directly on this worksheet. All formulas should be linked directly to the source on previous worksheets.

c. Using Excel's outlining feature, create an outline on the statement of cash flows that, when collapsed, shows only the subtotals for each section.

d. Suppose that sales were $2,850,000 in 2014 rather than $2,625,000. What is the 2014 net income and retained earnings?

e. Undo the changes from part d, and change the tax rate to 40%. What is the 2014 net income and retained earnings?

2. Using the data from the previous problem:

a. Create a common-size income statement for 2013 and 2014. This statement should be created on a separate worksheet with all formulas linked directly to the income statement.

b. Create a common-size balance sheet for 2013 and 2014. This statement should be created on a separate worksheet with all formulas linked directly to the balance sheet.

c. Create a common-size statement of cash flows for 2014 that can be switched between using sales and the 2013 cash balance in the denominator.

3. Download the file named "Chapter 2 Problem 3.xlsx" from the text support Web site. (www.cengage.com/finance/mayes)

a. Fill in the blanks on the financial statements for Winter Park Web Design with formulas. Some of the formulas will require links to data given in other worksheets in the workbook.

b. Create a common-size income statement and balance sheet using your answers from above. Using the techniques you have learned in this chapter, you should be able to do these statements in less than one minute with formatting that is identical to the original worksheets.

Internet Exercise

1. Choose your own company and repeat the analysis from Problems 1 and 2. You can get the data from MSN Money at http://money.msn.com/investing. To retrieve the data for your company, go to the Stocks area and enter the ticker symbol. Then, under Financials in the menu on the left side, choose the statement type.

   a. On the page that appears, click on the link for the Income Statement and copy the data to a new worksheet. Reformat the data so that it is more readable, and insert formulas in place of the numbers where possible.

   b. Repeat part a for the Balance Sheet.

   c. Create a common-size income statement and balance sheet based on the data from parts a and b.

| CHAPTER 3 | *The Cash Budget* |

After studying this chapter, you should be able to:

1. *Explain the purpose of the cash budget and how it differs from an income statement.*

2. *Calculate a firm's expected total cash collections and disbursements for a particular month.*

3. *Calculate a firm's expected ending cash balance and short-term borrowing needs.*

4. *Demonstrate how Excel can be used to determine the optimal timing of major cash expenditures.*

5. *Use the Scenario Manager to evaluate different assumptions in a model.*

6. *Use the debugging tools that Excel provides to find and fix errors in formulas.*

Of all the topics covered in this book, perhaps no other task benefits so much from the use of spreadsheets as the cash budget. As we'll see, the cash budget can be a complex document with many interrelated entries. Manually updating a cash budget, especially for a large firm, is not a chore for which one volunteers. However, once the initial cash budget is set up in a spreadsheet, updating and playing "what if" becomes very easy.

A *cash budget* is simply a listing of the firm's anticipated cash inflows and outflows over a specified period. Unlike a pro forma income statement (discussed in Chapter 5), the cash budget includes only actual cash flows. For example, depreciation expense (a noncash expense) does not appear on the cash budget, but principal payments on debt obligations (which are not on the income statement) do. Because of its emphasis on cash income and expenditures, the cash budget is particularly useful for planning short-term borrowing and the timing of expenditures. As with all budgets, another important benefit of the cash budget comes from reconciling actual after-the-fact cash flows with those from the forecast.

We'll see that a cash budget is composed of three parts:

1. The worksheet area, where we will do some preliminary calculations;

2. A listing of each of the cash inflows (collections) and outflows (disbursements); and

3. Calculation of the ending cash balance and short-term borrowing needs.

We are simplifying things somewhat. In reality, many of the given variables in this chapter would come from other budgets. For example, a firm would usually have at least a sales budget from which the sales forecasts are taken, a salary budget, a capital expenditure budget, and so on. All of these different budgets would be created before the final cash budget and require a great deal of thought and research. The cash budget worksheet would then pull values from those other budgeting worksheets.

Throughout the chapter, we will create a complete cash budget for June to September 2015 for Bithlo Barbecues, a small manufacturer of barbecue grills. The financial staff of the firm has compiled the following set of assumptions and forecasts to be used in the cash budgeting process:

1. Actual and expected sales through October are as given in Table 3-1 on page 75.

2. 40% of sales are for cash. Of the remaining 60% of sales, 75% is collected in the following month and 25% is collected two months after the sale.

3. Raw materials inventory purchases are equal to 50% of the following month's sales (e.g., June purchases are 50% of expected July sales). 60% of purchases are paid for in the month following the purchase, and the remainder are paid in the following month.

4. Wages are forecasted to be equal to 20% of expected sales.

5. Payments on leases for equipment are $10,000 per month.

6. Interest payments of $30,000 on long-term debt are due in June and September.

7. A $50,000 dividend will be paid to shareholders in June.

8. Tax prepayments of $25,000 will be paid in June and September.

9. $200,000 is scheduled to be paid in July for a capital investment, but management is flexible on the scheduling of this outlay.

10. Bithlo Barbecues must keep a minimum cash balance of $15,000 by agreement with its bank. Its cash balance at the end of May was $20,000.

The Worksheet Area

The worksheet area is not necessarily a part of the cash budget. However, it is useful because it summarizes some of the most important calculations in the budget. This section includes a breakdown of expected sales, collections on accounts receivable, and payments for materials (inventory) purchases. This section could, perhaps should, be included on a separate worksheet along with all of the assumptions. Alternatively, the values could be drawn from separate budget worksheets (e.g., the expected sales figure could be linked to the sales budget worksheet, which would include a sales forecast for each product line). It might also include some other preliminary calculations. Because our model is small, we will keep all of the assumptions and preliminary calculations on one worksheet.

Open a new workbook and rename Sheet1 to Cash Budget. Like any other financial statement, we begin the cash budget with the titles. In A1 enter: Bithlo Barbecues; in A2 type: Cash Budget; and in A3 enter: For the Period June to September 2015. Center these titles across columns A to I. Next, enter the names of the months from Exhibit 3-1 in C4:I4 using the AutoFill feature (see page 11).

EXHIBIT 3-1
CASH BUDGET HEADINGS

	A	B	C	D	E	F	G	H	I
1					Bithlo Barbecues				
2					Cash Budget				
3				For the Period June to September 2015					
4			April	May	June	July	August	September	October

Using Date Functions

As we will see, a cash budget spreadsheet is ideally suited for reuse in future budget cycles. After all, why should you recreate the entire worksheet just because the dates and numbers will be different in the future? With a little bit of planning, we can set up the worksheet to make it easy to use for future budgets.

Let's start by considering how we enter the dates into row 4. Instead of typing the names of the months, we can automate them with formulas. In particular, we would like to be able to change the date in C4 and have the other dates automatically update. To do so, we will need to use the **DATE** function in combination with the **YEAR**, **MONTH**, and **DAY** functions.

Recall that Excel treats dates as the number of days that have elapsed since January 1, 1900. The **DATE** function calculates the serial number for any date and is defined as:

DATE(*YEAR, MONTH, DAY*)

For example, enter the formula =Date(2015,2,4) into a blank cell (say, K4). This will return 42,039, which is the serial number for February 4, 2015. This number can be formatted using any built-in or custom date format to be displayed as a date instead of an integer. In fact, Excel will automatically apply the Short Date format to the result.

We can also reference a cell that contains a date and extract the year, month, or day using the appropriately named functions:

YEAR(*SERIAL_NUMBER*)

MONTH(*SERIAL_NUMBER*)

DAY(*SERIAL_NUMBER*)

In each case, *SERIAL_NUMBER* represents a date serial number. For example, type =Year(K4) into K5 and the result will be 2015. Similarly, =Month(K4) would return 2, and =Day(K4) would return 4.

With that as background, enter 4/1/2015 into C4. This is the date that will control the others. In D4 enter the formula: =DATE(YEAR(C4),MONTH(C4)+1,DAY(C4)). That formula looks at the date in the cell C4 and returns a date that is exactly one month later. Now copy the formula from D4 to E4:I4.

If you now change the date in C4, the others will update automatically. Note also that, because we are using dates instead of text, we can use these cells as the basis for calculations. For example, an entry in the budget might vary depending on the month of the year. We can now calculate that automatically so that it is always correct, no matter how the dates change. Now apply the custom number format "mmmm" to the values in C4:I4 so that only the month names are displayed.

Calculating Text Strings

It is often useful to calculate text results, just as we calculate numeric results. For example, it would be helpful if the heading in A3, which shows the relevant period for the cash budget, was updated when the date in C4 is changed. We can accomplish this by using string concatenation and the **TEXT** function.

Concatenation is the process of joining two or more text strings into one. Excel has a built-in function to perform this task:

CONCATENATE(*TEXT1, TEXT2, ...*)

but it is rarely used. Instead, the & operator is used because it performs the same task and is much more economical to type. For example, type Hello into K8 and World into K9. In

K10 enter the formula: =K8&" "&K9 and the result will be the string Hello World. Note that to produce a space between the words, we had to include an empty string.

The **TEXT** function takes a number (or the result of a formula) as an argument and converts it to text with a particular number format. It is defined as:

$$\text{TEXT}(\textit{VALUE, FORMAT\_TEXT})$$

where *VALUE* is the number and *FORMAT_TEXT* is a custom number format mask (see page 51).

Finally, enter the formula: ="For the Period "&TEXT(E4,"mmmm")&" to "&TEXT(H4,"mmmm yyyy") into A3. Now change the date in C4 a few times to understand how it works.

Sales and Collections

The starting point for a cash budget is the sales forecast. Many of the other forecasts in the cash budget are driven (at least indirectly) by this forecast. The sales forecast has been provided for us by Bithlo's marketing department in Table 3-1. In A5 enter the label Sales, and then copy the expected sales from the table into C5:I5 in your worksheet.

TABLE 3-1
BITHLO BARBECUES ACTUAL AND EXPECTED SALES FOR 2015[*]

Month	Sales
April	291,000
May	365,000
June	387,000
July	329,000
August	238,000
September	145,000
October	92,000

* April and May sales are actual.

Note that sales have a strong seasonal component. In this case, barbecuing is mostly a summer phenomenon, and we expect that sales will peak in June before falling dramatically in the fall and winter months. Such seasonality is important in many types of business: for example, sales in the fourth quarter (October to December) may be 30% or more of annual sales for many retailers.[1] Seasonal patterns must be included in your sales forecast if your cash budget is to be accurate.

At most firms, a portion of sales are made on credit. It is therefore important to know how quickly the sales can be collected. For Bithlo Barbecues, experience has shown that about 40% of its sales are cash and 60% are on credit. Of the 60% of sales made on credit, about 75% will be collected during the month following the sale and the remaining 25% will be collected two months after the sale. Therefore, 45% (= 0.60 × 0.75) of total sales will be collected in the following month, and 15% (= 0.60 × 0.25) will be collected in two months.[2]

Our goal is to determine the total collections in each month. In A6 type: Collections:, and then in A7 enter the label: Cash. This will indicate the cash sales for the month. In A8 enter: First Month to indicate collections from the sales made in the previous month. In A9 enter: Second Month to indicate collections on sales made two months earlier. Because our estimates of the collection percentages may change, it is important that they not be entered directly into formulas. Instead, enter these percentages in B7:B9.

Because the budget is for June to September, we will begin our estimates of collections in E7. (April and May sales are included here only because we need to reference sales from the two previous months to determine the collections from credit sales.) To calculate the cash collections for June, we multiply the expected June sales by the percentage of cash sales, so enter: =E5*$B7 into E7. To calculate collections from cash sales for the other months, simply copy this formula to F7:H7.

Collections on credit sales can be calculated similarly. In E8, we will calculate June collections from May sales with the formula: =D5*$B8. Copy this formula to F8:H8. Finally, collections from sales two months ago, in E9, can be calculated with the formula: =C5*$B9. After copying this formula to F9:H9, calculate the total collections in row 10 for each month by using the **SUM** function. Check your numbers against those in Exhibit 3-2 and format your worksheet to match. This is a good time to save your workbook.

Purchases and Payments

In this section of the worksheet area, we calculate the payments made for inventory purchases. Bithlo Barbecues purchases inventory (equal to 50% of sales) the month before the sale is made. For example, June inventory purchases will be 50% of expected July sales. However, it does not pay for the inventory immediately. Instead, 60% of the purchase price is paid in the following month, and the other 40% is paid two months after the purchase.

---

1. As an example, at Target Corp. fourth-quarter revenues averaged 31.10% of full year sales in the years 2004 to 2013. The comparable first-quarter average was only 22.71%.
2. For simplicity, we assume that 100% of sales will be collected. Most firms would include an allowance for "bad debts" or returns based on historical patterns.

EXHIBIT 3-2
CALCULATING COLLECTIONS AND PAYMENTS IN THE WORKSHEET AREA

	A	B	C	D	E	F	G	H
1				Bithlo Barbecues				
2				Cash Budget				
3			For the Period June to September 2015					
4			April	May	June	July	August	September
5	Sales		291,000	365,000	387,000	329,000	238,000	145,000
6	*Collections:*							
7	Cash	40%			154,800	131,600	95,200	58,000
8	First Month	45%			164,250	174,150	148,050	107,100
9	Second Month	15%			43,650	54,750	58,050	49,350
10	**Total Collections**				**362,700**	**360,500**	**301,300**	**214,450**
11	Purchases	50%	182,500	193,500	164,500	119,000	72,500	46,000
12	*Payments:*							
13	First Month	60%			116,100	98,700	71,400	43,500
14	Second Month	40%			73,000	77,400	65,800	47,600
15	**Total Payments**				**189,100**	**176,100**	**137,200**	**91,100**

We first need to calculate the amount of inventory purchased in each month. As noted, this is 50% of the following month's sales. So in A11 type: Purchases and in B11 enter: 50%. We will calculate April purchases in C11 with the formula: =$B11*D5. Copying this formula to D11:H11 completes the calculation of purchases.

Credit purchases are not cash outflows, so we need to calculate the actual cash payments for inventory in each month. This is very similar to the way we calculated total cash collections. First, enter labels. In A12 type: Payments:. In A13 and A14 enter: First Month and Second Month, respectively, and enter: Total Payments in A15. Now enter 60% in B13 and 40% in B14. In June, Bithlo Barbecues will pay for 60% of purchases made in May, so the formula in E13 is: =$B13*D11. Copy this to F13:H13 to complete the first month's payments. To calculate the June payment for April purchases in E14, use the formula: =$B14*C11. Copy this to F14:H14 and then calculate the total payments for each month in row 15.

At this point, your worksheet should look like the one in Exhibit 3-2. Check your numbers carefully to make sure that they agree with those in the exhibit. To clarify the logic of these formulas, examine Exhibit 3-3, which is the same as Exhibit 3-2, except it has arrows drawn in to show the references for June.

Because this portion of the cash budget contains only preliminary calculations, it isn't necessary that it be visible at all times. Therefore, we can hide it using Excel's group and outline feature as discussed on page 62. Select rows 5:16 and then go to the Data tab. In the

EXHIBIT 3-3
THE WORKSHEET AREA OF A CASH BUDGET

	A	B	C	D	E	F	G	H
1				Bithlo Barbecues				
2				Cash Budget				
3				For the Period June to September 2015				
4			April	May	June	July	August	September
5	Sales		291,000	365,000	387,000	329,000	238,000	145,000
6	Collections:							
7	Cash	40%			154,800	131,600	95,200	58,000
8	First Month	45%			164,250	174,150	148,050	107,100
9	Second Month	15%			43,650	54,750	58,050	49,350
10	Total Collections				362,700	360,500	301,300	214,450
11	Purchases	50%	182,500	193,500	164,500	119,000	72,500	46,000
12	Payments:							
13	First Month	60%			116,100	98,700	71,400	43,500
14	Second Month	40%			73,000	77,400	65,800	47,600
15	Total Payments				189,100	176,100	137,200	91,100

Outline group, click the upper portion of the Group button and then collapse the outline. When it is necessary to view this area we can simply expand the outline.

↳ Collections and Disbursements

This section of the cash budget is the easiest to set up in a spreadsheet because there are no complex relationships between the cells as there are in the worksheet area. The collections and disbursements area is very much like a cash-based income statement. However, note that there are no noncash expenses listed, and certain items (e.g., principal payments) that are not on the income statement will be on the cash budget. We need to list all of the actual cash flows that are expected for each month, whether they are on the income statement or not.

We will begin by summarizing the cash collections for each month. Enter the label: Collections in A17. In E17:H17, the formulas simply reference the total collections that were calculated in E10:H10. So, for example, the formula in E17 is: =E10. Copy this formula to F17:H17. Had there been other cash inflows expected, for example proceeds from a loan, then they would also be listed in this section.

In A18, enter the label: Less Disbursements:. The first cash outflow that we will enter is the inventory payment, which was calculated in the worksheet area. Enter Inventory Payments as the label in A19 and the formula in E19 is: =E15. Wages are assumed to be equal to 20% of sales. In A20 add the label: Wages and in B20 type: 20%, which will be

EXHIBIT 3-4
COLLECTIONS AND DISBURSEMENTS

	A	B	C	D	E	F	G	H
1				Bithlo Barbecues				
2				Cash Budget				
3				For the Period June to September 2015				
4			April	May	June	July	August	September
17	Collections				362,700	360,500	301,300	214,450
18	*Less Disbursements:*							
19	Inventory Payments				189,100	176,100	137,200	91,100
20	Wages	20%			77,400	65,800	47,600	29,000
21	Lease Payment				10,000	10,000	10,000	10,000
22	Interest				30,000	0	0	30,000
23	Dividend (Common)				50,000	0	0	0
24	Taxes				25,000	0	0	25,000
25	Capital Outlays				0	200,000	0	0
26	**Total Disbursements**				**381,500**	**451,900**	**194,800**	**185,100**

used to calculate the expected monthly wage expense. The formula to calculate wages in E20 is: =$B20*E5. Now copy these formulas to F20:H20. By now, you should be able to finish this section by entering the remaining labels and numbers as pictured in Exhibit 3-4.

There are a couple of points to note about this portion of the cash budget. First, we have assumed that the only cash inflows are from selling the firm's products. In other cases, however, it is possible that the firm might plan to sell some assets or bonds or stock. Any of these actions would bring cash into the firm and should be included under collections.

Second, we have included dividend payments, which do not appear on the income statement, on row 23. The reason that they are on the cash budget is that dividends represent a very real cash expenditure for the firm. They don't appear on the income statement because dividends are paid from after-tax dollars. In other problems, there may be other similar outlays, such as a principal payment to be made on a loan. Remember, the cash budget is not an income statement. For the cash budget, we do not use accrual accounting; we include all cash inflows and outflows when they are expected to occur, whether they will be on the income statement or not.

Finally, Bithlo Barbecues has scheduled capital outlays of $200,000 in July. Even though they are paying the full cost in July, it is unlikely that they would be allowed to expense this entire amount during 2015. Instead, the income statement would reflect the depreciation of these assets over a longer period of time. Regardless of tax laws or accounting conventions, it is important to include all expected cash inflows and outflows on the cash budget when they are scheduled to occur.

Calculating the Ending Cash Balance

This last section of the cash budget calculates the expected ending cash balance at the end of each month. This is an important part of the cash budget because it helps the manager understand how the firm's cash balance will fluctuate and thus its short-term borrowing needs. Knowing the borrowing requirements in advance allows managers to arrange for financing before they need it and provides the time necessary to evaluate possible alternatives. Managers can also use this information to determine the best timing for major expenditures.

TABLE 3-2
CALCULATING THE ENDING CASH BALANCE

	Beginning Cash Balance
+	Total Collections
−	Total Disbursements
=	Unadjusted Cash Balance
+	Current Borrowing
=	Ending Cash Balance

Table 3-2 shows the series of calculations necessary to determine the firm's ending cash balance. Essentially, this is the same procedure we saw in Table 2-2 on page 58 with the addition of short-term borrowing. In the next section we will add a few steps to this calculation, but the basic procedure is always as outlined in Table 3-2.

We have already made most of the calculations necessary to complete the cash budget. Before we finish this last section, however, we need to add another detail. The management of Bithlo Barbecues has decided that they would like to keep a minimum cash balance of $15,000 to meet any unexpected expenses. If the projected cash balance falls below this amount, they will need to borrow to bring the balance back to this minimum. In A32 enter the label: Notes:. We will use cells below A32 to list important assumptions about our cash budget. The first of these is the minimum cash balance requirement. In A33 enter the label: Minimum Acceptable Cash and in B33 enter: 15,000.

In cells A27:A31 enter the labels as shown in Exhibit 3-5. (Notice that this is exactly the same as was outlined in Table 3-2.) We start with the ending cash balance in May. Enter: 20,000 into D31. The ending cash balance for the month is simply the unadjusted cash balance plus current borrowing, so the formula in E31 is: =SUM(E29:E30). This formula will be the same for each month, so copy it across to F31:H31.

EXHIBIT 3-5
ENDING CASH BALANCE CALCULATION

	A	B	C	D	E	F	G	H
1				Bithlo Barbecues				
2				Cash Budget				
3				For the Period June to September 2015				
4			April	May	June	July	August	September
27	Beginning Cash Balance				20,000	15,000	15,000	121,500
28	Collections - Disbursements				(18,800)	(91,400)	106,500	29,350
29	Unadjusted Cash Balance				1,200	(76,400)	121,500	150,850
30	Current Borrowing				13,800	91,400	0	0
31	**Ending Cash Balance**			20,000	15,000	15,000	121,500	150,850
32	Notes:							
33	Minimum Acceptable Cash	15,000						

The beginning cash balance for any month is the same as the ending cash balance from the previous month. Therefore, we can simply reference the previous month's ending cash balance calculation. In E27 enter the formula: =D31 and copy this across to F27:H27. At this point, your beginning cash balance for each month, except for June, will be 0 because we have not yet entered any formulas in E28:H30.

Because we have already calculated the total collections and total disbursements, there is no need to have separate rows for those calculations in this section. Instead, we will calculate the net collections for June in E28 with the formula: =E17-E26. Copy this formula to F28:H28. For June, the result is −$18,800, which indicates that the firm expects to spend more than it will collect. In other words, the cash balance is expected to decline by $18,800 in June. This decline will be reflected in the unadjusted cash balance.

The unadjusted cash balance is what the cash balance would be if the firm did not have any short-term borrowing during the month. We add the beginning cash balance and the net collections for the month. The formula in E29 is: =SUM(E27:E28). The result is $1,200, which is less than the firm's minimum acceptable cash balance of $15,000. Therefore, Bithlo Barbecues will need to borrow $13,800 to bring the balance up to this minimum.

How did we determine that the firm needs to borrow $13,800? It is probably obvious to you, even without giving it much thought. However, you need to think it through carefully to create a formula that will work under all circumstances. We could use the following equation:

$$\text{Current Borrowing} = \text{Minimum Cash} - \text{Unadjusted Cash} \tag{3-1}$$

In this case we find that Bithlo Barbecues needs to borrow:

$$\$13,800 = \$15,000 - \$1,200$$

Equation (3-1) works in this case, but it is not appropriate in all circumstances. Suppose, for example, that the unadjusted cash balance had been $20,000. This would suggest that the firm needs to borrow –$5,000, which is absurd.[3] In a case such as this, we would like to see current borrowing at 0.

The calculation that we need can be stated as follows: "**If** the unadjusted cash balance is less than the minimum, **then** we borrow an amount equal to minimum cash – unadjusted cash. **Otherwise**, current borrowing is zero." With the formulas that we have used so far, this type of calculation is impossible. However, Excel has a built-in function that can handle situations where the result depends on some condition—the **I**F statement.

The **I**F statement returns one of two values, depending on whether a statement is true or false:

$$\textbf{\textit{I}}\text{F} \ (\textit{\textbf{LOGICAL\_TEST}}, \ \textit{\textbf{VALUE\_IF\_TRUE}}, \ \textit{VALUE\_IF\_FALSE})$$

LOGICAL_TEST is any statement that can be evaluated as being either true or false (i.e., boolean), and **VALUE_IF_TRUE** and *VALUE_IF_FALSE* are the return values that depend on whether **LOGICAL_TEST** was true or false. If you are familiar with computer programming, you will recognize this as the equivalent of the If–Then–Else construct that is supported by most programming languages.

The formula to calculate the firm's borrowing needs for June, in E30, is: `=IF(E29<=$B33,$B33-E29,0)`. Because the unadjusted cash balance is only $1,200, the result should indicate the need to borrow $13,800 as we found earlier. Copy this formula to F30:H30 to complete the calculation of current borrowing. Notice that, because of large positive net collections, the firm does not need to borrow funds in August or September.

We have already entered formulas for the ending cash balance in each month. You should now check your numbers and formatting against those in Exhibit 3-5.

Repaying Short-Term Borrowing

In the previous section, we calculated the amount that the firm needs to borrow each month, but it wasn't repaid when excess cash was available. For example, in August the firm is expecting to have a large unadjusted cash balance that could be used to reduce the loan balance. It should be obvious that keeping the outstanding short-term loan balance as small as possible is a good idea.

---

3. Unless, of course, you assume that negative borrowing is the same as investing. But we will consider investing excess funds in the next section.

Before altering our formulas to account for loan repayment, we need to know the cumulative outstanding loan balance at the end of each month. Select row 32 and insert a row. In A32 enter the label: Cumulative Borrowing. In D32 enter the formula: =C32+D30, which determines the cumulative loan balance by adding the previous balance to any new borrowing during the month. Copy this formula across E32:H32.

We can now change the formula in E30 so that it incorporates repayment. Note that the *VALUE_IF_FALSE* part of the formula was set to 0 if the firm doesn't need to borrow. This is where we will calculate the amount to repay whenever there is excess cash.

Look at the unadjusted cash balance for August in Exhibit 3-5. This is the first month in which the firm has a short-term loan balance and also excess cash. How much can they afford to pay back without going below the minimum cash balance? Obviously, they can repay the entire $105,200. However, we can't just assume that repaying the entire loan will always be the correct decision as that will sometimes leave the firm with a cash balance below the minimum, or negative. Instead, we need to figure out which is smaller: the loan balance or the amount of excess cash. In order to do this we will use the **MIN** function, which returns the smallest of the arguments and is defined as:

$$\text{MIN}(\textit{NUMBER1, NUMBER2, ...})$$

In E30 our new formula is: =IF(E29<=$B34,$B34-E29,-MIN(D32,E29-$B$34)). Note that the second part of the IF statement will be triggered only if there is excess cash available, and that it will never overpay the loan. That is, Current Borrowing will be 0 whenever there is excess cash without a loan balance.

At this point, the managers of Bithlo Barbecues know that they will need to arrange to borrow $13,800 before June and $91,400 before July. It is also obvious that they will have enough cash to pay off these borrowings in August. Your worksheet should look like the one in Exhibit 3-6.

Using the Cash Budget for What-If Analysis

Besides being useful for planning the firm's short-term borrowing needs, the cash budget can be useful in timing collections and expenditures. For example, suppose that the firm is concerned about the amount of borrowing that will be necessary in June and July. What we may want to do is to see what happens if we make certain changes in our assumptions.

EXHIBIT 3-6
A COMPLETED SIMPLE CASH BUDGET

	A	B	C	D	E	F	G	H
1				Bithlo Barbecues				
2				Cash Budget				
3				For the Period June to September 2015				
4				April	May	June	July	August	September
17	Collections					362,700	360,500	301,300	214,450
18	*Less Disbursements:*								
19	Inventory Payments					189,100	176,100	137,200	91,100
20	Wages	20%				77,400	65,800	47,600	29,000
21	Lease Payment					10,000	10,000	10,000	10,000
22	Interest					30,000	0	0	30,000
23	Dividend (Common)					50,000	0	0	0
24	Taxes					25,000	0	0	25,000
25	Capital Outlays					0	200,000	0	0
26	**Total Disbursements**					381,500	451,900	194,800	185,100
27	Beginning Cash Balance					20,000	15,000	15,000	16,300
28	Collections - Disbursements					(18,800)	(91,400)	106,500	29,350
29	Unadjusted Cash Balance					1,200	(76,400)	121,500	45,650
30	Current Borrowing					13,800	91,400	(105,200)	0
31	**Ending Cash Balance**			20,000	15,000	15,000	16,300	45,650
32	Cumulative Borrowing			0	13,800	105,200	0	0

One way that the firm may be able to reduce borrowing needs is to try to speed up collections on sales and to slow down the payments for inventory purchases (it will effectively be borrowing from suppliers instead of the bank). Suppose that the firm is able to collect 50% of sales during the first month, thereby reducing collections in the second month to 10%. Furthermore, assume that it can slow down its payments for inventory purchases to 50% in the first month after the purchase instead of the current 60%.

Change B8 to 50%, B9 to 10%, B13 to 50%, and B14 to 50%. You will see that borrowing will fall in June to $9,000 from $13,800. Borrowing in July will rise to $93,200 from $91,400. Therefore, the total amount of borrowing will decrease from the original $105,800 to $102,200. This has two benefits: It reduces the interest cost of borrowing (which we will consider in the next section), and it shifts that interest expense to a later point in time. Of course, there may also be an opportunity cost in the form of lost discounts due to paying suppliers later, and customers may go to competitors who offer better credit terms. Before moving on, make sure to change the percentages back to their original values.

As another example, consider Bithlo Barbecues' $200,000 capital expenditure currently planned for July 2015. This expenditure is the primary cause of the borrowing needed in July. Indeed, without this $200,000 outlay, the firm wouldn't need to borrow in July.

Assuming that there is some flexibility in scheduling this outlay, in which month should the expenditure be made? The answer, of course, depends on a number of factors, but we might decide to make the decision based on minimizing borrowing needs. That is, schedule the project such that the firm's short-term borrowing needs are minimized. This might be especially important if the firm expected borrowing needs in excess of its line of credit in a given month.

You can experiment a bit by changing the month in which the capital expenditure is made. First, however, it would be helpful to know the maximum expected borrowing for the four-month period. To do this we can make use of the **MAX** function, which is similar to **MIN** except that it returns the largest of the arguments:

$$\text{MAX}(NUMBER1, \ NUMBER2, \ \dots)$$

In J32, enter the formula: =MAX(D32:H32) to calculate maximum borrowing. Now, by moving the capital expenditure to different months, you should be able to verify the numbers in Table 3-3.

TABLE 3-3
OPTIMAL SCHEDULING FOR A CAPITAL EXPENDITURE

Month of Outlay	Total Four-Month Borrowing
June	$213,800
July	105,200
August	13,800
September	13,800

Obviously, by this criteria, the best time to schedule the outlay would be in either August or September. Before continuing, be sure to move the $200,000 outlay back to July.

The Scenario Manager

In the previous section, we performed what has come to be called a "What if?" analysis. That is, we changed the timing of the large capital expenditure to see what would happen to the total amount of borrowing for the period. The problem with doing it "by hand" as we did is that you lose the original results of your analysis after it is done. Also, every person who looks at your spreadsheet will need to perform that same analysis. Excel provides a better way—the Scenario Manager.

This tool allows us to store several scenarios (alternative input variables) in the spreadsheet and to display them at will. Once the scenario inputs are defined, we simply select a scenario from the list and Excel will enter the appropriate numbers into the spreadsheet and recalculate. Figure 3-1 shows the Scenario Manager dialog box before any scenarios have been created.

FIGURE 3-1
SCENARIO MANAGER DIALOG BOX WITH NO SCENARIOS DEFINED

What-If
Analysis ▾

To launch this tool, go to the Data tab. In the Data Tools group, click the What-If Analysis button and then choose **S**cenario Manager. When the dialog box is displayed, we can create our four scenarios. To begin, click the **A**dd button. In the next dialog box enter: Expenditure in June for the Scenario **n**ame. The Changing **c**ells are those cells that will contain different numbers under each scenario. In this case, they will be the capital outlay for each month, so enter: E25:H25 and click the OK button.

You will now be prompted to enter values for each of the changing cells for this scenario. Because our first scenario calls for the expenditure to be made in June, enter 200000 in the first box and 0 in each of the others. The Scenario Values dialog box should look like that in Figure 3-2.

FIGURE 3-2
SCENARIO VALUES DIALOG BOX FOR JUNE EXPENDITURE

Click the **A**dd button to create the next scenario. Repeat these steps until you have four scenarios with the expenditure occurring in different months.

Note that the Scenario Values dialog box prompts you for values by using the cell addresses as labels. That can be confusing, especially if the cells are not visible on the screen. One way to make this situation better is to use defined names for the cells, as was discussed in Chapter 1 (page 9). Close the Scenario Manager and then select E25. On the Formulas tab, click the Define Name button. Now, type June in the **N**ame edit box. Select the worksheet name from the **S**cope drop-down list to limit this name to this worksheet and then click the OK button. Name the other cells similarly. Launch the Scenario Manager and select the "Expenditure in June" scenario. Click the **E**dit button, then the OK button on the Edit Scenario dialog, and your Scenario Values dialog box should look like the one in Figure 3-3.

▤ Define Name ▾

FIGURE 3-3
SCENARIO VALUES DIALOG BOX WITH DEFINED NAMES

Many of the other tools supplied with Excel work with range names in a similar way. This is a useful trick to remember as it can simplify entering data. As we will see shortly, using range names will also improve the Scenario Summary sheets. After creating your scenarios, the Scenario Manager dialog box will look like the one in Figure 3-4.

FIGURE 3-4
SCENARIO MANAGER DIALOG BOX WITH FOUR SCENARIOS

To display a particular scenario, simply select it from the list and click the **S**how button. Excel will alter the contents of your changing cells to reflect the values that you entered. Of course, the entire worksheet will be recalculated and you can see the results of the selected scenario. Note that to be able to scroll around and see the entire worksheet you must click the Close button on the Scenario Manager dialog box. Take a look at the results of each scenario, but remember to reset the scenario to "Expenditure in July" (our default case) before continuing. If you forget to reset to the default scenario, Excel will always display the last chosen scenario. This can cause confusion when you later open your workbook.

Being able to quickly change between scenarios is quite helpful, but the real advantage of the Scenario Manager is its ability to summarize the results of all of your scenarios. In this case, we would like to compare the total borrowing that results under each scenario to determine the best time for the expenditure. Recall that we added a formula in J32 to calculate the maximum borrowing for the period. Before continuing, define a name for this cell such as "Max_Borrowing." (Remember that we use the underscore in place of a space because spaces are not allowed in range names.)

Return to the Scenario Manager and click on the S**u**mmary button. You will be asked to enter **R**esult cells. A result cell is a cell (or several cells) that shows the end result of each scenario. In this case, we are interested in maximum borrowing, so enter: J32 as the **R**esult cell and click the OK button. Excel will now create a new worksheet that summarizes your scenario results. For our scenarios, the results are in Exhibit 3-7. Note that these results are exactly the same as those in Table 3-3.

EXHIBIT 3-7
SCENARIO SUMMARY

	A	B	C	D	E	F	G	H
1								
2		Scenario Summary						
3				Current Values:	Expenditure in June	Expenditure in July	Expenditure in August	Expenditure in September
5		Changing Cells:						
6		June		0	200,000	0	0	0
7		July		200,000	0	200,000	0	0
8		August		0	0	0	200,000	0
9		September		0	0	0	0	200,000
10		Result Cells:						
11		Max_Borrowing		105,200	213,800	105,200	13,800	13,800
12		Notes: Current Values column represents values of changing cells at						
13		time Scenario Summary Report was created. Changing cells for each						
14		scenario are highlighted in gray.						

Column D contains the values that were active when the scenario summary was created. In most cases that will just be a repeat of one of the existing scenarios. It is a good practice to make sure that one of your scenarios reflects the default assumptions so that you can return to the defaults easily. In this example, the numbers in columns D and F are identical, so column D can be safely deleted.

Adding Interest and Investment of Excess Cash

In the previous section you created a basic cash budget for Bithlo Barbecues. In this section we will refine the calculation of the ending cash balance by considering two additional factors. First, we will add interest payments on borrowed funds and then we will consider the investment of excess cash.

Before beginning, let's create a copy of the previous cash budget in the same workbook. Right-click the sheet tab labeled "Cash Budget" and select **M**ove or Copy… from the menu. In the dialog box make sure to check the box labeled **C**reate a copy and select "(move to end)" from the list. The copied sheet will now be named Cash Budget (2). Right-click the sheet tab and rename the new sheet to Complex Cash Budget.

Next, we will need to make a few additions to the notes at the bottom of the worksheet. We will now assume that Bithlo Barbecues will invest any cash in excess of $40,000. In A35 add the label: Maximum Acceptable Cash and in B35 enter: 40,000. Furthermore, the firm will have to pay interest on its short-term borrowings and will earn interest on invested funds. In A36 type: Borrowing Rate (Annual) and in B36 enter: 8%. In A37 add the label: Lending Rate (Annual) and enter: 6% in B37.

Because we are working with monthly time periods, we need to convert these annual rates into monthly rates of interest. So, in C36 and C37 enter the label: Monthly. We will convert the annual rate to a monthly rate by dividing by 12. In D36 enter the formula: =B36/12, and copy this to D37.[4] You should see that the monthly borrowing rate is 0.67%, and the monthly lending rate is 0.50%.

Insert

We are now ready to expand the cash budget to include investing and the interest expense and income. Before entering any new formulas we need to insert a few new rows. Select row 23 (the dividend), and then click the upper half of the Insert button on the Home tab. This will insert a row above the selection. In A23 enter the label: Short-Term Interest Expense (Inc.). Next, select row 32 (the ending cash balance), insert a row, and enter: Current Investing into A32. Finally, select row 35 and insert a row. In A34 change the label to: Cumulative Borrowing (Investing) and in A35 type: Cumulative Interest Expense (Inc.). We need to keep track of the cumulative amount that is borrowed/invested so that we can calculate the monthly short-term interest expense/income.

We will enter the formula to calculate the cumulative amount of borrowing (investing) in D34. Positive amounts will represent borrowing, while negative numbers will represent investing. To calculate the *cumulative* amount, add the previous period's cumulative amount to current borrowing and subtract current investing. For May, in D34, the formula is: =C34+D31-D32, and the result should be 0. Copy this formula to E34:H34. Note that at this point the result for each month should be equal to the cumulative current borrowing.

Short-term interest expense (income) can now be calculated by multiplying the cumulative amount of borrowing (investing) from the previous month by the appropriate interest rate. So, in E23 we will use an **IF** statement to determine which rate to use. If the cumulative amount of borrowing (investing) is positive, we will multiply it by the borrowing rate. Otherwise, use the lending rate. The formula for June, E23, is: =IF(D34>0,D34* $D$39,D34*$D$40). For June, because the firm has not had previous borrowing or lending, the result should be 0. Copy this across to F23:H23.

We can now calculate the cumulative interest expense (income) in E35. To do this, we simply add the previous month's interest expense (income) to the current month's interest expense (income). For June, the formula is: =D35+E23. This formula should be copied across to F35:H35. The only purpose of this row is to help evaluate the results of a scenario that we will examine later. At this point, your worksheet should resemble the one in Exhibit 3-8.

---

4. Entering the 12 into the denominator might seem to violate our prohibition on entering numbers into formulas. However, there will always be 12 months in a year, so this number will never change.

EXHIBIT 3-8
THE WORKSHEET WITH INTEREST CALCULATIONS

	A	B	C	D	E	F	G	H
1				Bithlo Barbecues				
2				Cash Budget				
3				For the Period June to September 2015				
4				April	May	June	July	August	September
17	Collections					362,700	360,500	301,300	214,450
18	Less Disbursements:								
19	Inventory Payments					189,100	176,100	137,200	91,100
20	Wages	20%				77,400	65,800	47,600	29,000
21	Lease Payment					10,000	10,000	10,000	10,000
22	Interest					30,000	0	0	30,000
23	Short-term Interest Expense (Inc.)					0	92	702	0
24	Dividend (Common)					50,000	0	0	0
25	Taxes					25,000	0	0	25,000
26	Capital Outlays					0	200,000	0	0
27	**Total Disbursements**					**381,500**	**451,992**	**195,502**	**185,100**
28	Beginning Cash Balance					20,000	15,000	15,000	15,506
29	Collections - Disbursements					(18,800)	(91,492)	105,798	29,350
30	Unadjusted Cash Balance					1,200	(76,492)	120,798	44,856
31	Current Borrowing					13,800	91,492	(105,292)	0
32	Current Investing								
33	**Ending Cash Balance**				20,000	15,000	15,000	15,506	44,856
34	Cumulative Borrowing (Investing)				0	13,800	105,292	0	0
35	Cumulative Interest Expense (Inc.)				0		92	794	794
36	Notes:								
37	Minimum Acceptable Cash	15,000							
38	Maximum Acceptable Cash	40,000							
39	Borrowing Rate (Annual)	8%	Monthly	0.67%					
40	Lending Rate (Annual)	6%	Monthly	0.50%					

Calculating Current Borrowing

Determining the amount of current borrowing and current investing is the most complex part of this cash budget. We have already calculated current borrowing, but because we are now considering investments and interest, the formula will need to be changed. For current borrowing, the logic can be explained this way: "If the unadjusted cash balance is less than the minimum acceptable cash, then borrow enough to bring the balance to the minimum. However, if the firm has some investments, reduce the amount of borrowing by the amount of the investments (or total borrowing needs, whichever is less). If the unadjusted cash balance is greater than the minimum and the firm has previous borrowing, then use the cash above the minimum to reduce the outstanding borrowing." Writing a formula to implement this logic is complex, and it should be built in small pieces. After each piece, verify the result and then add on the next piece.

Writing this formula requires the use of nested **IF** statements. That is, we embed additional **IF** statements within the first. In pseudocode this is:

If Unadjusted Cash < Minimum Cash then {Firm needs to raise funds}
    If Cumulative Borrowing (Investing) < 0 then {Firm has investments it can sell}
        Current Borrowing = Max(Minimum Cash + Cumulative Borrowing (Investing) – Unadjusted Cash, 0)
    Else Current Borrowing = Minimum Cash – Unadjusted Cash {Must Borrow it all}
Else {Firm doesn't need to raise funds}
    If Cumulative Borrowing (Investing) > 0 then {Use excess funds to reduce previous borrowings}
        Current Borrowing = –Min(Cumulative Borrowing (Investing), Unadjusted Cash – Minimum Cash)
    Else Current Borrowing = 0
End If

The formula to calculate current borrowing in June, E31, is:
`=IF(E30<$B$37,IF(D34<0,MAX($B$37+D34-E30,0),$B$37-E30),` `IF(D34>0,-MIN(D34,E30-$B$37),0))`. Type this formula carefully, and then copy it to F31:H31. Note that we have also used the built-in **MAX** and **MIN** functions as discussed earlier in the chapter. In this formula, the **MAX** function is required to be sure that we don't end up with negative borrowing if the investments are more than sufficient to cover cash needs (i.e., we don't want to sell all of the investments if we don't need to). The **MIN** function is used when the firm has excess cash and has some outstanding loans to pay off. It finds the minimum of either (1) the cumulative amount of borrowing outstanding or (2) the difference between the unadjusted cash balance and the minimum acceptable cash balance. Note that we had to negate the result of the **MIN** function in order to get the correct result.

Using the Formula Auditing Tools to Avoid Errors

Sometimes the logic you need to solve a problem can get a bit complicated, as above. It is important to carefully think it through and build your formulas one small piece at a time. In this way we can slowly build up to a large, complex formula that always works. That's exactly how the above formula was created. However, no matter how careful you are in building a complex formula there is always the possibility of errors creeping in. Fortunately, there are several ways to identify these errors before they become serious problems (i.e., cost you or your company real money).

One of the best ways to avoid errors is to thoroughly test your formulas. The easiest way to do this is to change some numbers that the formula depends on and make sure that you are still getting correct answers. For example, we might temporarily change our ending cash balance in May. Then, carefully work through the ending cash balance calculations to make sure that they are working correctly.

Finding errors in the first version of a complex formula is very common. Fortunately, Excel provides several tools to help find and correct the cause. In the following subsections, we will take a short detour from our example to discuss these tools.

Using the F9 Function Key

One of Excel's first, most useful, and probably least known debugging tools is the F9 function key. Normally, pressing F9 causes a worksheet to recalculate, but when you use it in the formula bar it shows the contents of a cell address or the result of a calculation. For example, select E31 and highlight the first condition in the **IF** statement as shown in Figure 3-5.

FIGURE 3-5
USING THE F9 KEY IN THE FORMULA BAR

Before pressing the F9 key:

| × | ✓ | *fx* | =IF(E30<$B$37,IF(D34<0,MAX($B$37+D34-E30,0),$B$37-E30),IF(D34>0,-MIN(D34,E30-$B$37),0)) | ∨ |

After pressing F9 we see that the condition is true:

| × | ✓ | *fx* | =IF(TRUE,IF(D34<0,MAX($B$37+D34-E30,0),$B$37-E30),IF(D34>0,-MIN(D34,E30-$B$37),0)) | ∨ |

When you press F9, Excel evaluates the expression "E30<$B$37" and then reports that the result is true (E30 is, in fact, less than B37). Note that we also could have highlighted just the "E30" part of this expression and, after pressing F9, Excel would show that the value in E30 is equal to 1,200. Now, applying the same technique to the other part of the expression would show that B37 is equal to 15,000. At this point, the first part of the formula would show as "1200<15000" which is obviously true. This technique is very useful for checking parts of a formula to make sure they are accurate.

One important caveat is that if you now press Enter to return to the worksheet, your formula will be changed to include the results instead of reverting to the cell addresses. It is crucial to press the Esc key rather than Enter in order to avoid locking in the changes you've made.

Color-Coded Cell Addresses

Another member of the error-checking toolkit is the use of color coding in formulas. When you create or edit a formula, Excel colors the cell addresses and highlights each of those cells in that same color. This makes it easy to see which cells are being used. If you notice that you've used an incorrect cell or range, you can grab the colored outline and expand, contract, or move it to another location. This will change the appropriate cell or range of cells in your formula.

Formula Auditing Tools

The tools in the Formula Auditing group help you to trace errors, step through a calculation sequence, and watch the result in one cell as you edit another. To access these tools, click the Formulas tab of the Ribbon and look for the group shown in Figure 3-6.

FIGURE 3-6
THE FORMULA AUDITING TOOLBAR

🔻 Trace Precedents   🔣 Show Formulas
🔻 Trace Dependents   ⚠ Error Checking ▾
🔻 Remove Arrows ▾   ⓕ Evaluate Formula

Formula Auditing

Tracing Precedent and Dependent Cells

The three buttons on the left side of the Formula Auditing group are for tracing precedent or dependent cells. A precedent cell is one upon which a formula depends, while a dependent cell is one that depends on the result of the formula in the active cell. If the active cell contains a formula, clicking Trace Precedents will display arrows from the precedent cells. The arrows in Exhibit 3-3 (page 78) were created in this way. The Trace Dependents icon works in the same way, except that the arrows point to dependent cells.

To remove all of the arrows click the Remove Arrows button, or save the file. Note that this button is also a drop-down list that allows you to remove only the precedent or dependent arrows.

Background Error Checking

Number Stored as Text
Convert to Number
Help on this error
Ignore Error
Edit in Formula Bar
Error Checking Options...

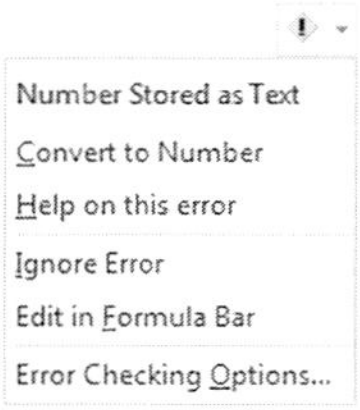

Unless this option is disabled, Excel will examine the worksheet for common types of errors as you work. If background error checking is on, a green triangle will appear in the upper left corner of the cell along with a Smart Tag that explains the error and offers a solution. Errors in logic cannot, of course, be detected, but it can identify many other types of errors.

Be aware that in some cases Excel will think that you've made an error when you have not. Don't automatically accept the proposed fix. If this happens repeatedly, you can tell Excel to stop checking for that type of error, or turn off background error checking completely. To change the error checking rules, go to the Formulas area in Options from the File tab.

The Watch Window

When working on a large worksheet, it is common to find yourself changing a value in one location and then scrolling to another to check the result. The Watch Window is a powerful tool that helps speed up formula debugging by letting you watch a distant cell without having to scroll to it. It even works with cells in other worksheets, but only in the same workbook. To activate this tool, click on the Watch Window button in the Formula Auditing group.

FIGURE 3-7
THE WATCH WINDOW

Once the Watch Window is displayed, you can choose one or more cells to watch by clicking the Add Watch button and choosing the cell. In Figure 3-7, we have selected E31. With this window displayed you can scroll to any part of the worksheet, change a cell value, and see what happens to E31. Note that if you close the Watch Window (or even save and close the workbook), the watch cells are not cleared. That allows you to open it again to continue watching the cell.

The Evaluate Formula Tool

Finally, perhaps the best feature for formula debugging is the Evaluate Formula tool. This tool lets you step through a formula piece by piece as Excel evaluates it. It works much like the F9 function key, except that it will step through the entire formula one step at a time. To activate this tool, click the Evaluate Formula button shown in Figure 3-6.

Figure 3-8 shows the Evaluate Formula dialog box with the formula in E31 ready to be evaluated. Note that E30 is underlined, indicating that it will be evaluated first. Simply click the **E**valuate button and "E30" will be replaced with "1200." Now, $B$37 will be underlined and ready to be evaluated. You can continue to click the **E**valuate button to work through the entire formula.

FIGURE 3-8
THE EVALUATE FORMULA TOOL

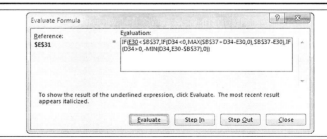

An additional feature is the Step **I**n function. For those expressions that themselves are the result of a formula, you can "step in" to the previous formula and evaluate it. For example, D34 is actually the result of the formula =C34+D31−D32. When D34 is underlined, clicking the Step In button will allow you to evaluate this formula and then return to evaluating the rest of the original formula.

One of the most difficult tasks in the process of building a spreadsheet model is making sure that it works correctly under all conditions. Using the tips and tools discussed here can make the job much simpler. Let's now return to our cash budgeting example.

Calculating Current Investing

If Bithlo Barbecues has cash in excess of the maximum ($40,000 in this case), then the excess cash should be invested in short-term securities. This is the essential idea behind the current investing item. Note that because we have added the Current Investing line, we must adjust our ending cash balance formula to take investing into account. The correct formula, in E33, is: =SUM(E30:E31)-E32. That is, our ending cash balance is now going to be the Unadjusted Cash Balance plus Current Borrowing minus Current Investing. (Investing is a cash outflow so it must be subtracted.) Copy this formula to F33:H33.

The current borrowing formula (page 92) was constructed so that the firm will first sell any existing short-term investments before borrowing. Therefore, if the sum of the unadjusted cash balance and current borrowing is less than the minimum required cash, the firm needs to sell some investments. Otherwise, if the unadjusted cash balance plus current borrowing is greater than the maximum acceptable cash, the firm must invest the excess.

To implement this logic we will again use nested **IF** statements. We also need to use the **AND** function, which allows us to evaluate several conditions instead of just one. This function will return true if, and only if, *all* of the arguments are true. If even one argument is false, then the function will return false.[5] The **AND** statement is defined as follows:

$$\text{AND}(LOGICAL1, LOGICAL2, ...)$$

In this function, *LOGICAL1*, *LOGICAL2*, and so on, are up to 255 arguments, each of which can be evaluated as true or false. We will use this function to determine if both of the following conditions are true: (1) unadjusted cash + current borrowing is less than the minimum cash, and (2) cumulative borrowing (investing) is negative (meaning that the firm has investments).

The formula that we will use to calculate the amount of current investing, in E32, is: =IF(AND(E30+E31<$B$37,D34<0),E30+E31-$B$37,IF(E30+E31>$B$38, E30+E31-$B$38,0)). Enter this formula and copy it across to F32:H32. Again, this is a complex formula, but it can be broken down into more understandable components:

---

5. Excel also has an **OR** function, which is defined similarly. However, it will return true when one, or more, of the arguments is true.

If Unadjusted Cash + Borrowing < Minimum Cash **AND** Cumulative Borrowing (Investing) < 0 then
    Current Investing = Unadjusted Cash + Borrowing – Minimum Cash
Else
    If Unadjusted Cash + Borrowing > Maximum Cash then
        Current Investing = Unadjusted Cash + Borrowing – Maximum Cash
    Else
        Current Investing = 0
End.

Your cash budget should now resemble that in Exhibit 3-9.

EXHIBIT 3-9
CALCULATING THE CASH BALANCE WITH BORROWING AND INVESTING

	A	B	C	D	E	F	G	H
1					Bithlo Barbecues			
2					Cash Budget			
3					For the Period June to September 2015			
4				April	May	June	July	August	September
28	Beginning Cash Balance				20,000	15,000	15,000	15,506
29	Collections - Disbursements				(18,800)	(91,492)	105,798	29,350
30	Unadjusted Cash Balance				1,200	(76,492)	120,798	44,856
31	Current Borrowing				13,800	91,492	(105,292)	0
32	Current Investing				0	0	0	4,856
33	**Ending Cash Balance**			20,000	15,000	15,000	15,506	40,000
34	Cumulative Borrowing (Investing)			0	13,800	105,292	0	(4,856)
35	Cumulative Interest Expense (Inc.)				0	92	794	794
36	Notes:							
37	Minimum Acceptable Cash	15,000						
38	Maximum Acceptable Cash	40,000						
39	Borrowing Rate (Annual)		8% Monthly	0.67%				
40	Lending Rate (Annual)		6% Monthly	0.50%				

Working Through the Example

In order to understand the complex cash budget, you must work through it line by line. In this section, we will do just that. Follow along in Exhibit 3-9.

June (column E): The unadjusted cash balance in June is projected to be only $1,200. Because this is less than the $15,000 minimum, the firm needs to raise funds. In this case it has no investments to sell, so it must borrow $13,800 to bring the ending cash balance to $15,000.

July (column F): The firm is projecting that it will be overdrawn by $76,492. Again, it has no investments to sell and must borrow an additional $91,492. Note that the cumulative borrowing is now $105,292.

August (column G): The firm is projecting an unadjusted cash balance of $120,798, well in excess of the maximum allowable cash. Before investing the excess, however, it needs to pay off the $105,292 of existing short-term debt. In this case, the firm can pay off the entire balance and still remain above the minimum cash requirement. However, after paying down the loans, its cash balance is not high enough to cause investment of excess funds.

September (column H): The firm is projecting that the unadjusted cash balance will be $44,856. In this case, there is no borrowing balance, so the $4,856 in excess of the maximum allowable cash can be invested and the ending cash balance will be $40,000. Note that the Cumulative Borrowing (Investing) in H34 is negative, indicating that the funds represent investments.

In any complex worksheet, such as this one, it is important that you work through the calculations by hand to check the results. Never accept the output until you are sure that it is absolutely correct. With this in mind, let's make two changes: First, set the maximum acceptable cash in B38 to $15,000. Now, set the unadjusted cash balance for May to $20,000 and copy E31:E33 to D31:D33. Make sure that this portion of your worksheet is the same as that in Exhibit 3-10, and then carefully go over the worksheet.

EXHIBIT 3-10
CASH BALANCE AFTER CHANGING MAXIMUM CASH TO $15,000

	A	B	C	D	E	F	G	H
1				Bithlo Barbecues				
2				Cash Budget				
3				For the Period June to September 2015				
4				April	May	June	July	August	September
28	Beginning Cash Balance					15,000	15,000	15,000	15,000
29	Collections - Disbursements					(18,775)	(91,492)	105,798	29,353
30	Unadjusted Cash Balance				20,000	(3,775)	(76,492)	120,798	44,353
31	Current Borrowing				0	13,775	91,492	(105,267)	0
32	Current Investing				5,000	(5,000)	0	531	29,353
33	**Ending Cash Balance**				**15,000**	**15,000**	**15,000**	**15,000**	**15,000**
34	Cumulative Borrowing (Investing)				(5,000)	13,775	105,267	(531)	(29,884)
35	Cumulative Interest Expense (Inc.)					(25)	67	769	766
36	Notes:								
37	Minimum Acceptable Cash	15,000							
38	Maximum Acceptable Cash	15,000							
39	Borrowing Rate (Annual)		8% Monthly	0.67%					
40	Lending Rate (Annual)		6% Monthly	0.50%					

May (column D): The unadjusted cash balance is greater than the minimum cash, so it does not need to borrow. In fact, it has $5,000 more than the maximum allowable cash that can be invested. The ending cash balance is $15,000.

June (column E): The firm is projecting the unadjusted cash balance to be –$3,775, but it does not borrow $18,775 because it has $5,000 in investments from May that reduce the borrowing need to only $13,775. Current Investing, therefore, is –$5,000.

July (column F): The unadjusted cash balance is projected to be –$76,492 and there are no investments that can be sold. Therefore, the firm must borrow $91,492. The cumulative borrowing is now $105,267.

August (column G): The firm is expected to have a large surplus of funds, which can be used to pay off the entire loan balance. Furthermore, it will have $531 in excess of the maximum allowable cash that is available to invest.

September (column H): The unadjusted cash balance is expected to be $44,353, which is $29,353 in excess of the maximum. This amount can be invested.

You are encouraged to experiment by changing values throughout the cash budget to see what happens. In particular, changing the projected sales and/or the payment schedule can be very enlightening. For example, suppose that Bithlo Barbecues' management decides to slow down payments for inventory purchases. Specifically, assume that it decides to pay only 40% in the month after the purchase and 60% two months after the purchase. You should find that this is not as good an idea as it sounds. Table 3-4 shows Cumulative Borrowing (Investing) before and after the change, assuming that the maximum cash is still $15,000. Note that the firm would end up borrowing a little more under this scenario, and the total interest paid would be higher.

TABLE 3-4
CUMULATIVE BORROWING (INVESTING)

Month	Before	After
May	(5,000)	(5,000)
June	13,775	11,575
July	105,267	108,852
August	(531)	12,178
September	(29,984)	(7,791)
Cumulative Interest Expense Through September	766	859

Summary

In this chapter, we have seen that the cash budget is simply a listing of the firm's expected *cash* inflows and outflows over a period of time. Cash budgets are useful in determining the firm's short-term borrowing and investing needs as well as scheduling transactions. Furthermore, it can be used when forecasting the financial statements. The cash budget is composed of three sections: (1) the worksheet area; (2) a listing of collections and disbursements; and (3) the ending cash balance calculation. We also saw how Excel's Scenario Manager tool can greatly simplify "What if?" analysis and display a table of the results.

One of the most important lessons in this chapter is that complex spreadsheets should be built up from simpler spreadsheets. In other words, start by building a simple version of the worksheet that covers the basics, and then gradually add the complex details. In this chapter, we started with a very simple cash budget, then added borrowing, interest on borrowing, and finally investing and the interest on invested funds. This method will make building the worksheet much easier and it will be less likely to contain errors. If you do find errors, we have covered some of the tools that Excel provides to help you find and fix them quickly. The Watch Window and Evaluate Formula tools are especially helpful in this regard.

TABLE 3-5
FUNCTIONS INTRODUCED IN THIS CHAPTER

Purpose	Function	Page
Calculate a date serial number	DATE(*YEAR*, *MONTH*, *DAY*)	74
Extract year from a date	YEAR(*SERIAL_NUMBER*)	74
Extract month from a date	MONTH(*SERIAL_NUMBER*)	74
Extract day from a date	DAY(*SERIAL_NUMBER*)	74
Join text strings	CONCATENATE(*TEXT1*, *TEXT2*, ...)	74
Convert a number to formatted text	TEXT(*VALUE*, *FORMAT_TEXT*)	75
Return a value based on a logical test	IF(*LOGICAL_TEST*, *VALUE_IF_TRUE*, *VALUE_IF_FALSE*)	82
Determines the minimum of a list of arguments	MIN(*NUMBER1*, *NUMBER2*, ...)	83
Determines the maximum of a list of arguments	MAX(*NUMBER1*, *NUMBER2*, ...)	85
Returns true only if all arguments are true	AND(*LOGICAL1*, *LOGICAL2*, ...)	96
Returns true if any argument is true	OR(*LOGICAL1*, *LOGICAL2*, ...)	96

Problems

1. Lakewood Laser SkinCare's ending cash balance as of January 31, 2015 (the end of its fiscal year 2014) was $15,000. Its expected cash collections and payments for the next six months are given in the following table.

Month	Collections	Payments
February	$24,750	$29,100
March	27,450	31,200
April	34,050	32,400
May	43,650	36,450
June	48,750	40,050
July	54,000	40,800

   a. Calculate the firm's expected ending cash balance for each month.

   b. Assuming that the firm must maintain an ending cash balance of at least $12,000, how much must they borrow during each month?

   c. If the firm must pay 5% annual interest on its short-term borrowing, what are your ending cash balances for each month?

   d. What are the ending cash balances if the firm uses any cash in excess of the minimum to pay off its short-term borrowing in each month?

2. Loblaw Manufacturing has asked you to create a cash budget in order to determine its borrowing needs for the June to October period. You have gathered the following information.

Month	Sales	Other Payments
June 2015	$223,600	$104,000
July	184,600	97,500
August	157,300	91,000
September	120,900	65,000
October	98,800	58,500
November	105,300	

April and May sales were $149,500 and $175,500, respectively. The firm collects 25% of its sales during the month, 60% the following month, and 15% two months after the sale. Each month it purchases inventory equal to 60% of the next month's expected sales. The company pays for 40% of its inventory purchases in the same month and 60% in the following month. However, the firm's suppliers give it a 2% discount if it pays during the same month as the purchase. A minimum cash balance of $25,000 must be maintained each month, and the firm pays 4% annually for short-term borrowing from its bank.

a. Create a cash budget for June to October 2015. The cash budget should account for short-term borrowing and payback of outstanding loans as well as the interest expense. The firm ended May with a $30,000 unadjusted cash balance.

b. Bob Loblaw, the president, is considering stretching out its inventory payments. He believes that it may be less expensive to borrow from suppliers than from the bank. He has asked you to use the Scenario Manager to see what the total interest cost for this time period would be if the company paid for 0%, 10%, 30%, or 40% of its inventory purchases in the same month. The remainder would be paid in the following month. Create a scenario summary, and describe whether the results support Bob's beliefs.

3. Camp and Fevurly Financial Planners have forecasted revenues for the first six months of 2015, as shown in the following table.

Month	Revenue	Month	Revenue
November 2014	$38,400	March	24,000
December	36,000	April	30,400
January 2015	20,000	May	32,000
February	21,600	June	36,000

The firm collects 60% of its sales immediately, 39% one month after the sale, and 1% are written off as bad debts two months after the sale. The firm assumes that wages and benefits paid to clerical personnel will be $7,000 per month while commissions to sales associates average 25% of collectable sales. Each of the two partners is paid $5,000 per month or 20% of net sales, whichever is greater. Commissions and partner salaries are paid one month after the revenue is earned. Rent expense for their office space is $3,500 per month, and lease expense for office equipment is $800. Utilities average $250 per month, except in May and June when they average only $150. The ending cash balance in December 2014 was $12,000.

a. Create a cash budget for January to June 2015, and determine the firm's ending cash balance in each month assuming that the partners wish to maintain a minimum cash balance of $10,000.

b. Camp and Fevurly are thinking of obtaining a line of credit from their bank. Based on their expectations for the first six months of the year, what is the minimum amount that would be necessary? Round your answer to the next highest $1,000 and ignore interest charges on short-term debt. (Hint: Look up the ROUNDUP function in the online help.)

c. Create three scenarios (best case, base case, and worst case) assuming that revenues are 10% better than expected, exactly as expected, or 10% worse than expected. What is the maximum that the firm would need to borrow to maintain its minimum cash balance in all three cases? Use the Scenario Manager, and create a summary of your results. Would this change your answer in part b?

4. You were recently hired to improve the financial condition of Idaho Springs Hardware, a small chain of three hardware stores in Colorado. On your first day the owner, Chuck Vitaska, told you that the biggest problem facing the firm has been periodic unexpected cash shortages that have made it necessary for him to delay wage payments to his employees. Having recently received a degree in finance, you immediately realize that your first priority is to develop a cash budget and to arrange for a short-term borrowing agreement with the firm's bank. After looking at the firm's past financial records, you developed a sales forecast for the remainder of the year, as is presented in the following table.

Month	Sales	Month	Sales
June 2015	$68,200	October	64,900
July	80,300	November	51,700
August	83,600	December	45,100
September	77,000		

In addition to the seasonality of sales, you have observed several other patterns. Individuals account for 40% of the firm's sales, and they pay in cash. The other 60% of sales are to contractors with credit accounts, and they have up to 60 days to pay. As a result, about 20% of sales to contractors are paid one month after the sale, and the other 80% is paid two months after the sale. Each month the firm purchases inventory equal to about 45% of the following month's sales. About 30% of this inventory is paid for in the month of delivery, while the remaining 70% is paid one month later.

Each month the company pays its hourly employees a total of $10,000, including benefits. Its salaried employees are paid $14,000, also including benefits. In the past, the company had to borrow to build its stores and for the initial inventories. This debt has resulted in monthly interest payments of $4,000 and monthly principal payments of $221. On average, maintenance at the stores is expected to cost about $800 per month, except October to December when snow removal costs will add about $200 per month. Sales taxes are 7% of quarterly sales and must be paid in June, September, and December. Other taxes are also paid during those months and are expected to be about 4% of quarterly sales in each of those months. The owner wishes to maintain a cash balance of at least $12,000 to limit the risk of cash shortages. The cash balance at the end of May is expected to be $15,000 (before any borrowing or investing).

a. Create a simple cash budget for Idaho Springs Hardware for June to December. Note that your records indicate that sales in April and May were $56,100 and $62,700, respectively. January 2016 sales are expected to be $39,600. What would be the ending cash balances if the firm does not borrow to maintain its $12,000 minimum?

b. Now assume that the firm can borrow from the bank at a rate of 6% per annum to maintain its liquidity and meet its required minimum cash balance. In addition, if the firm has funds in excess of the minimum, it will use the excess to pay off any previous balance.

c. While negotiating a line of credit, the firm's bank offered to sweep any cash in excess of the minimum into a money market fund that will return an average of 4% per year after expenses. If you accept this offer, how will it affect the firm's ending cash balances and need to borrow in each month? Note that the firm must have paid off all short-term loans before any excess cash can be invested, and invested funds will be used instead of borrowing when needed.

d. After completing the cash budget, you begin to think of ways to further reduce the firm's borrowing needs. One idea that comes to mind is changing the firm's credit policy with contractors because they seem to always pay at the last minute. Three scenarios come to mind: (1) In the best case, contractors are required to pay for 100% of their purchases during the month after the sale. You believe that this would cause a 5% decline in sales. (2) In the base case, everything remains as already outlined. (3) In the worst case, contractors would be required to pay for 100% of their purchases during the month after the sale, and you believe that this would cause a 20% drop in sales. You decide to use the Scenario Manager to evaluate these scenarios. To summarize the impact of the change, you will examine the impact on the firm's maximum borrowing needs and cumulative net interest cost (after accounting for investment earnings). In your opinion, should the firm change its credit policy?

CHAPTER 4

Financial Statement Analysis Tools

After studying this chapter, you should be able to:

1. *Describe the purpose of financial ratios and who uses them.*

2. *Define the five major categories of ratios (liquidity, efficiency, leverage, coverage, and profitability).*

3. *Calculate the common ratios for any firm by using income statement and balance sheet data.*

4. *Use financial ratios to assess a firm's past performance, identify its current problems, and suggest strategies for dealing with these problems.*

5. *Calculate the economic profit earned by a firm.*

In previous chapters, we have seen how the firm's basic financial statements are constructed. In this chapter, we will see how financial analysts can use the information contained in the income statement and balance sheet for various purposes.

Many tools are available for use when evaluating a company, but some of the most valuable are financial ratios. Ratios are an analyst's microscope; they allow us to get a better view of the firm's financial health than just looking at the raw financial statements. A ratio is simply a comparison of two numbers by division. We could also compare numbers by subtraction, but a ratio is superior in most cases because it is a measure of relative size. Relative measures are more easily compared to previous time periods or to other firms than changes in dollar amounts.

Ratios are useful to both internal and external analysts of the firm. For internal purposes, ratios can be useful in planning for the future, setting goals, and evaluating the performance of managers. External analysts use ratios to decide whether or not to grant credit, to monitor financial performance, to forecast financial performance, and to decide whether to invest in the company.

We will look at many different ratios, but you should be aware that these are, of necessity, only a sampling of the ratios that might be useful. Furthermore, different analysts may calculate ratios slightly differently, so you will need to know exactly how the ratios are calculated in a given situation. The keys to understanding ratio analysis are experience and an analytical mind.

We will divide our discussion of the ratios into five categories based on the information provided:

1.   *Liquidity ratios* describe the ability of a firm to meets its short-term obligations. They compare current assets to current liabilities.

2.   *Efficiency ratios* describe how well the firm is using its investment in various types of assets to produce sales. They may also be called asset management ratios.

3.   *Leverage ratios* reveal the degree to which debt has been used to finance the firm's asset purchases. These ratios are also known as debt management ratios.

4.   *Coverage ratios* are similar to liquidity ratios in that they describe the ability of a firm to pay certain expenses.

5.   *Profitability ratios* provide indications of how profitable a firm has been over a period of time.

One additional category, relative value ratios, will be discussed in Chapter 8 on page 254. Before we begin the discussion of individual financial ratios, open your Elvis Products International workbook from Chapter 2, and add a new worksheet named "Ratios."

Liquidity Ratios

The term "liquidity" refers to the speed with which an asset can be converted into cash without large discounts to its value. Some assets, such as accounts receivable, can easily be converted into cash with only small discounts. Other assets, such as buildings, can be converted into cash very quickly only if large price concessions are given. We therefore say that accounts receivable are more liquid than buildings.

All other things being equal, a firm with more liquid assets will be more able to meet its maturing obligations (e.g., its accounts payable and other short-term debts) than a firm with fewer liquid assets. As you might imagine, creditors are particularly concerned with a firm's ability to pay its bills. To assess this ability, it is common to use the current ratio and/or the quick ratio.

The Current Ratio

Generally, a firm's current assets are converted to cash (e.g., collecting on accounts receivable or selling its inventories) and this cash is used to retire its current liabilities. Therefore, it is logical to assess a firm's ability to pay its bills by comparing the size of its current assets to the size of its current liabilities. The current ratio does exactly this. It is defined as:

$$\text{Current Ratio} = \frac{\text{Current Assets}}{\text{Current Liabilities}} \tag{4-1}$$

Obviously, the higher the current ratio, the higher the likelihood that a firm will be able to pay its bills. So, from the creditor's point of view, higher is better. However, from a shareholder's point of view this is not always the case. Current assets usually have a lower expected return than do fixed assets, so the shareholders would like to see that only the minimum amount of the company's capital is invested in current assets. Of course, too little investment in current assets could be disastrous for both creditors and owners of the firm.

We can calculate the current ratio for 2014 for EPI by looking at the balance sheet (Exhibit 2-2, page 50). In this case, we have:

$$\text{Current Ratio} = \frac{1,290.00}{540.20} = 2.39 \text{ times}$$

meaning that EPI has 2.39 times as many current assets as current liabilities. We will determine later whether this is sufficient or not.

Exhibit 4-1 shows the beginnings of our "Ratios" worksheet. Enter the labels as shown. We can calculate the current ratio for 2014 in B5 with the formula: =`'Balance Sheet'!B8/ 'Balance Sheet'!B17`. After formatting to show two decimal places, you will see that the current ratio is 2.39. Copy the formula to C5.

EXHIBIT 4-1
RATIO WORKSHEET FOR EPI

	A	B	C
1	Elvis Products International		
2	Ratio Analysis for 2013 and 2014		
3	Ratio	2014	2013
4	Liquidity Ratios		
5	Current Ratio	2.39x	2.33x

Notice that we have applied a custom number format (see page 51 to refresh your memory) to the result in B5. In this case, the custom format is 0.00"x". Any text that you include in quotes will be shown along with the number. However, the presence of the text in the display does not affect the fact that it is still a number and may be used for calculations. As an experiment, in B6 enter the formula: =B5*2. The result will be 4.78 just as if we had not applied the custom format. Now, in B7 type: 2.39x and then copy the formula from B6 to B8. You will get a #VALUE! error because the value in B7 is a text string, not a number. This is one of the great advantages to custom number formatting: We can have both text and numbers in a cell and still use the number for calculations. Delete B6:B8 so that we can use the cells in the next section.

The Quick Ratio

Inventories are often the least liquid of the firm's current assets.[1] For this reason, many believe that a better measure of liquidity can be obtained by excluding inventories. The result is known as the quick ratio (sometimes called the acid-test ratio) and is calculated as:

$$\text{Quick Ratio} = \frac{\text{Current Assets} - \text{Inventories}}{\text{Current Liabilities}} \qquad (4\text{-}2)$$

For EPI in 2014 the quick ratio is:

$$\text{Quick Ratio} = \frac{1,290.00 - 836.00}{540.20} = 0.84 \text{ times}$$

Notice that the quick ratio will always be less than the current ratio, unless the firm has no inventory. This is by design. However, a quick ratio that is too low relative to the current ratio may indicate that inventories are higher than they should be. As we will see later, this

---

1. That is why you so often see 50% off sales when firms are going out of business.

can only be determined by comparing the ratio to previous periods or to similar companies in the same industry.

We can calculate EPI's 2014 quick ratio in B6 with the formula: =('Balance Sheet'!B8-'Balance Sheet'!B7)/'Balance Sheet'!B17. Copying this formula to C6 reveals that the 2013 quick ratio was 0.85. Be sure to remember to enter a label in column A for all of the ratios.

Efficiency Ratios

Efficiency ratios, also called asset management ratios, provide information about how well the company is using its assets to generate sales. For example, if two firms have the same level of sales, but one has a lower investment in inventories, we would say that the firm with lower inventories is more efficient with respect to its inventory management.

There are many different types of efficiency ratios that could be defined. However, we will illustrate five of the most common.

Inventory Turnover Ratio

The inventory turnover ratio measures the number of dollars of sales that are generated per dollar of inventory. It can also be interpreted as the number of times that a firm replaces its inventories during a year. It is calculated as:

$$\text{Inventory Turnover Ratio} = \frac{\text{Cost of Goods Sold}}{\text{Inventory}} \tag{4-3}$$

Note that it is also common to use sales in the numerator. Because the only difference between sales and cost of goods sold is a markup (i.e., profit margin), this causes no problems. In addition, you will frequently see the average level of inventories throughout the year in the denominator. Whenever using ratios, you need to be aware of the method of calculation to be sure that you are comparing "apples to apples."

For 2014, EPI's inventory turnover ratio was:

$$\text{Inventory Turnover Ratio} = \frac{3,250.00}{836.00} = 3.89 \text{ times}$$

meaning that EPI replaced its inventories about 3.89 times during the year. Alternatively, we could say that EPI generated $3.89 in sales for each dollar invested in inventories. Both interpretations are valid, though the latter is probably more generally useful.

To calculate the inventory turnover ratio for EPI, enter the formula: =`'Income Statement'!B6/'Balance Sheet'!B7` into B8 and copy this formula to C8. Notice that this ratio has deteriorated somewhat from 4 times in 2013 to 3.89 times in 2014. Generally, high inventory turnover is considered to be good because it means that the opportunity costs of holding inventory are low, but if it is too high the firm may be risking inventory outages and the loss of customers.

Accounts Receivable Turnover Ratio

Businesses grant credit to customers for one main reason: to increase sales. It is important, therefore, to know how well the firm is managing its accounts receivable. The accounts receivable turnover ratio (and the average collection period) provides us with this information. It is calculated by:

$$\text{Accounts Receivable Turnover Ratio} = \frac{\text{Credit Sales}}{\text{Accounts Receivable}} \qquad \text{(4-4)}$$

For EPI, the 2014 accounts receivable turnover ratio is (assuming that all sales are credit sales):

$$\text{Accounts Receivable Turnover Ratio} = \frac{3,850.00}{402.00} = 9.58 \text{ times}$$

So each dollar invested in accounts receivable generated $9.58 in sales. In cell B9 of your worksheet, enter: =`'Income Statement'!B5/'Balance Sheet'!B6`. The result is 9.58, which is the same as we found above. Copy this formula to C9 to get the 2013 accounts receivable turnover ratio.

Whether or not 9.58 is a good accounts receivable turnover ratio is difficult to know at this point. We can say that higher is generally better, but too high might indicate that the firm is denying credit to creditworthy customers (thereby losing sales). If the ratio is too low, it would suggest that the firm might be having difficulty collecting on its sales. We would have to see if the growth rate in accounts receivable exceeds the growth rate in sales to determine whether the firm is having difficulty in this area. We can see that is the case by looking at the common-size balance sheet in Exhibit 2-6 on page 57. Accounts receivable has grown from 23.91% of sales to 24.35%; a slight increase, but an increase nonetheless.

Average Collection Period

The average collection period (also known as days sales outstanding, or DSO) tells us how many days, on average, it takes to collect on a credit sale. It is calculated as follows:

$$\text{Average Collection Period} = \frac{\text{Accounts Receivable}}{\text{Credit Sales}/360} \tag{4-5}$$

Note that the denominator is simply credit sales per day.[2] In 2014, it took EPI an average of 37.59 days to collect on their credit sales:

$$\text{Average Collection Period} = \frac{402.00}{3,850.00/360} = 37.59 \text{ days}$$

We can calculate the 2014 average collection period in B10 with the formula: =`'Balance Sheet'!B6/('Income Statement'!B5/360)`. Copy this to C10 to find that in 2013 the average collection period was 36.84 days, which was slightly better than in 2014.

Note that this ratio actually provides us with the same information as the accounts receivable turnover ratio. In fact, it can easily be demonstrated by simple algebraic manipulation:

$$\text{Accounts Receivable Turnover Ratio} = \frac{360}{\text{Average Collection Period}}$$

Or alternatively:

$$\text{Average Collection Period} = \frac{360}{\text{Accounts Receivable Turnover Ratio}}$$

Because the average collection period is (in a sense) the inverse of the accounts receivable turnover ratio, it should be apparent that the inverse criteria apply to judging this ratio. In other words, lower is usually better, but too low may indicate lost sales.

Many firms offer a discount for fast payment in order to get customers to pay more quickly. For example, the credit terms on an invoice might specify 2/10n30, which means that there is a 2% discount for paying within 10 days otherwise the entire balance is due in 30 days. Such a discount is very attractive for customers, but whether it makes sense for a particular firm is for them to decide. Remember that accounts receivable represents short-term loans made to customers, and those funds have an opportunity cost. Regardless, offering a discount will almost certainly reduce the average collection period and increase the accounts receivable turnover. You should always compare the average collection period to the credit terms that the company offers its customers.

---

2. The use of a 360-day year dates back to the days before computers. It was derived by assuming that there are 12 months, each with 30 days (known as a "Banker's Year"). You may also use 365 days; the difference is irrelevant as long as you are consistent.

Fixed Asset Turnover Ratio

The fixed asset turnover ratio describes the dollar amount of sales that are generated by each dollar invested in fixed assets. It is given by:

$$\text{Fixed Asset Turnover} = \frac{\text{Sales}}{\text{Net Fixed Assets}} \qquad \text{(4-6)}$$

For EPI, the 2014 fixed asset turnover is:

$$\text{Fixed Asset Turnover} = \frac{3{,}850.00}{360.80} = 10.67 \text{ times}$$

So, EPI generated $10.67 in revenue for each dollar invested in fixed assets. In your "Ratios" worksheet, entering: `='Income Statement'!B5/'Balance Sheet'!B11` into B11 will confirm that the fixed asset turnover was 10.67 times in 2014. Again, copy this formula to C11 to get the 2013 ratio.

Note that because we use net fixed assets in the denominator, a firm can improve its fixed asset turnover ratio by simply delaying the replacement of its long-term assets. As accumulated depreciation increases net fixed assets will decrease, all other things being the same. However, this is a short-term gimmick since those assets will eventually wear out.

Total Asset Turnover Ratio

Like the other ratios discussed in this section, the total asset turnover ratio describes how efficiently the firm is using all of its assets to generate sales. In this case, we look at the firm's total asset investment:

$$\text{Total Asset Turnover} = \frac{\text{Sales}}{\text{Total Assets}} \qquad \text{(4-7)}$$

In 2014, EPI generated $2.33 in sales for each dollar invested in total assets:

$$\text{Total Asset Turnover} = \frac{3{,}850.00}{1{,}650.80} = 2.33 \text{ times}$$

This ratio can be calculated in B12 on your worksheet with: `='Income Statement'!B5/'Balance Sheet'!B12`. After copying this formula to C12, you should see that the 2013 value was 2.34, essentially the same as 2014.

We can interpret the asset turnover ratios as follows: Higher turnover ratios indicate more efficient usage of the assets and are therefore preferred to lower ratios. However, you should be aware that some industries will naturally have lower turnover ratios than others. For example, a consulting business will almost surely have a very small investment in fixed assets and therefore a high fixed asset turnover ratio. On the other hand, an electric utility will have a large investment in fixed assets and a low fixed asset turnover ratio. This does not mean, necessarily, that the utility company is more poorly managed than the consulting firm. Rather, each is simply responding to the demands of their very different industries.

EXHIBIT 4-2
EPI'S EFFICIENCY RATIOS

	A	B	C
1	Elvis Products International		
2	Ratio Analysis for 2013 and 2014		
3	Ratio	2014	2013
7	Efficiency Ratios		
8	Inventory Turnover	3.89x	4.00x
9	A/R Turnover	9.58x	9.77x
10	Average Collection Period	37.59 days	36.84 days
11	Fixed Asset Turnover	10.67x	9.95x
12	Total Asset Turnover	2.33x	2.34x

At this point, this part of your worksheet should resemble the one in Exhibit 4-2. Notice that we have applied the custom format, discussed above, to most of these ratios. In B10 and C10, however, we used the custom format `0.00" days"` because the average collection period is measured in days.

Leverage Ratios

In physics, leverage refers to a multiplication of force. Using a lever and fulcrum, you can press down on one end of a lever with a given force and get a larger force at the other end. The amount of leverage depends on the length of the lever and the position of the fulcrum. In finance, leverage refers to a multiplication of changes in profitability measures. For example, a 10% increase in sales might lead to a 20% increase in net income.[3] The amount of leverage depends on the amount of debt that a firm uses to finance its operations, so a firm that uses a lot of debt is said to be "highly leveraged."

Leverage ratios describe the degree to which the firm uses debt in its capital structure. This is important information for creditors and investors in the firm. Creditors might be concerned that a firm has too much debt and will therefore have difficulty in repaying loans. Investors might be concerned because a large amount of debt can lead to high volatility in

---

3. As we will see in Chapter 6, this would mean that the degree of combined leverage is 2.

the firm's earnings. However, most firms use some debt. This is because the tax deductibility of interest can increase the wealth of the firm's shareholders. We will examine several ratios that help to determine the amount of debt that a firm is using. How much is too much depends on the nature of the business.

The Total Debt Ratio

The total debt ratio measures the total amount of debt (long-term and short-term) that the firm uses to finance its assets:

$$\text{Total Debt Ratio} = \frac{\text{Total Liabilities}}{\text{Total Assets}} = \frac{\text{Total Assets} - \text{Total Equity}}{\text{Total Assets}} \qquad (4\text{-}8)$$

Calculating the total debt ratio for EPI, we find that debt financing makes up about 58.45% of the firm's capital structure:

$$\text{Total Debt Ratio} = \frac{964.81}{1,650.80} = 58.45\%$$

The formula to calculate the total debt ratio in B14 is: =`'Balance Sheet'!B19/'Balance Sheet'!B12`. The result for 2014 is 58.45%, which is higher than the 54.81% in 2013.

The Long-Term Debt Ratio

Many analysts believe that it is more useful to focus on just the long-term debt (LTD) instead of total debt. The long-term debt ratio is the same as the total debt ratio, except that the numerator includes only long-term debt:

$$\text{Long-Term Debt Ratio} = \frac{\text{Long-Term Debt}}{\text{Total Assets}} \qquad (4\text{-}9)$$

EPI's long-term debt ratio is:

$$\text{Long-Term Debt Ratio} = \frac{424.61}{1,650.80} = 25.72\%$$

In B15, the formula to calculate the long-term debt ratio for 2014 is: =`'Balance Sheet'!B18/'Balance Sheet'!B12`. Copying this formula to C15 reveals that in 2013 the ratio was only 22.02%. Obviously, EPI has increased its long-term debt at a faster rate than it has added assets.

The Long-Term Debt to Total Capitalization Ratio

Similar to the previous two ratios, the long-term debt to total capitalization ratio tells us the percentage of long-term sources of capital[4] that is provided by long-term debt (LTD). It is calculated by:

$$\text{LTD to Total Capitalization} = \frac{\text{LTD}}{\text{LTD} + \text{Preferred Equity} + \text{Common Equity}} \qquad \text{(4-10)}$$

For EPI, we have:

$$\text{LTD to Total Capitalization} = \frac{424.61}{424.61 + 685.99} = 38.23\%$$

Because EPI has no preferred equity, its total capitalization consists of long-term debt and common equity. Note that common equity is the total of common stock and retained earnings. We can calculate this ratio in B16 of the worksheet with: `='Balance Sheet'!B18/('Balance Sheet'!B18+'Balance Sheet'!B22)`. In 2013 this ratio was only 32.76%.

The Debt to Equity Ratio

The debt to equity ratio provides exactly the same information as the total debt ratio, but in a slightly different form that some analysts prefer:

$$\text{Debt to Equity} = \frac{\text{Total Debt}}{\text{Total Equity}} \qquad \text{(4-11)}$$

For EPI, the debt to equity ratio is:

$$\text{Debt to Equity} = \frac{964.81}{685.99} = 1.41 \text{ times}$$

In B17, this is calculated as: `='Balance Sheet'!B19/'Balance Sheet'!B22`. Copy this to C17 to find that the debt to equity ratio in 2013 was 1.21 times.

To see that the total debt ratio and the debt to equity ratio provide the same information, realize that:

$$\frac{\text{Total Debt}}{\text{Total Equity}} = \frac{\text{Total Debt}}{\text{Total Assets}} \times \frac{\text{Total Assets}}{\text{Total Equity}} \qquad \text{(4-12)}$$

---

4. Some analysts will include notes payable and the LTD due in one year in total capitalization.

but from rearranging equation (4-8) we know that:

$$\frac{\text{Total Assets}}{\text{Total Equity}} = \frac{1}{1 - \text{Total Debt Ratio}} \qquad (4\text{-}13)$$

so, by substitution we have:

$$\frac{\text{Total Debt}}{\text{Total Equity}} = \frac{\text{Total Debt}}{\text{Total Assets}} \times \frac{1}{1 - \dfrac{\text{Total Debt}}{\text{Total Assets}}} \qquad (4\text{-}14)$$

We can convert the total debt ratio into the debt to equity ratio without any additional information (the result is not exact due to rounding):

$$\frac{\text{Total Debt}}{\text{Total Equity}} = 0.5845 \times \frac{1}{1 - 0.5845} = 1.41$$

The Long-Term Debt to Equity Ratio

Once again, many analysts prefer to focus on the amount of long-term debt that a firm carries. For this reason, many analysts like to use the long-term debt to total equity ratio:

$$\text{Long-Term Debt to Equity} = \frac{\text{LTD}}{\text{Preferred Equity} + \text{Common Equity}} \qquad (4\text{-}15)$$

EPI's long-term debt to equity ratio is:

$$\text{Long-Term Debt to Equity} = \frac{424.61}{685.99} = 61.90\%$$

The formula to calculate EPI's 2014 long-term debt to equity ratio in B18 is: =`'Balance Sheet'!B18/'Balance Sheet'!B22`. After copying this formula to C18, note that the ratio was only 48.73% in 2013.

This portion of your worksheet should now look like the one in Exhibit 4-3.

Coverage Ratios

The coverage ratios are similar to liquidity ratios in that they describe the quantity of funds available to "cover" certain expenses. We will examine two very similar ratios that describe the firm's ability to meet its interest payment obligations. In both cases, higher ratios are desirable to a degree. However, if they are too high, it may indicate that the firm is under-utilizing its debt capacity and therefore not maximizing shareholder wealth.

EXHIBIT 4-3
EPI'S LEVERAGE RATIOS

	A	B	C
1	**Elvis Products International**		
2	**Ratio Analysis for 2013 and 2014**		
3	**Ratio**	**2014**	**2013**
13	**Leverage Ratios**		
14	Total Debt Ratio	58.45%	54.81%
15	Long-term Debt Ratio	25.72%	22.02%
16	LTD to Total Capitalization	38.23%	32.76%
17	Debt to Equity	1.41x	1.21x
18	LTD to Equity	61.90%	48.73%

The Times Interest Earned Ratio

The times interest earned ratio measures the ability of the firm to pay its interest obligations by comparing earnings before interest and taxes (EBIT) to interest expense:

$$\text{Times Interest Earned} = \frac{\text{EBIT}}{\text{Interest Expense}} \tag{4-16}$$

For EPI in 2014, the times interest earned ratio is:

$$\text{Times Interest Earned} = \frac{149.70}{76.00} = 1.97 \text{ times}$$

In your worksheet, the times interest earned ratio can be calculated in B20 with the formula: `='Income Statement'!B11/'Income Statement'!B12`. Copy the formula to C20 and notice that this ratio has declined rather precipitously from 3.35 in 2013.

The Cash Coverage Ratio

EBIT does not really reflect the cash that is available to pay the firm's interest expense. That is because a noncash expense (depreciation) has been subtracted in the calculation of EBIT. To correct for this deficiency, some analysts like to use the cash coverage ratio instead of times interest earned. The cash coverage ratio (also known as the EBITDA coverage ratio) is calculated as:

$$\text{Cash Coverage Ratio} = \frac{\text{EBIT} + \text{Noncash Expenses}}{\text{Interest Expense}} \tag{4-17}$$

The calculation for EPI in 2014 is:

$$\text{Cash Coverage Ratio} = \frac{149.70 + 20.00}{76.00} = 2.23 \text{ times}$$

Note that the cash coverage ratio will always be higher than the times interest earned ratio. The difference depends on the amount of depreciation expense and therefore the amount and age of fixed assets.

The cash coverage ratio can be calculated in cell B21 of your "Ratios" worksheet with: =('Income Statement'!B11+'Income Statement'!B10)/'Income Statement'!B12. In 2013, the ratio was 3.65.

EXHIBIT 4-4
EPI'S COVERAGE RATIOS

	A	B	C
1	Elvis Products International		
2	Ratio Analysis for 2013 and 2014		
3	Ratio	2014	2013
19	Coverage Ratios		
20	Times Interest Earned	1.97x	3.35x
21	Cash Coverage Ratio	2.23x	3.65x

Profitability Ratios

Investors, and therefore managers, are particularly interested in the profitability of the firms that they own. As we'll see, there are many ways to measure profits. Profitability ratios provide an easy way to compare profits to earlier periods or to other firms. Furthermore, by simultaneously examining the first three profitability ratios, an analyst can discover categories of expenses that may be out of line.

Profitability ratios are the easiest of all the ratios to analyze. Without exception, high ratios are preferred. However, the definition of high depends on the industry in which the firm operates. Generally, firms in mature industries with lots of competition will have lower profitability measures than firms in faster growing industries with less competition. For example, grocery stores will have lower profit margins than computer software companies. In the grocery business, a net profit margin of 3% would be considered quite good. That same margin would be abysmal in the software business, where 15% or higher is common.

The Gross Profit Margin

The gross profit margin measures the gross profit relative to sales. It indicates the amount of funds available to pay the firm's expenses other than its cost of sales. The gross profit margin is calculated by:

$$\text{Gross Profit Margin} = \frac{\text{Gross Profit}}{\text{Sales}} \qquad \text{(4-18)}$$

In 2014, EPI's gross profit margin was:

$$\text{Gross Profit Margin} = \frac{600.00}{3,850.00} = 15.58\%$$

which means that cost of goods sold consumed about 84.42% ($= 1 - 0.1558$) of sales revenue. We can calculate this ratio in B23 with: `='Income Statement'!B7/ 'Income Statement'!B5`. After copying this formula to C23, you will see that the gross profit margin has declined from 16.55% in 2013.

The Operating Profit Margin

Moving down the income statement, we can calculate the profits that remain after the firm has paid all of its operating (nonfinancial) expenses.

The operating profit margin is calculated as:

$$\text{Operating Profit Margin} = \frac{\text{Net Operating Income}}{\text{Sales}} \qquad \text{(4-19)}$$

For EPI in 2014:

$$\text{Operating Profit Margin} = \frac{149.70}{3,850.00} = 3.89\%$$

The operating profit margin can be calculated in B24 with the formula: `='Income Statement'!B11/'Income Statement'!B5`. Note that this is significantly lower than the 6.09% from 2013, indicating that EPI seems to be having problems controlling its operating costs.

The Net Profit Margin

The net profit margin relates net income to sales. Because net income is profit after all expenses, the net profit margin tells us the percentage of sales that remains for the shareholders of the firm (either dividends or retained earnings):

$$\text{Net Profit Margin} = \frac{\text{Net Income}}{\text{Sales}} \tag{4-20}$$

The net profit margin for EPI in 2014 is:

$$\text{Net Profit Margin} = \frac{44.22}{3,850.00} = 1.15\%$$

which can be calculated on your worksheet in B25 with: =`'Income Statement'!B15/ 'Income Statement'!B5`. This is lower than the 2.56% in 2013. If you take a look at the common-size income statement (Exhibit 2-5, page 56), you can see that profitability has declined because cost of goods sold, SG&A expense, and interest expense have risen more quickly than sales.

Taken together, the three profit margin ratios that we have examined show a company that may be losing control over its costs. Of course, high expenses mean lower returns for investors, and we'll see this confirmed by the next three profitability ratios.

Return on Total Assets

The total assets of a firm are the investment that the shareholders have made. Much like you might be interested in the returns generated by your investments, analysts are often interested in the return that a firm is able to get from its investments. The return on total assets is:

$$\text{Return on Total Assets} = \frac{\text{Net Income}}{\text{Total Assets}} \tag{4-21}$$

In 2014, EPI earned about 2.68% on its assets:

$$\text{Return on Total Assets} = \frac{44.22}{1,650.80} = 2.68\%$$

For 2014, we can calculate the return on total assets in cell B26 with the formula: =`'Income Statement'!B15/'Balance Sheet'!B12`. Notice that this is more than 50% lower than the 5.99% recorded in 2013. Obviously, EPI's total assets increased in 2014 at a faster rate than its net income (which actually declined).

Return on Equity

While total assets represent the total investment in the firm, the owners' investment (common stock and retained earnings) usually represent only a portion of this amount (some is debt). For this reason, it is useful to calculate the rate of return on the shareholder's invested funds. We can calculate the return on (total) equity as:

$$\text{Return on Equity} = \frac{\text{Net Income}}{\text{Total Equity}} \tag{4-22}$$

Note that if a firm uses no debt, then its return on equity will be the same as its return on assets. The more debt a firm uses, the higher its return on equity will be relative to its return on assets (see DuPont Analysis on page 124).

In 2014, EPI's return on equity was:

$$\text{Return on Equity} = \frac{44.22}{685.99} = 6.45\%$$

which can be calculated in B27 with: `='Income Statement'!B15/'Balance Sheet'!B22`. Again, copying this formula to C27 reveals that this ratio has declined from 13.25% in 2013.

Return on Common Equity

For firms that have issued preferred stock in addition to common stock, it is often helpful to determine the rate of return on just the common stockholders' investment:

$$\text{Return on Common Equity} = \frac{\text{Net Income Available to Common}}{\text{Common Equity}} \tag{4-23}$$

Net income available to common is net income less preferred dividends. In the case of EPI, this ratio is the same as the return on equity because it has no preferred shareholders:

$$\text{Return on Common Equity} = \frac{44.22 - 0}{685.99} = 6.45\%$$

For EPI, the worksheet formula for the return on common equity is exactly the same as for the return on equity.

DuPont Analysis

The return on equity (ROE) is important to both managers and investors. The effectiveness of managers is often measured by changes in ROE over time, and their compensation may be tied to ROE-based goals. Therefore, it is important that they understand what they can do to improve the firm's ROE and that requires knowledge of what causes changes in ROE over time. For example, we can see that EPI's return on equity dropped precipitously from 2013 to 2014. As you might imagine, both investors and managers are probably trying to figure out why this happened. The DuPont system is one way to look at this problem.

The DuPont system is a way to break down the ROE into its components so that management can understand how to improve the firm's ROE. Let's first take another look at the return on assets (ROA):

$$\text{ROA} = \frac{\text{Net Income}}{\text{Total Assets}} = \frac{\text{Net Income}}{\text{Sales}} \times \frac{\text{Sales}}{\text{Total Assets}} \qquad \text{(4-24)}$$

So, the ROA shows the combined effects of profitability (as measured by the net profit margin) and the efficiency of asset usage (the total asset turnover). Therefore, ROA could be improved by increasing profitability or by using assets more efficiently.

As mentioned earlier, the amount of leverage that a firm uses is the link between ROA and ROE. Specifically:

$$\text{ROE} = \frac{\text{Net Income}}{\text{Equity}} = \frac{\text{Net Income}}{\text{Total Assets}} \times \frac{\text{Total Assets}}{\text{Equity}} \qquad \text{(4-25)}$$

Note that the second term in (4-25) is sometimes called the "equity multiplier" and from (4-13) we know it is equal to:

$$\frac{\text{Total Assets}}{\text{Total Equity}} = \frac{1}{1 - \text{Total Debt Ratio}} = \frac{1}{1 - \dfrac{\text{Total Debt}}{\text{Total Assets}}} \qquad \text{(4-26)}$$

Substituting (4-26) into (4-25) and rearranging, we have:

$$\text{ROE} = \frac{\text{Net Income}}{\text{Total Assets}} \div \left(1 - \frac{\text{Total Debt}}{\text{Total Assets}}\right) \qquad \text{(4-27)}$$

We can now see that the ROE is a function of the firm's ROA and the total debt ratio. If two firms have the same ROA, the one using more debt will have a higher ROE.

We can make one more substitution to completely break down the ROE into its components. Because the first term in (4-27) is the ROA, we can replace it with (4-24):

$$ROE = \cfrac{\dfrac{\text{Net Income}}{\text{Sales}} \times \dfrac{\text{Sales}}{\text{Total Assets}}}{1 - \dfrac{\text{Total Debt}}{\text{Total Assets}}} \qquad\text{(4-28)}$$

Or, to simplify it somewhat:

$$ROE = \frac{\text{Net Profit Margin} \times \text{Total Asset Turnover}}{1 - \text{Total Debt Ratio}} \qquad\text{(4-29)}$$

To prove this to yourself, in A30 enter the label: DuPont ROE. Now, in B30 enter the formula: =(B25*B12)/(1-B14). The result will be 6.45% as we found earlier. Note that if a firm uses no debt then the denominator of equation (4-29) will be 1, and the ROE will be the same as the ROA.

Extended DuPont Analysis

We can take the decomposition of ROE one step further by breaking the net profit margin into three components:

1. The *operating profit margin*, which measures the basic profitability from the firm's day-to-day operations;

2. The *interest burden*, which measures the impact of interest expense on pre-tax earnings; and

3. The *tax burden*, which shows the impact of taxes on overall earnings.

We have already discussed the operating profit margin in equation (4-19) on page 121. The interest burden is calculated as:

$$\text{Interest Burden} = \frac{\text{Earnings Before Taxes}}{\text{Earnings Before Interest and Taxes}} = \frac{\text{EBT}}{\text{EBIT}} \qquad\text{(4-30)}$$

and the tax burden is calculated as:

$$\text{Tax Burden} = \frac{\text{Net Income}}{\text{Earnings Before Taxes}} = \frac{\text{NI}}{\text{EBT}} \qquad\text{(4-31)}$$

Multiplying these three ratios together gives us the net profit margin:

$$\text{Net Profit Margin} = \frac{\text{Net Income}}{\text{Sales}} = \frac{\text{EBIT}}{\text{Sales}} \times \frac{\text{EBT}}{\text{EBIT}} \times \frac{\text{NI}}{\text{EBT}} \qquad\text{(4-32)}$$

Finally, if we substitute equation (4-32) into the numerator of (4-28), we have:

$$\text{Extended DuPont ROE} = \frac{\dfrac{\text{EBIT}}{\text{Sales}} \times \dfrac{\text{EBT}}{\text{EBIT}} \times \dfrac{\text{NI}}{\text{EBT}} \times \dfrac{\text{Sales}}{\text{Total Assets}}}{1 - \dfrac{\text{Total Debt}}{\text{Total Assets}}} \qquad (4\text{-}33)$$

The extended DuPont system for calculating the ROE, equation (4-33), tells us that the return on equity is a function of operating profitability, the interest rate, the tax rate, the efficiency with which the firm uses its assets, and the amount of debt that it uses. At this point, this part of your worksheet should resemble Exhibit 4-5.

EXHIBIT 4-5
EPI's PROFITABILITY RATIO AND DuPONT ROE

	A	B	C
1	Elvis Products International		
2	Ratio Analysis for 2013 and 2014		
3	Ratio	2014	2013
22	Profitability Ratios		
23	Gross Profit Margin	15.58%	16.55%
24	Operating Profit Margin	3.89%	6.09%
25	Net Profit Margin	1.15%	2.56%
26	Return on Total Assets	2.68%	5.99%
27	Return on Equity	6.45%	13.25%
28	Return on Common Equity	6.45%	13.25%
29			
30	DuPont ROE	6.45%	13.25%

Analysis of EPI's Profitability Ratios

Obviously, EPI's profitability has slipped rather dramatically in the past year. The sources of these declines can be seen most clearly if we look at all of EPI's ratios.

The gross profit margin in 2014 is lower than in 2013, but not significantly (at least compared to the declines in the other ratios). The operating profit margin, however, is significantly lower in 2014 than in 2013. This indicates potential problems in controlling the firm's operating expenses, particularly SG&A expenses. The other profitability ratios are lower than in 2013 partly because of the "trickle down" effect of the increase in operating expenses. However, they are also lower because EPI has taken on a lot of extra debt in 2014, resulting in interest expense increasing faster than sales. This can be confirmed by examining EPI's common-size income statement (Exhibit 2-5, page 56).

Finally, the DuPont analysis of the firm's ROE has shown us that it could be improved by any of the following: (1) increasing the net profit margin; (2) increasing the total asset turnover; or (3) increasing the amount of debt relative to equity. Our ratio analysis has shown that operating expenses have grown considerably, leading to the decline in the net profit margin. Reducing these expenses should be the primary objective of management. Because the total asset turnover ratio is near the industry average, as we'll soon see, it may be difficult to increase this ratio. However, the firm's inventory turnover ratio is considerably below the industry average and inventory control may provide one method of improving the total asset turnover. An increase in debt is not called for because the firm already has somewhat more debt than the industry average.

Financial Distress Prediction

The last thing that any investor wants to do is to invest in a firm that is nearing a bankruptcy filing or about to suffer through a period of severe financial distress. Starting in the late 1960s and continuing today, scholars and credit analysts have spent considerable time and effort trying to develop models that could identify such companies in advance. The best-known of these models was created by Professor Edward Altman in 1968. We will discuss Altman's original model and a later one developed for privately held companies.

The Original Z-Score Model[5]

The Z-score model was developed using a statistical technique known as *multiple discriminant analysis*. This technique creates a quantitative model that places a company into one of two (or more) groups depending on the score. If the score is below the cutoff point, it is placed into group 1 (soon to be bankrupt), otherwise it is placed into group 2. In fact, Altman also identified a third group that fell into a so-called gray zone. These companies could go either way, but should definitely be considered greater credit risks than those in group 2. Generally, the lower the Z-score, the higher the risk of financial distress or bankruptcy.

The original Z-score model for publicly traded companies is:

$$Z = 1.2X_1 + 1.4X_2 + 3.3X_3 + 0.6X_4 + X_5 \qquad \text{(4-34)}$$

---

5. See E. Altman, "Financial Ratios, Discriminant Analysis and the Prediction of Corporate Bankruptcy," *Journal of Finance*, September 1968. The models discussed in this section are from an updated version of this paper written in July 2000: E. Altman, "Predicting Financial Distress of Companies: Revisiting the Z-Score and ZETA Models." This paper can be obtained from http://www.defaultrisk.com/pp_score_14.htm.

where the variables are the following financial ratios:

X_1 = net working capital/total assets

X_2 = retained earnings/total assets

X_3 = EBIT/total assets

X_4 = market value of all equity/book value of total liabilities

X_5 = sales/total assets

Altman reports that this model is 80–90% accurate if we use a cutoff point of 2.675. That is, a firm with a Z-score below 2.675 can reasonably be expected to experience severe financial distress, and possibly bankruptcy, within the next year. The predictive ability of the model is even better if we use a cutoff point of 1.81. There are, therefore, three ranges of Z-scores:

Z < 1.81	Bankruptcy predicted within one year
1.81 < Z < 2.675	Financial distress, possible bankruptcy
Z > 2.675	No financial distress predicted

We can easily apply this model to EPI in the Ratios worksheet. However, first note that we haven't supplied information regarding the market value of EPI's common stock. In A31, enter the label: Market Value of Equity and in B31 enter 884,400. The market value of the equity is found by multiplying the share price by the number of shares outstanding. Next, enter: Z-Score into A32, and in B32 enter the formula:

```
=1.2*('Balance Sheet'!B8-'Balance Sheet'!B17)/'Balance Sheet'
!B12+1.4*('Balance Sheet'!B21/'Balance Sheet'!B12)+3.3*('Income
Statement'!B11/'Balance Sheet'!B12)+0.6*(B31/'Balance Sheet'
!B19)+('Income Statement'!B5/'Balance Sheet'!B12).
```

If you've entered the equation correctly, you will find that EPI's Z-score in 2014 is 3.92, which is safely above 2.675, so bankruptcy isn't predicted.

The Z-Score Model for Private Firms

Because variable X_4 in equation (4-34) requires knowledge of the firm's market capitalization (including both common and preferred equity), we cannot easily use the model for privately held firms. Estimates of the market value of these firms can be made, but the result is necessarily very uncertain. Alternatively, we could substitute the book value of equity for its market value, but that wouldn't be correct. Most publicly traded firms trade for several times their book value, so such a substitution would seem to call for a new coefficient for X_4. In fact, all of the coefficients in the model changed when Altman reestimated it for privately held firms.

The new model for privately held firms is:

$$Z' = 0.717X_1 + 0.847X_2 + 3.107X_3 + 0.420X_4 + 0.998X_5 \qquad \text{(4-35)}$$

where all of the variables are defined as before, except that X_4 uses the book value of equity instead of market value. Altman reports that this model is only slightly less accurate than the one for publicly traded firms when we use the new cutoff points shown below.

$Z' < 1.21$	Bankruptcy predicted within one year
$1.23 < Z' < 2.90$	Financial distress, possible bankruptcy
$Z' > 2.90$	No financial distress predicted

If we treat EPI as a privately held firm, its Z-score for 2014 is 3.35 and for 2013 is 3.55. These scores show that EPI is not likely to file for bankruptcy anytime soon.

Using Financial Ratios

Calculating financial ratios is a pointless exercise unless you understand how to use them. One overriding rule of ratio analysis is this: *A single ratio provides very little information and may be misleading.* You should never draw conclusions from a single ratio. Instead, several ratios and other information should support any conclusions that you make.

With that precaution in mind, there are several ways that ratios can be used to draw important conclusions.

Trend Analysis

Trend analysis involves the examination of ratios over time. Trends, or the lack of trends, can help managers gauge their progress toward a goal. Furthermore, trends can highlight areas in need of attention. While we don't really have enough information on Elvis Products International to perform a trend analysis, it is obvious that many of its ratios are moving in the wrong direction.

For example, all of EPI's profitability ratios have declined in 2014 relative to 2013, some rather dramatically. Management should immediately try to isolate the problem areas. For example, the gross profit margin has declined only slightly, indicating that increasing materials costs are not a major problem, though a price increase may be called for. The operating profit margin has fallen by about 36%, and since we can't blame increasing costs of goods sold, we must conclude that operating costs have increased at a more rapid rate than revenues. The common-size income statement (Exhibit 2-5, page 56) shows that the culprit is SG&A expense. This increase in operating costs has led, to a large degree, to the decline in the other profitability ratios.

One potential problem area for trend analysis is seasonality. We must be careful to compare similar time periods. For example, many firms generate most of their sales during the holidays in the fourth quarter of the year. For this reason they may begin building inventories in the third quarter when sales are low. In this situation, comparing the third-quarter inventory turnover ratio to the fourth-quarter inventory turnover would be misleading.

Comparing to Industry Averages

Aside from trend analysis, one of the most beneficial uses of financial ratios is to compare similar firms within a single industry. This can be done by comparing to industry average ratios, which are published by organizations such as the Risk Management Association (RMA) and Standard & Poor's. Industry averages provide a standard of comparison so that we can determine how well a firm is performing relative to its peers.

Consider Exhibit 4-6, which shows EPI's ratios and the industry averages for 2014. You can enter the industry averages into your worksheet starting in D3 with the label: Industry 2014. Now select D5:D28, type 2.70 into D5, and then press the Enter key. Notice that the active cell will change to D6 when the Enter key is pressed. This is an efficient method of entering a lot of numbers because your fingers never have to leave the number keypad. It is especially helpful when entering numbers into multiple columns and discontiguous cells.

It should be obvious that EPI is not being managed as well as the average firm in the industry. From the liquidity ratios, we can see that EPI is less able to meet its short-term obligations than the average firm, though they are probably not in imminent danger of missing payments. The efficiency ratios show us that EPI is not managing its assets as well as would be expected, especially inventories. It is also obvious that EPI is using substantially more debt than its peers. The coverage ratios indicate that EPI has less cash to pay its interest expense than the industry average. This is due to carrying more than average debt. Finally, all of these problems have led to subpar profitability measures, which seem to be getting worse, rather than better.

It is important to note that industry averages may not be appropriate in all cases. In many cases, it is probably more accurate to define the "industry" as the target company's most closely related competitors. This group is probably far smaller (maybe only three to five companies) than the entire industry as defined by the 4-digit SIC code. The newer 6-digit NAICS code[6] improves, but doesn't eliminate, this situation.

6. North American Industry Classification System. This system was created by the U.S. Census Bureau and its Canadian and Mexican counterparts in 1997 and is replacing the SIC codes. See http://www.census.gov/eos/www/naics/ for more information.

EXHIBIT 4-6
EPI'S RATIOS VS. INDUSTRY AVERAGES

	A	B	C	D
1	Elvis Products International			
2	Ratio Analysis for 2013 and 2014			
3	Ratio	2014	2013	Industry 2014
4	Liquidity Ratios			
5	Current Ratio	2.39x	2.33x	2.70x
6	Quick Ratio	0.84x	0.85x	1.00x
7	Efficiency Ratios			
8	Inventory Turnover	3.89x	4.00x	7.00x
9	A/R Turnover	9.58x	9.77x	10.70x
10	Average Collection Period	37.59 days	36.84 days	33.64 days
11	Fixed Asset Turnover	10.67x	9.95x	11.20x
12	Total Asset Turnover	2.33x	2.34x	2.60x
13	Leverage Ratios			
14	Total Debt Ratio	58.45%	54.81%	50.00%
15	Long-term Debt Ratio	25.72%	22.02%	20.00%
16	LTD to Total Capitalization	38.23%	32.76%	28.57%
17	Debt to Equity	1.41x	1.21x	1.00x
18	LTD to Equity	61.90%	48.73%	40.00%
19	Coverage Ratios			
20	Times Interest Earned	1.97x	3.35x	2.50x
21	Cash Coverage Ratio	2.23x	3.65x	2.80x
22	Profitability Ratios			
23	Gross Profit Margin	15.58%	16.55%	17.50%
24	Operating Profit Margin	3.89%	6.09%	6.25%
25	Net Profit Margin	1.15%	2.56%	3.50%
26	Return on Total Assets	2.68%	5.99%	9.10%
27	Return on Equity	6.45%	13.25%	18.20%
28	Return on Common Equity	6.45%	13.25%	18.20%

Company Goals and Debt Covenants

Financial ratios are often the basis of company goal setting. For example, a CEO might decide that one goal of the firm should be to earn at least 15% on equity (ROE = 15%). Obviously, whether or not this goal is achieved can be determined by calculating the return on equity. Further, by using trend analysis, managers can gauge progress toward meeting goals, and they can determine whether the goals are realistic or not.

Another use of financial ratios can be found in covenants to loan contracts. When companies borrow money, the lenders (bondholders, banks, or other lenders) place restrictions on the company, very often tied to the values of certain ratios. For example, the lender may require that the borrowing firm maintain a current ratio of at least 2.0. Or, it may require that the firm's total debt ratio not exceed 40%. Whatever the restrictions, it is important that the firm monitor its ratios for compliance, or the loan may be due immediately.

Automating Ratio Analysis

Ratio analysis is as much art as science, and different analysts are likely to render somewhat different judgments on a firm. Nonetheless, you can have Excel do a rudimentary analysis for you. Actually, the analysis could be made quite sophisticated if you are willing to put in the effort. The technique that we will illustrate is analogous to creating an expert system, though we wouldn't call it a true expert system at this point.

An *expert system* is a computer program that can diagnose problems or provide an analysis by using the same techniques as an expert in the field. For example, a medical doctor might use an expert system (such as IBM's Watson) to diagnose a patient's illness. The doctor would tell the system about the symptoms and the expert system would consult its rules to generate a likely diagnosis.

Building a true ratio analysis expert system in Excel would be very time consuming, and there are better tools available. However, we can build a very simple system using only a few functions. Our system will analyze each ratio separately and will only determine whether a ratio is "Good," "Ok," or "Bad." To be really useful, the system would need to consider the interrelationships between the ratios, the industry that the company is in, and so on. We leave it to you to improve the system.

As a first step in developing our expert system, we need to specify the rules that will be used to categorize the ratios. In most cases, we have seen that the higher the ratio the better. Therefore, we would like to see that the ratio is higher in 2014 than in 2013 and that the 2014 ratio is greater than the industry average.

We can use Excel's built-in **IF** statement to implement our automatic analysis. Recall that the **IF** statement returns one of two values, depending on whether a statement is true or false:

$$\text{IF}(\textbf{\textit{LOGICAL\_TEST}}, \textbf{\textit{VALUE\_IF\_TRUE}}, \textit{VALUE\_IF\_FALSE})$$

Where **LOGICAL_TEST** is any statement that can be evaluated as true or false, and **VALUE_IF_TRUE** and *VALUE_IF_FALSE* are the return values, which depend on whether **LOGICAL_TEST** was true or false.

We actually want to make two tests to determine whether a ratio is "Good," "Ok," or "Bad." First, we will test to see if the 2014 ratio is greater than the 2013 ratio. To do this, we divide the 2014 value by the 2013 value. If the result is greater than 1, then the 2014 ratio is higher than the 2013 ratio. Using only this test, our formula for the current ratio would be: `=IF(B5/C5>=1,"Good","Bad")` in E5. In this case, the result should be "Good" because the 2014 value is greater than the 2013 value. If you copy this formula to E6, the result will be "Bad" because the 2014 quick ratio is lower than the 2013 quick ratio.

We can modify this formula to also take account of the industry average. If the 2014 ratio is greater than the 2013 ratio **and** the 2014 ratio is greater than the industry average, then the ratio is "Good." To accomplish this we need to use the **AND** function. This function will return true only if all arguments are true:

$$\text{AND}(\textbf{\textit{LOGICAL1}}, \textit{LOGICAL2}, \ldots)$$

In this function, ***LOGICAL1*** and *LOGICAL2* are the arguments to be evaluated as either true or false. You can have up to 255 arguments, but only one is required. The modified function in E5 is now: `=IF(And(B5/C5>=1,B5/D5>=1),"Good","Bad")`. Now, the ratio will only be judged as "Good" if both conditions are true. Note that they are not for the current ratio, so the result is "Bad."

One final improvement can be made by adding "Ok" to the possible outcomes. We will say that the ratio is "Ok" if the 2014 value is greater than the 2013 value, **or** the 2014 value is greater than the industry average. We can accomplish this by nesting a second **IF** statement inside the first in place of "Bad." For the second **IF** statement, we need to use Excel's **OR** function:

$$\text{OR}(\textbf{\textit{LOGICAL1}}, \textit{LOGICAL2}, \ldots)$$

This function is identical to the **AND** function, except that it returns true if any of its arguments are true. The final form of our equation is: `=IF(AND(B5/C5>=1,B5/D5>=1),"Good",IF(OR(B5/D5>=1,B5/C5>=1),"Ok","Bad"))`. For the current ratio, this will evaluate to "Ok." You can now evaluate all of EPI's ratios by copying this formula to E6:E28.

One more change is necessary. Recall that for leverage ratios, lower is generally better. Therefore, change all of the ">=" to "<=" in E14:E18. You also need to make the same change in E10 for the average collection period. Your worksheet should now resemble that shown in Exhibit 4-7.

EXHIBIT 4-7
EPI'S RATIOS WITH AUTOMATIC ANALYSIS

	A	B	C	D	E
1		Elvis Products International			
2		Ratio Analysis for 2013 and 2014			
3	Ratio	2014	2013	Industry 2014	Analysis
4	Liquidity Ratios				
5	Current Ratio	2.39x	2.33x	2.70x	Ok
6	Quick Ratio	0.84x	0.85x	1.00x	Bad
7	Efficiency Ratios				
8	Inventory Turnover	3.89x	4.00x	7.00x	Bad
9	A/R Turnover	9.58x	9.77x	10.70x	Bad
10	Average Collection Period	37.59 days	36.84 days	33.64 days	Bad
11	Fixed Asset Turnover	10.67x	9.95x	11.20x	Ok
12	Total Asset Turnover	2.33x	2.34x	2.60x	Bad
13	Leverage Ratios				
14	Total Debt Ratio	58.45%	54.81%	50.00%	Bad
15	Long-term Debt Ratio	25.72%	22.02%	20.00%	Bad
16	LTD to Total Capitalization	38.23%	32.76%	28.57%	Bad
17	Debt to Equity	1.41x	1.21x	1.00x	Bad
18	LTD to Equity	61.90%	48.73%	40.00%	Bad
19	Coverage Ratios				
20	Times Interest Earned	1.97x	3.35x	2.50x	Bad
21	Cash Coverage Ratio	2.23x	3.65x	2.80x	Bad
22	Profitability Ratios				
23	Gross Profit Margin	15.58%	16.55%	17.50%	Bad
24	Operating Profit Margin	3.89%	6.09%	6.25%	Bad
25	Net Profit Margin	1.15%	2.56%	3.50%	Bad
26	Return on Total Assets	2.68%	5.99%	9.10%	Bad
27	Return on Equity	6.45%	13.25%	18.20%	Bad
28	Return on Common Equity	6.45%	13.25%	18.20%	Bad

You should see that nearly all of EPI's ratios are judged to be "Bad." This is exactly what our previous analysis has determined, except that Excel has done it automatically. There are many changes that could be made to improve on this simple ratio analyzer, but we will leave that job as an exercise for you.

Economic Profit Measures of Performance

Economic profit is the profit earned in excess of the firm's costs, including its implicit opportunity costs (primarily its cost of capital). Accounting profit (net income), however, measures profit as revenues minus all of the firm's explicit costs. It takes into account a firm's cost of debt capital (interest expense), but it ignores the implicit cost of the firm's equity capital. The concept of economic profit is an old one, but it has been revived by consulting firms promising to improve the financial performance and executive compensation practices of their clients.[7] Some large firms have switched to various measures of economic profit—some with good results and some not. In any case, the method has generated a lot of interest, and we will include a short discussion of measuring economic profit in this section.

The basic idea behind economic profit measures is that the firm cannot increase shareholder wealth unless it makes a profit in excess of its cost of capital.[8] Because we will be taking account of the cost of capital explicitly, we cannot use the normal accounting measures of profit directly. The adjustments to the financial statements vary depending on the firm and who is doing the calculations. At the moment, there is no completely accepted standard. With this in mind, we will present a simplified economic profit calculation.

Mathematically, economic profit is:

$$\begin{aligned} \text{Economic Profit} &= \text{NOPAT} - \text{After-tax cost of operating capital} \\ &= \text{NOPAT} - (\text{Total Net Operating Capital} \times \text{WACC}) \end{aligned}$$
(4-36)

where NOPAT is net operating profit after taxes. The after-tax cost of operating capital is the dollar cost of all interest-bearing debt instruments (i.e., bonds and notes payable) plus the dollar cost of preferred and common equity. Generally, the firm's after-tax cost of capital (a percentage amount) is calculated and then multiplied by the amount of operating capital to obtain the dollar cost.

To calculate the economic profit, we must first calculate NOPAT, total operating capital, and the firm's cost of capital. For our purposes in this chapter, the cost of capital will be given (see Chapter 10 for the calculations). NOPAT is the after-tax operating profit of the firm:

$$\text{NOPAT} = \text{EBIT}(1 - \text{tax rate})$$
(4-37)

Note that the NOPAT calculation does not include interest expense because it will be explicitly accounted for when we subtract the cost of all capital.

Total operating capital is the sum of non-interest-bearing current assets and net fixed assets, less non-interest-bearing current liabilities. We ignore interest-bearing current assets because

---

7. The leader in this effort is the consulting firm Stern Stewart and Company who refer to economic profit by the copyrighted name Economic Value Added (EVA).

8. Economic profit is also measured by net present value (NPV), which is introduced in Chapter 11. The primary difference is that in this chapter we are trying to calculate the actual economic profit that was earned over some previous time period (usually the previous year). NPV measures the expected economic profit of a future investment.

they are not operating assets, and we ignore interest-bearing current liabilities (e.g., notes payable) because the cost of these liabilities is included in the cost of capital.

We will demonstrate the calculation of economic profit using the Elvis Products International data for 2013 and 2014. Make sure that the workbook containing EPI's financial statements is open, and insert a new worksheet for our economic profit calculations. Set up your new worksheet as shown in Exhibit 4-8, and rename the sheet "Economic Profit."

EXHIBIT 4-8
ECONOMIC PROFIT CALCULATION FOR EPI

	A	B	C
1	Elvis Products International		
2	Economic Profit Calculations		
3		2014	2013
4	Tax Rate	40%	40%
5	NOPAT		
6	Total Operating Capital		
7	After-tax Cost of Capital	13%	13%
8	Dollar Cost of Capital		
9	Economic Profit		

Note that we are assuming that the firm's cost of capital is 13%, and the tax rate should be pulled from the income statement with the formula: =' Income Statement' ! $B18. All of the other numbers must be calculated as discussed above.

Recall that NOPAT is simply EBIT times 1 – the tax rate, so in B5 enter the formula: =' Income Statement' !B11*(1-B4). You should see that EPI has generated an after-tax operating profit of $89,820 in 2014. Copy this formula to C5 to get the NOPAT for 2013.

The next step is to calculate the amount of operating capital. Because EPI has no short-term investments, we merely add current assets to net fixed assets and then subtract current liabilities less notes payable. In B6 enter the formula: =' Balance Sheet' !B8+' Balance Sheet' !B11-(' Balance Sheet' !B17-' Balance Sheet' !B15). Your result should show that the total operating capital for 2014 was $1,335,600. Copy the formula to C6.

To calculate the dollar cost of capital in B8, enter the formula: =B7*B6; copy this to C8. Recall that economic profit is simply NOPAT minus the dollar cost of capital, so we can calculate the economic profit in B9 with the formula: =B5-B8. You should find that EPI earned an economic profit of –$83,808 in 2014. Copy this formula to C9, and you will see that EPI's economic profit in 2013 was –$28,876.

This example shows how misleading accounting measures of profit (particularly net income) can be. In this case, EPI reported profits in both 2013 and 2014, but it was actually reducing shareholder wealth over the past two years. This mirrors the results from our ratio analysis. EPI's management has not been doing a good job, at least over this period. Your economic profit worksheet should now look like the one shown in Exhibit 4-9.

EXHIBIT 4-9
EPI'S COMPLETED ECONOMIC PROFIT WORKSHEET

	A	B	C
1	Elvis Products International		
2	Economic Profit Calculations		
3		2014	2013
4	Tax Rate	40%	40%
5	NOPAT	89,820	125,460
6	Total Operating Capital	1,335,600	1,187,200
7	After-tax Cost of Capital	13%	13%
8	Dollar Cost of Capital	173,628	154,336
9	Economic Profit	(83,808)	(28,876)

Summary

In this chapter, we have seen how various financial ratios can be used to evaluate the financial health of a company and therefore the performance of the managers of the firm. You have also seen how Excel can make the calculation of ratios quicker and easier than doing it manually. We looked at five categories of ratios: *Liquidity ratios* measure the ability of a firm to pay its bills; *efficiency ratios* measure how well the firm is making use of its assets to generate sales; *leverage ratios* describe how much debt the firm is using to finance its assets; *coverage ratios* tell how much cash the firm has available to pay specific expenses; and *profitability ratios* measure how profitable the firm has been over a period of time.

We have also seen how Excel can be programmed to do a rudimentary ratio analysis automatically, using only a few of the built-in logical functions. Table 4-1 provides a summary of the ratio formulas presented in this chapter. Finally, we looked at the concept of economic profit and how it can give a much clearer picture of a firm's financial health than traditional accounting profit measures.

TABLE 4-1
SUMMARY OF FINANCIAL RATIOS

Name of Ratio	Formula	Page
Liquidity Ratios		
Current Ratio	$\dfrac{\text{Current Assets}}{\text{Current Liabilities}}$	109
Quick Ratio	$\dfrac{\text{Current Assets} - \text{Inventories}}{\text{Current Liabilities}}$	110
Efficiency Ratios		
Inventory Turnover	$\dfrac{\text{Cost of Goods Sold}}{\text{Inventory}}$	111
Accounts Receivable Turnover	$\dfrac{\text{Credit Sales}}{\text{Accounts Receivable}}$	112
Average Collection Period	$\dfrac{\text{Accounts Receivable}}{\text{Annual Credit Sales}/360}$	113
Fixed Asset Turnover	$\dfrac{\text{Sales}}{\text{Net Fixed Assets}}$	114
Total Asset Turnover	$\dfrac{\text{Sales}}{\text{Total Assets}}$	114
Leverage Ratios		
Total Debt Ratio	$\dfrac{\text{Total Debt}}{\text{Total Assets}}$	116
Long-Term Debt Ratio	$\dfrac{\text{Long-Term Debt}}{\text{Total Assets}}$	116
LTD to Total Capitalization	$\dfrac{\text{LTD}}{\text{LTD} + \text{Preferred Equity} + \text{Common Equity}}$	117
Debt to Equity	$\dfrac{\text{Total Debt}}{\text{Total Equity}}$	117
LTD to Equity	$\dfrac{\text{LTD}}{\text{Preferred Equity} + \text{Common Equity}}$	118

TABLE 4-1 (CONTINUED)
SUMMARY OF FINANCIAL RATIOS

Name of Ratio	Formula	Page
Coverage Ratios		
Times Interest Earned	$\dfrac{\text{EBIT}}{\text{Interest Expense}}$	119
Cash Coverage Ratio	$\dfrac{\text{EBIT + Noncash Expenses}}{\text{Interest Expense}}$	119
Profitability Ratios		
Gross Profit Margin	$\dfrac{\text{Gross Profit}}{\text{Sales}}$	121
Operating Profit Margin	$\dfrac{\text{Net Operating Income}}{\text{Sales}}$	121
Net Profit Margin	$\dfrac{\text{Net Income}}{\text{Sales}}$	122
Return on Total Assets	$\dfrac{\text{Net Income}}{\text{Total Assets}}$	122
Return on Equity	$\dfrac{\text{Net Income}}{\text{Total Equity}}$	123
Return on Common Equity	$\dfrac{\text{Net Income Available to Common}}{\text{Common Equity}}$	123
DuPont Analysis of ROE	$\dfrac{\text{Net Profit Margin} \times \text{Total Asset Turnover}}{1 - \text{Total Debt Ratio}}$	125

TABLE 4-2
FUNCTIONS INTRODUCED IN THIS CHAPTER

Purpose	Function	Page
Return a value dependent on test	**IF(*LOGICAL_TEST*, *VALUE_IF_TRUE*, *VALUE_IF_FALSE*)**	132
Returns true if all arguments true	**AND(*LOGICAL1*, *LOGICAL2*, ...)**	133
Returns true if one argument is true	**OR(*LOGICAL1*, *LOGICAL2*, ...)**	133

Problems

1. Copy the Mike Owjai Manufacturing financial statements from Problem 1 in Chapter 2 into a new workbook.

   a. Set up a ratio worksheet similar to the one in Exhibit 4-6, page 131, and calculate all of the ratios for Mike Owjai Manufacturing.

   b. Identify at least two areas of potential concern using the ratios. Identify at least two areas that have shown improvement.

   c. In 2014 Mike Owjai Manufacturing's ROE increased. Explain, in words, why this increase occurred using the DuPont method from equation (4-29). Now use the extended DuPont method from (4-33).

   d. Mike Owjai Manufacturing has shown an accounting profit in each of the past two years. Calculate the economic profit for these years and compare it to net income. The WACC is 11%.

   e. Using Altman's model for privately held firms, calculate the Z-score for Mike Owjai Manufacturing. Does it appear that the firm is in imminent danger of bankruptcy?

2. A computer problem at Southglenn Photography Studios has resulted in incomplete financial statements. Management of the company has asked you to see if you can fill in the missing data.

Southglenn Photography Studios
Income Statement
For the Year Ended December 31, 2014

	2014
Sales	Ratio
Cost of Goods Sold	Ratio
Gross Profit	Formula
Operating Expenses	141,000
Earnings Before Interest and Taxes	Formula
Interest Expense	Ratio
Earnings Before Taxes	Formula
Taxes	Formula
Net Income	Ratio
Notes: Tax Rate	30%

Southglenn Photography Studios
Balance Sheet
As of December 31, 2014

	2014
Assets	
Cash	1,500
Accounts Receivable	Ratio
Inventories	136,500
Total Current Assets	Formula
Gross Fixed Assets	378,000
Accumulated Depreciation	Formula
Net Fixed Assets	Ratio
Total Assets	450,000
Liabilities and Owner's Equity	
Accounts Payable	66,000
Short-term Bank Notes	Formula
Total Current Liabilities	Ratio
Long-term Debt	Ratio
Common Equity	Ratio
Total Liabilities and Owner's Equity	Formula

a. Recreate the financial statements as shown using formulas with the ratios given below to fill in the cells with the word "Ratio." Use the **ROUND** function to round each of these answers to the nearest $10.

Ratio	Value
Current Ratio	0.898550
Inventory Turnover*	2.109890
A/R Turnover	10.000000
Fixed Asset Turnover	1.818180
LTD To Equity	0.395350
Times Interest Earned	2.786890
Net Profit Margin	0.047688
Return on Total Assets	0.050870
Return on Equity	0.131440

* Uses Cost of Goods Sold in numerator.

b. Complete the financial statements by using formulas that refer to existing data to fill in the remaining cells.

Internet Exercise

1. Choose your own company and repeat the analysis from Problem 1. You can get the data from MSN Money at http://money.msn.com/investing. To retrieve the data for your company, enter the ticker symbol to get a quote. Now under Financials on the left select the annual income statement. Highlight the entire data section and copy. Now paste this data directly into a new worksheet. The data will be pasted in HTML format and a Smart Tag will appear that will allow you to either "Keep Source Formatting" or "Match Destination Formatting." Experiment to see which one you like best. Repeat these steps for the balance sheet.

CHAPTER 5

Financial Forecasting

After studying this chapter, you should be able to:

1. *Explain how the "percent of sales" method is used to develop pro forma financial statements and how to construct such statements in Excel.*

2. *Use circular references to perform iterative calculations.*

3. *Use the* **TREND** *function for forecasting sales or any other trending variables.*

4. *Perform a regression analysis with Excel's built-in regression tools.*

5. *Determine if a variable is statistically significant in a regression analysis.*

Forecasting is an important activity for a wide variety of business people. Nearly all of the decisions made by financial managers are made on the basis of forecasts of one kind or another. For example, in Chapter 3 we've seen how the cash budget can be used to forecast short-term borrowing and investing needs. Every item in the cash budget is itself a forecast. Further, the ratios that we saw in Chapter 4 can be combined with forecasts to help achieve company goals. In this chapter, we will examine several methods of forecasting. The first, the percent of sales method, is the simplest. We will also look at more advanced techniques, such as regression analysis.

The Percent of Sales Method

Forecasting financial statements is important for a number of reasons. Among these are planning for the future and providing information to the company's investors. The simplest method of forecasting income statements and balance sheets is the percent of sales method. This method has the added advantage of requiring relatively little data to make a forecast.

The fundamental premise of the percent of sales method is that some, but not all, income statement and balance sheet items maintain a constant relationship with the level of sales. For example, if the cost of goods sold has averaged 65% of sales over the last several years, we would assume that this relationship would hold for the next year. If sales are expected to be $10 million next year, our cost of goods forecast would be $6.5 million (10 million × 0.65 = 6.5 million).

Of course, this method assumes that the forecasted level of sales is already known. There are two primary methods of forecasting sales. The *top-down* method relies on forecasts of macroeconomic variables (e.g., GDP, inflation rates) and of the condition of the industry as a whole. These expectations are then converted into a sales forecast for the entire firm, and sales targets for each division or product. The *bottom-up* method involves discussions with customers to determine the expected demand for each product and expectations regarding prices, which are then summed to calculate a firm-wide sales forecast. Of course, firms can use a combination of the two methods. We will take the sales forecast as a given.

Forecasting the Income Statement

As an example of income statement forecasting, consider the Elvis Products International (EPI) statements that you created in Chapter 2. The income statement is recreated here in Exhibit 5-1. Recall that we have used a custom number format to display this data in thousands of dollars, but that the full-precision numbers are there. Open the workbook that you created for Chapter 2, and make a copy of the Income Statement worksheet. Rename the new worksheet to PF Income Statement, where PF stands for *pro forma*.[1]

The level of detail that you have in an income statement will affect the number of items that will fluctuate directly with sales. In general, we will proceed through the income statement line by line asking the question, "Is it likely that this item will change proportionally with sales?" If the answer is yes, then we calculate the percentage of sales and multiply the result by the sales forecast for the next period. Otherwise, we will take one of two actions: Leave the item unchanged, or use other information to change

---

1. *Pro forma* is a Latin word that, for our purposes, can be interpreted to mean "as if." That is, these forecasted financial statements are presented as if the forecast time period has already happened.

the item.[2] If you don't know the answer, then you can create a chart that compares the item to sales over the last several quarters or years. It should be obvious if there is a relationship, though you may need to use some of the statistical tools, discussed on page 156, to determine the form of the relationship.

EXHIBIT 5-1
EPI's INCOME STATEMENTS FOR 2013 AND 2014

	A	B	C
1	Elvis Products International		
2	Income Statement		
3	For the Year Ended Dec. 31, 2014 ($ in 000's)		
4		*2014*	*2013*
5	Sales	3,850.00	3,432.00
6	Cost of Goods Sold	3,250.00	2,864.00
7	*Gross Profit*	*600.00*	*568.00*
8	Selling and G&A Expenses	330.30	240.00
9	Fixed Expenses	100.00	100.00
10	Depreciation Expense	20.00	18.90
11	*EBIT*	*149.70*	*209.10*
12	Interest Expense	76.00	62.50
13	*Earnings Before Taxes*	*73.70*	*146.60*
14	Taxes	29.48	58.64
15	*Net Income*	*44.22*	*87.96*

For EPI, only one income statement item will clearly change with sales: the cost of goods sold. Another item, SG&A (selling, general, and administrative) expense, is an aggregation of many things, some of which will probably change with sales and some that won't. For our purposes we choose to believe that, on balance, SG&A will change along with sales (that is, we assume that SG&A is mostly variable costs).

Changes in the other items are not directly related to a change in sales in the short term. Depreciation expense, for example, depends on the amount and age of the firm's fixed assets. Interest expense is a function of the amount and maturity structure of debt in the firm's capital structure. These items may, and probably will, change but we will need additional information to forecast them. Taxes depend directly on the firm's taxable income, though this indirectly depends on the level of sales. All of the other items on the income statement are calculated directly.

2. For example, if you know that the lease for the company's headquarters building has a scheduled increase, then you should be sure to include this information in your forecast for fixed costs.

Insert

Before getting started with the forecast, insert a column to the left of column B. Select a cell in column B and click the Insert button on the Home tab and then choose Insert Sheet Columns. Note that a Smart Tag will appear that will give you three choices: (1) Format Same As Left; (2) Format Same As Right; or (3) Clear Formatting. Choose the second option so that the custom number formats and column width will automatically be applied. So that we can experiment later if we choose, enter 40% for the tax rate in B18 and C18.

To generate our income statement forecast, we first determine the percentage of sales for each of the prior years for each item that changes. In this case, for 2014 we have:

$$\text{Cost of Goods Sold 2014 Percentage of Sales} \qquad \frac{\$3,250,000}{3,850,000} = 0.8442 = 84.42\%$$

$$\text{SG\&A Expense 2014 Percentage of Sales} \qquad \frac{\$330,300}{3,850,000} = 0.0858 = 8.58\%$$

The 2013 percentages (83.45% and 6.99%, respectively) can be found in exactly the same manner. We now calculate the average of these percentages over the past few years, and use this average as our estimate of the 2015 percentage of sales. The forecast is then found by multiplying these percentages by next year's sales forecast. Assuming that sales are forecasted to be $4,300,000 in 2015 we have:

$$\text{Cost of Goods Sold 2015 Forecast} \qquad \$4,300,000 \times 0.8393 = 3,609,108$$

$$\text{SG\&A Expense 2015 Forecast} \qquad \$4,300,000 \times 0.0779 = 334,803$$

To calculate the arithmetic average in Excel use the **AVERAGE** function, which is defined as:

Average(*NUMBER1*, *NUMBER2*, ...)

where *NUMBER1* is required, and you may have as many as 255 numbers or ranges.

Exhibit 5-2 shows a forecast of the complete 2015 income statement. To create this forecast in your worksheet, in B4 enter: `2015`.[3] Because the 2015 income statement will be calculated in exactly the same way as 2014, the easiest way to proceed is to copy C5:C15 into B5:B15. This will save you from entering formulas to calculate subtotals (e.g., EBIT) and will apply the cell borders. Insert a row above row 17, and in A16 type: `*Forecast`.

---

3. We have chosen to apply a custom format so that the number has an asterisk to indicate a footnote that informs the reader that these are forecasts. The custom format is `#"*"`.

EXHIBIT 5-2
PERCENT OF SALES FORECAST FOR 2015

	A	B	C	D
1	**Elvis Products International**			
2	**Pro-forma Income Statement**			
3	**For the Year Ended Dec. 31, 2014**			
4		*2015**	*2014*	*2013*
5	Sales	4,300.00	3,850.00	3,432.00
6	Cost of Goods Sold	3,609.11	3,250.00	2,864.00
7	*Gross Profit*	*690.89*	*600.00*	*568.00*
8	Selling and G&A Expenses	334.80	330.30	240.00
9	Fixed Expenses	100.00	100.00	100.00
10	Depreciation Expense	25.00	20.00	18.90
11	*EBIT*	*231.09*	*149.70*	*209.10*
12	Interest Expense	80.80	76.00	62.50
13	*Earnings Before Taxes*	*150.29*	*73.70*	*146.60*
14	Taxes	60.12	29.48	58.64
15	*Net Income*	*90.17*	*44.22*	*87.96*
16	* Forecast			
17				
18	Notes:			
19	Tax Rate	40%	40%	
20	Additional Depreciation	5.00		
21	Interest Rate	11.70%		

First, in B5 enter the sales forecast: 4,300,000. Now, we can calculate the 2015 cost of goods forecast in B6 with the formula: =AVERAGE(C6/C$5,D6/D$5)*B$5. This formula calculates the average of the cost of goods as a percentage of sales for the last two years and then multiplies it by the sales forecast. The result should be as shown above. Now copy this formula and paste it into B8 (using Paste Special Formulas to avoid pasting the underline) to get the forecast for SG&A expense.

Instead of performing the entire calculation in cells B6 and B8, we could have used a *helper column*. A helper column is used to do intermediate calculations and is sometimes useful. In this case, we could have calculated the average percentage of sales for each item in, say, column K. We would then use these values to perform the final calculation in column B. For example, K6 might contain the formula: =AVERAGE(C6/C$5,D6/D$5). Then the formula in B6 would be: =K6*B$5. This technique would allow you to easily see the average percentages (as in a common-size income statement) that are being used to generate the forecast. Although this might be useful, it can be an inefficient use of the spreadsheet unless it is necessary and may be confusing to others who view your work.

147

Assume that we do not have any information regarding changes in fixed expenses, so copy the value from C9. However, we have been informed that the firm intends to invest $50,000 in fixed assets in 2015. This will cause depreciation expense to rise by $5,000. We need to document this assumption, so in A20 type: Additional Depreciation, and in B20 enter: 5,000. We will come back to add a formula in B20 in the next section. Don't forget to apply the same custom number format to this cell that we used in the others.

The formula to calculate depreciation expense in B10 is: =C10+B20. Because we don't yet know how the firm will finance these investments, leave the interest expense at the same level as 2014. To calculate the taxes, in B14, use the formula: =B19*B13. Your worksheet should now look like the one in Exhibit 5-2, page 147.

Forecasting Assets on the Balance Sheet

We can forecast the balance sheet in exactly the same way as the income statement, with some major exceptions. For those items that can be expected to vary directly with sales, our formulas will be similar to those we have already seen. We will explain how to handle the other items below. Make a copy of the Balance Sheet and rename it PF Balance Sheet.

Create the percent of sales balance sheet for 2015 by selecting column B and inserting a new column. Change the heading to say Pro Forma Balance Sheet so that it is clear that we are working with a forecast. In B4 type the label: 2015. As before, apply a custom number format to display an asterisk after the number. Like we did with the income statement, we will move, line by line, through the balance sheet to determine which items will vary with sales.

The firm's cash balance is the first, and perhaps the most difficult, item with which we need to work. Does the cash balance vary, in constant proportion, with sales? Your first response might be, "Of course it does. As the firm sells more goods, it accumulates cash." This line of reasoning neglects two important facts. The firm has other things to do with its cash besides accumulating it, and because cash is a low-return asset, firms should seek to minimize the amount of their cash balance.[4] For these reasons, even though the cash balance will probably change, it probably will not change by the same percentage as sales and cash levels tend to be volatile. Therefore, we will simply use the cash balance from 2014 as our forecast, so enter: =C5 into cell B5.

The next two items, accounts receivable and inventory, are much easier. Both of these are likely to fluctuate roughly in proportion to sales. Using the same methodology that we used for the pro forma income statement, we will find the average percentage of sales for the past

---

4. Within reason, of course. Firms need some amount of cash to operate, but the amount needed does not necessarily vary directly with the level of sales.

New Arrange
Window All

two years and multiply that amount by our sales forecast for 2015. For accounts receivable, the formula in B6 is: =AVERAGE(C6/'PF Income Statement'!C$5,D6/'PF Income Statement'!D$5)*'PF Income Statement'!$B$5. Instead of typing the references to the pro forma income statement, it is easier to insert them by displaying both the income statement and the balance sheet and selecting the appropriate cells with the mouse. Click the View tab and select New Window. This will create an additional view of the workbook. Next, click on the Arrange All button and choose how you would like the worksheets arranged. In the second view, change to the PF Income Statement worksheet. Now that both worksheets are visible, it is easier to select cells. Because we will use the same formula for inventory, we can simply copy this formula down to B7. Total current assets in B8 is a calculated value, so we can copy the formula directly from cell C8.

In B9, we have the 2015 gross plant and equipment. This is the historical purchase price of the buildings and equipment that the firm owns. As noted earlier, the firm plans to make net new investments of $50,000 in 2015. We will document this assumption by entering Net Addition to Plant and Equipment in A28 and 50,000 in B28. The formula in B9 is: =C9+B28. Note that this increase is not necessarily due to the expected increase in sales. Although gross fixed assets may rise or fall in any given year, most companies always operate with spare capacity so the changes are not, in the short run, directly related to sales.

We now need to calculate the additional depreciation. We will assume that the expected life of the new equipment is 10 years and that it will be depreciated using the straight-line method to a salvage value of zero. In A29 enter the label: Life of New Equipment in Years, and in B29 enter 10. In A30 enter: New Depreciation (Straight-line). In B30 we will calculate the depreciation using the SLN function, which is defined as:

$$\text{SLN}(\textit{COST, SALVAGE, LIFE})$$

where the arguments are defined as you would expect. In B30 enter: =SLN(B28,0,B29). The additional depreciation expense will be $5,000. Now, return to the pro forma income statement where we will enter a formula in B20: ='PF Balance Sheet'!B30. This last step allows us to change the amount of the new investment and have the additional depreciation expense reflected on the pro forma income statement.

Now, return to the pro forma balance sheet. Accumulated depreciation will definitely increase in 2015 but not because of the forecasted change in sales. Instead, accumulated depreciation will increase by the amount of the depreciation expense for 2015. To determine the accumulated depreciation for 2015, we will add 2015's depreciation expense to 2014's accumulated depreciation. The formula is: =C10+'PF Income Statement'!B10.

To complete the asset side of the balance sheet, we note that both net fixed assets and total assets are calculated values. We can simply copy the formulas from C11:C12 and paste them into B11:B12.

Forecasting Liabilities on the Balance Sheet

Once the assets are completed, the rest of the balance sheet is comparatively simple because we can mostly copy formulas already entered. Before continuing, however, we need to distinguish among the types of financing sources. We have already seen that the types of financing that a firm uses can be divided into three categories:

- Current liabilities
- Long-term liabilities
- Owner's equity

These categories are not sufficiently distinguished for our purposes here. Instead, we will divide the liabilities and equity of a firm into two categories:

- *Spontaneous sources of financing*—These are the sources of financing that arise during the ordinary course of doing business. One example is accounts payable. After a credit account is established with a supplier, no additional work is required to obtain credit; it just happens spontaneously when the firm makes a purchase. Note that not all current liabilities are spontaneous sources of financing (e.g., short-term notes payable, long-term debt due in one year).

- *Discretionary sources of financing*—These are the financing sources that require a large effort on the part of the firm to obtain. In other words, the firm must make a conscious decision to obtain these funds. Furthermore, the firm's upper-level management will use its *discretion* to determine the appropriate type of financing to use. Examples of this type of financing include any type of bank loan, bonds, preferred stock, and common stock (but not retained earnings).

Generally speaking, spontaneous sources of financing can be expected to vary directly with sales. Changes in discretionary sources, on the other hand, will not have a direct relationship with changes in sales. We always leave discretionary sources of financing unchanged for reasons that will soon become clear.

Returning now to our forecasting problem, the first item to consider is accounts payable. As noted above, accounts payable is a spontaneous source of financing and will, therefore, change directly with sales. To enter the formula, all that is necessary is to copy the formula from one of the other items that we have already completed. Copy the contents of B6 (or B7, it doesn't matter which) and paste it into B14. The result should indicate a forecasted accounts payable of $189.05.

The next item to consider is the short-term notes payable. Because this is a discretionary source of financing, we will leave it unchanged from 2014. In reality, we might handle this item differently if we had more information. For example, if we knew that the notes would be retired before the end of 2015, we would change our forecast to zero. Alternatively, if the payments on the notes include both principal and interest, our forecast would be the 2014 amount less principal payments that we expect to make in 2015. Because we are leaving it unchanged, the formula in B15 is: =C15.

If we assume that the "other current liabilities" item represents primarily accrued expenses, then it is a spontaneous source of financing. We can, therefore, simply copy the formula from B14 and paste it into B16. The forecasted amount is $163.38.

Long-term debt, in B18, and common stock, in B20, are both discretionary sources of financing. We will leave these balances unchanged from 2014. In B18 the formula is: =C18 and in B20 the formula is: =C20.

The final item that we must consider is retained earnings. Recall that retained earnings accumulates over time. That is, the balance in any year is the accumulated amount that has been added in previous years plus any new additions. The amount that will be added to retained earnings is given by:

$$\text{Change in Retained Earnings} = \text{Net Income} - \text{Dividends}$$

where the dividends are those paid to both the common and preferred stockholders. The formula for retained earnings will require that we reference forecasted 2015 net income from the income statement and the dividends from the statement of cash flows (see Exhibit 2-7, page 59). Note that we are assuming that 2015 dividends will be the same as the 2014 dividends. We can reference these cells in exactly the same way as before, so the formula is: =C21+'PF Income Statement'!B15+'Statement of Cash Flows'!B19. The results should show that we are forecasting retained earnings to be $297.04 in 2015.

At this point, you should go back and calculate the subtotals in B17, B19, and B22. Finally, we calculate the total liabilities and owner's equity in B23 with =B19+B22.

Discretionary Financing Needed

Sharp-eyed readers will notice that our pro forma balance sheet does not balance. Although this appears to be a serious problem, it actually represents one of the purposes of the pro forma balance sheet. The difference between total assets and total liabilities and owner's equity is referred to as *discretionary financing needed* (DFN, also called additional funds needed or required new funds). In other words, this is the amount of discretionary financing that the firm thinks it will need to raise in the next year. Because of the amount of time and effort required to raise these funds, it is important that the firm be aware of its needs well in advance. The pro forma balance sheet fills this need. Frequently, the firm will find that it is forecasting a higher level of assets than liabilities and equity. In this case, the managers would need to arrange for more liabilities and/or equity to finance the level of assets needed to support the volume of sales expected. This is referred to as a *deficit* of discretionary funds. If the forecast shows that there will be a higher level of liabilities and equity than assets, the firm is said to have a *surplus* of discretionary funds. Remember that, in the end, the balance sheet must balance. The "plug figure" necessary to make this happen is the DFN.

We should add an extra line at the bottom of the pro forma balance sheet to calculate the DFN. Type Discretionary Financing Needed in A25, and in B25 add the formula =B12-B23. This calculation tells us that EPI expects to need $38,119.50 (displayed as 38.12 with the custom number format) more in discretionary funds to support its forecasted level of assets. In this case, EPI is forecasting a deficit of discretionary funds. Apply the custom number format to this number and to the rest of the balance sheet.

EXHIBIT 5-3
EPI'S PRO FORMA BALANCE SHEET FOR 2015

	A	B	C	D
1	**Elvis Products International**			
2	**Pro Forma Balance Sheet**			
3	**As of Dec. 31, 2014**			
4	*Assets*	*2015**	*2014*	*2013*
5	Cash and Equivalents	52.00	52.00	57.60
6	Accounts Receivable	444.51	402.00	351.20
7	Inventory	914.90	836.00	715.20
8	*Total Current Assets*	*1,411.40*	*1,290.00*	*1,124.00*
9	Plant & Equipment	577.00	527.00	491.00
10	Accumulated Depreciation	191.20	166.20	146.20
11	*Net Fixed Assets*	*385.80*	*360.80*	*344.80*
12	*Total Assets*	*1,797.20*	*1,650.80*	*1,468.80*
13	*Liabilities and Owner's Equity*			
14	Accounts Payable	189.05	175.20	145.60
15	Short-term Notes Payable	225.00	225.00	200.00
16	Other Current Liabilities	163.38	140.00	136.00
17	*Total Current Liabilities*	*577.43*	*540.20*	*481.60*
18	Long-term Debt	424.61	424.61	323.43
19	*Total Liabilities*	*1,002.04*	*964.81*	*805.03*
20	Common Stock	460.00	460.00	460.00
21	Retained Earnings	297.04	225.99	203.77
22	*Total Shareholder's Equity*	*757.04*	*685.99*	*663.77*
23	*Total Liabilities and Owner's Equity*	*1,759.08*	*1,650.80*	*1,468.80*
24	* Forecast			
25	Discretionary Financing Needed	38.12	Deficit	
26				
27	Notes:			
28	Net Addition to Plant & Equipment	50.00		
29	Life of New Equipment in Years	10		
30	New Depreciation (Straight-line)	5.00		

To make clear that this amount is a deficit (note that the sign is the opposite of what might be expected when using that word), we can have Excel inform us whether we will have a surplus or deficit of discretionary funds. Use an **IF** statement and realize that if the DFN is a positive number, then we have a deficit; otherwise we have a surplus or DFN is zero. So the formula in C25 is: `=IF(B25>0,"Deficit", IF(B25<0,"Surplus", "Balanced"))`.[5] Your balance sheet should now resemble that in Exhibit 5-3.

Using Iteration to Eliminate DFN

Circular errors result when a formula refers back to itself, either directly or indirectly through another formula. A simple example would be if the formula in B18 was =B18. Excel cannot calculate this because the result depends on itself (it is self-referential). In most cases, this is undesirable even if the formula eventually converges to a solution. However, there are circumstances that are necessarily self-referential and cannot be solved in any other way.

For example, if we wish to eliminate the DFN deficit, then the firm must raise that amount of money. Suppose that any discretionary funds will be raised with long-term debt. Simply adding $38.12 to the long-term debt in B18 will not quite solve the problem because that will lead to other changes. Specifically, additional long-term debt will increase interest expense resulting in lower net income. In turn, this will reduce retained earnings and still leave us with a (smaller) deficit of funding. This new DFN can then be added to long-term debt again, setting off the same chain of calculations. We repeat this cycle as many times as necessary until DFN is equal to zero (or within some allowable tolerance).

By default, Excel will not allow such calculations because the result may not converge. This would lead to an infinite loop of calculations that would tie up your computer in an endless series of calculations. However, if we know that the result will converge (as it will in this case) we can enable these kinds of self-referential, or iterative, calculations. To do so, click Options in the File tab and then go to Formulas. Check the Enable iterative calculation option. Note that we can set the maximum number of iterations as well as the convergence criteria. The default settings will cause the calculation to stop after 100 iterations or if the change in the result is 0.001 or less. Because we should need only a few iterations, leave these at their default settings.

Before we can eliminate the DFN, we need to make a few changes to the pro forma income statement and balance sheet. On the pro forma income statement, we need to add an interest rate. In A21 add the label: `Interest Rate` and then type `11.70%` into B21. This will

---

5. You could also design a custom number format. One possible format is: `#,###.00, "Deficit";#,###.00, "Surplus"`. The benefits of this approach are that you don't need to use a separate cell and you don't need to enter a formula.

allow us to calculate the total interest expense as the amount of debt changes. In B12 we will calculate the interest expense for 2015 with the formula: =B21*('PF Balance Sheet'!B15+'PF Balance Sheet'!B18). Note that the interest expense is 11.70% of the sum of short-term notes payable and long-term debt. At this point, the value in B12 should be the same as before (76.00).

On the pro forma balance sheet, we need to add our self-referential formula. Our goal is to have the long-term debt (in B18) increase by the amount of the DFN (in B25). However, we can't just set the formula in B18 to =B25. If we did, then the long-term debt would be 38.12, which would lead to a bigger DFN. This would then cause the debt to grow and the DFN to shrink, which would then cause the debt to shrink and the DFN to grow. It will never converge and will bounce back and forth until it hits the limit on the number of iterations.

To solve this problem by hand, we would start with the current amount of long-term debt (424.61) and then add the DFN to that. This will increase long-term debt, increase interest expense, lower net income, and reduce retained earnings leading to a lower DFN. We now start over again by adding the new DFN amount to long-term debt and the cycle will repeat. If we do this three or four times, DFN will get very close to zero. It may take 20 or 30 cycles for DFN to converge to exactly zero.[6]

Fortunately, we don't have to do this by hand. With the right formula for long-term debt, we can make the amount accumulate over many cycles. In B18 enter the formula: =B18+B25. This formula will take the current amount of long-term debt and add the DFN. This will lead to a chain of calculations that will lead to lower DFN. This amount will then be added to the long-term debt, and so on. Eventually, it will converge so that DFN equals zero and long-term debt is 465.61. Note also that interest expense is 80.80, net income is 90.17, and retained earnings is 294.16. The pro forma balance sheet should now look similar to the one in Exhibit 5-4 on page 155, except that we have a couple of important modifications to make.

This whole process will occur very rapidly, and you may not even see the changes taking place. It will be instructive to step through the process one iteration at a time. To do this, go to the Formulas tab in Options and set the Maximum Iterations to 1 (the default is 100). Now, reenter the formula in B18 (you must do this to reset the calculation). You should see that long-term debt is now 0.00, and DFN is 465.61. To step through the calculation, simply press the F9 key. This will cause the workbook to recalculate one cycle of the iterative formula. Long-term debt will now be 465.61 and DFN will be −32.69. Press F9 again to repeat the calculation and you will see how the numbers change. Keep pressing F9 until

---

6. You are strongly urged to try doing this by hand. This exercise will greatly improve your understanding of the process.

DFN goes to zero for several keystrokes. Make sure to go back and reset the maximum number of iterations to 100 or more before continuing.

Let's now improve our iterative calculations a bit. It is very helpful to have the capability to enable or disable the iterative calculations. This can be done as discussed above, but that is tedious. Instead, we can use a cell value (0 or 1) combined with **IF** statements to do the job. In A31, enter: Iteration and in B31 enter: 0. This will disable iteration, while a 1 will enable iteration. Now, in B18 change the formula for long-term debt so that it is: =IF(B31=1,B18+B25,C18). If iteration is turned on (B31 = 1) then the formula will be the same as before. If iteration is off then long-term debt will be the same as it was in 2014. It can also be helpful to have a note appear when iteration is on. So, in C31 enter the formula: =IF(B31=1,"Iteration is ON","").

EXHIBIT 5-4
THE PRO FORMA BALANCE SHEET AFTER ITERATION

	A	B	C	D
1	Elvis Products International			
2	Pro Forma Balance Sheet			
3	As of Dec. 31, 2014			
4	*Assets*	*2015**	*2014*	*2013*
5	Cash and Equivalents	52.00	52.00	57.60
6	Accounts Receivable	444.51	402.00	351.20
7	Inventory	914.90	836.00	715.20
8	*Total Current Assets*	*1,411.40*	*1,290.00*	*1,124.00*
9	Plant & Equipment	577.00	527.00	491.00
10	Accumulated Depreciation	191.20	166.20	146.20
11	*Net Fixed Assets*	*385.80*	*360.80*	*344.80*
12	*Total Assets*	*1,797.20*	*1,650.80*	*1,468.80*
13	*Liabilities and Owner's Equity*			
14	Accounts Payable	189.05	175.20	145.60
15	Short-term Notes Payable	225.00	225.00	200.00
16	Other Current Liabilities	163.38	140.00	136.00
17	*Total Current Liabilities*	*577.43*	*540.20*	*481.60*
18	Long-term Debt	465.61	424.61	323.43
19	*Total Liabilities*	*1,043.04*	*964.81*	*805.03*
20	Common Stock	460.00	460.00	460.00
21	Retained Earnings	294.16	225.99	203.77
22	*Total Shareholder's Equity*	*754.16*	*685.99*	*663.77*
23	*Total Liabilities and Owner's Equity*	*1,797.20*	*1,650.80*	*1,468.80*
24	* Forecast			
25	Discretionary Financing Needed	0.00	Balanced	
26	Total Accumulated DFN	41.00		
27				
28	Notes:			
29	Net Addition to Plant & Equipment	50.00		
30	Life of New Equipment	10		
31	New Depreciation (Straight Line)	5.00		
32	Iteration	1	Iteration is ON	

One final change is necessary. We would like to know exactly how much new financing is required. It should be clear that the original $38.12 is not the correct answer because each time that we iterate we add more long-term debt. So, we need a cell to calculate the accumulated DFN. Select row 26 and insert a new row. Now, in A26 enter the label: Total Accumulated DFN, and in B26 enter the formula: =IF(B32=1,B26+B25,B25). If iteration is on, this formula will keep track of the additions to DFN. Otherwise, it will be equal to the DFN without iteration. Experiment by changing B32 to 0 and back to 1 to see the effect of these changes.

This worksheet could be further refined in several ways. As one example, instead of raising all of the DFN using long-term debt, we could allocate some of it to new equity. In this case, we might use the long-term debt ratio to determine how much should be long-term debt. The balance would be allocated to equity. Note that additional equity would result in more dividends, which would complicate the situation a bit.

Using circular references should be the last resort. They should be used only when absolutely necessary, as in this case. If your calculation does not converge to a single value, then Excel will eventually stop trying to calculate it and you will have wrong answers. Furthermore, this technique is quite calculation intensive and will cause recalculation of a large spreadsheet to slow to a crawl. If at all possible, you should try to find another method of solving the problem that doesn't involve circular references.[7]

Other Forecasting Methods

The primary advantage of the percent of sales forecasting method is its simplicity. There are many other more sophisticated forecasting techniques that can be implemented in a spreadsheet program. In the rest of this chapter, we will look at techniques based on linear regression analysis.

Linear Trend Extrapolation

Suppose that you were asked to perform the percent of sales forecast for EPI. The first step in that analysis requires a sales forecast. Because EPI is a small company, nobody regularly makes such forecasts and you will have to generate your own. Where do you start?

Your first idea might be to see if there has been a clear trend in sales over the past several years and to extrapolate that trend, if it exists, to 2015. To see if there has been a trend, you

---

7. For an alternative to iterative calculations, see T. Arnold and P.C. Eismann, "Debt Financing Does NOT Create Circularity Within Pro Forma Analysis," *Advances in Financial Education,* Vol 6, Summer 2008, pp. 96–102.

first gather data on sales for EPI for the past five years. Table 5-1 presents the data that you have gathered. Add a new worksheet to your EPI workbook and rename it "Trend Forecast" so that it can be easily identified. Enter the data from Table 5-1 into your worksheet beginning in A1.

TABLE 5-1
EPI SALES FOR 2010 TO 2014

Year	Sales
2010	1,890,532
2011	2,098,490
2012	2,350,308
2013	3,432,000
2014	3,850,000

The easiest way to see if there has been a trend in sales is to create a chart that plots the sales data versus the years. Select A1:B6, and then insert a scatter chart[8] by clicking the Insert tab, then Insert Scatter (X,Y) or Bubble Chart, and choosing "Scatter with Straight Lines and Markers" as the type. Once the chart is created, click the Chart Elements button and insert the title: EPI Sales for 2010 to 2014. Your worksheet should resemble Exhibit 5-5.

EXHIBIT 5-5
EPI TREND FORECAST WORKSHEET

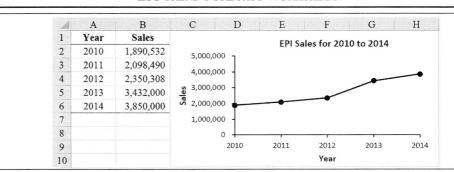

Examining the chart leads to the conclusion that sales have definitely been increasing over the past five years, but not at a constant rate. There are several ways to generate a forecast from this data, even though the sales are not increasing at a constant rate.

---

8. A line chart would also work. However, because our x-axis labels (years) are numeric, a scatter chart is the better choice.

One method is to let Excel draw a linear trend line. That is, let Excel fit a straight line to the data and extrapolate that line to 2015 (or beyond). The line generated is in the form of:

$$Y = mX + b$$

which you should recognize as the same equation used in algebra courses to describe a straight line. In this equation, m is the slope and b is the intercept.

To determine the parameters for this line (m and b) Excel uses regression analysis, which we will examine later. To generate a forecast based on the trend, we need to use the **TREND** function which is defined as:

TREND(*KNOWN_Y'S***,** *KNOWN_X'S*, *NEW_X'S*, *CONST*)

In the **TREND** function definition, ***KNOWN_Y'S*** is the range of the data that we wish to forecast (the dependent variable) and *KNOWN_X'S* is the optional range of data (the independent variables) that we want to use to determine the trend in the dependent variable.[9] Because the **TREND** function is generally used to forecast a time-based trend, *KNOWN_X'S* will usually be a range of years, though it can be any set of consecutive numbers (e.g., 1, 2, 3,...). *NEW_X'S* is a continuation of the *KNOWN_X'S* for which we don't yet know the value of the dependent variable. *CONST* is a boolean (True/False) variable that tells Excel whether or not to include an intercept in its calculations (generally this should be set to true or omitted).

To generate a forecast for 2015, first enter 2015 into A7. This will provide us with the *NEW_X'S* value that we will use to forecast 2015 sales. Next, enter the **TREND** function as: =TREND(B$2:B$6,A$2:A$6,A7,TRUE) into B7. The result is a sales forecast of $4,300,000, which is the same sales forecast that we used in the percent of sales forecasting method for the financial statements.

We can extend our forecast to 2016 and 2017 quite easily. To do this, first enter 2016 into A8 and 2017 into A9. Now copy the formula from B7 to B8:B9. You should see that the forecasted sales for 2016 and 2017 are $4,825,244 and $5,350,489, respectively.

Adding Trend Lines to Charts

An interesting feature of charts in Excel is that we can tell Excel to add a trend line to the chart. Adding this line requires no more work than making a menu choice; we do not have to calculate the data ourselves. To add a trend line to our chart, right-click the data series in the

---

9. While *KNOWN_X'S* and *NEW_X'S* are technically optional arguments, they should not be omitted in most cases. If both are omitted, then **TREND** returns an array of values on the trend line instead of the next forecasted value. In this case, if you neglect to array enter (Ctrl+Shift+Enter) and select multiple cells then the result will be the first value that is on the trend line.

chart and then choose Add Trendline from the shortcut menu to see the default linear trend line. In the Format Trendline panel, you can set the formatting options for the line. You can also show trend lines that aren't linear. For example, if sales had been increasing at an increasing rate, you might want to fit an exponential trend instead of a linear one. Excel also offers five other trend lines that it can calculate, including a moving average of user-determined length.

Excel can even do a forecast automatically in the chart, though you will not get the actual numerical forecast using this method. First, right-click the data series and choose **F**ormat Trendline. Before closing the Format Trendline panel, look at the Forecast section and set **F**orward to 1 unit. After clicking on the Close button, you will see a trend line that extends to 2015. We could also extend the forecast to 2016 or 2017 by setting **F**orward to 2 or 3.

If you decide that you no longer want to see the trend line, simply right-click on it and choose **D**elete from the shortcut menu.

Recall that we said that Excel generates the equation for the trend line and uses this equation to make the forecast. We can have Excel show this equation on the chart by selecting the appropriate options. Right-click on the trend line and choose **F**ormat Trendline from the shortcut menu. Near the bottom of the panel click on Display **E**quation on Chart. Click on the Close button and you should see the equation appear on the chart.

The equation that Excel displays, using scientific notation, is:

$$y = 525245x - 1\text{E}+09$$

which is Excel's way of saying:

$$y = 525{,}245x - 1{,}000{,}000{,}000$$

However, you should be suspicious of rounding problems any time you see scientific notation. In some cases the rounding isn't important, but in this case it is. We can fix the problem by right-clicking on the equation and choosing **F**ormat Trendline Label from the shortcut menu. Apply another format in the Label Options section and you should now see that the equation is:

$$y = 525{,}244.60x - 1{,}054{,}067{,}869.20$$

We can see that this equation does indeed generate the forecast for 2015 by substituting 2015 for x in the equation. At this point, your worksheet should look like the one in Exhibit 5-6.

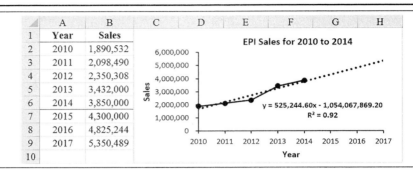

EXHIBIT 5-6
EPI TREND FORECAST WORKSHEET

Regression Analysis

The term *regression analysis* (also known as ordinary least squares or OLS regression) is a sophisticated-sounding term for a rather simple concept: fitting the best line to a data set. As simple as it sounds, the mathematics behind regression analysis is beyond the scope of this chapter. Excel can easily handle quite complex regression models, and we will make use of Excel's regression tools without delving too deeply into the underlying mathematics.

As we've noted, regression analysis is a technique for fitting the best line to a data set: a very powerful tool for determining the relationship between variables and for forecasting. You could simply plot the data and draw a line that appears to best fit the data, but there is no guarantee that the line you draw is actually the best line. Furthermore, you would have to guess at the parameters. In regression analysis, the best line is defined as the one that minimizes the sum of the squared errors (SSE). The errors are the difference between the actual data points and those predicted by the model.

In our previous example, we used regression analysis (disguised within the TREND function) to forecast EPI's level of sales for 2015. Aside from forecasting, the second major use of regression analysis is to understand the relationship between variables. In this section, we will see how to use Excel's regression tool to make a forecast.[10]

10. The regression tool is not a built-in function in the same sense as TREND. Instead, it is a part of the data analysis tools included with Excel. There is a regression function, LINEST. However, this function is more complex to use because it returns an array of values instead of a single value. Furthermore, the return values are not labeled. See the online help for more information.

Consider the following example in which we will make use of regression analysis to try to get an alternative forecast of next year's cost of goods sold for EPI. Table 5-2 provides the historical data for sales and cost of goods sold.

TABLE 5-2
EPI'S HISTORICAL SALES AND COST OF GOODS

Year	Sales	Cost of Goods
2010	$ 1,890,532	$ 1,570,200
2011	2,098,490	1,695,694
2012	2,350,308	1,992,400
2013	3,432,000	2,864,000
2014	3,850,000	3,250,000

Note that the data for the variables must be in columns when using the regression tool. Excel will misinterpret the data if it is in rows.

Recall that we previously calculated the average percentage of sales for 2013 and 2014 and used that average to generate our forecast for 2015. Suppose, however, that you are concerned that there may possibly be a more systematic relationship between sales and cost of goods sold. For example, it is entirely possible that as sales rise, cost of goods sold will rise at a slower rate. This may be due to efficiencies in the production process, quantity discounts on materials, and so on. Alternatively, there may be another relationship, or none at all. Regression analysis can help us to gain a better understanding of the historical relationship and, hopefully, generate better forecasts of the future cost of goods sold.

Before running the regression, let's create a chart of the data to help get a visual picture of the historical relationship. Enter the data from Table 5-2 into a new worksheet beginning in cell A1. Now select B1:C6 and create a scatter chart of the data.

To facilitate our visualization, change the scale on each axis as follows: Right-click the y-axis and choose **F**ormat Axis. On the Axis Options tab, under Bounds, change the Minimum to 1,000,000, the Maximum to 4,000,000, and the Major unit to 1,000,000. Repeat those settings for the x-axis. This will ensure that the scale of each axis is the same, which makes it much easier to see the relationship between our two variables. Note that you will probably need to change the width of the chart so that the distance between tick marks is the same on the x-axis as on the y-axis. This can be done in the Size group on the Chart Tools Format tab of the Ribbon.

FIGURE 5-1
CHART OF COST OF GOODS SOLD VS. SALES

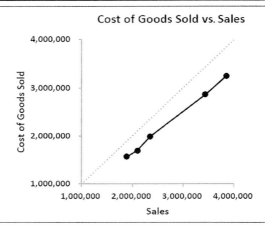

The chart in Figure 5-1 shows what appears to be a fairly consistent relationship. Furthermore, the slope of the line is something less than 45 degrees so we know that a change in sales of $1 will lead to a change of less than $1 in cost of goods sold (as we would expect). We can't know the exact relationship just by reading the chart, but we can run a regression analysis on the data to find the exact slope and intercept of the best-fitting line for this data.

Excel provides several functions to calculate the parameters of a regression equation. For example, the **INTERCEPT**, **SLOPE**, and **LINEST** functions all return the parameters of a regression line, while the **TREND** and **FORECAST** functions use linear regression to generate forecasts. There are also functions for nonlinear regression (e.g., **GROWTH** and **LOGEST**).

However, Excel also includes another method that we will cover here: the regression tool in the Analysis ToolPak add-in. This tool works very much like any statistical program that you may have used. It will ask for the data and then output a table of the regression results, including diagnostic data that is used to determine whether the relationship between the variables is statistically significant.

Make sure that the Analysis ToolPak add-in is installed and enabled on your PC. Click the File tab and go to Options, and then click Add-Ins. Look for Analysis ToolPak under "Active Application Add-ins." If it is listed, then the add-in is ready to use. If it isn't, then check to see if it is listed under "Inactive Application Add-ins." If so, then you will need to enable the add-in by clicking the **G**o button and then placing a check mark next to the add-in name. If you don't see the add-in listed in either location, then you will need to do a custom install from the Office 2013 installation media.

Data Analysis

To run the regression tool, click the Data Analysis button on the Data tab. Next, select Regression from the list of analysis tools that are available. Figure 5-2 shows the dialog box with the data ranges and other options already entered.

Before running the analysis, we need to determine the theoretical relationship between the variables of interest. In this case, we are hypothesizing that the level of sales can be used to predict the cost of goods sold. Therefore, we say that the cost of goods sold is dependent on sales. So the cost of goods sold is referred to as the dependent (Y) variable, and sales is the independent (X) variable.[11] Our mathematical model is:

$$\text{Cost of Goods Sold}_t = \alpha + \beta(\text{Sales}_t) + \tilde{e}_t \tag{5-1}$$

where α is the intercept, β is the slope, and $\tilde{e}_t$ is the random error term in period t.

FIGURE 5-2
THE REGRESSION TOOL FROM THE ANALYSIS TOOLPAK

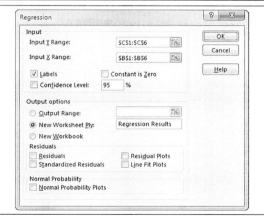

There are many options on this dialog box, but for our simple problem we are only concerned with four of them. First, we need to tell Excel where the dependent (Y) variable data are located. In the "Input **Y** Range" edit box enter $\$C\$1:\$C\$6$. In the "Input **X** Range" edit box enter $\$B\$1:\$B\$6$. Because we have included the labels in our input ranges, we must make sure to check the **L**abels box.[12] Finally, we want to tell Excel to create

---

11. Many regression models have more than one X variable. These models are known as multiple regressions and Excel can handle them just as easily as our example. The only restriction is that your X variables must be in a single contiguous range.

12. Be careful with the Labels checkbox. If you check it when you have not selected any labels, then Excel will assume that the first data points are labels and they will be excluded from the regression.

a new worksheet within the current workbook for the output. Click the radio button to the left of "New Worksheet **P**ly:" in the Output options section, and type `Regression Results` in the edit box to name the new worksheet.

After clicking the OK button, Excel will calculate the regression statistics and create a new worksheet named "Regression Results." We could also have Excel enter the output in the same worksheet by specifying the desired **O**utput Range. (Beware that Excel has a minor bug. When you click on the radio button for any of the output options, the cursor will return to the edit box for the Y range. Before selecting your output range, you must click in the proper edit box, otherwise you will overwrite your Y range.)

EXHIBIT 5-7
REGRESSION RESULTS

	A	B	C	D	E	F	G
1	SUMMARY OUTPUT						
2							
3	*Regression Statistics*						
4	Multiple R	99.91%					
5	R Square	99.83%					
6	Adjusted R Square	99.77%					
7	Standard Error	35,523.08					
8	Observations	5					
9							
10	ANOVA						
11		*df*	*SS*	*MS*	*F*	*Significance F*	
12	Regression	1	2,205,960,110,239.81	2,205,960,110,239.81	1,748.14	0.00	
13	Residual	3	3,785,666,908.99	1,261,888,969.66			
14	Total	4	2,209,745,777,148.80				
15							
16		*Coefficients*	*Standard Error*	*t Stat*	*P-value*	*Lower 95%*	*Upper 95%*
17	Intercept	(63,680.8247)	58,134.6760	(1.0954)	0.3534	(248,691.3096)	121,329.6601
18	Sales	0.8583	0.0205	41.8108	0.0000	0.7929	0.9236

Exhibit 5-7 shows the output of the regression tool (it has been reformatted to make it a bit easier to read). The output may appear to be complex if you are not familiar with regression analysis. However, we are primarily concerned with the part of the output that gives the parameters of the regression line.[13] In cells B17:B18 are the parameters of the regression equation. If we substitute these numbers into equation (5-1) we find:

$$\text{Cost of Goods Sold}_t = -63,680.8247 + 0.8583(\text{Sales}_t) + \tilde{e}_t$$

---

13. We are not trying to minimize the importance of this other output. On the contrary, it would be foolish to attempt to use regression methods for any important purpose without understanding the model completely. We are merely trying to illustrate how Excel can be used for this type of analysis as simply as possible.

The equation tells us that, all other things being equal, each $1 increase in sales will on average lead to an $0.8583 increase in cost of goods sold.

Statistical Significance

Before we use this equation to make our forecast, we should make sure that there is a statistically significant relationship between the variables. If the relationship is not significant, then any forecast would be of dubious quality. Furthermore, in a multiple regression it is possible that some X variables are significant while others are not.

We will begin by looking at the R Square (R^2) in cell B5. The R^2 is the coefficient of determination and tells us the proportion of the total variation in the dependent variable that is explained by the independent variable(s). In this case, changes in sales are able to explain nearly 100% of the variability in the cost of goods sold. That is a stronger relationship than you will normally find, but it indicates that this equation is likely to work very well, as long as we have a good forecast of next years' sales.

It is important to understand that R^2 does not indicate statistical significance. Indeed, it can be increased by simply adding an additional independent variable; even a random variable. This problem can be avoided by using the adjusted R^2, which modifies the original R^2 to account for the number of independent variables. The adjusted R^2 will only increase if the additional variables actually improve the predictive abilities of the model.

To judge the statistical significance of the individual X variables, we look at the t-statistics for our regression coefficients (D18; normally we aren't too concerned with the significance of the intercept). Usually we want to know whether a coefficient is statistically distinguishable from zero (i.e., "statistically significant"). Note that the magnitude of the coefficient is not the issue. If the coefficient for sales is significantly different from zero, then we know that sales is useful in predicting cost of goods sold. The t-statistic tells us how many standard errors the coefficient is away from zero. The higher this number, the more confidence we have that the coefficient is different from zero. In this case, the t-statistic is 41.81. A general rule of thumb is that, for large samples, a t-statistic greater than about 2.00 is significant at the 95% confidence level or more. Even though we don't have a large sample, we can be quite sure that the coefficient for sales is significant. Note that we can also use the p-value (E18) to determine the exact confidence level. Simply subtract the p-value from 1 to find the confidence level. Here, the p-value is 0.00003, so we are essentially 100% (actually, 99.997%) confident that our coefficient is significant.

In a multiple regression analysis we can judge the significance of the entire model, as opposed to individual variables, by looking at the F statistic. A high F statistic indicates that the model is significant. To judge the F statistic without consulting statistical tables, Excel provides the Significance F in F12. As with the p-value, discussed above, the closer this value is to 0 the better the model. Generally, we look for Significance F to be less than 0.05.

In the case of a single X variable, the F statistic provides the same information as the t-statistic. Like the adjusted R^2, the F statistic will only increase if additional variables add value to the model.

We are very confident that the coefficient for sales is not zero, but we don't know for sure if the correct value is 0.8583. That number is simply the best point estimate given our set of sample data. Note that in F18:G18 we have numbers labeled "Lower 95%" and "Upper 95%." This gives us a range of values between which we can be 95% sure that the true value of this coefficient lies. In other words, we can be 95% confident that the true change in cost of goods sold per dollar change in sales is between $0.7929 and $0.9236. Of course, there is a small chance (5%) that the true value lies outside of this range.[14]

As an aside, note that the 95% confidence range for the intercept contains 0. This indicates that we cannot statistically distinguish the intercept coefficient from zero. This is also confirmed by the rather high p-value, and low t-statistic, for the intercept. However, because we are merely using this model for forecasting, the significance of the intercept is not important.

We are now quite confident that our model is useful for forecasting cost of goods sold. To make a forecast for the 2015 cost of goods sold, we simply plug the 2015 sales forecast into the equation:

$$\text{Cost of Goods Sold}_{2015} = -63,680.82 + 0.8583(4,300,000) = 3,626,854.68$$

Recall that using the percent of sales method our forecast for 2015 cost of goods sold was $3,609,107.56. Our regression result agrees fairly closely with this number, so either number is probably usable for a forecast. However, note that both of these methods depend critically on our sales forecast. Without a good forecast of sales, all of our other forecasts are questionable.

To generate this forecast yourself, return to your worksheet with the data from Table 5-2. In A7 enter: `2015` for the year and in B7 enter the sales forecast of `4,300,000`. Now, calculate the forecast by using the regression output. The equation in C7 is: `='Regression Results'!B17+'Regression Results'!B18*B7`.

As we did with the **TREND** function, we can replicate this regression directly in the chart that was completed earlier. Right-click on data series and choose Add Trendline. Now, place the equation on the chart. Your worksheet should now look like the one in Exhibit 5-8.

14. Again, we are using quite a small sample with only five observations. This reduces our confidence somewhat and widens the 95% confidence interval. It would be preferable to use higher frequency data such as quarterly sales and cost of goods sold.

EXHIBIT 5-8
COMPLETED REGRESSION WORKSHEET WITH FORECAST

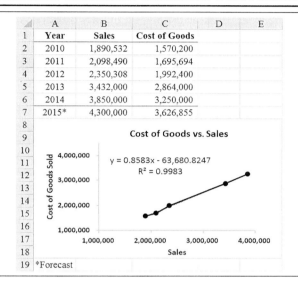

	A	B	C	D	E
1	**Year**	**Sales**	**Cost of Goods**		
2	2010	1,890,532	1,570,200		
3	2011	2,098,490	1,695,694		
4	2012	2,350,308	1,992,400		
5	2013	3,432,000	2,864,000		
6	2014	3,850,000	3,250,000		
7	2015*	4,300,000	3,626,855		

Cost of Goods vs. Sales

$y = 0.8583x - 63,680.8247$
$R^2 = 0.9983$

19 *Forecast

Using Built-in Functions for Regression Parameters

As noted earlier, Excel has several functions that can perform regression analysis directly in the worksheet without needing to use the Analysis ToolPak add-in. These functions are convenient, though they do not provide the statistics that we need to evaluate the statistical significance of the coefficients.

The chart in Exhibit 5-8 shows a more or less linear relationship, so we can use the **INTERCEPT** and **SLOPE** functions to find the parameters of the regression equation. These functions do exactly what their names imply, and are defined as:

INTERCEPT(*KNOWN_Y'S*, *KNOWN_X'S*)

SLOPE(*KNOWN_Y'S*, *KNOWN_X'S*)

On the same worksheet that you used for Exhibit 5-8 enter the labels `Intercept` and `Slope` into cells E2:E3. In F2, enter the formula: `=INTERCEPT(C2:C6,B2:B6)` and in F3 enter: `=SLOPE(C2:C6,B2:B6)`. You will find that you get the same results as above. To use these results to forecast cost of goods sold in C7, enter: `=F2+F3*B7`. Check to be sure that your answer matches that in Exhibit 5-8.

Summary

In this chapter, we have examined three methods of forecasting financial statements and variables. We used the percent of sales technique to forecast the firm's income statement and balance sheet based upon an estimated level of sales. We used a time-trend technique to forecast sales as an input to the percent of sales method. Finally, we looked at regression analysis to help generate a better forecast of the cost of goods sold by using the relationship between that and sales over the past five years.

We have barely scratched the surface of forecasting methodologies. However, we hope that this chapter has stimulated an interest in this important subject. If so, be assured that Excel, either alone or through an add-in program, can be made to handle nearly all of your forecasting problems. Please remember that any forecast is almost assuredly wrong. We can only hope to get reasonably close to the actual future outcome. How close you get depends upon the quality of your model and the inputs to that model.

TABLE 5-3
FUNCTIONS INTRODUCED IN THIS CHAPTER

Purpose	Function	Page
Calculate an arithmetic average	**Average(*NUMBER1*, *NUMBER2*, …)**	146
Calculate straight-line depreciation	**SLN(*COST*, *SALVAGE*, *LIFE*)**	149
Forecast future outcomes based on a time trend	**TREND(*KNOWN_Y'S*, *KNOWN_X'S*, *NEW_X'S*, *CONST*)**	158
Find the intercept of a regression equation	**INTERCEPT(*KNOWN_Y'S*, *KNOWN_X'S*)**	167
Find the slope of a regression equation	**SLOPE(*KNOWN_Y'S*, *KNOWN_X'S*)**	167

Read 3.3.2016

☑ Check Box when all highlighted notes are copied.

Problems

1. Using the data in the student spreadsheet file P&G.xlsx (to find the student spreadsheets for *Financial Analysis with Microsoft Excel*, seventh edition, go to www.cengagebrain.com) forecast the June 30, 2014, income statement and balance sheet for Procter & Gamble. Use the percent of sales method and the following assumptions: (1) Sales in FY 2014 will be $85,000; (2) The tax rate will be 25.24%; (3) Each item that changes with sales will be the five-year average percentage of sales; (4) No preferred dividends will be paid; and (5) The common dividend payout ratio will be 50% of income available to common stockholders. Use your judgment on all other items.

   a. What is the discretionary financing needed in 2014? Is this a surplus or deficit?

   b. Assume that the DFN will be absorbed by long-term debt and that the total interest rate is 4.38% of LTD. Set up an iterative worksheet to eliminate it.

   c. Create a chart of cash vs. sales and add a linear trend line. Is the cash balance a consistent percentage of sales? Does the relationship fit your expectations?

   d. Use the regression tool to verify your results from part c. Is the trend statistically significant? Use at least three methods to show why or why not.

   e. Turn off iteration, and use the Scenario Manager to set up three scenarios:
      1) *Best Case* — Sales are 5% higher than expected.
      2) *Base Case* — Sales are exactly as expected.
      3) *Worst Case* — Sales are 5% less than expected.
      What is the DFN under each scenario?

2. Use the same data as in Problem 1.

   a. Recalculate the percentage of sales income statement, but this time use the TREND function to forecast other income and interest expense.

   b. Recalculate the percentage of sales balance sheet, but this time use the TREND function to forecast cash, gross property plant and equipment, goodwill, intangible assets, and other long-term assets.

    c.   Do these new values appear to be more realistic than the original values? Does this technique make sense for each of these items? Might other income statement or balance sheet items be forecasted in this way?

3.   The spreadsheet file "Chapter 5 Problem 3.xlsx" (to find the student spreadsheets for *Financial Analysis with Microsoft Excel*, seventh edition, go to www.cengagebrain.com) contains monthly total returns for the S&P 500 index (using SPY as a proxy), Cypress Semiconductor (CY), and Fidelity Contrafund (FCNTX) from February 2009 to February 2014.

    a.   Create a scatter plot to show the relationship between the returns on CY and the S&P 500. Describe, in words, the relationship between the returns of CY and the S&P 500. Estimate the slope of a regression equation of this data. Repeat for FCNTX.

    b.   Add a linear trend line to the chart, and place the equation and R^2 on the chart. Does this equation confirm your guess from part a? How much of the variability in CY returns can be explained by variability in the broad market? Repeat for FCNTX.

    c.   Using the Analysis ToolPak add-in, run a regression analysis on this data. Your dependent variable is the CY returns, and the independent variable is the S&P 500 returns. Does this confirm the earlier results? The slope coefficient is CY's beta. Is the beta of this stock statistically significant? Explain.

    d.   Repeat part c using the returns on FCNTX and the S&P 500. Compare the R^2 from both regressions. What conclusions can you draw from the difference?

Internet Exercises

1.   Because you are reading this after the end of Procter & Gamble's fiscal year 2014, how do your forecasts from the previous problems compare to the actual FY 2014 results? Does it appear that more information would have helped to generate better forecasts? Insert Procter & Gamble's actual sales for 2014 into your forecast. Does this improve your forecast of earnings?

2. Choose your own company and repeat Problem 3. The data can be easily obtained from Yahoo! Finance (http://finance.yahoo.com). Enter a ticker symbol and get a stock price quote. On the left side of the page click the link for "Historical Prices." Set the dates for a five-year period and the frequency to monthly. Click the link at the bottom of the page to load the data into Excel. Now, repeat the steps using the ticker symbol SPY (an exchange traded fund that mimics the S&P 500). Now, combine the monthly closing prices onto one worksheet and calculate the monthly percentage changes. You should now have the data necessary to answer the questions from Problem 3. Note that to improve your results, you can also get the dividends and calculate the monthly total returns.

CHAPTER 6

Break-Even and Leverage Analysis

After studying this chapter, you should be able to:

1. *Differentiate between fixed and variable costs.*

2. *Calculate operating, cash, and total break-even points, and find the number of units that need to be sold to reach a target level of EBIT.*

3. *Define the terms "business risk" and "financial risk," and describe the origins of each of these risks.*

4. *Use Excel to calculate the DOL, DFL, and DCL, and explain the significance of each of these risk measures.*

5. *Explain how the DOL, DFL, and DCL are related to the break-even points.*

In this chapter, we will consider the decisions that managers make regarding the cost structure of the firm. These decisions will, in turn, impact the decisions they make regarding methods of financing the firm's assets (i.e., its capital structure) and pricing the firm's products.

In general, we will assume that the firm faces two kinds of costs:

1. *Variable costs* are those costs that are expected to change at the same rate as the firm's sales. Variable costs are constant per unit, so as more units are sold, the total variable costs rise. Examples of variable costs include sales commissions, costs of raw materials, hourly wages, and so on.

173

2. *Fixed costs* are those costs that are constant regardless of the quantity produced, over some relevant range of production. Total fixed cost per unit will decline as the number of units increases. Examples of fixed costs include rent, salaries, depreciation, and so on.

Figure 6-1 illustrates these costs.[1]

FIGURE 6-1
TOTAL FIXED AND TOTAL VARIABLE COSTS

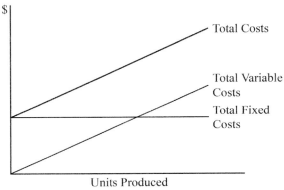

Break-Even Points

We can define the *break-even point* as the level of sales (either units or dollars) that causes profits, however measured, to equal zero. Most commonly, we define the break-even point as the unit sales required for earnings before interest and taxes (EBIT) to be equal to zero. This point is often referred to as the *operating break-even point*.

Define Q as the quantity sold, P as the price per unit, V as the variable cost per unit, and F as total fixed costs. With these definitions, we can say:

$$Q(P - V) - F = \text{EBIT} \tag{6-1}$$

which is a standard income statement relationship.

---

1. Most firms will also have some semi-variable costs that are fixed over a certain range of output, but will change if output rises above that level. For simplicity, we will assume that these costs are fixed.

If we set EBIT in equation (6-1) to zero, we can solve for the break-even quantity (Q^*):

$$Q^* = \frac{F}{P - V} \tag{6-2}$$

Assume, for example, that a firm is selling widgets for $30 per unit while variable costs are $20 per unit and fixed costs total $100,000. In this situation, the firm must sell 10,000 units to break even:

$$Q^* = \frac{100,000}{30 - 20} = 10,000 \text{ units}$$

The quantity $P - V$ is often referred to as the *contribution margin* per unit, because this is the amount that each unit sold contributes to covering the firm's fixed costs. Using equation (6-1), you can verify that the firm will break even if it sells 10,000 widgets:

$$10,000(30 - 20) - 100,000 = 0$$

We can now calculate the firm's break-even point in dollars by simply multiplying Q^* by the price per unit:

$$\$BE = P \times Q^* \tag{6-3}$$

In this example, the result shows that the firm must sell $300,000 worth of widgets to break even.

Note that we can substitute equation (6-2) into (6-3):

$$\$BE = P \times \frac{F}{(P - V)} = \frac{F}{(P - V)/P} = \frac{F}{CM\%} \tag{6-4}$$

So, if we know the contribution margin as a percentage of the selling price (CM%), we can easily calculate the break-even point in dollars. In the previous example, CM% is 33.33%, so the break-even point in dollars must be:

$$\$BE = \frac{100,000}{0.3333} = \$300,000$$

which confirms our earlier result.

Calculating Break-Even Points in Excel

We can, of course, calculate break-even points in Excel. Consider the income statement for Spuds and Suds, a very popular sports bar that serves only one product: A plate of gourmet french fries and a pitcher of imported beer for $16 per serving. The income statement is presented in Exhibit 6-1.

EXHIBIT 6-1
INCOME STATEMENT FOR SPUDS AND SUDS

	A	B
1	**Spuds and Suds**	
2	**Income Statement**	
3	**For the Year Ended Dec. 31, 2014**	
4		**2014**
5	Sales	$ 2,500,000
6	Less: Variable Costs	1,500,000
7	Less: Fixed Costs	400,000
8	*Earnings Before Interest and Taxes*	*600,000*
9	Less: Interest Expense	100,000
10	*Earnings Before Taxes*	*500,000*
11	Taxes	200,000
12	*Net Income*	*300,000*
13		
14	Less: Preferred Dividends	100,000
15	*Net Income Available to Common*	*200,000*
16	Common Shares Outstanding	1,000,000
17	*Earnings per Share*	*$ 0.20*
18		
19	**Assumptions**	
20	Price per Unit	$ 16.00
21	Unit Sales	156,250
22	Variable Costs as a Percent of Sales	60%
23	Tax Rate	40%

Before calculating the break-even point, enter the labels into a new worksheet as shown in Exhibit 6-1. Because we will be expanding this example, it is important that you enter formulas where they are appropriate. Before doing any calculations, enter the numbers in B20:B23.

We will first calculate the dollar amount of sales (in B5) by multiplying the per unit price by the number of units sold: =B20*B21. Variable costs are always 60% of sales (as shown in B22), so the formula in B6 is: =B22*B5. Both fixed costs (in B7) and interest expense (in B9) are constants, so they are simply entered directly. The simple subtraction and multiplication required to complete the income statement through B12 should be obvious.

In B14:B17, we have added information that is not immediately useful, but the figures will become central when we discuss operating and financial leverage. In cell B14, we have added preferred dividends, which will be subtracted from net income. The result (in B15) is net income available to the common shareholders. Preferred dividends are simply input into B14, and the formula in B15 is: =B12-B14. In B16, enter the number of common shares outstanding: 1,000,000. Earnings per share is then calculated as: =B15/B16 in cell B17.

Now we can calculate the break-even points. In cell A25 enter the label: Operating Break-even Point (Units). Next, copy this label to A26, and change the word "Units" to Dollars. In B25, we can calculate the break-even point in units using equation (6-2). The formula is: =B7/(B20-B6/B21). Notice that we have to calculate the variable cost per unit by dividing total variable costs (B6) by the number of units sold (B21). You can see that Spuds and Suds must sell 62,500 units in order to break even and that they are well above this level. We can calculate the break-even point in dollars simply by multiplying the unit break-even point by the price per unit. In B26, enter the formula: =B25*B20. You will see that the result is $1,000,000.

Other Break-Even Points

Recall that we found the break-even point by setting EBIT, in equation (6-1), equal to zero. However, there is no reason that we can't set EBIT equal to any amount that we might desire. For example, if we define $EBIT_{Target}$ as the target level of EBIT, we find that the firm can earn the target EBIT amount by selling:

$$Q^*_{Target} = \frac{F + EBIT_{Target}}{P - V}$$

(6-5)

Consider that Spuds and Suds might want to know the number of units that they need to sell in order to have EBIT equal $800,000. Mathematically, we can see that:

$$Q^*_{800,000} = \frac{400,000 + 800,000}{16 - 9.60} = 187,500 \text{ units}$$

need to be sold to reach this target. You can verify that this number is correct by typing 187,500 into B21 and checking the value in B8. To return the worksheet to its original values, press Ctrl+Z or reenter 156,250 into B21.

We can do the same thing, with more flexibility, by modifying our worksheet. Select row 22 and insert a new row. In A22 enter the label: Target EBIT and in B22 enter: 800,000. In A29 type: Units to Meet EBIT Target and then in B29 enter the formula: =(B7+B22)/(B20-B6/B21). The result will be 187,500 units as before. However, we can now easily change the target EBIT and see the unit sales required to reach the goal. Your worksheet should now look like the one in Exhibit 6-2.

EXHIBIT 6-2
BREAK-EVEN POINTS

	A	B
1	Spuds and Suds	
2	Income Statement	
3	For the Year Ended Dec. 31, 2014	
4		2014
5	Sales	$ 2,500,000
6	Less: Variable Costs	1,500,000
7	Less: Fixed Costs	400,000
8	Earnings Before Interest and Taxes	600,000
9	Less: Interest Expense	100,000
10	Earnings Before Taxes	500,000
11	Taxes	200,000
12	Net Income	300,000
13		
14	Less: Preferred Dividends	100,000
15	Net Income Available to Common	200,000
16	Common Shares Outstanding	1,000,000
17	Earnings per Share	$ 0.20
18		
19	Assumptions	
20	Price per Unit	$ 16.00
21	Unit Sales	156,250
22	Target EBIT	$ 800,000
23	Variable Costs as a Percent of Sales	60%
24	Tax Rate	40%
25		
26	Operating Break-even Point (Units)	62,500
27	Operating Break-even Point (Dollars)	1,000,000
28		
29	Units to Meet EBIT Target	187,500

Recall from page 48 that we defined cash flow as net income plus noncash expenses. We do this because the presence of noncash expenses (principally depreciation) in the accounting numbers distort the actual cash flows. We can make a similar adjustment to our break-even calculations by setting $EBIT_{Target}$ equal to the negative of the depreciation expense. This results in a type of break even that we refer to as the *cash break-even point*:

$$Q^*_{Cash} = \frac{F - \text{Depreciation}}{P - V} \qquad (6\text{-}6)$$

Note that the cash break-even point will always be lower than the operating break-even point because we don't have to cover the depreciation expense.

Similarly, we can calculate the break-even point in terms of earnings per share (i.e., where EPS = 0):

$$Q^*_{\text{Total}} = \frac{F + \text{Interest Exp.} + \dfrac{PD}{(1-t)}}{P - V} \tag{6-7}$$

Note that we are adding both interest expense and preferred dividends back to fixed costs to get the total fixed costs (operating and financial). Preferred dividends are not tax deductible, so we adjust them to determine the number of pre-tax dollars that are needed to pay the preferred dividends after taxes.

In A29 enter: `Total Break-even Point (Units)`, and in B29 enter the formula: `=(B7+B9+B14/(1-B25))/(B20-B6/B21)`. You should see that sales of 104,166.67 units will lead to EPS being equal to zero.

Using Goal Seek to Calculate Break-Even Points

As we've shown, the break-even point can be defined in numerous ways, and we don't even need to define it in terms of EBIT. For example, in equation (6-7) we showed a formula to calculate how many units need to be sold to break even in terms of earnings per share. However, we don't really need an equation and you may someday want to define break-even in terms for which we haven't derived an equation.

Excel has a tool, called *Goal Seek,* to help with problems like this.[2] To use Goal Seek, you must have a target cell with a formula and another cell on which it depends. For example, earnings per share in B17 depends indirectly on the unit sales in B21. So, changing B21 changes B17. When we use Goal Seek, we'll simply tell it to keep changing B21 until B17 equals zero.

What-If
Analysis ▾

Launch the **G**oal Seek tool by choosing What-If Analysis on the Data tab. In the dialog box, the S**e**t Cell is the cell that you want to take on a particular value, To **v**alue is the target value, and the By **c**hanging cell is the cell that can be changed until the target cell takes on the desired value. Essentially, Goal Seek mimicks what you might do if you were using trial and error to find the number of units to make EPS equal to zero.

Fill in the dialog box as shown in Figure 6-2 and click the OK button. You should find that, as we calculated above, unit sales of 104,166.67 will cause EPS to be equal to zero. You can experiment with this tool to find the other break-even points. Set B21 back to 156,250.

---

2. For more complicated problems, use the Solver add-in.

FIGURE 6-2
THE GOAL SEEK TOOL

Leverage Analysis

In Chapter 4 (page 115), we defined leverage as a multiplication of changes in sales into even larger changes in profitability measures. Firms that use large amounts of operating leverage will find that their EBIT will be more variable than firms that do not. We would say that such a firm has high *business risk*. Business risk is one of the major risks faced by a firm and can be defined as the variability of EBIT.[3] The more variable a firm's revenues, relative to its costs, the more variable its EBIT will be. Also, the likelihood that the firm won't be able to pay its expenses will be higher. As an example, consider a software company and a grocery chain. It should be apparent that the future revenues of the software company are much more uncertain than those of the grocery chain. This uncertainty in revenues causes the software company to have a much greater amount of business risk than the grocery chain. The software company's management can do little about this business risk; it is simply a function of the industry in which they operate. Software is not a necessity of life. People do, however, need to eat. For this reason, the grocery business has much lower business risk.

Business risk results from the environment in which the firm operates. Such factors as the competitive position of the firm in its industry, the state of its labor relations, and the variability of demand for its products all affect the amount of business risk a firm faces. In addition, as we will see, the degree to which the firm's costs are fixed (as opposed to variable) will affect the amount of business risk. Many of the components of business risk are beyond the control of the firm's managers. However, managers do have some control. For example, when making investment decisions managers may be able to choose between

---

3. The use of EBIT for this analysis assumes that the firm has no extraordinary income or expenses. Extraordinary items are one-time events that are not a part of the firm's ordinary business operations. If the firm does have these items, use its net operating income (NOI) instead of EBIT.

labor-intensive and capital-intensive production methods, or they may choose between methods that have differing levels of fixed costs.

In contrast, the amount of *financial risk* is determined directly by management. Financial risk refers to the probability that the firm will be unable to meet its fixed financing obligations (which includes both interest and preferred dividends). Obviously, all other things being equal, the more debt a firm uses to finance its assets, the higher its interest cost will be. Higher interest costs lead directly to a higher probability that the firm won't be able to pay. Furthermore, the use of debt financing concentrates the firm's business risk onto fewer shareholders, making the stock riskier. Because the amount of debt is determined by managerial choice, the financial risk that a firm faces is also determined by management.

Managers need to be aware that they face both business risk and financial risk, and that both affect the stock's beta. Therefore, these risks also affect the value of the stock and the firm's cost of capital. If they are in an industry with high business risk, they should control the overall amount of risk by limiting the amount of financial risk that they face. Alternatively, firms that face low levels of business risk can better afford more financial risk.

We examine these concepts in more detail by continuing with our Spuds and Suds example.

The Degree of Operating Leverage

Earlier we mentioned that a firm's business risk can be measured by the variability of its earnings before interest and taxes. If a firm's operating costs are all variable, then any variation in sales will be reflected by exactly the same variation in EBIT. However, if a firm has some fixed operating expenses then EBIT will be more variable than sales. We refer to this concept as *operating leverage*.

We can measure operating leverage by comparing the percentage change in EBIT to a given percentage change in sales. This measure is called the *degree of operating leverage* (DOL):

$$\text{DOL} = \frac{\%\Delta \text{ in EBIT}}{\%\Delta \text{ in Sales}} \tag{6-8}$$

So, if a 10% change in sales results in a 20% change in EBIT, we would say that the DOL is 2. As we will see, this is a symmetrical concept. As long as sales are increasing, a high DOL is desirable. However, if sales begin to decline, a high DOL will result in EBIT declining at an even faster pace than sales.

To make this concept more concrete, let's extend the Spuds and Suds example. Assume that management believes that unit sales will increase by 10% in 2015. Furthermore, they expect that variable costs will remain at 60% of sales and fixed costs will stay at $400,000. Copy B4:B27 to C4:C27. Now, insert a row above the tax rate in row 24. Enter the label: Projected Sales Growth, and in C24 enter: 10%. We need to have the 2015 unit sales in C21, so enter: =B21*(1+C24) into C21. (Note that you have just created a percent of sales income statement forecast for 2015, just as we did in Chapter 5.) Change the label in C4 to 2015 and you have completed the changes.

Before continuing, notice that the operating break-even points (C27:C28) have not changed. This will always be the case if fixed costs are constant and variable costs are a constant percentage of sales. The break-even point is always driven by the level of fixed costs.

Because we wish to calculate the DOL for 2014, we first need to calculate the percentage changes in EBIT and sales. In A32 enter the label: % Change in Sales from Prior Year, and in A33 enter: % Change in EBIT from Prior Year. To calculate the percentage changes, enter: =C5/B5-1 in cell C32 and then: =C8/B8-1 in C33. You should see that sales increased by 10%, while EBIT increased by 16.67%. According to equation (6-8), the DOL for Spuds and Suds in 2014 is:

$$DOL = \frac{16.67\%}{10.00\%} = 1.667$$

So, any change in sales will be magnified by 1.667 times in EBIT. To see this, recall that the formula in C21 increased the 2014 unit sales by 10%. Temporarily, change the value in C24 to 20%. You should see that if sales increase by 20%, EBIT will increase by 33.33%. Recalculating the DOL, we see that it is unchanged:

$$DOL = \frac{33.33\%}{20.00\%} = 1.667$$

Furthermore, if we change the value in C24 to -10%, so that sales decline by 10%, we find that EBIT declines by 16.67%. In this case the DOL is:

$$DOL = \frac{-16.67\%}{-10.00\%} = 1.667$$

So leverage is indeed a double-edged sword. You can see that a high DOL would be desirable as long as sales are increasing, but very undesirable when sales are decreasing. Unfortunately, most businesses don't have the luxury of altering their DOL immediately before a change in sales.

Calculating the DOL with equation (6-8) is actually more cumbersome than is required. With that equation we needed to use two income statements. However, a more direct method of calculating the DOL is to use the following equation:

$$DOL = \frac{Q(P - V)}{Q(P - V) - F} = \frac{\text{Sales} - \text{Variable Costs}}{\text{EBIT}} \qquad (6\text{-}9)$$

For Spuds and Suds in 2014, we can calculate the DOL using equation (6-9):

$$DOL = \frac{2,500,000 - 1,500,000}{600,000} = 1.667$$

which is exactly as we found with equation (6-8).

Continuing with our example, enter the label: Degree of Operating Leverage in A36. In B36, we will calculate the DOL for 2014 with the formula: =(B5-B6)/B8. You should get the same result as before. If you copy the formula from B36 to C36, you will find that in 2015 the DOL will decline to 1.57. We will examine this decline in the DOL later.

Before continuing, it is worth discussing a refinement of the formula in B36. The formula that we entered could potentially cause a division by zero (#DIV/0!) error if EBIT is zero (that is, if the firm is operating exactly at its break-even point). We could use an **IF** statement to avoid this error. If EBIT = 0, then the function will return #N/A (Not Available) as the result. This is better than having a #DIV/0! error or simply returning zero or a blank as the result. Returning a zero can throw off the results of other formulas. For example, the **COUNT** function would count a zero, but not an #N/A. To return #N/A as a result in the case of an error, we can use the **NA** function. This function takes no arguments, but you must put a closed pair of parentheses after it:

$$NA(\ )$$

Instead of using an **IF** statement and calculating the formula twice, we can modify the formula in B36 as follows: =IFERROR((B5-B6)/B8,NA()). Note that we have used the **IFERROR** function to check if the result will be an error. This function will return the first argument if it doesn't result in an error, or the second if it does. It is defined as:

$$\text{IFERROR}(VALUE,\ VALUE\_IF\_ERROR)$$

where *VALUE* is any statement or formula that can be evaluated by Excel. This technique is useful anytime a formula could result in an error that might render any dependent formulas incorrect. It is better to see a result of #N/A than to see an incorrect result.

Your worksheet should now appear similar to the one in Exhibit 6-3.

EXHIBIT 6-3
SPUDS AND SUDS BREAK-EVEN AND LEVERAGE WORKSHEET

	A	B	C
1	Spuds and Suds		
2	Income Statement		
3	For the Year Ended Dec. 31, 2014		
4		2014	2015*
5	Sales	$2,500,000	$2,750,000
6	Less: Variable Costs	1,500,000	1,650,000
7	Less: Fixed Costs	400,000	400,000
8	Earnings Before Interest and Taxes	600,000	700,000
9	Less: Interest Expense	100,000	100,000
10	Earnings Before Taxes	500,000	600,000
11	Taxes	200,000	240,000
12	Net Income	300,000	360,000
13			
14	Less: Preferred Dividends	100,000	100,000
15	Net Income Available to Common	200,000	260,000
16	Common Shares Outstanding	1,000,000	1,000,000
17	Earnings per Share	$ 0.20	$ 0.26
18			
19	Assumptions		
20	Price per Unit	$ 16.00	$ 16.00
21	Unit Sales	156,250	171,875
22	Target EBIT	$ 800,000	
23	Variable Costs as a Percent of Sales	60%	60%
24	Projected Sales Growth		10%
25	Tax Rate	40%	40%
26			
27	Operating Break-even Point (Units)	62,500	62,500
28	Operating Break-even Point (Dollars)	1,000,000	1,000,000
29	Total Break-even Point (Units)	78,125	78,125
30	Units to Meet EBIT Target	187,500	
31			
32	% Change in Sales from Prior Year		10.00%
33	% Change in EBIT from Prior Year		16.67%
34			
35			
36	Degree of Operating Leverage	1.67	1.57

The Degree of Financial Leverage

Financial leverage is similar to operating leverage, but the fixed costs that we are interested in are the fixed financing costs. These are the interest expense and preferred dividends.[4]

---

4. Preferred stock, as we'll see in Chapter 8, is a hybrid security, similar to both debt and equity securities. How it is treated is determined by one's goals. When discussing financial leverage, we treat preferred stock as if it were a debt security.

We can measure financial leverage by relating percentage changes in EPS to percentage changes in EBIT. This measure is referred to as the *degree of financial leverage* (DFL):

$$DFL = \frac{\%\Delta \text{ in EPS}}{\%\Delta \text{ in EBIT}} \tag{6-10}$$

For Spuds and Suds, we have already calculated the percentage change in EBIT, so all that remains is to calculate the percentage change in EPS. In A34 add the label: `% Change in EPS from Prior Year`, and in C34 add the formula: `=C17/B17-1`. Note that EPS is expected to increase by 30% in 2015 compared to only 16.67% for EBIT. Using equation (6-10) we find that the degree of financial leverage employed by Spuds and Suds in 2014 is:

$$DFL = \frac{30.00\%}{16.67\%} = 1.80$$

Therefore, any change in EBIT will be multiplied by 1.80 times in earnings per share. Like operating leverage, financial leverage works both ways. When EBIT is increasing, EPS will increase even more. And when EBIT decreases, EPS will decline by a larger percentage.

As with the DOL, there is a more direct method of calculating the DFL:

$$DFL = \frac{Q(P - V) - F}{Q(P - V) - \left(F + \text{Interest Exp.} + \dfrac{PD}{(1 - t)}\right)} = \frac{EBIT}{EBT - \dfrac{PD}{(1 - t)}} \tag{6-11}$$

In equation (6-11), PD is the amount of preferred dividends paid by the firm, and t is the tax rate. The second term in the denominator, $PD/(1 - t)$, requires some explanation. Because preferred dividends are paid out of after-tax dollars, we must determine how many *pre-tax* dollars are required to meet this expense. In this case, Spuds and Suds pays taxes at a rate of 40%, so they require $166,666.67 in pre-tax dollars in order to pay $100,000 in preferred dividends:

$$\frac{100,000}{(1 - 0.40)} = 166,666.67$$

We can use equation (6-11) in the worksheet to calculate the DFL for Spuds and Suds. In cell A37, enter the label: `Degree of Financial Leverage`. In B37, enter: `=IFERROR(B8/(B10-B14/(1-B25)),NA())`. You should find that the DFL is 1.80, which is the same as we found by using equation (6-10). Copying this formula to C37 reveals that in 2015 we expect the DFL to decline to 1.62.

The Degree of Combined Leverage

Most firms make use of both operating and financial leverage. Because they are using two types of leverage, it is useful to understand the combined effect. We can measure the total leverage employed by the firm by comparing the percentage change in sales to the percentage change in earnings per share. This measure is called the *degree of combined leverage* (DCL):

$$DCL = \frac{\%\Delta \text{ in EPS}}{\%\Delta \text{ in Sales}} \tag{6-12}$$

Because we have already calculated the relevant percentage changes, it is a simple matter to determine that the DCL for Spuds and Suds in 2014 was:

$$DCL = \frac{30.00\%}{10.00\%} = 3.00$$

Therefore, any change in sales will be multiplied threefold in EPS. Recall that we earlier said that the DCL was a combination of operating and financial leverage. You can see this if we rewrite equation (6-12) as follows:

$$DCL = \frac{\%\Delta \text{ in EPS}}{\%\Delta \text{ in Sales}} = \frac{\%\Delta \text{ in EBIT}}{\%\Delta \text{ in Sales}} \times \frac{\%\Delta \text{ in EPS}}{\%\Delta \text{ in EBIT}}$$

Therefore, the combined effect of using both operating and financial leverage is multiplicative rather than simply additive. Managers should take note of this and use caution in increasing one type of leverage while ignoring the other. They may end up with more total leverage than anticipated. As we have just seen, the DCL is the product of DOL and DFL, so we can rewrite equation (6-12) as:

$$DCL = DOL \times DFL \tag{6-13}$$

To calculate the DCL for Spuds and Suds in your worksheet, first enter the label: `Degree of Combined Leverage` into A38. In B38, enter the formula: `=B36*B37`, and copy this to C38 to find the expected DCL for 2015. At this point, the lower part of your worksheet should look like Exhibit 6-4.

EXHIBIT 6-4
SPUDS AND SUDS WORKSHEET WITH THREE MEASURES OF LEVERAGE

	A	B	C
27	Operating Break-even Point (Units)	62,500	62,500
28	Operating Break-even Point (Dollars)	1,000,000	1,000,000
29	Total Break-even Point (Units)	104,167	104,167
30	Units to Meet EBIT Target	187,500	
31			
32	% Change in Sales from Prior Year		10.00%
33	% Change in EBIT from Prior Year		16.67%
34	% Change in EPS from Prior Year		30.00%
35			
36	Degree of Operating Leverage	1.67	1.57
37	Degree of Financial Leverage	1.80	1.62
38	Degree of Combined Leverage	3.00	2.54

Extending the Example

Comparing the three leverage measures for 2014 and 2015 shows that in all cases the firm will be using less leverage in 2015. Recall that the only change in 2015 was that sales were increased by 10% over their 2014 level. The reason for the decline in leverage is that fixed costs (both operating and financial) have become a smaller portion of the total costs of the firm. This will always be the case: *As sales increase above the break-even point, leverage will decline regardless of the measure that is used.*

We can see this by extending our Spuds and Suds example. Suppose that management is forecasting that sales will increase by 10% each year for the foreseeable future. Furthermore, because of contractual agreements, the firm's fixed costs will remain constant through at least 2018. In order to see the changes in the leverage measures under these conditions, copy C4:C38 and paste into D4:F38. This will create pro forma income statements for three additional years. Change the labels in D4:F4 to 2016, 2017, and 2018.

You should see that the DOL, DFL, and DCL are all decreasing as sales increase. This is easier to see if we create a chart. Select A36:F38 and then create a Line chart of the data. Be sure to set B4:F4 as the x-axis labels by right-clicking the chart and choosing Select Data. Under Horizontal (Category) Axis Labels click the Edit button and select the range. You should end up with a chart that resembles the one in Figure 6-3.

FIGURE 6-3
CHART OF VARIOUS LEVERAGE MEASURES AS SALES INCREASE

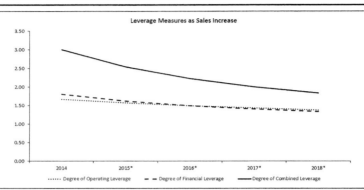

Obviously, as we stated earlier, the amount of leverage declines as the sales level increases. One caveat to this is that in the real world, fixed costs are not necessarily the same year after year. Furthermore, variable costs do not always maintain an exact percentage of sales. For these reasons, leverage may not decline as smoothly as depicted in our example. However, the general principle is sound and should be understood by all managers.

Linking Break-Even Points and Leverage Measures

While it may not be obvious, there is a connection between the break-even points and the various measures of leverage that we have defined. In this section we will reveal the links.[5]

Recall our definition of the operating break-even point in equation (6-2), page 175. Using that definition, we can solve for fixed costs (F):

$$F = Q^*_{\text{Operating}} \times (P - V) \qquad \textbf{(6-14)}$$

Substituting the definition of F from (6-14) into our definition of the DOL in (6-9) from page 182 results in:

$$\text{DOL} = \frac{Q(P - V)}{Q(P - V) - Q^*_{\text{Operating}}(P - V)} = \frac{Q}{Q - Q^*_{\text{Operating}}} \qquad \textbf{(6-15)}$$

---

5. See Zivney, T. & Goebel. J. (2013), The Relationship Between the Breakeven Point and Degrees of Leverage, *Advances in Financial Education*, 11, pp. 122–126. I expand on that to include preferred dividends when calculating the DFL.

So, we can clearly see (as was shown in Figure 6-3) that as sales rise above the operating break-even point, the DOL will decline.

In a similar fashion, we can derive the DFL in terms of the total break-even point as defined in equation (6-7), page 179. First, solve for the total fixed operating and financial costs:

$$F + \text{Interest Exp.} + \frac{\text{PD}}{(1-t)} = Q_{\text{Total}}^* \times (P - V) \tag{6-16}$$

Now, substitute into equation (6-11) on page 185:

$$\text{DFL} = \frac{Q(P-V) - Q_{\text{Operating}}^*(P-V)}{Q(P-V) - Q_{\text{Total}}^*(P-V)} = \frac{Q - Q_{\text{Operating}}^*}{Q - Q_{\text{Total}}^*} \tag{6-17}$$

Finally, recall from equation (6-13) on page 186 that the DCL is the product of the DOL and DFL. Therefore, using the results from (6-15) and (6-17):

$$\text{DCL} = \frac{Q}{Q - Q_{\text{Operating}}^*} \times \frac{Q - Q_{\text{Operating}}^*}{Q - Q_{\text{Total}}^*} = \frac{Q}{Q - Q_{\text{Total}}^*} \tag{6-18}$$

So, the degree of combined leverage will decline as the unit sales rises above the total break-even point.

To verify that these results are correct, return to your worksheet and copy the labels from A36:A38 and paste them into A41:A43. In B41 enter the formula: =B21/(B21-B27) to calculate the DOL. In B42 enter: =(B21-B27)/(B21-B29) for the DFL. Finally, in B43 enter: =B21/(B21-B29) for the DCL. You should find that all of your answers match those that were previously calculated.

Summary

We started this chapter by discussing the firm's operating break-even point. The break-even point is determined by a product's price and the amount of fixed and variable costs. The amount of fixed costs also played an important role in the determination of the amount of leverage a firm employs. We studied three measures of leverage:

1. The *degree of operating leverage* (DOL) measures the degree to which the presence of fixed costs multiplies changes in sales into even larger changes in EBIT.

2. The *degree of financial leverage* (DFL) measures the change in EPS relative to a change in EBIT. Financial leverage is a direct result of managerial decisions about how the firm should be financed.

3. The *degree of combined leverage* (DCL) provides a measure of the total leverage used by the firm. This is the product of the DOL and DFL.

We also introduced the Goal Seek tool, which is very useful whenever you know the result that you want but not the input value required to get that result.

TABLE 6-1
FUNCTIONS INTRODUCED IN THIS CHAPTER

Purpose	Function	Page
Return #N/A	NA( )	183
Determine if a formula returns an error value	IFERROR(*VALUE*, *VALUE_IF_ERROR*)	183

TABLE 6-2
SUMMARY OF EQUATIONS

Name	Equation	Page
Operating Break-Even Level in Units	$Q^*_{\text{Operating}} = \dfrac{F}{P - V}$	175
Operating Break-Even Level in Dollars	$\$BE = P \times Q^*_{\text{Operating}} = \dfrac{F}{\text{CM\%}}$	175
Cash Break-Even Point in Units	$Q^*_{\text{Cash}} = \dfrac{F - \text{Depreciation}}{P - V}$	178
Total Break-Even Point where EPS = 0	$Q^*_{\text{Total}} = \dfrac{F + \text{Interest Exp.} + \dfrac{PD}{(1 - t)}}{P - V}$	179
Degree of Operating Leverage (DOL)	$\text{DOL} = \dfrac{\%\Delta \text{ in EBIT}}{\%\Delta \text{ in Sales}} = \dfrac{Q(P - V)}{Q(P - V) - F}$	181
Degree of Financial Leverage (DFL)	$\text{DFL} = \dfrac{\%\Delta \text{ in EPS}}{\%\Delta \text{ in EBIT}} = \dfrac{\text{EBIT}}{\text{EBT} - \dfrac{PD}{(1 - t)}}$	185
Degree of Combined Leverage (DCL)	$\text{DCL} = \dfrac{\%\Delta \text{ in EPS}}{\%\Delta \text{ in Sales}} = \text{DOL} \times \text{DFL}$	186

Problems

1. Meyerson's Bakery is considering the addition of a new line of pies to its product offerings. It is expected that each pie will sell for $15 and the variable costs per pie will be $9. Total fixed operating costs are expected to be $20,000. Meyerson's faces a marginal tax rate of 35%, will have interest expense associated with this line of $3,000, and expects to sell about 4,000 pies in the first year.

   a. Create an income statement for the pie line's first year. Is the line expected to be profitable?

   b. Calculate the operating break-even point in both units and dollars.

   c. How many pies would Meyerson's need to sell in order to achieve EBIT of $15,000?

   d. Use the Goal Seek tool to determine the selling price per pie that would allow Meyerson's to break even in terms of its net income.

   e. Calculate the DOL, DFL, and DCL for the new pie line.

2. Income Statements for Xcel Energy from 2011 to 2013 appear below.

Xcel Energy Incorporated
Annual Income Statements
For the Years 2011 to 2013 ($ in millions)

	2011	2012	2013
Revenue	10,655	10,128	10,915
Cost of revenue	5,186	4,534	5,135
Gross profit	*5,469*	*5,594*	*5,780*
Operation and maintenance	2,140	2,176	2,274
Depreciation and amortization	891	926	978
Other operating expenses	656	669	681
Operating income	*1,782*	*1,823*	*1,848*
Interest Expense	591	602	575
Other income	119	134	160
Income before income taxes	*1,310*	*1,355*	*1,432*
Provision for income taxes	468	450	484
Net income	*841*	*905*	*948*
Preferred dividend	7	-	-
Net income available to common shareholders	*834*	*905*	*948*
Basic Shares Outstanding	485	488	496
Basic EPS	1.72	1.86	1.91
Tax Rate	35.73%	33.21%	33.80%

   a. Enter the data into your worksheet. Assume that Cost of Revenue and Operation and Maintenance costs are variable. Depreciation and Other operating expenses are fixed costs. Ignore Other income when calculating EBT for the questions below.

b. Given that Xcel Energy is a power company, would you expect that it would have more operating leverage or financial leverage?

c. Calculate the degree of operating leverage for each year using the assumptions from part a.

d. Calculate the degree of financial leverage for each year.

e. Calculate the degree of combined leverage for each of the three years. Does it appear that Xcel's leverage measures have been increasing or decreasing over this period?

f. Create a line chart that shows how the various leverage measures have changed over this three-year period.

3. The following is information for three local auto dealers:

	Bell's Domestics	Junior's Used	Europe's Best	Industry Average
Average Selling Price	$34,650	$26,730	$51,480	$29,700
Unit Sales	1,350	1,665	765	1,125
Interest Expense	742,500	990,000	2,970,000	1,485,000
Variable Costs (% of Sales)	60%	45%	40%	48%
Fixed Costs	9,000,000	6,300,000	18,000,000	9,900,000
Preferred Dividends	900,000	0	540,000	270,000
Common Shares	4,500,000	7,200,000	2,700,000	6,300,000

a. Using the information given in the above table, construct income statements for each company and the industry average. Assume that each company faces a tax rate of 35%.

b. Calculate the break-even points and the degrees of operating, financial, and combined leverage for each company and the industry average.

c. Compare the companies to each other and the industry average. What conclusions can you draw about each operation?

Internet Exercise

1. Following the instructions from Internet Exercise 2 in Chapter 5, get the income statements for the company of your choice for the past three years from MSN Money. Now repeat the analysis from Problem 2. What differences do you note between the leverage measures for your company and Xcel Energy?

CHAPTER 7

The Time Value of Money

After studying this chapter, you should be able to:

1. *Explain the concept of the time value of money.*

2. *Calculate the present value and future value of a stream of cash flows using Excel.*

3. *Explain the types of cash flows encountered in financial analysis and how to adjust for each type in making time value calculations in Excel.*

4. *Differentiate between the alternative compounding periods, and use Excel to compare present and future values under different compounding schemes.*

"A bird in the hand is worth more than two in the bush." That old aphorism, when translated into the language of finance, becomes "A dollar today is worth more than a dollar tomorrow." Intuitively, it probably makes sense, but why? Stated very simply, you can take that dollar today and invest it with the expectation of having more than a dollar tomorrow.

Because money can be invested to grow to a larger amount in the future, we say that money has a "time value." This concept of a time value of money underlies much of the theory of financial decision making, and you will be required to understand this material in order to complete the remaining chapters.

Future Value

Imagine that you have $1,000 available to invest. If you earn interest at the rate of 10% per year, then you will have $1,100 at the end of one year. The mathematics behind this example is quite simple:

$$1,000 + 1,000(0.10) = 1,100$$

In other words, after one year you will have your original $1,000 (the *principal* amount) plus the 10% interest earned on the principal. Because you won't have the $1,100 until one year in the future, we refer to this amount as the *future value*. The amount that you have today, $1,000, is referred to as the *present value*. If, at the end of the year, you choose to make the same investment again, then at the end of the second year you will have:

$$1,000 + 1,000(0.10) + 100(0.10) + 1,000(0.10) = 1,210$$

The $1,210 at the end of the second year can be broken down into its components: the original principal, the first year's interest, the interest earned in the second year on the first year's interest, and the second year's interest on the original principal. Note that we could restate the second year calculation to be:

$$1,100 + 1,100(0.10) = 1,210$$

Or, by factoring out the 1,100 we get:

$$1,100(1 + 0.10) = 1,210$$

Notice that in the second year the interest is earned on both the original principal and the interest earned during the first year. The idea of earning interest on previously earned interest is known as *compounding*. This is why the total interest earned in the second year is $110 versus only $100 the first year.

Returning to our original one-year example, we can generalize the formula for any one-year investment as follows:

$$FV_1 = PV + PV(i)$$

where FV_1 is the future value at the end of year 1, PV is the present value, and i is the one-year interest rate (compounding rate). The above equation is not in its simplest form. We can factor PV from both terms on the right-hand side, simplifying the future value equation to:

$$FV_1 = PV(1 + i) \qquad \text{(7-1)}$$

Recall that in our two-year example, we earned interest on both the principal and interest from the first year. In other words, the first year FV became the second year PV. Symbolically, the second year FV is:

$$FV_2 = FV_1(1 + i)$$

Substituting $PV(1 + i)$ for FV_1 and simplifying, we have:

$$FV_2 = PV(1 + i)(1 + i) = PV(1 + i)^2$$

We can actually further generalize our future value equation. Realize that the exponent (on the right-hand side) is the same as the subscript (on the left-hand side) in the future value equation. When we were solving for the future value at the end of the first year, the exponent was 1. When we were solving for the future value at the end of the second year, the exponent was 2. In general, the exponent will be equal to the number of the period for which we wish to find the future value.

$$FV_N = PV(1 + i)^N \tag{7-2}$$

Equation (7-2) is the basis for all of the time value equations that we will look at in the sections ahead. Using this version of the equation, you can see that investing $1,000 for two years at 10% per year will leave you with $1,210 at the end of two years. In other words:

$$FV_2 = 1,000(1.10)^2 = 1,210$$

Using Excel to Find Future Values

It is easy enough to calculate future values with a hand calculator, especially a financial calculator. But, as we will see in the sections and chapters ahead, it is often necessary to use future values in worksheets. Excel makes these calculations easy with its **Fv** function:

$$\textbf{Fv}(\textit{RATE, NPER, PMT, PV, TYPE})$$

There are five arguments to the **Fv** function. *RATE* is the interest rate per period (year, month, day, etc.), *NPER* is the total number of periods, and *PV* is the present value. *PMT* and *TYPE* are included to handle annuities (a series of equal payments, equally spaced over time), which we will deal with later. For the problem types we are currently solving, we will set both *PMT* and *TYPE* to 0.[1]

---

1. The *TYPE* argument tells Excel whether the cash flows occur at the end (0) or beginning (1) of the period.

EXHIBIT 7-1
FUTURE VALUE OF A SINGLE CASH FLOW

	A	B
1	**Future Value Calculations**	
2	Present Value	1,000.00
3	Years	1
4	Rate	10%
5	Future Value	

Let's set up a simple worksheet to calculate the future value of a single sum. Starting with a blank worksheet, enter the labels and numbers as shown in Exhibit 7-1.

We want to use the **Fv** function to calculate the future value of $1,000 for one year at 10% per year. In B5 enter the formula: `=FV(B4,B3,0,-B2,0)`. The result, $1,100, is exactly the same as we found earlier. Note that we have entered –B2 for the *Pv* argument. The reason for the negative sign is because Excel realizes that either the *Pv* or the *Fv* must be a cash outflow. If we had not used the negative sign, the result (*Fv*) would have been negative. Users of financial calculators will recognize this as the *cash flow sign convention*.

You can now experiment with different values for the arguments. Try replacing the 1 in B3 with a 2. Excel immediately updates the result in B5 with $1,210, just as we found in the second part of our example. To see just how powerful compounding can be, insert 30 into B3. The result, $17,449.40, indicates that each $1,000 invested at 10% per year will grow to $17,449.40 after just 30 years. If we double the investment in B2 to $2,000, then we should double the future value. Try it; you should get a result of $34,898.80, exactly twice what we got with a $1,000 investment. In general, any money invested for 30 years at 10% per year will grow to 17.449 times its initial value. To see even more powerful examples of compounding, try increasing the interest rate.

Present Value

Our future value equation can be solved for any of its variables. We may wish to turn our example problem around to solve for the present value. Suppose that the problem is restated as, "What initial investment is required so that you will accumulate $1,210 after two years if you expect to earn an interest rate of 10% per year?" In this case, we want to solve for the present value—we already know the future value.

Mathematically, all that we need to do is to solve the future value equation (7-2) for the present value:

$$PV = \frac{FV_N}{(1+i)^N} \qquad \text{(7-3)}$$

Of course, we already know that the answer must be $1,000:

$$PV = \frac{1,210}{(1.10)^2} = 1,000$$

In Excel, we can solve problems of this type by using the built-in **Pv** function:

$$PV(RATE, NPER, PMT, FV, TYPE)$$

The arguments to the **Pv** function are exactly the same as those for the **Fv** function, except that *PV* is replaced by *FV*. For this example, modify your worksheet by entering data into cells D1:E5 as shown in Exhibit 7-2.

EXHIBIT 7-2
PRESENT VALUE OF A SINGLE CASH FLOW

	A	B	C	D	E
1	**Future Value Calculations**			**Present Value Calculations**	
2	Present Value	1000.00		Future Value	$1,100.00
3	Years	1		Years	1
4	Rate	10%		Rate	10%
5	Future Value	$1,100.00		Present Value	

In cell E5 place the formula: =PV(E4,E3,0,-E2,0). Again, we enter the future value reference as negative so that the present value result will be positive. The result will be $1,000, exactly as expected.

We have purposely constructed our future value and present value examples side by side in the worksheet to demonstrate that present value and future value are inverse functions. Let's change our worksheet to make this concept clear. We want to link the references in the present value function to the cells used in the future value function. This will allow changes in the future value arguments to change the present value arguments. First, select E2 and enter: =B5, in E3 type: =B3, and in E4 enter: =B4. Now, regardless of the changes made to the future value side of the worksheet, the present value should be equal to the value in B2. Try making some changes to the inputs in B2, B3, and B4. No matter what changes you make, the calculated present value (in E5) is always the same as the present value input in B2. This is because the present value and future value are inverse functions of each other.

Annuities

Thus far, we have examined the present and future values of single cash flows (also referred to as *lump sums*). These are powerful concepts that will allow us to deal with more complex cash flows. *Annuities* are a series of nominally equal cash flows, equally spaced in time. Examples of annuities abound. Your car payment is an annuity, so is your mortgage (or rent) payment. If you don't already, you may someday own annuities as part of a retirement program. The cash flow pictured in Figure 7-1 is another example.

FIGURE 7-1
A TIMELINE FOR AN ANNUITY CASH FLOW

How do we find the value of a stream of cash flows such as that pictured in Figure 7-1? The answer involves the *principle of value additivity*. This principle says that "the value of a stream of cash flows is equal to the sum of the values of the components." As long as the cash flows occur at the same time, they can be added together. Therefore, if we can move each of the cash flows to the same time period (any time period), we can add them to find the value as of that time period. Cash flows can be moved around in time by compounding or discounting.

Present Value of an Annuity

One way to find the present value of an annuity is to find the present value of each of the cash flows separately and then add them together. Equation (7-4) summarizes this method:

$$PV_A = \sum_{t=1}^{N} \frac{Pmt_t}{(1+i)^t} \tag{7-4}$$

where PV_A is the present value of the annuity, t is the time period, N is the total number of payments, Pmt_t is the payment in period t, and i is the discount rate.

Of course, this equation works fine for any annuity (or any stream of cash flows), but it can be very tedious for annuities with more than just a few payments. Imagine finding the current balance (i.e., present value) of a mortgage with more than 300 payments to go before it is paid off! We can find a closed-form solution (the above equation is an "open-form" solution because the number of additions is indefinite) by taking the summation:

$$PV_A = Pmt\left[\frac{1 - \dfrac{1}{(1+i)^N}}{i}\right] \tag{7-5}$$

where all terms are as previously defined. Notice that we have dropped the subscript t because this solution does not depend on our taking the present values separately. Instead, because each payment is the same, we can value the entire stream of cash flows in one step.

Let's find the present value of the cash flow pictured in Figure 7-1. Assuming that the discount rate for this cash flow is 8%, the equation is:

$$PV_A = 100\left[\frac{1 - \dfrac{1}{(1.08)^5}}{0.08}\right] = 399.27$$

This means that if you were to deposit $399.27 into an account today that pays 8% interest per year, you could withdraw $100 at the end of each year and be left with a balance of $0.00 at the end of the five years.

Recall from our earlier discussion of single cash flows that we can use Excel's built-in **Pv** function to find present values. To recap, the **Pv** function is defined as:

$$\textbf{Pv}(\textit{RATE, NPER, PMT, FV, TYPE})$$

When dealing with single cash flows we set *PMT* and *TYPE* to 0. Those arguments are used only in the case of annuities. *PMT* will be set to the dollar amount of the periodic payment. *TYPE* is an optional binary (0 or 1) variable that controls whether Excel assumes the payment occurs at the end (0) or the beginning (1) of the period. For the time being, we will assume that all payments occur at the end of the period (i.e., they are *regular* annuities).

EXHIBIT 7-3
PRESENT VALUE OF AN ANNUITY

	A	B
1	**Present Value of an Annuity**	
2	Payment	100
3	Interest Rate	8%
4	Number of Payments	5
5	Present Value	

Set up a worksheet with the data pictured in Exhibit 7-3 in cells A1:B5. In B5 we wish to find the present value of the annuity presented in Figure 7-1, so enter: =PV(B3,B4,B2,0,0). Note that we have entered the payment as a positive number and the result is –$399.27. The interpretation is that if you were to make a deposit (a cash outflow) of $399.27 today, you could make a withdrawal of (a cash inflow) $100 each year for the next five years. Had we made the payment (B2) negative instead, the present value would have been a positive $399.27. The answer is the same, except for the sign, but the interpretation is different. In this case, the interpretation is that if you were to take out a loan of $399.27 (a cash inflow) today, you would need to repay $100 (a cash outflow) per year for each of the next five years to retire the loan.

We can, of course, experiment with various arguments. For example, suppose that instead of five withdrawals of $100 each you wanted to make ten withdrawals of $50 each. How much would you need to deposit into this account in order to deplete the account after 10 withdrawals? Change the number of payments in B4 to: 10 and the payment in B2 to: 50. After these changes, you will see that an initial deposit of only $335.50 will allow you to achieve your goal.

Returning now to our original example, reset the payment amount to: 100 and the number of payments to: 5. How much would you have to deposit if you want to make your first withdrawal today, rather than one year from today? (An annuity that begins paying immediately is known as *annuity due*.) To answer this question, realize that the only thing we have changed is the timing of the first withdrawal. We will still make a total of five withdrawals of $100 each, but they occur at the beginning of each period. In B5, change the *TYPE* argument to 1, from 0 originally, so that the formula is now: =PV(B3,B4,B2,0,1). The result is –$431.21, indicating that, because the first withdrawal occurs immediately, you will have to make a larger initial deposit. Note that the amount of the deposit must be larger because you will not earn the first year's interest before making the first withdrawal.

Another way to look at this is that we are effectively depositing $331.21 (= $431.21 deposit –$100 withdrawal) in order to be able to make four future withdrawals of $100 each. To see that this is the case, change the **Pv** formula back to its original form (set *TYPE* = 0) and change the number of payments to 4. The present value is then shown to be $331.21, exactly as claimed.

Future Value of an Annuity

Imagine that you have recently begun planning for retirement. One of the attractive options available is to set up a traditional Individual Retirement Account (IRA). What makes the IRA so attractive is that you can deposit up to $5,500 per year, and the investment gains will accrue tax free until you begin to make withdrawals after age 59½. Furthermore, depending on your situation, the IRA deposits may reduce your taxable income.

To determine the amount that you will have accumulated in your IRA at retirement, you need to understand the future value of an annuity. Recalling the principle of value additivity, we could simply find the future value of each year's investment and add them together at retirement. Mathematically this is:

$$FV_A = \sum_{t=1}^{N} Pmt_t(1 + i)^{N-t} \qquad (7\text{-}6)$$

Alternatively, we could use the closed-form solution of equation (7-6):

$$FV_A = Pmt\left[\frac{(1 + i)^N - 1}{i}\right] \qquad (7\text{-}7)$$

Assume that you are planning on retirement in 30 years. If you deposit $5,500 each year into an IRA account that will earn an average of 7.5% per year, how much will you have after 30 years? Because of the large number of deposits, equation (7-7) will be easier to use than equation (7-6), though we could use either one. The solution is:

$$FV_A = 5,500\left[\frac{(1.075)^{30} - 1}{0.075}\right] = 568,696.71$$

As usual, Excel provides a built-in function to handle problems such as this one. The **Fv** function, which we used to find the future value of a single sum earlier, will also find the future value of an annuity. Its use is nearly identical to the **Pv** function; the only difference is the substitution of **Pv** for **Fv**. Set up a new worksheet like the one in Exhibit 7-4.

EXHIBIT 7-4
FUTURE VALUE OF AN ANNUITY

	A	B
1	**Future Value of an Annuity**	
2	Payment	5,500
3	Interest Rate	7.50%
4	Number of Payments	30
5	Future Value	

In B5 place the formula: =FV(B3,B4,-B2,0,0). The result of $568,696.71 agrees exactly with the result from the formula. What if that amount is less than what you had hoped for? One solution is to start making the investments this year, rather than next (i.e., the beginning of this period rather than the end of this period). To see the effect of this change all that needs to be done is to change the *TYPE* argument to 1 so that the formula is now:

=FV(B3,B4,-B2,0,1). That minor change in your investment strategy will net you about $42,652 extra at retirement. Perhaps a better alternative is to accept a little extra risk (we assume that you are young enough that this makes sense) by investing in stock mutual funds that will return an average of about 10% per year over the 30-year horizon. In this case, still assuming that you start investing right now, you will have $995,188.84 at retirement. Significantly better! The extra 2.5% return each year added more than $400,000 to your retirement fund. This is the magic of compounding.

Solving for the Annuity Payment

Suppose that you want to know the amount that must be deposited in order to accumulate a given sum after a number of years. For example, assume that you are planning to purchase a house five years from now. Because you are currently a student, you will begin saving for the $10,000 down payment one year from today. How much will you need to save each year, if your savings will earn interest at a rate of 4% per year? Figure 7-2 diagrams the problem.

FIGURE 7-2
A TIMELINE FOR ANNUAL SAVINGS TO OBTAIN $10,000 IN FIVE YEARS

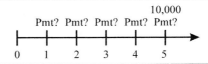

In this case, we wish to solve for the payment that you would have to make each year. The future value of the annuity is already known, so the **FV** function would be inappropriate. What we need is Excel's **PMT** function:

$$\text{PMT}(\textit{RATE, NPER, PV, FV, TYPE})$$

The arguments for the **PMT** function are similar to those for the **PV** and **FV** functions, except that it has *PV* and *FV* arguments in place of the *PMT* argument.

Enter the information from Exhibit 7-5 into cells A1:B6 of a new worksheet. In cell B6 enter the **PMT** function: =PMT(B5,B4,-B2,B3,0). The result indicates that you will have to save $1,846.27 per year (a cash outflow) in order to accumulate $10,000 for the down payment in five years.

EXHIBIT 7-5
ANNUITY PAYMENT WHEN PV OR FV IS KNOWN

	A	B
1	**Solving for an Annuity Payment**	
2	Present Value	0
3	Future Value	10,000
4	Number of Payments	5
5	Interest Rate	4.00%
6	Annual Payment Amount	

The **PMT** function allows *both PV* and *FV* to be inputs. In the previous example, it was assumed that *PV* was 0. However, let's suppose that you have recently inherited $3,000 from your uncle and that you want to use this money to begin saving now for that down payment. Because the $3,000 will grow to only $3,649.96 after five years at 4% per year (this can be verified by using the worksheet created for Exhibit 7-1), you will still need to save some amount every year. How much will you need to save each year? To find out, simply set the present value, in B2, to 3,000 leaving the other values unchanged. Because the initial investment *reduces* the total amount that you need to save to $6,350.04 (why?), your annual saving requirement is reduced to $1,172.39.

Solving for the Number of Periods in an Annuity

Solving for the present value, future value, and payment for annuities are fairly simple problems. That is, the formulas are straightforward and easy to apply. Solving for the number of periods, N, is not as obvious mathematically. To do so requires knowledge of logarithms. If you know the present value of the annuity, then solving equation (7-5) for N we get:

$$N = \frac{\ln\left(1 - \frac{iPV_A}{Pmt}\right)}{-\ln(1 + i)} \qquad (7\text{-}8)$$

where $\ln(\cdot)$ is the natural logarithm operator. If you know the future value, then solving equation (7-7) for N results in:

$$N = \frac{\ln\left(1 + \frac{iFV_A}{Pmt}\right)}{\ln(1 + i)} \qquad (7\text{-}9)$$

Return now to our original example of saving for the down payment for a house. Recall that it was determined that by saving $1,846.27 per year you could afford the down payment after five years, assuming no initial investment. Set up the worksheet in Exhibit 7-6.

EXHIBIT 7-6
NUMBER OF ANNUITY PAYMENTS WHEN PV OR FV IS KNOWN

	A	B
1	**Solving for N in an Annuity**	
2	Present Value	$0
3	Future Value	10,000.00
4	Annual Payment	1,846.27
5	Annual Rate	4.00%
6	Number of Years	

We can solve this problem using equation (7-9) and the built-in **LN** function:[2]

$$\text{LN}(NUMBER)$$

In B6 enter the formula: =LN(B5*B3/B4+1)/LN(1+B5). The result is five years as we would expect.

Excel also offers the built-in **NPER** function, which also works with lump sums, to solve problems of this type directly. This function is defined as:

$$\text{NPER}(RATE, PMT, PV, FV, TYPE)$$

where all of the arguments are as previously defined. To use this function, you must know the payment, per period interest rate, and either the present value or future value or both.

Because we want to solve for the number of periods, insert the **NPER** function into B6: =NPER(B5,-B4,-B2,B3,0). Notice that both the *PV* and *PMT* arguments are made negative in this function. Again, this is because of the cash flow sign convention. In this case, we wish to be able to withdraw the future value (a cash inflow and, therefore, positive) and deposit the *PV* and *PMT*s (cash outflows, therefore negative). The result is five years, exactly as we would expect. If you enter the $3,000 inheritance into B2, then you will have the down payment in only 3.39 years.

---

2. Logarithms are often useful tools, and Excel offers functions to handle them. In addition to **LN**, the other logarithm functions are **LOG10** and **LOG**. The former calculates the base 10 logarithm, and the latter can calculate a logarithm with any base.

Solving for the Interest Rate in an Annuity

Unlike the present value, future value, payment, and number of periods, there is no closed-form solution for the rate of interest of an annuity. The only way to solve this problem is to use a trial-and-error approach, perhaps an intelligent one such as the Newton–Raphson technique or the bisection method.[3]

Excel, however, offers the **RATE** function that will solve for the interest rate. It is defined as:

$$\text{RATE}(\textit{NPer, Pmt, Pv, Fv, Type, Guess})$$

where the arguments are as defined earlier, and *GUESS* is your optional first guess at the correct answer. Ordinarily, the *GUESS* can be safely omitted.

> Suppose that you are approached with an offer to purchase an investment that will provide cash flows of $1,500 per year for 10 years. The cost of purchasing this investment is $10,500. If you have an alternative investment opportunity, of equal risk, that will yield 8% per year, which one should you accept?

There are actually several ways that a problem such as this could be solved. One method is to realize that 8% is your opportunity cost of funds and should therefore be used as your discount rate. Using the worksheet created in Exhibit 7-3 we find that the present value (i.e., current worth to you) of the investment is only $10,065.12. Because the price ($10,500) is greater than the value, you should reject the investment and accept your alternative.[4]

Another method of solving this dilemma is to compare the yields (i.e., compound annual return) offered by the investments. All other things being equal, the investment with the highest yield should be accepted. We already know that your alternative investment offers an 8% yield, but what is the yield of your new opportunity?

Create a new worksheet and enter the data as shown in Exhibit 7-7. Note that we are entering the PV, in B2, as a negative number in order to allow the function to work regardless of the direction of the cash flows. This is to maintain flexibility so that you can change the numbers in the worksheet without editing the function. Just remember to use the correct signs.

---

3. These are powerful techniques for solving this type of problem. The bisection method, briefly, involves choosing two initial guesses at the answer that are sure to bracket the true answer. Each successive guess is halfway between the two previous guesses that bracket the solution. The Newton–Raphson technique requires calculus and is beyond the scope of this book. For more information, consult any numerical methods textbook.

4. Note that we are simply comparing the cost of the investment to its perceived benefit (present value). If the cost is greater than the benefit, the investment should be rejected. We will expand on this method in future chapters.

EXHIBIT 7-7
YIELD ON AN ANNUITY

	A	B
1	**Solving for *i* in an Annuity**	
2	Present Value	-10,500
3	Future Value	0
4	Annual Payment	1,500
5	Number of Years	10
6	Annual Rate	

In B6 place the function: =RATE(B5,B4,B2,B3,0,0.1). The result is 7.07% per year, so you should reject the new investment in favor of the alternative that offers 8% per year. This is the same result we obtained with the present value methodology, as expected. Later, we will see that this will always be the case when comparing mutually exclusive investment opportunities.[5]

Deferred Annuities

Not all annuities begin their payments during the year following the analysis period. For example, if you are planning for your retirement, you will probably start by determining the amount of income that you will need each year during retirement. However, if you are a student, you will probably not retire for many years. Your retirement income, then, is an annuity that won't begin until you retire. In other words, it is a *deferred annuity.* How do we determine the value of a deferred annuity?

Assume that you own a time machine (made of a super-strong futuristic metal that can withstand the gravitational forces of a black hole in space). This machine can transport you to any time period that you choose. If we use this time machine to transport you to the year just prior to retirement, then valuing the stream of retirement income becomes a simple matter. Just use Excel's **Pv** function as we did earlier. The year before the first withdrawal is now considered to be year 0, the first year of retirement is year 1, and so on. Figure 7-3 demonstrates this time-shifting technique.

---

5. Mutually exclusive investment opportunities are those in which you may choose one investment or the other, but not both. That is, the choice of one precludes you also choosing the other.

FIGURE 7-3
TIME-SHIFTING AS A FIRST STEP IN SOLVING DEFERRED ANNUITY PROBLEMS

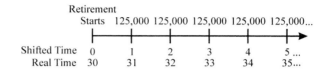

In constructing Figure 7-3, we have assumed that you will retire 30 years from now, and will require an income of $125,000 per year during retirement. If we further assume that you will need your retirement income for 35 years and expect to earn 6% per year, then you will need to have accumulated $1,812,280.80 by year 30 to provide this income. In other words, $1,812,280.80 is the present value, at year 30, of $125,000 per year for 35 years at 6%. You can use the worksheet created for Exhibit 7-3 to verify these numbers.[6]

The problem in Figure 7-3 is that knowing the amount that we will need 30 years from now doesn't directly tell us how much we need to save today. The present value function in Excel, or the PV_A equation (7-5), must be thought of as a transformation function. That is, it transforms a series of payments into a lump sum. That lump sum ($1,812,280.80 in our example) is then placed *one period before the first payment occurs*. In our earlier examples, the annuities began payment at the end of period 1, so the present value was at time period 0 (one period earlier than period 1). In the current example, the present value is at time period 30, also one period before the first payment.

In order to determine the amount that we need to invest today, we must treat the required savings at retirement as a future value. This sum must then be discounted back to period 0. For example, if we assume that you can earn 8% per year before retirement, then you would need to invest $180,099.63 today in order to meet your retirement goals.

Exhibit 7-8 presents a simple worksheet to determine the investment required today in order to provide a particular income during retirement. Open a new worksheet and enter the data and labels from Exhibit 7-8.

---

6. Although $125,000 per year may seem like a lot of money, we arrived at this figure by assuming that you would need $50,000 per year in today's dollars. We then adjusted that amount for an average inflation rate of 3% per year for 31 years to arrive at $125,000. In fact, that won't be enough because inflation will continue during retirement. So, your retirement income will need to rise each year to keep pace with inflation. We will deal with this in the next section.

EXHIBIT 7-8
PLANNING FOR RETIREMENT

	A	B
1	**Retirement Worksheet**	
2	Annual Retirement Income Need	125,000
3	Years until Retirement	30
4	Years in Retirement	35
5	Rate of Return before Retirement	8.00%
6	Rate of Return during Retirement	6.00%
7	Savings Required at Retirement	
8	Investment Required Today	
9	Annual Investment Required	

To complete our retirement worksheet, we need to enter functions into cells B7:B9. Recall that the first step in our retirement income problem was to determine the present value of your retirement income at period 30. To do this in our worksheet, enter the **Pv** function into B7: =PV(B6,B4,-B2,0,0). The result, $1,812,280.80, tells us that you will need to have saved this amount in order to provide the income indicated in B2 for the number of years indicated in B4. To determine the amount that you would need to invest today (a lump sum), you need to determine the present value, at time period 0, of the amount in B7. To do this, in B8 enter the formula: =PV(B5,B3,0,-B7,0). As before, the amount required today is $180,099.63.

Another feature of the retirement planning worksheet is that it will calculate the annual savings required to reach your goal. To make Excel do this calculation, we need to use the **PMT** function. In B9 enter: =PMT(B5,B3,0,-B7,0). The result is $15,997.79, which means that if you can save this amount each year for the next 30 years, and earn an average of 8% interest each year, you will reach your goal. As difficult as that may be, it is much easier than investing the lump sum today.

We have ignored the effects of inflation and taxes on your retirement planning for this worksheet. But if we assume that you save the amount in B9 in a tax-deferred account, the results are a bit more realistic. Experiment with this worksheet. You may be surprised at the difficulty of saving for a comfortable retirement.

Graduated Annuities

Previously, we defined an annuity as a series of nominally equal cash flows, equally spaced in time. However, not everything that is called an annuity has equal cash flows each period.

For example, it is common today for people to invest a lump sum today in exchange for a series of payments that will escalate over time to maintain constant purchasing power. An insurance company may offer such an investment opportunity to retirees who are concerned about inflation in the future, and some lotteries offer an "annuitized" payout that increases each year.

Return to our example in the previous section. Your stated goal was to receive $125,000 each year for the 35 years that you expect to spend in retirement. However, if your income doesn't rise each year then your purchasing power will decline dramatically by the end of the 35 years. In fact, if inflation averages 3% per year, your income in the last year will have the same purchasing power as only about $44,423 (about one-third as much as needed) would have had at the beginning of your retirement. Clearly, then, it would be beneficial if your retirement income would grow to keep up with the rate of inflation.

Present Value of a Graduated Annuity

Suppose that you expect inflation to be 3% per year during retirement, so you have revised your retirement income needs so that your income grows by 3% each year. Figure 7-4 shows the revised timeline.

FIGURE 7-4
RETIREMENT INCOME GROWING AT 3% PER YEAR

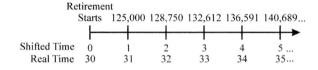

How do we find the present value of such a cash flow stream? It would appear that we cannot use the **Pv** function because it assumes that all of the cash flows are the same in each period. That leaves us with the fallback position of using the principle of value additivity. In other words, calculate the present value of each cash flow separately, and then add them together to get the total present value. This method requires a table that lists all of the cash flows and the use of equation (7-4) on page 200.

Fortunately, if we can assume that the growth rate of the cash flows will be constant, as it is in this case, then there is a closed-form solution for the present value of a graduated annuity when the first payment occurs one period from now:

$$PV_{GA} = \frac{Pmt_1}{i-g}\left[1 - \left(\frac{1+g}{1+i}\right)^N\right]$$

(7-10)

where Pmt_1 is the first cash flow, i is the interest rate, g is the growth rate, and N is the number of cash flows.

$$PV_{GA} = \frac{125,000}{0.06 - 0.03}\left[1 - \left(\frac{1.03}{1.06}\right)^{35}\right] = 2,641,257.55$$

As before, if we assume that you will earn 6% per year during retirement and your withdrawals grow 3% per year to keep up with inflation, then you will need to accumulate $2,641,257.55 in order to meet your income goals.

We can use the **Pv** function to calculate the same result, but only after modifying the interest rate. In the case of a graduated annuity we have two rates: a discount rate and a growth rate. These rates work against each other, so you might expect that we could use a "net" interest rate. In this case that would be 6% – 3% = 3%, but that won't work properly because interest rates compound. In other words, they are multiplicative instead of additive. Therefore, we need a slightly more complicated formula:

$$\text{Net Rate} = \frac{(1 + i)}{(1 + g)} - 1 \tag{7-11}$$

Instead of subtracting, we need to divide. In this case, the net interest rate is:

$$\text{Net Rate} = \frac{1.06}{1.03} - 1 \cong 0.02913$$

One final adjustment is necessary; we must also divide the result of the **Pv** function by $(1 + g)$. This adjustment effectively changes the payment at period 1 into its inflation-adjusted value at period 0.

We can now easily modify the retirement worksheet presented in Exhibit 7-8 to handle our new assumption regarding inflation. Make a copy of that worksheet, and then select row 5 and insert a new row. In A5 enter the label: Expected Inflation Rate, and in B5 enter: 3%. Now, we need to change the formula in B8 to: =-PV((1+B7)/(1+B5)-1,B4,B2)/(1+B5). You will see that the result is $2,641,257.55, exactly the same as before. Furthermore, the results in B9:B10 have automatically updated to include our new assumption. As you can see, you will now need to save $23,315.53 per year before retirement. That is about $7,318 more per year than the original projection, but this will allow you to maintain constant purchasing power during retirement. Exhibit 7-9 shows the new retirement planning worksheet.

EXHIBIT 7-9
PLANNING FOR RETIREMENT ADJUSTED FOR INFLATION

	A	B
1	**Retirement Worksheet with Growing Income**	
2	Annual Retirement Income Need	125,000
3	Years until Retirement	30
4	Years in Retirement	35
5	Expected Inflation Rate	3.00%
6	Rate of Return before Retirement	8.00%
7	Rate of Return during Retirement	6.00%
8	Savings Required at Retirement	$2,641,257.55
9	Investment Required Today	$262,481.13
10	Annual Investment Required	$23,315.53

In this example, the annuity payments begin at the end of the period. However, in many cases (such as lotteries) the first cash flow occurs immediately. This type of cash flow is called a *graduated annuity due*. We can easily modify equation (7-10) using the principal of value additivity to handle cash flows that start immediately.

Realize that we can treat a graduated annuity due as a regular graduated annuity with one less payment plus an additional payment today:

$$PV_{GAD} = Pmt_0 + \frac{Pmt_0(1+g)}{i-g}\left[1 - \left(\frac{1+g}{1+i}\right)^{N-1}\right] \qquad (7\text{-}12)$$

where Pmt_0 is the cash flow that occurs immediately. Again, we can use the interest rate adjustment from equation (7-11) in the **Pv** function. In this case, we need to use only the interest rate adjustment and set the *TYPE* argument to 1. So, if you plan to start withdrawals on the day of your retirement, you can change the formula in B8 to: `=-PV((1+B7)/(1+B5)-1,B4,B2,0,1)`. Because you will be making the first withdrawal one year earlier, you will need to have accumulated $2,799,733 at retirement, and you will need to save more each year.

Because equations (7-10) and (7-12) are complex, we have written an add-in function to do the calculations. An add-in function is similar to a built-in function, but you must have the add-in installed and open to use the function.[7] The FAME_PVGA function is defined as:

FAME_PVGA(*PMT, NPER, GROWTHRATE, DISCRATE, BEGEND*)

---

7. You can download the Famefncs.xlam add-in from the official Web site www.cengagebrain.com. Installation of the add-in is described in Chapter 1 on page 25.

Where **PMT** is the first cash flow, **NPER** is the number of cash flows, **GROWTHRATE** is the rate at which the cash flows grow over time, and **DISCRATE** is the required return. *BEGEND* is an optional argument that specifies if the cash flow occurs at the end (0) or beginning (1) of the period. (Note that *BEGEND* works just like the *TYPE* argument in the built-in **PV** function.)

Using this add-in function, you can replace the formula in B8 with: `=FAME_PVGA(B2,B4,B5,B7,0)`. You will get the same answer, but it is a bit easier to use the add-in function.

Future Value of a Graduated Annuity

Recall that the principle of value additivity states that we can find the value of a series of cash flows by moving the cash flows to a given period and then summing them together. The resulting lump sum is economically equivalent to the original series of cash flows. We can make use of this fact (further illustrated in the next section) to derive a formula for the future value of a graduated annuity. Specifically, we will first find the present value using equation (7-10) and then multiply it by $(1 + i)^N$. After simplifying, the formula for the future value of a graduated annuity is:

$$FV_{GA} = \frac{Pmt_1(1+i)^N}{i-g}\left[1-\left(\frac{1+g}{1+i}\right)^N\right]$$

(7-13)

Let's look at an example:

> Imagine that you are going to make an investment of $1,000 next year and then increase your investment each year by 6% per year for four additional years. If you can earn 8% per year on your investment, how much will you have accumulated at the end of year 5?

Using equation (7-13) we can see that the answer is $6,555.13:

$$FV_{GA} = \frac{1,000(1.08)^5}{0.08-0.06}\left[1-\left(\frac{1.06}{1.08}\right)^5\right] = 6,555.13$$

As before, we have created a user-defined function to do this calculation:

FAME_FVGA(PMT, NPER, GROWTHRATE, DISCRATE, BEGEND)

All of the arguments are defined identically to those for the **FAME_PVGA** function.

Uneven Cash Flow Streams

Annuities are very neat from a cash flow point of view, but most investments don't have cash flows that are the same in each period. When the cash flows are different in each period, we refer to them as *uneven cash flow streams*. Investments of this type are not as easy to deal with, though conceptually they are the same.

Recall our discussion of the principle of value additivity. This principle says that as long as cash flows occur in the same period, we can add them together to determine their combined value. The principle applies to any time period, not just to time period 0. So, to determine the present value of an uneven stream of cash flows, one option is to determine the present value of each cash flow separately, and then add them together. The same technique applies to the future value of an uneven stream. Simply find the future value of each cash flow separately, and then add them together.

Excel's **Pv** and **Fv** functions cannot be directly used for uneven cash flow streams because they assume equal (annuity) payments or a lump sum (though they can be used as array functions). Set up the worksheet in Exhibit 7-10 and we'll see what needs to be done.

EXHIBIT 7-10
PV AND FV FOR UNEVEN CASH FLOWS

	A	B
1	**Uneven Cash Flow Streams**	
2	Year	Cash Flow
3	1	1,000
4	2	2,000
5	3	3,000
6	4	4,000
7	5	5,000
8	Interest Rate	11.00%
9	Present Value	
10	Future Value	

First, we want to solve for the present value of the cash flows in B3:B7. To do this, we will use the net present value (NPV) function. This function will be especially valuable for capital budgeting in Chapter 11. The **NPV** function is defined as:

$$\text{NPV}(\textbf{\textit{RATE}}, \textbf{\textit{VALUE1}}, \textit{VALUE2}, ...)$$

where **RATE** is the per period rate of return (i.e., the discount rate), **VALUE1** is the first cash flow (or range of cash flows), *VALUE2* is the second cash flow, and so on. Excel will accept up to 255 cash flows in the list. To find the present value of the cash flows, enter: =NPV(B8,B3:B7) into B9.[8] Note that we have entered the cash flows as a range, rather than as individual values. Excel will accept the arguments either way, though a range is generally easier to enter. The result is $10,319.90. To verify this result, you can find the present value of each cash flow at 11% per year and then add them together.

Finding the future value of an uneven stream is a bit more difficult because Excel has no built-in function to perform this calculation. Recall, however, the principle of value additivity. If we can get all of the cash flows into the same period, we can add them together and then move the result to the desired period. Figure 7-5 shows this solution.

FIGURE 7-5
FINDING THE FUTURE VALUE OF AN UNEVEN CASH FLOW STREAM

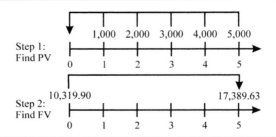

First, we find the present value of the uneven stream of cash flows, perhaps using the **NPV** function, and then we find the future value of the present value of the cash flows. The easiest way to implement this method in Excel is to use the **NPV** function *nested* within the **FV** function. A nested function is one that is used as an input to another function. In B10 enter: =FV(B8,A7,0,-NPV(B8,B3:B7),0). The future value is found to be $17,389.63. Notice that we have used the **NPV** function inside the **FV** function. As an alternative, we could have entered –B9 for the present value argument because we have already calculated it, but the result would be the same. Using nested functions can often simplify a worksheet by making use of fewer cells, though the formulas tend to be more complex.

Solving for the Yield in an Uneven Cash Flow Stream

Often in financial analysis, it is necessary to determine the yield of an investment given its price and cash flows. For example, we have seen that one way to choose between alternative investments is to compare their yields, and we will see more examples in Chapter 11. This

---

8. If you are familiar with the definition of Net Present Value (NPV), you should know that Excel's NPV function does not calculate the NPV as it is normally defined. Instead, it merely calculates the present value of uneven cash flows. This is covered in more depth in Chapter 11.

was easy when dealing with annuities and lump-sum investments, where we could use the **RATE** function. But, what about the case of uneven cash flow investments? We will use the worksheet in Exhibit 7-11 to find out.

EXHIBIT 7-11
YIELD ON AN UNEVEN CASH FLOW STREAM

	A	B
1	**Yield of Uneven Cash Flows**	
2	Year	Cash Flow
3	0	(10,319.90)
4	1	1,000
5	2	2,000
6	3	3,000
7	4	4,000
8	5	5,000
9	Yield	

To solve for the yield in problems such as this, we need to make use of the **IRR** (internal rate of return) function. The IRR is defined as the rate of return that equates the present value of future cash flows with the cost of the investment ($10,319.90 in this problem). In Excel, the **IRR** function is defined as:

$$\text{IRR}(VALUES, GUESS)$$

where **VALUES** is a range of cash flows (including the cost), and *GUESS* is the optional first guess at the correct interest rate. We will study this function in depth in Chapter 11, but for now we will just make use of it.

Before we find the solution, notice a couple of things about the worksheet. The cash flows are listed separately, so we cannot use the **IRR** function like we used the **FV**, **PV**, and **PMT** functions. Also, we must include the cost of the investment as one of the cash flows. To find the yield on this investment, insert into B9: =IRR(B3:B8,0.10). The result is 11%, which means that if you purchase this investment you will earn a compound annual rate of 11%.

We have used one form of the **IRR** function in B9. Another option is to omit the *GUESS* (0.10 in our example). In this case, either form will work. Sometimes, however, Excel will not be able to converge on a solution without a *GUESS* being specified. Remember that this is essentially a trial-and-error process, and sometimes Excel needs a little help to go in the right direction.

A few situations may cause an error when using the **IRR** function. One that we've already discussed is that Excel may not converge to a solution. In this case, you can usually find the answer by supplying Excel with a different *GUESS*. Another occurs if you have no negative cash flows. As an example, change the purchase price to a positive 10,319.90. Excel will return the #NUM! error message indicating that there is a problem. In this case the problem is that your return is infinite (why?). A third problem can result from more than one negative cash flow in the stream. In general, there will be one solution to the problem for each sign change in the cash flow stream. In our original example, there is only one sign change (from negative to positive after the initial purchase.)

Nonannual Compounding Periods

There is no reason why we should restrict our analyses to investments that pay cash flows annually. Many investments make payments (e.g., interest) semiannually, monthly, daily, or even more frequently. Everything that we have learned to this point still applies, with only a minor change.

Recall our basic time value of money formula (7-2):

$$FV_N = PV(1 + i)^N$$

Originally, we defined i as the annual rate of interest and N as the number of years. Actually, i is the periodic rate of interest and N is the total number of periods. As an example, i might be the weekly interest rate and N the total number of weeks for which we will hold the investment. Because rates are usually quoted in terms of simple (i.e., not compounded) annual rates, we can restate our basic formula as:

$$FV_N = PV\left(1 + \frac{i}{m}\right)^{Nm} \tag{7-14}$$

where i is the annual rate, N is the number of years, and m is the number of periods per year. Because there are 52 weeks in a year ($m = 52$), we would calculate the weekly rate as the annual rate divided by 52. Similarly, the number of weeks would be calculated by multiplying the number of years (perhaps a fractional number of years) by 52.

Excel can handle nonannual compounding just as easily as annual compounding. Just enter the rate and number of periods adjusted for the length of the compounding period. Let's look at an example.

Assume that you are shopping for a new bank to set up a savings account. As you start shopping, you notice that all of the banks offer the same stated annual interest rate, but different compounding periods.

To help make your decision, you set up the worksheet in Exhibit 7-12.

EXHIBIT 7-12
NONANNUAL COMPOUNDING PERIODS

	A	B
1	**Nonannual Compounding Worksheet**	
2	Initial Investment	1,000.00
3	Simple Annual Rate of Interest	10.00%
4	Term of Investment (Years)	1
5	**First National Bank**	
6	Periods per Year	1
7	Future Value	$1,100.00
8	**Second National Bank**	
9	Periods per Year	2
10	Future Value	$1,102.50
11	**Third National Bank**	
12	Periods per Year	12
13	Future Value	$1,104.71

Notice that all of the banks are advertising a 10% annual rate. The only difference is how often they credit the interest to your account (i.e., the frequency of compounding). Being economically rational, you will choose the bank that will provide the highest balance at the end of the year. To determine the end-of-year balances, enter the **Fv** formula in B7: =FV($B$3/B6,$B$4*B6,0,-$B$2). Copy the formula from B7 to both B10 and B13. Note that we have again made use of nested functions. In this case, the rate is defined as the annual rate *divided* by the number of periods in a year, and the number of periods is the number of years *times* the number of periods in a year.

The choice is clear. You should choose the Third National Bank because it offers the highest end-of-year balance ($1,104.71). All other things being equal, the more frequent the compounding, the higher your future value will be. To see this more clearly, set up the worksheet shown in Exhibit 7-13.

To finish the worksheet, use the **Fv** formula in C6: =FV(B$3/B6,B6*$B$4,0,-B$2) and copy it down to the other cells. It is important that you insert the dollar signs as indicated so that the references to the present value and interest rate remain fixed when copying.

EXHIBIT 7-13
COMPARING VARIOUS NONANNUAL COMPOUNDING PERIODS

	A	B	C
1	**Nonannual Compounding Periods**		
2	Present Value	1,000	
3	Annual Rate	10.00%	
4	Years	1	
5	**Frequency**	**Periods/Year**	**FV**
6	Annual	1	
7	Semiannual	2	
8	Quarterly	4	
9	Bimonthly	6	
10	Monthly	12	
11	Biweekly	26	
12	Weekly	52	
13	Daily	365	

As before, more frequent compounding leads to higher future values. Furthermore, the future value increases at a decreasing rate as the number of compounding periods increases. This can be seen more easily if we create a chart of the future values. Select the labels in A5:A14 and the numbers in C5:C14 (remember, you can select discontiguous ranges by holding down the Ctrl key while dragging the mouse). Note that you are selecting one extra row because we will use this worksheet again later to add one more data point. Now, click the Insert tab and create a Column chart formatted as shown in Exhibit 7-14.

EXHIBIT 7-14
NONANNUAL COMPOUNDING RESULTS

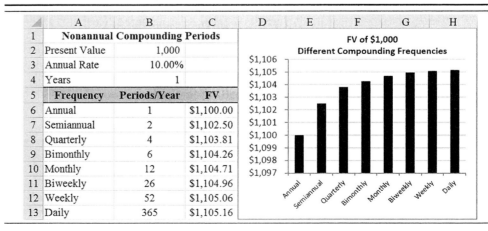

	A	B	C
1	**Nonannual Compounding Periods**		
2	Present Value	1,000	
3	Annual Rate	10.00%	
4	Years	1	
5	**Frequency**	**Periods/Year**	**FV**
6	Annual	1	$1,100.00
7	Semiannual	2	$1,102.50
8	Quarterly	4	$1,103.81
9	Bimonthly	6	$1,104.26
10	Monthly	12	$1,104.71
11	Biweekly	26	$1,104.96
12	Weekly	52	$1,105.06
13	Daily	365	$1,105.16

Effective Annual Interest Rates

Another way that we can look at the results of changing the compounding frequency is by calculating the *effective annual interest rate* (EAR). The EAR is the rate that is actually earned when compounding is more frequent than annual. It is calculated as:

$$EAR = \left(1 + \frac{i}{m}\right)^m - 1 \tag{7-15}$$

where i is the simple (or stated) annual rate and m is the number of compounding periods per year.

Return to our example of the three banks, in Exhibit 7-12, all of which were promising a 10% interest rate. The Second National Bank was compounding interest semiannually, so it was offering an effective annual rate of 10.25%:

$$EAR = \left(1 + \frac{0.10}{2}\right)^2 - 1 = 0.1025$$

Excel offers the **EFFECT** function to calculate the effective annual interest rate:

EFFECT(*NOMINAL_RATE, NPERY*)

where ***NOMINAL_RATE*** is the stated annual interest rate and ***NPERY*** is the number of compounding periods per year. To calculate the EAR being offered by the Second National Bank, return to that worksheet and enter the formula: =EFFECT($B$3,B9). You should get a result of 10.25% as above. Doing the same for the Third National Bank will return an EAR of 10.47% per year.

Less commonly, you will know the EAR and need to determine the simple (or nominal) annual rate. In these cases you can use the **NOMINAL** function:

NOMINAL(*EFFECT_RATE, NPERY*)

where ***EFFECT_RATE*** is the EAR. Applying this function to the EARs that were just calculated will return 10% for all three banks.

Continuous Compounding

We have seen that more frequent compounding leads to higher future values. However, our examples extended this idea only as far as daily compounding. There is no reason that we can't also compound every half-day, every hour, or even every minute. In fact, this concept can be extended to the smallest imaginable time period: the instant. This type of compounding is referred to as *continuous compounding*.

Continuous compounding is an extension of what we have seen already. To recap, recall that we changed the basic future value function:

$$FV_N = PV\left(1 + \frac{i}{m}\right)^{Nm}$$

The more frequently we compound, the larger m is going to be. For example, with semiannual compounding $m = 2$, but with daily compounding $m = 365$. What if we set m equal to infinity? We can't do that because i/∞ is effectively equal to zero. Instead we can take the limit as m approaches infinity. When we do this, we get:

$$\lim_{m \to \infty} FV_N = PVe^{iN} \tag{7-16}$$

where e is the base of the natural logarithm and is approximately equal to 2.718.

Excel does not offer functions to solve for the present or future value when compounding is continuous. However, we can easily create the formulas using the **EXP** function, which raises e to a specified power.[9] This function is defined as:

EXP(*NUMBER*)

Using the worksheet in Exhibit 7-14, we can add in cell C14: =B2*exp(B3*B4). Because we assumed a one-year period, the power to which e is raised is simply the interest rate. Add the label: Continuous in A14 and the worksheet is complete. Continuous compounding doesn't offer much of an increase over daily compounding. The advantage gets larger as the amount invested grows, but it would take huge sums to make a significant difference. Note that we can get a good approximation of continuous compounding by using the **EFFECT** function with a large number for *NPERY*. To see this, change the formula in C14 to: =B2*(1+EFFECT(B3,100000)) and notice that the answer is essentially the same.

We can also calculate the present value of a continuously compounded sum. All that needs to be done is to solve equation (7-16) for PV:[10]

$$\lim_{m \to \infty} PV = FV_N e^{-iN} \tag{7-17}$$

---

9. e is the base of the natural logarithm, so $\exp(\cdot)$ is the inverse of $\ln(\cdot)$. In other words, $\exp(\ln(x)) = x$.

10. Many students find that the continuous compounding equations are easier to recall if we change the notation slightly. Specifically, let P be the present value, F be the future value, r is the annual rate of interest, and T is the number of years (which can be fractional). With this notation, equation (7-16) becomes: $F = Pe^{rT}$, and equation (7-17) becomes: $P = Fe^{-rT}$. This is easier because the formulas can be pronounced. For example, equation (7-16) is pronounced "Pert."

Summary

In this chapter, we have discussed the concept of the time value of money. Present value represents the amount of money that needs to be invested today in order to purchase a future cash flow or stream of cash flows. Future value represents the amount of money that will be accumulated if we invest known cash flows at known interest rates. Further, we have discussed various types of cash flows. Annuities are equal cash flows, equally spaced through time. Graduated annuities are similar to normal annuities, but the cash flows grow by a certain amount each period. Uneven cash flows are those in which the periodic cash flows are not equal.

Before continuing with future chapters, you should be comfortable with these concepts. Practice by changing the worksheets presented in this chapter until you develop a sense for the type of results that you will obtain.

TABLE 7-1
FINANCIAL FUNCTIONS USED IN THIS CHAPTER

Purpose	Function	Page
Find the future value	FV(*RATE, NPER, PMT, PV, TYPE*)	197
Find the present value	PV(*RATE, NPER, PMT, FV, TYPE*)	199
Payment of an annuity	PMT(*RATE, NPER, PV, FV, TYPE*)	204
Number of periods	NPER(*RATE, PMT, PV, FV, TYPE*)	206
Natural logarithm	LN(*NUMBER*)	206
Yield of an annuity	RATE(*NPER, PMT, PV, FV, TYPE, GUESS*)	207
Present value of a graduated annuity	FAME_PVGA(*PMT, NPER, GROWTHRATE, DISCRATE, BEGEND*)	213
Future value of a graduated annuity	FAME_FVGA(*PMT, NPER, GROWTHRATE, DISCRATE, BEGEND*)	214
Present value of unequal cash flows	NPV(*RATE, VALUE1, VALUE2,…*)	215
Yield of uneven cash flows	IRR(*VALUES, GUESS*)	211
Effective Annual Rate	EFFECT(*NOMINAL_RATE, NPERY*)	221
Nominal Annual Rate	NOMINAL(*EFFECT_RATE, NPERY*)	221
Raise *e* to a power	EXP(*NUMBER*)	222

☑ Check Box when all highlighted notes are copied

READ 8/9/2016

Problems

1. Upon starting your new job after college, you've been confronted with selecting the investments for your 401(k) retirement plan. You have four choices for investing your money:

   - A money market fund that has historically returned about 1% per year.
   - A long-term bond fund that has earned an average annual return of 4.5%.
   - A conservative common-stock fund that has earned 6.5% per year.
   - An aggressive common-stock fund that has earned 11% per year.

   a. If you were to contribute $5,500 per year for the next 35 years, how much would you accumulate in each of the above funds?

   b. Now, change your worksheet so that it allows for less than annual investments (monthly, biweekly, etc.). Your total annual investment will remain unchanged, but it may be made in smaller, but more frequent, amounts.

   c. Set up a scenario analysis that shows your accumulated value in each fund if you were to invest quarterly, monthly, biweekly, and weekly. Create a scenario summary of your results.

   d. What relationship do you notice between the frequency of investment and the future value? Create a Column chart of the results that more clearly shows the outcome from more frequently investing.

2. Given the following set of cash flows:

Period	Cash Flow
1	$ 45,000
2	40,000
3	35,000
4	30,000
5	25,000

   a. If your required rate of return is 7% per year, what is the present value of the above cash flows? Future value?

b. Now, suppose that you are offered another investment that is identical, except that the cash flows are reversed (i.e., cash flow 1 is 25,000, cash flow 2 is 30,000, etc.). Is this worth more, or less, than the original investment? Why?

c. If you paid $130,000 for the original investment, what average annual rate of return would you earn? What return would you earn on the reversed cash flows?

d. Still assuming that your required return is 7%, would you be willing to purchase either of these investments? Explain why, or why not.

3. Your five-year-old daughter has just announced that she would like to attend college. The College Board has reported that the average cost of tuition, room, board, and other expenses at public four-year colleges is $18,391 in the 2013–2014 academic year.[11] The cost has risen 3.2% over the last year. You believe that you can earn a rate of 8% on investments to meet this goal.

a. If costs continue to rise at 3.2% per year, how much will it cost for the first year of tuition in 13 years?

b. Assuming that you plan to have enough money saved in 13 years to cover all four years of college costs, how much will you need to have accumulated by that time? Note that the tuition, room, and board is a graduated annuity growing 3.2% per year, and assume that you will pay all costs at the beginning of each year.

c. If you were to invest a lump sum today in hopes of covering your daughter's college costs, how much would you have to invest?

d. If you decided to invest annually instead, how much would you have to invest each year? What if you make investments monthly?

e. You just learned of a $10,000 inheritance and plan to invest it in your daughter's college fund. Given this new source of funds, how much will you now have to invest each year?

---

11. See http://trends.collegeboard.org/college_pricing/ for the full results.

4. You have decided to invest in a small commercial office building that has one tenant. The tenant has a lease that calls for annual rent payments of $20,000 per year for the next three years. However, after that lease expires you expect to be able to increase the rent by 5% per year for the next seven years. You plan to sell the building for $300,000 ten years from now.

   a. Create a table showing the projected cash flows for this investment assuming that the next lease payment will be made in one year.

   b. Assuming that you need to earn 11% per year on this investment, what is the maximum price that you would be willing to pay for the building today? Use the **NPV** function.

   c. Notice that the cash flow stream starts out as a three-year regular annuity, but it then changes into a seven-year graduated annuity plus a lump sum in year 10. Use the principal of value additivity to calculate the present value of the cash flows.

   d. Suppose that the current owner of the building is asking $200,000 for the building. If you paid this price, what annual rate of return would you earn? Should you buy the building at this price?

5. Congratulations! You have just won the State Lottery. The lottery prize was advertised as an annuitized $105 million paid out in 30 equal annual payments beginning immediately. The annual payment is determined by dividing the advertised prize by the number of payments. You now have up to 60 days to determine whether to take the cash prize or the annuity.

   a. If you were to choose the annuitized prize, how much would you receive each year?

   b. The cash prize is the present value of the annuity payments. If interest rates are 4.5%, how much will you receive if you choose the cash option?

   c. Now suppose that, as many lotteries do, the annuitized cash flows will grow by 3% per year to keep up with inflation, but they still add up to $105 million. In this case, the first payment will be $2,207,022.23 today. If you took the cash prize instead, how much would you receive (before taxes)?

CHAPTER 8   *Common Stock Valuation*

After studying this chapter, you should be able to:

1. *Differentiate among the definitions of "value," and explain the importance of intrinsic value in making financial decisions.*

2. *Explain how intrinsic value is calculated by considering the size, timing, and perceived riskiness of the cash flows.*

3. *Explain the concept of "required rate of return," and calculate this rate using the Capital Asset Pricing Model (CAPM).*

4. *Use several discounted cash flow (DCF) models to value a common stock.*

5. *Use relative valuation models, especially for stocks that do not meet the assumptions of DCF models.*

Determining the value of financial assets is important to both investors and corporate financial managers. The obvious reason is that nobody wants to pay more than an asset is worth, because such behavior would lead to lower returns. Less obvious, but equally important, is that we can draw some valuable conclusions from the observed prices of assets. We will examine one of these conclusions in detail in Chapter 10 when we use the market value of corporate securities to determine the required rate of return on investments.

In this chapter we will look at several models that can be used to determine the value of a share of common or preferred stock.

What Is Value?

The term "value" has many different meanings depending on the context in which it is used. For our purposes, there are four important types of value.

Most generally, value can be defined as the amount that a willing and able buyer agrees to pay for an asset to a willing and able seller. In order to establish the value of an asset, it is important that both the buyer and seller be willing and able. Otherwise, no legitimate transaction can take place, and value cannot be determined without a voluntary exchange. Notice that we did not say that the value of an asset is always the same as its price. Price and value are distinct, though related, concepts. The price of an asset can be greater than its value (in which case we say that the asset is overvalued), less than its value (undervalued), or equal to its value (fairly valued).

Book value is the price of an asset less its accumulated depreciation. Depreciation is a systematic method of accounting for the reduction in the value of an asset over its useful life. Because of the systematic nature of depreciation (i.e., it is determined in advance according to some well-defined formula), book value does not necessarily fairly represent the actual market value of the asset. Because of this and other distortions of value, so-called value investors exist. These investors seek out the stocks of companies that they believe to be undervalued, in hopes that the market will eventually recognize the true value of the company.

Intrinsic value is the value of an asset to a particular investor. Intrinsic value can be determined by calculating the present value of the expected future cash flows *at that investor's required rate of return*. Because we use the investor's required rate of return in the calculation, and because each investor has different preferences and perceptions, intrinsic value is unique to each individual. Without these differences in intrinsic values, markets would not function smoothly.

Market value is the price of an asset as determined in a competitive marketplace. The market price is the price that the marginal investor is willing to pay and will fluctuate (sometimes wildly) throughout the trading day. Investors will purchase assets with market values below their intrinsic values (undervalued assets) and sell assets with market values above their intrinsic values (overvalued assets). It is easy to determine the market value of securities traded in the public markets, but not so easy for many other types of assets. Houses, for example, are traded only rarely, so it is difficult to determine their true market value. In these cases, we must rely on estimates of market value made by experts (e.g., appraisers).

Unless otherwise modified, or obvious from the context, all references to the term "value" from this point forward will refer to the individual's intrinsic value.

Fundamentals of Valuation

As noted earlier, the intrinsic value of an asset is the present value of the expected future cash flows provided by the asset. Mathematically, intrinsic value is given by:

$$V = \sum_{t=1}^{N} \frac{Cf_t}{(1+i)^t} \tag{8-1}$$

where Cf_t is the expected cash flow in period t and i is the required rate of return for the investor performing the calculation.[1] If N is finite, then the last cash flow will include the expected selling price of the asset.

The most important components of value are likely to be the size and timing of the expected cash flows. The larger the expected cash flows and the more quickly they are to be received, the higher the value will be. In other words, there is a positive relationship between the size of the cash flows and value and a negative relationship between the time until the cash flows are received and value.

The other component of value is the investor's required rate of return. The required return is affected by the rates of return offered by competing investment vehicles and the riskiness of the investment. For example, if bonds are offering higher returns than stocks, we would expect that the prices of stocks would drop (and the prices of bonds would rise) as investors moved their money out of stocks and into bonds. This would occur because investors would recognize that bonds are less risky than stocks, and they would raise their required returns for stocks. Because an increase in the required return will decrease value, investors would sell stocks, thereby driving down the prices. This process would continue until the prices of stocks had fallen enough and bond prices risen enough, so that the expected returns reverted to the equilibrium relationship.

To determine the value of a security, then, we must first determine three things:

1. What are the expected future cash flows?
2. When will the cash flows occur?
3. What is the required rate of return for this particular stream of cash flows?

As we discuss the methods of valuing securities, keep these ideas in mind as they are the fundamentals of all security valuation.

---

1. At this point, we will assume that all future cash flows are known with certainty. In Chapter 12, we will examine what happens when future cash flows are uncertain.

Determining the Required Rate of Return

As mentioned earlier, one of the determinants of the required return for any stream of cash flows is the perceived riskiness of those cash flows. We will leave an in-depth discussion of risk for Chapter 12, but for now we will assume that the risk of a security is known.

In general, each investor can be classified by risk preference into one of three basic categories:

1. **Risk Averse**—The risk-averse investor prefers less risk for a given rate of return. The risk averter can be encouraged to accept nearly any level of risk, but only if the rate of return is expected to compensate him fairly. In other words, he must be paid in order to accept risk.

2. **Risk Neutral**—The risk-neutral investor is indifferent to the level of risk. His required rate of return will not change, regardless of the risk involved.

3. **Risk Lover**—The risk-loving investor will actually lower his required rate of return as the risk increases. In other words, he is willing to pay to take on extra risk.

Under ordinary circumstances, we assume that all investors are risk averse and must receive a higher rate of return in order to accept a higher risk. Realize, however, that even investors in the same category can have different risk preferences, so two risk-averse investors will likely have different required returns for the same asset.

FIGURE 8-1
THEORETICAL RISK-RETURN TRADE-OFF FOR TWO RISK-AVERSE INVESTORS

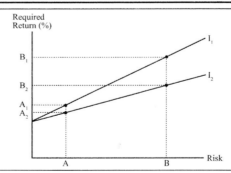

Figure 8-1 illustrates the ex-ante (expected) risk-return trade-off for two risk-averse investors. We know they are risk averse because the lines have a positive slope. In this case, security B is riskier than A and therefore has the higher expected return for both investors. Investor I_1 can be seen to be more risk averse than I_2 because the slope of the risk-return line is steeper. In other words, the risk premium grows at a faster rate for I_1 than it does for I_2.

A Simple Risk Premium Model

An easy method of determining the required rate of return for a security can be derived by assuming that the relationship pictured in Figure 8-1 is constant. If this is the case, then we can define the expected rate of return for an asset as a base rate (y-axis intercept) plus a premium that is based on the riskiness of the security. In equation form:

$$E(R_i) = \text{Base Rate} + \text{Risk Premium}$$

where $E(R_i)$ is the expected rate of return for security i, the base rate is the rate of return on some benchmark security, and the risk premium is subjectively determined (though it must be greater than zero).

The problem with this model is that it is entirely subjective. Both the security chosen to provide the base rate and the risk premium are defined by the individual using the model. For example, one individual might choose the rate of return on bonds issued by his company as the base rate, while another might choose the average rate paid on AAA-rated corporate bonds. Furthermore, because of individual differences in risk preferences, each individual is likely to assign a different value to the risk premium. Obviously, what is needed is a more objective approach that applies to the entire market instead of just to individual investors if we are to develop an explanation of security values.

CAPM: A More Scientific Model

The Capital Asset Pricing Model (CAPM) provides us with a more objective version of the simple risk premium model for determining expected returns. For our purposes, we can consider the CAPM to be a version of the simple risk premium model, with its inputs more rigorously defined. The CAPM is given by (we will see how to derive this equation in Chapter 13):

$$E(R_i) = R_f + \beta_i[E(R_m) - R_f] \tag{8-2}$$

where R_f is the risk-free rate of interest, β_i is a measure of the riskiness of security i relative to the riskiness of the market portfolio, and $E(R_m)$ is the expected rate of return on the market portfolio.

In the CAPM, R_f serves as the base rate of interest. It is defined as the rate of return on a security with zero risk. Sometimes R_f is referred to as the "pure time value of money," or, in other words, the rate of return earned for delaying consumption but not accepting any risk. Because it is risk-free, we know R_f with certainty in advance. Ordinarily, R_f is assumed to be the rate of return on a U.S. Treasury security with time to maturity equal to the expected holding period of the security in question. Treasury securities are chosen as a proxy for the theoretical risk-free rate because they are free of default risk and are therefore the closest of all securities to being truly risk-free.

The second term in the CAPM is the risk premium and is more complex. The market portfolio is a portfolio that contains all risky assets. Because no such portfolio exists, it is usually proxied by a stock index such as the S&P 500, which serves as a sort of benchmark against which other portfolios are measured. Subtracting the risk-free rate of return from the expected market return gives the expected market risk premium, which can be thought of as the risk premium of an average risk security. Beta (β) is an index of systematic risk.[2] It measures the risk of a particular security *relative* to the market portfolio. If a stock has a beta of 2, then we could say that the stock is twice as risky as the market portfolio. If it is twice as risky, then common sense (and the CAPM) tells us that the risk premium for this stock should be twice that of the market. Likewise, a stock with a beta of 0.5 should carry half of the risk premium of the market.

So the CAPM is no more than a sophisticated version of the simple risk premium model, which applies to all assets. With this in mind, we can redraw the risk-return trade-off graph (known as the security market line) in Figure 8-2.

FIGURE 8-2
THE SECURITY MARKET LINE

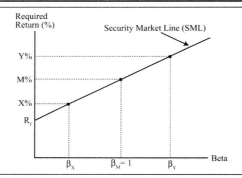

To see the CAPM in action, consider the following example:

> As a security analyst for Dewey, Cheatham, and Howe Securities you are preparing a report detailing your firm's expectations regarding two stocks for the year to come. Your report is to include the expected returns for these stocks and a graph illustrating the expected risk-return trade-off.

2. In the world of CAPM, there are two types of risk: systematic and unsystematic. Systematic risk is the market-related risk that affects all assets. An example would be unexpected changes in interest rates. Unsystematic risk is the company-specific risk such as the risk of a strike or of losing a major contract. As we will see in Chapter 13, through proper diversification, unsystematic risk can often be eliminated from a portfolio.

Other analysts at DCH have informed you that the firm expects the S&P 500 to earn a return of 11% in the year ahead, and that the risk-free rate is 5%. According to Morningstar, the betas for stocks X and Y are 0.5 and 1.5, respectively. What are the expected returns for X and Y?

To work this example, open a new workbook and enter the data so that it resembles the worksheet in Exhibit 8-1.

EXHIBIT 8-1
CALCULATING EXPECTED RETURNS WITH THE CAPM

	A	B	C	D	E
1		The Security Market Line			
2		Risk-free	X	Market	Y
3	Beta	0.00	0.50	1.00	1.50
4	Expected Return	5.00%		11.00%	

Before continuing, it is important to understand some of these inputs. The example problem did not mention the betas of the risk-free asset or of the market portfolio. How did we know that the beta of the risk-free asset is 0? Recall that beta measures the riskiness of the asset *relative to the market*. Because the risk-free asset has no risk, by definition, any measure of risk must be equal to zero. By definition, the market has a beta of 1.00 because the risk is measured relative to the market itself.

To complete this example, we need to enter the formula for the CAPM, equation (8-2), into C4 and E4. In C4 enter: =$B$4+C3*($D$4-$B$4) and then copy this cell to E4. You should see that security X has an expected return of 8% and Y has an expected return of 14%. Notice that the expected return of X is not one-half that of the market, nor is the expected return of Y 50% greater than that of the market. Instead, it is the risk premium of these securities that is one-half (for X) or one and one-half (for Y) the risk premium of the market. The portion of the expected return that comes from delaying consumption (the risk-free rate) is the same for both securities.

Finally, we can create a graph of the security market line (SML) with these data points. Select B3:E4 and then click the Insert Scatter (X,Y) button on the Insert tab. Choose a scatter chart with straight lines and markers. The betas in the first row will be placed on the x-axis automatically.

You can experiment with the SML by changing the expected return for the market or the risk-free rate. You will notice that the slope of the SML changes as you change the market risk premium. In other words, the slope changes as market participants become more, or less, risk averse. At this point, your worksheet should match the one in Exhibit 8-2.

EXHIBIT 8-2
EXPECTED RETURNS AND THE SECURITY MARKET LINE

	A	B	C	D	E
1		The Security Market Line			
2		Risk-free	X	Market	Y
3	Beta	0.00	0.50	1.00	1.50
4	Expected Return	5.00%	8.00%	11.00%	14.00%
5					
6		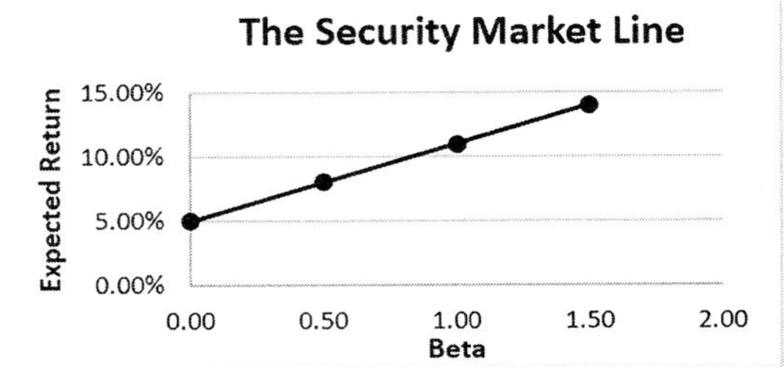 **The Security Market Line**			
7					
8					
9					
10					
11					
12					
13					
14					

Valuing Common Stocks

The first question to ask when attempting to value any security is, "What are the expected cash flows?" In the case of common stocks, there are two types of cash flows: dividends and the price received at the time of the sale. Consider the following problem:

Suppose that you are interested in purchasing shares of the common stock of the XYZ Corporation. XYZ recently paid a dividend of $2.40, and you expect that this dividend will continue to be paid into the foreseeable future. Furthermore, you believe (for reasons that will become clear) that you will be able to sell this stock in three years for $20 per share. If your required return is 12% per year, what is the maximum amount that you should be willing to pay for a share of XYZ common stock?

To clarify the problem, it helps to examine it in terms of a timeline as in Figure 8-3.

FIGURE 8-3
TIMELINE FOR XYZ COMMON STOCK

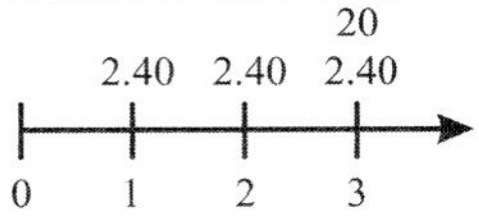

```
                        20
            2.40  2.40  2.40
        ├─────┼─────┼─────┼────────►
        0     1     2     3
```

Calculating the value of this stock is a simple matter of calculating the present value of its cash flows (equation (8-1)). Given that your required return is 12%, the intrinsic value must be:

$$V = \frac{2.40}{1.12} + \frac{2.40}{(1.12)^2} + \frac{2.40 + 20}{(1.12)^3} = 20$$

If the stock is currently selling for $24 (the market value), would you purchase any shares? Obviously not, because the market value exceeds your intrinsic value by $4. If you did purchase the shares, and your cash flow expectations were realized, your average annual rate of return would be less than your required return.

Of course, the XYZ example problem is somewhat contrived because there is no way to know, for sure, what the dividends and selling price are going to be in the future. With dividends this is not so much of a problem, because firms tend to have a somewhat stable dividend policy and are reluctant to cut dividends. The advanced knowledge of the selling price is a different matter. It is impossible to know exactly what the market price will be tomorrow and even more difficult to know the price three years hence.

The Constant-Growth Dividend Discount Model

To eliminate these problems, we can make a couple of assumptions. The first assumption is that dividends will grow at a constant rate.[3] With this assumption, knowing the most recent dividend (D_0) is equivalent to knowing all future dividends. Also assume that we have an infinite holding period. In other words, we will never sell the stock, so we don't have to worry about forecasting the selling price. While this second assumption may sound ludicrous, we will see that it is little more than a mathematical trick that allows us to develop a model.

These assumptions lead to a model for the valuation of common stock that is known as the constant-growth dividend discount model (DDM) or the *Gordon Growth Model*. Recall that we have defined the value of a common stock as the present value of future dividends plus the present value of the selling price. Because the stock will never be sold, due to the infinite holding period, the model becomes:

$$V_{CS} = \frac{D_1}{(1 + k_{CS})} + \frac{D_2}{(1 + k_{CS})^2} + \frac{D_3}{(1 + k_{CS})^3} + \cdots + \frac{D_\infty}{(1 + k_{CS})^\infty}$$

---

3. Note that this is not an assumption that the dividend stream will always get larger. The growth rate could be negative, in which case the dividends would be shrinking over time. Furthermore, the growth rate could be zero, which means that the dividends are constant.

where V_{CS} is the value of the common stock, the D's are the dividends in each period, and k_{CS} is the required return.[4] Because the dividends are growing at a constant rate, they can be expressed as a function of the most recently paid dividend (D_0):

$$V_{CS} = \frac{D_0(1+g)}{(1+k_{CS})} + \frac{D_0(1+g)^2}{(1+k_{CS})^2} + \frac{D_0(1+g)^3}{(1+k_{CS})^3} + \cdots + \frac{D_0(1+g)^\infty}{(1+k_{CS})^\infty}$$

This equation can be restated in closed form as:

$$V_{CS} = \frac{D_0(1+g)}{k_{CS}-g} = \frac{D_1}{k_{CS}-g} \tag{8-3}$$

Returning to the example, realize that XYZ's dividend growth rate is 0% (i.e., the dividend stream is not growing). Therefore, the value of a share is:

$$V_{CS} = \frac{2.40(1+0)}{0.12-0} = 20$$

which is exactly the same value as was found when assuming that you knew the value of the stock three years hence.

To see how you knew that the value of the stock would be $20 in three years, we can again use the time-shifting technique from Figure 7-3 (page 209). Let's look at another example.

> Suppose you are interested in purchasing a share of the common stock of the ABC Corporation. ABC has not recently paid any dividends, nor is it expected to for the next three years. However, ABC is expected to begin paying a dividend of $1.50 per share four years from now. In the future, that dividend is expected to grow at a rate of 7% per year. If your required return is 15% per year, what is the maximum amount that you should be willing to pay for a share of ABC common stock?

In order to determine the value of ABC common stock as of today (period 0), we must first find the value as of some future time period. The constant-growth DDM can be used at any time period and will always provide the value of the stock at the time period that is one period before the dividend which is used in the numerator:

$$V_N = \frac{D_{N+1}}{(k_{CS}-g)} \tag{8-4}$$

---

4. k_{CS} is the same as i, but is the more common notation for this model. This notation also helps to distinguish between the investor's required return for the different securities issued by the firm.

FIGURE 8-4
VALUING ABC COMMON STOCK WITH TIME-SHIFTING

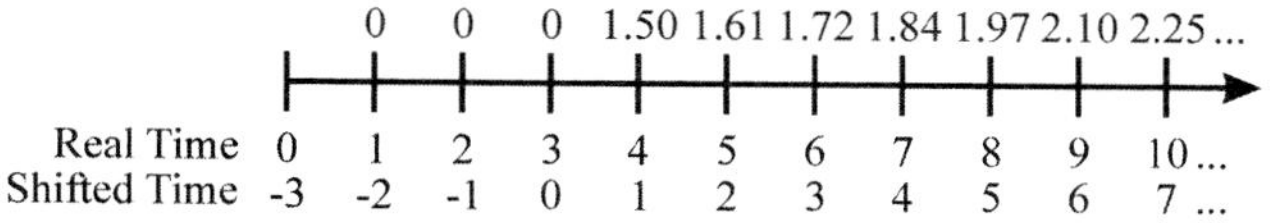

	0	0	0	1.50	1.61	1.72	1.84	1.97	2.10	2.25 ...

```
          ├──┼──┼──┼──┼──┼──┼──┼──┼──┼──►
Real Time   0   1   2   3   4   5   6   7   8   9  10...
Shifted Time -3  -2  -1   0   1   2   3   4   5   6   7 ...
```

For this particular problem, the future time period we choose is somewhat arbitrary as long as it is period 3 or later (but period 3 is the easiest). In this case, let's find the value as of period 3 (using the period 4 dividend):

$$V_3 = \frac{D_4}{k_{CS} - g} = \frac{1.50}{0.15 - 0.07} = 18.75$$

So we know that the stock will be worth $18.75 per share three years from today. Remembering that the value of a stock is the present value of its cash flows and that the only relevant cash flow in this case is the value at year 3 (which encapsulates the value of all future dividends), the value as of today must be:

$$V_0 = \frac{18.75}{1.15^3} = 12.33$$

We could also begin the valuation process at period 5 (or any other period). In this case, the value at period 5 (using the period 6 dividend) is:

$$V_5 = \frac{1.72}{0.15 - 0.07} = 21.50$$

Next, find the present value of all future cash flows (in this case: D_4, D_5, and V_5):

$$V_0 = \frac{1.50}{1.15^4} + \frac{1.61 + 21.50}{1.15^5} = 12.35$$

The $0.02 difference in values is due to rounding. Incidentally, note that had we only discounted back to period 3, the value at that time would have been $18.75.

Earlier we said that the assumption of an infinite holding period was not as ludicrous as it sounds. Let's examine this assumption in more detail. Open a new worksheet and enter the labels as shown so that it matches the fragment of a worksheet in Exhibit 8-3.

EXHIBIT 8-3
WORKSHEET TO TEST THE INFINITE HOLDING PERIOD ASSUMPTION

	A	B	C	D	E
1	Infinite Holding Period Assumption				
2	Period	Dividends	Present Value	Growth Rate	7%
3	1	0.00		Req. Return	15%
4	2	0.00			
5	3	0.00			
6	4	1.50			
7	5	1.61			
8	6	1.72			
9	7	1.84			
10	8	1.97			
11	9	2.10			
12	10	2.25			

Fill ▾   Note that the series of numbers representing the periods extends from 1 to 120 in cells A3:A122. To easily input these numbers, enter a 1 in A3 and then click the Fill button in the Editing group on the Home tab, and choose Series from the drop-down menu. In the Series dialog box, set the Step value to 1 and the Stop value to 120. Also be sure to set the series Type to Linear and Series in to Columns. The dialog box should look like Figure 8-5.

FIGURE 8-5
THE SERIES DIALOG BOX

In this worksheet, we want to calculate the value of the stock with various numbers of dividends included. From the example problem, we know that ABC will first pay a dividend of $1.50 in period 4 and that the dividend will grow at a 7% (cell E2) rate each year. Before continuing, enter the dividends into the worksheet as follows: First, enter a 0 for each of the first three dividends. For period 4, enter: 1.50 in B6. In B7, we want to calculate the period 5 dividend, so enter: =B6*(1+E$2). Now copy this formula to each cell in the range

B8:B122. To make sure that the copy was successful, note that the value in B122 should be 3,842.46 (the power of compounding!).

Now, in C3:C122, we want to find the cumulative present values of the dividends as we add more and more of them. We will use the **NPV** function to calculate the present values of the dividends. In C3 enter: =NPV(E$3,B$3:B3). The dollar sign will effectively freeze the first cell reference, so if we copy this formula down the range will expand. Copy the formula over the range C4:C122. Column C gives the value of the stock if we include only the dividends through the selected period. For example, the value in C20 ($8.15) is the value of the stock if we consider only the first 18 dividends. Similarly, the value in C50 ($11.85) is the value of the stock if we consider only the first 48 dividends.

Notice how the present value of the dividends converges to the value of the stock ($12.33) as we include more and more dividends in the calculation. It is not necessary to include more than about 120 dividends because the present value of all dividends beyond that point is effectively zero. This is easier to see if we create a graph of the values versus the number of dividends. Highlight the ranges A3:A122 and C3:C122. Now click the Insert tab and choose a scatter chart with straight lines and no markers.

EXHIBIT 8-4
THE INFINITE HOLDING PERIOD IS JUST FOR SIMPLICITY

	A	B	C	D	E	F	G	H	I
1	**Infinite Holding Period Assumption**								
2	Period	Dividends	Present Value	Growth Rate	7%				
3	1	0.00	$0.00	Req. Return	15%				
4	2	0.00	$0.00						
5	3	0.00	$0.00						
6	4	1.50	$0.86						
7	5	1.61	$1.66						
8	6	1.72	$2.40						
9	7	1.84	$3.09						
10	8	1.97	$3.73						
11	9	2.10	$4.33						
12	10	2.25	$4.89						
13	11	2.41	$5.40						
14	12	2.58	$5.89						
15	13	2.76	$6.33						

The Value of ABC Common Stock as More Dividends are Included

Your worksheet should now resemble the one in Exhibit 8-4, except that we have added a dotted line to represent the known value of the stock ($12.33). If you wish to add the same dotted straight line, remember that it only takes two points to define a line. So, choose an empty area of the worksheet, say D6:E7. In D6 enter 0, and in D7 enter 120. These cells represent the two x values for the line. In E6 calculate the value of the stock with the formula: =B6/(E3-E2)/(1+E3)^3. In E7 enter: =E6 because the y values for the line are the same (that's what makes it horizontal). Finally, right-click in the chart and choose Select Data. Click the Add button, and select D6:D7 for the x values and E6:E7 for the y values. Note that in Exhibit 8-4 we have moved the chart so that it hides the data for this line because it doesn't need to be visible.

The Two-Stage Growth Model

Assuming that the dividends will grow at a constant rate forever is convenient from a mathematical perspective, but it isn't very realistic. Other dividend-based valuation models have been developed, which are more true to life. For example, there is a two-stage growth model that allows for a period of supra-normal growth followed by constant growth forever.[5] In addition, there are several three-stage models which modify the two-stage model to allow for some pattern of decline into the constant-growth stage. All of these models are more complex than the constant-growth model, but keep in mind that they are still present value calculations. The only thing that has changed is the pattern of the future cash flows.

The two-stage valuation model allows for the dividend to grow at one rate for several periods and then to grow at a (usually, but not necessarily) slower rate from that point onward. This is a much more realistic model because a firm's dividends may be growing at a fast rate now, but that rate of growth is unlikely to be continued forever. All companies will eventually mature and find that their earnings growth slows so their dividend growth rate must slow as well. The two-stage model assumes that the change in the dividend growth rate will happen instantaneously at some point.

Let g_1 represent the dividend growth rate from period 1 to n, and g_2 be the dividend growth rate for the remainder of time. Assuming that $D_0 \neq 0$, $g_1 \neq k_{CS}$, and $g_2 < k_{CS}$, the model is:

$$V_{CS} = \frac{D_0(1 + g_1)}{k_{CS} - g_1}\left[1 - \left(\frac{1 + g_1}{1 + k_{CS}}\right)^n\right] + \frac{\dfrac{D_0(1 + g_1)^n(1 + g_2)}{k_{CS} - g_2}}{(1 + k_{CS})^n} \tag{8-5}$$

Note that the first term in equation (8-5) is simply the present value of the first n dividends growing at a rate of g_1 (a graduated annuity, see equation (7-10) on page 211). The second term is the present value of all the remaining dividends growing at a constant rate of g_2. This is exactly the same procedure we used earlier to value ABC's common stock, except that ABC not only had two growth rates (0% and 7%), but also was not originally paying a dividend.[6] Note that if $g_1 = g_2$ then equation (8-5) simplifies to equation (8-3).

---

5. Actually, the growth rate in the first phase can be less than the long-run constant rate.

6. Note that we cannot use equation (8-5) in that case because D_0 was equal to $0.00. Plugging in $0.00 for D_0 would give a value of $0.00 for the stock.

To demonstrate the use of this model, let's use an example.

> Oviedo Paper, Inc. is a major producer of paper products. Due to its immensely popular new stationery product, analysts expect that the firm's earnings and dividends will grow at a rate of 15% per year for the next five years. After that, analysts expect that the firm's growth rate will decline to its historical value of 8% per year as competitors launch similar products. If Oviedo Paper recently paid a dividend (D_0) of $0.35 and your required return is 12%, what is the value of the stock today?

To find the value, use equation (8-5):

$$V_{CS} = \frac{0.35(1.15)}{0.12 - 0.15}\left[1 - \left(\frac{1.15}{1.12}\right)^5\right] + \frac{\dfrac{0.35(1.15)^5(1.08)}{0.12 - 0.08}}{(1.12)^5} = 12.68$$

While quite long, we can use the formula: `=B2*(1+B3)/(B6-B3)*(1-((1+B3)/(1+B6))^B5)+((B2*(1+B3)^B5*(1+B4))/(B6-B4))/(1+B6)^B5` to verify that the value is $12.68 per share. We could also use the **Pv** function to value the dividends in the first growth phase (see page 211 for the technique), though it doesn't really simplify things in this case since we still have to value the constant-growth phase with a formula.

Because this equation is quite tedious, and Excel has no built-in function for this model, we have written a user-defined function to do the calculations. Make sure that you have the FameFncs.xlam add-in installed so that you have access to the function. Now, return to your original workbook and open a new worksheet. The user-defined function we will use is called **FAME_TwoStageValue** and is defined as:

FAME_TwoStageValue(*DIV1*, *ReqRate*, *GrowthRate1*, *GrowthRate2*, *G1Periods*)

where ***DIV1*** is the dividend to be paid at the end of period 1, ***ReqRate*** is the required return, ***GrowthRate1*** and ***GrowthRate2*** are the two growth rates, and ***G1Periods*** is the length of the first growth period.

Set up your new worksheet to look like the one in Exhibit 8-5. To get the value in B8, use the Insert Function dialog box. Choose the User Defined category, and then select **FAME_TwoStageValue** from the list. After entering the appropriate addresses, the formula in B8 should be: `=FAME_TwoStageValue(B2*(1+B3),B6,B3,B4,B5)`. Note that to get the dividend at period 1 (***DIV1***), we need to multiply the period 0 dividend by 1 + B3, which is the first growth rate. Your answer in B8 should confirm the calculations we made using equation (8-5).

As noted earlier, if both growth rates are the same (i.e., we have a single, constant-growth rate), then this model will give the same value as equation (8-3). Let's assume that the long-run growth rate is 8%. Change the value in B3 to 8%, and you will see that the constant-growth value of the stock is $9.45. Obviously, then, the higher initial growth rate in the early years adds a bit over $3 per share in value to the stock.

EXHIBIT 8-5
THE TWO-STAGE GROWTH MODEL

	A	B
1	**Oviedo Paper Valuation**	
2	Dividend 0	0.35
3	Growth Rate 1	15%
4	Growth Rate 2	8%
5	Period 1 Length	5
6	Required Return	12%
7		
8	Two-Stage Value of Stock	$ 12.68

Three-Stage Growth Models

There are any number of growth phases that could be assumed for a firm's dividends, but three is the typical limit used in practice. In this section, we will see three different three-stage models, each of which makes slightly different assumptions about how the growth rate changes. The three-stage growth models are very similar in concept to the two-stage model. The difference is that the two-stage model assumes that the change in the growth rate occurs instantaneously, whereas the three-stage models assume a more gradual decline in the growth rate over some period. This is a more realistic assumption. Figure 8-6 shows a comparison of the growth rate assumptions compared to the two-stage model.

FIGURE 8-6
MULTI-STAGE GROWTH MODELS

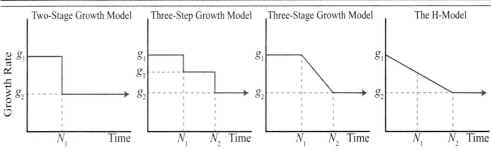

The Three-Step Model

The three-step model is very similar to the two-stage model, except that it has a transition phase with constant growth (generally between g_1 and g_2, but it could be any rate). Therefore, we have three steps: two graduated annuities followed by a constant-growth perpetuity, which is how we will value the stock. Assuming that $D_0 \neq 0$, $g_1 \neq k_{CS}$, $g_T \neq k_{CS}$, and $g_2 < k_{CS}$, the three-step model is given by:

$$
V_{CS} = \frac{D_0(1+g_1)}{k_{CS}-g_1}\left[1-\left(\frac{1+g_1}{1+k_{CS}}\right)^n\right] + \frac{D_0(1+g_1)^n(1+g_t)\left[1-\left(\frac{1+g_t}{1+k_{CS}}\right)^T\right]}{(k_{CS}-g_t)(1+k_{CS})^n}
$$

$$
+ \frac{D_0(1+g_1)^n(1+g_t)^T(1+g_2)}{(k_{CS}-g_2)(1+k_{CS})^{n+T}}
$$

(8-6)

where g_t is the growth rate during the transition step, T is the length of the transition step, and all other variables are as previously defined. While equation (8-6) looks intimidating, it is just the present value of this particular pattern of cash flows.

Again, because of the length of equation (8-6), we have written a user-defined function to perform the calculations:

FAME_THREESTEPVALUE(*DIV1*, *REQRATE*, *GROWTHRATE1*, *TRANSGROWTHRATE*, *GROWTHRATE2*, *G1PERIODS*, *TRANSPERIODS*)

where the arguments are the same as for **FAME_TWOSTAGEVALUE**, except for the inclusion of another growth rate (***TRANSGROWTHRATE*** is the growth rate during the transition phase).

Let's change our worksheet to assume that there will now be a three-year transition period with a growth rate of 10% per year. Modify your worksheet by inserting a row above row 4, and entering `Transition Growth Rate` in A4, and `10%` in B4. Insert another row above row 7 and enter `Transition Period Length` in A7, and `3` in B7. In A11, enter the label: `Three-Step Value of Stock`.

In B11 enter: `=FAME_ThreeStepValue(B2*(1+B3),B8,B3,B4,B5,B6,B7)`. You should find that the value of the stock using this model is $13.27 per share, which is about $0.59 higher than the two-stage model due to the higher average growth rate.

The Three-Stage Model

The three-stage model differs from the three-step model because it assumes that the growth rate declines linearly in each year of the transition period. So, instead of one rate in the transition phase, the growth rate is different in each year as can be seen in Figure 8-6.

The declining growth rate complicates the model because we have to calculate each dividend during the transition phase. The formula is:

$$V_{CS} = \frac{D_0(1+g_1)}{k_{CS}-g_1}\left[1 - \left(\frac{1+g_1}{1+k_{CS}}\right)^n\right] + \sum_{t=n+1}^{n+T} \frac{D_{t-1}(1+g_t)}{(1+k_{CS})^t} + \frac{D_{n+T}(1+g_2)}{(k_{CS}-g_2)(1+k_{CS})^{n+T}} \quad \text{(8-7)}$$

where all variables are as previously defined, and the transition phase goes from period $n+1$ to $n+T$. Note that T is the length of the transition phase. The growth rates in the transition are given by:

$$g_t = g_1 - (g_1 - g_2)\frac{(t-n)}{T}$$

Because of the changing growth rates during the transition, this model is very difficult to use in a spreadsheet without a user-defined function. Therefore, we have included one:

FAME_THREESTAGEVALUE(*DIV1*, *REQRATE*, *GROWTHRATE1*, *GROWTHRATE2*, *G1PERIODS*, *TRANSPERIODS*)

where all arguments are the same as in the **FAME_TWOSTAGEVALUE** function, except for *TRANSPERIODS*, which is the length of the transition phase.

Our spreadsheet already has all of the needed information, so we only need to add a label and the calculation. In A12 enter the label: `Three-Stage Value of Stock`, and in B12 enter: `=FAME_ThreeStageValue(B2*(1+B3),B8,B3,B5,B6,B7)`. You should find that the value using this model is $13.38, slightly higher than the result of the three-step model.

The H-Model

Because of the complexity of the three-stage model (as well as the three-step model), Fuller and Hsia developed the *H-Model* as an approximation.[7] This model assumes that the growth rate declines linearly from the first period to the beginning of the constant-growth phase. The "H" in the name refers to the "halfway" point between now and the constant-growth phase. Mathematically, the H-Model is given by:

$$V_{CS} = \frac{D_0}{k_{CS}-g_2}[(1+g_2) + (n+T/2)(g_1 - g_2)] \quad \text{(8-8)}$$

where H is often substituted for the $(n+T/2)$ term.

---

7. Russel J. Fuller and Chi-Cheng Hsia, "A Simplified Common Stock Valuation Model," *Financial Analysts Journal*, September–October 1984.

Note that equation (8-8) looks quite similar to the constant-growth equation (8-3). The difference is that rather than using a single growth rate, the term in brackets in the H Model represents a factor by which the constant-growth model must be multiplied to account for the higher initial growth rates.

It should be obvious that the average growth rate in the H-Model will be higher than the average growth rate in the two-stage model. For this reason, the H-Model will always give a somewhat higher valuation than the two-stage model. How much higher depends on the length of the transition period. It will tend to be near the values given by the three-step and three-stage models (sometimes higher, sometimes lower).

Let's return to our example using Oviedo Paper, Inc. Recall that the growth rate will transition from 15% to 8% over a three-year period. That makes the time in the first stage five years (n), and the transition phase (T) equals three. Using equation (8-8), we find that the value of the stock is:

$$V_{CS} = \frac{0.35}{0.12 - 0.08}[1.08 + (5 + 3/2)(0.15 - 0.08)] = 13.43$$

As with the other models, we have written a user-defined function to do the calculations for the H-Model. This function is defined as:

FAME_HModelValue(*DIV1*, *REQRATE*, *GROWTHRATE1*, *GROWTHRATE2*,
G1PERIODS,TRANSPERIODS)

All of the function's arguments are the same as before. Note that even though equation (8-8) uses D_0, we have set up the function to ask for D_1 for consistency with the other user-defined functions.

In A13 enter: H-Model Value of Stock. In B13, use the Insert Function dialog box to enter the function (note that you will have to scroll down in the dialog box to enter the last argument). It is: =FAME_HModelValue(B2*(1+B3),B9,B3,B5,B6,B8). As you can see in Exhibit 8-6, the three-year transition period adds $0.75 to the value of the stock as compared to the two-stage model.

Ultimately, it's important to remember that all of these common stock valuation models are nothing more than present value functions. Each uses a different assumption about the growth pattern of the dividends, but they are still present value calculations. When faced with a problem that doesn't fit the assumptions of any of these models, simply forecast the dividends in the future using whatever growth assumptions are appropriate. Then, calculate the present value of the future dividends using the **NPV** function. This is the method that was used to find the value of ABC common stock in the example problem on page 236.

EXHIBIT 8-6
MULTI-STAGE DIVIDEND GROWTH MODEL RESULTS

	A	B
1	**Oviedo Paper Valuation**	
2	Dividend 0	0.35
3	Growth Rate 1	15%
4	Transition Growth Rate	10%
5	Growth Rate 2	8%
6	Period 1 Length	5
7	Transition Period Length	3
8	Required Return	12%
9		
10	Two-Stage Value of Stock	$ 12.68
11	Three-Step Value of Stock	$ 13.27
12	Three-Stage Value of Stock	$ 13.38
13	H-Model Value of Stock	$ 13.43

Alternative Discounted Cash Flow Models

As noted previously, the value of a stock is given by the present value of its expected future cash flows—that is, the dividends that it will pay. However, we can restructure these models in a way that provides some additional insight into the valuation process. The two models presented in this section do just that.

The Earnings Model

Imagine a company that pays out 100% of its earnings as dividends. In this case, the dividend is equal to earnings per share (EPS), and the growth rate must be 0% because it is investing only enough (through the depreciation charge) to maintain the assets it currently owns. Using the constant-growth dividend discount model with $g = 0\%$, equation (8-3), the value of the common stock would be:

$$V_{CS} = \frac{EPS_1}{k}$$

This is the value of the stock if the firm doesn't reinvest and therefore doesn't grow. Most firms do reinvest at least some of their earnings, so the value of the stock must be equal to the value if it doesn't grow plus the present value of its future growth opportunities (*PVGO*):

$$V_{CS} = \frac{EPS_1}{k} + PVGO \tag{8-9}$$

The future earnings growth rate will be driven by the rate of return that is generated by the reinvested earnings (the ROE). If we let b = the retention ratio and r = the return on equity, then the growth rate (g) will be:[8]

$$g = br \tag{8-10}$$

Incidentally, recall the extended DuPont method of calculating the ROE from Chapter 4 on page 125. From this, we know that the growth rate depends on the operating profit margin, the interest rate on debt, the tax rate, the efficiency with which the firm uses its assets, and the amount of debt that it has in addition to its dividend payout ratio. Thus, the value of the stock always depends on how well-run the firm is.

The value of the stock will increase only if the firm's ROE (r) is greater than its required return (k). In other words, if the firm generates a positive net present value (NPV).[9] *PVGO* is equal to the present value of the future NPVs generated by the reinvested earnings (*RE*). If we assume that the NPV is a perpetuity and that it will grow at a constant rate of g, then:

$$PVGO = \sum_{t=1}^{\infty} \frac{NPV_t}{(1+k)^t} = \frac{NPV_1}{k-g} \tag{8-11}$$

The NPV in any given year is the present value of the earnings generated by the investment less the cost of the investment. Mathematically, the NPV is given by:

$$NPV_1 = \frac{RE_1 \times r}{k} - RE_1$$

By substituting this result into equation (8-11), it can be rewritten as:

$$PVGO = \frac{\dfrac{RE_1 \times r}{k} - RE_1}{k-g} = \frac{RE_1\left(\dfrac{r}{k} - 1\right)}{k-g} \tag{8-12}$$

Now substitute equation (8-12) into equation (8-9) and we have the earnings model:

$$V_{CS} = \frac{EPS_1}{k} + \frac{RE_1\left(\dfrac{r}{k} - 1\right)}{k-g} \tag{8-13}$$

This model is important because it directly links the company's ROE to the value of the stock. Specifically, note that the stock price can only rise if $r > k$. In fact, if $r < k$ (the

---

8. Note that if b = 0% (100% payout ratio), then g must also be 0%.

9. Net present value is discussed in detail in Chapter 11 beginning on page 345.

company earns less than its required return), then the value of the stock will fall. Let's look at an example:

> Analysts expect that Aurora Foods will earn $1.40 per share in the coming year and pay a dividend of $0.49 per share. Historically, the firm's ROE has been 15%, and its required return on investments is 12%. What is the value of the stock?

Note that RE_1 will be equal to $EPS_1 - D_1$, or $0.91 per share, and that the retention ratio is 65%. The growth rate is $0.65 \times 0.15 = 0.0975$. So, using equation (8-13), we see that the value of the stock is:

$$V_{CS} = \frac{1.40}{0.12} + \frac{0.91\left(\frac{0.15}{0.12} - 1\right)}{0.12 - 0.0975} = 11.67 + 10.11 = 21.78$$

We can create a worksheet that will make it easy to change the assumptions in the problem. Exhibit 8-7 shows the worksheet.

EXHIBIT 8-7
THE EARNINGS MODEL

	A	B
1	**Aurora Foods Valuation**	
2	Earnings per Share	1.40
3	Dividend	0.49
4	ROE	15.00%
5	Required Return	12.00%
6		
7	Retained Earnings	0.91
8	Retention Ratio	65.00%
9	Growth Rate	9.75%
10		
11	Value without Growth	$11.67
12	Value of Growth Opportunities	$10.11
13	Value of Stock	$21.78

The values given in the example are in B2:B5. In B7:B9 are the intermediate calculations that need to be done before using the model. Retained earnings is calculated in B7 with the formula: =B2-B3. The retention ratio, in B8, is found with: =1-B3/B2, and the growth rate is: =B4*B8.

We have chosen to separate the components of the value into cells B11:B12 to highlight them separately. In B11 add the formula: =B2/B5. The value of the growth opportunities is given in B12 by the formula: `=B7*(B4/B5-1)/(B5-B9)`. The total value of the stock is the sum of B11:B12. You should find that it is $21.78, exactly as we found earlier.

Using this worksheet, you can experiment with some of the assumptions. In particular, notice that if you change the ROE so that it is less than the required return then the value of the growth opportunities will be negative. For example, if you change the ROE to 10%, then the value of the growth opportunities is –$2.76 and reduces the total value of the stock to $8.91. This demonstrates that growth just for the sake of growth doesn't make economic sense; only profitable growth opportunities are worth pursuing.

Using Data Tables

Instead of randomly plugging numbers into the spreadsheet to understand how this model works, we can use an Excel feature known as a *data table*. Essentially, a data table tells Excel to plug various numbers into the model and recalculate the result. To see how this works, set up a data table to calculate the growth rate and stock value as the ROE changes.

In D2 enter the label: ROE, and then in D3:D8 enter a series of numbers from 10% to 20% in 2% increments. In E2:F2 we need formulas that Excel will use to calculate the results of changing the ROE. Because we already have our model set up, we can simply reference the growth rate and stock value. In E2 enter: `=B9` and in F2 enter: `=B13`. Apply a custom number format of just the name. Excel will plug the new ROEs into B4, and then record the values from B9 and B13 in the data table. This will not affect your original model at all.

To create the data table, select D2:F8 (the data table range) and then choose Data Table from the What-If Analysis button on the Data tab. Since our ROEs are in a column, we will enter B4 as the Column input cell. After clicking the OK button, you should see the data table populated with the results. Exhibit 8-8 shows the data table that was created.

EXHIBIT 8-8
A DATA TABLE SHOWING GROWTH RATE AND VALUE AS ROE CHANGES

	D	E	F
2	**ROE**	**Growth Rate**	**Value of Stock**
3	10%	6.50%	8.91
4	12%	7.80%	11.67
5	14%	9.10%	16.90
6	16%	10.40%	30.63
7	18%	11.70%	163.33
8	20%	13.00%	(49.00)

Note that the stock value rises as ROE increases, until the growth rate exceeds the required return. At that point, the model fails and says that the value is negative.

Before leaving the earnings model, note that it is mathematically equivalent to the constant-growth dividend discount model. In this case, the company will pay a dividend of $0.49 next year, and its growth rate is 9.75%. Therefore, the value of the stock must be $21.78:

$$V_{CS} = \frac{0.49}{(0.12 - 0.0975)} = 21.78$$

The Free Cash Flow Model

Free cash flow is defined as total operating cash flow after taxes less the reinvestment in operating assets that is required to maintain the firm's growth rate.[10] Recall from our discussion of economic profit in Chapter 4 (see page 134) that we defined net operating profit after tax (NOPAT) as:

$$\text{NOPAT} = \text{EBIT}(1 - \text{tax rate})$$

We can now define *after-tax operating cash flow* as:

$$\text{After-Tax Operating Cash Flow} = \text{NOPAT} + \text{Noncash Expenses}$$

Where "noncash expenses" are depreciation, amortization, and sometimes other noncash charges. Operating cash flow (after tax) is the cash flow available for the firm to reinvest in assets and/or pay out to investors (interest, principal, dividends, share repurchases). Therefore, operating cash flow belongs to both the creditors and the shareholders of the firm.

As was noted earlier, all firms must reinvest in the business to maintain a positive growth rate. To calculate the required investment in operating assets, we first forecast the level of operating assets for the next period (see Chapter 5) and then calculate the current level of those assets. The difference is the required investment:

$$\Delta \text{ Operating Assets} = \Delta \text{ NOWC} + \Delta \text{ Operating Fixed Assets}$$

where NOWC is net operating working capital (operating current assets less operating current liabilities). Note that we are referring to operating assets as defined on page 135. Therefore, we need to exclude any nonoperating assets and current liabilities (e.g., marketable securities and notes payable) from our calculations. We will account for these nonoperating items later.

---

10. Free cash flow is a non-GAAP financial metric, so definitions can vary. Some are very complex and some are quite simple. For example, Morningstar defines it as Cash Flows from Operations less in Capital Expenditures. Both numbers are available on the statement of cash flows.

If we subtract the required reinvestment in operating assets from the operating cash flow, then we have free cash flow (FCF):

$$\text{Free Cash Flow} = \text{Operating Cash Flow} - \Delta \text{ Operating Assets} \qquad \text{(8-14)}$$

This free cash flow belongs to all of the firm's capital providers. Therefore, the value of the firm's operating assets is the present value of the future free cash flows, discounted at the firm's WACC. However, we have omitted any nonoperating assets from our calculations, and these assets have value too. For this reason, we must add the value of these nonoperating assets to the present value of the FCF in order to arrive at the value of the entire firm:[11]

$$V_F = \sum_{t=1}^{\infty} \frac{FCF_t}{(1 + WACC)^t} + \text{Nonoperating Assets} \qquad \text{(8-15)}$$

where WACC is the firm's weighted average cost of capital. Now, if we assume (as we did for dividends in earlier models) that the FCF will grow at a constant rate (g) forever, then the value of the entire firm (V_F) is:

$$V_F = \frac{FCF_1}{(WACC - g)} + \text{Nonoperating Assets} \qquad \text{(8-16)}$$

Note that we can make other assumptions about the growth pattern of FCF. For example, we might forecast FCF for each year over the next five years and assume constant growth thereafter. In that case, we would use the general non-constant-growth model developed earlier. Or, we could assume that it will grow in two or three stages. In those cases, we could use the two-stage or one of the three-stage models to find the present value, instead of the single-stage constant-growth model, for the first term in equation (8-16).

Ultimately, we are trying to get to the per share value of the common stock. The value of the entire firm is also given by:

$$V_F = V_D + V_P + V_C \qquad \text{(8-17)}$$

where V_D is the market value of the debt, V_P is the value of the preferred equity, and V_C is the value of the common equity. Note that equation (8-17) is nothing more than a restatement of the familiar balance sheet equation:

$$\text{Total Assets} = \text{Total Liabilities} + \text{Total Equity}$$

except that equation (8-17) is stated in terms of current market values instead of book values.

---

11. Note that value of the nonoperating assets is the PV of their future cash flows. However, especially for short-term investments, the values on the balance sheet are very close to their market value.

If we substitute equation (8-16) into equation (8-17) and solve for V_C, then we have the free cash flow model:

$$V_C = \frac{FCF_1}{(WACC - g)} + \text{Nonoperating Assets} - V_D - V_P \qquad \textbf{(8-18)}$$

Equation (8-18) gives the total market value of the common equity. Typically, however, we want to know the per share value. For this reason, we would divide V_C by the number of common shares outstanding.

To make this clear, let's look at an example:

> Analysts project that Front Range Mountaineering Supplies will generate pre-tax operating profits (EBIT) of $160,000 in the coming year. The firm will have $40,000 in depreciation expense and a tax rate of 30%. Management has told analysts that it expects to make net new investments of $30,000 in operating assets over the next year. It has $25,000 in marketable securities on the books, and the market value of its debt is $450,000. The analysts believe that the WACC is 12% and that free cash flow can grow at about 7% per year. If the company has 350,000 common shares outstanding, what is the intrinsic value per share?

First, note that NOPAT is equal to:

$$\text{NOPAT} = 160,000(1 - 0.30) = 112,000$$

and by adding the depreciation expense we get the operating cash flow after tax:

$$\text{Operating Cash Flow} = 112,000 + 40,000 = 152,000$$

Now, free cash flow is equal to the operating cash flow less the change in total operating assets:

$$\text{Free Cash Flow} = 152,000 - 30,000 = 122,000$$

Using equation (8-18), the total market value of the firm's equity, after adding the marketable securities and subtracting the market value of the debt, is:

$$V_C = \frac{122,000}{0.12 - 0.07} + 25,000 - 450,000 = 2,015,000$$

Finally, to find the per share value of the stock we divide by the number of common shares outstanding:

$$V_C = \frac{2,015,000}{350,000} = 5.76$$

Exhibit 8-9 shows a worksheet for performing the valuation. The data in A3:B11 are taken directly from the example problem. Once the data and labels are entered, the formulas are quite simple. As we did earlier, the first step is to calculate NOPAT in B13 with the formula: =B3*(1-B5). Operating cash flow, in B14, is: =B13+B4 and free cash flow is: =B14-B6.

Again, the value of the entire firm, including debt, is the present value of the free cash flow plus the value of the nonoperating assets. We assume that free cash flow is growing at a constant rate forever, so the formula in B17 is: =B15/(B9-B10)+B7. To calculate the value of the firm's equity in B18, we subtract debt: =B17-B8. Finally, the per share value of the stock is determined by dividing the market value of the equity by the number of shares outstanding: =B18/B11. The result is $5.76 per share, exactly as we got from the formulas.

EXHIBIT 8-9
FREE CASH FLOW VALUATION MODEL

	A	B
1	**Front Range Mountaineering Supplies**	
2	**Free Cash Flow Valuation Model**	
3	EBIT	160,000
4	Depreciation	40,000
5	Tax Rate	30%
6	Change in Op Cap	30,000
7	Non-Operating Assets	25,000
8	Market Value of Debt	450,000
9	WACC	12%
10	Growth in FCF	7%
11	Shares Outstanding	350,000
12		
13	NOPAT	112,000
14	Operating Cash Flow	152,000
15	Free Cash Flow	122,000
16		
17	Value of Firm	2,465,000
18	Value of Equity	2,015,000
19	Per Share Value	5.76

We have assumed that the company is in a constant-growth phase, but this may not be correct for less mature companies. In that case, an analyst will typically create a model of the company over the next five years or so and then assume constant growth after that. In this case, the non-constant-growth model should be used. The procedure is similar to that shown in Figure 8-4, except that we substitute free cash flow estimates for the dividends and get the value of the entire firm instead of the value of the stock. At that point, proceed as we did earlier by adding the current value of nonoperating assets and subtracting the current value of the debt to get the market value of the equity.

Relative Value Models

The models presented earlier are generally known as DCF (discounted cash flow) models. Although these models are commonly used by analysts, they rely on forecasts of future cash flows that are often very uncertain. We can mitigate that problem somewhat by using scenario analysis, with several alternative growth rates giving a range of values. However, we can also use a different kind of model altogether: *relative value models*.

Relative value models provide a way to value a stock relative to other similar stocks using valuation ratios such as the Price to Earnings (P/E) ratio. These models have two major advantages: They are easy to use, and they can be used to value stocks for which the DCF models fail. For example, it is difficult to use the dividend discount models for stocks that don't currently pay a dividend and may not for the foreseeable future. However, as long as the company has positive earnings, you can use the P/E model. If the company is losing money, then you can (with great care) use the Price to Sales (P/S) or Price to Book Value (P/B) models instead.

The P/E ratio is defined as the current stock price divided by the expected earnings per share over the next year:

$$\text{Price to Earnings} = \frac{\text{Price per Share}}{\text{Earnings per Share}} \tag{8-19}$$

The essential idea is that the P/E ratio tells us how much investors are willing to pay for each dollar of expected earnings. Therefore, all we need is an estimate of earnings and a "justified" P/E ratio. For two identical companies, the P/E ratio should be the same. No two companies are ever identical, but if they are similar (in the same industry and share other characteristics), then their P/E ratios should be in the same general area. The justified P/E ratio is often calculated by averaging the P/E ratios of comparable firms. To value a stock using this model, we merely multiply the expected earnings by the justified P/E ratio:

$$V = EPS_1 \times PE \tag{8-20}$$

Any differences in P/E ratios should be explained by differences in perceived risk or growth rates. If we substitute equation (8-3) into the numerator of equation (8-19), then we can see how the growth rate and required return (which is influenced by risk from a number of sources) affect the P/E ratio:

$$\text{P/E} = \frac{D_1/(k_{CS}-g)}{EPS_1} \tag{8-21}$$

Note that a higher required return, as would be used for a riskier firm, will lead to a lower P/E ratio. Also, a company with a higher growth rate should have a higher P/E ratio. Now we can determine if a stock is undervalued or overvalued by comparing its P/E ratio to the average of its peers. If it has a higher than average P/E that doesn't seem to be justified by lower risk or higher growth, then the stock is overvalued relative to its peers. We can also compare the current P/E to the historical average for the firm to determine if it undervalued or overvalued compared to the past.

Now suppose that the company doesn't have any earnings. A negative P/E ratio is meaningless, so we can't use that model. However, we can use the P/S ratio or the P/B ratios instead. In addition to the above ratios, several others can be used. For example, the Enterprise Value to EBIT (or EBITDA) ratio is commonly used by analysts, particularly to compute the takeover value of a company. *Enterprise value* is defined as the market value of the firm's equity (stock price times shares outstanding) plus the market value of debt less the amount of cash and equivalents on the balance sheet.

The relative value models are very commonly used by analysts these days, but they are not without their drawbacks. One of the problems is that there is no way to know what absolute value of a P/E ratio is appropriate. Instead, the models are relative. Therefore, if you are comparing one company to several other overvalued stocks, you will come up with a value that is too high. Another problem is that no two companies are the same, and it can be difficult to figure out whether valuation differences are due to expectations about risk, growth rates, or both. Finally, the relationship that should exist between earnings growth, risk, and P/E ratio is not clear and may change over time. Still, used with caution, relative value models can be used to validate the results of a DCF analysis.

Preferred Stock Valuation

Preferred stock is a kind of hybrid security. It represents an ownership claim on the assets of the firm, like common stock, but holders of preferred stock do not benefit from increases in the firm's earnings and they generally cannot vote in corporate elections, like bonds. Further, like a bond, preferred stock generally pays a fixed dividend payment each period. Also, like a common stock, there is no predefined maturity date, so the life of a share of preferred stock is effectively infinite.

With the complex nature of preferred stock, it is natural to assume that it must be difficult to value. As we will see, preferred stock valuation is actually quite easy. To see how we can derive the valuation formula for preferred stock, consider the following example:

> The XYZ Corporation has issued preferred stock that pays a 10% annual dividend on its $50 par value. If your required return for investments of this type is 12%, what is the maximum amount that you should be willing to pay for a share of XYZ preferred?

As usual, the first step in valuing preferred stock is to determine the cash flows. In the case of XYZ preferred, we have an infinite stream of dividends that are 10% of the par value. That is, we have a perpetual annuity, or perpetuity, of $5 per year. Figure 8-7 illustrates the expected cash flows for XYZ preferred stock.

FIGURE 8-7
TIMELINE FOR XYZ PREFERRED STOCK

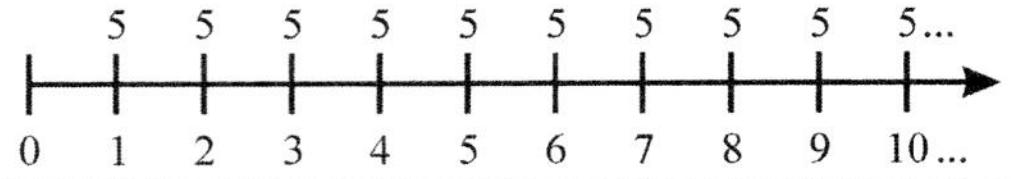

One way that we can arrive at a valuation formula for preferred stock is to realize that the cash flows resemble those of common stock. Preferred stock pays a dividend and never matures, just like common stock. The only difference, as far as the cash flows are concerned, is that the dividend never changes. In other words, the growth rate is zero. Therefore, we can say that the value of preferred stock is:

$$V_P = \frac{D_0(1+g)}{k_P - g}$$

But because the growth rate is 0, we can simplify this to:

$$V_P = \frac{D}{k_P} \qquad \text{(8-22)}$$

Notice that the subscript has been dropped on the dividend because all dividends are equal.

As an alternative, we can value the preferred stock as an annuity with an infinite life using equation (7-5). In this case, we have:

$$V_P = D\left[\frac{1 - \dfrac{1}{(1 + k_P)^\infty}}{k_P}\right] = D\left[\frac{1 - \dfrac{1}{\infty}}{k_P}\right]$$

But any number divided by infinity is effectively equal to 0, so this equation reduces to:[12]

$$V_P = \frac{D}{k_P}$$

which is exactly the same as equation (8-22).

---

12. Actually, we can't divide by infinity. Instead, we should take the limit as N approaches infinity.

So, for valuation purposes, regardless of whether we treat preferred stock like common stock or perpetuity, we arrive at exactly the same valuation formula. To find the value of a share of preferred stock, we simply need to divide its dividend payment by our required rate of return. Therefore, the value of XYZ's preferred stock must be:

$$V_P = \frac{5}{0.12} = 41.66$$

You can prove this by recreating Exhibit 8-4 (page 239), with all of the dividends set to 5.

Summary

The valuation process is important to both financial managers and investors. As we will see in future chapters, understanding the valuation process is crucial to making sound financial decisions.

In this chapter, we found that the value of a security depends on several factors:

- The size of the expected future cash flows
- The timing of the expected cash flows
- The perceived riskiness of the expected cash flows

Once the cash flows and required rate of return have been determined, we can value the security by finding the present value of its future cash flows. The dividend discount models differ only in the expected pattern of dividend growth. They all reduce to the present value of future cash flows to the stockholders.

We also derived the earnings model, which is important because it shows that the firm must make productive investments (ROE > k) in order to increase the stock price. The free cash flow model shows that the value of the entire firm is the present value of the expected future operating cash flows less expected investments.

Finally, we examined relative value models. These models do not rely (at least directly) on the present value of future cash flows. Instead, they attempt to value a stock much like houses are valued: by looking at "comparables" and then assuming that the valuation should be similar, though some adjustments can be made.

☑ Check Box after copying highlighted Notes

TABLE 8-1
SELECTED FORMULAS USED IN THIS CHAPTER

Valuation	Formula	Page
Constant-growth common stock	$V_{CS} = \dfrac{D_0(1+g)}{k_{CS}-g} = \dfrac{D_1}{k_{CS}-g}$	236
Two-stage growth common stock	$V_{CS} = \dfrac{D_0(1+g_1)}{k_{CS}-g_1}\left[1-\left(\dfrac{1+g_1}{1+k_{CS}}\right)^n\right] + \dfrac{\dfrac{D_0(1+g_1)^n(1+g_2)}{k_{CS}-g_2}}{(1+k_{CS})^n}$	240
H-Model common stock	$V_{CS} = \dfrac{D_0}{k_{CS}-g_2}[(1+g_2)+(n+T/2)(g_1-g_2)]$	244
Earnings Model	$V = \dfrac{EPS_1}{k} + \dfrac{RE_1\left(\dfrac{r}{k}-1\right)}{k-g}$	247
Free Cash Flow Model	$V_C = \dfrac{FCF_1}{(WACC-g)} + \text{Nonoperating Assets} - V_D - V_P$	252
Preferred stock	$V_P = \dfrac{D}{k_P}$	256

TABLE 8-2
FUNCTIONS INTRODUCED IN THIS CHAPTER

Purpose	Function	Page
Two-stage model	FAME_TwoStageValue(*DIV1*, *REQRATE*, *GROWTHRATE1*, *GROWTHRATE2*, *G1PERIODS*)	241
Three-step model	FAME_THREESTEPVALUE(*DIV1*, *REQRATE*, *GROWTHRATE1*, *TRANSGROWTHRATE*, *GROWTHRATE2*, *G1PERIODS*, *TRANSPERIODS*)	243
Three-stage model	FAME_ThreeStageValue(*DIV1*, *REQRATE*, *GROWTHRATE1*, *GROWTHRATE2*, *G1PERIODS*, *TRANSPERIODS*)	245
H-Model	FAME_HModelValue(*DIV1*, *REQRATE*, *GROWTHRATE1*, *GROWTHRATE2*, *G1PERIODS*, *TRANSPERIODS*)	245

Problems

1. Bob's Rawhide Company has a dividend payout ratio of 30%. Next year it will earn $2.50 per share and have a return on equity of 15%. The shareholders' required return is 12%.

   a. Calculate the company's growth rate of EPS.

   b. Using the earnings model, what is the value of the stock?

   c. Construct a data table that shows how the growth rate and value of the stock will change if the ROE ranges between 10% and 20%, in 1% increments. Now, using that data, create a scatter chart to show the relationship between the value of the stock and the ROE. Is the relationship linear? At what point does the model break down?

   d. Using the constant-growth dividend discount model, what is the value of the stock?

2. As an analyst at Churnem & Burnem Securities, you are responsible for making recommendations to your firm's clients regarding common stocks. After gathering data on Denver Semiconductors, you have found that its dividend has been growing at a rate of 5% per year to the current (D_0) $0.60 per share. The stock is now selling for $20 per share, and you believe that an appropriate rate of return for this stock is 9% per year.

   a. If you expect that the dividend will grow at a 5% rate into the foreseeable future, what is the highest price at which you would recommend purchasing this stock to your clients?

   b. Suppose now that you believe that the company's new product line will cause much higher growth in the near future. Your new estimate is for a three-year period of 15% annual growth to be followed by a return to the historical 5% growth rate. Under these new assumptions, what is the value using the two-stage dividend growth model?

   c. You now realize that it is likely that the growth will transition from 15% down to 5% gradually, rather than instantaneously. If you believe that the transition will take five years, what is the value of the stock? Use the three-stage and H-Model valuation methods.

   d. For each of the answers from above, create an **IF** statement that shows whether the stock is undervalued, overvalued, or fairly valued.

e. Create a data table showing the stock value using the two-stage, three-stage, and H-Model for long-run growth rates between 0% and 10% in 1% increments. Use an XY Scatter chart to visualize the results.

3. The Miracle Clean Company has some new products that it expects to lead to high growth in the near future. It has given analysts the following forecasts for the next three years:

	2015	2016	2017
Depreciation	20,250	28,350	36,450
EBIT	168,750	195,750	222,750
Investment in Operating Assets	47,000	34,000	15,000

The firm's debt has a current market value of $600,000 and it has $50,000 in marketable securities. There are 100,000 common shares outstanding. The expected tax rate is 35%, and the WACC is estimated to be 12%.

a. Calculate the free cash flow for each of the next three years.

b. After 2017 free cash flow growth is expected to slow to 8% per year permanently. What is the value of the stock today?

c. Without the new products, free cash flow in 2015 would be $63,000 and it would grow at 8% per year forever. What is the value of the stock if the new products aren't introduced?

Internet Exercise

1. Using the Yahoo! Finance Web site (http://finance.yahoo.com) get the current price and five-year dividend history for Intel. To gather this data, enter the ticker symbol (INTC) in the search box at the top of the page, and select Intel Corporation from the list. Record the current price from this page. Now, at the left side of the quote page, click on the Historical Prices link. To get a table of previous dividends, select Dividends Only at the top of the table, set the Start Date to five years before today's date, and click the Get Prices button. Click the Download to Spreadsheet link at the bottom of the table to download a file with this data. You may have the choice of either saving the file or opening it directly in Excel. It is easier to let it open in Excel. Otherwise, save the .csv (comma separated variables) file, and then open it with Excel. It shouldn't need any further processing other than some formatting. You now have the dividends in a worksheet.

   a. Because INTC pays dividends quarterly, for each quarter calculate the percentage change in the dividends. Now, calculate the compound quarterly growth rate of the dividends using the **GEOMEAN** function.

   b. Now, annualize the quarterly dividend growth rate.

   c. Calculate the intrinsic value of the stock using a 14% required rate of return and the calculated annual growth rate. Use the sum of the most recent four dividends as D_0.

   d. Now assume that INTC's dividend growth rate will remain the same for the next five years, and then fall to 75% of its current rate. What is the value of the stock using the two-stage dividend discount model?

   e. If the dividend growth rate begins declining immediately from the current level to its long-term rate over 20 years (15-year transition plus the initial 5 years), what is the value of the stock according to the H-Model? What is the value using the three-stage model? Use the same assumptions as in part d.

   f. How does the calculated intrinsic value compare to the actual market price of the stock for each of the models used? Use an **IF** statement to display whether the stock is undervalued, overvalued, or fairly valued. Would you buy the stock at its current price?

CHAPTER 9 — *Bond Valuation*

After studying this chapter, you should be able to:

1. *Calculate the value of a bond using formulas and built-in functions.*
2. *Describe the factors that determine the price of a bond.*
3. *Calculate the various bond return measures in Excel.*
4. *Create a U.S. Treasury yield curve using live data from the Internet.*
5. *Understand and demonstrate Malkiel's five bond pricing theorems.*
6. *Calculate duration and convexity, and use them to make investment decisions.*

Fixed-income securities have long been an important source of capital for governments and corporations, and a relatively secure investment for both individual and institutional investors (pension funds, mutual funds, and insurance companies, to name a few). Bonds are secure for investors because they are contractual obligations of the issuer. In the case of corporate bonds, they are much safer than common stock of the same firm because in the event of liquidation the bondholders will be paid before the shareholders.

Bonds are the focus of this chapter, but you should understand that much of the material in this chapter applies to any kind of cash flow. For example, we can calculate the duration of a mortgage, common stock, and so on.

Bond Valuation

A bond is an interest-bearing security that obligates the issuer to pay the bondholder periodic interest payments and to repay the principal at maturity. Discounted securities are typically short-term debt obligations that do not pay interest.[1] Instead, they are sold for less than face value and redeemed for the full face value at maturity. Bonds and discounted securities are valued in the same manner as most other securities. That is, the value of a bond is the present value of its future cash flows.

For a bond the cash flows consist of periodic (usually semiannual) interest payments and the return of the principal at maturity. The cash flow at maturity will therefore consist of both the last interest payment and the principal repayment. Often, but not always, the principal (usually called the *face value*) of the bond is $1,000. For a four-year semiannual payment bond the timeline is shown in Figure 9-1.

FIGURE 9-1
TIMELINE FOR A FOUR-YEAR BOND WITH SEMIANNUAL INTEREST PAYMENTS

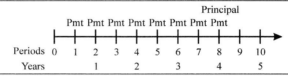

As Figure 9-1 makes clear, a bond consists of two types of cash flows: an annuity (the interest payments) and a lump sum (the principal). Recalling the principle of value additivity from Chapter 7, we know that this stream of cash flows can be valued by adding the present values of its components. For a bond, the value (V_B) is given by:

$$V_B = Pmt\left[\frac{1 - \dfrac{1}{(1 + k_B)^N}}{k_B}\right] + \frac{FV}{(1 + k_B)^N} \tag{9-1}$$

where *Pmt* is the periodic interest payment, k_B is the periodic required rate of return for the bond, N is the number of periods, and FV is the face value. The first term in equation (9-1) is the present value of the stream of interest payments, and the second is the present value of the principal. A word of warning is in order: This formula is valid only on an interest payment date. We will soon discuss the adjustments necessary to fix this problem.

---

1. There are many types of discounted securities such as Treasury bills, commercial paper, certificates of deposit, and banker's acceptances. The term to maturity is typically less than one year.

Consider an example problem:

> Nanoterials, Inc. has issued bonds with 20 years to maturity, an 8% coupon rate, and $1,000 face value. If your required rate of return is 9% and the bonds pay interest semiannually, what is the value of these bonds?

Before solving this problem, some definitions are required. Historically, bonds were printed on ornately decorated paper with small detachable coupons around the edges. These coupons were to be presented to the issuer in order to collect the periodic interest payments. Because of this practice, the interest payment has come to be known as the *coupon payment*, and the rate of interest that the issuer has promised to pay is referred to as the *coupon rate*. The annual interest payment is determined by multiplying the *face value* (principal) by the coupon rate. For bonds that pay interest more frequently than annually, the annual interest payment is divided by the number of payments per year. Most often, interest is paid twice per year, so the annual interest payment must be divided by two.

For the Nanoterials bonds, the annual interest payment is $80 (= $0.08 \times 1,000$), but the semiannual payment is $40 (= $80 \div 2$). Furthermore, because the interest is paid twice per year, we must also adjust the required return and number of periods to a semiannual basis. The required return is 9% per year, which is 4.5% (= $0.09 \div 2$) per six-month period. Because there are 20 years to maturity, there are 40 (= 20×2) six-month periods to maturity. Therefore, the value of the bonds is:

$$V_B = 40 \left[\frac{1 - \dfrac{1}{1.045^{40}}}{0.045} \right] + \frac{1,000}{1.045^{40}} = 907.99$$

As you have probably guessed, we can use Excel's **Pv** function to find the value of this bond. Recall that this function allows for both annuity payments and a future value. Now, set up the worksheet shown in Exhibit 9-1.

EXHIBIT 9-1
BOND VALUATION USING THE PV FUNCTION

	A	B
1	**Bond Valuation**	
2	Time to Maturity (Years)	20
3	Coupon Rate	8.00%
4	Required Return	9.00%
5	Frequency	2
6	Face Value	$ 1,000

Notice that we have added the payment frequency in row 5. This will allow us to change the bond to annual, quarterly, or monthly payments, if necessary. To complete the worksheet, enter `Value` into A8, and then in B8 add the formula: `=PV(B4/B5,B2*B5,-B3*B6/B5,-B6)`. Take note of the fact that we have made adjustments for the semiannual nature of the payments. Specifically, the required return and payment amount have been divided by the frequency, and the time to maturity was multiplied by the frequency. Also, the payment amount and the face value were made negative so that the resulting bond value will be a positive number. As expected, the result is a value of $907.99.

Valuing Bonds Between Coupon Dates

As noted earlier, equation (9-1) works only on coupon payment dates (it is correct twice a year!). The cause of the problem is *accrued interest*. Specifically, interest does not compound between coupon dates. Instead, interest accrues equally on each day. For example, three months into a coupon period, the Nanoterials bond will have accrued (i.e., earned but not yet paid) interest equal to one-half of the full-period interest, or $20.

Before continuing, let's calculate the value of the bond at the end of period 1. Realize that after one period has elapsed, the bond will now have 39 periods remaining to maturity. The bond will be worth:

$$V_B = 40\left[\frac{1 - \dfrac{1}{1.045^{39}}}{0.045}\right] + \frac{1,000}{1.045^{39}} = 908.85$$

The price has increased by $0.86 (about 0.095%), but your required return is 4.5% per period. Where is the rest of your return? You have also earned $40 in interest, so your total income is $40.86, or 4.5% (= 40 869/07.99). Equation (9-1) assumes that the bond is being valued instantaneously after the interest payment is made. So, the total value of your investment, including interest earned, at the end of period 1 is $948.85. Note that we can also arrive at this price by using the future value formula:

$$907.99(1.045)^1 = 948.85$$

This provides the necessary clue to valuing bonds between coupon dates: If we value the bond as of the *previous coupon date* and then move it forward by the amount of time elapsed, we will find the total value of the bond. This is known as the invoice price (or *dirty price*) of the bond. It is the amount that you would actually pay, including the accrued interest, to the previous owner of the bond. However, bond dealers quote prices without the accrued interest (the *clean*, or quoted, price). If we subtract the accrued interest from the invoice price ($948.85), we get the quoted price ($908.85) at the end of period 1.

So, what is the value of the Nanoterials bond if two months (1/3 of a period) have elapsed since the last coupon was paid? The invoice price ($V_{B,Invoice}$) would be:

$$V_{B,Invoice} = \left(40 \left[\frac{1 - \dfrac{1}{1.045^{40}}}{0.045} \right] + \frac{1,000}{1.045^{40}} \right) (1.045)^{1/3} = 921.41$$

and, to get the quoted price ($V_{B,Quoted}$), we subtract the accrued interest:

$$V_{B,Quoted} = 921.41 - \frac{1}{3}(40) = 908.08$$

Note that if you change your worksheet to reflect the fact that there are 39 2/3 periods (19.83333 years) remaining, you will get the wrong answer ($908.27, off by about $0.19). We can fix this by modifying our worksheet. Make a copy of your bond valuation worksheet and change the label in A2 to Time to Maturity (Periods). In B2, enter 39 2/3 (Excel will interpret this as 39.666…). Switching to periods, rather than years, will make things a bit easier.

Before entering the formulas, we need to discuss the **ROUNDUP** function. This function rounds a number upward and is defined as:

ROUNDUP(*NUMBER, NUM_DIGITS*)

where ***NUMBER*** is the number to be rounded and ***NUM_DIGITS*** is the number of digits to round to. If ***NUM_DIGITS*** is negative, the ***NUMBER*** will be rounded to that power of 10. For example, $10^0 = 1$, so if ***NUM_DIGITS*** is 0 the number will be rounded to the next highest integer. If ***NUM_DIGITS*** is -1, the number will be rounded to the next highest 10, and so on. You are encouraged to experiment with this function until you understand how it works.

Now, change the label in A8 to Invoice Price. The formula, in B8, will be: =PV(B4/B5,ROUNDUP(B2,0),-B3*B6/B5,-B6)*(1+B4/B5)^(ROUNDUP(B2,0)-B2). This looks complicated, but the **ROUNDUP** function is being used to adjust the number of periods so that it is equal to the remaining number of periods as of the last coupon date. In this case, 39 2/3 gets rounded up to 40. The resulting invoice price is $921.41.

In A9 enter the label Accrued Interest, and then in B9 enter the formula: =(ROUNDUP(B2,0)-B2)*B3*B6/B5. Here, the first part of the formula calculates the fractional portion of the period that has elapsed and then multiplies that by the periodic coupon payment. Finally, to get the quoted price in B10, enter the formula: =B8-B9. The final answer is $908.08, exactly as we found earlier. Your new worksheet should look like the one in Exhibit 9-2.

EXHIBIT 9-2
VALUING A BOND BETWEEN COUPON DATES

	A	B
1	**Bond Valuation**	
2	Time to Maturity (Periods)	39 2/3
3	Coupon Rate	8.00%
4	Required Return	9.00%
5	Frequency	2
6	Face Value	$ 1,000
7		
8	Invoice Price	$921.41
9	Accrued Interest	13.33
10	Quoted Price	908.08

The worksheet that we have just created is complex, but it is actually too simple. In the real world, we need to worry about exact dates, not abstract periods. This leads to a couple of additional headaches that our worksheet can't handle. Fortunately, Excel has functions that can handle these situations without the need for complicated formulas.

Using Excel's Advanced Bond Functions

To find the value of a coupon-bearing bond, Excel provides the **PRICE** function. Note that, unlike the **PV** function or equation (9-1), the **PRICE** function works even on nonpayment dates and returns the quoted price of the bond. The **PRICE** function is defined as:

PRICE(*SETTLEMENT, MATURITY, RATE, YLD, REDEMPTION, FREQUENCY, BASIS*)

SETTLEMENT is the date on which money and securities actually change hands,[2] and *MATURITY* is the date on which the last coupon payment is made and the principal is returned. Excel uses the system date format to determine if what you have entered is a date. The Windows date format can be changed in the Control Panel if necessary, but most users will accept the default for their country. In the United States, the default is the Month/Day/Year format, so Excel will recognize, say, 2/4/2015 as February 4, 2015, and treat it as a date. You could also enter this date as Feb 4, 2015, and Excel will convert it to a date. Unrecognized date formats are treated as text strings. Dates are converted to a number that represents the number of days since January 1, 1900 (or January 1, 1904, on the Macintosh). In the 1900 date system the serial number 1 corresponds to January 1, 1900. In the 1904 date system the

---

2. Settlement is generally three business days after the trade. This policy is known as T+3. For government securities, settlement is T+1.

serial number 1 corresponds to January 2, 1904 (January 1, 1904, is 0). To see the actual serial number, you can use the General number format. The difference in date systems is important to those transferring files from PCs to Macs. Using serial numbers makes date math quite simple. For example, you can determine the number of days between two dates with simple subtraction.[3] Also, note that the date serial number is independent of the date format applied.

RATE is the annual coupon rate and *YLD* is the annual required rate of return. In Excel functions, rates are always entered in decimal form, which is different from the convention for financial calculators. If the coupon rate is 10%, you must enter it as 0.10, although Excel will convert a number followed by a percent sign (%) to this format. The effect of the percent sign is to cause Excel to divide the preceding number by 100.

REDEMPTION is the amount to be received per $100 of face value when the bond is redeemed. It is important to realize that the redemption price can be different than the face value of the bond. This would be the case, for example, if the bond was called by the issuer. Calling a bond issue is very similar to refinancing a mortgage, in that the issuer usually wishes to reissue debt at a lower interest rate. There is often a premium paid to bondholders when bonds are called, and this premium plus the face value is the redemption price. If a bond issue has a 4% call premium, then *REDEMPTION* would be set to 104. For noncallable bonds, this will be set to 100.

FREQUENCY is the number of coupons paid in a year. Most often this will be 2, though other values are possible. Excel will return the #NUM! error if *FREQUENCY* is any value other than 1, 2, or 4 (annual, semiannual, or quarterly). Note that bonds that pay interest on a monthly basis, while rare, do exist.[4] This function does not work with such bonds.

BASIS describes the assumption regarding the number of days in a month and year. Historically, different financial markets have made different assumptions regarding the number of days in a month and a year. Corporate, agency, and municipal bonds are priced assuming that there are 30 days in a month and 360 days in a year (a "bankers year"). Treasury bonds are priced assuming a 365-day year (366 days in a leap year) and the actual

---

3. As an interesting demonstration of the power of serial date numbers and custom formatting, consider the following: To determine exactly how old you are, enter your birth date in a blank cell of a worksheet, say A1. In A2 enter the formula: =TODAY()-A1. The **TODAY()** function returns the serial number of the current date. Now, choose the Custom category in the Number Format dialog box and type the following format in the <u>T</u>ype box: y" years,"m" months, and "d" days" and click on OK.

4. For example, GE Capital has a 3.6% bond that matures on 8/15/2031 and pays monthly coupons. The CUSIP number is 36966TGG1. Monthly payment bonds are most often issued by firms in the financial services industry.

number of days in a month.[5] Excel allows for five possibilities [days per month/days per year (code)]:

- 30/360 (0, or omitted)
- actual/actual (1)
- actual/360 (2)
- actual/365 (3)
- European 30/360 (4)

Any number greater than 4 will result in an error. For corporate and municipal bonds in the United States, use a basis of 0, and for U.S. Treasury bonds use a basis of 1.

It is easy to determine the number of days between two dates using both the actual/actual and 30/360 day count techniques. Recall that Excel stores dates as a serial number that represents the number of days since January 1, 1900. Therefore, we can calculate the actual number of days between any two dates using simple subtraction, even in a leap year. For the 30/360 day count basis, Excel provides the **DAYS360** function:

$$\text{DAYS360}(\textit{START\_DATE}, \textit{END\_DATE}, \textit{METHOD})$$

where the first two arguments are obvious, and *METHOD* is an optional argument specifying whether to use the U.S. (0, or omitted) or European (1) standard. You can see the difference between actual/actual and 30/360 by entering two dates, at least a few months apart. For our purposes, the basis is unlikely to make a difference in the calculated price. However, if you are trading in large numbers of bonds, the basis can make a significant difference.

To see how the **PRICE** function works, open a new worksheet and enter the data displayed in Exhibit 9-3, which is taken from the example. The settlement date should be entered by simply typing the date as it appears. As noted earlier, Excel will automatically recognize it as a date. Recall that the Nanoterials bonds mature in 20 years. We have assumed that the settlement date is 2/15/2015 and that the maturity date is 2/15/2035. In actual practice, the maturity date of the bond could be found in the indenture, by asking a broker, or by viewing the appropriate Form 424B2 in the SEC's Edgar database.[6]

The current value of the bond can now be found by entering the function: =PRICE(B2,B3,B4,B5,B6/B6*100,B7,B8)/100*B6 in B10. Because the **PRICE** function returns the price as a percentage of the face value (90.799), we must divide by 100

---

5. For more information on day count conventions, see *Standard Securities Calculation Methods*, by John J. Lynch, Jr., and Jan H. Mayle, Securities Industry Association, 1986.

6. This site may be accessed at http://www.sec.gov/edgar/searchedgar/companysearch.html. Select the company of interest, and then enter 424B2 into the Filing Type box in the search area. Note that older bonds may not be in the system.

EXHIBIT 9-3
BOND VALUATION WORKSHEET USING THE PRICE FUNCTION

	A	B
1	**Bond Valuation**	
2	Settlement Date	2/15/2015
3	Maturity Date	2/15/2035
4	Coupon Rate	8.00%
5	Required Return	9.00%
6	Face Value	1000
7	Frequency	2
8	Basis	0
9		
10	Value	$ 907.99

and multiply by the face value in order to convert it to a dollar amount. The result is $907.99, exactly as we found manually. Notice that we have not made any adjustment for the fact that the bond pays interest semiannually. Excel automatically makes this adjustment for you based on the function's **FREQUENCY** argument.

What is the value of the bond two months after the settlement date? Earlier, we found that the quoted price was $908.08, but that required a complicated formula using both the **PV** and **ROUNDUP** functions. The **PRICE** function will automatically calculate the quoted price between coupon dates, so all we need to do is set the settlement date to 4/15/2015 in B2. The answer is $908.08, as we found earlier.

Bond Return Measures

Most often, investors don't decide to buy a bond just because the price is below some calculated intrinsic value. Instead, they will examine available alternative investments and compare bonds on the basis of the returns that they offer. There are several ways to calculate the returns offered by bonds. In this section, we will cover three return measures for bonds and two additional measures for discounted debt securities.

Before starting, modify your worksheet by entering Return Measures in A11. This will serve to separate these results from the previous calculations.

Current Yield

The current yield is defined as the annual coupon payment divided by the current price of the bond:

$$CY = \frac{\text{Annual Pmt}}{V_B} \qquad (9\text{-}2)$$

The current yield is a rough measure of the return earned over the next year. We say that it is rough because it ignores compounding and the change in price which may occur over the life of the bond. The current yield measures the income yield only; like a stock's dividend yield, it ignores capital gains.

Excel has no built-in function to calculate the current yield, but it is a simple matter to write the formula yourself. On your worksheet, move to A12 and type: Current Yield. Now, in B12 enter: =(B4*B6)/B10. In our example the current yield is 8.81%, which is, in fact, the return that you would earn over the next year if you received $80 in interest on an investment of $907.99. However, if interest rates remain unchanged over the year, the value of the bond will increase to $909.75. The capital gain of $1.76 is ignored in the current yield calculation. Note that when a bond is selling at a discount to its face value, the current yield will understate the total return. If the bond is selling at a premium, then the current yield will overstate the total return.

Yield to Maturity

The *yield to maturity* is the compound annual rate of return that can be expected if the bond is held to maturity. The yield to maturity is not without its problems as a return measure, but it is superior to the current yield because it accounts for both interest payments and capital gains. It is also more complex to calculate.

Essentially, the yield to maturity is found by taking the bond price as given and solving the valuation equation for the required return (k_B).[7] No method exists, however, to solve directly for the yield to maturity. The yield can be found by using a trial-and-error approach, but it is a bit tedious. Excel makes the yield calculation simple with its built-in **YIELD** function, which is defined as:

YIELD(*SETTLEMENT, MATURITY, RATE, PR, REDEMPTION, FREQUENCY, BASIS*)

All of the variables are the same as previously defined with the exception of *PR*, which is the price of the bond as a percentage of the face value.

---

7. It should be noted that for most purposes, the terms "required return" and "yield to maturity" can be used interchangeably and often are. However, there is a slight, but important, difference between the terms. Specifically, the required return is specified by the investor and can be different for other investors. The yield to maturity is not under the control of the investor; instead it is merely a function of the current bond price and cash flows promised from the bond. As such, the yield to maturity will be the same regardless of who calculates it.

To make the calculation, first place the label: `Yield to Maturity` in A13 and then enter: `=YIELD(B2,B3,B4,B10/B6*100,B6/B6*100,B7,B8)` in B13. Note that the only difference from the **PRICE** function is that we replaced *YLD* with the current price of the bond as a percentage of par. In this case, we had to convert the bond price (in B10) back to a percentage of par by dividing it by the face value and multiplying by 100. The result, as should be expected, is 9%.

We could also use the **RATE** function (see page 207) to find the yield to maturity if we assume that the settlement date is also an interest payment date for the bond. This technique is especially useful if you don't know the exact settlement and maturity dates for the bond, and if you are calculating the yield on a payment date. Rather than replace our **YIELD** function, we'll simply insert the **RATE** function in B14 so that we can compare the results. In A14 type the label `Yield Using Rate Function`. In B14 enter the function: `=RATE(YEARFRAC(B2,B3,B8)*B7,B4*B6/B7,-B10,B6)*B7`.

In order to use this function, we've had to embed several calculations. For the number of periods, we are using the **YEARFRAC** function, which calculates the fraction of a year between any two dates using an appropriate day count basis. This function is defined as:

$$\text{YEARFRAC}(\textit{START\_DATE}, \textit{END\_DATE}, \textit{METHOD})$$

YEARFRAC returns the number of years between the settlement and maturity dates, and we then multiply by the payment frequency to get the number of periods. The payment amount is simply the coupon rate times the face (redemption) value divided by two. You'll note that after annualizing the result by doubling (because it pays semiannually), the answer is the same 9% as before. Again, it is important to remember that the **RATE** function will provide the correct answer only on a payment date. If the bond is between payment dates, then use the **YIELD** function.

As mentioned earlier, there are a few potential problems with the yield to maturity. Implicit in the calculation are some key assumptions: (1) that you hold the bond to maturity; and (2) that you reinvest the cash flows for the rest of the life of the bond at a rate equal to the yield to maturity. Note that if market returns change, and you have to sell the bond before it matures, you will receive a price that is different than you expected. This is known as *price risk*. Furthermore, if market rates change, you will be reinvesting the cash flows at a different rate than expected. This is known as *reinvestment risk*. Either or both of these factors can cause your actual return to be different from the yield to maturity that was calculated when you purchased the bond. Thus, the combination of price and reinvestment risk is known as *interest rate risk* (see page 289 for more information).

EXHIBIT 9-4
CURRENT YIELD AND YIELD TO MATURITY

	A	B
1	**Bond Valuation**	
2	Settlement Date	2/15/2015
3	Maturity Date	2/15/2035
4	Coupon Rate	8.00%
5	Required Return	9.00%
6	Face Value	1000
7	Frequency	2
8	Basis	0
9		
10	Value	$ 907.99
11	**Return Measures**	
12	Current Yield	8.81%
13	Yield to Maturity	9.00%
14	Yield Using Rate Function	9.00%

Yield to Call

One other common measure of return is the *yield to call*. As noted earlier, many issuers reserve the right to buy back the bonds that they sell if it serves their interests. In most cases, bonds will be called if interest rates drop substantially so that the firm will save money by refinancing at a lower rate. If we calculate the yield to maturity assuming that the bond will be called at the first opportunity, we will have calculated the yield to call. Because it is common to have a contractual obligation to pay a premium over par value if the bonds are called, this must be taken into account in our calculation. Note that the call schedule specifies the exact call dates (typically, once per year on an anniversary date) and the premiums on those dates. The premiums typically fall over time to zero.

In order to make this calculation, we must add a couple of lines to our worksheet. First, insert a row above row 4. To do this, highlight row 4 and click the top of the Insert button on the Home tab. Now, in A4 type: First Call Date to indicate that this is the first date at which the firm has the option of calling the bonds. In B4 enter: 2/15/2020. This date reflects the fact that the first call date is often a few years after the issue date (which we are assuming is the same as the settlement date in this case). Next, insert a row above row 8 and label it in A8: Call Price. Cell B8 will be the price at which the bonds can be called, in this case 5% over par value, so enter: 1050. In A17, enter the label: Yield to Call.

Finally, we will calculate the yield to call in B17 with the formula: =YIELD(B2,B4,B5, B12/B7*100,B8/B7*100,B9,B10). This is exactly the same formula as the yield to maturity, except that we have changed the maturity date to the call date and the redemption

EXHIBIT 9-5
BOND VALUATION WORKSHEET WITH YIELD TO CALL ADDED

	A	B
1	**Bond Valuation**	
2	Settlement Date	2/15/2015
3	Maturity Date	2/15/2035
4	First Call Date	2/15/2020
5	Coupon Rate	8.00%
6	Required Return	9.00%
7	Face Value	1000
8	Call Price	1050
9	Frequency	2
10	Basis	0
11		
12	Value	$ 907.99
13	**Return Measures**	
14	Current Yield	8.81%
15	Yield to Maturity	9.00%
16	Yield Using Rate Functi	9.00%
17	Yield to Call	11.23%

value to the call price. Note that the call premium plus the earlier receipt of the face value has caused the yield to call to be 11.23%. Of course, the issuer would never call the bond under these circumstances because interest rates have risen since the bond was originally issued. Your worksheet should now resemble the one in Exhibit 9-5.

Make-Whole Call Provisions

The type of call provision that we have demonstrated is known as a *regular call* feature, and was typical until about 15 years ago. Recently, though, most callable corporate bonds have been issued with a *make-whole call* feature.[8] In a regular call the bond is typically called at a price below market value because interest rates have declined (i.e., the price is above the face value plus the call premium). Thus, investors are worse off than if the bond hadn't been called. In a make-whole call, however, the call provision specifies that investors will be paid the present value of all remaining cash flows, or the par value, whichever is greater. The discount rate used in the calculation is the current Treasury rate with a maturity equal to the remaining life of the bond plus a spread—typically 15 to 50 basis points, depending on credit rating. The spread is specified in the bond's indenture and is set at issuance.

8. For more in-depth discussion, see Mann, S. V., & Powers, E. A. (2003). "Indexing a Bond's Call Price: An Analysis of Make-Whole Call Provisions," *Journal of Corporate Finance*, 9, 535–554.

Using this method, investors are no worse off than if the bond hadn't been called. Because the make-whole call feature makes calling a bond more expensive for the issuer, it is only rarely invoked. However, the bonds are continuously callable, on short notice, as opposed to only once a year. When calculating the yield to call with a make-whole call feature, the **REDEMPTION** argument of the **YIELD** function would be calculated using the **PRICE** function, with its **YLD** argument being equal to the Treasury rate plus the spread.

Returns on Discounted Debt Securities

Not all debt instruments are bonds of the type that we have discussed earlier. Money market securities are short-term, high-quality, debt instruments sold on a discounted basis. That is, they do not pay interest; instead, they are sold for less than their face value. Because the full face value is returned to the investor at maturity, the interest is the difference between the face value and the purchase price. Examples of this type of security would include U.S. Treasury Bills, commercial paper, banker's acceptances, and short-term municipals.

Returns on discounted securities are usually quoted on a bank discount basis. The bank discount rate (*BDR*) is calculated as follows:

$$BDR = \frac{FV - P_0}{FV} \times \frac{360}{M} \tag{9-3}$$

where *FV* is the face value of the security, P_0 is the purchase price, and *M* is the number of days until maturity. For example, if you purchase a 26-week (181-day) T-Bill for $985, the bank discount rate is:

$$BDR = \frac{1,000 - 985}{1,000} \times \frac{360}{181} = 0.02983 = 2.983\%$$

We can calculate the bank discount rate in Excel using the **DISC** function:

DISC(*SETTLEMENT, MATURITY, PR, REDEMPTION, BASIS*)

All of the variables are as previously defined. To see how this function works, insert a new worksheet into your workbook and enter the data in Exhibit 9-6.

Notice that both the redemption value and purchase price are entered as a percentage of par, though we could enter the actual values. In B8 enter the **DISC** function as: `=DISC(B2,B3,B5,B4,2)`. Note that we have set the *BASIS* to 2 because equation (9-3) uses the actual/360 day count convention. The answer is 2.983%, exactly as we calculated using the equation.

EXHIBIT 9-6
CALCULATING THE BANK DISCOUNT RATE

	A	B
1	**Discount Securities**	
2	Settlement Date	2/15/2015
3	Maturity Date	8/15/2015
4	Redemption Value	100
5	Purchase Price	98.50
6	Days to Maturity	181
7		
8	Bank Discount Rate	2.983%

The bank discount rate is the method used to quote discount securities in the market. However, it does have a couple of problems: (1) It uses the face value as the basis for calculating the return, but you have only paid the purchase price, not the face value. (2) It assumes that there are only 360 days in a year, instead of 365 (366 in a leap year). We can solve these problems by calculating the bond equivalent yield:

$$BEY = BDR \times \frac{FV}{P_0} \times \frac{365}{360} = \frac{FV - P_0}{P_0} \times \frac{365}{M} \tag{9-4}$$

The bond equivalent yield is simply a "fixed" version of the bank discount rate: We are using the purchase price as the basis for calculating the return and changing the day count convention to actual/actual. This allows us to compare the yield to yields on coupon-bearing bonds. In this example the bond equivalent yield is:

$$BEY = 0.02983 \times \frac{1,000}{985} \times \frac{365}{360} = \frac{1,000 - 985}{985} \times \frac{365}{181} = 0.03071 = 3.071\%$$

As you might expect, Excel has a built-in function to calculate the bond equivalent yield:

YIELDDISC(*SETTLEMENT, MATURITY, PR, REDEMPTION, BASIS*)

In A9 of your worksheet enter the label: Bond Equivalent Yield, and in B9 enter the formula: =YIELDDISC(B2,B3,B5,B4,1). Note that the *BASIS* is set to 1 (actual/actual) in this case. The answer is 3.071% as we found using the equation.

The U.S. Treasury Yield Curve

A yield curve is a chart that shows yields across the maturity spectrum and is useful for giving investors an idea of the yields that are currently available in the market. Professionals use the U.S. Treasury yield curve,[9] along with information about yield spreads for various types of bonds, to determine the required yield on the bonds that they are trying to value.

We can create yield curves for different types of securities (e.g., Treasuries, corporates, municipals). One should be careful that the securities used to construct the yield curve differ as little as possible, except for term to maturity. U.S. Treasury securities are almost ideal for this purpose because they are all free of default risk. In this section, we will show how to construct a U.S. Treasury yield curve using data that is freely available on the Internet.

Excel provides tools that can be used to obtain data directly from databases, text files, or Web sites. For our purposes, we wish to use the Web Query tool to gather data from a table on a Web site. Specifically, we will use a Web Query to get data on Treasury yields from the U.S. Department of the Treasury. This query can be refreshed (automatically or manually) to grab the most recent data from the site.

Open a new workbook, select the Data tab, and then click the From Web button in the Get External Data group. This will launch the New Web Query dialog box, which includes a browser that we can use to navigate to a Web page. In the address bar of the browser, enter the URL: `http://www.treasury.gov/resource-center/data-chart-center/interest-rates/Pages/TextView.aspx?data=yield` and you should see the page load. Scroll down until you see the table containing the yield curve data for the last five days as shown in Figure 9-2.

To import one or more tables from the page, you will simply click the arrows at the left of the table. Select the table by clicking the yellow arrow and then click the **I**mport button to pull the data into cell A2 of your worksheet. You have now created a link to this table, and it can be refreshed at any time by clicking the Refresh All button in the Connections group on the Data tab. By default, every time you open this workbook the query will pull the new data from the Web site. You can change the settings for the Web Query by right-clicking the data and choosing D**a**ta Range Properties.

---

9. Technically, we should use a curve constructed from the yields available on U.S. Treasury coupon STRIPS. This data is available from the *Wall Street Journal* at http://online.wsj.com/mdc/public/page/2_3020-tstrips.html. Unfortunately, it cannot be accessed directly from Excel in the manner demonstrated here. Instead, it must be copied and pasted.

FIGURE 9-2
THE WEB QUERY DIALOG BOX

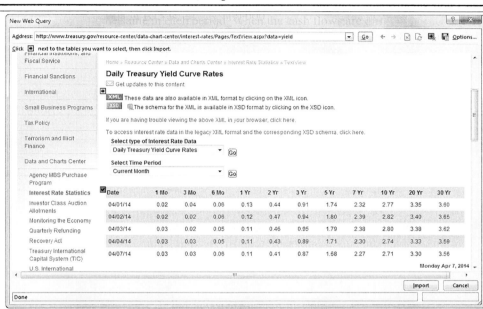

We can now format the table and create the yield curve chart. In order to have the data points properly spaced on the chart, we need to convert the maturities from text (e.g., 1 Month) to numbers. We cannot place formulas inside the query results (A1:L7), so we will create the data for our chart to the right of the query results. You could also place these calculations on another worksheet. In O3:P13 enter the number of years. For example, in O3 enter 0.0833 because three months is equal to 0.0833 years. Do the same for the other maturities (e.g., 0.5 for 6 months). In P3:P13 we will calculate today's yields. So, in P3 enter: =B7/100 and format the result as a percentage. Repeat this for each of the other maturities.

If you are going to apply formatting to the query, as shown earlier, be aware that refreshing the query can remove the formatting. To avoid this, right-click within the data range and choose Data Range Properties. Make sure that the Preserve cell formatting option is checked.

Finally, select O3:P13 and insert a scatter chart with straight lines and markers. For the chart title, use a text formula in P1: ="U.S. Treasury Yield Curve "&CHAR(10)& TEXT(A7,"m/dd/yyyy"). (The Char(10) inserts a new line character.) Insert a chart title, select it, and then click on cell P1. The result should look like Exhibit 9-7.

EXHIBIT 9-7
THE U.S. TREASURY YIELD CURVE USING A WEB QUERY

	A	B	C	D	E	F	G	H	I	J	K	L
1						US Treasury Bonds						
2	Date	1 mo	3 mo	6 mo	1 yr	2 yr	3 yr	5 yr	7 yr	10 yr	20 yr	30 yr
3	4/1/2014	0.02%	0.04%	0.06%	0.13%	0.44%	0.91%	1.74%	2.32%	2.77%	3.35%	3.60%
4	4/2/2014	0.02%	0.02%	0.06%	0.12%	0.47%	0.94%	1.80%	2.39%	2.82%	3.40%	3.65%
5	4/3/2014	0.03%	0.02%	0.05%	0.11%	0.46%	0.95%	1.79%	2.38%	2.80%	3.38%	3.62%
6	4/4/2014	0.03%	0.03%	0.05%	0.11%	0.43%	0.89%	1.71%	2.30%	2.74%	3.33%	3.59%
7	4/7/2014	0.03%	0.03%	0.06%	0.11%	0.41%	0.87%	1.68%	2.27%	2.71%	3.30%	3.56%

U.S. Treasury Yield Curve 4/07/2014

Bond Price Sensitivities

As should be clear, bond values are a function of several variables: coupon rate, face value, term to maturity, and the required return. It is useful to understand how changes in these variables lead to changes in bond prices because these relationships help identify investment strategies and guide the choices that corporations make when making capital structure decisions.

Burton Malkiel set forth, and rigorously proved, five bond pricing theorems that will help us understand how bond prices react to changing circumstances:[10]

1. Bond prices move inversely with interest rates.

2. For a given change in yield, long-term bond prices will change more than short-term bond prices.

---

10. B. G. Malkiel, "Expectations, Bond Prices, and the Term Structure of Interest Rates," *Quarterly Journal of Economics*, May 1962, pp. 197–218.

3.   The sensitivity of bond prices to yield changes increases at a decreasing rate as term to maturity increases.

4.   For a given change in yields, bond prices will respond asymmetrically. That is, bond prices will rise more when rates fall than they will fall when rates rise.

5.   High-coupon bonds are less sensitive to changes in yields than are low-coupon bonds.

In this section, we will examine these theorems in detail.

Changes in the Required Return

Because the value of a bond is the present value of its future cash flows, you probably expect that the value will increase as the interest rate declines, and vice versa. And you would be correct. Let's examine this idea to fix it in your mind and to point out a factor which you may not have considered.

Return to the bond valuation worksheet (Exhibit 9-5). We want to create a new section on this worksheet that will show the value of the bond at various interest rates. Move to A20 and enter: YTM, and in B20 enter: Bond Value. Starting in A21, we want a column of interest rates ranging from 1% to 15% in steps of 1% (i.e., 0.01). Create this data series using the Fill Series command on the Home tab. In B21 we need the value of the bond, using 1% as the required return. Using the **PRICE** function, this can be done with the formula: =PRICE(B$2,B$3,B$5,A21,B$7/B$7*100,B$9,B$10)/100*B$7. This is the same formula as we used previously in B12, except that we have replaced the rate with the value in A21. Further, we have added dollar signs to fix most of the cell references so that they do not change as we copy this formula down. The interest rate is not fixed because we want it to change in each row. Copy the formula over the range B22:B35.

If you now create a scatter chart with the yield on the x-axis and the bond value on the y-axis, your worksheet should look similar to the one in Exhibit 9-8. We have embellished our graph to show the current price and the required rate of return. If you wish to add the same dotted straight lines, remember that it takes only two points to define a line. We need two lines, one horizontal and one vertical. Choose an empty area of the worksheet, say E20:F24. In E20 enter 0, and in E21 enter: =B6. These cells represent the two x values for the horizontal line. In F20:F21 enter: =B12 (the current price) for the y coordinates. Create the points for the vertical line in a similar fashion using cells E23:F24. Finally, right-click in the chart and choose Select Data. Click the Add button, and add a new data series using the newly entered data. You can also copy and Paste Special in the chart.

If you wish to replicate the data labels on the chart in Exhibit 9-8, simply click once on the new data series, and then click a second time on one of the end points. This will select only

EXHIBIT 9-8
BOND VALUE FOR VARIOUS REQUIRED RETURNS

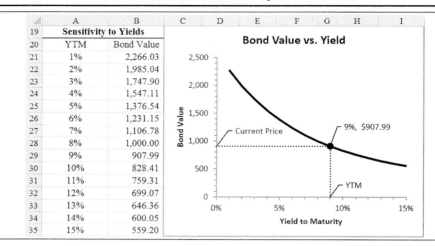

	A	B
19	**Sensitivity to Yields**	
20	YTM	Bond Value
21	1%	2,266.03
22	2%	1,985.04
23	3%	1,747.90
24	4%	1,547.11
25	5%	1,376.54
26	6%	1,231.15
27	7%	1,106.78
28	8%	1,000.00
29	9%	907.99
30	10%	828.41
31	11%	759.31
32	12%	699.07
33	13%	646.36
34	14%	600.05
35	15%	559.20

one point on the line. Right-click the point and choose Add Data La**b**el (there is no need to choose it a second time from the flyout menu). Next, right-click the data label and choose **F**ormat Data Labels. In the Format Data Label panel under Label Options, you can choose the options that you wish to display. Note that "Leader Lines" are the lines that connect the data point to the label.

Confirming Malkiel's first theorem, we can see that the price is inversely related to the required return. Furthermore, the relationship is not linear; instead it is convex to the origin. As we will see, this nonlinear relationship (known as *convexity*) also demonstrates the fourth theorem.

Move the chart to the right so that column C is exposed. In C20 enter the label: Change. In C21:C35 we want to enter the change in the bond price from the current price. In other words, the numbers in this range will be the gain or loss that would be experienced if you purchased the bond and then interest rates changed from the original 9% to the value in column A. In C21 enter the formula: =B21-$B$29 (which will fix the subtracted price at B29). Now copy the formula down the entire range.

Figure 9-3 shows how the bond price will change. Examine cells C21:C35 in your worksheet carefully. In particular, notice that the price changes are not symmetric. For example, if the yield falls by 4% (to 5%), the price rises by $468.55. However, if the rate rises by 4% (to 13%), the price falls by only $261.63. In other words, as yields drop the price rises by more than it falls if yields rise a similar amount. This confirms Malkiel's fourth theorem.

FIGURE 9-3
BOND VALUE VS. REQUIRED RETURN

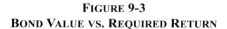

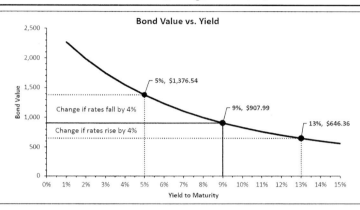

Changes in Term to Maturity

As a bond approaches its maturity date, the price must approach its face value (ignoring accrued interest). Because a bond can sell at a premium (above face value), at face value, or at a discount (below face value), investors may realize a capital loss, no gain or loss, or a capital gain if they hold the bond to maturity.

To see how the price changes as maturity approaches, move to A37 and enter the labels so that your worksheet resembles the one in Exhibit 9-9. Create a series in A39:A59 from 20 down to 0. Use the Fill Series command with a step value of –1. Notice that we have included a column for a second bond. Copy the original data (in B2:B11) and place it in C2:C11. The only difference between the two bonds is the required return. For the second bond, set the required return to 7% and notice that the price of this bond is $1,106.78. This allows us to compare bonds selling at a discount and premium as they move toward maturity.[11]

In B39, we want to enter the **PRICE** function for the first bond, allowing only the time to maturity to change. The formula to do this is: =PRICE(B$2,EDATE(B$2,$A39*12), B$5,B$6,B$7/B$7*100,B$9,B$10)/100*B$7. Because the second argument is the maturity date, we must calculate it based on the number of years that is given in A39.

---

11. This is a contrived situation. The "law of one price" guarantees that identical cash flows, with the same level of risk, will have identical prices and thus identical yields. If this situation actually existed, arbitrageurs would buy Bond 1 (driving its price up) and short sell Bond 2 (driving its price down) until the prices were the same.

EXHIBIT 9-9
BOND PRICES VS. TIME TO MATURITY

	A	B	C
37	**Sensitivity to Time to Maturity**		
38	Years to Maturity	Bond 1	Bond 2
39	20	907.99	1,106.78
40	19	909.75	1,104.21
41	18	911.67	1,101.45
42	17	913.77	1,098.50
43	16	916.06	1,095.34
44	15	918.56	1,091.96
45	14	921.29	1,088.34
46	13	924.27	1,084.45
47	12	927.52	1,080.29
48	11	931.08	1,075.84
49	10	934.96	1,071.06
50	9	939.20	1,065.95
51	8	943.83	1,060.47
52	7	948.89	1,054.60
53	6	954.41	1,048.32
54	5	960.44	1,041.58
55	4	967.02	1,034.37
56	3	974.21	1,026.64
57	2	982.06	1,018.37
58	1	990.64	1,009.50
59	0	1,000.00	1,000.00

To do this we used the **EDATE** function, which returns a date that is a number of months after the *START_DATE*:

$$\text{EDATE}(\textit{START\_DATE}, \textit{MONTHS})$$

In this case, we are using the settlement date for the *START_DATE*, and the number of months is the number of remaining years to maturity multiplied by 12 to convert it to months. Copy this formula to C39 to find the price of the second bond and then copy both of these down the entire range. Note that the **PRICE** function will return a #NUM! error when the term to maturity is 0. Therefore, in B59 and C59 enter the formula: =B$7 to get the face value. The numbers in your worksheet should be the same as those in Exhibit 9-9.

Notice that the first bond slowly increases in price as the time to maturity declines. The second bond's price, however, slowly decreases as time to maturity declines. This demonstration assumes that yields remain constant for the next 20 years. In actuality, required yields change on a daily basis, so the change in price will not be as smooth as the worksheet shows.

To see this more clearly, create a scatter chart of this data by selecting A38:C59. Once the chart is created, you may want to adjust the scale of the y-axis. Right-click the y-axis and choose **F**ormat Axis. Now set the Minimum edit box to 850. This will change the scale so that the origin of the y-axis is at 850, effectively magnifying the area of the chart that we are interested in. Note that we have also added a line to indicate the par value of the bond. In cell D39 enter 1000 and copy it down to the rest of the range. Now, right-click the chart and choose S**e**lect Data. Click the **A**dd button and add a series with A39:A59 as the x values, and D39:D59 as the y values. After adding labels to the chart, this part of your worksheet should look like Figure 9-4.

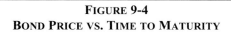

FIGURE 9-4
BOND PRICE VS. TIME TO MATURITY

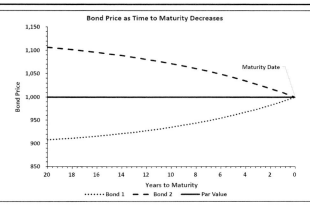

Comparing Two Bonds with Different Maturities

When investors decide to purchase bonds, they have myriad choices, including many combinations of term to maturity and coupon rates. Malkiel's second theorem says that long-term bond prices will change more than short-term bond prices when yields change. To see this, make a copy of A1:C12 from your worksheet and paste it into a new worksheet.

Our first goal is to set up the worksheet so that both bonds are identical, and then we will change the maturity date of the second bond. Previously, the only difference between the bonds was the required return. So, change that to 9% for the second bond (cell C6). Now, set the maturity date for the second bond, in C3, to 2/15/2025. It is now a 10-year bond, while the first is a 20-year bond. Set up the rest of the worksheet as shown in Exhibit 9-10.

In B15:C16 we will calculate the prices of the two bonds at the yields given in A15:A16. This will allow us to see how the prices change at different yields. In B15, enter the formula: =PRICE(B$2,B$3,B$5,$A15,B$7/B$7*100,B$9,B$10)/100*B$7, and then copy it to the other cells. In B17:C17 we want to calculate the price changes, so the formula

EXHIBIT 9-10
PRICE CHANGES WITH DIFFERENT MATURITIES

	A	B	C
1	**Bond Valuation**		
2	Settlement Date	2/15/2015	2/15/2015
3	Maturity Date	2/15/2035	2/15/2025
4	First Call Date	2/15/2020	2/15/2020
5	Coupon Rate	8.00%	8.00%
6	Required Return	9.00%	9.00%
7	Redemption Value	1,000	1,000
8	Call Price	1,050	1,050
9	Frequency	2	2
10	Basis	0	0
11			
12	Value	$ 907.99	$ 934.96
13			
14	**Yield**	**Bond 1**	**Bond 2**
15	9%		
16	12%		
17	Price Change		
18	Percentage Change		

in B17 is: =B16-B15. Copy that to C17. Finally, calculate the percentage change in B18 with: =B16/B15-1 and copy that formula to C18.

Notice that our starting yield is 9%, as before. If you purchased either bond and then rates instantaneously rose to 12% the prices would fall by $208.92 (–23.01%) and $164.36 (–17.58%), respectively. Recall that the bonds are identical, except for their terms to maturity. The price of Bond 1 fell by more because it is a longer term bond. Now, change the yield in A16 to 6%, so that the prices will now rise. Note that the price of Bond 1 rises by more than the price of Bond 2, as expected.

Now, change the maturity date on Bond 2 to 2/15/2020, so that it has only five years to maturity. Note how the price of Bond 2 now changes by even less than it did as a 10-year bond. This is just as Malkiel's second theorem claims: Long-term bond prices will change by more (in percentage terms) than short-term bonds when yields change.

Malkiel's third theorem says that the sensitivity to yield changes increases at a decreasing rate as maturity lengthens. This means that, for example, when compared to a 20-year bond, a 30-year bond isn't that much more sensitive to yield changes. However, a 10-year bond will be considerably less sensitive to yield changes than the 20-year bond.

We can see this in our worksheet very easily. Bond 1 will serve as our point of comparison. First, change the maturity of Bond 2 to 2/15/2025, and note that its price will rise by 22.87% when yields fall from 9% to 6%. This compares to a 35.59% for Bond 1, which has 10 additional years to maturity. That is a difference of about 12.72%.

Now, change the maturity date of Bond 2 (in C3) to 2/15/2045. Note that the price change is 42.37%. That is a difference of only 6.78% compared to Bond 1. Finally, change the maturity date to 2/15/2055. Table 9-1 shows the results.

TABLE 9-1
CHANGES IN PRICE WHEN YIELDS DROP FROM 9% TO 6%

Maturity Date (Term)	Change in Price	Difference from 20-Year Bond
2/15/2025 (10)	22.87%	12.72%
2/15/2035 (20)	35.59%	0.00%
2/15/2045 (30)	42.37%	6.78%
2/15/2055 (40)	45.94%	10.35%

This confirms Malkiel's third theorem. While longer term bonds change more when yields change, the sensitivity decreases as the term increases. So, the difference in interest rate sensitivity between a 30-year and a 40-year bond is much less than the difference between a 10-year and a 20-year bond.

Comparing Two Bonds with Different Coupon Rates

The fifth theorem says that high-coupon bonds are less sensitive to yield changes than low-coupon bonds. We can use a slightly modified version of our worksheet to demonstrate this theorem. Make a copy of the previous worksheet, and reset the maturity date of Bond 2 to 2/15/2035. Change the coupon rate of Bond 2 to 4%, so that the bonds are identical, except that Bond 2 has a lower coupon rate.

Again, we will modify the yield in A16 to see how the changing yields affect the prices of bonds with different coupon rates. Enter 12% in A16, and notice that Bond 2 (with a lower coupon rate) has a larger percentage loss than Bond 1 (with a higher coupon rate). Now, change A15 to 6% and see that Bond 2 shows a greater percentage gain than Bond 1. Exhibit 9-11 shows this result.

In both cases, Bond 1 actually had a larger change in dollar terms. However, that is misleading because the price of Bond 2 starts out at a much lower price (only $539.96) because of its lower coupon rate. It is the percentage change that matters most, so this confirms theorem five.

EXHIBIT 9-11
PRICE CHANGES WITH DIFFERENT COUPON RATES

	A	B	C
1	**Bond Valuation**		
2	Settlement Date	2/15/2015	2/15/2015
3	Maturity Date	2/15/2035	2/15/2035
4	First Call Date	2/15/2020	2/15/2020
5	Coupon Rate	8.00%	4.00%
6	Required Return	9.00%	9.00%
7	Redemption Value	1,000	1,000
8	Call Price	1,050	1,050
9	Frequency	2	2
10	Basis	0	0
11			
12	Value	$ 907.99	$ 539.96
13			
14	**Yield**	**Bond 1**	**Bond 2**
15	9%	907.99	539.96
16	6%	1,231.15	768.85
17	Price Change	323.16	228.89
18	Percentage Change	35.59%	42.39%

Duration and Convexity

We have just demonstrated that long-term bonds and those with low coupon rates are much more sensitive to changes in yields than are short-term bonds and those with high coupon rates. This suggests a trading strategy for bond investors: *If you believe that interest rates will rise, you should move into short-term bonds with high coupon rates. On the other hand, if you think that rates will fall, you should move into long-term bonds with low coupon rates.*

Investors frequently make such directional trades based on interest rate forecasts. However, there are many combinations of coupon rates and maturities. Suppose that you have to choose between two bonds: a long-term bond with a high coupon rate or a short-term bond with a low coupon rate. Which bond will lose less if interest rates rise? Which one will gain more if rates fall? In other words, which bond has the most interest rate risk?

Duration

It is difficult to answer those questions without doing the actual calculations. However, in 1938 Frederick Macaulay developed a measure of interest rate risk that can answer this question.[12] *Duration* is a weighted average of the time to receive the cash flows of the bond in present value terms.

Duration combines the effects of maturity, coupon rate, and yield into a single number that we can use to measure the interest rate sensitivity of a bond. The longer the duration, the greater the interest rate risk of the bond. As you might imagine, this allows investors to immediately determine which bond will better suit their portfolio, given their expectations about future interest rate movements.

Mathematically, Macaulay's duration is calculated as:

$$D_{Mac} = \frac{\sum_{t=1}^{N} \frac{Pmt_t}{(1 + YTM)^t}(t)}{V_B}$$ (9-5)

where Pmt_t is the cash flow in period t, YTM is the per period (usually semiannual) yield to maturity, and V_B is the current price. The fractional part of the numerator is the present value of each cash flow as a percentage of the bond's price, which serves as the weighting in the average, and t is the number of periods until each cash flow is received. As with equation (9-1), this formula is only accurate on a payment date.

Let's calculate the Macaulay duration (D_{Mac}) of Bond 1 from our previous example:

$$D_{Mac} = \frac{\frac{40}{1.045^1}(1) + \frac{40}{1.045^2}(2) + \frac{40}{1.045^3}(3) + \cdots + \frac{1040}{1.045^{40}}(40)}{907.99} = 19.67 \text{ periods}$$

Note that the semiannual payment is $40, the semiannual yield is 4.5% (= 9%/2), and the current bond price is $907.99. This results in a duration of 19.67 semiannual periods. Duration is actually expressed in years, so we need to divide the result by the payment frequency. Therefore, the Macaulay duration of Bond 1 is 9.83 years.

Excel has a built-in function called, naturally, **DURATION**:

DURATION(*SETTLEMENT, MATURITY, COUPON, YLD, FREQUENCY, BASIS*)

---

12. F. R. Macaulay, *Some Theoretical Problems Suggested by the Movements of Interest Rates, Bond Yields and Stock Prices in the United States Since 1856.* New York: National Bureau of Economic Research, 1938.

Using the worksheet from Exhibit 9-11, let's calculate the duration of both bonds. In A20 type the label: Macaulay Duration, and in B20 enter the formula: =DURATION(B2, B3,B5,B6,B9,B10). Now copy the formula to C20 to find the duration of Bond 2.

Duration is accurate only for very small changes in the yield, so change the yield in A16 to 10%, so that the change in yield is 1%. The duration of Bond 1 is 9.83 years, and for Bond 2 it is 11.45 years. Note that as we left things, the only difference between the two bonds is the coupon rate. In this case, Bond 2 has a longer duration so it should be more sensitive to interest rate changes than Bond 1. If you look at the percentage changes in row 18, you will see that Bond 2 does change more than Bond 1.

EXHIBIT 9-12
CALCULATING THE MACAULAY DURATION

	A	B	C
1	**Bond Valuation**		
2	Settlement Date	2/15/2015	2/15/2015
3	Maturity Date	2/15/2035	2/15/2035
4	First Call Date	2/15/2020	2/15/2020
5	Coupon Rate	8.00%	4.00%
6	Required Return	9.00%	9.00%
7	Redemption Value	1,000	1,000
8	Call Price	1,050	1,050
9	Frequency	2	2
10	Basis	0	0
11			
12	Value	$ 907.99	$ 539.96
13			
14	**Yield**	**Bond 1**	**Bond 2**
15	9.0%	907.99	539.96
16	10.0%	828.41	485.23
17	Price Change	(79.58)	(54.73)
18	Percentage Change	-8.76%	-10.14%
19			
20	Macaulay Duration	9.83	11.45

If you make changes to the coupon rates and maturity dates, you will see how the duration changes. Pay particular attention to the fact that the bond with the longer duration always has the bigger percentage price change. So, you can see that duration can be a useful tool for investors trying to gauge interest rate risk.

Modified Duration

If you paid careful attention to the previous exercise, you may have noticed that the Macaulay duration is close to the percentage change in the bond's price. In our original example, changing the yield in A16 to 10% from the original 9% caused a –8.76% change in the price of Bond 1. That isn't too different from the duration of 9.83 years. So, the duration can be used to estimate the percentage change in the value if interest rates change by 1%.

We can get a closer approximation to the percentage change in the bond price by using the *modified duration* (D_{Mod}):

$$D_{Mod} = \frac{D_{Mac}}{\left(1 + \dfrac{YTM}{m}\right)} \tag{9-6}$$

where *m* is the payment frequency. In this case, the modified duration of Bond 1 is:

$$D_{Mod} = \frac{9.83}{\left(1 + \dfrac{0.09}{2}\right)} = 9.41$$

Excel has the **MDURATION** function to calculate modified duration. It is defined as:

MDURATION(*SETTLEMENT, MATURITY, COUPON, YLD, FREQUENCY, BASIS*)

All of the arguments are identical to those in the **DURATION** function. Let's add this function to our worksheet. In A21 the label is: Modified Duration, and in B21 the formula is: =MDURATION(B2,B3,B5,B6,B9,B10). This gives the same result that we got from the equation above. Now copy this formula to C21.

This is closer to the percentage change in the bond's price, but it still isn't very accurate for a 1% change in the yield. The reason is that the approximation holds only for very small changes in yields (it is a linear approximation to a nonlinear function). For small yield changes, we can get a very good approximation by using the following formula:

$$\% \text{ Change in Price} \approx -D_{Mod} \times \Delta YTM \tag{9-7}$$

If we change the yield by 0.10% (say, from 9% to 9.1%), then the price of Bond 1 will change by:

$$\% \text{ Change in Price} \approx -9.41 \times 0.001 = -0.0094 = -0.94\%$$

This is very close to the actual price change of –0.934%. We can easily see this in our worksheet. First, change the yield in A16 to 9.10%. Now, in A22 add the label: `Predicted % Change`, and in B22 the formula is: `=-B21*($A16-$A15)`. Copy that formula to C22, and then notice how similar the values in B22:C22 are to the exact calculations in B18:C18.

EXHIBIT 9-13

CALCULATING THE PERCENTAGE PRICE CHANGE USING MODIFIED DURATION

	A	B	C
1		**Bond Valuation**	
2	Settlement Date	2/15/2015	2/15/2015
3	Maturity Date	2/15/2035	2/15/2035
4	First Call Date	2/15/2020	2/15/2020
5	Coupon Rate	8.00%	4.00%
6	Required Return	9.00%	9.00%
7	Redemption Value	1,000	1,000
8	Call Price	1,050	1,050
9	Frequency	2	2
10	Basis	0	0
11			
12	Value	$ 907.99	$ 539.96
13			
14	**Yield**	**Bond 1**	**Bond 2**
15	9.0%	907.99	539.96
16	9.1%	899.51	534.09
17	Price Change	(8.48)	(5.87)
18	Percentage Change	-0.93%	-1.09%
19			
20	Macaulay Duration	9.83	11.45
21	Modified Duration	9.41	10.96
22	Predicted % Change	-0.94%	-1.10%

Visualizing the Predicted Price Change

The modified duration is the slope of the price/yield function (at the current price and yield) divided by the price of the bond. In calculus, we would write the formula as:

$$D_{Mod} = \frac{\partial P / \partial Y}{P} \qquad \text{(9-8)}$$

That is, modified duration is equal to the partial derivative of the price function with respect to the yield, divided by the price. The slope of the price/yield curve, at any particular point, is given by the numerator of equation (9-8). We can calculate the slope by multiplying the modified duration by the price of the bond:

$$\text{Slope} = D_{Mod} \times P = \frac{\text{Rise}}{\text{Run}} \qquad \text{(9-9)}$$

Recalling from your math classes that the slope of a line is defined as "rise over run," you will see that equation (9-9) gives a hint as to how we can visualize the modified duration in a chart. We will simply create a chart of the price/yield relationship and then add a chart of a line with the same slope that is tangent to the curve at a point representing the current price and yield. The slope of the tangent line is given by equation (9-9), so we simply construct a line with the same slope that also passes through the point that represents the current price and yield. This line will show the predicted price for any yield that you choose.

We have already created a chart of the price/yield function in Exhibit 9-8 (page 282). Return to that worksheet and make a copy of it so that we can add a line to the chart. We need only two points to draw the line, but it is helpful to have a third point in this case. The middle point will be the current price and yield. The two end points will be offsets from this point. Starting in H1, enter the text shown in Exhibit 9-14.

EXHIBIT 9-14
DATA FOR TANGENT LINE

	H	I	J
1	**Predicted Price Change Line**		
2	Slope	8,544.09	
3	High Point	3%	1,420.64
4	Mid Point	9%	907.99
5	Low Point	15%	395.35

In I2, we calculate the slope of our line as described in equation (9-9): =MDURATION(B2, B3,B5,B6,B9,B10)*B12. The x values, which are simply three yields, are in column I. The "High Point" in I3 is the bond yield less 6%: =B6-0.06. The 6% offset is an arbitrary amount to extend the line leftward. Similarly, in I5 enter: =B6+0.06. This will extend the line rightward. In I4 enter: =B6 for the mid point. In column J we have the y values for the line. In J3 enter the formula: =($I$4-I3)*$I$2+$B$12 and copy it down. This gives us the prices on the line with the slope that was calculated in I2.

To add this line to the chart, right-click the chart and choose Select Data. Add a new series with the x values in I3:I5 and the y values in J3:J5. The result should look like Figure 9-5.

We can now change the yield and see how it affects the slope of the line. For example, decreasing the yield (in B6) will result in the line having a greater slope. So, when yields decrease, modified duration (and Macaulay duration) will increase. Conversely, increasing the yield will result in a flatter line, implying a lower modified duration.

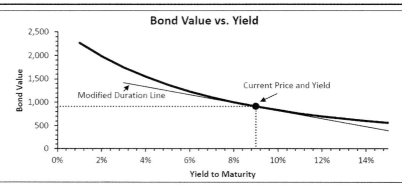

FIGURE 9-5
PRICE PREDICTED BY CHANGE IN YIELD

Convexity

As noted earlier, equation (9-7) works well only for small changes in the yield. The reason is that it is a linear approximation to a nonlinear function. Take another look at Figure 9-5, and recall that the price/yield function is curved. More specifically, it is convex to the origin. Notice how our straight line approximation departs from the price/yield function for large changes in the yield. A measure of this curvature is called *convexity*, and it can be used to improve our approximation of the change in price. Convexity (C) can be calculated with:

$$C = \frac{\dfrac{1}{(1 + YTM)^2}\left[\displaystyle\sum_{t=1}^{N}\dfrac{Pmt_t}{(1 + YTM)^t}(t^2 + t)\right]}{V_B} \tag{9-10}$$

Again, as usual, YTM is the per period yield to maturity, and equation (9-10) works only on a payment date. We can calculate the convexity of Bond 1 as follows:

$$C = \frac{\dfrac{1}{1.045^2}\left[\dfrac{40}{1.045^1}(1^2 + 1) + \dfrac{40}{1.045^2}(2^2 + 2) + \cdots + \dfrac{1{,}040}{1.045^{40}}(40^2 + 40)\right]}{907.99} = 545.92$$

As with the duration, we need to convert the convexity to an annual number. To do this, we divide by the payment frequency squared. So, the annual convexity is:

$$C = \frac{545.92}{2^2} = 136.48$$

What does this number mean? Technically, convexity is the second derivative of the price function with respect to the yield, divided by the price of the bond. Therefore, it can be thought of as the rate of change of the bond's duration. In practice, it is just a measure of the degree of curvature in the price/yield function. The higher the convexity, the more curved the function.

Unfortunately, Excel does not have a built-in function to calculate convexity. However, we have included the **FAME_CONVEXITY** function in the Famefncs.xlam add-in. It will calculate convexity on a payment date and is defined as:

FAME_CONVEXITY(*SETTLEMENT*, *MATURITY*, *FV*, *COUPON*, *YLD*, *FREQUENCY*)

where all of the arguments are as before, except that *FV* is the face value of the bond.

Return to the worksheet created for Exhibit 9-13 (page 292). Select row 22 in your worksheet and insert a new row. In A22 enter: Convexity. Now, enter the formula: =FAME_Convexity(B2,B3,B7,B5,B6,B9) in B22. Copy this formula to C22. The convexity of Bond 1 is 136.48, and for Bond 2 it is 174.52.

We can use the convexity to improve our approximation of the percentage change in price because it accounts for the curvature of the price/yield function. To do this, we will modify equation (9-7) as follows:

$$\% \text{ Change in Price} \approx -D_{Mod} \times \Delta YTM + \frac{1}{2}C \times \Delta YTM^2 \qquad \textbf{(9-11)}$$

In your worksheet, change the formula in B22 to: =-B21*($A16-$A15)+0.5*B22* ($A16-$A15)^2, and copy this formula to C22. Note that our approximation is now correct to two decimal places. For bigger changes in the yield, the approximation improves dramatically over using only modified duration. For example, change the yield in A16 to 10%, and notice how close the approximation is to the exact result. Exhibit 9-15 shows the final worksheet.

Convexity is not only useful for improving the estimate of the percentage change in bond prices. Frankly, with computers we can easily calculate the exact change. Instead, convexity is very useful when comparing bonds that have the same, or similar, durations. The more convex bond will gain more, or lose less, if yields change. Therefore, more convexity is preferred to less.

EXHIBIT 9-15
USING CONVEXITY TO IMPROVE THE ESTIMATED PRICE CHANGE

	A	B	C
1	**Bond Valuation**		
2	Settlement Date	2/15/2015	2/15/2015
3	Maturity Date	2/15/2035	2/15/2035
4	First Call Date	2/15/2020	2/15/2020
5	Coupon Rate	8.00%	4.00%
6	Required Return	9.00%	9.00%
7	Redemption Value	1,000	1,000
8	Call Price	1,050	1,050
9	Frequency	2	2
10	Basis	0	0
11			
12	Value	$907.99	$539.96
13			
14	Yield	Bond 1	Bond 2
15	9.0%	907.99	539.96
16	10.0%	828.41	485.23
17	Price Change	(79.58)	(54.73)
18	Percentage Change	-8.76%	-10.14%
19			
20	Macaulay Duration	9.83	11.45
21	Modified Duration	9.41	10.96
22	Convexity	136.48	174.52
23	Predicted % Change	-8.73%	-10.09%

Summary

We have seen that the value of a bond is a function of its term to maturity, coupon rate, required return, and face value. More specifically, as with other securities, the value of a bond is the present value of its future cash flows. The required return (yield) relative to the coupon rate determines whether the bond sells at par value or at a discount or premium to par. We have seen how to determine the value of a bond either on or between payment dates using the **Pv** and **PRICE** functions.

The rate of return that is expected for a bond may be computed in several ways. The current yield measures only the income portion of the return, while the yield to maturity takes both income and capital gains (or losses) into account. Therefore, the yield to maturity is superior to the current yield for most purposes. When a bond is callable by the issuer, the yield to call informs us about the return that would be earned if the bond is called at the next call date.

Interest rate risk comprises both price risk and reinvestment rate risk. If yields rise, then prices will fall. However, rising yields also mean that interest payments can be reinvested at higher returns. Duration can be used as a measure of the sensitivity of a bond's value to changes in interest rates. The longer the duration, the more the bond price will fluctuate in response to changing rates. Duration takes account of the term to maturity, the coupon rate, and the yield to determine interest rate sensitivity.

Convexity measures the curvature of the price/yield relationship. When comparing bonds with identical durations, more convexity equates to less risk. We can also use convexity to improve estimates of the change in a bond's price when yields change.

TABLE 9-2
FORMULAS USED IN THIS CHAPTER

Purpose	Formula	Page
Value of a bond on a coupon date	$V_B = Pmt\left[\dfrac{1 - \dfrac{1}{(1+k_B)^N}}{k_B}\right] + \dfrac{FV}{(1+k_B)^N}$	264
Current Yield	$CY = \dfrac{\text{Annual Pmt}}{V_B}$	272
Bank Discount Rate	$BDR = \dfrac{FV - P_0}{FV} \times \dfrac{360}{M}$	276
Bond Equivalent Yield	$BEY = BDY \times \dfrac{FV}{P_0} \times \dfrac{365}{360} = \dfrac{FV - P_0}{P_0} \times \dfrac{365}{M}$	277
Macaulay Duration	$D_{Mac} = \dfrac{\sum_{t=1}^{N} \dfrac{Pmt_t}{(1+YTM)^t}(t)}{V_B}$	289
Modified Duration	$D_{Mod} = \dfrac{D_{Mac}}{\left(1 + \dfrac{YTM}{m}\right)}$	291

TABLE 9-2 (CONTINUED)
FORMULAS USED IN THIS CHAPTER

Purpose	Formula	Page
% Change in Price using D_{Mod}	$\text{% Change in Price} \approx -D_{Mod} \times \Delta YTM$	291
Convexity	$C = \dfrac{\dfrac{1}{(1 + YTM)^2}\left[\displaystyle\sum_{t=1}^{N}\dfrac{Pmt_t}{(1 + YTM)^t}(t^2 + t)\right]}{V_B}$	294
% Change in Price using convexity	$\text{% Change in Price} \approx -D_{Mod} \times \Delta YTM + \dfrac{1}{2}C \times \Delta YTM^2$	295

TABLE 9-3
FUNCTIONS INTRODUCED IN THIS CHAPTER

Purpose	Function	Page
Round a number up, away from 0	ROUNDUP(*NUMBER*, *NUM_DIGITS*)	267
Value of a bond	PRICE(*SETTLEMENT*, *MATURITY*, *YLD*, *REDEMPTION*, *FREQUENCY*, *BASIS*)	268
Count Days using the 30/360 Method	DAYS360(*START_DATE*, *END_DATE*, *METHOD*)	270
Yield to maturity of a bond	YIELD(*SETTLEMENT*, *MATURITY*, *RATE*, *PR*, *REDEMPTION*, *FREQUENCY*, *BASIS*)	272
Calculate the Fraction of a Year using a Day Count Method	YEARFRAC(*START_DATE*, *END_DATE*, *METHOD*)	273
Bank Discount Rate	DISC(*SETTLEMENT*, *MATURITY*, *PR*, *REDEMPTION*, *BASIS*)	276
Bond Equivalent Yield	YIELDDISC(*SETTLEMENT*, *MATURITY*, *PR*, *REDEMPTION*, *BASIS*)	277

TABLE 9-3 (CONTINUED)
FUNCTIONS INTRODUCED IN THIS CHAPTER

Purpose	Function	Page
Find a date months after a specified date	EDATE(*START_DATE*, *MONTHS*)	284
Macaulay Duration	DURATION(*SETTLEMENT*, *MATURITY*, *COUPON*, *YLD*, *FREQUENCY*, *BASIS*)	289
Modified Duration	MDURATION(*SETTLEMENT*, *MATURITY*, *COUPON*, *YLD*, *FREQUENCY*, *BASIS*)	291
Convexity on a payment date	FAME_CONVEXITY(*SETTLEMENT*, *MATURITY*, *FV*, *COUPON*, *YLD*, *FREQUENCY*)	295

Problems

1. As an investor, you are considering an investment in the bonds of the Front Range Electric Company. The bonds pay interest quarterly, will mature in 12 years, and have a coupon rate of 3.25% on a face value of $1,000. Currently, the bonds are selling for $800.

    a. If your required return is 5.40% for bonds in this risk class, what is the highest price you would be willing to pay? (Use the **Pv** function.)

    b. What is the current yield of these bonds?

    c. What is the yield to maturity on these bonds if you purchase them at the current price? (Use the **RATE** function.)

    d. If you hold the bonds for one year, and interest rates do not change, what total rate of return will you earn, assuming that you pay the market price? Why is this different from the current yield and YTM?

    e. If the bonds can be called in three years with a call premium of 4% of the face value, what is the yield to call on these bonds? (Use the **RATE** function.)

    f. Now assume that the settlement date for your purchase is 7/30/2015, the maturity date is 7/30/2027, and the first call date is 7/30/2018. Using the **PRICE** and **YIELD** functions recalculate your answers to parts a, c, and d.

    g.   If market interest rates remain unchanged, do you think it is likely that the bond will be called in three years? Why or why not?

    h.   Create a chart that shows the relationship of the bond's price to your required return. Use a range of 0% to 15% in calculating the prices.

2.   After recently receiving a bonus, you have decided to add some bonds to your investment portfolio. You have narrowed your choice down to the following bonds (assume semiannual payments):

	Bond A	Bond B	Bond C
Settlement Date	2/15/2015	2/15/2015	2/15/2015
Maturity Date	8/15/2025	5/15/2035	6/15/2045
Coupon Rate	5.00%	7.50%	8.00%
Market Price	$987	$1,040	$1,098
Face Value	$1,000	$1,000	$1,000
Required Return	5.25%	7.00%	7.25%

    a.   Using the **PRICE** function, calculate the intrinsic value of each bond. Are any of the bonds currently undervalued? How much accrued interest would you have to pay for each bond?

    b.   Calculate the current yield of each bond. Is this the total return that you would earn each year? If you were on a fixed income, would you care about this number?

    c.   Using the **YIELD** function, calculate the yield to maturity of each bond using the current market prices. How do the YTMs compare to the current yields of the bonds?

    d.   Calculate the duration and modified duration of each bond. Create a chart that shows both measures versus term to maturity. Does duration increase linearly with term? If not, what relationship do you see?

    e.   Which bond would you rather own if you expect market rates to fall by 2% for all bonds? What if rates will rise by 2%? Why?

3. On April 10, 2014, the U.S. Treasury issued three T-Bills, and they had issued a one-year T-Bill on April 3, 2014:

	4-Week	13-Week	26-Week	52-Week
Issue Date	4/10/2014	4/10/2014	4/10/2014	4/3/2014
Maturity Date	5/8/2014	7/10/2014	10/9/2014	4/2/2015
Face Value per $100	100	100	100	100
Price per $100	99.998056	99.992417	99.974722	99.873611

a. Calculate the bank discount rate for each security using the formulas given in the chapter and using the **DISC** function.

b. Calculate the bond equivalent yield for each security using the formulas given in the chapter and using the **YIELDDISC** function.

c. Find the most recent T-Bill auction results from: https://www.treasurydirect.gov/instit/annceresult/annceresult.htm. Note that you will need to click the CUSIP numbers to get the auction prices. Repeat parts a and b.

Internet Exercise

1. Using the FINRA Advanced Bond Search tool (http://finra-markets.morningstar.com/BondCenter/Screener.jsp?type=advanced), find an AAA-rated noncallable corporate bond with at least 12 years to maturity. Click the link to get more detailed information on your bond, and then set up a worksheet to answer the following questions. Note that because we are using corporate bonds, the basis should be set to 0 (30/360).

a. Calculate the value of the bond using the **PRICE** function.

b. Calculate the current yield.

c. Calculate the yield to maturity using the **YIELD** function.

d. Calculate the duration of the bond using the **DURATION** function, and the modified duration using **MDURATION**. If interest rates rise by 1%, how much will the price change?

CHAPTER 10

The Cost of Capital

After studying this chapter, you should be able to:

1. Define "hurdle rate" and show how it relates to the firm's weighted average cost of capital (WACC).

2. Calculate the WACC using both book- and market-value weights.

3. Calculate component costs of capital with flotation costs and taxes.

4. Explain how and why a firm's WACC changes as total capital requirements change.

5. Use Excel to calculate the "break-points" in a firm's marginal WACC curve, and graph this curve in Excel.

Suppose that you are offered an investment opportunity that you believe will earn a return of 8%. If your required rate of return is 10%, would you make this investment? Clearly not. Even though you might earn a profit, in the accounting sense of the word, you wouldn't be making as much as required to make the investment attractive. Presumably, you have other investment alternatives, with similar risk, that will earn your required return. So, 10% is the opportunity cost of your funds, and you will reject investments that earn less than this rate. This rate is also known as your cost of capital, and corporations use the concept every day to make investment decisions.

Knowledge of a firm's cost of capital is vital if managers are to make appropriate decisions regarding the use of the firm's funds. Without this knowledge, poor investments may be made that actually reduce shareholder wealth. In this chapter, you will learn what the cost of capital is and how to calculate it.

The Appropriate "Hurdle" Rate

A firm's required rate of return on investments is often referred to as the *hurdle rate* because all projects must earn a rate of return high enough to clear this rate. Otherwise, while the project may earn an accounting profit (covering its operating and interest costs), it may not earn enough to cover its cost of equity. It will, therefore, earn a negative economic profit and reduce shareholder wealth. But what is the appropriate rate to use when evaluating investment opportunities? Let's look at an example:

> The managers of Rocky Mountain Motors (RMM) are considering the purchase of a new tract of land that will be held for one year. The purchase price of the land is $10,000. RMM's capital structure is currently made up of 40% debt, 10% preferred stock, and 50% common equity. Because this capital structure is considered to be optimal, any new financing will be raised in the same proportions. RMM must raise the new funds as indicated in Table 10-1.

TABLE 10-1
FUNDING FOR RMM'S LAND PURCHASE

Source of Funds	Amount	Dollar Cost	After-Tax Cost
Debt	$ 4,000	$ 280	7%
Preferred Stock	1,000	100	10%
Common Stock	5,000	600	12%
Total	10,000	980	9.8%

> Before making the decision, RMM's managers must determine what required rate of return will simultaneously satisfy all of their capital providers. What is the minimum rate of return that will accomplish this goal?

Looking at the third column of Table 10-1, it is clear that the total financing cost is $980. So, the project must generate at least $980 in excess of its cost in order to cover the financing costs. This represents a minimum required return of 9.8% on the investment of $10,000. Table 10-2 shows what would happen under three alternative rate of return scenarios.

TABLE 10-2
ALTERNATIVE SCENARIOS FOR RMM

Rate of Return	8%	9.8%	11%
Total Funds Available	$ 10,800	$ 10,980	$ 11,100
Less: Debt Costs	4,280	4,280	4,280
Less: Preferred Costs	1,100	1,100	1,100
Available to Common Shareholders	5,420	5,600	5,720

Recall that the common shareholders' required rate of return is 12% on the $5,000 that they provided. This means that the shareholders expect to get back at least $5,600. If RMM earns only 8%, the common shareholders will receive only $5,420, $180 less than required. We assume that the common shareholders have alternative investment opportunities (with equal risk) that would return 12%. Therefore, if the project can return only 8%, the best decision for managers to make would be to allow the common shareholders to hold on to their money. In other words, the project should be rejected.

On the other hand, if the project is expected to return 9.8%, the common shareholders will receive exactly the amount that they require. If the project returns 11%, they will be more than satisfied. Under these latter two scenarios the project should be accepted because shareholder wealth will be either increased by the amount required ($600) or increased by more than required ($720).[1]

The Weighted Average Cost of Capital

It still remains to determine, in a general way, what required rate of return will simultaneously satisfy all of the firm's stakeholders. Recall that 40% of RMM's funds were provided by the debt holders. Therefore, 40% of this minimum required rate of return must go to satisfy the debt holders. For the same reason, 10% of this minimum required rate of return must go to satisfy the preferred stockholders, and 50% will be required for the common stockholders.

In general, the minimum required rate of return must be a weighted average of the individual required rates of return on each form of capital provided. Therefore, we refer to this minimum required rate of return as the *weighted average cost of capital* (WACC). The WACC can be found as follows:

---

1. The difference between the amount that is available to the common shareholders and the amount required is known as the net present value (*NPV*). This concept will be explored in Chapter 11.

$$WACC = w_d k_d + w_P k_P + w_{cs} k_{cs} \qquad (10\text{-}1)$$

where the w's are the weights of each source of capital and the k's are the costs (required returns) for each source of capital. In the case of RMM, the WACC is:

$$WACC = 0.40(0.07) + 0.10(0.10) + 0.50(0.12) = 0.098 = 9.80\%$$

which is exactly the required return that we found earlier.

Determining the Weights

The weights that one uses in the calculation of the WACC will obviously affect the result. Therefore, an important question is, "Where do the weights come from?" Actually, there are three possible answers to this question. Perhaps the most obvious answer is to find the weights on the balance sheet.

The balance sheet weights (usually referred to as the *book-value* weights) can be obtained by the following procedure: Find the total long-term debt, total preferred equity, and the total common equity. Add together each of these to arrive at the grand total of the long-term sources of capital. Finally, divide each component by the grand total to discover the percentage that each source is of total capital. Table 10-3 shows these calculations for RMM.

TABLE 10-3
CALCULATION OF BOOK-VALUE WEIGHTS FOR RMM

Source of Capital	Total Book Value	Percentage of Total
Long-Term Debt	$ 400,000	40%
Preferred Equity	100,000	10%
Common Stock	500,000	50%
Grand Total	1,000,000	100%

The problem with book-value weights is that they represent the weights as they were when the securities were originally sold. That is, the book-value weights represent historical weights. The calculated WACC would better represent current reality if we used the present weights. Because the market constantly revalues the firm's securities, and we assume that the capital markets are efficient, we can find the weights by using the current market values of the securities.

The procedure for determining the *market-value weights* is similar to that used to find the book-value weights. First, determine the total market value of each type of security. Total the results and then divide the market value of each source of capital by the total to determine the weights.

TABLE 10-4
CALCULATION OF MARKET-VALUE WEIGHTS FOR RMM

Source	Price per Unit	Units	Total Market Value	Percentage of Total
Debt	$ 904.53	400	$ 361,812	31.14%
Preferred	100.00	1,000	100,000	8.61%
Common	70.00	10,000	700,000	60.25%
Totals			1,161,812	100.00%

Table 10-4 shows RMM's current capital structure in market-value terms. Note that, in market-value terms, the percentage of common equity has risen considerably, while the percentages of debt and preferred equity have fallen. Using these weights we can see that their WACC is:

$$WACC = 0.3114(0.07) + 0.0861(0.10) + 0.6025(0.12) = 0.1027 = 10.27\%$$

The third type of weights that may be used are the *target capital structure* weights. If management believes that the current capital structure is less than optimal, then they may have an optimal capital structure in mind. Presumably, over time, the firm will raise capital in a manner that ultimately results in the firm achieving its target capital structure. These target weights are ideal for calculating the WACC because we care most about the cost of capital over the life of a project.

In this example, the book-value WACC and the market-value WACC are quite close together. This is not always the case. Whenever possible, use the target weights or the market-value weights to determine the WACC.

WACC Calculations in Excel

We can easily set up a worksheet to do the calculations for the WACC as in Table 10-4. To do this, first copy the data from Table 10-4 into a new worksheet, starting with the headings in A1.

In column D we want to calculate the total market value of the securities, which is the price times the number of units outstanding. So, in D2 enter: =B2*C2 and copy the formula down to D3 and D4. Cell D5 should have the total market value of the securities, so enter: =Sum(D2:D4). In column E we need the percentage that each security represents of the total market value. These are the weights that we will use to calculate the WACC. In E2 enter: =D2/D$5 and copy down to E3 and E4. As a check, calculate the total in E5.

Next, we want a column for the after-tax costs of each source of capital and the WACC. In F1 enter the label: After-Tax Cost. Now, in F2:F4 enter the after-tax cost of each component from Table 10-1. We could calculate the WACC in F5 with the formula: =E2*F2+E3*F3+E4*F4. Even easier would be to use the **SUMPRODUCT** function, which is defined as:

$$\text{SUMPRODUCT}(\textit{ARRAY1}, \textit{ARRAY2}, \ldots)$$

where *ARRAY1*, *ARRAY2*, and so on, are up to 255 ranges. This function multiplies the corresponding values in each array and then adds together the results. It is perfect for calculating weighted averages. we can calculate the WACC in cell F5 with the formula: =SUMPRODUCT(E2:E4,F2:F4).[2]

The completed worksheet appears in Exhibit 10-1. Note that the WACC is exactly as we calculated earlier. You are encouraged to experiment by changing the market prices of the securities to see how the weights and the WACC change.

EXHIBIT 10-1
WORKSHEET TO CALCULATE RMM'S WACC

	A	B	C	D	E	F
1	Source	Price	Units	Total Market Value	% of Total	After-tax Cost
2	Debt	$904.53	400	$ 361,812	31.14%	7.00%
3	Preferred	100.00	1,000	100,000	8.61%	10.00%
4	Common	70.00	10,000	700,000	60.25%	12.00%
5	Totals			$ 1,161,812	100.00%	10.27%

Calculating the Component Costs

Up to this point, we have taken the component costs of capital as a given. In reality, these costs are anything but given, and, in fact, change continuously. How we calculate these costs is the subject of this section.

To begin, note that the obvious way of determining the required rates of return is to simply ask capital providers what their required rate of return is for the particular security that they

---

2. We could also use an array formula: =SUM(E2:E4*F2:F4); just remember to press Ctrl+Shift+Enter when entering this formula.

own. For all but the most closely held of firms, this would be exceedingly impractical and you would likely get some outlandish responses. However, there is a way by which we can accomplish the same end result.

Recall from Chapter 8 that the market value of a security is equal to its intrinsic value to the marginal investor. Further, if investors are rational, they will buy (sell) securities as the expected return rises above (falls below) their required return. Therefore, we can say that the investors in the firm "vote with their dollars" on the issue of the firm's cost of capital. This force operates in all markets.[3] So at any given moment, the price of a security will reflect the overall required rate of return for that security. All we need, then, is a method of converting the observed market prices of securities into required rates of return.

Because we have already discussed the valuation of securities (common stock, preferred stock, and bonds), you should recall that a major input was the investor's required rate of return. As we will see, we can simply take the market price as a given and then solve the valuation equations for the required rate of return.

The Cost of Common Equity

Because of complexities in the real world, finding a company's cost of common equity is not always straightforward. In this section, we will look at two approaches to this problem, both of which we have seen previously in other guises.

Using the Dividend Discount Model

Recall that a share of common stock is a perpetual security, which we assume will periodically pay a cash flow that grows over time. We have previously demonstrated that the present value of such a stream of cash flows is given by equation (8-3):

$$V_{CS} = \frac{D_0(1 + g)}{k_{CS} - g} = \frac{D_1}{k_{CS} - g}$$

assuming an infinite holding period and a constant rate of growth for the cash flows.

If we know the current market price of the stock, we can use this knowledge to solve for the common shareholder's required rate of return. Simple algebraic manipulation will reveal that this rate of return is given by:

$$k_{CS} = \frac{D_0(1 + g)}{V_{CS}} + g = \frac{D_1}{V_{CS}} + g \tag{10-2}$$

---

3. Anybody who isn't convinced should check the history of stock prices for companies such as Lehman Brothers and VeraSun Energy. They were falling long before the firms filed for bankruptcy.

Note that this equation says that the required rate of return on common equity is equal to the sum of the expected dividend yield and the growth rate of the dividend stream. We could also use any of the other common stock valuation models (see Chapter 8), though solving for the required return is slightly more complicated.

Using the CAPM

Not all common stocks will meet the assumptions of the dividend discount models. In particular, many companies do not pay dividends. An alternative approach to determining the cost of equity is to use the *Capital Asset Pricing Model* (CAPM).

The CAPM gives the expected rate of return for a security if we know the risk-free rate of interest, the market risk premium, and the riskiness of the security relative to the market portfolio (i.e., the security's beta). The CAPM, you will recall, is the equation for the security market line:

$$E(R_i) = R_f + \beta_i(E(R_m) - R_f)$$

Assuming that the stockholders are all price-takers, their expected return is the same as the firm's required rate of return.[4] Therefore, we can use the CAPM to determine the required rate of return on equity.

The Cost of Preferred Equity

Preferred stock, for valuation purposes, can be viewed as a special case of the common stock, with the growth rate of dividends equal to zero. We can carry this idea to the process of solving for the preferred stockholders' required rate of return. First, recall that the value of a share of preferred stock was given by equation (8-22):

$$V_P = \frac{D}{k_P}$$

As with common stock, we can algebraically manipulate this equation to solve for the required return if the market price is known:

$$k_P = \frac{D}{V_P} \qquad \text{(10-3)}$$

---

4. A price-taker cannot materially affect the price of an asset through individual buying or selling. This situation generally exists in the stock market because most investors are small when compared to the market value of the firm's common stock.

The Cost of Debt

Finding the cost of debt is more difficult than finding the cost of either preferred or common equity because there is no formula (except for trivial cases). Instead, we must use an algorithm. The process is similar: Get the market price of the security, and then find the discount rate that makes the present value of the expected future cash flows equal to the current price. This rate is the same as the yield to maturity (see page 272). However, we cannot directly solve for this discount rate. Instead, we must use an iterative trial-and-error process.

Recall that the value of a bond is given by equation (9-1):

$$V_B = Pmt \left[\frac{1 - \frac{1}{(1 + k_d)^N}}{k_d} \right] + \frac{FV}{(1 + k_d)^N}$$

The problem is to find k_d such that the equality holds between the left and right sides of the equation. Suppose that, as in Exhibit 10-1, the current price of RMM's bonds is $904.53, the coupon rate is 10%, the face value of the bonds is $1,000, and the bonds will mature in 10 years. If the bonds pay interest annually, our equation looks as follows:

$$904.53 = 100 \left[\frac{1 - \frac{1}{(1 + k_d)^{10}}}{k_d} \right] + \frac{1,000}{(1 + k_d)^{10}}$$

We must make an initial, but intelligent, guess as to the value of k_d. Because the bond is selling at a discount to its face value, we know that the yield to maturity (k_d) must be greater than the coupon rate. Therefore, our first guess should be something greater than 10%. If we choose 12% we will find that the price would be $886.99, which is lower than the actual price. Our first guess was incorrect, but we now know that the answer must lie between 10% and 12%. The next logical guess is 11%, which is the halfway point. Inserting this for k_d we get a price of $941.11, which is too high, but not by much. Further, we have narrowed the range of possible answers to those between 11% and 12%. Again, we choose the halfway point, 11.5%, as our next guess. This results in an answer of $913.48. Continuing this process we will eventually find the correct answer to be 11.67%.[5]

---

5. The method presented here is known as the bisection method. Briefly, the idea is to quickly bracket the solution and to then choose as the next approximation the answer that is exactly halfway between the previous possibilities. This method can lead to very rapid convergence to the solution if a good beginning guess is used.

Of course, as we will soon see, we can use Excel's **RATE** or **YIELD** function instead of manually solving for the before-tax cost of debt.

Making an Adjustment for Taxes

Notice that the answer that we found for the cost of debt, 11.67%, is not the same as that listed in Exhibit 10-1. Because interest is a tax-deductible expense, interest payments actually cost the firm less than the full amount of the payment. In this case, if RMM were to make an interest payment of $116.70, and the marginal tax rate is 40%, it would cost them only $70.02 (= $116.70 \times (1 - 0.40)$). Observe that $70.02 / 1,000 \approx 0.07$, or 7%, which is the after-tax cost of debt listed in Exhibit 10-1.

In general, we need to adjust the cost of debt to account for the deductibility of the interest expense by multiplying the before-tax cost of debt (i.e., the yield to maturity) by $1 - t$, where t is the marginal tax rate.[6] Note that we do not make the same adjustment for the cost of common or preferred equity because dividends are not tax deductible.

Using Excel to Calculate the Component Costs

A general principle that we have relied on in constructing our worksheets is that we should make Excel do the calculations whenever possible. We will now make changes to our worksheet in Exhibit 10-1 to allow Excel to calculate the component costs of capital.

The After-Tax Cost of Debt

We cannot calculate any of the component costs on our worksheet without adding some additional information. We will first add information which will be used to calculate the after-tax cost of debt. Beginning in A7 with the label: Additional Bond Data, add the information from Table 10-5 into your worksheet. For simplicity, we assume that the bonds pay interest annually.

---

6. This is just a close approximation, but close enough for most purposes because the cost of capital is an estimate anyway. It would be more accurate to use the after-tax cash flows in the equation. This will result in the after-tax cost of debt with no adjustment required and will differ slightly from that given earlier. Due to uncertainty regarding future tax rates, this is unlikely to be more "exact."

TABLE 10-5
ADDITIONAL DATA FOR CALCULATING THE COST OF DEBT FOR RMM

Additional Bond Data	
Tax Rate	40%
Coupon Rate	10%
Face Value	$1,000
Maturity	10

With this information entered, we now need a function to find the cost of debt. Excel provides two built-in functions that will do the job: **RATE** and **YIELD**. We have already seen both of these functions. Because **YIELD** (defined on page 272) requires more information than we have supplied for this example, we will use **RATE**. Recall that **RATE**, which works only on a payment date, will solve for the yield for an annuity-type stream of cash flows and allows for a different present value and future value. Specifically, **RATE** is defined as:

RATE(*NPER*, *PMT*, *PV*, *FV*, *TYPE*, *GUESS*)

We will be supplying both a *PV* and an *FV*. Specifically, *PV* is the current bond price and *FV* is the face value of the bond. In F2 enter the **RATE** function as: =RATE(B11,B9*B10, -B2,B10). The result is 11.67%, which we found to be the pre-tax cost of debt. Remember that we must also make an adjustment for taxes, so we need to multiply by 1 − *t*. The final form of the formula in F2 then is: =RATE(B11,B9*B10,-B2,B10)*(1-B8), and the result is 7.00%. If we knew the settlement and maturity dates, then the **YIELD** function would be a better choice because it works on any date. With the new bond information, your worksheet should resemble Exhibit 10-2.

EXHIBIT 10-2
RMM WORKSHEET WITH ADDITIONAL BOND DATA

	A	B	C	D	E	F
1	Source	Price	Units	Total Market Value	% of Total	After-tax Cost
2	Debt	$ 904.53	400	$ 361,812	31.14%	7.00%
3	Preferred	100.00	1,000	100,000	8.61%	10.00%
4	Common	70.00	10,000	700,000	60.25%	12.00%
5	Totals			$ 1,161,812	100.00%	10.27%
6						
7	**Additional Bond Data**					
8	Tax Rate	40%				
9	Coupon Rate	10%				
10	Face Value	$ 1,000				
11	Maturity	10				

The Cost of Preferred Stock

Compared to calculating the after-tax cost of debt, finding the cost of preferred stock is easy. We need to add only one piece of information: the preferred dividend. In C7 type: Additional Preferred Data. In C8 type: Dividend and in D8 enter: 10.

We know from equation (10-3) that we need to divide the preferred dividend by the current price of the stock. Therefore, the equation in F3 is: =D8/B3.

The Cost of Common Stock

To calculate the cost of common stock, we need to know the most recent dividend and the dividend growth rate in addition to the current market price of the stock. In E7 type: Additional Common Data. In E8 type: Dividend 0 and in F8 enter: 3.96. In E9 enter the label: Growth Rate and in F9 enter: 6%.

Finally, we will use equation (10-2) to calculate the cost of common stock in F4. Because we know the most recent dividend (D_0) we need to multiply that by $1 + g$. The formula in F4 is: =(F8*(1+F9))/B4+F9, and the result is 12% as we found earlier.

As you will see, we have not yet completed the calculation of the component costs for RMM. We have left out one crucial piece which we will discuss in the next section. At this point, your worksheet should resemble that in Exhibit 10-3.

EXHIBIT 10-3
RMM COST OF CAPITAL WORKSHEET

	A	B	C	D	E	F
1	Source	Price	Units	Total Market Value	% of Total	After-tax Cost
2	Debt	$904.53	400	$ 361,812	31.14%	7.00%
3	Preferred	100.00	1,000	100,000	8.61%	10.00%
4	Common	70.00	10,000	700,000	60.25%	12.00%
5	Totals			$ 1,161,812	100.00%	10.27%
6						
7	**Additional Bond Data**		**Additional Preferred Data**		**Additional Common Data**	
8	Tax Rate	40%	Dividend	$ 10.00	Dividend 0	$ 3.96
9	Coupon Rate	10%			Growth Rate	6%
10	Face Value	$ 1,000				
11	Maturity	10				

The Role of Flotation Costs

Any action that a corporation takes has costs associated with it. Up to this point, we have implicitly assumed that securities can be issued without cost, but this is not the case. Selling securities directly to the public is a complicated procedure, generally requiring a lot of management time as well as the services of an *investment bank*. An investment bank is a firm that serves as an intermediary between the issuing firm and the public, which usually buys the securities from the firm at a discount (the *underwriting spread*). In addition to forming the underwriting syndicate to sell the securities, the investment banker also functions as a consultant to the firm. As a consultant, the investment banker usually advises the firm on the pricing of the issue and is responsible for preparing the registration statement for the Securities and Exchange Commission (SEC).

The cost of the investment banker's services and other costs of issuance are referred to as *flotation costs*. (The term derives from the fact that the process of selling a new issue is generally referred to as floating a new issue.) Flotation costs add to the total cost of the new securities to the firm, so we must increase the component cost of capital to account for them.

There are two methods of accounting for flotation costs. The most popular method is the cost of capital adjustment. Under this method, the market price of new securities is *decreased* by the per unit flotation costs. This results in the net amount that the company receives from the sale of the securities. The component costs are then calculated in the usual way except that the net amount received, not the market price, is used in the equation.

The second, less common, method is the investment cost adjustment. Under this methodology, we increase the initial outlay for the project under consideration to account for the total flotation costs. Component costs are then calculated as we did earlier. The primary disadvantage of this technique is that, because it assigns all flotation costs to one project, it implicitly assumes that the securities used to finance a project will be retired when the project is completed.[7]

Because it is more common, and its assumptions are more realistic, we will use the cost of capital adjustment technique. When flotation costs are included in the analysis, the equations for the component costs are given in Table 10-6.

---

7. For more information on both methods, see E. F. Brigham and L. C. Gapenski, "Flotation Cost Adjustments," *Financial Practice and Education*, Vol. 1, No. 2, Fall/Winter 1991, pp. 29–34.

TABLE 10-6
COST OF CAPITAL EQUATIONS WITH FLOTATION COST ADJUSTMENT

Component	Equation*
Cost of new common equity	$k_{CS} = \dfrac{D_0(1+g)}{V_{CS}-f} + g = \dfrac{D_1}{V_{CS}-f} + g$
Cost of preferred equity	$k_P = \dfrac{D}{V_P-f}$
Pre-tax cost of debt (solve for k_d)	$V_B - f = Pmt\left[\dfrac{1 - \dfrac{1}{(1+k_d)^N}}{k_d}\right] + \dfrac{FV}{(1+k_d)^N}$

* In these equations, the flotation costs (*f*) are a dollar amount per unit. It is also common for flotation costs to be stated as a percentage of the unit price.

Adding Flotation Costs to Our Worksheet

We can easily incorporate the adjustment for flotation costs into our worksheet. All that we need to do is change the references to the current price in each of our formulas to the current price minus the per unit flotation costs. These costs are given in Table 10-7.

TABLE 10-7
FLOTATION COSTS AS A PERCENTAGE OF SELLING PRICE FOR RMM

Security	Flotation Cost
Bonds	1%
Preferred Stock	2%
Common Stock	5%

Enter the information from Table 10-7 into your worksheet. For each security, we have added the information at the end of the "Additional information" section. For example, in A12 enter: Flotation Cost and then in B12 enter: 1%, which is the flotation cost for bonds. Add similar entries for preferred and common stock.

To account for flotation costs, change your formulas to the following:

F2   =RATE(B11,B9*B10,-B2*(1-B12),B10)*(1-B8)

F3   =D8/(B3*(1-D9))

F4   =(F8*(1+F9))/(B4*(1-F10))+F9

Once these changes have been made, you will notice that the cost of each component has risen. The overall WACC has increased from 10.27% to 10.51% as a result of the flotation costs. Your worksheet should now resemble the one shown in Exhibit 10-4.

EXHIBIT 10-4
COST OF CAPITAL WORKSHEET WITH FLOTATION COSTS

	A	B	C	D	E	F
1	Source	Price	Units	Total Market Value	% of Total	After-tax Cost
2	Debt	$ 904.53	400 $	361,812	31.14%	7.10%
3	Preferred	100.00	1,000	100,000	8.61%	10.20%
4	Common	70.00	10,000	700,000	60.25%	12.31%
5	Totals			$ 1,161,812	100.00%	10.51%
6						
7	**Additional Bond Data**		**Additional Preferred Data**		**Additional Common Data**	
8	Tax Rate	40%	Dividend	$ 10.00	Dividend 0	$ 3.96
9	Coupon Rate	10%	Flotation Cost	2%	Growth Rate	6%
10	Face Value	$1,000.00			Flotation Cost	5%
11	Maturity	10				
12	Flotation Cost	1%				

The Cost of Retained Earnings

We have shown how to calculate the required returns for purchasers of new common equity, preferred stock, and bonds, but firms also have another source of long-term capital: retained earnings. Is there a cost to such internally generated funding, or is it free? Consider that managers generally have two options as to what they do with the firm's internally generated funds. They can either reinvest them in profitable projects or return them to the shareholders in the form of dividends or a share repurchase. Because these funds belong to the common shareholders alone, the definition of a "profitable project" is one that earns at least the common shareholder's required rate of return. If these funds will not be invested to earn at least this return, they should be returned to the common shareholders. So there is a cost (an opportunity cost) to internally generated funds: the cost of common equity.

Note that the only difference between retained earnings (internally generated common equity) and new common equity is that the firm must pay flotation costs on the sale of new common equity. Because no flotation costs are paid for retained earnings, we can find the cost of retained earnings in the same way we did before learning about flotation costs. In other words,

$$k_{RE} = \frac{D_0(1 + g)}{V_{CS}} + g = \frac{D_1}{V_{CS}} + g \qquad \text{(10-4)}$$

This notion of an opportunity cost for retained earnings is important for a couple of reasons. Most importantly, managers should be disabused of the notion that the funds on hand are "free." As you now know, there is a cost to these funds, and it should be accounted for when making decisions. In addition, there may be times when a project that otherwise appears to be profitable is really unprofitable when the cost of retained earnings is correctly accounted for. Accepting such a project is contrary to the principle of shareholder wealth maximization and will result in the firm's stock price falling.

The Marginal WACC Curve

A firm's WACC is not constant. Changes can occur in the WACC for a number of reasons. As a firm raises more and more new capital, its WACC will likely increase due to an increase in supply relative to demand for the firm's securities. Furthermore, total flotation costs may increase as more capital is raised. Additionally, no firm has an unlimited supply of projects that will return more than the cost of capital, so the risk that new funds will be invested unprofitably increases.

We will see in Chapter 11 that these increases in the WACC play an important role in determining the firm's optimal capital budget. For the remainder of this chapter, we will concentrate on determining the WACC at varying levels of total capital.

Finding the Break-Points

We can model a firm's marginal WACC curve with a *step function*. This type of function resembles a staircase when plotted. They are commonly used as a linear (though discontinuous) approximation to nonlinear functions. The accuracy of the approximation improves as the number of steps increases.

Estimating the marginal WACC (MCC) curve is a two-step process:

1. Determine the levels of total capital at which the marginal WACC is expected to increase. These points are referred to as *break-points*.

2. Determine the marginal WACC at each break-point.

Figure 10-1 illustrates what a marginal WACC curve might look like for RMM. Notice that the break-points are measured in terms of dollars of total capital. In this section, we will estimate where these break-points are likely to occur and the WACC at the break-points.

FIGURE 10-1
THE MARGINAL WACC (MCC) CURVE AS A STEP FUNCTION

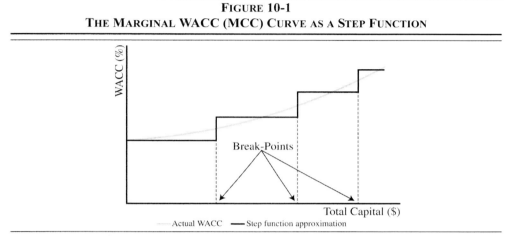

After consulting with their investment bankers, the managers of RMM have determined that they can raise new money at the costs indicated in Table 10-8. Open a new worksheet and enter the data from Table 10-8 beginning in cell A1. The percentages in the "% of Total" column should be referenced from the worksheet that was created for Exhibit 10-4.

TABLE 10-8
ROCKY MOUNTAIN MOTORS INFORMATION

Source	% of Total	Amounts That Can Be Sold	Marginal After-Tax Cost
Common	60.25%	Up to 100,000	12.31%
		100,001 to 500,000	15.00%
		More than 500,000	17.00%
Preferred	8.61%	Up to 50,000	10.20%
		More than 50,000	13.00%
Debt	31.14%	Up to 250,000	7.10%
		More than 250,000	8.00%

Note that you should enter just the numbers from the "Amounts That Can Be Sold" column. You can define custom formats, so the numbers are displayed with the text. This allows us to have the text and still use the numbers for the calculations that follow. For example, you can format the first cell as "Up to "#,##0 (which will cause the number to be displayed as shown in the table). The second number (500,000) can be formatted with "100,001 to "#,##0 so that it will display as shown.

RMM feels that its current capital structure is optimal, so any new money will be raised in the same proportions. For example, if the firm decides to raise $200,000 in total capital, then $120,500 (60.25% of $200,000) will come from common equity, $62,280 (31.14%) will be debt, and $17,220 (8.61%) will be preferred equity.

Using the information in Table 10-8, we can determine the location of the break-points in RMM's marginal WACC curve. To do this, first realize that a break will occur whenever the cost of an individual source of capital changes because that will cause the WACC to rise. There will be a break-point associated with the issuance of $100,000 in common stock, for example. But recall that break-points are measured in dollars of total capital. So the question is, "How do we convert this $100,000 in common stock into the amount of total capital?"

Because the capital will be raised in constant proportions, we can use the following equation:

$$\$ \text{ Total Capital } = \frac{\$ \text{ Common Stock}}{\% \text{ Common Stock}} \tag{10-5}$$

In this case, we can see that if RMM raised $100,000 in new common stock, then it must have raised $165,973 in total capital. Using equation (10-5):

$$\$165,973 \approx \frac{\$100,000}{0.6025}$$

We can use this information to see that if RMM issued $100,000 in new common stock, then it must also have raised $51,684 (= $165,973 × 0.3114) in new debt, and $14,290 (= $165,973 × 0.0861) in new preferred stock.

To locate all of the break-points, all we need to do is find the points at which the cost of each source of capital changes, and then convert those into dollars of total capital using the same idea as expressed in equation (10-5).

Table 10-9, using the information from Table 10-8, shows how to find these break-points.

TABLE 10-9
FINDING THE BREAK-POINTS IN RMM'S MARGINAL WACC CURVE

Source	Calculation*	Break-Point
Common Stock	100,000 / 0.6025	$ 165,973
Common Stock	500,000 / 0.6025	829,866
Preferred Stock	50,000 / 0.0861	580,906
Debt	250,000 / 0.3114	802,773

* The weights are rounded to four decimal places. The actual
calculation uses the weights as calculated in Exhibit 10-4.

In your worksheet enter Break-Points in cell E1. The first break-point is associated with the $100,000 level of new common stock. In E2, enter the formula =C2/B$2. The result is $165,973, exactly as we found in Table 10-9. Copy this formula to E3. In E5 the formula is: =C5/B$5. In E7 your formula will be: =C7/$B$7. Note that the denominator changes as the source of the break-point changes.

The next step is to determine the WACC at each of the break-points. To find the WACC we must convert each break-point into its components and then determine the cost of each component. There are a number of ways we might approach this problem in the worksheet. Because we would ultimately like to generate a chart of the marginal WACC, we will set up a table that shows the amount of total capital, the cost of each component, and the WACC at that level of total capital.

Begin by entering the labels in A10:E10. In A10 enter: Total Capital. In B10: Cost of Equity. In C10: Cost of Preferred. In D10: Cost of Debt. In E10: WACC. Now, in A11, enter 0 for the starting total capital. In A12, we want to enter the first break-point. We could just reference E2, which has the smallest break-point, but that may not be the smallest of the break-points if the weights or other data change. To ensure that A12 always has the smallest break-point, we should use the SMALL function:

SMALL($ARRAY$, K)

where $ARRAY$ is a range of numbers and K is the position that you want to return. In A12, enter: =SMALL(E2:E7,1) to get the smallest of the break-points. In A13, enter =SMALL(E2:E7,2) to get the second smallest break-point, and so on. To finish this series with a round number, in A16 enter: =ROUNDUP(MAX(E2:E7),-5). This will round the largest break-point up to the next $100,000.

Next, we will determine the cost of each source for each level of total capital. In B11, we need to find the cost of equity at $0 of total capital. To facilitate later copying, we will set up a nested **IF** statement. In this case, the formula is: =IF(A11*$B$2<=$C$2,$D$2, IF(A11*$B$2<=$C$3,$D$3,$D$4)). In words, this formula says, "If the amount of total capital (in A11) times the percentage of common stock (B2) is less than or equal to $100,000 (C2) then the cost is 12.31% (D2). Otherwise, if the amount is less than or equal to $500,000 then the cost is 15% (D3). Otherwise, the cost is 17% (D4)."

We use similar, but less complicated, formulas to determine the cost of preferred stock and debt at each level of total capital. For preferred stock, enter the formula: =IF(A11*$B$5 <=$C$5,$D$5,$D$6) into C11. In D11 enter the formula: =IF(A11*$B$7<=$C$7, $D$7,$D$8) to determine the appropriate cost of debt. At this point, the cost of each source of funds should be at its lowest level.

Finally, we can calculate the marginal WACC (in E11), with the formula: =$B$2*B11+ $B$5*C11+$B$7*D11. This formula calculates a weighted average of the costs calculated in B11:D11. Make sure that you have entered the formulas exactly as given, and then copy them down through B12:E16. Your worksheet should now match the one in Exhibit 10-5.

EXHIBIT 10-5
THE WACC AT EACH BREAK-POINT

	A	B	C	D	E
1	**Source**	**% of Total**	**Max Level**	**After-tax Cost**	**Break-points**
2	Common	60.25%	Up to 100,000	12.31%	165,973
3			100,001 500,000	15.00%	829,866
4			More than 500,000	17.00%	
5	Preferred	8.61%	Up to 50,000	10.20%	580,906
6			More than 50,000	13.00%	
7	Debt	31.14%	Up to 250,000	7.10%	802,773
8			More than 250,000	8.00%	
9					
10	**Total Capital**	**Cost of Equity**	**Cost of Preferred**	**Cost of Debt**	**WACC**
11	0	12.31%	10.20%	7.10%	10.51%
12	165,973	12.31%	10.20%	7.10%	10.51%
13	580,906	15.00%	10.20%	7.10%	12.13%
14	802,773	15.00%	13.00%	7.10%	12.37%
15	829,866	15.00%	13.00%	8.00%	12.65%
16	900,000	17.00%	13.00%	8.00%	13.85%

Creating the Marginal WACC Chart

Recall that we want to create a chart of the marginal cost of capital, approximated by a step function. To create this chart, we need the WACCs and the break-points created earlier. Select A10:A16 and then hold down the Ctrl key while selecting E10:E16. Insert a scatter chart with straight lines.[8] We don't need, or want, markers for this chart.

FIGURE 10-2
THE MARGINAL WACC CURVE FOR RMM

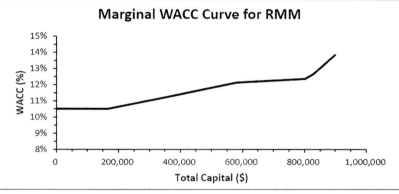

The chart in Figure 10-2 obviously does not depict a perfect step function, as shown in Figure 10-1. With a little trick, we can easily change this chart into a perfect step function.

First, realize that we want the line to be perfectly vertical at each break-point. In order to do that, we must have two y values (WACC) corresponding to each particular x value (amount of total capital). However, if we use the exact break-point twice, then our calculated WACC will be the same. To get the WACC to increase, we need to increase the break-point by a very tiny amount. To see this, select row 13 and insert a new row. Now, in A13 enter the formula: =A12+0.01. Then copy the other formulas in row 12 down to row 13. The WACC in E13 is now higher than that in E12. Take a look at your chart and notice that you now have a nice step for the first break-point. If you zoomed far enough into the chart, you would see that the step is slightly sloped, but at normal size the slope isn't visible.

Repeat these steps with the other three break-points, and then your chart should look like the one in Exhibit 10-6.

---

8. The most common error in making this type of chart correctly is choosing the wrong type of scatter chart. If you choose a scatter chart with smoothed lines, the result will be a little too smooth. Try it. Also note that you will not get a good step function using a line chart.

EXHIBIT 10-6
RMM's MARGINAL WACC CURVE AS A STEP FUNCTION

	A	B	C	D	E
	A	**B**	**C**	**D**	**E**
10	**Total Capital**	**Cost of Equity**	**Cost of Preferred**	**Cost of Debt**	**WACC**
11	0	12.31%	10.20%	7.10%	10.51%
12	165,973	12.31%	10.20%	7.10%	10.51%
13	165,973	15.00%	10.20%	7.10%	12.13%
14	580,906	15.00%	10.20%	7.10%	12.13%
15	580,906	15.00%	13.00%	7.10%	12.37%
16	802,773	15.00%	13.00%	7.10%	12.37%
17	802,773	15.00%	13.00%	8.00%	12.65%
18	829,866	15.00%	13.00%	8.00%	12.65%
19	829,866	17.00%	13.00%	8.00%	13.85%
20	900,000	17.00%	13.00%	8.00%	13.85%

Marginal WACC Curve for RMM

Summary

We began this chapter with a discussion of the appropriate required rate of return to use in the evaluation of a company's scarce capital resources. We demonstrated that a weighted average of the cost of each source of capital would be sufficient to simultaneously satisfy all of the providers of capital. In addition, we showed that the costs of the sources of capital can be found by simply inverting the valuation equations from Chapters 8 and 9 and including flotation costs (except for retained earnings). Finally, we saw that the firm's marginal WACC changes as the amount of total capital changes. We showed how to determine the location of the break-points and how to plot the marginal WACC curve as a step function.

☑ Check Box After copying Highlighted Notes

TABLE 10-10
FUNCTIONS INTRODUCED IN THIS CHAPTER

Purpose	Function	Page
Calculate the sum of the product of corresponding cells	SUMPRODUCT(*ARRAY1*, *ARRAY2*, ...)	308
Return the *K*th smallest number in a range	SMALL(*ARRAY*, *K*)	321

Problems

1. The Dempere Imports Company's EPS in 2014 was $1.85, and in 2009 it was $1.12. The company's payout ratio is 40%, and the stock is currently valued at $62.35. Flotation costs for new equity will be 12%. Net income in 2015 is expected to be $15 million.

    The company's investment banker estimates that it could sell 10-year semiannual bonds with a coupon rate of 7%. The face value would be $1,000 and the flotation costs for a bond issue would be 3%. The market-value weights of the firm's debt and equity are 30% and 70%, respectively. The firm faces a 35% tax rate.

    a. Based on the five-year track record, what is Dempere's EPS growth rate? What will the dividend be in 2015?

    b. Calculate the firm's cost of retained earnings and the cost of new common equity.

    c. Calculate the break-point associated with retained earnings.

    d. What is the firm's after-tax cost of new debt?

    e. If Dempere's after-tax cost of debt is 6%, what is the WACC with retained earnings? With new common equity?

    f. Create a scatter chart that shows the firm's marginal WACC as a step function. The x-axis should go to at least $20 million. Be sure to fully label the chart, including a data label with leader lines that shows the value of the break-point.

2. TRM Consulting Services currently has the following capital structure:

Source	Book Value	Quantity
Common Stock	$ 25,000,000	1,250,000
Preferred Stock	5,000,000	100,000
Debt	8,600,000	8,600

New debt would mature on June 30, 2040, have a coupon rate of 8%, and would be sold for their par value of $1,000. The bonds pay interest semiannually, and flotation costs would be 2% of the selling price. The bonds would be issued on June 30, 2015.

The preferred stock pays a $7 dividend annually and is currently valued at $67.50 per share. Flotation costs on new preferred equity would be 4% of the price.

The common stock, which can be bought for $28.00, has experienced a 6% annual growth rate in dividends and is expected to pay a $1.60 dividend next year. Flotation costs on new common equity would be 8%. The stock has a beta of 1.25, the risk-free rate is 3%, and the expected market risk premium is 7%.

In addition, the firm expects to generate $150,000 of retained earnings. Assume that TRM's marginal tax rate is 35%.

a. Set up a worksheet with all of the data from the problem in a well-organized input area.

b. Calculate the book-value weights for each source of capital.

c. Calculate the market-value weights for each source of capital.

d. Calculate the component costs of capital (i.e., debt, preferred equity, retained earnings, and new common equity). Use the **YIELD** function (see page 277) when finding the after-tax cost of debt. Use the CAPM to find the cost of retained earnings, and the constant growth model for new common equity.

e. Calculate the weighted average costs of capital using both the market-value and book-value weights with retained earnings and also new common equity.

3. Suppose that TRM Consulting Services has discussed its need for capital with its investment bankers. The bankers have estimated that TRM can raise new funds in the capital markets under the following conditions:

Source	Range	After-Tax Cost
Retained Earnings	Up to 150,000	11.75%
Common Equity	Up to 1,000,000	12.21%
	1,000,001 to 3,000,000	12.80%
	More than 3,000,000	13.20%
Preferred Equity	Up to 200,000	10.80%
	More than 200,000	11.05%
Debt	Up to 1,000,000	5.32%
	1,000,001 to 2,000,000	6.00%
	More than 2,000,000	6.50%

a. Using the information from the previous problem, calculate each of the break-points, including the break-point due to retained earnings.

b. Create a chart of TRM's marginal WACC curve using the market-value weights. Make sure that it is a perfect step function.

Internet Exercise

1. Using the Yahoo! Finance Web site (http://finance.yahoo.com) get the current price and five-year dividend history for PPG Industries, Inc. (NYSE: PPG). Use the same procedure as in the Internet Exercise of Chapter 8 to gather this data. In addition, get the beta for PPG from its profile page on Yahoo! Finance, and the five-year U.S. Treasury yield (ticker: ^FVX). Note that you will need to divide the index value by 100 to get the yield.

a. Calculate the annualized dividend growth rate from the five-year dividend history using the same procedure as in Chapter 8.

b. Using the stock's current price, dividend, and growth rate, calculate the cost of retained earnings for PPG.

c. Assuming that the average market return over the next five years will be 8%, calculate the cost of retained earnings using the CAPM. Use the actual beta and five-year Treasury yield (risk-free rate) in the model.

d. To get your final estimate of the cost of retained earnings, simply average the results from parts b and c.

CHAPTER 11

Capital Budgeting

After studying this chapter, you should be able to:

1. *Identify the relevant cash flows in capital budgeting.*

2. *Demonstrate the use of Excel in calculating the after-tax cash flows used as inputs to the various decision-making techniques.*

3. *Calculate depreciation expense using the straight-line method and MACRS.*

4. *Compare and contrast the six major capital budgeting decision techniques (payback period, discounted payback, NPV, PI, IRR, and MIRR).*

5. *Explain scenario analysis, and show how it can be done in Excel.*

6. *Use Solver to find the firm's optimal capital budget under capital rationing.*

Capital budgeting is the term used to describe the process of determining how a firm should allocate scarce capital resources to available long-term investment opportunities. Some of these opportunities are expected to be profitable, while others are not. Because the goal of the firm is to maximize shareholder's wealth, the financial manager is responsible for selecting only those investments that are expected to increase shareholder wealth. As we will see, capital budgeting is simply a comparison of costs versus benefits; and only projects where the benefit equals or exceeds the cost should be accepted.

The techniques that you will learn in this chapter have wide applicability beyond corporate asset management. Lease analysis, bond refunding decisions, mergers and acquisition analysis, corporate restructuring, and new product decisions are all examples of where these techniques are used. On a more personal level, decisions regarding mortgage refinancing, renting versus buying, and choosing a credit card are but a few examples of where these techniques are useful.

On the surface, capital budgeting decisions are simple. If the benefits exceed the costs, then the project should be accepted, otherwise it should be rejected. Unfortunately, quantifying costs and benefits is not always straightforward. We will examine this process in this chapter and then extend it to decision making under conditions of uncertainty in Chapter 12.

Estimating the Cash Flows

Before we can determine whether an investment will increase shareholder wealth or not, we need to estimate the cash flows that it will generate. Although this is usually easier said than done, there are some general guidelines to keep in mind. There are two important conditions that a cash flow must meet in order to be included in our analysis.

The cash flows must be:

1. *Incremental*—The cash flows must be in addition to those that the firm already has. For example, a firm may be considering an addition to an existing product line. But the new product may cause some current customers to switch from another of the firm's products. In this case, we must consider both the cash flow increase from the new product and the cash flow decrease from the existing product. In other words, only the net new cash flows are considered.

2. *After-tax*—The cash flows must be considered on an after-tax basis. The shareholders are not concerned with before-tax cash flows because they can't be reinvested or paid out as dividends until the taxes have been paid. Remember that the relevant tax rate is the marginal tax rate because we are evaluating additional cash flows.

But we should disregard cash flows that are:

1. *Sunk costs*—These are cash flows that have occurred in the past and cannot be recovered, regardless of the investment decision. Because value is defined as the present value of the expected *future* cash flows, we are only concerned with the future cash flows. Therefore, sunk costs are irrelevant for capital budgeting purposes.

2. *Financing costs*—The cost of financing is obviously important in the analysis, but it will be implicitly included in the discount rate used to evaluate the profitability of the project. Explicitly including the dollar

amount of financing costs (e.g., extra interest expense) would amount to double-counting. For example, suppose that you discovered an investment that promised a sure 15% return. If you could borrow money at 10% to finance the purchase of this investment, it obviously makes sense because you will earn 5% over your cost. Notice that the dollar interest cost is implicitly included because you must earn at least 10% to cover your financing costs.

With these points in mind, we can move on to discuss the estimation of the relevant cash flows. We will classify all cash flows as a part of one of the three groups illustrated in Figure 11-1.

FIGURE 11-1
TIMELINE ILLUSTRATING PROJECT CASH FLOWS

The Initial Outlay

The *initial outlay* (abbreviated IO in Figure 11-1) represents the net up-front cost of the project. Though we will presume that the initial outlay occurs at time period 0 (today), there are many cases, perhaps most, in which the cost of a project is spread out over several periods. For example, the contractor in large construction projects is usually paid some percentage when construction begins, with additional monies being paid as the project reaches various stages of completion. Furthermore, there is usually some delay between the analysis phase of a project and its implementation. So to be technically correct, the initial outlay actually occurs over some near-term future time period.

The initial outlay comprises several cash flows. It is impossible to enumerate all of the components for all possible projects, but we will provide some basic principles. The most obvious is the cash outlay required to purchase the project. The prices of a piece of machinery or of a building are clear examples. There are other components however. Any shipping expenses, labor costs to install machinery, or initial employee training costs should be included. Together, the costs to get a project up and running are referred to as the *depreciable base* for the project because this is the amount that we will depreciate over the life of the project.

There may also be cash flows that serve to reduce the initial outlay. For example, in a replacement decision (e.g., replacing an existing machine with a newer model) there is often some salvage value for the old machine. This amount will be deducted from the initial outlay. However, there may be taxes associated with the sale of the old equipment. Whenever an asset is sold for an amount that differs from its book value, there are tax consequences. If an asset is sold for more than its book value, tax is owed on the difference. If it is sold for less than book value, the difference is used to offset the firm's taxable income, thus resulting in a tax savings. These extra taxes (tax savings) will increase (decrease) the initial outlay.

Finally, there may be costs that are not at all obvious. For example, suppose that a company is considering an investment in a new machine that is substantially faster than the older model currently being used. Because of the extra speed, the company may find that it needs to increase its investment in raw materials. The portion of the cost of these extra raw materials that is financed by long-term sources of funds should be included as an increase in the initial outlay because they would not be purchased unless the project is undertaken. This cost is referred to as the change in net operating working capital (NOWC).

The calculation of the initial outlay can be summarized by the following equation:

IO = Price of Project + Shipping + Installation + Training – (Salvage Value – Taxes on Salvage) + ΔNOWC

Again, every project is different. The formula given is merely a summary of the possible components of the initial outlay. The key is to focus on any nonoperating cash flows that occur at the beginning of the project's life.

The Annual After-Tax Operating Cash Flows

Calculating the initial outlay, as complicated as it may appear, is relatively easy compared with accurately calculating the annual after-tax operating cash flows (ATCF). The reason is that we really can't be sure of the cash flows in the future. For the time being, we will assume that we do know exactly what the future cash flows will be, and in Chapter 12 we will consider the complications of uncertainty.

Generally, the annual after-tax cash flows are made up of five components, but not necessarily all five:

1. *Additional revenue*—New or improved products can lead to net new revenue. Remember that we must consider only the incremental revenues.

2. *Cost savings*—There may be some savings that will accompany the acceptance of a project. For example, the firm may decide to replace a manually operated machine with a fully automated version. Part of the savings would be the salary and benefits of the operators of the old machine. Other savings might come from lower maintenance costs, lower power consumption, or fewer defects.

3. *Additional expenses*—Instead of purchasing a fully automated machine, the firm might opt for a process that is more labor intensive. This would allow the company more flexibility to adjust to changes in the market, but the extra labor costs must be considered when determining the cash flows.

4. *Investments in net operating working capital*—If sales are expected to increase each year, then it is likely that net operating working capital will also increase each year. These investments represent negative cash flows and must be included.

5. *Additional depreciation benefits*—Whenever the asset mix of the firm changes, there is likely to be a change in the amount of depreciation expense. Because depreciation expense is a noncash expense that serves to reduce taxes, we need to consider the tax savings, or extra taxes, due changes in depreciation expense.

We must be careful to remember that the only relevant cash flows are those that are after-tax and incremental. Keeping this in mind, we can summarize the calculation of the after-tax cash flows as follows:

ATCF = (ΔRevenues + Savings – Expenses) × (1 – tax rate) + (ΔDepreciation × tax rate) – ΔNOWC

Or, equivalently, we could write that equation as follows:

ATCF = (ΔRevenues – ΔNet Expenses – ΔDepreciation) × (1 – tax rate) + ΔDepreciation – ΔNOWC

The difference is whether we treat the depreciation tax benefit explicitly, or implicitly. The second version looks rather like the income statement, except that it only has incremental operating cash flows. For this reason, we refer to it as an *operating cash flow statement*. We will demonstrate this method in Chapter 12.

The Terminal Cash Flow

The terminal cash flow consists of those nonoperating cash flows that occur only in the final time period of the project. Normally, there will also be operating cash flows that occur during this period, but we have categorized those as the final period after-tax cash flows. The terminal cash flow will consist of things such as the expected salvage value of the new machine, any tax effects associated with the sale of the machine, recovery of any investments in net working capital, and perhaps some shut-down costs.

TCF = Recovery of ΔNOWC – (Shut-down Expenses × (1 – tax rate)) + Salvage Value – Taxes on Salvage of New Machine

Estimating the Cash Flows: An Example

Throughout this chapter, we will demonstrate the concepts with the following example.

> The Supreme Shoe Company is considering the purchase of a new, fully automated machine to replace a manually operated one. The machine being replaced, now five years old, originally had an expected life of 10 years, is being depreciated using the straight-line method from $40,000 down to $0 and can now be sold for $22,000. It takes one person to operate the machine and he earns $29,000 per year in salary and benefits. The annual costs of maintenance and defects on the old machine are $6,000 and $4,000, respectively. The replacement machine being considered has a purchase price of $75,000 and an expected salvage value of $15,000 at the end of its five-year life. There will also be shipping and installation expenses of $6,000. Because the new machine would work faster, investment in net working capital would increase by a total of $3,000. The company expects that annual maintenance costs on the new machine will be $5,000 while defects will cost $2,000.

> Before considering this project, the company undertook an engineering analysis of current facilities to determine if other changes would be necessitated by the purchase of this machine. The study cost the company $5,000 and determined that existing facilities could support this new machine with no other changes. In order to purchase the new machine, the company would have to take on new debt of $30,000 at 10% interest, resulting in increased interest expense of $3,000 per year. The required rate of return for this project is 15% and the company's marginal tax rate is 34%. Furthermore, management has determined that the maximum allowable time to recover its investment is three years. Is this project acceptable?

For this type of problem, it is generally easiest to separate the important data from the text. This is true regardless of whether you are doing problems by hand or with a spreadsheet program. Of course, a spreadsheet offers many advantages that we will examine later. For now, open a new worksheet and enter the data displayed in Exhibit 11-1.

Notice that in creating Exhibit 11-1 we have simply listed all of the relevant data from the Supreme Shoe problem. There are also some minor calculations entered. Remember, it is important that you set up your worksheets so that Excel does all of the possible calculations for you. This will allow us to more easily experiment with different values (i.e., perform a "what-if" analysis) or change assumptions later.

We have left the cost of the engineering study out of our model. Because the $5,000 was spent before our analysis, it is considered to be a sunk cost. That is, there is no way to recover that money, so it is irrelevant to any future decisions. Adding this to the cost of the project would unnecessarily penalize the project. Furthermore, we haven't considered the $3,000 in extra interest expense that will be incurred each year. The money spent to finance a project must be ignored because we will account for it in the required return. In addition, Supreme Shoe has decided to take on the debt for 10 years, which is longer than the expected life of the new machine. Therefore, it wouldn't be correct to apply all of the interest expense to this one project.

EXHIBIT 11-1
RELEVANT CASH FLOWS FOR SUPREME SHOE

	A	B	C	D
1		The Supreme Shoe Company		
2		Replacement Analysis		
3		*Old Machine*	*New Machine*	*Difference*
4	Price	40,000	75,000	
5	Shipping and Install	0	6,000	
6	Original Life	10	5	
7	Current Life	5	5	
8	Original Salvage Value	0	15,000	
9	Current Salvage Value	22,000	0	
10	Book Value	20,000	81,000	
11	Increase in Raw Materials	0	3,000	
12	Depreciation	4,000	13,200	(9,200)
13	Salaries	29,000		29,000
14	Maintenance	6,000	5,000	1,000
15	Defects	4,000	2,000	2,000
16	Marginal Tax Rate	34.00%		
17	Required Return	15.00%		

We calculate the book value of the current machine in B10 because the book value and the salvage value together will determine the tax liability from the sale of this machine. Book value is calculated as the difference between the depreciable base and the accumulated depreciation. In this instance, the depreciable base is found by adding B4 and B5. The accumulated depreciation is the annual depreciation expense times the number of years of the original life that have passed. In our worksheet this is B12*(B6–B7). So the formula in B10 is: =B4+B5-B12*(B6-B7). For informational purposes, copy the formula to C10.

The difference column presents the savings that the new machine will provide. The formulas are simply the difference between the expenses of the current machine and those of the proposed machine. In D12 place the formula: =B12-C12 and then copy it to cells D13:D15. To avoid confusion, we only calculate differences for the relevant cells. Your worksheet should now resemble Exhibit 11-1.

Calculating Straight-Line Depreciation Expense

Supreme Shoe uses the straight-line method for analysis purposes. Straight-line depreciation applies depreciation equally throughout the expected useful life of the project and is calculated as follows:

$$\frac{\text{Depreciable Base} - \text{Salvage Value}}{\text{Useful Life}}$$

Excel has built-in functions for calculating depreciation in five different ways: straight-line (**SLN**), double-declining balance (**DDB**), fixed-declining balance (**DB**), sum of the years' digits (**SYD**), and variable-declining balance (**VDB**). We will use the **VDB** function to calculate MACRS depreciation in the next section. Because Supreme Shoe uses the straight-line method, we will use the **SLN** function that is defined as:

$$\text{SLN}(\textbf{\textit{COST}}, \textbf{\textit{SALVAGE}}, \textbf{\textit{LIFE}})$$

where **COST** is the depreciable base of the asset, **SALVAGE** is the estimated salvage value, and **LIFE** is the number of years over which the asset is to be depreciated.

Recall that the depreciable base includes the price of the asset plus the shipping and installation costs. For the old machine, then, in cell B12 enter: =SLN(B4+B5,B8,B6). Because the annual depreciation will be calculated the same way for the new machine, simply copy the formula in B12 to C12.

Calculating Depreciation Expense Using MACRS

An alternative to using straight-line depreciation is MACRS (Modified Accelerated Cost Recovery System). As the name suggests, MACRS accelerates the depreciation allowance compared to straight-line. This allows companies to receive the tax savings from depreciation more quickly, which improves the profitability of a project.

Unlike straight-line depreciation, MACRS doesn't directly use the economic life of an asset to determine the recovery period. Instead, the IRS provides guidance on the types of assets that fall into the allowable recovery periods.[1] Also, all assets are depreciated to a terminal value of zero, so an estimated salvage value is unnecessary for MACRS purposes.

For recovery periods that are 10 years or less, MACRS starts by depreciating at twice the straight-line rate. For the 15- and 20-year classes, the rate is 150% of straight-line. MACRS switches to the straight-line rates when that becomes advantageous. One complication is the

---

1. Most assets will fall into the 3-, 5-, 7-, 10-, 15-, or 20-year classes. Some assets may be depreciated over longer periods. See IRS Publication 946 at http://www.irs.gov/publications/p946/ch04.html.

half-year convention, which assumes that the asset was acquired exactly half way through the year, regardless of the actual date. This means that the first year's depreciation is only half of what it would otherwise be and that there is an extra half-year of depreciation at the end of the class life. That is, an asset is actually depreciated over a period that is one year longer than the class life.

TABLE 11-1
MACRS PERCENTAGES BY CLASS LIFE

Year	3-Year	5-Year	7-Year	10-Year
1	33.33%	20.00%	14.29%	10.00%
2	44.45%	32.00%	24.49%	18.00%
3	14.81%	19.20%	17.49%	14.40%
4	7.41%	11.52%	12.49%	11.52%
5		11.52%	8.93%	9.22%
6		5.76%	8.92%	7.37%
7			8.93%	6.55%
8			4.46%	6.55%
9				6.56%
10				6.55%
11				3.28%

The IRS provides tables of percentages for each year's depreciation, as shown in Table 11-1. We could use the **VLOOKUP** function to find the correct percentage and calculate a given year's depreciation. This function performs a vertical lookup in the first column of a table and then returns the result from that row in the specified column. **VLOOKUP** is defined as:

VLOOKUP(*LOOKUP_VALUE*, *TABLE_ARRAY*, *COL_INDEX_NUM*, *RANGE_LOOKUP*)

where **LOOKUP_VALUE** is the value to look for in the first column, **TABLE_ARRAY** is the address of the table data, **COL_INDEX_NUM** is the column from which the result should be returned, and *RANGE_LOOKUP* is an optional argument that tells the function to return an exact or approximate match. As an example, assume that a copy of Table 11-1 is located in A2:E12, and we wish to find the percentage for the third year of a project in the 7-year class. We could use this function: =VLOOKUP(3,A2:E12,4). This would find 3 in the first column and then return 17.49% from the fourth column. That percentage would then be multiplied by the depreciable base to determine the depreciation amount.

We can calculate the depreciation more easily (no table required) and accurately using Excel's **VDB** function. VDB stands for "variable-declining balance," and this function allows us to specify the rate at which the depreciable base is written off. It also allows us to switch to straight-line depreciation in the period where that would be advantageous. The **VDB** function is defined as:

VDB(*COST, SALVAGE, LIFE, START_PERIOD, END_PERIOD, FACTOR, NO_SWITCH*)

The *COST, SALVAGE,* and *LIFE* arguments are the same as in the **SLN** function. The *START_PERIOD* and *END_PERIOD* arguments must be specified because this function can be used to calculate the accumulated depreciation between two periods. *FACTOR* specifies the rate of decline (1 for straight-line, 2 for double-declining balance, etc.), and *NO_SWITCH* is an optional argument that specifies whether to switch over to straight-line or not.

For MACRS, *SALVAGE* is always 0, *LIFE* is equal to the class life, *FACTOR* will be 2 (or 1.5 for 15- or 20-year classes), and we can omit *NO_SWITCH*. Because of the half-year convention, specifying the starting and ending periods is a bit complicated. For the first year, the start period must be 0, and end period must be 0.50. For the last year, the start period is the year minus 1.50, and the end period is the class life. For the periods in between, the starting period is the year minus 1.5, and the ending period is the year minus 0.5. So, for example, in the second year *START_PERIOD* would be 0.5 and *END_PERIOD* would be 1.5.

For the moment, assume that the example project was being depreciated using the MACRS 3-year class. Enter the data shown in Exhibit 11-2.

EXHIBIT 11-2
MACRS CALCULATIONS

	H	I	J	K	L	M
8		MACRS Calculations				
9	Class	3				
10	Depreciable Base	81,000				
11	**Year**	**1**	**2**	**3**	**4**	**5**
12	MACRS	27,000	36,000	12,000	6,000	0

To calculate the MACRS depreciation for year 1, enter this formula in I12: `VDB($I$10, 0,$I$9,MAX(0,I11-1.5),MIN($I$9,I11-0.5),2)`. Notice that we can calculate the starting period using the **MAX** function. It will return 0 in year 1, 0.5 in year 2, and so on. We calculate the ending period using the **MIN** function. It will return either the class life or the year minus 0.5, whichever is less. This way, we can just copy the formula across and get the correct depreciation for each year.

If you copy the formula to M12, which is beyond the class life, then you will get a #NUM! error message. The **VDB** function will return an error if you try to calculate depreciation after the asset is fully depreciated. We can get around this problem by wrapping the function in the **IFERROR** function. This function will test a calculation for an error. If no error is found, it will return the result of the calculation. Otherwise, it will return an alternate value that you specify. This function is defined as:

IfError(*Value, Value_if_Error*)

In this case, we wish to return a zero if the asset has been fully depreciated. So, in I12 enter: `=IFERROR(VDB($I$10,0,$I$9,MAX(0,I11-1.5),MIN($I$9,I11-0.5),2),0)`. Now copy that across J12:M12, and your results should match those shown in Exhibit 11-2. Try extending the formula to more cells and changing the MACRS class in I9.

Because the above formula is hard to remember, we have provided a user-defined function named **Fame_Macrs** in the Famefncs.xlam add-in. It will calculate MACRS depreciation for class lives from 3 to 20 years and is defined as:

Fame_Macrs(*Cost, MacrsClass, Year, Table*)

where *Table* is an optional argument that tells the function whether to use the exact calculation or the table percentages. This function, like **Vdb**, will return an error for periods beyond the class life. If you have the add-in installed, you can replace the formula in I12 with: `=IFERROR(FAME_MACRS($I$10,$I$9,I11,0),0)`.

Because the Supreme Shoe Company uses straight-line depreciation for project evaluation, we will return to that method for the remainder of this chapter.

Calculating the Relevant Cash Flows

Return now to the example problem with the data as presented in Exhibit 11-1 (page 335). We will use that data to calculate the cash flows that we will need to use when evaluating this potential investment.

The initial outlay consists of the price of the new machine, the shipping and installation costs, and the salvage value of the old machine and any taxes that might be due from that sale. We will calculate the initial outlay in B19 as: `=-(C4+C5-B9+(B9-B10)*B16+C11)`. The formula is less complex than it looks. The first three terms simply represent the total cost of the new machine less the salvage value of the old machine. The next part of the formula calculates the tax due on the sale of the old machine. Notice that if the book value were less than the salvage value, this formula will add a negative value thus reducing the initial outlay. Finally, we add the increase in net working capital because this investment would not be necessary unless the new machine was purchased.

Next, we need to calculate the annual after-tax cash flows for this project. We will separate the calculation of the depreciation tax benefit from the other cash flows because it is informative to see the savings generated by the increased depreciation (also because, as we will see in Chapter 12, the depreciation tax benefit is a less risky cash flow than the others). In B20 we calculate the annual after-tax savings as: =SUM(D13:D15)*(1-B16). We have used the **SUM** function because it is more compact than simply adding the three cell addresses individually. Also, if we later discover any other savings (or extra costs), we can insert them into the range and the formula will automatically reflect the change. Note that this project will not have any impact on overall revenues.

The depreciation tax benefit represents the savings in taxes that we will have because of the extra depreciation expense. Remember that depreciation is a noncash expense so that the only result of increasing depreciation is to reduce taxes and thereby increase cash flow. To calculate the depreciation tax benefit in cell B21, enter the formula: =-D12*B16. We make the depreciation amount negative because the change in depreciation in D12 is negative (indicating extra expense). In B22 we total the annual after-tax savings and the depreciation tax benefit with the formula: =SUM(B20:B21).

Finally, the terminal cash flow consists of any nonoperating cash flows that occur only in the final period. For the Supreme Shoe project, the additional cash flows are the after-tax salvage value and the recovery of the investment in raw materials. In this case, there is no tax consequence of salvaging the machine for $15,000 because that is the same as the book value, but we will calculate the taxes regardless because we may later wish to make changes. The formula in B23 is: =C8-(C8-(SUM(C4:C5)-C12*C6))*B16+C11.

Don't forget that the terminal cash flow is only the nonoperating part of the total cash flow in year 5. We will have to add on the annual after-tax cash flow (operating cash flows) in year 5 before analyzing the profitability of the project. At this point, your worksheet should resemble the one shown in Exhibit 11-3.

EXHIBIT 11-3
CASH FLOWS FOR SUPREME SHOE

	A	B
18	**Cash Flows**	
19	Initial Outlay	(62,680)
20	Annual After-Tax Savings	21,120
21	Depreciation Tax Benefit	3,128
22	Total ATCF	24,248
23	Terminal Cash Flow	18,000

Making the Decision

We are now ready to make a decision as to the profitability of this project. Financial managers have a number of tools at their disposal to evaluate profitability. We will examine six of these. Before beginning the analysis, examine the timeline presented in Figure 11-2, which summarizes the cash flows for the Supreme Shoe replacement decision.

FIGURE 11-2
TIMELINE FOR THE SUPREME SHOE REPLACEMENT DECISION

The Payback Method

The payback method answers the question, "How long will it take to recoup the initial investment?" If the answer is less than or equal to the maximum allowable period, the project is considered to be acceptable. If the payback period is longer than is acceptable, then the project is rejected. Note that the payback period serves as a kind of break-even period, and thus provides some information regarding the liquidity of the project under analysis.

There are two ways to calculate the payback period. The easiest method, which we can use for the Supreme Shoe problem, is used when the cash flows are an annuity. To calculate the payback for these types of cash flows, simply divide the initial outlay by the annuity payment:

$$\text{Payback Period} = \frac{\text{Initial Outlay}}{\text{Annuity Payment}}$$

For Supreme Shoe, the cash flows are not strictly an annuity, except for the first four years. If the payback period is less than four years, then we can use this method. For this project, the payback period is calculated as:

$$\text{Payback Period} = \frac{62,680}{24,248} = 2.58 \text{ years}$$

Because Supreme Shoe requires that projects have a maximum payback period of three years, the replacement machine is acceptable by this criteria. In A25, enter the label:

`Payback Period` and in B25 enter the formula: `=-B19/B22`. Your result should be 2.58 years.

An alternative way to calculate the payback period, which must be used if the cash flows are not an annuity, subtracts the cash flows from the initial outlay until the outlay is recovered. This method is much easier to demonstrate than to describe. So let's look at the Supreme Shoe problem using this method. Table 11-2 illustrates this procedure.

TABLE 11-2
CALCULATING THE PAYBACK PERIOD

	Calculation	Comments	Cumulative Payback
	62,680	Initial outlay	
−	24,248	minus first cash flow	1 year
=	38,432	left to be recovered	
−	24,248	minus second cash flow	2 years
=	14,184	left to be recovered	2 years < payback < 3 years

At this point, we know that the payback period must be between two and three years and that the remainder will be recovered during the third year. Assuming that the cash flow in year 3 is earned evenly through the year, we can simply divide the amount yet to be recovered by the cash flow in year 3 to arrive at the fraction of the year required to recover this amount. In this case, it will take 0.58 years (= $14,184 \div 24,248$). Add this to the two years that we have already counted, and we arrive at 2.58 years, exactly as before.

Although the payback period makes a great deal of sense intuitively, it is not without its problems. Specifically, the principal problem is that the payback method ignores the time value of money. You know, from the discussion of time value in Chapter 7, that we cannot simply add cash flows that occur in different time periods. Furthermore, it should be obvious that most investments become increasingly attractive as the firm's required return (WACC) falls and less attractive when the required return rises. However, the payback period doesn't change when the WACC changes. We will address this problem shortly.

A second difficulty with the payback period is that it does not take all of the cash flows into account. Because it ignores all cash flows beyond the payback period, it can lead to less than optimal decisions. Suppose, for example, that the year 5 cash flow for the Supreme Shoe project was −$100,000 instead of $42,248. The payback period is still 2.58 years, which suggests that it should be accepted, but anybody taking even a cursory look at the cash flows would reject the project immediately. This second problem will be remedied when we look at the NPV, PI, IRR, and MIRR techniques.

The Discounted Payback Period

We can fix the time value of money problem by using the *discounted payback period*. This method is identical to the payback period, except that we use the present value of the cash flows instead of the nominal values. Because present values are always less than nominal values, the discounted payback period will always be longer than the regular payback period.

For Supreme Shoe, the discounted payback period is 3.53 years. Calculating this number is slightly more difficult than calculating the regular payback period because the present values of the cash flows are different in each period. For this reason, we must use the method shown in Table 11-2 to calculate the discounted payback period.[2]

Because Excel does not have a payback function, we have included one in the Famefncs.xlam add-in.[3] It contains a function called **FAME_PAYBACK** that can be used exactly like a built-in function, as long as the add-in is active. The function is defined as:

$$\text{FAME\_PAYBACK}(\textit{CASHFLOWS}, \textit{RATE})$$

where **CASHFLOWS** is a contiguous range of cash flows, and *RATE* is the optional discount rate to be used to calculate the present values of the cash flows. If *RATE* is left out the default discount rate is 0%, so this function will calculate the regular payback period. Be aware that the initial outlay (i.e., the first cash flow in the list) must be negative, or else you will get unpredictable results. All other cash flows may be either positive or negative.

Before using the **FAME_PAYBACK** macro, and the other functions that we will be using later, we need to set up a table of cash flows. In cells C18:D24 set up the following table:

EXHIBIT 11-4
CASH FLOWS FOR CALCULATING THE DISCOUNTED PAYBACK PERIOD

	C	D
18	**Period**	**Cash Flows**
19	0	(62,680)
20	1	24,248
21	2	24,248
22	3	24,248
23	4	24,248
24	5	42,248

---

2. In the case where all of the nominal cash flows are equal (an annuity), we could use the **NPER** function. This function calculates the number of periods that an annuity must pay to have the present value of the cash flows equal to the price. We can also use this function to calculate the regular payback period for an annuity if we set the discount rate to zero.

3. Please see "Using User-Defined Functions" on page 25 to learn more about the add-in.

In order to set up the table in Exhibit 11-4, very little data input is required because most of the data already exists or can be calculated. Start by typing the column labels in cells C18 and D18. To enter the period numbers, in cell C19 type a zero and then select the range

⬇ Fill ▾ C19:C24. Click the Fill button on the Home tab and then choose <u>S</u>eries. Click on OK when the dialog box appears (the default options should work fine). This command will enter a series of numbers starting with the first number in the selected range. It can be very helpful in situations where you need a list of consecutive numbers or dates.

The cash flows are most easily entered by using references to the cells where the original calculations exist. Entering the numbers in this way, rather than retyping them, will later allow us to experiment with various scenarios. In cell D19 enter: =B19 to capture the initial outlay. In cell D20 we need the first cash flow, so enter: =B$22. Note that the dollar sign will freeze the cell reference so that it will remain at row 22 when we copy it. Copy the formula from D20 to the range D21:D23, and note that the value is the same in each cell as it was in D20. Finally, to get the total cash flow for year 5 (in D24) enter: =B22+B23. Remember that the cash flow in the final year of the life of a project is the sum of its annual after-tax cash flow and the terminal cash flow. In the timeline pictured in Figure 11-2, we showed these cash flows separately, but we must add them together in Exhibit 11-4 for the following analysis.

Calculating the discounted payback period is a simple matter. In cell B26 enter the formula: =FAME_Payback(D19:D24,B17). The discounted payback period is 3.53 years, which is longer than the maximum acceptable payback. You should verify this result by hand.

Using the three-year benchmark in this case would be incorrect because it was presumably determined under the assumptions of the regular payback period. Some allowance must be made for the fact that the discounted payback period will always be greater than the regular payback period. Suppose then that management decides that the discounted payback must be 3.75 years or less to be acceptable. With the new criteria, the project is acceptable under both payback methods.

However, the benefit of the discounted payback period technique is that the acceptability of a project will change as required returns change. If the required return should rise to 18%, the discounted payback period will rise to 3.80 years and the project would be rejected. Because the regular payback period ignores the time value of money it would still suggest that the project is acceptable, regardless of the required return. Try changing the required return in B17 to verify this for yourself.

Note that the discounted payback period still ignores cash flows beyond the period where payback is achieved. All of the remaining techniques that we will introduce are considered to be superior because they recognize the time value of money and all of the cash flows are considered in the analysis.

Net Present Value

Neither the regular payback period nor the discounted payback period is an economically correct decision criterion. Even with the discounted payback method we are ignoring cash flows beyond the payback period. How then can the financial analyst make the correct decision? In this section, we will cover the net present value decision criteria, which is the most theoretically correct method.

Most people would agree that purchasing an asset for less than its value is a good deal. Further, purchasing an asset for exactly its value isn't bad. What most people try to avoid is purchasing an asset for more than its value.[4] If we define value as the present value of future cash flows (see Chapter 8), then the net present value (NPV) represents the excess value (i.e., economic profit) captured by purchasing an asset. More specifically:

$$NPV = PVCF - IO = Value - Cost$$

Or more mathematically:

$$NPV = \sum_{1\,=\,t}^{N} \frac{CF_t}{(1 + i)^t} - IO \tag{11-1}$$

There are a couple of important things to note about the NPV. Most importantly, because value can be greater than, equal to, or less than cost, the NPV can be greater than, equal to, or less than zero. If the value is less than the cost, the NPV will be negative, and the project will be rejected. Otherwise, the project will be accepted because the value is greater than (or equal to) the cost. In the latter case, the wealth of the shareholders will be increased (or at least unchanged) by the acceptance of the project. So NPV really represents the change in shareholder wealth that accompanies the acceptance of an investment. Because the goal of management is to maximize shareholder wealth, they must accept all projects where the NPV is greater than or equal to zero.

Why does NPV represent a change in shareholder wealth? To see this important point, remember that any cash flows in excess of expenses accrue to the common stockholders of the firm. Therefore, any project that generates cash flows sufficient to cover its costs will result in an increase in shareholder wealth. Consider the following example:

> Huey and Louie are considering the purchase of a lemonade stand that
> will operate during the summer months. It will cost them $100 to build

---

4. Theoretically, nobody would ever purchase an asset for more than it is worth to them at the time the decision is made. Purchasing an asset proves, *ipso facto*, that the cost is, at most, equal to the value to that individual at that moment (assuming a voluntary exchange).

and operate the stand. Because they have only $50 of their own (common equity) they will need to raise the additional capital elsewhere. Huey's father agrees to loan the pair $30 (debt) with the understanding that they will repay him a total of $33 at the end of the summer. The other $20 can be raised in a preferred stock offering to several of the other kids in the neighborhood. The preferred stock is sold with the promise to pay a $3 dividend at the end of the summer. Huey and Louie would have to earn at least $10 in order to compensate them for their time, effort, and money invested. Assuming that the stand will be demolished, and all capital returned, at the end of the summer, should they undertake this project?

The answer to this question depends on the cash flows that Huey and Louie expect the lemonade stand to generate. Note that the weighted average cost of capital is 16%:

$$WACC = 0.30\left(\frac{3}{30}\right) + 0.20\left(\frac{3}{20}\right) + 0.50\left(\frac{10}{50}\right) = 0.16$$

The three scenarios in Table 11-3 will demonstrate the possibilities.

TABLE 11-3
POSSIBLE SCENARIOS FOR THE LEMONADE STAND

	Scenario 1 16% Return	Scenario 2 20% Return	Scenario 3 8% Return
Total cash inflow after operating expenses and taxes	$116	$120	$108
Less cost of debt	(33)	(33)	(33)
Less cost of preferred stock	(23)	(23)	(23)
Less cost of common equity	(60)	(60)	(60)
Remainder to common stockholders (NPV)	0	4	−8

Notice that the required returns of each of the stakeholders is unchanged in each scenario. The only variable is the cash inflow after operating expenses and taxes (NOPAT). In the first scenario, all of the capital providers are exactly satisfied, even Huey and Louie get the $10 return that they have demanded. Therefore, the project is acceptable, and it has a net present value of zero (as indicated by the remainder). Under the second scenario, everybody is satisfied and there is an extra $4 that goes directly to Huey and Louie (the shareholders). This is an example of a positive NPV.

Finally, in scenario 3, the debtholder and the preferred stockholders are satisfied, but there is a shortfall of $8 that will reduce Huey and Louie's return to only $2. Notice that in the last case, the return to the common stockholders is positive (i.e., they get back $2 more than they invested), but less than required. This is an example of a negative NPV and will cause Huey and Louie to reject the project.[5]

Returning now to our Supreme Shoe example, the NPV of this project can be determined by taking the present value of the after-tax cash flows and subtracting the initial outlay. In this case, performing the calculations by hand poses no great difficulty. However, Excel can calculate the NPV just as easily and allow us to experiment later. You have already made use of the built-in **NPV** function in Chapter 7. At that point, we did not make clear the misleading nature of this function. It does not really calculate the NPV as we have defined it. Instead, it simply calculates the present values of the cash flows as of one period before the first cash flow. It is vitally important that you understand this point before using this function.

To use the **NPV** function for this problem, insert: =NPV(B17,D20:D24)+B19 into B27. We do *not* include the initial outlay in the **NPV** function. Instead, we use the **NPV** function to determine the present value of the cash flows and then add the (negative) initial outlay to this result. The net present value is shown to be $27,552.24, so the project is acceptable.

An alternative method is to include the initial outlay and then adjust the result. In this case, the present value would be as of time period –1, so multiplying by (1 + WACC) will bring it to time period 0. The alternative, then, is to place the formula: =NPV(B17, D19:D24)*(1+B17) into B27. This will give exactly the same result.

The Profitability Index

The beauty of the net present value is that it reports the dollar increase in shareholder wealth that would result from acceptance of a project. Mostly, this is desirable, but there is one problem: Comparing projects of differing size can be misleading when a firm is operating with a fixed amount of investment capital. If both projects are acceptable and mutually exclusive, the larger project will likely have a higher NPV. The *profitability index* (PI) is a measure of the dollar benefit per dollar of cost ("bang for the buck"). PI is calculated by:

$$PI = \frac{\$\ \text{Benefit}}{\$\ \text{Cost}} = \frac{\sum_{t=1}^{N} \frac{CF_t}{(1+i)^t}}{IO} = \frac{PVCF}{IO} \tag{11-2}$$

---

5. We are talking about the economic costs, not just the accounting costs. Economists consider the cost of the equity and other opportunity costs. Accounting costs ignore the cost of equity and other opportunity costs. Therefore, NPV is the same thing as the *economic profit* generated by the project.

As indicated in the equation, the benefit is calculated as the present value of the after-tax cash flows and the cost is the initial outlay. Obviously, if the PI is greater than or equal to 1, the project is acceptable because the benefits exceed, or at least equal, the costs. Otherwise, the benefits are less than the costs and the project would be rejected. The profitability index will always result in the same accept/reject answer as NPV.

There are two ways that we can calculate the PI in Excel. The most apparent is to use the **NPV** function and to divide that result by the initial outlay. In other words, in B28 type: =NPV(B17,D20:D24)/-B19. This will give 1.4396 as the result, indicating that the project is acceptable. The alternative is to make use of the following relationship:

$$NPV = PVCF - IO$$

Or by rearranging we get:

$$PVCF = NPV + IO$$

Therefore, because we have already calculated the NPV in B27, we can calculate the PI with: =(B27-B19)/-B19. This method will be slightly faster because Excel doesn't have to recalculate the present values. In all but the largest problems, the increase in speed probably won't be noticeable on a PC, but the technique is especially helpful when doing problems by hand.

The Internal Rate of Return

The *internal rate of return* (IRR) provides a measure of the compound average annual rate of return that a project will provide. If the IRR equals, or exceeds, the required return for a project, the project will be accepted. Because it is a measure of the percentage return, many analysts prefer it to the other methods that we have discussed, but there are problems with the IRR.

The IRR is the discount rate that makes the net present value equal to zero. An alternative, but equivalent, definition is that the IRR is the discount rate that equates the present value of the cash flows to the initial outlay. In other words, the IRR is the discount rate that makes the following equality hold:

$$IO = \sum_{t=1}^{N} \frac{CF_t}{(1 + IRR)^t} \tag{11-3}$$

Unfortunately, in most cases there is no closed-form method for solving for the IRR. The primary method of solving this equation is an iterative trial-and-error approach. Although this may sound tedious, generally a solution can be found within three or four iterations if some intelligence is used. However, there is little need for this procedure because Excel has a built-in function that performs this operation.

The built-in **RATE** function in Excel will find the IRR for an annuity type of cash flow stream, but it cannot accept a series of uneven cash flows. To deal with uneven cash flows, Excel provides the **IRR** function that is defined as:

$$\text{IRR}(\textit{VALUES}, \textit{GUESS})$$

where *VALUES* is the contiguous range of cash flows and *GUESS* is the optional initial guess at the true IRR. The cash flow stream must include at least one negative cash flow, or else the IRR would be infinite (why?). Because solving for the IRR is an iterative process, it is possible that Excel will not converge to a solution. Excel will indicate this situation by displaying #NUM! in the cell rather than an answer. If this error occurs, one possible solution is to change your *GUESS* until Excel can converge to a solution.

To calculate the IRR for the Supreme Shoe example, enter: =IRR(D19:D24) into B29. The result is 30.95%, which is greater than the WACC of 15%. So the project is acceptable.

At this point, let's try an experiment to prove our definition of the IRR. Recall that the IRR was defined as the discount rate that makes the NPV equal zero. To prove this, temporarily change the value in B17 to: =B29. Notice that the net present value in B27 changes to $0.00, which proves the point. Note also that the profitability index changes to 1.00. Before continuing, change the required return back to its original value of 15%.

Problems with the IRR

The internal rate of return is a popular profitability measure because, as a percentage, it is easy to understand and easy to compare to the required return. However, the IRR suffers from several problems that could potentially lead to less-than-optimal decisions. In this section, we will discuss these difficulties and solutions where they exist.

Earlier, we mentioned that the NPV will almost always lead you to the economically correct decision. Unfortunately, the IRR and NPV will not always lead to the same decision when projects are mutually exclusive. *Mutually exclusive* projects are those where the selection of one project precludes the acceptance of another. When projects being compared are mutually exclusive, a ranking conflict may arise between the NPV and IRR.[6] In other words, the NPV method may suggest that Project A be accepted, while the IRR may suggest Project B. If you can't select both, which profitability measure do you believe?

---

6. This is not a problem with independent projects because all independent projects with a positive NPV (IRR > WACC) will be accepted, so ranking is not required.

There are two causes of this type of problem: (1) The projects are of greatly different sizes; or (2) the timing of the cash flows is different. To see the size problem more clearly, consider the following question: "Would you rather earn a 100% return on a $10 investment (Project A), or a 10% return on a $1,000 investment (Project B)?" Obviously, most of us would be more concerned with the dollar amounts and would choose the 10% return because that would provide $100 versus only $10 in the other case. The solution to this problem is actually quite simple. If you can raise $1,000 for Project B, then the correct comparison is not between A and B, but between B and A plus whatever you could do with the other $990 (call it Project C) that is available if you choose Project A. If Project C would return 10%, then you could earn $109 by investing in both A and C, which is preferable to investing in B.

The timing problem is more difficult to deal with. Suppose you are given the task of evaluating the two mutually exclusive projects in Table 11-4, with a 10% required return.

TABLE 11-4
CASH FLOW TIMING CAN CAUSE A RANKING CONFLICT

Period	Project A	Project B	Project C (= A – B)
0	(1,000)	(1,000)	0
1	0	400	(400)
2	200	400	(200)
3	300	300	0
4	500	300	200
5	900	200	700
NPV	$291.02	$248.70	$42.32
IRR	17.32%	20.49%	12.48%

Which would you choose? Obviously there is a conflict because Project A would be selected under the NPV criteria, but Project B would be selected by the IRR criteria. We can use logic similar to that used for the size problem to see that NPV is the correct criteria. If Project B is accepted, we must reject Project A and the differential cash flows (Project C). If the differential cash flows provide a positive NPV, then they should not be rejected. In effect, what we are arguing is that Project A is equivalent to Project B plus the differential cash flows. So choosing between these projects is effectively deciding whether the differential cash flows are profitable or not. Conveniently, all that we really need to do is accept the project with the highest NPV. Note that Project A would be preferred as long as the discount rate is less than 12.48%. At higher discount rates, Project B would be preferred. A useful tool for these kinds of problems is the NPV profile chart, which is introduced on page 354.

Yet another problem with the IRR is that there may be more than one IRR. Specifically, because the general equation for the IRR is an Nth degree polynomial, it will potentially have as many as N solutions. In the usual case, where there is one cash outflow followed by several inflows, there will be only one solution. However, when there are net cash outflows in the outlying periods (*nonnormal cash flows*), we may be able to find more than one solution. In particular, there can be, at most, one real solution per sign change in the cash flow stream.[7]

FIGURE 11-3
NONNORMAL CASH FLOWS MAY HAVE MULTIPLE IRRS

Consider, as an example, the cash flows depicted in Figure 11-3. Solving for the IRR in this example will lead to three solutions: 207.82%, –31.54%, and –76.27%. The answer that you get from Excel will depend on the initial *GUESS* that you supply. If you don't provide Excel with a *GUESS*, it will give –31.54% as the answer. Any *GUESS* of 11.8% or greater will get an answer of 207.82%, and a guess of –68.35% will get an answer of –76.27%. It is impossible to say which of these answers is correct because all will result in an NPV of zero if used as the discount rate (try it!). So, even though these IRRs are mathematically correct, they have no economic meaning. The IRR should be ignored whenever there are multiple results.

The Modified Internal Rate of Return

An easy solution to the problems of the IRR is to simply use the NPV instead. This is not likely to please everyone, however. Despite its problems, executives continue to prefer the IRR to the NPV because, as a percentage, it is easy to compare to the firm's cost of capital. To understand how we can use an IRR-type calculation and still arrive at correct answers requires that you understand the root cause of the problems with the IRR.

Implicit in the calculation of the IRR is the assumption that the cash flows are reinvested at the IRR. In other words, the IRR method assumes that as each cash flow is received, it is reinvested for the remaining life of the project at a rate that is the same as the IRR.[8] For projects with a very high or very low IRR, this assumption is likely to be violated. If the cash flows are reinvested at some other rate, the actual average annual rate of return will be different than the IRR. To see this assumption at work, consider again our Supreme Shoe

---

7. The interested reader is advised to study Descartes' Rule of Signs.

8. This also explains why we cannot solve directly for the IRR: We must know the IRR to know the reinvestment rate, and without knowing the reinvestment rate we can't solve for the IRR.

project. The timeline is pictured in Figure 11-4 with the explicit reinvestment of the cash flows at the IRR of 30.945%.

FIGURE 11-4
SUPREME SHOE CASH FLOWS WITH EXPLICIT REINVESTMENT AT THE IRR

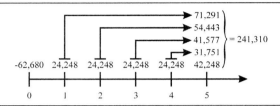

Assuming that the cash flows are reinvested at 30.945% per year, at the end of year 5 Supreme Shoe will have accumulated $241,310 from its original investment of $62,680. The compound average annual return, then, must be:

$$\sqrt[5]{\frac{241,310}{62,680}} - 1 \approx 30.945\%$$

which is exactly the same as the IRR. Note that we have used the geometric mean, equation (1-1) from Chapter 1, though you could use the **RATE** function.

It seems unlikely that Supreme Shoe can earn a rate this high over a five-year period. If we change the reinvestment rate to a more reasonable 15% (the WACC), then we have the timeline in Figure 11-5.

FIGURE 11-5
SUPREME SHOE CASH FLOWS WITH EXPLICIT REINVESTMENT AT 15%

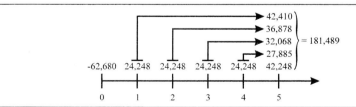

In this case, Supreme Shoe will have accumulated only $181,489 by the end of the fifth year. Its average annual rate of return with a 15% reinvestment rate will be:

$$\sqrt[5]{\frac{181,489}{62,680}} - 1 \approx 23.69\%$$

which is substantially lower than the 30.95% IRR. When we calculate the average annual return with a reinvestment rate that is different than the IRR, we refer to it as the *modified internal rate of return*, or MIRR. For Supreme Shoe, the MIRR is 23.69%, which is greater than the required return of 15%, so the project should be accepted.

Excel has a built-in function to calculate the MIRR. The function is defined as:

MIRR(*VALUES*, *FINANCE_RATE*, *REINVEST_RATE*)

where *VALUES* is the range of cash flows, *FINANCE_RATE* is the required rate of return, and *REINVEST_RATE* is the rate at which the cash flows are to be reinvested. To calculate the MIRR in your Supreme Shoe worksheet, enter: =MIRR(D19:D24,B17,B17) into B30. Exactly as we calculated earlier, the answer is 23.69%. In this example, we have used the same rate for the required return and the reinvestment rate. This is normally the appropriate assumption to make (it is the same assumption that is implicit within the NPV calculation). But if you have other information that suggests a different reinvestment rate, then that different rate should be used.

An alternative calculation method shows the relationship between the profitability index (and therefore the NPV) and the MIRR:[9]

$$MIRR = \sqrt[N]{PI} \times (1 + WACC) - 1 = \sqrt[N]{\left(\frac{NPV}{IO} + 1\right)} \times (1 + WACC) - 1 \qquad \textbf{(11-4)}$$

So, for this example we have:

$$MIRR = \sqrt[5]{1.4396} \times 1.15 - 1 = 0.2369$$

This method will not give the same answer as Excel's **MIRR** function if you have nonnormal cash flows, given the way that we have defined PI [see equation (11-2) on page 347]. That is because there is more than one methodology for calculating MIRR and PI when you have cash outflows after the initial outlay. Excel calculates the MIRR by finding the discount rate that equates the present value of the outflows to the future value of the cash inflows.

The methodology used in equation (11-4) is different from the one used by Excel. It finds the discount rate that equates the initial outlay to the future value of all other cash flows, regardless of the sign. This methodology, while different, is just as valid and is preferred by some (your author included). Both methodologies will give the same accept/reject decision (though different numbers for nonnormal cash flows), and this useful equation will always give the same answer as Excel's **MIRR** function when you have normal cash flows.

---

9. See T. Arnold and T. Nixon, "An Easy Method to Introduce MIRR into Introductory Finance," *Advances in Financial Education*, Vol 11 (2013), pp. 70–74.

Sensitivity and Scenario Analysis

Probably the most important benefit of using a spreadsheet program is that it allows us to play "what-if" games with the data. That is, we can experiment with different values to determine how our results would change if there are changes in the assumptions.

NPV Profile Charts

One useful technique that we can use is referred to as the *NPV profile*. This is simply a chart of the NPV at various discount rates. The analyst can determine, at a glance, how sensitive the NPV is to the assumed discount rate. To create an NPV profile chart, we merely set up a range of discount rates and NPV calculations and then create a chart.

To create an NPV profile chart for Supreme Shoe, let's create a range of discount rates from 0% to 35% in 5% increments. Move to cell A36 and enter: 0. To create the range of discount rates, select A36:A43 and then click Fill on the Home tab and then choose Series. In the dialog box, change the Step Value to: 0.05 (you could type 5% instead) and then click the OK button. You should now have a range of discount rates from 0% to 35%. We will use these rates in our NPV calculations.

To calculate the NPV at each discount rate, enter: =NPV(A36,D$20:D$24)+D$19 in B36. This is exactly the same formula as in B27, except that we have added a few dollar signs to freeze the references and we changed the discount rate to reference A36. Copying this formula to B37:B43 will calculate the NPV at each discount rate. Note that the NPV becomes negative at a discount rate somewhere between 30% and 35%. Of course, we knew this already because the IRR is 30.95%. Finally, to create the chart select the A36:B43 and insert a scatter chart with straight lines. Your worksheet should now resemble Exhibit 11-5.

EXHIBIT 11-5
NPV PROFILE FOR SUPREME SHOE

	A	B	C	D	E	F	G
34	**NPV Profile Data**						
35	Required Return	NPV					
36	0%	$76,560.00					
37	5%	$56,404.62					
38	10%	$40,415.58					
39	15%	$27,552.24					
40	20%	$17,070.16					
41	25%	$8,427.90					
42	30%	$1,225.62					
43	35%	($4,836.13)					

Observe that the chart clearly shows the IRR is just over 30%. This is the point where the NPV line crosses the x-axis of the NPV profile chart. Furthermore, it is obvious that for any discount rate below 30% the project has a positive NPV; thus it is acceptable. In fact, it is obviously acceptable at any reasonable discount rate.

Typically, an NPV profile chart is used to compare two mutually exclusive projects. Whenever there is a ranking conflict, the NPV profiles will cross at a rate at which the firm would be indifferent between the two projects. You can try this by entering the data for projects A and B from Table 11-4 and then creating an NPV profile chart for the projects.

FIGURE 11-6
NPV PROFILE CHART FOR TWO PROJECTS

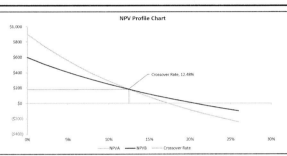

This "crossover rate," where the NPVs are the same, can be found by calculating the IRR of the difference between the cash flows of the two projects. If you placed the cash flows for the projects into B2:C7, then this formula will calculate the crossover rate: =IRR(B2:B7–C2:C7). Note that this is the rate found in the lower right corner of Table 11-4 on page 350.

Scenario Analysis

Excel contains a very powerful tool called the *Scenario Manager* that helps in analyzing the effects of different assumptions. Scenario Manager can be used to toggle your worksheet between various alternative scenarios, or it can create a summary of the effects of changing the assumptions. We will create three scenarios in which the estimates of maintenance and defect costs are different than expected. The three scenarios are listed in Table 11-5.

TABLE 11-5
THREE POSSIBLE SCENARIOS FOR SUPREME SHOE

	Best Case	**Expected Case**	**Worst Case**
Maintenance	$ 2,000	$ 5,000	$ 8,000
Defects	1,000	2,000	5,000

In the Best Case scenario, both maintenance and defects are lower than those in the Expected Case (which represents the original estimates). In the Worst Case, both are higher than expected. Because we are going to be changing our assumed values for maintenance and defects, it will be helpful to first define range names for these cells. Select C14 and then click the Formulas tab and choose Define Name. Assign the name Maintenance to this cell, give a worksheet-level scope, and enter a comment about its purpose. Now define the name Defects for cell C15 (see page 9 for a discussion of named ranges).

What-If
Analysis ▾

The Scenario Manager can be found by clicking the What-If Analysis button on the Data tab. Because no scenarios are defined at this point, the first dialog box will ask you to click the Add button to define your scenarios. In this case, we want the maintenance and defect estimates to change, so click the Add button and then enter: Best Case for the scenario name. Click in the Changing cells edit box, highlight cells C14:C15, and then click the OK button.

The next dialog box will ask you to supply the new values for the changing cells like in Figure 11-7. In the edit box labeled "Maintenance:" enter: 2000 and in the edit box labeled "Defects:" type: 1000. Note that this dialog box prompts you for the values using the names that we earlier defined for these cells. If you didn't define the names, then you will be prompted with the cell addresses instead of names.

FIGURE 11-7
THE SCENARIO VALUES DIALOG BOX

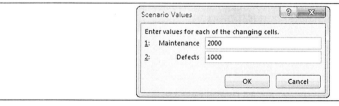

Click the Add button to enter the next scenario. Now, repeat these steps for the other two cases using the names "Expected Case" and "Worst Case" and the appropriate values from Table 11-5.

Figure 11-8 shows how the dialog box will look when you have entered all three scenarios.

At this point, you can change the worksheet to display the scenario of your choice by highlighting the name of the case and clicking the Show button. For example, if you highlight "Worst Case" and click the Show button, the maintenance and defect cells will change and the worksheet will update. You can now see the effects of these changes on the cash flows and profitability measures (e.g., the NPV is $14,277.70 under the Worst Case scenario).

FIGURE 11-8
THE SCENARIO MANAGER

Return to the original data by choosing "Expected Case" from the list and pressing the Show button. This type of flexibility is one of the promised results of proper worksheet design. Scenario analysis will not work properly unless you are diligent about using formulas, rather than retyping values, whenever possible.

It would be nice to see a summary of the different scenarios, and we can do just that. But first, exit from the Scenario Manager and define a name for each cell in B25:B30 so that the output will be easier to understand. Now, bring back the Scenario Manager and click the Summary button. When the Scenario Summary dialog box appears, select cells B25:B30 for the Result cells and click OK. Excel will then automatically create a new worksheet that displays the changed values and the resulting profitability measures. Exhibit 11-6 shows the summary worksheet.

We have defined three simple scenarios, but other problems may require more scenarios or more changing variables. You can define as many scenarios as your PC's memory will hold, but only the first 251 will be displayed on the scenario summary worksheet. There is also a limit of 32 changing cells per scenario. Note that you can safely delete the "Current Values" column since it shows the same data as our "Expected Case." It is a good idea to always define a scenario that uses the default values so that you can easily return the spreadsheet to the original values.

EXHIBIT 11-6
SCENARIO SUMMARY REPORT FOR SUPREME SHOE

Scenario Summary				
	Current Values:	Best Case	Expected Case	Worst Case
Changing Cells:				
Maintenance	5,000	2,000	5,000	8,000
Defects	2,000	1,000	2,000	5,000
Result Cells:				
Payback_Period	2.58	2.33	2.58	3.09
Discounted_Payback	3.53	3.08	3.53	4.25
NPV	27,552.24	36,401.93	27,552.24	14,277.70
PI	1.44	1.58	1.44	1.23
IRR	30.95%	35.85%	30.95%	23.41%
MIRR	23.69%	26.03%	23.69%	19.82%

The Optimal Capital Budget

How large a firm's capital budget should be is a serious problem that confronts financial managers. One solution that is often chosen is capital rationing. *Capital rationing* is the arbitrary limiting of the amount of capital available for investment purposes. This solution is, in theory, contrary to the goal of the firm. In order to maximize shareholder wealth, the firm must accept all positive NPV projects. Remember that a positive NPV project is one that will cover the cost of financing (i.e., the weighted average cost of capital). In effect, a positive NPV project is self-liquidating, so there should be no problem raising the required funds to make the investment. No matter how much must be raised, as long as positive NPV projects exist, a firm should continue to invest until the cost of investing exceeds the benefits to be gained.[10]

Optimal Capital Budget Without Capital Rationing

We have seen in the previous chapter that a firm's weighted average cost of capital will increase as the amount of capital to be raised increases. We can make use of this fact to determine exactly what a firm's optimal capital budget should be in the absence of capital rationing. Briefly, we rank all projects by their IRR and compare this ranking to the marginal WACC schedule.

---

10. From your economics classes, recall that to maximize profits a firm should continue to produce until the marginal cost equals the marginal revenue. This is the same idea, but in a different context. Furthermore, we are evaluating costs and benefits in present value terms and, as we will see in Chapter 12, we are taking risk into account.

Recall the Rocky Mountain Motors (RMM) example from Chapter 10, and create a copy of the worksheet used for Exhibit 10-6 (page 324). Assume that RMM has found ten potential new projects, each of which would be profitable at their current WACC of 10.51% (i.e., all have IRRs > 10.51%). The projects are listed in Table 11-6.

TABLE 11-6
ROCKY MOUNTAIN MOTORS PROJECTS

Cost	Cumulative Cost	IRR
$445,529	$445,529	15.02%
439,207	884,736	15.87%
407,769	1,292,505	16.51%
396,209	1,688,714	16.16%
271,477	1,960,191	15.38%
201,843	2,162,034	11.69%
189,921	2,351,955	13.82%
146,661	2,498,616	12.19%
138,298	2,636,914	11.48%
74,950	2,711,864	13.00%

Enter the data from Table 11-6 into your RMM worksheet beginning with the labels in A22:C22. The cumulative cost can be calculated by entering: =SUM(A$23:A23) into B23 and then copying the formula to the other cells. The first step in determining the optimal capital budget is to sort all of the projects by their IRR. Select A22:C32 and click the Sort & Filter button on the Home tab. Because we want to sort based on the third column (instead of the first column, which is the default), we need to choose Custom Sort from the menu. Choose IRR from the "Sort by" list and Largest to Smallest in the Order list. This sorted list of IRRs is known as the Investment Opportunity Schedule (IOS).

Next, we want to add the project IRRs to the marginal WACC chart created earlier (see Exhibit 10-6 on page 324). To add the new data, right-click in the chart area and choose Select Data from the shortcut menu. In the dialog box, click on the **A**dd button to create a new data series. For the Series **n**ame type: IOS, and then enter B23:B32 for the **X** Values and C23:C32 for the **Y** Values. Finally, notice that the MCC schedule goes out only to $900,000, but the IOS extends out to over $2,700,000. To fix this, change the value in A20 to: 3,000,000. Your worksheet should look like the one in Exhibit 11-7.

A→Z
Sort &
Filter ▾

EXHIBIT 11-7
MARGINAL WACC AND THE IOS FOR RMM

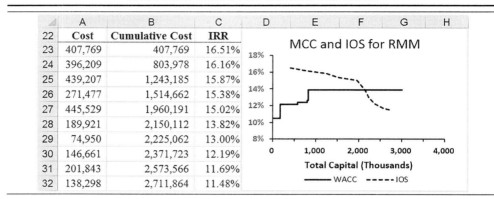

	A	B	C	D E F G H
22	**Cost**	**Cumulative Cost**	**IRR**	
23	407,769	407,769	16.51%	
24	396,209	803,978	16.16%	
25	439,207	1,243,185	15.87%	
26	271,477	1,514,662	15.38%	
27	445,529	1,960,191	15.02%	
28	189,921	2,150,112	13.82%	
29	74,950	2,225,062	13.00%	
30	146,661	2,371,723	12.19%	
31	201,843	2,573,566	11.69%	
32	138,298	2,711,864	11.48%	

As was shown on page 323, we can make the IOS line into a step function. The process is exactly the same as before: We must add additional data points for the cumulative cost and IRR, so that we have two points at each change in the IRR. Once that is finished we can simply edit the data series by right-clicking the IOS and choosing Select Data from the menu. Now, edit the X and Y data ranges to the new ones. Once complete, your chart should look like the one in Exhibit 11-8.

The optimal capital budget without capital rationing is the level of total capital at which the marginal WACC schedule and the IOS cross. In this case, that would be $1,960,191. In other words, the five projects with the highest IRRs should be selected.

EXHIBIT 11-8
COMPLETED MCC AND IOS CHART

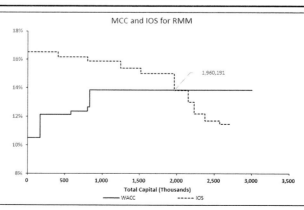

Optimal Capital Budget Under Capital Rationing

Though technically irrational, capital rationing is common. How then can we determine the optimal capital budget in the presence of restricted capital? In this situation, we need to find the combination of projects that maximizes the total net present value subject to the capital spending constraint.

This can be a tedious exercise when there are a large number of positive NPV projects from which to choose. For example, assume that we have four positive NPV projects available. At a minimum we must select one project, but we can select up to four. If we look at every possible combination of these four projects, then we will examine 16 possible combinations. As the number of projects grows, the number of combinations grows even faster. In general, there are 2^N possible combinations, where N is the number of positive NPV projects. Note that negative NPV projects are excluded from this calculation and further consideration because we cannot increase the total NPV by adding a negative NPV project.[11]

Excel provides a tool called the *Solver* that can be used in any type of constrained maximization or minimization problem. The Solver provides a dialog box in which you specify a cell to be optimized, the cells that may be changed, and the constraints under which the Solver must operate. It then finds the optimal solution. Let's look at an example.

> Because of declining demand for high-pressure frammis valves, the Frammis Valve Corporation of America (FVCA) is considering expanding into a number of other businesses. The managers of FVCA have determined that it has 13 potential new investments (see Exhibit 11-9). The total cost of these investments would be $7,611,990, but they are limited to a maximum total investment of only $3,000,000. Your job is to determine the combination of the projects the company should choose.

Because there are 13 acceptable projects, you will have to examine each of the 8,192 ($= 2^{13}$) possible combinations and determine which provides the highest total NPV, while keeping the total cost less than $3,000,000. This problem is obviously going to be time consuming if you have to do it by hand. Enter the data from Exhibit 11-9 into a new worksheet beginning in cell A4.

To solve this problem, we need a way to determine the sum of the costs and NPVs for only those projects that are selected. Because each project will either be selected or not, this is a perfect use for a *binary variable*. A binary variable can take on one of two values, most commonly 0 or 1. We will set up a column with 0s and 1s, where 1 indicates that a project is selected, and 0 indicates rejection. Your worksheet should resemble that in Exhibit 11-9.

---

11. Strictly speaking, this is not always true. Under a multi-period capital budgeting scenario with multi-period cash flow constraints, it is possible that adding negative NPV projects could increase the total NPV if they provide needed cash flows at the right time.

EXHIBIT 11-9
FVCA'S CAPITAL BUDGETING PROBLEM

	A	B	C	D
1	The Optimal Capital Budget			
2	Under Capital Rationing			
3	Project	Cost	NPV	Include
4	A	237,005	84,334	1
5	B	766,496	26,881	1
6	C	304,049	23,162	1
7	D	565,178	82,598	1
8	E	108,990	20,590	1
9	F	89,135	90,404	1
10	G	795,664	18,163	1
11	H	814,493	97,682	1
12	I	480,321	52,063	1
13	J	826,610	53,911	1
14	K	734,830	56,323	1
15	L	910,598	88,349	1
16	M	978,621	69,352	1
17	Total	7,611,990	763,812	13
18	Constraint	3,000,000		

Note that we have initially set each cell in D4:D16 to 1. Due to the nature of the problem, we cannot use an ordinary **Sum** function to total columns B and C. Recall that we want only the sum of the costs and NPVs of the projects that are to be selected. There are several ways to do this, but we will use array formula.[12]

An *array formula* is one that operates on each element in a range, but without specifying each element separately. Array formulas are therefore easier to write and save space. To calculate the total cost of the accepted projects in B17, we want to write a formula that multiplies the costs in column B by the corresponding 0 or 1 in column D and keeps a running total of the results. One way to do this is to write a formula such as: =B4*D4 + B5*D5 + B6*D6... However, this would be a long formula to enter. The equivalent array formula would be: =Sum(B4:B16*$D4:$D16). This is much shorter and easier to understand.

Excel will not understand this formula unless you enter it in a specific way. You must enter array formulas with the Shift+Ctrl+Enter key combination. After correctly entering an array formula, it will appear in the formula bar surrounded by a pair of curly braces ({}). The

---

12. We could also use the **SumIf** or **SumProduct** functions.

formula in B17 will be displayed as: {=SUM(B4:B16*$D4:$D16)}. Note that you do not type the braces. They are only displayed as an indicator that the formula is an array formula. If you see a #VALUE! error in B17, then you probably did not hold down Shift+Ctrl when pressing the Enter key. Copy the formula from B17 to C17, and your totals should be the same as those in Exhibit 11-9.

To restate the problem, we want to maximize the total NPV in C17 by changing the cells in D4:D16 subject to two constraints. The first constraint is that the total cost, in B17, must be less than or equal to 3,000,000. Next we must constrain the values in D4:D16 to be either 0 or 1, but they cannot take on any noninteger values (i.e., they must be binary values).

?→ Solver

Launch the Solver from the Analysis group on the Data tab.[13] In the Set Target Cell edit box enter: C17 and then click on the **M**ax radio button. This tells the Solver that we want to maximize the function in C17. Note that, under different circumstances, we could also minimize this formula or force it to a specific value. Next we need to tell Solver which cells it may change to find a solution. In the **B**y Changing Cells edit box enter: D4:D16.

The hardest part of solving many optimization problems is setting up the appropriate constraints. In this problem we have two constraints, and it will take only two statements to fully specify them. In other cases, it may take more than one statement to fully specify a single constraint. To add a constraint, click on the **A**dd button. This will bring up a second dialog box in which we can enter a cell reference (or range) and the constraint. Note that the dialog box contains a drop-down list in the center that describes the possible relationships. These are <=, =, >=, int, bin, and dif. The last three are all integer constraints. "int" tells the Solver that the values in the cells must be an integer, and "bin" that they must be either 0 or 1. "dif" is a type of integer constraint that allows you to specify that all cells in the range must be different.

Add the first constraint by entering B17 in the Cell Reference edit box, select <=, and enter B18 in the constraint exit box. This will make sure that the total cost is less than the $3,000,000 constraint. For the second constraint, we must constrain the cells in D4:D16 to be binary (0 or 1). Add this constraint and the problem is almost ready to solve.

Because of the large number of possible solutions, the default configuration of the Solver may not find the solution, or it may find a less than optimal solution. In the main Solver dialog box choose the Simplex LP method because this is a linear programming problem. Now, click on the O**p**tions button. This will bring up another dialog box containing the options that you can set. Most of these are beyond the scope of this text. Set the Max **T**ime to at least 500 seconds (higher if you have a very slow PC) and **I**terations to at least 500. These two options control how long the Solver will try to solve the problem (they are maximums,

---

13. If you don't see the Solver button, then you need to activate the Solver add-in. Click the File tab and then click Options. You can activate Solver from the Add-Ins section.

and Solver will stop as soon as it finds the solution). Because our binary constraint is really an integer constraint, make sure that Ignore Integer Constraints is not checked and that Integer Optimality (%) is set to 0. The latter is a convergence tolerance requirement and the default of 5% is too loose to find the optimal solution in the problem.

FIGURE 11-9
THE SOLVER DIALOG BOX

Finally, to start the Solver working on the problem click the Solve button. When Solver finds the solution, it will present you with a dialog box that asks if you would like to save the solution or return to the original values. If you choose to save the optimal solution, your worksheet will resemble the one in Exhibit 11-10. Note that projects A, C, D, F, H, and L are selected; we know this because they have a 1 in the Include column.

One final point about the Solver: You can easily change the constraint of $3,000,000 to any other value and then run the Solver again. Because the Solver settings are saved, you do not need to reenter the data every time.

EXHIBIT 11-10
THE OPTIMAL SOLUTION FOR THE FVCA CAPITAL BUDGET

	A	B	C	D
1	The Optimal Capital Budget			
2	Under Capital Rationing			
3	Project	Cost	NPV	Include
4	A	237,005	84,334	1
5	B	766,496	26,881	0
6	C	304,049	23,162	1
7	D	565,178	82,598	1
8	E	108,990	20,590	0
9	F	89,135	90,404	1
10	G	795,664	18,163	0
11	H	814,493	97,682	1
12	I	480,321	52,063	0
13	J	826,610	53,911	0
14	K	734,830	56,323	0
15	L	910,598	88,349	1
16	M	978,621	69,352	0
17	Total	2,920,458	466,529	6
18	Constraint	3,000,000		

Once the optimal solution is found you can save it as a named scenario and then use the Scenario Analysis tool to view all of the different scenarios. For example, we could create scenarios with total investment constraints of $3 million, $5 million, and $7 million. Once you've run the Solver with each of those constraints, choose What-If Analysis from the Data tab and view the scenarios. You can also create a scenario summary as shown in Exhibit 11-11. In this case, we have edited the worksheet a bit to label the result cells (B17:D17) and hidden the changing cells to improve readability.

EXHIBIT 11-11
SCENARIO SUMMARY FOR OPTIMAL CAPITAL BUDGETING PROBLEM

Scenario Summary	$3,000,000 Constraint	$5,000,000 Constraint	$7,000,000 Constraint
Changing Cells:			
Result Cells:			
Total Investment	2,920,458	4,919,171	6,816,326
Total NPV	466,529	641,695	745,649
Number of Projects	6	9	12

Other Techniques

For those who don't have a computer or the skills required to maximize the total NPV, other techniques can be used to approximate the optimal capital budget. The first is to select the projects with the highest profitability indices. You may have to discard some high PI projects, and you will likely not achieve the maximum NPV, but the solution can often be found with less work than maximizing NPV. As an alternative, we could choose the projects with the highest IRRs. However, this could be misleading if the projects are of greatly different sizes (as in the RMM example).

Summary

Capital budgeting is one of the most important functions of the corporate financial manager. In this chapter, we have seen how to calculate the relevant cash flows and how to evaluate those cash flows to determine the profitability of accepting the project. We have demonstrated six profitability measures that are summarized in Table 11-7.

TABLE 11-7
SUMMARY OF PROFITABILITY MEASURES

Profitability Measure	Acceptance Criteria
Payback Period	<= Maximum allowable period
Discounted Payback	<= Maximum allowable period
Net Present Value	>= 0
Profitability Index	>= 1
Internal Rate of Return	>= WACC
Modified IRR	>= WACC

In addition, we introduced the Scenario Analysis and Solver tools provided by Excel. The Scenario Analysis tool allows us to easily compare the outcomes based on various inputs. The Solver allows us to find optimal values for a cell in a model.

☑ Check Box after Copying Notes

TABLE 11-8
FUNCTIONS INTRODUCED IN THIS CHAPTER

Purpose	Function	Page
Calculate Straight-Line Depreciation	SLN(*COST*, *SALVAGE*, *LIFE*)	336
Vertical Lookup	VLOOKUP(*LOOKUP_VALUE*, *TABLE_ARRAY*, *COL_INDEX_NUM*, *RANGE_LOOKUP*)	337
Calculate Variable Depreciation	VDB(*COST*, *SALVAGE*, *LIFE*, *START_PERIOD*, *END_PERIOD*, *FACTOR*, *NO_SWITCH*)	338
Handle Errors	IFERROR(*VALUE*, *VALUE_IF_ERROR*)	339
Calculate MACRS Depreciation	FAME_MACRS(*COST*, *MACRSCLASS*, *YEAR*, *TABLE*)	339
Calculate the Payback Period	FAME_PAYBACK(*CASHFLOWS*,*RATE*)	343
Calculate the IRR	IRR(*VALUES*,*GUESS*)	349
Calculate the MIRR	MIRR(*VALUES*, *FINANCE_RATE*, *REINVEST_RATE*)	353

Problems

1. You are considering an investment in two projects, A and B. Both projects will cost $100,000, and the projected cash flows are as follows:

Year	Project A	Project B
1	$ 6,250	$ 45,000
2	18,750	33,750
3	35,000	25,000
4	43,750	18,750
5	50,000	12,500

a. Assuming that the WACC is 8%, calculate the payback period, discounted payback period, NPV, PI, IRR, and MIRR. If the projects are mutually exclusive, which project should be selected?

b. Create an NPV profile chart for projects A and B. What is the exact crossover rate for these two projects?

2. The Ocean City water park is considering the purchase of a new log flume ride. The cost to purchase the equipment is $3,500,000, and it will cost an additional $250,000 to have it installed. The equipment has an expected life of 6 years, and it will be depreciated using a MACRS 7-year class life. Management expects to run about 150 rides per day, with each ride averaging 25 riders. The season will last for 120 days per year. In the first year, the ticket price per rider is expected to be $4.00, and it will be increased by 4% per year. The variable cost per rider will be $1.40, and total fixed costs will be $320,000 per year. After six years, the ride will be dismantled at a cost of $115,000 and the parts will be sold for $450,000. The cost of capital is 12%, and its marginal tax rate is 35%.

    a. Calculate the initial outlay, annual after-tax cash flow for each year, and the terminal cash flow.

    b. Calculate the NPV, IRR, and MIRR of the new equipment. Is the project acceptable?

    c. Create a Data Table that shows the NPV, IRR, and MIRR for MACRS classes of 3, 5, 7, 10, 15, and 20 years. What do you conclude about the speed of depreciation and the profitability of an investment?

    d. Using the Goal Seek tool, calculate the minimum ticket price that must be charged in the first year in order to make the project acceptable.

3. Arroy Snackfoods is considering replacing a five-year-old machine that originally cost $50,000. It was being depreciated using straight-line to an expected salvage value of zero over its original 10-year life, and could now be sold for $40,000. The replacement machine would cost $190,000 and have a five-year expected life. It would be depreciated using the MACRS 5-year class life. The actual expected salvage value of this machine after 5 years is $20,000. The new machine is expected to operate much more efficiently, saving $10,000 per year in energy costs. In addition, it will eliminate one salaried position saving another $45,000 annually. The firm's marginal tax rate is 35% and the WACC is 9%.

    a. Set up an operating cash flow statement, and calculate the payback, discounted payback, NPV, IRR, and MIRR of the replacement project. Should the project be accepted?

    b. At what discount rate would you be indifferent between keeping the existing equipment and purchasing the new equipment?

4. Chicago Turkey is considering a new turkey farm to service its western region stores. The stores currently require 650,000 turkeys per year, and they are purchased from various local turkey farms for an average price of $8 per bird. The managers believe that their new farm would lower the cost per bird to $7, while maintaining the average selling price of $10 per bird. However, due to the centralized structure of this operation, shipping expenses will increase to $1.25 per bird from the current $1.00. The firm will need to increase its inventory of live turkeys by $45,000. It will cost $150,000 to purchase the land and $300,000 to construct the buildings and purchase equipment. In addition, labor expense will rise by $250,000 per year. The buildings and equipment will be depreciated using the straight-line method over five years to a salvage value of $100,000. After five years, the company will sell the farm for $300,000 ($100,000 for the buildings and equipment, $200,000 for the land). The firm's marginal tax rate is 35%, and note that land is not depreciable.

   a. Calculate the initial outlay, after-tax cash flows, and terminal cash flow for this project.

   b. If the WACC is 11%, calculate the payback period, discounted payback period, NPV, PI, IRR, and MIRR.

   c. Management is uncertain about several of the variables in your analysis and have asked you to provide three different scenarios.

Scenario	Labor Expense	Salvage Value of Buildings	Salvage Value of Land
Best Case	$200,000	$150,000	$300,000
Expected Case	250,000	100,000	200,000
Worst Case	350,000	20,000	40,000

   Create a scenario analysis showing the profitability measures for this investment using the information in the table above. (Note: The salvage value of the buildings is the actual forecasted salvage value, not that used for depreciation.)

5. The Chief Financial Officer of Eaton Medical Devices has determined that the firm's capital investment budget will be $5,000,000 for the upcoming year. Unfortunately, this amount is not sufficient to cover all of the positive NPV projects available to the firm.

Project	Cost	NPV
A	$922,775	$106,728
B	488,486	50,524
C	1,432,913	244,053
D	892,192	77,709
E	166,844	15,277
F	1,159,674	66,922
G	2,697,950	107,166
H	239,625	69,015
I	1,777,453	52,614
J	884,841	49,296

You have been asked to choose which investments should be made.

a. Using the Solver, determine which of the above projects should be included in the budget if the firm's goal is to maximize shareholder wealth. (Note: Set the Solver to use the Simplex LP method, and turn off the Ignore Integer Constraints setting.)

b. Now assume that the CFO has informed you that projects A and B are mutually exclusive, but one of them must be selected. Change your Solver constraints to account for this new information and find the new solution. (Use the same options as in part a.)

c. Ignore the constraints from part b. The CFO has now informed you that Project I is of great strategic importance to the survival of the firm. It must be accepted. Which projects should be accepted?

d. Explain why the different constraints in parts a, b, and c result in different results. Which one results in the highest total investment? Which one has the highest overall NPV?

e. If you rank the projects by profitability index and then select them until you reach a total cost near $5,000,000 do you get the same results as when optimizing by NPV? Use the **RANK.AVG** function to rank the projects by profitability index in descending order.

CHAPTER 12

Risk and Capital Budgeting

After studying this chapter, you should be able to:

1. *Define the five major statistical measures used in finance, and calculate them manually and in Excel.*

2. *Explain five techniques for incorporating risk into the capital budgeting decision process.*

3. *Perform sensitivity and scenario analysis with data tables and Scenario Manager.*

4. *Perform a Monte Carlo simulation to determine the expected NPV of an investment.*

Risk is a difficult concept to define, but most people recognize such obvious risks as swimming in shark-infested waters. If you consider risky situations for a moment, you will realize that the thing that they all have in common is uncertainty about the outcome and the possibility of a loss. Many times, we face the loss of life or money. In this chapter, we are concerned with the possibility of a financial loss. Specifically, we will say that the larger the possibility of loss, the larger the risk.

We will begin by attempting to measure the riskiness of an investment, and then we will consider how we can adjust our decision-making process to account for the risk that we have measured. In Chapter 13, we will see how we can reduce risk through diversification.

Review of Some Useful Statistical Concepts

Any situation that has an uncertain outcome can be said to have a *probability distribution*, which is simply a listing of the potential outcomes and their associated probabilities. A probability distribution is said to be *discrete* if there are a limited number of potential outcomes and *continuous* if an infinite number of possible outcomes can occur. Figure 12-1 illustrates both continuous and discrete probability distributions. Continuous probability distributions can be approximated by discrete distributions if we have enough possible outcomes. To keep things simple, in this chapter we will use only discrete distributions in our examples.

FIGURE 12-1
CONTINUOUS VS. DISCRETE PROBABILITY DISTRIBUTIONS

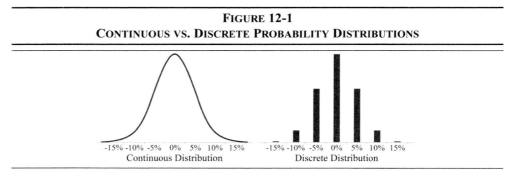

One type of probability distribution has numerous properties that make it especially attractive for our use: the *normal distribution*. In particular, the normal distribution can be completely described by its mean and variance, which will prove useful in our efforts to understand risk.

The Expected Value

The *expected value* of a distribution is a weighted average of all possible outcomes where the weights are the probabilities of occurrence. The expected value can be thought of as the most likely outcome or the average outcome if we could run an experiment thousands of times. For any discrete probability distribution, the expected value is given by:

$$E(X) = \sum_{t=1}^{N} \rho_t X_t$$ (12-1)

where $E(X)$ is the expected or most likely X, X_t is the tth possible outcome, and ρ_t is the probability that X_t will occur. For the normal distribution, the expected value is the same as the more familiar arithmetic mean.

To illustrate the calculation of the expected value, suppose that you have been offered an opportunity to participate in a game of chance. The rules of this particular game are such that you must pay $200 to play, and Table 12-1 describes the possible payoffs.

TABLE 12-1
PROBABILITY DISTRIBUTION FOR A GAME OF CHANCE

Probability	Cash Flow
0.25	$ 100
0.50	200
0.25	300

To determine whether you should play this game, we must compare the expected payoff to the cost of playing. If the expected cash flow exceeds your cost, then it makes sense to play. The expected cash flow, $E(Cf)$, of this game is:

$$E(Cf) = 0.25(100) + 0.50(200) + 0.25(300) = 200$$

so that you expect to break even after paying to play (this is known as a *fair bet* and would be rejected by a risk averse investor). Note that in actuality, if the game is played only once you could lose as much as $100 or win as much as $100 net of your cost of entry. However, the most likely outcome is a net gain of $0.00. The arithmetic mean of cash flows $(\overline{Cf})$ is:

$$\overline{Cf} = \frac{100 + 200 + 300}{3} = 200$$

and subtracting your cost, you can see that they are the same. Again, in this case, the expected value and the arithmetic mean are the same because the outcomes of this game are symmetrically distributed.

It is important to understand that many times the assumption of a symmetrical distribution is not accurate, and in this case the arithmetic mean and the expected value will not be the same. This is particularly true in many financial situations where your maximum loss is limited to 100% of the investment, but your potential gain is unlimited. This results in a distribution that is skewed to the right. In this type of situation it is often helpful to transform the data. For example, with financial assets we often calculate log-price relatives instead of the usual percentage changes:

$$\text{Log-Price Relative} = Ln\left(\frac{P_1}{P_0}\right) \tag{12-2}$$

where Ln is the natural logarithm operator, P_1 is the ending price, and P_0 is the beginning price. This transformation converts a skewed variable into a normally distributed variable, at least approximately, and allows us to use statistics that assume normality.

Measures of Dispersion

Whenever we use an expected value, it is useful to know how much, on average, the actual outcome might deviate from the expected outcome. The larger these potential deviations, the less confidence we have that the expected outcome, or something near it, will actually occur. Another way of saying this is that the larger the potential deviations from the expected value, the higher the probability of an outcome far away from the expected outcome.

Recall that we earlier said that high probabilities of loss indicate a high-risk situation. Therefore, when comparing distributions we can say that the distribution with the larger potential deviations has a higher probability of greater loss and so it is more risky.

The Variance and Standard Deviation

To measure risk, we need a way to measure the size of the potential deviations from the mean. One measure that we could use is the average deviation from the mean:

$$\overline{D} = \sum_{t=1}^{N} p_t(X_t - E(X)) \tag{12-3}$$

But the average deviation is, by definition, always zero. So we need another measure of dispersion that doesn't suffer from this flaw. We could calculate the average of the absolute values of the deviations, but historically we have used the *variance* and *standard deviation*. The variance is the average of the squared deviations from the mean and is calculated as:[1]

$$\sigma_X^2 = \sum_{t=1}^{N} p_t(X_t - E(X))^2 \tag{12-4}$$

Because we are squaring the deviations from the mean, and the result of squaring a number is always positive, the variance must be positive.[2] The larger the variance, the less likely it is that the actual outcome will be near the expected outcome and the riskier it is considered to be. Figure 12-2 illustrates this by comparing two normal distributions.

---

1. Note that in your beginning statistics class, you probably defined the population variance as:

$$\sigma_X^2 = \frac{1}{N} \sum_{t=1}^{N} (X_t - \overline{X})^2$$

Our definition is equivalent if we assume that all outcomes are equally likely.

2. It is possible that the variance could be zero, but only if just one possible outcome exists.

FIGURE 12-2
COMPARISON OF THE RISKINESS OF TWO DISTRIBUTIONS

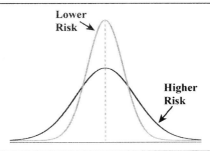

Returning to the example in Table 12-1, we can calculate the variance of possible outcomes as follows:

$$\sigma^2 = 0.25(100 - 200)^2 + 0.50(200 - 200)^2 + 0.25(300 - 200)^2 = 5,000$$

So the variance of possible outcomes is 5,000. But 5,000 in what units? In this case the units are squared dollars, an unusual unit of measurement to be sure. In order to make this measurement more understandable we take the square root of the variance, which gives us the *standard deviation* in the original units:

$$\sigma_X = \sqrt{\sigma_X^2} = \sqrt{\sum_{t=1}^{N} p_t (X_t - E(X))^2} \tag{12-5}$$

The standard deviation of potential outcomes in our game example is:

$$\sigma = \sqrt{5,000} = 70.71$$

which means that about 68% of all outcomes will be within one standard deviation of the mean (200 ± 70.71), and about 95.5% will be within two standard deviations (200 ± 141.42). Furthermore, it is exceedingly unlikely (<0.30%), but not impossible, that the actual outcome will fall beyond three standard deviations from the mean.[3]

---

3. This is known as the empirical rule. For nonnormal distributions, Chebyshev's Theorem gives similar (though not as precise) results.

The Coefficient of Variation

Suppose that after playing the original game, you are offered a chance to play the game again. This time, though, the game is 10 times larger and so is your cost to play. The possible outcomes are presented in Table 12-2.

TABLE 12-2
SAME GAME, BUT 10 TIMES LARGER

Probability	Cash Flow
0.25	$ 1,000
0.50	2,000
0.25	3,000

Is this game riskier than the old game? Let's look at the standard deviation to see:

$$\sigma = \sqrt{0.25(1,000 - 2,000)^2 + 0.50(2,000 - 2,000)^2 + 0.25(3,000 - 2,000)^2}$$
$$\sigma = 707.106$$

Because the standard deviation is 10 times larger, it appears that the new game is much riskier. Recall, however, that we said that high risk was associated with a high probability of loss. In the new game, your probability of loss is unchanged (25%). Since the probability of loss is unchanged, the risk should be the same.

Apparently the standard deviation has a scale problem. That is, larger numbers cause larger standard deviations, even if the relative dispersion is unchanged. The coefficient of variation handles the scale problem by dividing the standard deviation by the mean, so it is a measure of risk per unit of return:

$$\gamma_X = \frac{\sigma_X}{E(X)} \tag{12-6}$$

If the new game is truly riskier than the old game, it will have a higher coefficient of variation. Let's compare the coefficients of variation for both games:

$$\gamma_1 = \frac{70.7106}{200} = 0.3535$$

$$\gamma_2 = \frac{707.106}{2,000} = 0.3535$$

Because $\gamma_1 = \gamma_2$, both games must be equally risky. The coefficient of variation is useful any time the expected values of two distributions are significantly different. The standard deviation has no meaning without reference to the expected value. Because it provides a measure of risk relative to return, the coefficient of variation can always be used to compare investments without regard to the size of the investment.

Using Excel to Measure Risk

Now that we understand how risk can be evaluated, let's look at how Excel might be used to simplify the calculations. In this section, we will introduce several of Excel's built-in functions and user-defined functions that are contained in the file Famefncs.xlam. Before continuing, make sure that the add-in is enabled and open a new workbook, into which we will enter data from an example of a capital budgeting project.

The Freshly Frozen Fish Company Example

> The Freshly Frozen Fish Company currently markets frozen fish fillets and other related products. While seeking expansion ideas, management of the company decided to look into the possibility of a line of frozen catfish fillets. Entry into this business would require the purchase of an existing 80-acre catfish farm in western Alabama at a cost of $250,000 for the land and $400,000 for the buildings and equipment. The buildings and equipment will be depreciated using MACRS with a class life of 20 years. At the end of the five years, management anticipates that the farm will be sold for $550,000 ($350,000 for the land and $200,000 for the buildings and equipment).
>
> The marketing department estimates that the firm will be able to sell 200,000 pounds of fillets at an average wholesale price of $2.50 per pound during the first year. Unit demand is expected to grow at a rate of 8% annually thereafter. Variable operating expenses are expected to average 60% of gross sales, and fixed costs (not including depreciation) will be $80,000 per year. The company's marginal tax rate is 35% and its WACC is 10%.

Before we can determine the riskiness of this project, we must determine its cost and annual cash flows. Let's begin by entering all the data from the problem into the worksheet starting in cell A1. The easiest way to extract data from a problem such as this is to take it as it comes and enter it into the worksheet in that order, being careful to label every row. This way, you are less likely to overlook an important piece of data. That is exactly what we've done in Exhibit 12-1. If necessary, we can rearrange this table later.

Recall from Chapter 11 (page 331) that our first task is to determine the initial outlay. The example problem in that chapter was a little different than this one because it was a replacement problem. However, exactly the same techniques can be used to determine the cash flows. Just realize that in the case of this entirely new project we aren't replacing anything, so any cash flows associated with old equipment are set to zero. Otherwise, the methodology is exactly the same.

EXHIBIT 12-1
FRESHLY FROZEN FISH COMPANY INPUTS

	A	B
1	**Frozen Catfish Fillet Project Inputs**	
2	Cost of Land	250,000
3	Cost of Buildings & Equipment	400,000
4	MACRS Class	20
5	Life of Project (Years)	5
6	Terminal Value of Land	350,000
7	Terminal Value of Buildings & Equipment	200,000
8	First Year Catfish Sales (lbs)	200,000
9	Price per Pound	2.50
10	Unit Sales Growth Rate	8%
11	Variable Costs as % of Sales	60%
12	Fixed Costs	80,000
13	Tax Rate	35%
14	WACC	10%

Before continuing, let's take a little time to set up our calculation area on the worksheet. Realize that the annual after-tax cash flows are going to be different in each of the five years. To keep things as simple as possible, we will set up the calculations in an operating cash flow format, which is similar to an income statement but includes only operating cash flows. In A16 enter: `Annual Cash Flows for Frozen Catfish Fillet Project`, and center this title over A16:G16. Next, in B17 enter: 0 and use AutoFill to extend that to 5 in G17. Now apply a custom number format of: `"Year "0` to the range.

We have purposely simplified this example, so we have no shipping, installation, training, or construction costs. The initial outlay is simply the cost of the land and buildings. In A18 enter: `Initial Outlay`, and in B18 enter: `=-(B2+B3)`. This will give us the initial outlay as a negative number. The result is –$650,000.

Our next step is to calculate the annual after-tax cash flows for each year. As noted earlier, the cash flows will be different each year because sales and variable operating expenses are expected to increase every year by 8%. Additionally, the depreciation expense will differ each year because we are using MACRS instead of straight-line depreciation. We will calculate the ATCF for each year as:

$$\text{ATCF}_N = (S_N - V_N - F_N - D_N)(1 - t) + D_N$$

where S_N is the total revenue in year N, V_N is the total variable costs, F_N is the fixed costs, D_N is the annual depreciation expense, and t is the marginal tax rate. This is exactly the same equation as shown on page 333, except that it has been modified slightly to suit this problem. The operating cash flow statement uses this equation, but in a vertical format.

In A19 enter: Sales as the label. We will calculate the first year sales in C19 by multiplying unit sales (200,000 pounds) by the selling price ($2.50), so the equation is: =B8*B9. This gives us $500,000 in sales revenue for the first year. Each additional year's sales will be 8% greater than previous sales, so in D19 enter: =C19*(1+$B$10). Now copy this formula over the range E19:G19. As a check, note that under these assumptions sales will grow to $680,244.48 by year 5.

Next, to calculate the annual variable costs enter: =C19*$B$11 into C20, and copy it across D20:G20. In A20 enter: Variable Costs as the label for the row. In A21 enter: Fixed Costs for the label, and then in C21 enter: =$B$12. Copy this over D21:G21.

We will calculate the depreciation expense in row 22, so enter: Depreciation Expense in A22. Because we are using MACRS depreciation (see page 336), we will use the **FAME_MACRS** function included in the Famefncs.xlam add-in. Recall that this function is defined as:

FAME_MACRS(*Cost*, *MacrsClass*, *Year*, *Table*)

where *TABLE* is an optional argument that tells the function whether to use the exact calculation or the table percentages. In this case, we will use the exact calculation, so in C22 enter: =IFERROR(FAME_MACRS($B$3,$B$4,C17,FALSE),0). Remember that we cannot depreciate land, only the buildings and equipment. Note that we are referencing the year number in row 17, which explains why we used a custom number format in that row. Copy the formula from C22 to D22:G22. The depreciation expense will be $15,000 in year 1 and $22,853 in year 5.

We can now calculate the taxable cash flows in row 23. In A23 add the label: Taxable Cash Flows. Subtract the total costs from sales in C23 with the formula: =C19-SUM(C20:C22) and copy this across the other columns. In A24 enter the label: Taxes, and in C24 enter: =C23*$B$13 and copy it to D24:G24.

At this point, to get the ATCF we need to add back the depreciation expense that was previously subtracted. In A25 enter: Add: Depreciation as the label and then in C25: =C22. Copy this to the remaining cells, and then in A26 enter: Annual After-Tax Cash Flows. Finally, in C26 we can enter: =C23-C24+C25. Copy this to the other cells in D26:G26. The ATCF for year 1 should be $83,250.

The last cash flow that we must calculate is the terminal cash flow, so in A27 enter the label: Terminal Cash Flow. Recall that this is the sum of the nonoperating cash flows that occur at the end of the life of the project. In this problem, those would be the sale of the land and buildings as well as any taxes required on the gains. The land is not depreciable, so any gain on the sale of land is taxable. We will start building this formula in G27 by calculating the after-tax proceeds from selling the land with the formula: =B6-(B6-B2)*B13.

To calculate the tax on the buildings and equipment, we must first determine the book value in year 5 so that we can compare that to the salvage value. The book value is the original cost less the accumulated depreciation. If this is different from the salvage value, the difference is taxable. Therefore, the cash inflow from selling the buildings and equipment can be calculated with the formula: =B7-(B7-(B3-SUM(C22:G22)))*B13.

The terminal cash flow will be the sum of the after-tax cash flows received from selling the land and from selling the buildings. So, in G27 your formula is: =B6-(B6-B2)*B13+B7-(B7-(B3-SUM(C22:G22)))*B13.

In order to summarize our calculations, we will add one more row. In A28 enter: Total Annual Cash Flows. In B28 enter: =B18. In C28 enter: =C26+C27 and copy it across. Check your worksheet against that shown in Exhibit 12-2 to be sure that your calculations are correct.

EXHIBIT 12-2
CALCULATION OF THE ANNUAL AFTER-TAX CASH FLOWS

	A	B	C	D	E	F	G
16		Annual Cash Flows for Frozen Catfish Fillet Project					
17		Year 0	Year 1	Year 2	Year 3	Year 4	Year 5
18	Initial Outlay	(650,000)					
19	Sales		500,000	540,000	583,200	629,856	680,244
20	Variable Costs		300,000	324,000	349,920	377,914	408,147
21	Fixed Costs		80,000	80,000	80,000	80,000	80,000
22	Depreciation Expense		15,000	28,875	26,709	24,706	22,853
23	Taxable Cash Flows		105,000	107,125	126,571	147,236	169,245
24	Taxes		36,750	37,494	44,300	51,533	59,236
25	Add: Depreciation		15,000	28,875	26,709	24,706	22,853
26	Annual After-Tax Cash Flow		83,250	98,506	108,980	120,410	132,862
27	Terminal Cash Flow						543,650
28	Total Annual Cash Flows	(650,000)	83,250	98,506	108,980	120,410	676,512

At this point, we are ready to calculate the net present value to give a preliminary assessment of the merits of this project. In A30 enter: Net Present Value, and in B30 enter: =NPV(B14,C28:G28)+B28. The NPV is $91,272.55, which would seem to indicate that the project is acceptable. If you calculate the other profitability measures, you will find that the IRR is 13.77%, the MIRR is 12.93%, the profitability index is 1.14, the payback period is 4.35 years, and the discounted payback is 4.78 years.

Introducing Uncertainty

If we lived in a world of perfect certainty, the catfish fillet project would be accepted without question. After all, it appears that it will increase shareholder wealth by $91,272.55. Unfortunately, the world is not certain. Even in this simplified example, it should be clear that many sources of uncertainty may arise. For example, the marketing department doesn't really *know* that the firm will sell 200,000 pounds of catfish fillets in the first year. Likewise, it doesn't know that it will be able to get the assumed $2.50 per pound or that demand will grow at an annual rate of 8% per year. Consumer demand may be far less than expected. This could lead to a double whammy: Not only would unit demand be less than expected, but the wholesale price would likely be less than $2.50 per pound. Poor first year acceptance could also mean lower subsequent growth rates. These and many other uncertainties naturally result in uncertainty surrounding our expected annual cash flows that, in turn, results in uncertainty surrounding the estimated NPV.

In such an uncertain world, it is helpful to develop models that allow us to determine how much uncertainty surrounds our estimate of the NPV. For example, we might like to make an educated guess as to the probability that the NPV will actually turn out to be less than zero. The following sections will lead us to an answer to this question.

Sensitivity Analysis

As noted earlier, many uncertain variables exist in our catfish fillet example. In fact, we could say that virtually all of the variables are uncertain, as are many others that we have not explicitly considered. However, some of these variables have more of an impact on the NPV than others. Because it would take a lot of time and effort to generate precise forecasts of every variable, it is helpful to concentrate on only the most important variables. Sensitivity analysis is the tool that helps us to identify the variables that deserve the most attention.

The idea is to make small changes in variables, one at a time, and observe the effect on the NPV (or any other decision criteria). For example, we might change the selling price from $2.50 per pound to $2.25 (a change of –10%) and then calculate that the NPV would decline to $34,291.68. Record this fact and reset the selling price to its original value. Now, reduce the terminal value of the land to $315,000 (a change of –10%) and note that the NPV declines to $77,146.59. Reducing the selling price by 10% leads to a much bigger decline in the NPV than does a similar reduction in the terminal value of the land. Therefore, we should devote more resources to accurately determining the selling price, and not spend much time estimating the value of the land.

There are two problems with the procedure outlined earlier. First, by making only a single small change to each variable, we may miss nonlinear relationships. Second, carrying out this procedure for each uncertain variable would be cumbersome. We would have to change a variable, write down the resulting NPV, reset the variable to its original value, change another variable, write down the resulting NPV, and so on. To solve the first problem, we can simply make several changes in each variable, both up and down. For example, we could change the selling price per pound by –30% to +30% in, say, 10% increments. This, however, exacerbates the second problem by making the analysis even more onerous. Fortunately, Excel provides a solution.

Using Data Tables

A data table is an Excel tool that automatically performs the process described previously. To see how it works, let's set up a simple example. Suppose that we wish to see what happens to the expected NPV as the selling price varies from $1.50 to $3.50 per pound. To start, enter $1.50 in G5 and $2.00 in H5.[4] Now use AutoFill to create the rest of the price series. The next step is to enter a formula into F6. In this case, we are interested in the NPV, so we need to enter: =NPV(B14,C28:G28)+B28.

FIGURE 12-3
THE DATA TABLE DIALOG BOX

When we execute the data table command, Excel will automatically substitute the values from G5:K5 into our model (in cell B9) one at a time and record the resulting NPVs in the table. Select F5:K6 (this is the entire area of the table, including the NPV formula) and then choose Data Table... from the What-If Analysis button on the Data tab. In the resulting dialog box, type B9 into the Row input cell edit box as shown in Figure 12-3. After clicking the OK button, this section of your worksheet should look like the one in Exhibit 12-3.

The values in G6:K6 are the NPVs. For example, if the price per pound was $1.50 the NPV would be –$136,650.91. Similarly, if the price was $3.50 the NPV would be $319,196. If necessary, you can change any or all of the prices in row 5 and the table will automatically update.

---

4. The data table can be created anywhere on this worksheet, but it cannot be in another worksheet. You can get around this limitation by carefully constructing your formulas.

EXHIBIT 12-3
THE DATA TABLE FOR DIFFERENT PRICES

	F	G	H	I	J	K
4			NPV Sensitivity to Unit Prices			
5	Unit Price	$1.50	$2.00	$2.50	$3.00	$3.50
6		(136,650.91)	(22,689.18)	91,272.55	205,234.27	319,196.00

The original NPV formula in F6 is not a part of the table per se, and it might confuse some people. It is only there so that Excel knows what formula to use when calculating the table. We can easily hide this value by simply selecting F6 and changing the font color to white, or using a custom number format with just a semicolon. This will make the table easier to read.

Excel allows for other types of data tables than we have demonstrated here. The data table in Exhibit 12-3 is called a row-oriented one-variable table because our prices are in a row. If the prices were in a column instead, we could create a column-oriented one-variable table. To create a column-oriented table, the only difference is that you would enter the changing cell (B9) into the Column input cell edit box (see Figure 12-3). The result would be exactly the same, except for the orientation table. We can also create two-variable data tables that allow for two changing variables. The procedure is similar, but you should check the online help for the details.

Because we have more than one uncertain variable in our catfish fillet problem, we will need several data tables. It will also be helpful, for comparison purposes, to deviate a bit from the methodology described earlier. Specifically, we can set up several data tables based on percentage changes in our uncertain variables. This will make it easier to compare the result from a change in unit sales to the result from a change in the growth rate.

Let's start by changing the input area of the worksheet so that it can accommodate this type of sensitivity analysis more easily. In D5 enter: Sensitivity %, and then in D6:D11 enter: 0% in each cell. Change B6 so that it has a formula rather than a number: =350000*(1+D6). Now if we put 10% into D6, for example, the terminal value of the land will change from $350,000 to $385,000. Make similar changes in cells B7:B11 so that those values change as we change the corresponding percentages. Your input area should now look like the one in Exhibit 12-4. Note that we will be doing the sensitivity analysis on only six of the variables.

At this point, we can proceed in a similar manner as we did earlier. Let's first create a percentage-based data table for the terminal value of the land. Go to A38 and enter: Terminal Value of Land. In B38:H38 enter a series of numbers from –30% to +30% in 10% increments (–30%, –20%, –10%, etc.). In A39, enter the NPV function: =NPV(B14,C28:G28)+B28.

EXHIBIT 12-4
THE INPUT AREA SET UP FOR SENSITIVITY ANALYSIS

	A	B	C	D
1	**Frozen Catfish Fillet Project Inputs**			
2	Cost of Land	250,000		
3	Cost of Buildings & Equipment	400,000		
4	MACRS Class	20		
5	Life of Project (Years)	5		Sensitivity %
6	Terminal Value of Land	350,000		0%
7	Terminal Value of Buildings & Equipment	200,000		0%
8	First Year Catfish Sales (lbs)	200,000		0%
9	Price per Pound	2.50		0%
10	Unit Sales Growth Rate	8%		0%
11	Variable Costs as % of Sales	60%		0%
12	Fixed Costs	80,000		
13	Tax Rate	35%		
14	WACC	10%		

We have now set up the table and all that remains is to select it and execute the Data Table… command. In this case the row input cell is D6, which is the percentage that corresponds to the terminal value of the land. The data table will plug –30% into D6, which will change the terminal land value in B6 resulting in a different NPV. Next, it will plug in –20%, and so on.

Using the same procedure, create data tables for each of the uncertain variables, each time changing the row input cell (D7, D8, etc.). You should end up with six data tables as shown in Exhibit 12-5. Note that, as mentioned earlier, we have hidden the original NPV formula so that the table is easier to read.

Sensitivity Diagrams

Some people can look at the data tables and see at a glance that the most important variables are the unit sales, price per pound, and the variable cost as a percentage of sales. Others, however, find it helpful to create charts of the data. We can either create a separate chart for each variable or put all of the variables in one chart.

To create one chart that shows all of the variables, select B38:H39 and then Ctrl+click each of the NPV other series. Create a scatter chart and place it somewhere convenient in the worksheet. For this example problem, it turns out that some of the lines overlap, so it is impossible to tell them apart on the chart. This is not always the case. However, even when we don't have this problem, it can be much easier to see which variables are most important if they are all in separate charts. This is particularly true when we have a lot of variables.

EXHIBIT 12-5
DATA TABLES FOR THE UNCERTAIN VARIABLES

	A	B	C	D	E	F	G	H
37				Sensitivity Tables				
38	Terminal Value of Land	-30%	-20%	-10%	0%	10%	20%	30%
39		48,895	63,021	77,147	91,273	105,399	119,524	133,650
40								
41	Value of Buildings & Equipment	-30%	-20%	-10%	0%	10%	20%	30%
42		67,057	75,129	83,201	91,273	99,345	107,417	115,488
43								
44	First Year Catfish Sales (lbs)	-30%	-20%	-10%	0%	10%	20%	30%
45		(79,670)	(22,689)	34,292	91,273	148,253	205,234	262,215
46								
47	Price per Pound	-30%	-20%	-10%	0%	10%	20%	30%
48		(79,670)	(22,689)	34,292	91,273	148,253	205,234	262,215
49								
50	Unit Sales Growth Rate	-30%	-20%	-10%	0%	10%	20%	30%
51		66,954	74,941	83,046	91,273	99,620	108,091	116,686
52								
53	Variable Costs as % of Sales	-30%	-20%	-10%	0%	10%	20%	30%
54		347,686	262,215	176,744	91,273	5,801	(79,670)	(165,141)

Creating a separate chart for each variable is more time consuming, and you need to make sure that the scaling of the axes is the same in each chart so that you can compare the slopes. The advantage to this approach is that it is much easier to identify the individual data series. As can be seen in Figure 12-4, the lines with the steepest slopes are the same as those previously identified as the most important variables.

In order to make this comparison, it is vital that the axis scaling is identical in each chart. To make creating all of these charts easier, you can copy and paste the first one and then simply change the data ranges. To change the data series in a chart, right-click in the chart and choose Select Data... In the dialog box, select the series and then click the **E**dit button to change the data ranges.

An alternative to the visual approach is to use the **SLOPE** function to determine the slope of each line. This function calculates a regression equation and returns the slope. It is defined as:

$$\text{SLOPE}(\textit{KNOWN\_Y'S}, \textit{KNOWN\_X'S})$$

where **KNOWN_Y'S** and **KNOWN_X'S** are the Y and X data ranges, respectively. For our purpose, the Y variables are the NPVs and the X variables are the percentage changes. For example, we can use =SLOPE(B39:H39,B38:H38) to find that the slope of the line for the terminal land value is 141,259.60. This can then be numerically compared to the slopes of the other lines. The larger the slope, the more important the variable. Note that if any of the slopes might be negative, then it is helpful to use the **ABS** function to return the absolute

FIGURE 12-4
SENSITIVITY DIAGRAMS FOR EACH VARIABLE

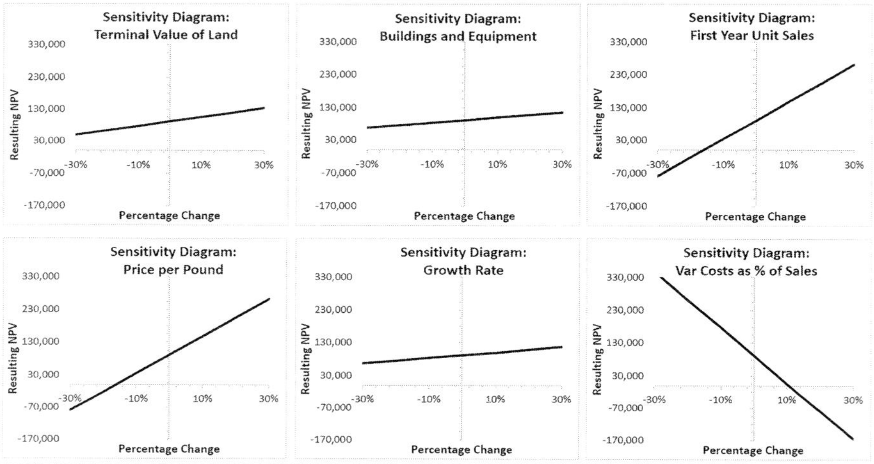

value of the slope. Adding this function to the formula will change it to: `=ABS(SLOPE(B39:H39,B38:H38))`. This allows us to compare magnitudes without regard to signs.

Clearly, the most important variables are the unit sales, price per pound, and the variable cost as a percentage of sales. These are the variables that we will use in our scenario analysis in the next section.

Scenario Analysis

The sensitivity analysis has identified the three most important variables, but we've only seen their impact on the NPV in isolation. A *scenario analysis* will allow us to see the combined effects of changing all of these variables simultaneously. Suppose that after seeing the sensitivity analysis report, a meeting was held to determine three possible scenarios. The best and worst cases are shown in Table 12-3 along with the base case, which represents the original expectations. It also shows the probability that each scenario will actually occur.

The worst-case scenario is one in which all of the variables are at their worst possible values. Similarly, the best case assumes that all of the variables take on their best possible values simultaneously. Although such outcomes are unlikely, they are useful for determining the extreme boundaries around the expected NPV. It is common to add a few additional, and more realistic, scenarios to these.

TABLE 12-3
THREE SCENARIOS

Variable	Worst Case 20%	Base Case 60%	Best Case 20%
Unit Sales	125,000	200,000	275,000
Price per Pound	$2.25	$2.50	$2.65
Variable Cost %	65%	60%	55%

Excel provides the Scenario Manager to help us analyze such scenarios. In Chapter 3 (page 85), we used the Scenario Manager to perform a sensitivity analysis to see the effect of the timing of a large capital expenditure on total borrowing. In Chapter 11 (page 355), we performed a scenario analysis to determine the combined effect of changing maintenance and defect costs on the profitability measures of a replacement project.[5]

In this section, we will again use the Scenario Manager, but our goal is to get a better understanding of the riskiness of the frozen catfish product. Specifically, we want to get an idea of the probability distribution around the expected NPV, especially the range of possible outcomes. Before using the Scenario Manager, it is helpful to define names for the changing cells. Set up the scenarios given in Table 12-3, and create a scenario summary report with the NPV as the result cell.

EXHIBIT 12-6
SCENARIO SUMMARY REPORT

	B	C	D	E	F
2	Scenario Summary				
3			Worst Case	Base Case	Best Case
5	Changing Cells:				
6		Catfish_Sales_Pounds	125,000	200,000	275,000
7		Price_Per_Pound	2.25	2.50	2.65
8		Var_Costs_Percent	65%	60%	55%
9	Result Cells:				
10		Net_Present_Value	$(198,083.40)	$ 91,272.55	$ 455,772.01

5. We could have used the Scenario Manager to do the sensitivity analysis, but that would have required 42 different scenarios. It is much easier to use data tables for sensitivity analysis, but they are not adequate for scenario analysis because data tables allow only (at most) two variables to change at the same time.

Exhibit 12-6 shows the scenario summary report, with the "Current Values" column deleted. Note that in the worst case, where the price and unit sales are low and variable costs are high, the NPV is significantly negative. On the other hand, the NPV is very high in the best case. So far, the scenario analysis has shown a risk of a negative NPV. However, we haven't yet quantified that risk.

Assume that the experts who defined the three scenarios were also asked to assign the probabilities of occurrence to each scenario. Feeling that the extreme scenarios are relatively unlikely, they assigned a probability of 20% to the best and worst cases. This leaves 60% for the base case. On your Scenario Summary worksheet, enter: Probabilities in C12, 20% in D12, 60% in E12, and 20% in F12. Figure 12-5 shows a histogram of the probability distribution.

FIGURE 12-5
PROBABILITY DISTRIBUTION OF NPV

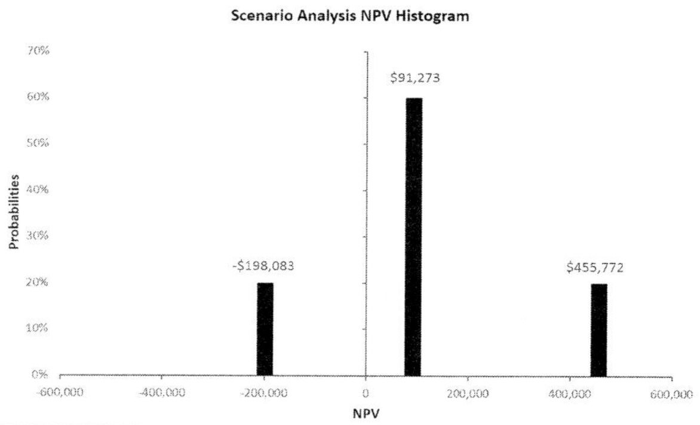

Calculating the Expected NPV from the Scenarios

With this information, we can now calculate the expected NPV for the project. Your first thought might be to try using the **AVERAGE** function. Recall from Chapter 1 that the **AVERAGE** function calculates the arithmetic (equally weighted) average of the observations. However, a glance at Figure 12-5 shows that the distribution is somewhat skewed to the right, and the possible outcomes are not all equally likely, so the average will overstate the expected value (as was discussed on page 373).

It would be more appropriate to calculate the expected value (see page 372). Recall that the expected value is found by multiplying each possible outcome by its associated probability and summing the results. In C13 of the Scenario Summary worksheet enter: Expected NPV. We can make this calculation in any of several different ways. For example, in D13 we could enter: =D10*D12+E10*E12+F10*F12, but that's not the best way. A better way would be to use an array formula: `=SUM(D10:F10*D12:F12)`, just remember to hold down the Shift+Ctrl keys when pressing the Enter key. Finally, we have supplied a user-defined function called **FAME_EXPVALUE** that will calculate the expected value of a probability distribution. It is defined as:

FAME_EXPVALUE(*VALUES*, *PROBABILITIES*)

where *VALUES* is the range of possible outcomes and ***PROBABILITIES*** is the range of probabilities. To use this function, make sure that the Famefncs.xlam add-in is installed and enabled, and then enter: `=Fame_ExpValue(D10:F10,D12:F12)` into D13. As an alternative, you can use the Insert Function dialog box that will list this function in the "User Defined" category.

Whichever way you choose to calculate it, the expected NPV for this project is $106,301.25. This means that, if our assumptions are correct, it is likely that this project is a good investment. If we could repeat this investment thousands of times under the same conditions, the average NPV would be $106,301.25. Unfortunately, we get only one chance, so it would be nice to know a little more about the dispersion of the possible outcomes around the expected value.

Calculating the Variance and Standard Deviation

The scenario summary report makes it obvious that a negative NPV is possible. The question to ask is, "How risky is this project, and what is the likelihood that the NPV will be negative?" The first step toward answering this question is to calculate one or more of the measures of dispersion (variance, standard deviation, or coefficient of variation) mentioned earlier in this chapter.

Excel provides two functions for calculating the variance of a range of numbers: **VARS** (or **VAR** if you are using the older functions) calculates a sample variance, while **VARP** (or **VARP**) calculates a population variance.[6] These functions are defined as:

VARS(*NUMBER1*, *NUMBER2*, ...)

and

VARP(*NUMBER1*, *NUMBER2*, ...)

---

6. The difference between a sample *statistic* and a population *parameter* is that the sample statistic includes an adjustment to account for the bias introduced because we aren't dealing with the full population. In this case, the adjustment is to divide by $N-1$ instead of N.

Again, we can substitute a range of numbers for the individual numbers in the definition. For our purposes, we should use **VAR.P** because we know the entire set of possible outcomes. In C14 enter: Variance, and in D14 enter: =VAR.P(D10:F10). The result is 71,568,179,048.23, which is a huge number!

One problem with this is that it ignores the probabilities that we assigned to the scenarios, and ignoring valuable information is never a good idea. To calculate the variance correctly, using all of the available information, we can use equation (12-4). Again, we have some choices about how to implement the equation. One way is to use an array formula: =SUM(D12:F12*(D10:F10-D13)^2). If you can remember the formula for the variance, this will give the correct answer of 43,091,482,025.75.

We can make this calculation much easier by using a user-defined function from Famefncs.xlam called **FAME_VAR**. This function, which will make use of the probabilities, is defined as:

$$\text{FAME\_VAR}(\textit{VALUES}, \textit{PROBABILITIES})$$

and the inputs are the same as with the **FAME_EXPVALUE** function. To use this function enter: =FAME_Var(D10:F10,D12:F12) into D14. Whether you use the array formula or the macro, you will get the correct answer of 43,091,482,025.75.

Of course, the problem with the variance is that it is difficult to interpret because the basic units (dollars) are squared. The standard deviation will correct this problem. As with the variance, Excel provides two functions: **STDEV.P** (or **STDEVP**) and **STDEV.S** (or **STDEV**). These functions are defined as:

$$\text{STDEV.P}(\textit{NUMBER1}, \textit{NUMBER2}, \dots)$$

and

$$\text{STDEV.S}(\textit{NUMBER1}, \textit{NUMBER2}, \dots)$$

However, these functions do not take into account the probabilities that have been provided.[7] Because we have already calculated the variance in D14, the easiest way to calculate the standard deviation is to enter: =SQRT(D14) into D15. Alternatively, we could use an array function or **FAME_STDDEV**:

$$\text{FAME\_STDDEV}(\textit{VALUES}, \textit{PROBABILITIES})$$

---

7. That's not to say that **VAR.S**, **VAR.P**, **STDEV.S**, and **STDEV.P** are useless functions. Anytime you don't have information regarding probabilities (say, historical data), or anytime you can safely assume that your data are normally distributed, they are very useful.

where the arguments are the same as with **FAME_VAR**. To use this function, enter: `=Fame_StdDev(D10:F10,D12:F12)` in D15. The result is 207,584.88.

Now we know quite a bit more about the distribution around the expected NPV. For example, we know that the 95.5% confidence interval for the NPV is from –$308,861 to $521,471 (plus or minus two standard deviations). Implied by that wide confidence interval is the fact that the probability of a negative NPV is quite high.

Calculating the Probability of a Negative NPV

Given the expected NPV and its standard deviation, we can calculate the probability of a negative NPV using a test statistic. Specifically, we would like to know the probability of the NPV being less than zero, so the test statistic is:

$$z = \frac{0 - \text{E}(NPV)}{\sigma_{NPV}} \tag{12-7}$$

Equation (12-7) tells us how many standard deviations 0 is away from the mean. Using the expected NPV and the standard deviation from the scenario analysis, we find:

$$z = \frac{0 - 106,301.25}{207,584.88} = -0.5121$$

This means that zero is 0.5121 standard deviations below the expected value. We can look up this value in a statistical table showing the area under a standard normal curve to determine the probability that the NPV is less than or equal to zero. Go ahead, pull out your dusty old statistics textbook, and you'll see that the probability is about 30.43% (–0.5121 isn't in the table, so look up –0.51 as an approximation).

Of course, we can automate this calculation. Excel provides the **NORM.S.DIST** (or **NORMSDIST**) function that calculates the area under a standard normal curve. This function is defined as:

$$\textbf{NORM.S.DIST}(z, \textit{CUMULATIVE})$$

where *z* is calculated as done earlier and measures the number of standard deviations above or below the expected value. *CUMULATIVE* tells the function whether to use the cumulative distribution function (true) or the probability mass function (false). In C16 enter: `Prob(NPV <= 0)` as the label, and in D16 enter: `=NORM.S.DIST((0-D13)/D15, TRUE)`. The result is that we have a 30.43% chance of the NPV being less than zero.

Obviously, we have learned a lot more about the nature of this project than we knew before. But, what are we to make of this 30% chance of a negative NPV? Should we accept the project because it has a positive expected NPV or reject it because there is a relatively high probability of a negative NPV? There is no easy answer. The individual decision maker must

EXHIBIT 12-7
COMPLETED SCENARIO SUMMARY WORKSHEET

	B	C	D	E	F
1					
2	Scenario Summary				
3			Worst Case	Base Case	Best Case
5	Changing Cells:				
6	Catfish_Sales_Pounds		125,000	200,000	275,000
7	Price_Per_Pound		2.25	2.50	2.65
8	Var_Costs_Percent		65%	60%	55%
9	Result Cells:				
10	Net_Present_Value	$	(198,083.40)	$91,272.55	$ 455,772.01
11					
12	Probabilities		20%	60%	20%
13	Expected NPV	$	106,301.25		
14	Variance	$ 43,091,482,025.75			
15	Standard Deviation		207,584.88		
16	Prob(NPV <= 0)		30.43%		

decide. However, this result certainly suggests that it would be prudent to go back and expend more effort to firm up the estimates of the uncertain variables, which would reduce the uncertainty surrounding the estimated NPV.

Monte Carlo Simulation

Still another method for dealing with risk is *Monte Carlo simulation*. A simulation is similar to a scenario analysis, but a computer generates thousands of scenarios automatically. Each of the uncertain variables in the model is assumed to be a random variable with a known probability distribution. So, we can create a scenario by randomly drawing a value for each of the uncertain variables from their probability distributions and plugging those numbers into the model. The model is then recalculated and the model outputs (e.g., NPV) are collected and stored. This process is then repeated thousands of times, resulting in thousands of potential NPVs.

From this long list of potential NPVs, we can get a much better understanding of the expected NPV of the project and the amount of uncertainty surrounding it. As we saw in the scenario analysis, we can learn about the range of potential NPVs, the standard deviation of the NPVs, and the probability that the NPV will actually turn out to be negative (or positive, depending on how you choose to look at it). Furthermore, instead of seeing just unlikely best- and worst-case scenarios, we can see many of the potential in-between scenarios. The result is that we better understand the risks of the project. An additional benefit of simulation over scenario analysis is that it should result in less uncertainty (standard deviation around the expected NPV) because we have many more, and more realistic, possible outcomes.

The key to getting good results from a simulation is to choose the correct probability distributions and correlation structure for the variables. This can be difficult and may require a good deal of judgment on the part of the analyst, especially when historical data is not available. On occasion, the analyst can use general principles or theoretical knowledge to determine the correct distribution of a variable. For example, any variable that is the product of two normally distributed variables will be lognormally distributed. Suppose that we need to make a guess at the distribution of total revenue. Because total revenue is the product of unit sales and the price per unit, and because it could be very large but never fall below zero, a lognormal distribution would seem to be appropriate.

Excel does not have any built-in simulation tools, though it does have a random number generator, and Data Tables can be made to do simple simulations. However, we have included an add-in to do simulations on the book's Web site. Download the add-in and save it on your PC. Install it through Excel Options in the same way that you have installed Famefncs.xlam. We will use this add-in to perform a Monte Carlo simulation on the catfish fillet problem. Make sure that your workbook is on the catfish fillet worksheet that you used to do the scenario analysis and then open the ExcelSim.xlam file.[8] When the add-in is active, a new "ExcelSim 2015" button will appear on the Data tab.

ExcelSim
2015
Simulation

Before beginning the simulation, let's define the problem. We have identified three important uncertain variables in the model: Unit sales in the first year, price per unit, and the variable costs as a percentage of sales. Further, let's assume that management has specified the probability distributions for each of these variables as shown in Table 12-4.

TABLE 12-4
PROBABILITY DISTRIBUTIONS FOR SIMULATION

Variable	Probability Distribution
Unit sales in pounds	Normal with mean 200,000 and standard deviation of 25,000.
Price per pound	Triangular with minimum of 2.25, most likely of 2.50, and maximum of 2.65.
Variable cost as % of sales	Uniform with minimum of 55% and maximum of 65%.

---

8. Please see the "ExcelSim 2015 Documentation" file on the Web site for more information on installing and using this add-in. Especially, note that the add-in is intended for educational purposes only. It is missing several features, such as the ability to specify correlations between variables, that make it inappropriate for real-world usage.

These distributions were chosen primarily to demonstrate three of the most commonly used distributions, but also with some logic. We assume that unit sales will tend to cluster around 200,000 pounds in the first year. Even though the distribution of unit sales will be skewed to the right (it can be very high, but not below 0), it was felt that the skewness will be so minor as to be safely ignored. Therefore, a normal distribution seems appropriate. A triangular distribution was chosen for the unit price because management feels confident that it can identify the minimum, maximum, and most likely prices but is not confident in choosing any particular distribution. Finally, a uniform distribution was chosen for variable costs because management feels that it could be anywhere between 55% and 65%, but isn't comfortable in saying that any one value is more likely than another. Figure 12-6 shows the distributions graphically.

FIGURE 12-6
GRAPHS OF PROBABILITY DISTRIBUTIONS

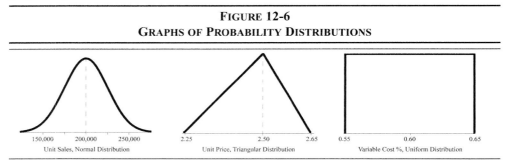

Again, make sure that your catfish fillet worksheet is open and then click the ExcelSim button on the Data tab. The main ExcelSim dialog box will appear. The first edit box is for the "Changing Cells." These are the cells that contain the uncertain variables (unit sales, etc.). Type B8, B9, B11 into this edit box, or you may select the cells with the mouse (hold down the Ctrl key as you click on each cell). Next we need to select the "Watch Cells," which are the cells that will be stored after each trial. In this case, we would like to keep track of the NPV for each trial, so enter B30 into the edit box. The "Watch Names" edit box is optional. You can use it to specify a cell that contains a descriptive label for each of the watch cells. Type A30 into this edit box.

At this point, all that remains is to tell ExcelSim how many trials to run and what to name the worksheet that will be created for the output (this is optional). Keep in mind that the more trials you run, the more accurate the simulation will be. The maximum number of iterations is 30,000 but we will run only 500 to keep the output more manageable. Type 500 into the "Iterations" edit box. Finally, enter Frozen Catfish Simulation into the "Sheet Name" edit box. If you choose not to enter a sheet name for the output, it will be named "Simulation Report" by default. Figure 12-7 shows the main dialog box with the data entered.

FIGURE 12-7
EXCELSIM MAIN DIALOG BOX

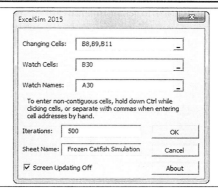

After clicking the OK button, you will be presented with the first of the distribution dialog boxes. These dialog boxes are where you will describe the probability distribution for the uncertain variables. There will be one for each changing cell. Note that if you have used defined names for the changing cells (as we have already done before running the scenario analysis), the names will be shown in the title bar. The first variable is the unit sales. Table 12-4 tells us that the distribution is normal with a mean of 200,000 and standard deviation of 25,000. So, select "Normal" from the distribution list. At this point, the dialog box will change to prompt you for a mean and standard deviation for the distribution. Enter 200,000 for the mean, and 25,000 for the standard deviation. Figure 12-8 shows the completed dialog box.

FIGURE 12-8
DISTRIBUTION DIALOG BOX FOR UNIT SALES

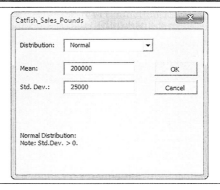

Click the OK button, and we will repeat this process for the other two changing cells. The next dialog box is for the unit price. Note that the dialog box is, at first, showing the exact settings as were previously entered. This is helpful if the distribution is the same, but we need to choose a different distribution. Choose a triangular distribution from the drop-down list. You will now be prompted for the left side, mode (or most likely), and right side of this distribution. Enter 2.25 for the left side, 2.50 for the mode, and 2.65 for the right side, as shown in Figure 12-9, and then click the OK button.

FIGURE 12-9
DISTRIBUTION DIALOG BOX FOR PRICE PER POUND

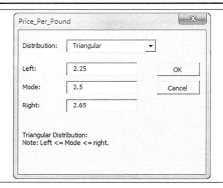

Finally, choose a uniform distribution for the variable costs. In this case, you will be asked to supply the lower and upper limits of the distribution. Because variable costs are expected to be somewhere between 55% and 65% of sales, enter 0.55 for the lower limit and 0.65 for the upper limit (Figure 12-10).

FIGURE 12-10
DISTRIBUTION DIALOG BOX FOR VARIABLE COSTS

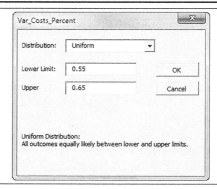

When you click the OK button, the simulation will begin to run. You can follow the progress by watching the status bar at the lower left corner of the Excel window. (If you re-run the simulation, uncheck the Screen Updating Off box and you can watch the spreadsheet change.) After a few seconds, a new worksheet containing the output will be displayed.

EXHIBIT 12-8
THE SIMULATION OUTPUT

	A	B
1	*Simulation Report by ExcelSim*	
2		Trial Results
3	Trial	Net Present Value
4	1	($69,885.48)
5	2	$17,504.43
6	3	$101,745.36
501	498	$58,417.18
502	499	$31,484.35
503	500	$31,393.53
504	Min	($112,714.17)
505	Max	$383,077.74
506	Mean	$87,407.76
507	Median	$81,766.56
508	Mode	#N/A
509	Avg Dev	65,955.84
510	Std Dev	80,766.19
511	Coef. Var.	0.92
512	Skewness	0.26
513	Kurtosis	(0.20)

The output consists of the 500 NPVs generated during the simulation and some descriptive statistics at the bottom. Exhibit 12-8 shows the results of the first three and last three trials (the rest are hidden to save space), as well as the summary statistics. Because these results are based on random draws from the probability distributions, your results will be somewhat different. However, the mean and standard deviation of the NPVs should be similar.

Just as we did with the output from the scenario analysis, we can draw some important conclusions from this data. It will also be useful to compare the results of the simulation to the scenario analysis. First, note that the mean NPV was $87,408, while the minimum and maximum NPVs were –$112,714 and $383,078, respectively. Second, the minimum and maximum NPVs are not as extreme as the worst-case and best-case NPVs from the scenario analysis. This suggests that the extra information provided by the simulation has reduced the uncertainty.

The standard deviation of the NPVs is $80,766, which is considerably less than the standard deviation from the scenario analysis. The reason for the reduction in uncertainty is that we have run many more scenarios, and most of them are not nearly as extreme as the best- and worst-case scenarios. The reduction in uncertainty is also reflected in the probability that the NPV is less than or equal to zero. Recall that we can use the **NORM.S.DIST** function to calculate this probability as we did for the scenario analysis. In D506 enter the label Prob(NPV <= 0), and in E506 enter the formula =NORM.S.DIST((0-B506)/ B510,TRUE). The result shows a 13.96% chance of a negative NPV (again, your results will vary depending on the mean and standard deviation from your simulation). We can also verify this by doing an actual count of the NPVs that are less than 0. Copy the label from D506 and paste it into D507. Excel has a useful function called **COUNTIF** that is defined as:

COUNTIF(RANGE, CRITERIA)

where **RANGE** is the range of numbers and **CRITERIA** is the particular counting rule that you wish to apply. In this case, we wish to count the number of NPVs that are less than or equal to 0, so in E507 enter the formula: =COUNTIF(B4:B503,"<=0")/500. From our simulation of 500 trials, there were 68 negative NPVs, or 13.60%, which conforms closely to the previous result.[9] So, the project appears to be far less risky than was suggested by the scenario analysis.

Finally, we can use Excel's built-in Histogram tool to get a visual look at the probability distribution. Click the Data Analysis button on the Data tab and choose the Histogram tool from the list. This will display the dialog box shown in Figure 12-11.

FIGURE 12-11
THE HISTOGRAM DIALOG BOX

---

9. The array formula =SUM((B4:B503<=0)*1)/500 will give the same result.

All you need to do is specify the <u>I</u>nput Range (B3:B503), check the <u>L</u>abels box, specify the <u>O</u>utput Range (D509), and select <u>C</u>hart Output. Excel will decide how to group the data and will create the histogram as shown in Figure 12-12.

FIGURE 12-12
HISTOGRAM OF NPVS FROM THE SIMULATION

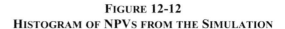
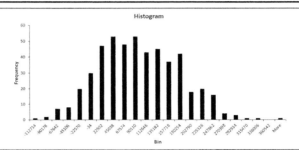

The Risk-Adjusted Discount Rate Method

Yet another method of incorporating risk into our capital budgeting decision process is to use a risk-adjusted discount rate (RADR). When we discussed how to determine the required rate of return in Chapter 8, we mentioned a model referred to as a "simple risk premium model." The RADR is an example of this model. Recall that the simple risk premium model was defined as:

$$\text{Required Return} = \text{Base Rate} + \text{Risk Premium}$$

and that the base rate and risk premium are subjectively determined. The idea behind this model is that the investor (or firm) has some minimum required return for tying up her funds to which a premium is added in order to compensate for risk. Projects with greater risk require larger risk premiums. In using the RADR technique, we will modify this model so that it becomes:

$$\text{RADR} = \text{WACC} + \text{Risk Premium}$$

Note that the risk premium is still subjectively determined, but the base rate is the firm's WACC. The correct discount rate for average risk projects is the WACC, but for riskier-than-average projects, a positive risk premium is added. This higher discount rate is meant to penalize the riskier project and will result in a lower, and possibly negative, NPV. If the project still has a positive NPV, then the project is expected to more than compensate the shareholders for the extra risk, and it should be accepted. For projects with less risk than average, the risk premium would be negative.

Normally, the risk premium will be determined according to a schedule that has been approved by the firm's upper management. This schedule will typically assign risk premiums according to the type of project. For example, if the firm is analyzing the possibility of replacing an existing machine, it would probably be considered a very low-risk project and the risk premium might be –2%. On the other hand, a new product line, such as the one we are examining in this chapter, would be considered quite risky and might require a 3% risk premium. Expansion of an existing and successful project would probably be considered an average risk and the WACC with no risk premium would be used as the discount rate. Ultimately, the risk premium will be determined by managerial judgment. This judgment may be based on experience, some statistical measure of risk, or the outcome of a scenario analysis or a Monte Carlo simulation.

In our Freshly Frozen Fish problem, suppose that management has determined that a 3% risk premium is required. Because the WACC for the firm is 10%, the required return for this project would be 13%. Plugging this rate into your frozen catfish fillet worksheet reveals that the risk-adjusted NPV is $17,379.29. The fact that the NPV is still positive suggests that this is a good investment. It will likely more than compensate shareholders for the extra risk.

We can also look at the IRR of the project and turn the question around. Instead of asking what risk premium is required, we can ask if the expected risk premium is sufficient. Under the original assumptions, the IRR was calculated to be 13.77%. Recall that the IRR is the discount rate that would result in the NPV being equal to zero. Because the IRR is 3.77% greater than the WACC, this is the expected risk premium. The project will obviously have a positive NPV for any risk premium up to 3.77%. Therefore, the question is, "Is an extra 3.77% per year enough of a risk premium to compensate for the extra risk of this project?" If the answer is "yes," then the project should be accepted.

The Certainty-Equivalent Approach

The problem with the RADR approach to adjusting for risk is that it combines two adjustments: one for risk and another for time. This approach implicitly assumes that risk is an increasing function of time. In many cases this may be true. Cash flow forecasts for a period of five years from now are generally less certain than are forecasts for next year. However, such is not necessarily the case. For example, suppose that a firm has a maintenance contract that calls for a major overhaul of a machine in three years. If the cost of this overhaul is specified in the contract, this is a very low-risk cost, even though it occurs in three years.

The *certainty-equivalent* (CE) approach separates the adjustments for time and risk. Where the RADR technique increases the discount rate to adjust for risk, the CE approach decreases the cash flow. To adjust for risk with the CE approach, we multiply the cash flow by the certainty-equivalent coefficient. The net result is the same: The cash flow is penalized for risk. To adjust for time, we discount the cash flows at the risk-free rate of interest. This is the basis for the theoretical superiority of the CE approach: It makes separate adjustments for risk and time, rather than the intermingled adjustments of the RADR.

Certainty-equivalent coefficients are determined as follows: Decision makers are asked what *certain* cash flow they would be willing to accept in exchange for the risky cash flow at some point in the future. The ratio of these cash flows determines the CE coefficient (α).

$$\alpha = \frac{\text{Riskless cash flow}}{\text{Risky cash flow}} \qquad \text{(12-8)}$$

As an example, assume that you are willing to accept $95 dollars for sure in place of a risky $100 one year from now. Your CE coefficient for this cash flow would be:

$$\alpha = \frac{95}{100} = 0.95$$

Riskier cash flows will be deflated with lower CE coefficients. In effect, this risky cash flow times $(1 - \alpha)$ is the amount that you would be willing to pay for an insurance policy to guarantee that you receive the risky cash flow (we are ignoring the time value of money for the moment). The CE coefficient will always be between 0 and 1, and will usually decrease with time because of increased risk. To use the CE approach, each cash flow is multiplied by the appropriate coefficient, α_n, and then the net present value is found using the risk-free rate of interest as the discount rate. The risk-free rate is used to discount the cash flows because all of the risk has been removed by the CE adjustment. Effectively, the CE technique converts a risky stream of cash flows into a risk-free stream of cash flows.

Let's remake our Freshly Frozen Fish worksheet to see how the CE approach works. First, make a copy of your worksheet. Now, in the new worksheet, change A14 to: `Risk-Free Rate`, and B14 to: `4%`. Assume that management has given you the CE coefficients shown in Table 12-5:

TABLE 12-5
FRESHLY FROZEN FISH CE COEFFICIENTS

Year	CE Coefficient (α)
0	1.00
1	0.95
2	0.90
3	0.85
4	0.80
5	0.75

Select rows 29 and 30 and then insert two new rows just below the annual cash flows. In A29 enter Certainty Equivalent Coefficients and then enter the CE coefficients from the table into B28:G28. In A30 enter Risk-Adjusted Cash Flows. In B30 enter the formula =B28*B29 and copy it across. To calculate the risk-adjusted NPV, in B32 enter the formula: =NPV(B14,C30:G30)+B30. Note that the risk-adjusted NPV is $89,737.37, which is very close to our previous result. We don't need to calculate the risk-adjusted cash flows in separate cells (B30:G30). Instead, we could calculate the NPV with the array formula: =NPV(B14,C28:G28*C29:G29)+B28. Just remember to enter that formula using Shift+Ctrl+Enter.

We can also calculate the IRR and MIRR of the risk-adjusted cash flows. The formula for the IRR in B33 is: =IRR(B30:G30). Similarly, the formula for the MIRR is: =MIRR(B30:G30,B14,B14). Remember that these measures must now be compared to the risk-free rate of interest, not to the firm's WACC. Because both are greater than the 4% risk-free rate, the project is acceptable. Exhibit 12-9 shows the completed worksheet.

EXHIBIT 12-9
THE CATFISH FILLET WORKSHEET USING THE CE METHOD

	A	B	C	D	E	F	G
16		Annual Cash Flows for Frozen Catfish Fillet Project					
17		Year 0	Year 1	Year 2	Year 3	Year 4	Year 5
18	Initial Outlay	(650,000)					
19	Sales		500,000	540,000	583,200	629,856	680,244
20	Variable Costs		300,000	324,000	349,920	377,914	408,147
21	Fixed Costs		80,000	80,000	80,000	80,000	80,000
22	Depreciation Expense		15,000	28,875	26,709	24,706	22,853
23	Taxable Cash Flows		105,000	107,125	126,571	147,236	169,245
24	Taxes		36,750	37,494	44,300	51,533	59,236
25	Add: Depreciation		15,000	28,875	26,709	24,706	22,853
26	Annual After-Tax Cash Flow		83,250	98,506	108,980	120,410	132,862
27	Terminal Cash Flow						543,650
28	Total Annual Cash Flows	(650,000)	83,250	98,506	108,980	120,410	676,512
29	Certainty Equivalent Coefficients	1.00	0.95	0.90	0.85	0.80	0.75
30	Risk-adjusted Cash Flows	(650,000)	79,088	88,656	92,633	96,328	507,384
31							
32	Net Present Value	$89,737.37					
33	Internal Rate of Return	7.52%					
34	Modified Internal Rate of Return	6.73%					

If the certainty equivalents and the RADR are correctly determined, the decision that results from both methods will usually be the same. However, the CE technique suffers from the need to understand the utility function of the decision maker and thus is very difficult to correctly implement in practice. At best, the CE coefficients could be found by interviewing the relevant decision maker as described earlier. Unfortunately, most modern corporations are owned by many shareholders and it is their risk preferences that we need to be concerned about, not those of some individual corporate officer. For this reason, the CE method is not generally used in practice.

Summary

We began this chapter with a discussion of risk and determined that it is roughly equivalent to the probability of a loss. The higher the probability of a loss, the higher the risk. We also found that we could measure risk in any of several ways, but that the standard deviation or coefficient of variation are the generally preferred methods.

Risk can be incorporated into the analysis of capital investments in many ways. We've demonstrated that sensitivity analysis is an important first step in order to identify the variables that most impact the NPV. Once identified, we can focus our efforts on getting good estimates of these variables. Next, we can perform a scenario analysis or a Monte Carlo simulation to better understand the uncertainty surrounding the expected NPV.

Although Monte Carlo simulation is beginning to be more widely used, the primary method of incorporating risk into capital budgeting is the risk-adjusted discount rate technique. This technique involves the addition of a premium to the WACC in order to account for the riskiness of the investment. We also discussed the certainty-equivalent method whereby the risky cash flows are deflated according to a decision maker's utility function. This method is superior to the RADR in theory, but is difficult to use in practice.

TABLE 12-6
FUNCTIONS INTRODUCED IN THIS CHAPTER*

Purpose	Function	Page
Calculate MACRS depreciation expense	FAME_MACRS(*COST, MACRSCLASS, YEAR, TABLE*)	379
Calculate the slope of a regression line	SLOPE(*KNOWN_Y'S, KNOWN_X'S*)	385
Calculate the expected value	FAME_EXPVALUE(*VALUES, PROBABILITIES*)	389
Calculate a population variance	VAR.P(*NUMBER1, NUMBER2, ...*)	389
Calculate a sample variance	VAR.S(*NUMBER1, NUMBER2, ...*)	389

TABLE 12-6 (**Continued**)
FUNCTIONS INTRODUCED IN THIS CHAPTER*

Purpose	Function	Page
Calculate variance when the probability distribution is known	FAME_VAR(*VALUES, PROBABILITIES*)	390
Calculate a population standard deviation	STDEV.P(*NUMBER1, NUMBER2, ...*)	390
Calculate a sample standard deviation	STDEV.S(*NUMBER1, NUMBER2, ...*)	390
Calculate standard deviation when the probabilities are known	FAME_STDDEV(*VALUES, PROBABILITIES*)	390
Calculate coefficient of variation when the probabilities are known	FAME_CV(*VALUES, PROBABILITIES*)	N/A
Calculate the area under a standard normal curve	NORM.S.DIST(*Z, CUMULATIVE*)	391
Count the numbers in a range that meet a specified criteria	COUNTIF(*RANGE, CRITERIA*)	398

*   All functions with names beginning in **FAME_** are macros supplied on the Famefncs.xlam add-in, which is available from the official Web site.

Problems

1. Telluride Tours is currently evaluating two mutually exclusive investments. After doing a scenario analysis and applying probabilities to each scenario, it has determined that the investments have the following distributions around the expected NPVs.

Probability	NPV_A	NPV_B
10%	−$30,600	−$11,475
20%	−7,650	1,913
40%	15,300	15,300
20%	38,250	28,688
10%	61,200	42,075

    Several members of the management team have suggested that Project A should be selected because it has a higher potential NPV. Other members have suggested that Project B appears to be more conservative and should be selected. They have asked you to resolve this question.

    a. Calculate the expected NPV for both projects. Can the question be resolved with this information alone?

    b. Calculate the variance and standard deviation of the NPVs for both projects. Which project appears to be riskier?

    c. Calculate the coefficient of variation for both projects. Does this change your opinion from part b?

    d. Calculate the probability of a negative NPV for both projects.

    e. Which project should be accepted? Why?

2. The Salida Salt Company is considering making a bid to supply the highway department with rock salt to drop on roads in the county duringthe winter. The contract will guarantee a minimum of 25,000 tons in each year, but the actual quantity may be above that amount if conditions warrant. Management believes that the actual quantity will average 40,000 tons per year. The firm will need an initial $2,300,000 investment in processing equipment to get the project started. The contract will last for five years and is not expected to be renewed. The accounting department has estimated that annual fixed costs will be $500,000 and that variable costs should be about $94 per ton of the final product. The new equipment

will be depreciated using MACRS with a class life of five years. At the end of the project, it is estimated that the equipment could be sold for $150,000. The marketing department estimates that the state will grant the contract at a selling price of $125 per ton, though it may get some lower bids if the contract is opened for competitive bidding. The engineering department estimates that the project will need an initial net working capital investment of $115,000. The firm's WACC is 12%, and the marginal tax rate is 35%.

a. Set up a worksheet containing all of the relevant information in this problem, and operating cash flow statement that shows the total annual cash flows for each year, including the initial outlay.

b. Calculate the payback period, discounted payback period, NPV, IRR, and MIRR of this project. Is the project acceptable?

c. If the state decides to open the project for competitive bidding, what is the lowest bid price that you can enter without reducing shareholder wealth? Explain why your answer is correct.

d. Perform a Monte Carlo simulation with 1,000 trials to determine the expected NPV and the standard deviation of the expected NPV. The uncertain variables and their probability distributions are given below. The quantity of rock salt sold should be simulated for each year independently of the others (i.e., it is five separate variables).

Variable	Distribution
Tons of rock salt in each year	Triangular with a minimum of 25,000, most likely of 40,000, and maximum of 50,000.
Variable cost per ton	Normal with a mean of $95 and a standard deviation of $5.
Salvage value of equipment	Uniform with a minimum of $70,000 and a maximum of $200,000.

e. Create a histogram showing the probability distribution of NPV.

f. Using the output of the simulation, what is the probability that the NPV will be less than or equal to zero? Would you suggest that the project be accepted?

3. Montrose Manufacturing is considering two potential investments. Each project will cost $115,000 and have an expected life of five years. The CFO has estimated the probability distributions for each project's cash flows as shown in the following table:

Probability	Potential Cash Flows	
	Project 1	Project 2
30%	$18,000	$15,000
40%	40,500	45,000
30%	54,000	69,000

The company believes that the probability distributions apply to each year of the five years of the projects' lives. Montrose Manufacturing uses the risk-adjusted discount rate technique to evaluate potential investments.

As a guide for assigning the risk premiums, the CFO has put together the following table based on the coefficient of variation.

Coefficient of Variation	Risk Premium
0.00	−1.50%
0.20	0.00%
0.30	1.00%
0.40	1.50%
0.50	2.50%

a. Calculate the expected cash flows, standard deviation, and coefficient of variation for each project.

b. If the firm's WACC for average risk projects is 10%, what is the appropriate risk-adjusted discount rate for each project? Use the **VLOOKUP** function to calculate the project WACC.

c. Using the appropriate discount rates, calculate the payback period, discounted payback period, NPV, PI, IRR, and MIRR for each project.

d. If the projects are mutually exclusive, which should be accepted? What if they are independent?

CHAPTER 13

Portfolio Statistics and Diversification

After studying this chapter, you should be able to:

1. *Define the concept of diversification and explain why it reduces risk.*

2. *Calculate the expected return and standard deviation of a portfolio with any number of securities.*

3. *Create a variance/covariance matrix using two different methods.*

4. *Explain the concept of the efficient frontier, and locate portfolios that are on the frontier so that they can be charted.*

5. *Explain why adding a risk-free asset into the universe of securities used to create the efficient frontier results in the CML and CAPM.*

6. *Use a utility function to identify the optimal portfolio for an investor.*

In the previous chapter, we examined investment risk in isolation. However, investments are rarely held in isolation. Instead, investors (whether individuals, money managers, or corporations) typically own many investments simultaneously. In a world without uncertainty, an investor would choose to own the investment that will provide the highest return over their holding period. In the real world, fraught with uncertainty, investors cannot possibly know which investment will provide the highest return, or even if an investment will earn a profit. Therefore, it makes sense to spread one's funds across several investments in the hope that some will be profitable enough to more than offset the losses of others. This is known as *diversification*, and it is the subject of the current chapter.

Portfolio Diversification Effects

A portfolio is a collection of assets. An individual's portfolio consists of all of the assets that the individual owns. For the manager of a mutual fund, the portfolio comprises all assets under management, whether they are stocks, bonds, real estate, another asset class, or a combination of asset classes. From the stockholder's point of view, a corporation is similar to a mutual fund. That is, a corporation is simply a portfolio of investments (projects) managed by a professional management team.

Why do investors, whether individuals or corporations, typically own portfolios that consist of more than one asset? Because a portfolio of multiple investments typically offers lower risk than owning a single asset. Often, a portfolio will have less risk than any of the individual investments that it contains. There may be a cost, in the form of a somewhat lower expected return when compared to the highest return alternative, but the overall risk/ return trade-off is improved. This reduction in risk is known as the diversification effect.

It will be helpful to examine the effect that the addition of risky assets has on the overall risk of the portfolio. Let's look at an example using stock selection (though the same concept applies to capital investment projects).

Suppose that you have $10,000 available for investment purposes. Your stockbroker has suggested that you invest in either stock A or stock B, but you are concerned about the riskiness of these stocks. During your investigation you gathered the historical returns for these stocks presented in Table 13-1.

TABLE 13-1
HISTORICAL ANNUAL RETURNS FOR A AND B

Year	Stock A Returns	Stock B Returns
2010	10.30%	10.71%
2011	−0.10%	25.00%
2012	23.30%	0.38%
2013	2.20%	26.20%
2014	14.00%	11.52%

To quantify your concerns about the riskiness of these stocks, you open a new worksheet and enter the data from Table 13-1.

Because both firms have had their ups and downs, you want to calculate the average annual return for the last five years. Further, to get a feeling for their riskiness, you want to calculate the standard deviation of these returns. Assuming that you have entered the data from Table

13-1 starting with the labels in row 1, you can calculate the average return for stock A in B7 with: =AVERAGE(B2:B6). Copying this to C7 will calculate the average return for stock B. Exhibit 13-1 shows that stock A has earned an average of 9.94% per year over the last five years, while stock B has earned 14.76% per year.[1] Note that because we are using historical returns we assume that all returns are equally likely, so we can use the built-in **AVERAGE** function instead of calculating a probability-weighted average.

Obviously, if the average historical return reflects the expected future average return, stock B is to be preferred. Recall, however, that higher returns are generally accompanied by higher risk. We can measure the riskiness of these returns with the standard deviation. To calculate the sample standard deviation of stock A's returns enter: =STDEV.S(B2:B6) in B8 and copy it to C8. We can use Excel's built-in formula in this case because we do not have information regarding the probability distribution of returns, so we assume that each one is equally likely. The results show that the standard deviation of returns is 9.43% for stock A and 10.83% for stock B.

EXHIBIT 13-1
RISK AND RETURN FOR STOCKS A AND B

	A	B	C
		Stock A	Stock B
1	Year	Returns	Returns
2	2010	10.30%	10.71%
3	2011	-0.10%	25.00%
4	2012	23.30%	0.38%
5	2013	2.20%	26.20%
6	2014	14.00%	11.52%
7	Expected Return	9.94%	14.76%
8	Standard Deviation	9.43%	10.83%

Now you have a problem. Stock B provides a higher return, but stock A is less risky. Which should you choose? The answer depends on your risk/return preferences. Investors who are very risk averse would likely prefer stock A, while others who are more risk willing would prefer stock B. Fortunately, you have another alternative.

Suppose that you decide to purchase both stocks instead of just one of them. You will put 50% of your funds in stock A and 50% in stock B. We can determine the returns that this portfolio would have earned in each year by calculating a weighted average of each stock's return. In D1, enter: Portfolio, and in D2, enter the formula: =0.5*B2+0.5*C2. This

---

1. We are calculating the arithmetic mean because it gives us the "typical" annual return. In this case, we have no interest in the geometric mean.

shows that our portfolio would have earned 10.51% in the year 2010. Copy this formula to each cell in the range D3:D6, and then copy the expected return formula from C7 to D7.

Notice that the expected portfolio return is 12.35%, exactly halfway between the returns on the individual stocks (remember that you put 50% into each stock). Now, let's see what happens to the standard deviation. Copy the formula from C8 to D8. Notice that the standard deviation of the portfolio is only 1.35%—significantly less than the standard deviation of either stock alone! This is a demonstration of the benefits of diversification. Exhibit 13-2 shows these results.

EXHIBIT 13-2
PORTFOLIO OF STOCKS A AND B

	A	B	C	D
		Stock A	Stock B	
1	Year	Returns	Returns	Portfolio
2	2010	10.30%	10.71%	10.51%
3	2011	-0.10%	25.00%	12.45%
4	2012	23.30%	0.38%	11.84%
5	2013	2.20%	26.20%	14.20%
6	2014	14.00%	11.52%	12.76%
7	Expected Return	9.94%	14.76%	12.35%
8	Standard Deviation	9.43%	10.83%	1.35%

Because the portfolio provides a higher return and less risk than stock A, you would certainly prefer the portfolio over stock A alone. We cannot, however, definitively say that you would prefer the portfolio to stock B. To determine which you would pick, we would need information regarding your risk/return preferences as indicated by your utility function (see page 436). In this case, most people would probably prefer the portfolio because the difference in returns is slight, but the difference in risk is relatively large.

Determining Portfolio Risk and Return

As you have seen in the previous example, combining assets into a portfolio (whether that portfolio consists of stocks or equipment or product lines) may result in the reduction of risk below that of any individual asset. You have also seen that the expected return for a portfolio will be between the lowest return asset and the highest return asset. In general, we can say that the expected return of a portfolio is a weighted average of the expected returns of the individual assets. The weights are given by the proportion of total portfolio value that each asset represents. In mathematical terms:

$$E(R_P) = \sum_{t=1}^{N} w_t E(R_t) \tag{13-1}$$

where w_t is the weight and $E(R_t)$ is the expected return of the tth asset. Equation (13-1) is applicable regardless of the number of assets in the portfolio. From the previous example, the expected return for the portfolio is:

$$E(R_P) = 0.5(0.0994) + 0.5(0.1476) = 0.1235 = 12.35\%$$

which is exactly the result we got when we calculated it in D7 using a different methodology. The difference with equation (13-1) is that we can use it without needing to know each year's returns. All that we need are the expected returns for each asset.

Portfolio Standard Deviation

While the expected return of the portfolio is a weighted average of the expected returns of the assets, the portfolio standard deviation is not so simple. If we calculated a weighted average of the standard deviations of stocks A and B, we would get:

$$\text{Weighted average } \sigma = 0.5(0.0943) + 0.5(0.1083) = 0.1013 = 10.13\%$$

But we know that the portfolio standard deviation is 1.35% from our previous calculations. Obviously, there is something else going on here.

What is going on is that we have ignored the *correlation* between these two stocks. Because the returns don't always move in exactly the same direction, some of the volatility in one stock tends to cancel out volatility in the other. Correlation describes how strongly the returns of two assets tend to move together through time. We can measure this with the correlation coefficient (r):

$$r_{X, Y} = \frac{\sum_{t=1}^{N} \rho_t (X_t - \bar{X})(Y_t - \bar{Y})}{\sigma_X \sigma_Y} \tag{13-2}$$

The correlation coefficient can range from -1 to $+1$. With perfect negative correlation, the returns always move in exactly the opposite direction. When returns always move in exactly the same direction, they are said to be perfectly positively correlated. Figure 13-1 illustrates the extremes that the correlation coefficient can have.

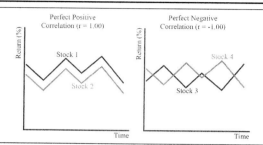

FIGURE 13-1
PERFECT POSITIVE AND PERFECT NEGATIVE CORRELATION

The extremes shown in Figure 13-1 are rarely seen in practice. Instead, the correlation for any two investments will be somewhere in between.[2] In fact, most investments tend to be positively correlated, but to varying degrees. This positive correlation is due to the fact that most investments tend to move in the same direction as the overall economy. However, industry and company-specific factors tend to lower the correlations. For example, imagine a furniture manufacturer is considering the purchase of another company. If that other company is also in the furniture business, then the correlation with the existing assets is likely to be quite high (close to 1). However, if the other company is in a completely unrelated industry, then the correlation is likely to be lower (though probably still positive).

A closely related way to measure the co-movement of returns is the *covariance*. The covariance is similar to the variance, except that we have two return series rather than one. The covariance is calculated as:

$$\sigma_{X,\,Y} = \sum_{t\,=\,1}^{N} \rho_t (X_t - \bar{X})(Y_t - \bar{Y})$$

(13-3)

Note that equation (13-3) is the numerator of equation (13-2). The covariance is a very useful statistic, but it is difficult to interpret because it is not scaled. The correlation coefficient is related to the covariance as follows:

$$r_{X,\,Y} = \frac{\sigma_{X,\,Y}}{\sigma_X \sigma_Y}$$

(13-4)

The correlation coefficient measures the same thing as the covariance, but it has been transformed so that it will always be between −1 and +1, which makes it much easier to

---

2. At the time of this writing, the average correlation between companies in the S&P 500 index was 31.83% based on the last three years of monthly returns.

interpret. However, the covariance has its advantages, especially when computing portfolio statistics because it reduces the number of calculations that must be done.

Assume that you wish to form a portfolio consisting of 50% in stock 1 and 50% in stock 2 (from Figure 13-1). Because these stocks are perfectly positively correlated, a plot of the portfolio returns would be exactly halfway between the plots of the returns for stocks 1 and 2. Your portfolio returns would be just as volatile as if you owned either stock alone. There is no diversification of risk when the correlation is perfectly positive.

On the other hand, a similar portfolio of stocks 3 and 4 would result in a substantial reduction in volatility. Notice that the volatility of the returns of stock 3 is canceled out by the volatility of the returns of stock 4. This is an extreme example, but the lesson is that whenever the correlation is less than +1, there will be some risk reduction.

The correlation is obviously important in the calculation of the portfolio risk. For a portfolio of two securities, the variance is given by:

$$\sigma_P^2 = w_1^2\sigma_1^2 + w_2^2\sigma_2^2 + 2w_1w_2r_{1,2}\sigma_1\sigma_2 \tag{13-5}$$

where the w's are the weights of each security, and $r_{1,2}$ is the correlation coefficient for the two securities. The standard deviation of a two-security portfolio is the square root of its variance:

$$\sigma_P = \sqrt{w_1^2\sigma_1^2 + w_2^2\sigma_2^2 + 2w_1w_2r_{1,2}\sigma_1\sigma_2} = \sqrt{\sigma_P^2} \tag{13-6}$$

Holding all other variables constant, it is clear that the lower the correlation ($r_{1,2}$) between the securities, the lower the risk of the portfolio will be. In other words, the lower the correlation, the greater the benefits of diversification.

Returning to our example with stocks A and B, we can calculate the correlation coefficient with Excel's built-in function **CORREL**. This function is defined as:

CORREL(*ARRAY1*, *ARRAY2*)

where *ARRAY1* and *ARRAY2* are the two ranges containing the stocks' returns. Before using the **CORREL** function, create a chart of the returns to see if you can guess the correlation coefficient. Select A1:C6 and then create a scatter chart of the returns.

Examining the chart, it is clear that when stock A's returns are high, stock B's returns are low, and vice versa. The correlation coefficient is obviously negative and probably near −1. We can confirm this by using the **CORREL** function. In B9, enter the formula: =CORREL(B2:B6,C2:C6). Note that the answer is −0.9741, so our suspicions are confirmed. This low correlation is the reason that the standard deviation of the portfolio is so low.

EXHIBIT 13-3
WORKSHEET DEMONSTRATING LOW CORRELATION BETWEEN STOCKS A AND B

	A	B	C	D	E	F	G	H	I
1	Year	Stock A Returns	Stock B Returns	Portfolio					
2	2010	10.30%	10.71%	10.51%					
3	2011	-0.10%	25.00%	12.45%					
4	2012	23.30%	0.38%	11.84%					
5	2013	2.20%	26.20%	14.20%					
6	2014	14.00%	11.52%	12.76%					
7	Exp. Ret.	9.94%	14.76%	12.35%					
8	Std. Dev.	9.43%	10.83%	1.35%					
9	Correlation	-97.41%							

Now copy D1:D6, select the chart, and then use Paste Special… to add the portfolio returns as a new data series. Your worksheet should now resemble that in Exhibit 13-3.

We can also calculate the portfolio standard deviation using the covariance instead of the correlation:

$$\sigma_P = \sqrt{w_1^2\sigma_1^2 + w_2^2\sigma_2^2 + 2w_1 w_2 \sigma_{1,2}}$$ (13-7)

Equation (13-7) is mathematically equivalent to equation (13-6), but is slightly easier to calculate. Referring back to equation (13-4), you can see that in order to calculate the correlation coefficient you must first calculate the covariance. That means that it is more computationally efficient to use the covariance.

Just as with the correlation, Excel has a built-in function to calculate the sample covariance:

COVARIANCE.S($ARRAY1$, $ARRAY2$)

We can calculate the covariance between the returns on stocks A and B in B10 with the formula: =COVARIANCE.S(B2:B6,C2:C6). The result is –0.00995. Using equation (13-7), the portfolio standard deviation is:

$$\sigma_P = \sqrt{0.5^2 \times 0.0943^2 + 0.5^2 \times 0.1083^2 + 2(0.5)(0.5)(-0.00995)} = 0.0135 = 1.35\%$$

Changing the Weights

In the example above, we set the weights such that half of your money was invested in stock A and the other half was invested in stock B. We can examine how the portfolio standard deviation changes as we change the weights of A and B. Place the following labels in your worksheet. In A13: Stock A, in B13: Stock B, and in C13: Port Std Dev. Enter a series in A14:A24 ranging from 100% down to 0% in increments of 10%. These will represent the weights allocated to stock A.

EXHIBIT 13-4
PORTFOLIO STANDARD DEVIATION AS WEIGHTS CHANGE

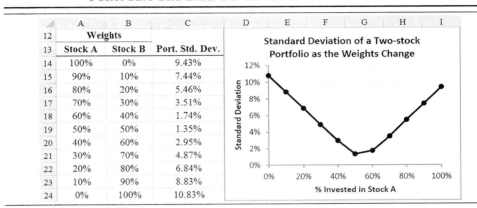

	A	B	C	D	E	F	G	H	I
12	Weights								
13	**Stock A**	**Stock B**	**Port. Std. Dev.**						
14	100%	0%	9.43%						
15	90%	10%	7.44%						
16	80%	20%	5.46%						
17	70%	30%	3.51%						
18	60%	40%	1.74%						
19	50%	50%	1.35%						
20	40%	60%	2.95%						
21	30%	70%	4.87%						
22	20%	80%	6.84%						
23	10%	90%	8.83%						
24	0%	100%	10.83%						

Because the weights must sum to 100%, we can calculate the weight of stock B in B14 with: =1-A14. The portfolio standard deviation, in cell C14, can be found using equation (13-7): =SQRT(A14^2*B8^2+B14^2*C8^2+2*A14*B14*$B$10). Now simply copy the formulas in B14:C14 down to the rest of the range. If you create a scatter chart of the data (use the ranges: A13:A24, C13:C24), your worksheet should resemble that in Exhibit 13-4.

It is instructive to examine the extremes in the chart in Exhibit 13-4. First, note that when 100% of your funds are allocated to stock A, the portfolio standard deviation is equal to that of stock A. Similarly, if 100% is allocated to stock B, the portfolio standard deviation is equal to that of stock B. Also, notice that the minimum standard deviation is achieved with about one-half of your funds allocated to each stock.[3]

The benefits of diversification in an individual's investment portfolio should be clear. By selecting securities that are less than perfectly positively correlated (in different industries, different countries, etc.) you can reduce risk significantly while reducing return slightly. Diversification works exactly the same way within corporations. A firm that invests in projects that are not perfectly correlated will reduce the volatility of its earnings. However, although diversification is undoubtedly a good idea for individuals, many believe that

---

3. The actual weights are 53.50% in stock A and 46.50% in stock B. We leave it as an exercise for you to find these weights using the Solver.

corporations should not seek to diversify. The reason is that the shareholders are perfectly capable of diversifying away company-specific risks on their own, and they can do it in a way that suits their unique purposes. On the other hand, a firm's managers, employees, and other stakeholders will benefit if the company diversifies because of a lower possibility of financial distress. Whether or not a firm should diversify is, however, an open question.

Portfolios with More than Two Securities

Obviously, we can create portfolios of more than two securities. Most individuals who own stocks own more than two. Corporations have many ongoing projects and multiple brands, and many mutual funds own hundreds of stocks and/or other securities.

Regardless of the number of securities in a portfolio, the expected return is always a weighted average of the individual expected returns. The standard deviation is, however, more complicated. Recall that when we were evaluating the standard deviation of the two-stock portfolio, we had to account for the covariance between the two stocks. Similarly, when we have a three-stock portfolio, we must account for the covariance between each pair of stocks. The standard deviation of a three-stock portfolio is thus given by (using the covariance form):

$$\sigma_P = \sqrt{w_1^2\sigma_1^2 + w_2^2\sigma_2^2 + w_3^2\sigma_3^2 + 2w_1w_2\sigma_{1,2} + 2w_1w_3\sigma_{1,3} + 2w_2w_3\sigma_{2,3}} \tag{13-8}$$

Obviously, the expression for the portfolio standard deviation gets to be cumbersome for more than two securities. To add a fourth security to equation (13-8) would require four additional terms. Therefore, when more than two securities are included, the expression is usually written as:

$$\sigma_P = \sqrt{\sum_{i=1}^{N}\sum_{j=1}^{N} w_i w_j r_{i,j}\sigma_i\sigma_j} \tag{13-9}$$

or, in the equivalent covariance form:

$$\sigma_P = \sqrt{\sum_{i=1}^{N}\sum_{j=1}^{N} w_i w_j \sigma_{i,j}} \tag{13-10}$$

Equations (13-9) and (13-10), while not exactly simple, will calculate the standard deviation of a portfolio of any number of securities.

Creating a Variance/Covariance Matrix

As we have seen, in order to calculate the standard deviation (or variance) of a portfolio, we need to know the weights allocated to each security, standard deviation (or variance) of each security, and the covariance between each pair of securities. We have already demonstrated how to calculate all of these items; however, the pairwise covariances are most easily displayed in a matrix. The variance/covariance matrix also makes the calculation of the portfolio standard deviation much easier.

EXHIBIT 13-5
STOCK RETURN DATA FOR VARIANCE/COVARIANCE MATRIX

	A	B	C	D	E
1	Year	LOON	UFO	SOP	LOL
2	2010	11.10%	17.38%	23.42%	1.48%
3	2011	-11.29%	-2.29%	-7.31%	9.73%
4	2012	21.72%	15.53%	8.26%	-1.08%
5	2013	16.38%	32.33%	14.28%	18.46%
6	2014	12.36%	-7.85%	9.47%	13.29%
7	Exp. Ret.	10.05%	11.02%	9.62%	8.38%
8	Std. Dev.	12.63%	16.19%	11.19%	8.13%

Excel has a built-in tool to create a variance/covariance matrix. Before seeing how it works, create a new worksheet with the returns for the four stocks shown in Exhibit 13-5 and rename it Stock Data. Be sure to calculate the expected returns and standard deviations because they will be required later.

FIGURE 13-2
THE COVARIANCE DIALOG BOX

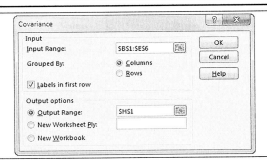

Data Analysis

To create the covariance matrix, click the Data Analysis button on the Data tab and then choose Covariance from the list. This will launch the dialog box shown in Figure 13-2.

Enter B1:E6 in the Input Range edit box. Notice that we have included the labels in the first row. This isn't required, but it makes the output easier to read. Make sure to check the Labels in first row box, otherwise you will get an error message. Place the output in H1.

Exhibit 13-6 shows the resulting covariance matrix. The covariance between any two stocks can be read at the intersection of the appropriate row and column. For example, cell J4 contains the covariance between UFO and SOP (0.0082). The numbers along the diagonal are the variances of the returns for each stock.[4]

EXHIBIT 13-6
THE POPULATION VARIANCE/COVARIANCE MATRIX

◢	H	I	J	K	L
1		*LOON*	*UFO*	*SOP*	*LOL*
2	LOON	0.0128			
3	UFO	0.0087	0.0210		
4	SOP	0.0078	0.0082	0.0100	
5	LOL	-0.0014	0.0004	-0.0012	0.0053

Note that the upper half of the matrix is empty. That is because the covariance matrix is symmetric, so those cells would be a mirror image of those in the lower diagonal. Unfortunately, Excel's covariance tool calculates the population covariances, and we are using sample covariances. So, this tool is not as useful as we would like. We will see how to fix this in the next section.

Using Matrix Algebra to Calculate the Variance/Covariance Matrix

Excel's covariance tool has three drawbacks: (1) It only creates the lower diagonal; (2) it only calculates population covariances; and (3) it only uses formulas for the variances. The last point means that the variance/covariance matrix won't update correctly if the returns are changed. To fix these problems, we could edit the matrix so that it uses formulas (the **COVARIANCE.S** function) in all of the cells or we could use matrix algebra.

Because Excel has built-in functions to do matrix calculations, it is straightforward to create the variance/covariance matrix using a single array formula. This has the benefit of eliminating the deficiencies of the covariance tool, and it is faster as well. Using matrix notation, the *sample* variance/covariance matrix (V) is calculated as:

---

4. The covariance of a variable with itself is the same as the variance of that variable.

$$V = \frac{D'D}{n-1} \qquad \text{(13-11)}$$

where D is the *difference matrix*, D' is the transpose of D, and n is the number of returns for each security. The difference matrix is a matrix of the returns less the expected return. Matrix multiplication can be done using the **MMULT** function:

$$\text{MMULT}(\textit{ARRAY1}, \textit{ARRAY2})$$

where both arguments are ranges on the worksheet or in memory. Following the rules of matrix algebra, the number of columns in *ARRAY1* must be equal to the number of rows in *ARRAY2*. We also need to calculate the transpose of the difference matrix, so we can use the **TRANSPOSE** function:

$$\text{TRANSPOSE}(\textit{ARRAY})$$

where *ARRAY* is a range on the worksheet or in memory. Because **MMULT** and **TRANSPOSE** inherently return multiple values, they are array functions. Therefore, you must select a range that will hold all of the output (instead of a single cell) and press Shift+Ctrl+Enter when entering them from the formula bar. This also means that you only need to enter the formula once to get all of the results.

Because we are using an array formula, we can calculate the difference array in memory, rather than creating it on the worksheet. To create the covariance matrix, select I2:L5 and then enter: `=MMULT(TRANSPOSE(B2:E6-B7:E7),(B2:E6-B7:E7))/4`. This will create the output shown in Exhibit 13-7. If you get a #VALUE! error instead, then you need to remember to enter the formula using Shift+Ctrl+Enter.[5]

EXHIBIT 13-7
THE SAMPLE VARIANCE/COVARIANCE MATRIX

	H	I	J	K	L
1		*LOON*	*UFO*	*SOP*	*LOL*
2	**LOON**	0.0160	0.0109	0.0097	-0.0018
3	**UFO**	0.0109	0.0262	0.0102	0.0004
4	**SOP**	0.0097	0.0102	0.0125	-0.0015
5	**LOL**	-0.0018	0.0004	-0.0015	0.0066

---

5. On the official Web site, http://www.cengagebrain.com/, you can download the cov-matrix.xlam add-in that creates a variance/covariance matrix with some additional capabilities and options. Once installed, it will appear on the Data tab.

This is similar to the output of the covariance tool, except that it is the full sample variance/covariance matrix and will update automatically if any of the returns are changed. It will also facilitate the calculation of the portfolio standard deviation in the next section.

In this example, because we are using historical data, we are assuming that all possible outcomes are equally likely. However, we often have probability distributions with unequal probabilities. In that case, assuming that the probabilities are in A2:A6, we would change the above formula to: =MMULT(TRANSPOSE(A2:A6*(B2:E6-B7:E7)),(B2:E6-B7:E7)). Try it by replacing each of the years in A2:A6 with 0.20 (20% probability). This will give the same population covariance matrix as Exhibit 13-6, but with the flexibility of changing the probabilities. Remember to reset the formula to match Exhibit 13-7 before continuing.

Calculating the Portfolio Standard Deviation

We have seen earlier that we can use equation (13-10) to calculate the portfolio standard deviation. However, the number of terms in that equation grows very quickly as the number of securities increases. It simply isn't practical to type in that equation if there are more than two or three securities. The total number of covariances (including variances) required in the formula is given by:

$$\text{Number of Covariances} = \frac{N(N+1)}{2} \tag{13-12}$$

Equation (13-12) counts only the lower half of the covariance matrix as shown in Exhibit 13-6 (there are $4(4+1)/2 = 10$ covariances). The full covariance matrix in Exhibit 13-7 requires N^2 covariances to fill the entire matrix.

Therefore, it is impractical to try to create a worksheet formula to calculate the portfolio standard deviation of a portfolio with more than a few securities. Not only would the formula be very long, but the chance of making an error is high. Therefore, we should either use matrix algebra or a user-defined function to do the calculation. We will demonstrate both techniques in this section.

We have all the data required to calculate the portfolio standard deviation, except for the weights. Let's begin by assuming that our portfolio will hold all four stocks in equal proportions (i.e., 25% in each). Starting in A10, set up the data as shown in Exhibit 13-8.

In any portfolio, the weights of the individual securities must sum to 100%. So, as a check, in B15 enter the formula: =SUM(B11:B14). To calculate the expected return of the portfolio in B16 enter: =SUM(TRANSPOSE(B11:B14)*$B$7:$E$7) as an array formula. Note that we need to transpose one of the ranges because their orientation differs. The expected return of the equally weighted portfolio is 9.77%.

EXHIBIT 13-8
CALCULATING THE PORTFOLIO STANDARD DEVIATION

	A	B
10	**Stock**	**Weights**
11	LOON	25.00%
12	UFO	25.00%
13	SOP	25.00%
14	LOL	25.00%
15	Sum Weights	
16	Exp Return	
17	Std Dev	

We can restate equation (13-10) to calculate the portfolio standard deviation in matrix notation:

$$\sigma_P = \sqrt{W'VW} \tag{13-13}$$

where W is the column vector (range) of weights, V is the variance/covariance matrix, and W' is the transpose of the weight vector. In B17 enter the formula: `=SQRT(MMULT(MMULT(TRANSPOSE(B11:B14),$I$2:$L$5),B11:B14))`. Remember to enter the formula using Shift+Ctrl+Enter because it is an array formula. You should find that the portfolio standard deviation is 8.56%.

Instead of using the matrix functions, we can use the **FAME_PORTVAR1** user-defined function from the Famefncs.xlam add-in. This function calculates the portfolio variance given the variance/covariance matrix and the weights. It is defined as:

FAME_PORTVAR1(*VARCOVMAT*,*WEIGHTS***)**

where ***VARCOVMAT*** is the variance/covariance matrix, and ***WEIGHTS*** is the range of weights for each security. To calculate the portfolio standard deviation in B17, replace the formula with: `=SQRT(FAME_PortVar1($I$2:$L$5,B11:B14))`. Your answer should be the same.

You can experiment by changing the weights to see how the expected return and standard deviation changes. There are an infinite number of portfolios that can be created from these stocks by varying the weights.

The Efficient Frontier

As noted above, an infinite number of portfolios can be constructed from any universe of securities. Some will be better than others. If we were to create a graph showing the risk and return combination for every possible portfolio, it would be known as the *feasible set*.

FIGURE 13-3
THE FEASIBLE SET AND EFFICIENT FRONTIER

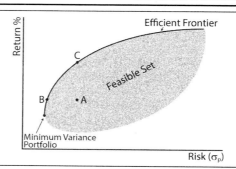

Figure 13-3 shows the feasible set and some additional information. Notice that portfolios A, B, and C are within the feasible set, so they could be created. However, portfolio B is on the edge of the feasible set and has the same expected return as A, but with less risk. Therefore, given a choice, any investor would prefer B over A. Similarly, portfolio C has the same amount of risk as A, but it has a much higher return. So, any investor would prefer C over A.

Portfolios B and C are both on the upper edge of the feasible set, which is known as the *efficient frontier*. Portfolios that are located on the efficient frontier will always be preferred over portfolios that are inside the feasible set because they offer either: (1) a higher return with the same risk; or (2) the same return with less risk. For this reason, investors will always choose from among the portfolios that lie on the efficient frontier.

Unless we know an investor's utility function, however, we cannot determine which portfolio on the efficient frontier would be chosen by that investor. For example, we cannot say whether you would prefer B or C (or some other portfolio on the efficient frontier) without knowing your utility function. We will examine the process of choosing the optimal portfolio with a utility function in a later section.

Finally, note the portfolio labeled "Minimum Variance Portfolio." This is the least risky portfolio that is located on the efficient frontier.

Locating Portfolios on the Efficient Frontier in Excel

Finding the portfolios that lie on the efficient frontier is a quadratic (nonlinear) optimization problem. Specifically, we want to find the set of portfolios that minimize the risk for each feasible expected return subject to two (sometimes three or more) constraints: (1) The sum of the weights must equal 1; (2) the calculated return must equal the specified target return; and, sometimes, (3) each of the weights must be between 0 and 1. The third constraint specifies that short sales are not allowed, which is a common constraint for individual and institutional investors. Also note that corporations cannot short sell their projects, so that constraint would often be appropriate. For our theoretical purposes, we will allow short sales and, therefore, disregard constraint 3. We will also assume that the proceeds from the shorted securities can be used to purchase more of the long positions.

In Chapter 11 (pages 361 to 365), we used the Solver to find the solution to an optimal capital budgeting problem. We can use the Solver for any type of optimization, so we will use it to locate a couple of the portfolios on the efficient frontier. Because the efficient frontier begins at the minimum variance portfolio, we will first solve for the set of weights for our four stocks that result in the smallest possible portfolio standard deviation, without regard to the return. This is the minimum variance portfolio that was pictured in Figure 13-3.

?→ Solver   Click the Solver button on the Data tab to get the Solver dialog box as shown in Figure 13-4.

FIGURE 13-4
USING THE SOLVER TO GET THE MINIMUM VARIANCE PORTFOLIO

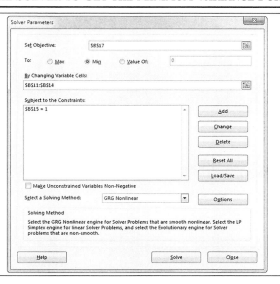

For the minimum variance portfolio, we are seeking to minimize the portfolio standard deviation in B17, so that is the Target Cell. Select the Mi**n** radio button so that the Solver will minimize the function. The **B**y Changing Variable Cells should be the weights in B11:B14. Now, click the **A**dd button so that we can add the constraint: B15 = 1. This assures that the weights will add up to 1 (i.e., 100% of your money will be invested).

Because we are solving a nonlinear optimization problem, we cannot use the Simplex LP solver as we did in Chapter 11. Instead, be sure to set the solving method to use the GRG Nonlinear solver. The default options should work fine, so we don't need to change them, but be sure that Ma**k**e Unconstrained Variables Non-Negative is not checked.

Make sure that your dialog box looks like the one in Figure 13-4 and then click the **S**olve button. After a few seconds, you should be notified that Solver has found a solution. Choose to keep that solution, and you will see that the expected return of the minimum variance portfolio is 8.84% and the standard deviation is 5.87%.[6]

We will follow an almost identical process to find one more portfolio on the efficient frontier. We only need one more because every portfolio on the frontier can be calculated directly from any two frontier portfolios.

We need to specify the target return for this other portfolio and add another constraint. First, copy B10:B17 across to column C. This will set up the formulas for the other portfolio. In C10 change the name of the portfolio to: `Max Return`.

Now that we have the cells set up, relaunch the Solver. Change the Target Cell to C17, the Changing Cells to C11:C14, and then change the existing constraint to: C15 = 1. We also need to add a new constraint so that: C16 = C7. This ensures that the calculated return (C16) is equal to our target return (C7) for this portfolio. The target return will be the same as that of the stock with the highest return (UFO in this example).[7] The main Solver dialog box should now look like the one in Figure 13-5.

---

6. When allowing short sales, as we are here, we can analytically solve for the weights of the minimum variance portfolio directly using:

$$\text{Min Var Weights} = \frac{V^{-1}e}{e'V^{-1}e}$$

where V^{-1} is the inverse of the variance/covariance matrix and e is a column vector of ones. See Grinold, R.C. & Kahn, R.N. (1995), *Active Portfolio Management*. Chicago: Irwin Professional Publishing.

7. This is just a convenience, and we could set it to any other value. In fact, because we are allowing short sales, just about any return is achievable in theory. If we did not allow short sales, then the highest achievable return would be equal to that of the highest returning stock.

FIGURE 13-5
SOLVING FOR THE WEIGHTS FOR PORTFOLIO 2

Click the Solve button and you should find that the standard deviation of the Max Return portfolio is 15.39%. Your worksheet should look like the one in Exhibit 13-9. The negative weights indicate stocks that should be sold short, with the proceeds being used to purchase more of the other stocks. Now compare the riskiness of the Max Return portfolio to that of UFO. Both have exactly the same expected return (11.02%), but our new portfolio achieves that return with less risk. This is a good example of diversification in action.

EXHIBIT 13-9
TWO EFFICIENT FRONTIER PORTFOLIOS

	A	B	C
		Min Var	Max
10	**Stock**	**Portfolio**	**Return**
11	LOON	15.55%	48.75%
12	UFO	-4.78%	76.66%
13	SOP	26.70%	-16.09%
14	LOL	62.52%	-9.31%
15	Sum Weights	100.00%	100.00%
16	Exp Return	8.84%	11.02%
17	Std Dev	5.87%	15.39%

Charting the Efficient Frontier

We have located two portfolios that are on the efficient frontier, and we could create a chart now. However, having only two portfolios will produce a line, not a smooth curve, so we will create several more before charting the frontier. Before beginning, select C10:C17 and move it to L10:L17 by dragging. This will give us some space to create the other portfolios.

We will now make use of a special property of portfolios on the efficient frontier: Every portfolio on the frontier is a combination of two other portfolios that are on the frontier, so the weights are a weighted average of the weights in the other two portfolios:

$$W_P = xW_{\text{Min Var}} + (1 - x)W_{\text{Max Return}} \tag{13-14}$$

We have the weights for two portfolios already, so we'll start by creating a portfolio that is exactly 90% invested in the Minimum Variance portfolio, and 10% invested in the Max Return portfolio (though we could use any two portfolios for which we know the weights). This will be located toward the left part of the efficient frontier.

In C9 enter the weight: 90%. Enter a formula to calculate the weight of LOON in C11: =C$9*$B11+(1-C$9)*$L11. You should see that LOON will have a weight of 18.87% in this new frontier portfolio. Copy this formula down through C14 to get the weights of the other stocks. The weight in row 9 is the proportion that is invested in the minimum variance portfolio, and the remainder of your funds will be invested in the maximum return portfolio.

To get the weights, returns, and standard deviations for the remaining portfolios, simply copy C11:C17 across to D11:K17. Your worksheet should match Exhibit 13-10.

EXHIBIT 13-10
WEIGHTS FOR PORTFOLIOS ON THE EFFICIENT FRONTIER

	A	B	C	D	E	F	G	H	I	J	K	L
9			90%	80%	70%	60%	50%	40%	30%	20%	10%	
10	Stock	Min Var Portfolio	Port 2	Port 3	Port 4	Port 5	Port 6	Port 7	Port 8	Port 9	Port 10	Max Return
11	LOON	15.55%	18.87%	22.19%	25.51%	28.83%	32.15%	35.47%	38.79%	42.11%	45.43%	48.75%
12	UFO	-4.78%	3.36%	11.51%	19.65%	27.80%	35.94%	44.08%	52.23%	60.37%	68.52%	76.66%
13	SOP	26.70%	22.42%	18.15%	13.87%	9.59%	5.31%	1.03%	-3.25%	-7.53%	-11.81%	-16.09%
14	LOL	62.52%	55.34%	48.16%	40.97%	33.79%	26.60%	19.42%	12.24%	5.05%	-2.13%	-9.31%
15	Sum Weights	100.00%	100.00%	100.00%	100.00%	100.00%	100.00%	100.00%	100.00%	100.00%	100.00%	100.00%
16	Exp Return	8.84%	9.06%	9.28%	9.50%	9.71%	9.93%	10.15%	10.37%	10.58%	10.80%	11.02%
17	Std Dev	5.87%	6.04%	6.52%	7.26%	8.18%	9.22%	10.36%	11.56%	12.81%	14.09%	15.39%

Once the portfolios are located, then creating a chart of the efficient frontier is as easy as creating a scatter chart. If you refer back to Figure 13-3, you will see that we want the expected returns on the y-axis and the standard deviations on the x-axis. Select A16:L17 and insert a scatter chart with straight lines and markers. At first, your chart will have the variables on the wrong axes, so we need to edit the chart to fix this problem.

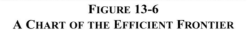

FIGURE 13-6
A CHART OF THE EFFICIENT FRONTIER

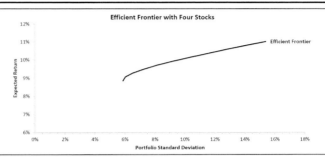

Right-click in the chart and choose S**e**lect Data... from the shortcut menu. In the Select Data Source dialog box, click the **E**dit button. Now change the Series **X** values so that it points to B17:L17. Change the Series **Y** values to B16:L16. This will "flip" the chart so that the values are on the correct axes. After adding the appropriate chart title and axis titles, your chart should look like the one in Figure 13-6.

The efficient frontier in the chart isn't quite a smooth curve. This is because we have only plotted 11 portfolios. If we had found, say, 20 portfolios with more of them near the apex of the curve, then it would be much smoother. Another way is to change the chart type to scatter with smooth lines. This is generally not recommended because it applies artificial smoothing to the data so that the chart is not necessarily a good representation of the data.

The Capital Market Line

So far, we have included only risky assets in the portfolios. Now imagine that a completely risk-free asset is also available. This is an asset that has a standard deviation of returns of zero, and its expected return is equal to the risk-free rate. Of course, this asset exists only in theory. In the real world, U.S. Treasury bills come closest to being risk-free assets because they are free of default risk. We will use a theoretical risk-free asset with an expected return of 7%. We are interested in seeing how the efficient frontier changes when a risk-free asset is added to the universe of securities.

To begin, create a copy of the worksheet that you used to create Exhibit 13-9. We will make a few modifications to include this additional asset. In F1 enter Risk-Free for the name of the asset and then enter 7% as the return for each year. Now copy E7:E8 to F7:F8 to calculate the expected return and standard deviation of the risk-free asset. This section of your worksheet should now look like the one in Exhibit 13-11.

EXHIBIT 13-11
DATA INCLUDING THE RISK-FREE ASSET

	A	B	C	D	E	F
1	Year	LOON	UFO	SOP	LOL	Risk-Free
2	2010	11.10%	17.38%	23.42%	1.48%	7.00%
3	2011	-11.29%	-2.29%	-7.31%	9.73%	7.00%
4	2012	21.72%	15.53%	8.26%	-1.08%	7.00%
5	2013	16.38%	32.33%	14.28%	18.46%	7.00%
6	2014	12.36%	-7.85%	9.47%	13.29%	7.00%
7	Exp. Ret.	10.05%	11.02%	9.62%	8.38%	7.00%
8	Std. Dev.	12.63%	16.19%	11.19%	8.13%	0.00%

We also need to add the risk-free asset to the variance/covariance matrix. In M1 and H6 enter the label: Risk-Free. Now select I2:M6 and enter the formula: =MMULT(TRANSPOSE(B2:F6-B7:F7),(B2:F6-B7:F7))/4. This is the same formula that we used previously, except that the ranges have been expanded to include the risk-free asset. The variance/covariance matrix is shown in Exhibit 13-12.

Note that the covariance (and correlation) of the risk-free asset with any other asset is 0. Because the returns on the risk-free asset don't vary, they certainly can't vary with the returns on any other asset. It is this fact that makes the risk-free asset so good for diversification purposes, as we will see shortly.

EXHIBIT 13-12
THE VARIANCE/COVARIANCE MATRIX WITH THE RISK-FREE ASSET

	H	I	J	K	L	M
1		LOON	UFO	SOP	LOL	Risk-Free
2	LOON	0.0160	0.0109	0.0097	-0.0018	0.0000
3	UFO	0.0109	0.0262	0.0102	0.0004	0.0000
4	SOP	0.0097	0.0102	0.0125	-0.0015	0.0000
5	LOL	-0.0018	0.0004	-0.0015	0.0066	0.0000
6	Risk-Free	0.0000	0.0000	0.0000	0.0000	0.0000

Finally, we need to add the risk-free asset into the portfolio section of the worksheet. Select row 15 and insert a new row. Type Risk-Free into A15, and then edit the formulas in B16, B17, and B18 so that they include the new data. The new formulas are:

B16:   =SUM(B11:B15)

B17:   =SUM(TRANSPOSE(B11:B15)*$B$7:$F$7)

B18:   =SQRT(MMULT(MMULT(TRANSPOSE(B11:B15),$I$2:$M$6),B11:B15))

Remember that the formulas in B17 and B18 are array formulas, so they must be entered using Shift+Ctrl+Enter.

Now, we will run the Solver exactly as before. Remember that we are allowing unlimited short sales because that is one of the assumptions made in the derivation of the capital market line (CML). Furthermore, we assume that any proceeds from short sales can be used to purchase additional long positions in other assets.

The minimum variance portfolio will be 100% invested in the risk-free asset because the portfolio standard deviation can never be below 0. Therefore, set the weights in B11:B14 to 0% and B15 to 100%. You should see that the expected return on this portfolio is 7% and the standard deviation is 0%. We don't need to use the Solver for this portfolio.

As before, we will minimize the standard deviation of the Max Return portfolio, so the Target Cell is L18. The Changing Cells are the weights in L11:L15. Because we are allowing short sales, we only need to set two constraints. The first is that the sum of the weights must equal 1, so click the **A**dd button and enter the constraint: L16 = 1. The second is that the calculated portfolio return must equal the target return (11.02%), so enter the constraint: L17 = C7.

FIGURE 13-7
SOLVER SETTINGS FOR THE MAX RETURN PORTFOLIO

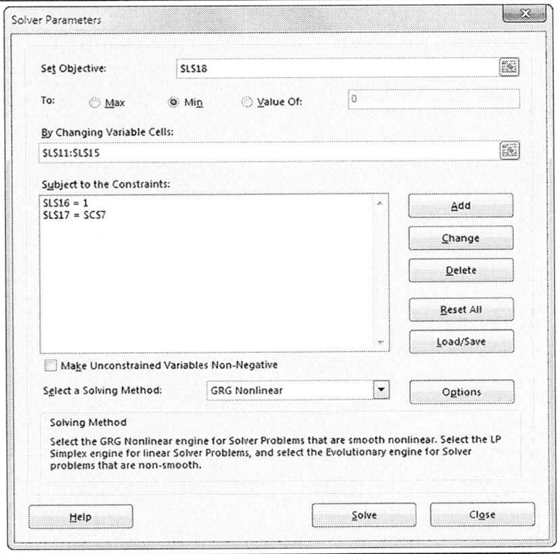

Make sure that your Solver dialog box matches the one shown in Figure 13-7, and then click the **S**olve button. You should find that the expected return for the Max Return portfolio is 11.02% and the standard deviation is 11.51%. The other portfolios should have updated automatically. Your worksheet should look like the one pictured in Exhibit 13-13.

EXHIBIT 13-13
PORTFOLIOS ON THE CML

	A	B	C	D	E	F	G	H	I	J	K	L
9			90%	80%	70%	60%	50%	40%	30%	20%	10%	
10	Stock	Min Var Portfolio	Port 2	Port 3	Port 4	Port 5	Port 6	Port 7	Port 8	Port 9	Port 10	Max Return
11	LOON	0.00%	3.92%	7.83%	11.75%	15.66%	19.58%	23.49%	27.41%	31.33%	35.24%	39.16%
12	UFO	0.00%	2.04%	4.08%	6.12%	8.16%	10.19%	12.23%	14.27%	16.31%	18.35%	20.39%
13	SOP	0.00%	3.19%	6.39%	9.58%	12.77%	15.96%	19.16%	22.35%	25.54%	28.74%	31.93%
14	LOL	0.00%	8.48%	16.96%	25.44%	33.92%	42.39%	50.87%	59.35%	67.83%	76.31%	84.79%
15	Risk-Free	100.00%	82.37%	64.75%	47.12%	29.49%	11.87%	-5.76%	-23.39%	-41.01%	-58.64%	-76.26%
16	Sum Weights	100.00%	100.00%	100.00%	100.00%	100.00%	100.00%	100.00%	100.00%	100.00%	100.00%	100.00%
17	Exp Return	7.00%	7.40%	7.80%	8.21%	8.61%	9.01%	9.41%	9.81%	10.22%	10.62%	11.02%
18	Std Dev	0.00%	1.15%	2.30%	3.45%	4.60%	5.75%	6.90%	8.05%	9.20%	10.35%	11.51%

Charting the Capital Market Line

We are now ready to create a chart of the CML. First, return to your efficient frontier worksheet and copy the chart of the efficient frontier (Figure 13-6). Now paste the chart into the CML worksheet. This will maintain the links to the original data, so the chart should look the same.

We want to add the CML to this chart so that we can compare the efficient frontier with the CML. Right-click in the chart and choose Select Data. Next, click the Add button so that we can add the new series. In the Series name edit box, type: = "CML" to name the series. For the Series X values select B18:F18, and for the Series Y values select B17:F17. Your chart should now look like the one in Figure 13-8.

FIGURE 13-8
CHART OF THE CML AND THE EFFICIENT FRONTIER

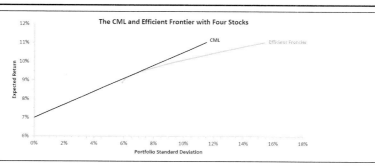

There are several important points to note about this chart. First, notice that the CML is a straight line. That is, adding a risk-free asset to our universe of securities creates a linear risk/return trade-off.

Second, notice that the CML provides a better risk/return trade-off than the efficient frontier. For any portfolio that lies on the efficient frontier, there is a superior portfolio on the CML. This is important because it means that if a risk-free asset (such as Treasury bills) is available, then investors will no longer choose portfolios from among those on the efficient frontier. Rather, they will choose a portfolio that lies on the CML.

Finally, notice that there is one point of commonality between the CML and the efficient frontier. The CML is tangent to the efficient frontier at the location of a very special portfolio known as the *market portfolio*. The market portfolio contains all risky assets (all four stocks in our example) in proportion to their market values. In other words, it is a capitalization-weighted portfolio.

The market portfolio does not hold the risk-free asset. Every other portfolio on the CML is made up of some portion of the risk-free asset and the market portfolio. Therefore, all investors will invest in a portfolio that holds the market portfolio and the risk-free asset (i.e., somewhere on the CML).

This means that the investment decision is the same for all investors—they all invest in the market portfolio. The only choice that they have to make is how much of the risk-free asset to own. This choice is known as the financing decision. A long position is equivalent to making a loan at the risk-free rate, while a short position in the risk-free asset is equivalent to borrowing at the risk-free rate and using the proceeds to purchase more of the market portfolio.

By introducing a risk-free asset, we have separated the investing and financing decisions. This is known as the *Tobin's separation theorem* and is illustrated in Figure 13-9.

FIGURE 13-9
THE CML AND THE SEPARATION THEOREM

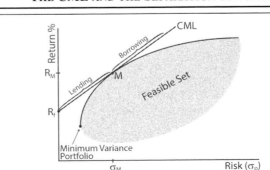

Identifying the Market Portfolio

The market portfolio plays a central role in modern portfolio theory. It would be helpful if we could identify its exact location on the efficient frontier. By looking at Figure 13-9, you should be able to see that the equation (in slope-intercept form) of the CML is:

$$E(R_P) = R_F + \frac{(R_M - R_F)}{\sigma_M}\sigma_P \qquad (13\text{-}15)$$

The slope of the CML is known as the *market price of risk* and is given by:

$$\text{Slope of CML} = \frac{(R_M - R_F)}{\sigma_M} \qquad (13\text{-}16)$$

The market price of risk is a measure of the excess return per unit of risk that is available in the market. Because the CML is a straight line, it has the same slope at every point. Therefore, we can generalize that to any portfolio by substituting for R_M and σ_M. This gives us the *Sharpe ratio*, which is a well-known portfolio performance metric. The equation for the Sharpe ratio is:

$$\text{Sharpe Ratio} = \frac{(R_P - R_F)}{\sigma_P} \qquad (13\text{-}17)$$

In Figure 13-8, it appears that the market portfolio is very close to portfolio 3 on the efficient frontier, but we don't know for sure what the weights are. We can find its exact position on the efficient frontier by using the Solver to find the weights for the portfolio that maximizes the Sharpe ratio.

The risk-free asset could be combined with any portfolio on the efficient frontier, with the resulting line known as a *capital allocation line*. Investors will prefer portfolios on the steepest capital allocation line, which is the one with the highest Sharpe ratio (i.e., the CML).

We will use M10:M19 to solve for the market portfolio. So, select L10:L19 and copy the range to M10:M19. Change the label in M10 to: `Market Portfolio`, and in A19 enter: `Sharpe Ratio`. In B19 enter the formula: `=IFERROR((B17-$B$17)/B18,0)` and then copy it across C19:M19. We are using the **IFERROR** function to avoid a #DIV/0! error for the minimum variance portfolio.

Our goal is to use the Solver to maximize the Sharpe ratio in M19 by changing the weights in M11:M15, subject to the constraints that M16 = 1, and M15 = 0 (the market portfolio does not hold the risk-free asset). Launch the Solver and set up the dialog box so that it matches Figure 13-10.

FIGURE 13-10
SOLVER DIALOG BOX TO FIND THE MARKET PORTFOLIO

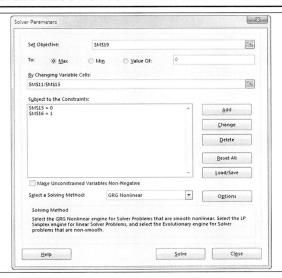

After running the Solver, you will find that the market portfolio has a Sharpe ratio of 0.3494, which is also the slope of the CML. Your output should match Exhibit 13-14 (some columns are hidden).

EXHIBIT 13-14
THE MARKET PORTFOLIO AND OTHERS ON THE EFFICIENT FRONTIER

	A	B	C	D	J	K	L	M
10	Stock	Min Var Portfolio	Port 2	Port 3	Port 9	Port 10	Max Return	Market Portfolio
11	LOON	0.00%	3.92%	7.83%	31.33%	35.24%	39.16%	22.21%
12	UFO	0.00%	2.04%	4.08%	16.31%	18.35%	20.39%	11.57%
13	SOP	0.00%	3.19%	6.39%	25.54%	28.74%	31.93%	18.11%
14	LOL	0.00%	8.48%	16.96%	67.83%	76.31%	84.79%	48.10%
15	Risk-Free	100.00%	82.37%	64.75%	-41.01%	-58.64%	-76.26%	0.00%
16	Sum Weights	100.00%	100.00%	100.00%	100.00%	100.00%	100.00%	100.00%
17	Exp Return	7.00%	7.40%	7.80%	10.22%	10.62%	11.02%	9.28%
18	Std Dev	0.00%	1.15%	2.30%	9.20%	10.35%	11.51%	6.53%
19	Sharpe Ratio	-	0.3494	0.3494	0.3494	0.3494	0.3494	0.3494

The market portfolio is located at the point of tangency between the CML and the efficient frontier because that is the point at which their slopes are equal. We have now exactly identified the market portfolio. We know how much of each stock it holds, and we know its return and standard deviation.

As noted earlier, the market portfolio is located very close to portfolio 3 on the efficient frontier. You can add it to the chart of the efficient frontier and CML (Figure 13-8). Right-click the chart and choose S**e**lect Data. Click the **A**dd button and set the Series **n**ame to `Market Portfolio`, the X value to the market portfolio's standard deviation, and the Y value to its expected return. Figure 13-11 shows the result.

FIGURE 13-11
THE MARKET PORTFOLIO WITH THE CML AND EFFICIENT FRONTIER

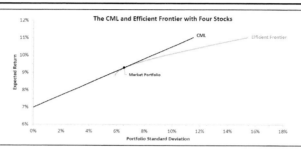

Utility Functions and the Optimal Portfolio

Each investor will prefer a different portfolio; which one depends upon their preferences regarding risk and return. As noted in Chapter 8, some investors are more tolerant of risk than others, and we would expect these investors to choose a riskier portfolio with a higher expected return. In order to identify the optimal portfolio we need to know the investor's utility function and degree of risk aversion. For our purposes, we will use the following utility function (which is just one of many possible utility functions):

$$E(U) = E(R) - \frac{1}{2}A\sigma^2 \tag{13-18}$$

where $E(R)$ is the expected return of the portfolio, σ^2 is the variance, and A is the coefficient of relative risk aversion ($-\infty \leq A \leq \infty$). When $A > 0$ the investor is risk averse, and higher values of A indicate greater risk aversion (i.e., less risk tolerance). When $A = 0$, the investor is risk neutral. Equation (13-18) will allow us to calculate the utility of a portfolio on the efficient frontier, and to find the portfolio that maximizes the utility for any given investor.

Charting Indifference Curves

An *indifference curve* shows all possible combinations of risk and return that would provide the same amount of utility for a given investor. We can rearrange equation (13-18) as follows:

$$E(R) = E(U) + \frac{1}{2}A\sigma^2 \tag{13-19}$$

which will allow us to specify levels of utility, risk aversion, and risk and then solve for the return. We can then plot the combinations that result in the specified level of utility. When we plot multiple indifference curves, we call it an *indifference map*.

Create a new worksheet and name it Indifference Curves. In A1 enter: Risk Aversion, and in B1 enter: 2.5. In A2 enter: Utility, and in B2:D2 enter 7%, 8%, and 9%. In A4:A19 enter a series going from 0 to 15% in 1% increments. In B4 enter the formula to calculate the return: =B$2+0.5*$B$1*$A4^2, and copy it over the range. Now copy the chart that you created for Figure 13-6 into this worksheet, and add each of the indifference curves. Your worksheet should look like the one in Exhibit 13-15.

We could add many more indifference curves, as there are an infinite number of them. However, we are seeking the portfolio on the efficient frontier that maximizes the expected utility for the investor. This portfolio will be located at the point where an indifference curve is tangent to the efficient frontier. Indifference curve 3 is close to the frontier, but outside of the feasible set. So, the investor cannot quite achieve that level of utility.

EXHIBIT 13-15
THE EFFICIENT FRONTIER AND THREE INDIFFERENCE CURVES

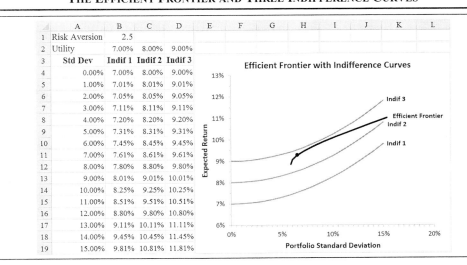

	A	B	C	D
1	Risk Aversion	2.5		
2	Utility	7.00%	8.00%	9.00%
3	**Std Dev**	**Indif 1**	**Indif 2**	**Indif 3**
4	0.00%	7.00%	8.00%	9.00%
5	1.00%	7.01%	8.01%	9.01%
6	2.00%	7.05%	8.05%	9.05%
7	3.00%	7.11%	8.11%	9.11%
8	4.00%	7.20%	8.20%	9.20%
9	5.00%	7.31%	8.31%	9.31%
10	6.00%	7.45%	8.45%	9.45%
11	7.00%	7.61%	8.61%	9.61%
12	8.00%	7.80%	8.80%	9.80%
13	9.00%	8.01%	9.01%	10.01%
14	10.00%	8.25%	9.25%	10.25%
15	11.00%	8.51%	9.51%	10.51%
16	12.00%	8.80%	9.80%	10.80%
17	13.00%	9.11%	10.11%	11.11%
18	14.00%	9.45%	10.45%	11.45%
19	15.00%	9.81%	10.81%	11.81%

To find the optimal portfolio, return to the worksheet that you used to create the CML. Copy M10:M19 over to column N. In A20 enter the label: Utility, and then in B20 enter the formula: =B17-0.5*'Indifference Curves'!$B$1*B18^2. Copy this across C20:N20 to calculate the utility for each portfolio.

Finally, launch the Solver and set it to maximize cell N20 by changing N11:N15 with a constraint of N16 = 1. You should find that the portfolio with the highest utility has an expected return of 11.88% and a standard deviation of 13.98%. This is the optimal portfolio for the investor with a risk aversion coefficient of 2.5. You can easily change the risk aversion coefficient and then find the optimal portfolio for a different investor.

Exhibit 13-16 shows the CML and the efficient frontier along with the indifference curve for the highest achievable level of utility (0.0944) for this investor. It was created in the same way as Exhibit 13-15, except that only the tangency indifference curve was calculated.

Notice that the optimal portfolio is well above the efficient frontier. This portfolio is only available because we added the risk-free asset. Without the risk-free asset, the optimal portfolio would have an expected return of 9.78% and utility of 0.0888. We leave it as an exercise for you to find this portfolio using the Solver.

EXHIBIT 13-16
OPTIMAL PORTFOLIO FOR THE INVESTOR

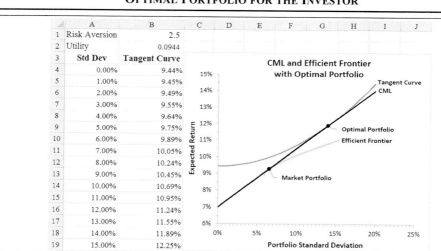

The Capital Asset Pricing Model

One of the best known models in finance is the capital asset pricing model (CAPM). In this section, we will see how to derive this model and its famous risk measure, beta (β). Recall that the market portfolio sits at the tangency point of the CML and the efficient frontier. So, at that point, the slopes are equal. The slope of the efficient frontier at point M is given by:

$$\text{Slope of frontier at M} = \frac{(R_P - R_M)\sigma_M}{(\sigma_{P,M} - \sigma_M^2)} \tag{13-20}$$

where R_P is the expected return on a portfolio, and $\sigma_{P,M}$ is the covariance between that portfolio and the market portfolio. If we now set equation (13-20) equal to equation (13-16), then we get:

$$\frac{(R_P - R_M)\sigma_M}{(\sigma_{P,M} - \sigma_M^2)} = \frac{(R_M - R_F)}{\sigma_M}$$

Now, cross multiply and simplify to solve for R_P and the solution is:

$$R_P = R_F + \frac{\sigma_{P,M}}{\sigma_M^2}(R_M - R_F) \tag{13-21}$$

Note that beta is defined as:

$$\beta_P = \frac{\sigma_{P,M}}{\sigma_M^2} \tag{13-22}$$

Finally, substitute (13-22) into (13-21) to get the familiar form of the CAPM with beta as its measure of risk:

$$R_P = R_F + \beta_P(R_M - R_F) \tag{13-23}$$

According to modern portfolio theory, there are two types of risk: (1) market (or systematic) risk; and (2) company-specific (or unsystematic) risk. Market risk is the risk associated with market-wide factors, such as unexpected changes in GDP or inflation rates. Market risk affects all investments to some degree. Company-specific risk factors (such as increased competition or employees going on strike) affect only individual investments. When we create a diversified portfolio, the risk that we are eliminating is the company-specific, or diversifiable, risk. Market risk cannot be diversified away.

The CAPM says that the portfolio return is equal to the risk-free rate plus a risk premium. The risk premium is determined by the product of the market risk premium and the portfolio beta. Beta is an index of market risk, so it tells us how sensitive the portfolio is to market risk factors. Note that the CAPM does not contain a risk premium associated with company-specific risk. Because company-specific risks can be diversified away, investors will not receive any additional return for holding a less than perfectly diversified portfolio.

The Security Market Line

When we create a chart of the CAPM equation, it is referred to as the security market line (SML). In this section, we will calculate the betas of our four stocks and create a chart of the SML. To begin, return to the worksheet that you used to create Exhibit 13-14.

We have already determined the weights of each of the stocks in the market portfolio and the expected return and standard deviation of that portfolio. We will now work backward to calculate the market portfolio's return in each year. In F1 enter the label: `Market`. Remember that the return on a portfolio is a weighted average of the returns of the individual securities. So, we can calculate the rate of return on the market portfolio in 2010 by entering: `=MMULT(B2:E2,$M$11:$M$14)` into F2. Copy that formula to F3:F6 to complete the calculation. Now we can copy E7:E8 to F7:F8 to get the expected return and standard deviation of the market portfolio. You should get the same values as we previously calculated in M16:M17.

We can calculate the betas for each of the stocks using equation (13-22). In A9 enter: `Beta`, and calculate the beta for LOON in B9 with the formula: `=COVARIANCE.S(B2:B6, $F$2:$F$6)/$F$8^2`. You should find that LOON's beta is 1.339. Now copy that formula across C9:F9 to calculate the other betas. Your worksheet should match the one in Exhibit 13-17.

EXHIBIT 13-17
BETAS FOR THE STOCKS AND THE MARKET PORTFOLIO

	A	B	C	D	E	F
1	Year	LOON	UFO	SOP	LOL	Market
2	2010	11.10%	17.38%	23.42%	1.48%	9.43%
3	2011	-11.29%	-2.29%	-7.31%	9.73%	0.58%
4	2012	21.72%	15.53%	8.26%	-1.08%	7.60%
5	2013	16.38%	32.33%	14.28%	18.46%	18.85%
6	2014	12.36%	-7.85%	9.47%	13.29%	9.95%
7	Exp. Ret.	10.05%	11.02%	9.62%	8.38%	9.28%
8	Std. Dev.	12.63%	16.19%	11.19%	8.13%	6.53%
9	Beta	1.339	1.763	1.151	0.603	1.000

To chart the SML, we will need to add the data for the risk-free asset. In A21 type: `Beta` and in A22 type: `Exp. Return`. In B20 enter: `Risk-Free`, in B21 enter: `0.000`, and in B22 enter: `7.00%`. Now copy the labels from B1:F1 and paste them into C20:G20. In C21 enter the formula: `=B9`, and in C22 enter: `=B7`. Copy the formulas from C21:C22 across D21:G22.

To create the chart, select A21:G22 and insert a scatter chart. Your chart should now look like the one in Figure 13-12.

FIGURE 13-12
THE SECURITY MARKET LINE

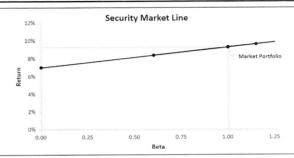

Summary

Diversification is the process of allocating capital across multiple investments in order to reduce the riskiness of the portfolio. Diversification reduces risk because assets are not perfectly positively correlated, so volatility in one asset tends to cancel out volatility in another. Therefore, it is important to choose assets that are not highly correlated.

We demonstrated that the expected return of a portfolio is a weighted average of the expected returns of the individual assets, but that the standard deviation is more complicated. When calculating the portfolio standard deviation, we have to include each of the pairwise covariances. We showed how to calculate the variance/covariance matrix and then how to use it to calculate the portfolio standard deviation.

We then discussed the efficient frontier and why investors will choose only from among the portfolios that are located on it. We used the Solver to find a sample of the portfolios on the efficient frontier and then created a chart of it.

Next, we added a risk-free asset to our universe of securities and showed how the efficient frontier changes into the CML. Portfolios on the CML provide a better risk/return trade-off than those on the efficient frontier. When a risk-free asset is available, investors will choose to hold it in some combination with the market portfolio. The exact portfolio chosen will depend upon the investor's utility function.

Finally, we derived the CAPM by equating the slopes of the CML and the efficient frontier. This provided us with an important way to view the risk/return trade-off and a measure of risk known as beta. Beta is an index of systematic risk and shows how sensitive an asset is to market risk factors. We also saw that if the CAPM is correct investors are only rewarded for taking on market risk. There is no reward for holding a less than perfectly diversified portfolio.

TABLE 13-2
FUNCTIONS INTRODUCED IN THIS CHAPTER*

Purpose	Function	Page
Calculate the correlation coefficient	**CORREL**(*ARRAY1*, *ARRAY2*)	415
Calculate the covariance	**COVARIANCE.S**(*ARRAY1*, *ARRAY2*)	416
Matrix multiplication	**MMULT**(*ARRAY1*, *ARRAY2*)	421
Matrix transpose	**TRANSPOSE**(*ARRAY*)	421
Calculate the portfolio variance	**FAME_PORTVAR1**(*VARCOVMAT*,*WEIGHTS*)	423
Calculate the portfolio variance	**FAME_PORTVAR2**(*CORRMAT*,*WEIGHTS*)	N/A
Calculate covariance using probabilities	**FAME_COVAR**(*VALUES1*, *VALUES2*, *PROBABILITIES*)	N/A
Calculate correlation using probabilities	**FAME_CORR**(*VALUES1*, *VALUES2*, *PROBABILITIES*)	N/A

*   All functions with names beginning in **FAME_** are macros supplied in the Famefncs.xlam add-in, which is available from the official Web site.

Problems

1.   You are considering an investment in the stock market and have identified two potential stocks (XYZ and ABC) to purchase. The historical returns for the past five years are shown in the table below.

Year	XYZ Returns	ABC Returns
2010	12.35%	22.28%
2008	17.01%	8.75%
2009	13.18%	17.78%
2010	8.51%	19.66%
2014	16.85%	4.03%

a. Calculate the average return and standard deviation of returns for each stock over the past five years. Which stock would you prefer to own? Would everyone make the same choice?

b. Calculate the correlation coefficient between the two stocks. Does it appear that a portfolio consisting of XYZ and ABC would provide good diversification?

c. Calculate the annual returns that would have been achieved had you owned a portfolio consisting of 50% in XYZ and 50% in ABC over the past five years.

d. Calculate the average return and standard deviation of returns for the portfolio. How does the portfolio compare with the individual stocks? Would you prefer the portfolio to owning either of the stocks alone?

e. Create a chart that shows how the standard deviation of the portfolio's returns changes as the weight of XYZ changes.

f. Using the Solver, what is the minimum standard deviation that could be achieved by combining these stocks into a portfolio? What are the exact weights of the stocks that result in this minimum standard deviation?

2. You have decided to investigate a number of exchange-traded funds (ETFs) in an attempt to build a diversified portfolio. You believe that the transportation, consumer goods, energy, financials, and health care sectors are the best in which to invest. To begin, you have gathered the monthly total returns for the last five years from some ETFs (IYT, IYK, IYE, IYF, IYH) in each of these sectors.

a. Download the Five ETFs Monthly Returns.xlsx file from the official Web site http://www.cengagebrain.com/. This contains the data for this, and the next two problems.

b. What are the average monthly returns and standard deviations for each of the ETFs?

c. Which performed best on a risk/return basis during this period? Which was the worst? Use the Sharpe ratio and assume that the risk-free rate averaged 0.165% per month during this period.

d. Create an equally weighted portfolio of all the ETFs. Calculate the expected return and standard deviation of this portfolio.

3. Using the ETF data from the previous problem:

    a. Create a sample variance/covariance matrix using the ETF returns. Use the matrix algebra functions or the **COVARIANCE.S** function. (Hint: The matrix function will be less work.)

    b. Using the Solver, find the weights for the minimum variance portfolio.

    c. Using the Solver, find the optimal weights for a portfolio with a return equal to that of the ETF with the highest return. Now, create 9 additional portfolios with returns between that of the minimum variance and maximum return portfolios.

    d. Create a chart of the efficient frontier. Now add a new series that shows the returns and standard deviations of the individual ETFs. How does the efficient frontier compare to the ETFs?

    e. Find the weights for the market portfolio. What is its return and standard deviation?

    f. Add the capital market line (CML) to your chart.

4. Do problem 3 again, but this time do not allow short sales (i.e., no negative weights).

    a. Create a new chart that shows the efficient frontiers from this problem and problem 3.

    b. From which frontier would you prefer to choose your investments?

5. You are considering investing in the following securities and have developed the probability distributions for their returns over the next year.

Economic Outlook	Probability	Expected Returns			
		OMG	BRB	NOOB	T-bills
Recession	0.10	–29%	–9%	16%	3%
Slow growth	0.20	–14%	3%	11%	3%
Average	0.40	14%	7%	4%	3%
Fast growth	0.20	23%	11%	–7%	3%
Boom	0.10	34%	14%	–14%	3%

    a. Calculate the expected return and standard deviation of each security.

b. Create a variance/covariance matrix for the four securities. See page 422 for an example of how to create a formula that uses probabilities instead of historical (equally weighted) data.

c. Using the Solver, create a set of 11 portfolios that make up the capital market line. Create a chart of the CML from your results, and add a plot of the original securities.

d. Find the weights of each security in the market portfolio by maximizing the Sharpe ratio.

e. How does the risk/return trade-off of the original securities compare to that available on the CML?

Internet Exercise

1. Choose two stocks from different industries that you think would have a low correlation. Get the closing prices for each month over the past five years for both stocks. To get the prices from Yahoo! Finance (http://finance.yahoo.com) follow the same procedure as was used in the Chapter 8 Internet Exercise to get the dividends, but this time select "Monthly" rather than "Dividends." Download the data into Excel.

a. Calculate the returns for both stocks in each month during the five-year period using log-price relatives (see equation (12-2) on page 373).

b. Calculate the average monthly return and standard deviation of monthly returns for each stock. Using only this information, which of the two stocks would you have preferred to own over this period?

c. Calculate the correlation coefficient for the two sets of returns using the **CORREL** function. Is it as low as you expected?

d. If the historical returns, standard deviations, and correlation fairly represent the future, calculate the expected return and standard deviation of a portfolio consisting of 50% invested in each stock. How does the portfolio compare with the individual stocks?

e. Using the Solver, find the weights for each stock that would result in the minimum portfolio standard deviation.

CHAPTER 14

Writing User-Defined Functions with VBA

After studying this chapter, you should be able to:

1. *Describe the two types of "macros" and explain the difference between them.*
2. *Identify and explain the parts of the VB editor.*
3. *Write your own VBA user-defined function for any given formula.*
4. *Write a user-defined function that allows for optional arguments.*
5. *Use the debugging tools that are available in the VB editor.*
6. *Create an Excel add-in program.*

Despite its hundreds of built-in functions, Excel doesn't always have the one you need. Fortunately, it does provide a method by which you can add your own functions to the program and use them in your worksheets.

In previous chapters, we have used several custom functions that extend Excel in ways that are useful. Those custom functions, known as *user-defined functions* (UDFs), are written in the Visual Basic for Applications (VBA) programming language. VBA is available in all of the Microsoft Office applications and in some third-party applications.

In this chapter, we will provide a brief demonstration of how to use VBA to create functions that meet your needs. If you have ever done any computer programming, you will find it easy to learn. If not, don't worry. If you can understand a mathematical formula, it is likely that you will be able to convert it into a user-defined function without much trouble after reading this chapter.

VBA is quite powerful and can be used for everything from something as simple as changing the formatting of a cell in a worksheet to writing complete applications that don't appear to be Excel worksheets, and everything in between.

Before continuing, be sure to enable the Developer tab in the Ribbon. Click the File tab and then go to Options. In the Customize Ribbon category, choose Main Tabs in the Customize the Ribbon drop-down on the right side of the dialog box and place a checkmark next to Developer in the right-side pane.

FIGURE 14-1
THE DEVELOPER TAB

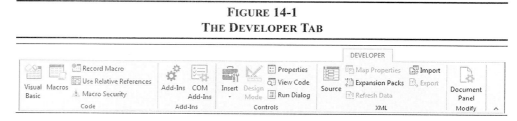

What Is a Macro?

In computer science, a *macro* is a word or keystroke that serves as a substitute for a long series of commands. Excel has many built-in macros of this type. For example, you can press Ctrl+B to make the font in a cell, or range, bold. This is a shortcut for the series of steps that would otherwise be required. When you press Ctrl+B, Excel will automatically perform all of those steps behind the scenes. This type of macro is known as a *keystroke macro*.

Although we can create VBA programs that replicate the functionality of keystroke macros, VBA is not, strictly speaking, a macro language. Instead, it is a fully functional object-oriented programming language. Still, in common usage, VBA programs are often called macros.

Two Types of Macros

In Excel, there are two types of macros. Closest to the traditional definition of keystroke macros are *procedure macros* (also known as subroutines). Procedure macros can do things such as activating another worksheet, opening a file, formatting a range of cells, and so on.

As an example, I have written a procedure macro called "ConvertIS" that I use to reformat income statements that are imported from a particular database. It does several things, very quickly and consistently, that would be time consuming to do manually:

1. Deletes several blank rows.

2. Sets the font size, borders, and background colors for each of the cells.

3. Changes some text to my preference.

Because the income statements from this database are all similar, this macro can be used on every income statement that I import.

Macros such as this one are more easily recorded than written from scratch. Excel has a macro recorder that will record everything that you do while recording and convert it into the VBA language. The recorded macro will be saved into a code module within the VB Editor. Once it is recorded, you can easily assign a key combination to run the macro, and you can edit it to make it better suit your purposes. Editing recorded macros is an excellent way to learn the VBA language. You can launch the macro recorder by clicking the Record Macro button on the Developer tab or by clicking the button in the status bar (below the sheet tabs).

Record Macro

Procedure macros can be incredibly useful, but they are not the focus of this chapter. Instead, we are more concerned with writing *functions*. Function macros (more correctly called *user-defined functions*) cannot modify Excel worksheets like procedure macros. Instead, all that they can do is to take some inputs (arguments), process them through an algorithm, and then return a result to the spreadsheet. User-defined functions (UDFs) are identical to the built-in functions like **SUM**, **PV**, **GEOMEAN**, and so on. The difference is that you can create your own UDFs that calculate results for which there are no built-in functions.

UDFs are useful for frequently used formulas that would require an excessive amount of time to type into a cell. A good example of this would be the **FAME_TWOSTAGEVALUE** function that is included in the Famefncs.xlam add-in. If you look back to equation (8-5) on page 240, you will see that this equation would be time consuming to accurately type into a cell. The UDF saves time and effort and assures accuracy.

In other cases, UDFs can calculate results that would be difficult, or impossible, to perform in a single cell formula. For example, try to write a worksheet formula to calculate the payback period for any set of cash flows. Although it is easy to write such a formula for a particular set of cash flows, making it generic enough to work for any stream of cash flows is much more difficult. In this case, it is far easier to write a UDF to do the job. That is exactly what the **FAME_PAYBACK** function does.

In the next section, we will introduce you to the VB editor that is used to create both types of macros. Later, we will focus on how to write your own UDFs.

The Visual Basic Editor

Visual
Basic

Visual Basic macros are not written in worksheets. Instead, they are created in the Visual Basic editor, which provides many useful tools for writing code, keeping track of it, and debugging it. The editor can be thought of as a word processor that was specifically designed for writing macros. You can open the editor by clicking the Visual Basic button on the Developer tab or by using Alt+F11. The Alt+F11 keystroke will allow you to easily move back and forth between Excel and the VB editor.

FIGURE 14-2
THE VISUAL BASIC EDITOR

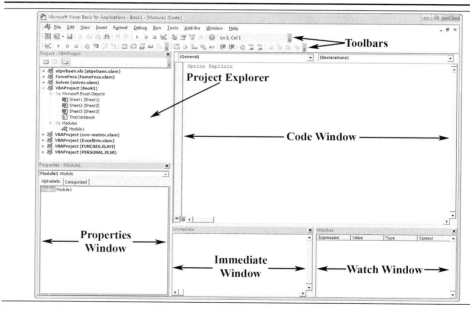

Figure 14-2 shows the VB editor with several useful windows open. Most of your work will be done in the Code Window, as that is where the macros are written. The Project Explorer allows you to choose the project and particular code module to work on. The Properties Window allows you to set properties (names, visibility, behavior) of code modules and worksheets. The Watch Window allows you to monitor the values of variables as you are debugging your code, much like the Watch Window in a spreadsheet as shown in Figure 3-7 (page 95). Finally, the Immediate Window is used like a scratchpad to test or evaluate lines of code that are typed into it. If these windows are not visible on the screen, you can enable them by selecting them in the <u>V</u>iew menu of the VB editor.

The Project Explorer

The Project Explorer shows a list of all the open VBA projects. A VBA project is part of an ordinary Excel workbook, but it may also have VBA code modules attached. Note that any VBA code that you write for a project is saved with the workbook, not in a separate file. However, you can easily export the code to a text file for backup purposes or so that you can import it into another workbook.

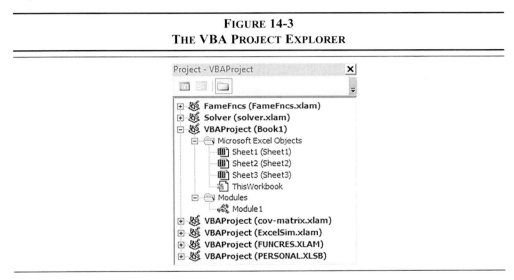

In Figure 14-3, you can see that there are seven open projects. Each one has a name and a collapsible outline to show or hide its components. Note that every open workbook will have an associated project, and every worksheet will have a code module. For example, you will see that Book1 is an open workbook with three worksheets.

The first project shown in Figure 14-3 is FameFncs.xlam, which contains one worksheet, the ThisWorkbook code module, and another code module named "FAME_Functions." All of this is hidden from the casual user. Because FameFncs.xlam is an add-in, even its worksheet is invisible outside of the VB editor, though it is available for macros to use for various purposes (it is storing the MACRS table for the **FAME_MACRS** function). ThisWorkbook is a special code module used for procedure macros that respond to workbook-level events, such as when there is a right-click, when the workbook is deactivated, or when the workbook is about to be closed.

The real work in FameFncs.xlam is done in the FAME_Functions code module. This is where the user-defined functions reside. To see what the functions look like, make sure that the Famefncs.xlam add-in is enabled. Now, open the VB editor and double-click on the FameFncs project. To see the code for all of the user-defined functions, simply double-click the FAME_Functions code module. The code will appear in the code window.

The Code Window

As mentioned above, the code window is a sort of specialized word processor. It has many features that are specially designed to make writing macros easier. For example, some of the text will be color-coded to make it easier to understand: Reserved keywords are shown in blue and comments are shown in green. Of course, this can be customized to your preferences.

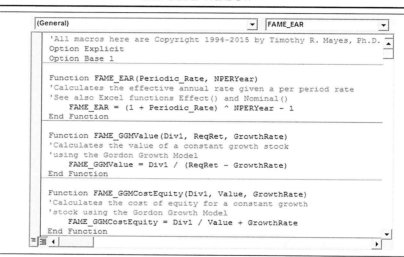

FIGURE 14-4
THE CODE WINDOW

Figure 14-4 shows the code window with three user-defined functions visible. These are three of the least complex UDFs in the add-in, but they contain all of the required elements to calculate and return a result to your worksheet. Even without any programming experience, you can probably understand what each function does because they are like Excel's built-in functions in that they take arguments, do calculations, and return a result.

Take note of the procedure drop-down list in the upper right corner of the editor. This list contains the names of all the procedures and functions in the current code module. By selecting a particular function from the list, you can immediately jump to the code for that function. This is especially useful if you prefer to use the code window in its Procedure View, which shows only one function at a time in the editor. Figure 14-4 shows the editor in its Full Module View, which shows the entire contents of the module. In this view, you can either jump directly to a function, or scroll through the code module until you find the one that you want to work on. The icons in the lower left corner are used to switch between the different views.

The Parts of a Function

Every user-defined function must have at least five elements in order to work:

1. The keyword "Function" at the beginning of the first line. This tells VBA that you are beginning a new function, as opposed to a procedure that begins with the keyword "Sub."

2. The name of the function. You can choose nearly any name for your functions, except that they must be unique within a code module. Also, the name cannot contain spaces and must not be a reserved keyword. The name will be used when calling the function from your worksheets, so make it meaningful.

3. A list of the function arguments, surrounded by parentheses. These arguments are the variables that must be passed to the function from your worksheet. Even if your function doesn't require any arguments, it still needs to have a set of closed parentheses after the function name.

4. An assignment of the result of the calculations to the name of the function. This tells VBA the value to return to the cell on your worksheet from which the function was called.

5. The last part is the "End Function" statement. This informs VBA that it has reached the end of the function.

This is nearly everything that you need to know in order to write simple functions. However, just as we suggested in Chapter 1 (page 36) that you should document the complex formulas in your spreadsheets, you should do the same with your user-defined functions. In VBA, you can use comments to provide explanations of how your functions work. Comments begin with an apostrophe and can contain any text that you require. Comments are ignored by VBA, but they are invaluable to the humans who may read your code. You cannot use too many comments, so make liberal use of them. This simple step will avoid many difficulties when you revisit your code in the future.

Writing Your First User-Defined Function

Let's begin by writing a very simple function to calculate a firm's net profit margin, which was the first worksheet formula discussed in Chapter 1. There is really no need for a function like this because it is so easy to create a worksheet formula to do the job, but it will serve as an easy starting point.

Start by opening a new workbook, and then open the VB editor. In the Project Explorer window, you should see a list of open VBA projects, including one named "VBAProject

(Book1)," or something similar. The part of the name in parentheses will match the name of the workbook, so it may be Book2 or Book3 depending on how many other workbooks you have opened previously in this session. Now, right-click on the project name and select Insert Module from the shortcut menu. This will insert a new code module named Module1 into your project. The code window will now be available to enter new code into this module, and the VB editor should look very much like Figure 14-2. Note that you can easily tell which code module you are working on by checking the text in the title bar of the editor.

Recall that the net profit margin is calculated by dividing sales by net income. We will call our user-defined function "NetProfitMargin," and it will require two arguments: net income and sales. The easiest way to begin a new function is to let the VB editor insert a function template for you, though you are free to do the typing for yourself. Choose Insert Procedure from the menu. This will launch the Add Procedure dialog box where you can specify some basic information about the function as shown in Figure 14-5.

FIGURE 14-5
THE ADD PROCEDURE DIALOG BOX

Make sure that you type the name and specify that the type of procedure is "Function." When you click the OK button, the following text will appear in the code window:[1]

```
Public Function NetProfitMargin()

End Function
```

All that remains is to type in the arguments after the function name and add the code to calculate the result. In this case, we need two arguments (inputs): net income and sales. We can name these arguments nearly anything, but it is best to use descriptive names. So, inside

---

1. The keyword "Public" indicates that the function may be called from outside the current module. Functions are public by default, so this is not required. You may also use the keyword "Private."

the parentheses type: `NetIncome, Sales`. Just like function names, the names of the arguments cannot contain spaces, though you could use an underscore character if you feel that it would improve readability (e.g., Net_Income). At this point, your function looks like this:

Public Function NetProfitMargin(NetIncome, Sales)

End Function

So far, the function doesn't actually do anything, but we can now call it from a worksheet. Set up the worksheet pictured in Exhibit 14-1 (this is the same as Exhibit 1-4, on page 18) and save it as "Chapter 14 Worksheets.xlsm."

EXHIBIT 14-1
MICROSOFT PROFITABILITY ANALYSIS WORKSHEET

	A	B	C	D	E	F	G
1		Microsoft Corporation Profitability Analysis					
2		(Millions of Dollars)					
3		2008 to 2013					
4		2013	2012	2011	2010	2009	2008
5	Sales	77,849.00	73,723.00	69,943.00	62,484.00	58,437.00	60,420.00
6	Net Income	21,863.00	16,978.00	23,150.00	18,760.00	14,569.00	17,681.00
7	Net Profit Margin	28.08%	23.03%	33.10%	30.02%	24.93%	29.26%

Source: Microsoft Corporation, Microsoft® Investor Relations, http://www.microsoft.com Retrieved: Nov 2013.

Now select B7 and bring up the Insert Function dialog box. Choose the User Defined category, and scroll down the list to NetProfitMargin and select it. This will launch the Function Arguments dialog box just as it would for any built-in Excel function. Notice how you are prompted for the arguments with the names that you supplied in the function definition. This is why it is important to give meaningful names to the arguments.

FIGURE 14-6
THE FUNCTION ARGUMENTS DIALOG BOX FOR NETPROFITMARGIN

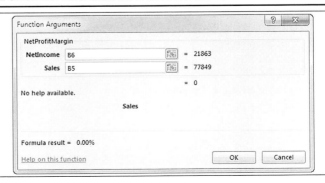

Enter B6 for NetIncome and B5 for Sales. When you press the OK button, the function will be inserted into cell B7 as =NetProfitMargin(B6,B5). However, the answer will be 0.00 because the function doesn't yet do any calculations.

Recall that every function must assign a value to the function name in order to return a value to the worksheet. Let's now add the calculation to our function:

```
Public Function NetProfitMargin(NetIncome, Sales)
    NetProfitMargin = NetIncome / Sales
End Function
```

In VBA, the "=" is the assignment operator.[2] That is, it assigns the value of the right-hand side to the variable on the left-hand side. In this case, we are assigning the result of dividing net income by sales to the name of the function. This is how we pass the result back to the worksheet.

Finally, let's add a comment that describes the purpose of the function so that anybody who reads the code can easily figure out what it does. Remember that comments are denoted by an apostrophe at the beginning of the comment:

```
Public Function NetProfitMargin(NetIncome, Sales)
'Calculates Net Profit Margin given Net Income and Sales
    NetProfitMargin = NetIncome / Sales
End Function
```

Return to your worksheet, and notice that the result is still 0.00. Whenever you change a function, you must force the worksheet to recalculate in order to see the new result. To do this, simply select B7, then click in the formula bar at the end of the formula, and then press the Enter key. You should now see that the result is 28.08%, exactly as we had originally calculated using a worksheet formula. You can now copy the formula to C7:G7.

The NetProfitMargin function is available for use in any workbook, as long as the workbook that contains the code is open. As an example, create a copy of this worksheet in a new workbook. Right-click on the sheet tab and choose **M**ove or Copy from the shortcut menu. In the "**T**o Book:" drop-down list, choose (new book), and make sure to check the "Create a copy" box.

The first thing you should notice in the new workbook is that the NetProfitMargin function returns the #NAME! error. This is because Excel doesn't recognize the name of the function because it isn't contained in this workbook. We need to change the reference to the function name so that it contains the name of the file that contains the function. We can do this either by re-entering the function using the Insert Function dialog box or by typing the full path and file name. It is easiest to reenter the function through the Insert Function dialog box.

---

2. It can also be used as a comparison operator to compare the values of two variables. For example, we can use a statement such as: If X = Y Then Z = 2*Y Else Z = 2*X

After you have done that, you should see that the formula now contains the file name as well as the name of the function: ='Chapter 14 Worksheets.xlsm'!NetProfitMargin(B6,B5).

Whenever you link to an external worksheet, or a function in an external worksheet, Excel needs to know the name and location of the file to which you are linking. This is so that it can find the function or data. If it cannot find the file, it will give the #NAME! error in every cell that contains a broken link and others that are dependent on those cells.

Typically, this problem arises because the source file has been moved or deleted. Save this new workbook, and then close both workbooks. Now, move "Chapter 14 Worksheets.xlsm" into a different directory. When you reopen the workbooks, you should see the #NAME! error in the new workbook. If you look at the formula, you will see a reference to "Chapter 14 Worksheets.xlsm," but the path to the file will be incorrect.

FIGURE 14-7
THE EDIT LINKS DIALOG BOX

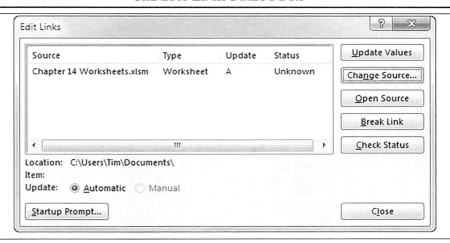

Edit Links

To fix this problem, choose Edit Links from the Data tab and tell Excel where to find "Chapter 14 Worksheets.xlsm." Figure 14-7 shows the Edit Links dialog box. Click on the Change Source button and then navigate to the file location. Be aware that the file that contains the function must also be opened in order for the function to recalculate.

As we will see later, one easy way around this problem is to create an Excel add-in from the workbook that contains your functions. As you know, add-ins can be "installed" through the Add-Ins dialog box so that they are always opened automatically when you start Excel. That way the functions contained within the add-in are also always available.

Writing More Complicated Functions

Normally, you won't write user-defined functions to do calculations that are easily done by writing worksheet formulas. Instead, you will probably write UDFs for longer formulas that you need to use repeatedly, perhaps in several different workbooks. In this section, we discuss several additional features of VBA that make more complex functions easy to write.

Variables and Data Types

A *variable* is temporary storage location that can be used to hold values until you need them again in your function. Variables can hold many different types of data and can be declared so as to hold only a specific data type (say, an integer value or a text string) or any of the data types supported by VBA (variant).

Because you will most likely be writing functions to do mathematical calculations, we have summarized the numerical data types in Table 14-1. VBA also supports many other types that may be useful. For example, variables that are declared to be the Boolean data type can be either true or false. We can manipulate dates with variables that are declared to be the Date data type. Finally, we can declare variables to be a String if they will hold text values.

TABLE 14-1
SOME OF VBA'S NUMERIC DATA TYPES[1]

Type Name	Numeric Range
Byte	0 to 255
Integer	–32,768 to 32,767
Long Integer	–2,147,483,648 to 2,147,483,647
Currency	–922,337,203,685,477.5808 to 922,337,203,685,477.5807
Single	-3.40×10^{38} to -1.40×10^{-45} for negative values; 1.40×10^{-45} to 3.40×10^{38} for positive values
Double	-1.79×10^{308} to -4.94×10^{-324} for negative values; 4.94×10^{-324} to 1.79×10^{308} for positive values
Variant	Variants can hold any data type, including numbers up to the range of a double. This is the most flexible data type and is the default type if a variable is not declared.

1 There are additional numeric data types, and some in the 64-bit version of Excel 2013 can handle larger numbers. For the full list, see http://msdn.microsoft.com/EN-US/library/office/gg251528.aspx.

It is good programming practice to announce the names and data types of variables before you use them so that memory can be set aside to hold them. This is known as *declaring* your variables and is done with the Dim statement. Consider the following examples:

Dim SmallNumber As Byte
Dim X As Integer, Y As Integer, Z As Integer
Dim BigNumber As Double
Dim UnknownType As Variant

There are several things to note about the declarations above. First, note that the Byte and Integer data types can only hold whole numbers. That is, we can assign them a value such as 1 or 19, but we cannot assign a value of 1.618 (a real number). We can assign either whole or real numbers to variables that are declared to be Single, Double, or Variant. If you don't know whether a variable will hold whole numbers or real numbers, it is generally best to declare them as Single. Secondly, notice that we can declare multiple variables with a single Dim statement. This saves space in your code and makes it easier to read. Finally, you don't have to declare variables before using them. If you use an undeclared variable, VBA will implicitly declare it to be a Variant so that it can hold any type of data that you may want to store. However, this is discouraged as it can lead to errors if your code implicitly expects a particular data type.

Declaring your variables has a couple of advantages: It makes your code less susceptible to errors, and it makes your functions run faster. Because of these advantages, it is a good idea to make VBA force you to declare all of your variables before using them with the *Option Explicit* statement at the beginning of the file. If you look back at Figure 14-4, you will see that I have used this statement at the beginning of the FameFncs.xlam code.[3]

It is important to understand the lifetime and scope of a variable. The *lifetime* of a variable defines whether or not the variable retains its value after the function exits. Most of the time, variables have a lifetime limited to the running time of the function in which they are used. Unless you use the keyword Static when declaring the variable, it will lose its value when the function completes its work. The *scope* of a variable determines whether its value can be read outside of a function or not. Variables that are declared within a function can only be read within the function itself: they are *local*. You can also use *global* variables outside of functions that will be visible to, and can be modified by, all functions within a module. It is usually best to use variables that have a local scope rather than global, but sometimes you will need a global variable that can be referenced by several functions.

3. The VBA editor can be made to automatically insert Option Explicit in every new module. To set this up, go to **T**ools and then **O**ptions. On the Editor tab, select Require Variable Declaration.

The If-Then-Else Statement

In Chapter 3 (page 82), we introduced Excel's **IF** statement, which returns one value or another depending on the result of a logical test. VBA has a similar, though more powerful, construct. As with the worksheet function, this is useful when a function needs to return different results depending on whether a particular condition is true or false. The If-Then-Else statement has two possible forms: the single-line form and the block form. A single-line statement looks like this:

If *condition is true* **Then** *do this* **Else** *do this instead*

For simple tests, the single-line format works well. The drawback is that you can only take one action if the condition is true, or one action if it is false. In other words, it works exactly like a single **IF** statement in a worksheet. The block form can take multiple actions and serially evaluate multiple conditions. The block form looks like this:

```
If condition is true Then
     do this first
     do this second
Else
     do this instead
End If
```

Notice that the block form must be terminated with the End If statement so that VBA knows that you are done with the If-Then-Else statement.

Let's create a function that calculates the present value of a lump sum (it will not handle annuities). Recall that the formula to calculate the present value of a lump sum is:

$$PV = \frac{FV}{(1 + i)^N}$$

where *FV* is the future value, *i* is the per period interest rate, and *N* is the number of periods. Let's call our function MyPV and it will require three arguments to represent the variables in the formula.

Return to the "Chapter 14 Worksheets.xlsm" file that we created earlier for the NetProfitMargin function. Open the VB editor and go to Module1. Now, click in the code window below the NetProfitMargin function, and type the following:

```
Public Function MyPV(FV, Rate, NPer)
'Calculates the present value of a lump sum
     MyPV = FV / (1 + Rate) ^ NPer
End Function
```

Can you think of any potential problems with this function? One very important thing to always keep in mind is that users are unpredictable. Therefore, it is helpful to try to anticipate everything and anything that they might do wrong. Switch back to your Excel workbook and create the worksheet pictured in Exhibit 14-2.

EXHIBIT 14-2
PRESENT VALUE WORKSHEET

	A	B
1	**Present Value Function Test**	
2	Future Value	1,000
3	Interest Rate	0.10
4	Number of Periods	5.00
5		
6	Present Value	

Select B6 and enter the formula: =MyPV(B2,B3,B4). You should find that the present value of $1,000 to be received five years from now at 10% is $620.92. You can easily verify that this is correct by using Excel's **Pv** function or your financial calculator.

So, what is wrong with the MyPV function? Notice that we entered the interest rate (in B3) in decimal form. That is, 10% is entered as 0.10. We have built our function on the implicit assumption that users will understand that they must enter percentages in this way. Suppose, however, that some hapless user doesn't understand this and enters 10 into B3 instead of 0.10. They probably don't realize it, but they are telling the function that the interest rate is 1,000% per period! Try it yourself and you will see that the answer is $0.0062. Not quite what the user expected.

We can anticipate this kind of error and handle it automatically with the function by using the If-Then-Else statement. Edit your function so that it looks like the one below:

```
Public Function MyPV(FV, Rate, NPer)
'Calculates the present value of a lump sum
'If Rate is greater than or equal to 1, it will be divided by 100
    If Rate >= 1 Then Rate = Rate / 100
    MyPV = FV / (1 + Rate) ^ NPer
End Function
```

Now, if the user puts any number greater than or equal to 1 into B3, the function will automatically assume that they meant it to be a percentage and automatically adjust. Return to your worksheet and force the function to recalculate. You will now get $620.92, exactly as you expected.

Note that we have done something that may be unexpected in the Then clause. We have assigned a different value to the Rate argument by modifying the Rate argument itself. This is a common programming technique to avoid declaring a variable that isn't really needed.

Instead, we could have declared a new variable to stand in for the rate. In this case, our function might look like this:

```
Public Function MyPV(FV, Rate, NPer)
'Calculates the present value of a lump sum
'If Rate is greater than or equal to 1, it will be divided by 100
Dim IntRate as Single
    If Rate >= 1 Then IntRate = Rate / 100 Else IntRate = Rate
    MyPV = FV / (1 + IntRate) ^ NPer
End Function
```

Note that we declared the variable IntRate to be the Single data type because it is a real number. There is no need to declare it as a Double because we would never need an interest rate as large as that data type can handle. Using the Single data type saves a small amount of memory. It is good practice to always use the smallest data type that will get the job done. Don't forget to replace Rate with IntRate in the last line of the function. If you do, you will get the wrong answer if a user types in 10 instead of 0.10. This is exactly the type of bug that can be difficult to spot in your code.

To make the function less subject to errors, we should take the further step of declaring the data types of our function arguments. This will make sure that the user doesn't call the function with, say, a text string instead of a number for the FV argument. It will also make sure that the user can only supply single cells as arguments, rather than ranges of cells. Change the function declaration to:

Public Function MyPV(FV As Single, Rate As Single, NPer As Single)

Now, return to your worksheet and force a recalculation of the function. It should still produce the correct answer. However, if you now change B4 to `Five` (a String value), you will get a #VALUE! error. In fact, you would get that error whether the arguments were declared or not. Still, with the arguments' data types specified, if the user passes the wrong data type the function will immediately return an error value. The function will not be executed at all, which may avoid other types of errors.

Looping Statements

Some kinds of formulas can be calculated only by cycling through the same calculation multiple times. An example would be any formula that has a summation sign, such as the expected value formula. The formula for calculating the expected value of a set of possible outcomes is:

$$E(X) = \sum_{t=1}^{N} \rho_t X_t$$

where $E(X)$ is the expected or most likely X, X_t is the tth possible outcome, and ρ_t is the probability that X_t will occur. You will no doubt recognize this as equation (12-1) from page 356. In order to do this calculation, we must cycle through each possible outcome and multiply it by its probability. We also need to keep a running total as we work through the calculation.

VBA has several statements that can loop through calculations such as this one. We will use the For...Next loop.[4] This looping statement requires a variable to serve as a counter so that it can keep track of how many times it goes through the loop. After each pass through the loop, the counter variable is incremented and then it returns to the beginning of the loop. If the counter still hasn't reached its ending value, then the calculation continues. As an example, consider the following code snippet:

```
X = 0
For t = 1 to 10
    X = X + t
Next t
```

In this case, the variable X is first assigned a value of 0 (this is known as *initializing* the variable), then it is increased with each of the 10 passes through the loop by the value of t. On the first pass, X will be set equal to 1. After the next pass (with $t = 2$), X will be equal to 3. This process will continue until t gets incremented to 11, at which point the loop will end and X will equal 55. Clearly, this kind of calculation is difficult to do with a normal worksheet formula, though we can sometimes achieve the result with an array formula or the **SUMPRODUCT** worksheet function.

VBA also has two kinds of Do...Loop. Do...Loops are similar to For...Next loops in that they will repeatedly run code, but their stopping condition is indeterminate. Do...While loops will continually run as long as the condition is true, whereas Do...Until loops will run as long as the condition is false (i.e., until it becomes true). With Do...Loops, it is possible that they will never run at all. The following code shows an example of a Do...While loop:

```
X = 0
Do While X < 10
    X = X + 1
Loop
```

This code simply increments the variable X by 1 each time through the loop as long as X is less than 10. If you change the first line so that X = 15, then the loop will never run at all. Similarly, if you replace the "While" with "Until" in the original code (with X = 0) then the loop won't be executed because the condition is true immediately. Note that it is possible for Do...Loops to run forever (an *infinite loop*), so you must be careful with them. To avoid

---

4. Open the VBA help and do a search for "looping through code" to see some examples of other looping constructs.

infinite loops, you can use the Exit Do statement within the loop. If you find your code stuck in an infinite loop, you can press the ESC key to get out of it.

Let's create a function to calculate the expected value of a variable using a For...Next loop, but first create the worksheet shown in Exhibit 14-3.

EXHIBIT 14-3
A WORKSHEET FOR THE EXPECTED VALUE FUNCTION

	A	B
1	**Probability**	**Value**
2	0.25	100
3	0.50	150
4	0.25	220
5	Expected Value	155

Return to Module1 in the VB editor and type in the following function:

```
Public Function ExpValue(Values As Range, Weights As Range)
'Calculates the expected value of a probability distribution
Dim t as Integer, VarCount As Integer
Dim EV As Single
    VarCount = Values.Count 'Number of values in the range
    EV = 0                  'Initialize variable
    For t = 1 To VarCount
        EV = EV + Values(t) * Weights(t)
    Next t
    ExpValue = EV
End Function
```

Aside from the For...Next loop, there are a couple of new things in this function. First, notice that we have declared our arguments to be of the Range data type. The Range data type represents a collection of worksheet cells, not a specific numeric type. It is a type of array and may contain one or more worksheet cells. Even though we expect that each of the values and weights will be of the Single data type, we cannot declare the arguments to be Single. Doing so would limit the function only one value and one weight. Secondly, notice that we have added comments at the end of some of the lines of code. This can be useful to save space and improve the readability of the code.

Now, take another look at the following line of code:

```
VarCount = Values.Count
```

Recall that we said that VBA is an object-oriented programming language. An object is a combination of VBA code and data that can be operated on as a single unit. In VBA an Excel workbook is an object (as are worksheets, ranges, cells, charts, and many other things), and it has certain *properties* that we can access (read or write to) programmatically. We can read the name of the workbook object as follows:

WbName = MyWorkbook.Name

Assuming that WbName is a String variable and MyWorkbook refers to a specific workbook object, this line of code will assign the name of the workbook to the string variable. We access object properties by using "dot notation." The .Name that appears after MyWorkbook tells VBA that we want to know the Name property of the workbook object. Most objects have at least several properties that we can access in this way.

In our ExpValue function, we have defined both of our arguments to be of the Range data type. Ranges are objects in VBA, so we can learn about their properties by using the dot notation. In this case, Values.Count tells VBA to look at the Values range that was passed as an argument and tell us how many cells are contained in the range.

We can also find out about the properties of the individual cells in a Range object. Each cell is also an object, so we can use dot notation to find the value that a cell holds. If we want to know the value of the second cell in the Values range, we could use the following code:

X = Values(2).Value

Assuming that the variable X is of the correct data type, this will assign the value of the second cell in the range to X. Note that the Value property is the default property of a cell object, so we could accomplish the same thing with this code:

X = Values(2)

In other words, to read the default property we don't need to use the .Value syntax. Now take another look at the line of code in our For…Next loop:

EV = EV + Values(t) * Weights(t)

Notice that we are referencing Values(t) and Weights(t). Depending on the value of t (our counter variable) this will read the values of the cells that are in the Values and Weights ranges. In our example problem, Values(2) is equal to 150 and Weights(2) is equal to 0.50. As the code cycles through the loop, the appropriate values and weights are read, multiplied together, and then added to EV so as to create a running sum of the results. The last line of code assigns EV to the function name to return the value to the worksheet cell.

Using Worksheet Functions in VBA

Excel has hundreds of built-in functions, and there is no need to recreate them for use in your VBA functions. Instead, we can use the WorksheetFunction object to call the built-in functions. For example, we could rewrite our MyPV function using this object instead of doing the PV calculation in the code. Copy the code that you entered earlier, and rename the function to MyPV2:

```
Public Function MyPV2(FV, Rate, NPer)
'Calculates the present value of a lump sum
'If Rate is greater than or equal to 1, it will be divided by 100
    If Rate >= 1 Then Rate = Rate / 100
    MyPV2 = –Application.WorksheetFunction.PV(Rate, NPer, 0, FV)
End Function
```

Note that the WorksheetFunction object is a child of the Application object, so we access it using dot notation as discussed above. This isn't strictly required, but it is good practice and can prevent some obscure errors. All, or nearly all, of Excel's built-in functions can be used in this manner. Using built-in functions in this way can make your functions easier to code and less likely to contain errors.

Using Optional Arguments

Many of Excel's built-in functions have optional arguments; that is, arguments that you do not need to supply for the function to work properly. For example, the **Pv** function requires that you supply the *RATE*, *NPER*, and *PMT* arguments, but the *FV* and *TYPE* arguments are optional. These optional arguments have default values that are used if they are not supplied when the function is called (both are set to 0).

VBA also allows functions to have optional arguments by using the *Optional* keyword prior to the argument name. Note that optional arguments must come at the end of the argument list. That is, once an argument is declared to be optional, then all following arguments must be optional as well. As we will see optional arguments can be given a default value, though they are not required.

Let's create a function to calculate net present value that properly handles the initial outlay (unlike the built-in NPV function as pointed out on page 347). Enter the following code in the same module as the other functions for this chapter:

```
Public Function NetPresentValue(Rate As Single, IO As Double, CF1 As Double,
Optional CF2 As Double = 0, Optional CF3 As Double = 0)
'Calculates the true net present value, unlike the built-in NPV function
    If IO > 0 Then IO = -IO
    NetPresentValue = CF1 / (1 + Rate) + CF2 / (1 + Rate) ^ 2 + CF3 / (1 + Rate) ^ 3 + IO
End Function
```

This function has some limitations. For example, it will only handle up to three cash flows. However, it demonstrates the use of optional arguments. Notice that both *CF2* and *CF3* are optional, and that they are assigned a value of 0 if they are not supplied. To see the function in action, create a new worksheet with the data shown in Exhibit 14-4.

EXHIBIT 14-4
USING THE NETPRESENTVALUE FUNCTION

	A	B
1	Discount Rate	10%
2		
3	**Period**	**Cash Flow**
4	0	(1,000)
5	1	500
6	2	700
7	NPV	33.06

To use the UDF in cell B7, enter: `=NetPresentValue(B1,B4,B5,B6)`. Notice that we have supplied all of the arguments except for CF3, which was automatically given a value of 0. You can verify that this answer is correct by using the built-in NPV function.

Using ParamArray for Unlimited Arguments

In the previous section, our NetPresentValue function was limited to only three cash flows. We can get around that limitation by using ParamArray for the last argument. Consider the code for NetPresentValue2:

```
Public Function NetPresentValue2(Rate As Single, IO As Double, ParamArray
CashFlows() As Variant)
'Calculates the true net present value, unlike the built-in NPV function
'This version allows an unlimited number of cash flows
Dim NumCashFlows As Integer
Dim i As Integer
Dim PresentValue As Double
    If IO > 0 Then IO = -IO
    NumCashFlows = UBound(CashFlows) - LBound(CashFlows) + 1 'Count cash flows
    PresentValue = 0
    For i = 0 To (NumCashFlows - 1)
        PresentValue = PresentValue + CashFlows(i) / (1 + Rate) ^ (i + 1)
    Next i
    NetPresentValue2 = PresentValue + IO    'Return the NPV
End Function
```

There are many changes in the function, but for our discussion here the most is in the function declaration. Notice that the last argument is: *ParamArray CashFlows() As Variant*. This says that we expect an array of arguments. An array is essentially a list of zero or more values that can be referenced by their index number (starting at 0 for the first item). In this case, the array will hold the cash flows that the user enters.

The function begins by declaring three variables, and then making sure that the initial outlay (IO) is a negative number. It then determines how many cash flows are in the CashFlows array by using the UBound and LBound functions. UBound gives the upper-bound of the array (i.e., the position of the last item in the array), while LBound gives the lower-bound (usually 0, but it can be 1). The rest of the function consists of a For…Loop that calculates the present value of the cash flows and then returns the NPV.

Using the worksheet created in Exhibit 14-4, you would call the function with: `=NetPresentValue2(B1,B4,B5,B6)`. You should get the same answer as before. If there were more than two cash flows, you would simply add them to the list of arguments. Note that this function cannot handle ranges from the spreadsheet as doing so would make it more complicated.

One important caution is that we have omitted any error checking on the cash flows. It is possible that the user could pass invalid values to the function. For example, if you called the function with: =NetPresentValue2(B1,B4,B5,B6,"string"), then the function would return a #VALUE! error. It would be better to catch this error within the function, but error handling is beyond the scope of this chapter.

Debugging VBA Code

It would be nice if we could write functions that always work perfectly under all conditions. Unfortunately, nobody is perfect and errors (bugs) in software are a regular occurrence. Therefore, it is important that you have some idea of the tools that are available to help you find the errors in your code.

The VB editor provides many tools for debugging code: breakpoints, the Watch Window, the Immediate Window, and several others. We will cover these tools in this section.

Breakpoints and Code Stepping

Typically, when a user-defined function is called from a worksheet, the code runs from beginning to end without interruption. However, if the function is returning incorrect answers, it would be helpful to be able to interrupt the code execution so that you can examine its current state. This is exactly what *breakpoints* allow us to do. Before a function runs, we can enter the VB editor and set a breakpoint on a particular line of code using the F9 function key or the **D**ebug **T**oggle Breakpoint menu choice. When the code is executed and reaches the line where the breakpoint is set, the code will stop running and the VB editor will appear. Figure 14-8 shows the code window with the code stopped at a breakpoint.

FIGURE 14-8
THE CODE WINDOW WITH A BREAKPOINT

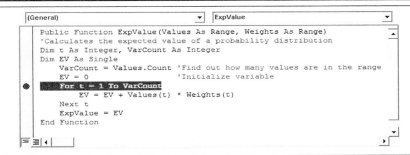

In the VB editor click on the line shown in Figure 14-8. Now press F9 to set the breakpoint. You will notice that the background of that line is now red to indicate that a breakpoint has been set. Return to the worksheet that you created in Exhibit 14-3 and force a recalculation of the ExpValue function. At this point, you should see the code window as it appears in Figure 14-8.

We can now easily examine the value of the variables. Simply move the mouse pointer over any variable and let it hover there for a few seconds. You should see a tag pop up that shows the current value of the variable at this point. If a variable hasn't yet been initialized, it may show up as "Empty" or it may simply give the wrong value. Move the mouse pointer over the VarCount variable, and it should say VarCount = 3. However, if you let the mouse hover over Values(t) it will show Values(t) = "Value" because right now the variable t is set to 0 (it hasn't yet been initialized by the For...Loop).

In Chapter 3 on page 95, we discussed the Evaluate Formula tool that allowed us to debug worksheet formulas by stepping through the calculations one at a time. The VB editor offers a similar stepping function that lets us go through the code line by line. In order to use this feature, you must first set a breakpoint so that the code stops executing on some line. We have already set and activated a breakpoint in the ExpValue function, so all we need to do is press the F8 function key. This will cause the current line of code to execute. Each time you press F8 the next line will be executed, and you can examine the values of the variables to verify that they are correct. If not, then you may be able to spot the source of the error. Being able to step line by line through the code is an invaluable tool when it comes to debugging functions. To remove the breakpoint, return to the line of code and press F9.

Once you have located the error in your code, you can stop execution by choosing **R**un **R**eset from the menu or by pressing the reset button on the toolbar. Edit the code and then run it again to check for additional errors.

The Watch Window

The Watch Window, pictured at the bottom of Figure 14-2, allows us to more easily keep track of the values of variables and expressions as we step through the code. To add a variable or expression to the Watch Window, right-click on it to bring up the Add Watch dialog box. Right-click on VarCount and choose **A**dd Watch.

FIGURE 14-9
THE ADD WATCH DIALOG BOX

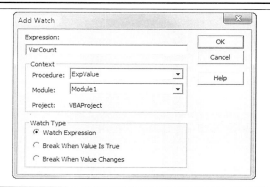

Figure 14-9 shows the Add Watch dialog box. Note that we can actually set three different types of watches. Typically, you will select Watch Expression, which will add the variable to the Watch Window where its value will be updated as you step through the code. The other two types set an automatic breakpoint either when the value is true or when it changes. Click the OK button to add VarCount to the Watch Window. Now, add a couple of other watches and step through the code.

FIGURE 14-10
THE WATCH WINDOW

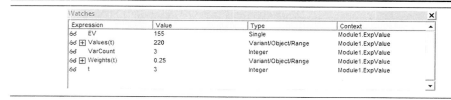

Figure 14-10 shows the Watch Window with the values of five variables immediately before the function exits. That is, the function has finished running, except that it hasn't yet returned the value to the worksheet. EV has a value of 155, which we know is the correct value to return. Notice that Values(t) and Weights(t) are ranges, so you can expand them in the Watch Window to look at their properties in detail by clicking the plus sign.

The Immediate Window

The Immediate Window allows us to query for the current value of a variable, reset a variable to a different value, or execute VBA commands. If the Immediate Window is not visible, select <u>V</u>iew <u>I</u>mmediate Window from the menu or press Ctrl+G on your keyboard.

The Immediate Window is mainly useful if we have triggered a breakpoint and code execution has been paused. Return to your worksheet and force a recalculation of the ExpValue function. Step through the For...Next loop exactly one time. In the Immediate Window type ?EV and then press the Enter key. This will generate a query for the value of the EV variable at this point in the code. You should see that it is equal to 25. This same value is displayed in the Watch Window because we previously set a watch for this variable.

Figure 14-11 shows the Immediate Window with two queries. The second one asks for the current value of Values(t). Note that we can put Values(t) into the Watch Window as well, but it won't display the current value because Values is a range variable.[5] The Immediate Window doesn't have this problem.

FIGURE 14-11
THE IMMEDIATE WINDOW

As mentioned above, we can also execute VBA commands. For example, we could change the value of EV by typing EV = 200 into the Immediate Window. Notice that we don't use the leading question mark if we want to execute a statement. Depending on where the code is when you execute this command, you will end up with a different result from the function. If you enter that command when t = 2, the function will ultimately return 255 as the result.

The Immediate Window can also be used when we aren't debugging code. It can be especially useful for testing snippets of code. For example, type ?Application.Name and then press enter. You should see that you are using an application called Microsoft Excel.

There are more debugging tools, but these should be enough to get you started. You may consult the online help to learn more about debugging your VBA code.

---

5. Actually, we can force the Watch Window to display the value by entering Values(t).Value, or by drilling down into the outline.

Creating Excel Add-Ins

Oftentimes, you will create user-defined functions (or procedures) that are primarily of use in a single workbook. If you aren't likely to use a function outside of that workbook, then it makes sense to write it in a code module attached to the workbook. This is what we have done above. However, if you want to use your functions in multiple workbooks, or make them available for others to use, then it is best to create an Excel add-in. This is exactly what I have done with the FameFncs.xlam add-in that is distributed with this book. Add-ins can be distinguished from regular Excel workbooks by the .xlam file extension, as opposed to .xlsm used for workbooks containing macros.

Add-ins are created from normal Excel workbooks, but they have several advantages:

1. If you distribute your functions in an add-in, users can install the add-in once through Excel Options and then never have to worry about opening the file again. As long as there is a checkmark next to the add-in's name in the Add-Ins dialog box, it will automatically be opened every time Excel is started. This means that your functions are always available to be used.

2. Referencing functions is less complicated if they are contained in an add-in. To access one of the above functions from another workbook, we must specify the name and full path to the workbook. For example, to call the MyPV function, we would have to use this formula: ='Chapter 14 Worksheets.xlsm'!MyPV(A1,A2,A3). However, if the function was in an active add-in, we could call the same function from any workbook with: =MyPV(A1,A2,A3).

3. The worksheets in an add-in are hidden from the user. This means less confusion on their part because they won't feel like they have to use your worksheets to use the functions.

4. It is easier to protect your code from prying eyes and restrict access to it. Because the workbook is hidden from the user, and you can protect the code with a password, users can't view or modify the code without your permission.

Fortunately, creating an add-in is very easy. First, you will open a new workbook and write your code, just as we have done above. Then, choose Save **A**s from the File tab, and then in the Save as type drop-down list, select the "Excel Add-In (*.xlam)" type. Make sure that you save the add-in in a location that you can remember.

You have now created an add-in. To use it, close your "Chapter 14 Worksheets.xlam" file, and then go to Options and then Add-**I**ns. Click the **G**o button, then the **B**rowse button in the Add-Ins dialog box, and then navigate to the directory where you saved the add-in. Finally, select the add-in file, click the OK button, and then make sure there is a checkmark next to the name. You can now use your functions in any workbooks that you create.

One last thing to note is that you can covert the add-in back into a normal workbook if you ever need to do so. Simply go into the VB Editor and select the ThisWorkbook module for your add-in. In the Properties Window set the "IsAddin" property to False and then save the workbook using the .xlsm format.

Best Practices for VBA

As with creating spreadsheets, there are some best practices that are good to follow when writing VBA code. In this section we will list some of them.

1. Remember that user-defined functions should not attempt to modify the formating or contents of any cell other than the one from which is was called. Doing so will create a #VALUE! error.

2. User-defined functions should accept as arguments all of the values that they need to do the calculation. Reading required values from the worksheet will create problems with recalculation because Excel won't know to recalculate the function when the referenced cell changes.

3. Declare all variables using the Dim statement at the beginning of each function. To be sure that none slip by, use Option Explicit at the top of each module. While you can declare variables anywhere within your function, it is best to do so at the top so that you always know where to check the types.

4. When declaring variables, be sure to give them an explicit type (e.g., Dim X as Integer). If you don't assign a type VBA will make it a variant, which gives you some flexibility, but at the cost of speed and memory efficiency.

5. Give all variables a descriptive name. This will help immensely when debugging your code. Many programmers go a step further and use a naming convention that also indicates the type of the variable. There are many such conventions; probably the most famous is Hungarian notation, which uses one or more letters at the beginning of the variable name. For example, iCounter (integer) or strName (string). Whatever convention you use, be consistent with it.

6. Indent your code for easier reading. If all lines of code start at the beginning of a line it can be difficult to follow the flow of the logic. Indenting also makes it much easier to identify different blocks of code.

7. Use comments liberally throughout your code. Ideally, you will have a comment at the top of each function that describes its purpose and defines each of the arguments. Many programmers also list their name and that date that the code was written. Furthermore, you should have a comment for each line of code where its purpose or method isn't clear at a glance.

8. Create a "library" of your commonly used functions. This will make it easier for you to find them when you want to reuse them for future projects. Your library can be a simple as a single text file that holds all of your useful functions, or it can be a more complex system.

9. Try not to create monolithic functions that do everything. Using single-purpose functions makes it easier to understand the code, locate errors, and reuse the functions elsewhere.

10. If your function will be writing large amounts of data to a worksheet, then disable screen updating with Application.ScreenUpdating = False. This will dramatically speed up the execution of the code. Reenable this setting prior to exiting the function with Application.ScreenUpdating = True.

11. Don't reinvent the wheel. Search your own code library and the Internet for code that does what you need. Not only is this faster, but the code that you find will most likely have been optimized.

12. Much like you should be doing with your spreadsheets, test your VBA code extensively before putting it to use.

Summary

In this chapter, we have provided a few short lessons in how to use the VB editor to write and debug user-defined formulas. We have discussed the components of the VB editor, the five requirements for a user-defined function that returns a value to the worksheet, several programming concepts, and the tools that are available for debugging your code. We covered the steps that are necessary to convert your code into an Excel add-in so that your functions can be used in any workbook, or even distributed to others who may find the functions useful. Finally, we discussed 12 "best practices" to use when writing VBA code.

Clearly, one short chapter in a textbook is not enough instruction for you to be completely comfortable working in VBA. Also, due to space constraints we didn't have time to discuss procedure macros or more advanced concepts. Hopefully, though, this chapter has taught you something useful and you will try your hand at writing some user-defined functions. If you want to learn more about VBA programming, I can recommend several very useful resources:

1. I am a big fan of John Walkenbach and can highly recommend any of his books. In particular, *Excel 2013 Power Programming with VBA* (Wiley, 2013) is excellent. I refer to it often when attempting something that I haven't done before, or don't do often.

2. Chip Pearson, of Pearson Software Consulting, LLC, has an excellent Web site devoted to Excel and VBA programming located at: http://www.cpearson.com/excel.htm.

3. Microsoft hosts user-to-user forums where you can search for answers or ask questions. Go to http://social.msdn.microsoft.com/Forums/en-US/home?forum=isvvba.

If those sources fail to answer your questions, there is always the World Wide Web. Do a search and you are almost guaranteed to find your answer or something else interesting.

Problems

1. Write a user-defined function to calculate a firm's return on equity using the DuPont method as defined by (4-29) on page 125. You will need the function to accept three arguments: the net profit margin, total asset turnover ratio, and the debt ratio. Now, write another function to calculate the extended DuPont ROE as defined in equation (4-33) on page 126. This second function will require five arguments: the operating profit margin, interest burden, tax burden, total asset turnover, and the debt ratio.

2. Create a user-defined function to calculate the value of a common stock using the earnings model that was introduced in Chapter 8 on page 246.

    a. What arguments will you need to accept in order to implement equation (8-13) exactly as it is displayed?

    b. Now change your function so that it requires the retention ratio, instead of the expected retained earnings.

    c. Use your function to solve parts a and b of problem 1 on page 259.

3. A stock's beta coefficient can be calculated using the following equation:

$$\beta_i = \frac{\sigma_{i, m}}{\sigma_m^2}$$

a. Write a user-defined function that can calculate the beta coefficient. The arguments to the function should be the covariance between the stock and market returns, and the variance of the market's returns. For example, **BETA(*COVAR AS SINGLE, MARKETVAR AS SINGLE*)**.

b. Rewrite your function so that it accepts ranges of returns and then calculates the beta directly from the returns. It should be defined as: **BETA(*STOCKRETURNS AS RANGE, MARKETRETURNS AS RANGE*)**. Your function should make use of Application.WorksheetFunction to calculate the covariance and variance (use Excel's **COVAR.S** and **VAR.S** functions). In the code, be sure to check to see if the number of stock returns is equal to the number of market returns. The function should return an error if the count of returns is not equal.

4. Write a user-defined function that calculates the average collection period with two arguments: accounts receivable, and annual credit sales, and assumes that there are 360 days per year.

    Now, write another version of the function that accepts an optional third argument that indicates whether to use 360 or 365 days in a year. This third argument should default to using a 360-day year. The second function should return an error value (look up CVErr in the help) if the user specifies any number other than 360 or 365 days per year.

CHAPTER 15

Analyzing Datasets with Tables and Pivot Tables

After studying this chapter, you should be able to:

1. *Use a sorted and filtered Excel table present only the information of interest.*
2. *Build a pivot table and use it to present data in specific ways.*
3. *Add, remove, and rearrange data fields in a pivot table.*
4. *Create calculated columns in tables and calculated fields in pivot tables.*
5. *Use pivot charts to illustrate trends in data from a pivot table.*

Businesses generate large amounts of data of all kinds, and somebody has to process it into a format that is usable for analysis and reporting. For example, a sales manager may have a spreadsheet (or database) that contains the details of every sale. These data might include the date, the name of the customer, the product, the price, and so on. Or, a financial planner may have a dataset that contains information on every mutual fund that she might recommend to a client. These data may include the name of the fund, its ticker symbol, several measures of performance and risk, and other useful information.

Whatever the dataset contains, the analyst needs to be able to quickly categorize it into useful groups, summarize it in various ways, and make calculations from the data.

Ultimately, the results will need to be presented in a report. Excel has a number of tools that can help, but our focus in this chapter will be on Excel tables and pivot tables.

Although you may think of the worksheet itself as a table, the term has a more specific meaning in Excel. A *table* is a data structure that contains related data and allows the user to more easily manage and update the dataset as new information arrives. For example, you can filter the dataset to show only those items that meet certain criteria, or sort the dataset by any field. Tables automatically grow as new data is added, and shrink if data is deleted. Furthermore, formulas and formatting in the table are automatically extended to new records that are added.

A *pivot table* is an even more flexible data structure that allows the analyst to quickly slice and dice a dataset into a useful report. For example, the financial planner from above might want to group all of the mutual funds by investment type (stocks, bonds, etc.), show the year-to-date return for each fund, and then calculate the average return by investment type. A pivot table makes this task fast and easy, even though the original dataset isn't sorted in that manner. Furthermore, it is easy to rearrange the pivot table to organize and present the same data differently; perhaps by fund family instead of by investment type.

Learning to use tables and pivot tables will dramatically increase your productivity and your understanding of the data. Because the datasets used in this chapter are large, workbooks containing the raw data are available on the official Web site for this book, http://www.cengagebrain.com/.

Creating and Using an Excel Table

Imagine that you are an investment advisor who invests in exchange-traded funds and exchange-traded notes (ETFs and ETNs, respectively) on behalf of your clients. You ask your assistant to gather data for all of the 763 funds on your approved list. The data will consist of the fund name, ticker symbol, legal structure, brand, advisor, category, star rating, average premium to NAV, size, returns for the last three years, expense ratio, correlation with benchmark, average daily volume, and some performance measures (alpha, beta, etc.). Your goal is to be able to comb through this data to find the funds that meet various criteria.

Exhibit 15-1 shows a small portion of the data in the ETF Data.xlsx workbook, which is available on the official Web site. Note how the data are organized. Data *fields* (name, ticker symbol, etc.) are in columns, and *records* (each individual fund) are in rows. The full dataset has 22 fields and 772 records, though some of them are duplicates. As useful as the dataset might be, it is simply too large to easily find data points or analyze the funds. Imagine scrolling through the data to find all of the bond funds or the funds provided by the Vanguard Group.

EXHIBIT 15-1
PARTIAL ETF DATASET

	A	B	C	F	H	I
	Fund Name	Ticker	Structure	Broad Category	Morningstar Rating	Premium to NAV %
1						
2	iShares MSCI All Country Asia ex Jpn Idx	AAXJ	ETF	Equity	2	-0.55%
3	iShares MSCI ACWI Index	ACWI	ETF	Equity	3	0.01%
4	iShares MSCI ACWI ex US Index	ACWX	ETF	Equity	3	-0.05%
5	BLDRS Asia 50 ADR Index	ADRA	UIT	Equity	1	-0.28%
6	BLDRS Developed Markets 100 ADR Index	ADRD	UIT	Equity	3	0.13%
7	BLDRS Emerging Markets 50 ADR Index	ADRE	UIT	Equity	2	-0.12%
8	BLDRS Europe 100 ADR Index	ADRU	UIT	Equity	2	0.17%
9	PowerShares DB Agriculture Short ETN	ADZ	ETN	Alternative		-10.30%
10	Market Vectors Africa Index ETF	AFK	ETF	Equity		0.22%
11	PowerShares DB Agriculture Dble Shrt ETN	AGA	ETN	Alternative		-16.45%
12	PowerShares DB Agriculture Long ETN	AGF	ETN	Commodities		-13.27%

Source: Based on data from Morningstar Direct

Table

As mentioned above, converting this data into an Excel table will allow you to easily manage the dataset. To create the table, simply select any cell within the data area (say, D9) and then choose Table from the Insert tab. Excel will make a guess as to the range that you want to use, and whether there are headings. It typically guesses correctly, but if it doesn't then you can easily select the correct range. Figure 15-1 shows the Create Table dialog box as it appears for this dataset.

FIGURE 15-1
THE CREATE TABLE DIALOG BOX

After clicking the OK button, you will see that Excel has applied some formatting and that there is a drop-down arrow button next to each field name. There is also a new contextual tab in the Ribbon that is labeled Design. On the Design tab, which is only visible when the active cell is in a table, you can choose a different style for the table if you don't like the default choice. Simply move the mouse pointer over the styles available in the Table Styles group until you find one that you like.

There are a few things on the Design tab that are not related to the look of the table. For example, you can rename the table, convert it back to an ordinary range of cells, create a pivot table, or add a slicer. We will look at pivot tables later in this chapter (see page 485).

EXHIBIT 15-2
PART OF THE ETF TABLE

	Fund Name	Ticker	Structure	Broad Category	Morningstar Rating	Premium to NAV %
58	iPath DJ-UBS Livestock TR Sub-Idx ETN	COW	ETN	Commodities		0.06%
59	IQ Real Return ETF	CPI	ETF	Allocation	2	-0.02%
60	Guggenheim China Technology ETF	CQQQ	ETF	Equity	3	-0.25%
61	Global Commodity Equity ETF	CRBQ	ETF	Equity	3	-0.23%
62	Guggenheim Spin-Off	CSD	ETF	Equity	5	0.07%
63	iShares 1-3 Year Credit Bond	CSJ	ETF	Fixed Income	3	0.16%
64	ProShares Large Cap Core Plus	CSM	ETF	Alternative	5	0.01%
65	Guggenheim Timber ETF	CUT	ETF	Equity	4	0.00%
66	Guggenheim Multi-Asset Income	CVY	ETF	Equity	4	0.05%
67	SPDR MSCI ACWI (ex-US)	CWI	ETF	Equity	3	0.11%
68	SPDR Nuveen Barclays Capital CA Muni Bd	CXA	ETF	Tax Preferred	2	-0.84%
69	WisdomTree Chinese Yuan Strategy	CYB	ETF	Alternative		-0.10%

Source: Based on data from Morningstar Direct

Another nice feature of tables is that the column headings will now replace the usual A, B, C headings as you scroll down the worksheet. As shown in Exhibit 15-2, this makes it easy to keep track of your fields in a large table.

Removing Duplicate Records from the Table

It isn't obvious at a glance, but our dataset contains nine duplicate records. This is quite a common occurrence, so the Design tab has a tool for removing such records. If you scroll down to row 148, you will see two ETFs from ALPS. Looking more closely, you will see that it is actually one fund listed twice. There are other duplicates as well, and they could be anywhere in the table so it would be difficult to remove them manually.

Remove
Duplicates

To permanently delete all of the duplicate records in the table, click the Remove Duplicates button on the Data tab (it is also on the Design tab). Because we only want to delete records that are exact matches in each field, make sure that all columns are selected in the dialog box and then click OK. You should see a message box saying that 9 duplicate records have been removed and that 763 remain.

 Advanced

If you had wanted to keep the duplicate records, but not see them, then you could have applied an Advanced Filter from the Data tab. Just be sure to check Unique records only at the bottom of the dialog box. Note that for the purposes of this chapter we have chosen to permanently remove the duplicates.

Filtering the Table

When you created the table, Excel automatically added an AutoFilter drop-down to each column header. By clicking the arrow for any column, you can perform operations to sort or filter the table in various ways. Figure 15-2 shows the drop-down for the Fund Name field.

FIGURE 15-2
THE AUTOFILTER FOR THE FUND NAME FIELD

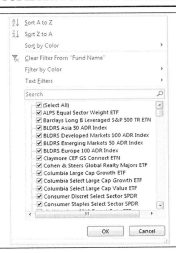

If you choose a Sort option, the entire table will automatically be sorted according to the data in the column to which the sort is applied. Note also that you can select or deselect any of the funds in the Search area. For example, to hide certain funds simply uncheck the boxes next to their names. They will remain in the table, but the rows will be hidden. To restore them, click Clear Filter From "Fund Name."

We can apply more advanced filtering techniques by applying a Text Filter. For example, suppose that you want to only see the funds that contain the word "Bond" in their name. Select Text Filters and choose the "Contains…" filter and then enter Bond into the dialog box. You should see that there are only 39 funds that meet this criteria.

We can easily add a second criteria to this filter by choosing Text Filters again and entering the text into the second box. For example, we could add a filter for fund names that contain both the word "Bond" and the word "Long." If you do this, you will find that there are only four that meet the criteria. Be sure to clear this filter before continuing.

It is important to note that the fund name isn't always indicative of its investment style. So, if you want to filter for all of the long-term bond funds, it would be better to filter on the Morningstar Category field. Click the drop-down arrow next to Morningstar Category, remove the checkmark from the (Select All) item, and then scroll down the list and select the Long-Term Bond and Long Government categories, as shown in Figure 15-3.

FIGURE 15-3
FILTERING FOR LONG-TERM BOND FUNDS

The result of this filter is that there are 12 long-term bond funds in the table. There may be some long-term bond funds that were missed because they didn't meet the criteria that were specified. For example, there are categories named "Muni California Long," "Muni National Long," and "Muni New York Long" that we could have selected. If you go back and select the latter two categories (you aren't interested in California bonds), you will find that there are five additional long-term bond funds. There may still be other funds that do not include the word "Long" in their category, in which case you would need to search further.

Sorting and Filtering Numeric Fields

The drop-downs for numeric fields are similar to those for text fields, except that they have a different set of numeric filters. We can extend our previous filter operation by choosing to Sort Largest to Smallest based on the Return 2013 field. You can see that 2013 was a bad year for these long-term bond funds.

In addition to the sort, we can also add a filter to the Return 2013 field. After sorting by total return, you will notice that some of the funds have dramatically outperformed others. You might wish to see only those funds that lost less than 10% in 2013. Click the Greater Than option after selecting Number Filters and enter -0.10 into the dialog box. You will see that 12 bonds meet these criteria.

EXHIBIT 15-3
LONG-TERM BOND ETFS SORTED AND FILTERED BY RETURN[1]

	A	B	C	D	F	G	M
1	**Fund Name** ▾	**Ticker** ▾	**Structure** ▾	**Branding Name** ▾	**Broad Category** ▾	**Morningstar Category** ▾	**Return 2013** ▾
25	SPDR Nuveen Barclays Capital Muni Bond	TFI	ETF	State Street	Tax Preferred	Muni National Long	-3.59%
34	SPDR Nuveen Barclays Capital NY Muni Bd	INY	ETF	State Street	Tax Preferred	Muni New York Long	-3.80%
125	PowerShares Build America Bond	BAB	ETF	PowerShares	Fixed Income	Long-Term Bond	-5.09%
285	iShares 7-10 Year Treasury Bond	IEF	ETF	iShares	Fixed Income	Long Government	-6.12%
311	PIMCO 7-15 Year U.S. Treasury Index ETF	TENZ	ETF	PIMCO	Fixed Income	Long Government	-6.18%
315	PowerShares Insured New York Muni Bond	PZT	ETF	PowerShares	Tax Preferred	Muni New York Long	-6.28%
433	PowerShares Insured National Muni Bond	PZA	ETF	PowerShares	Tax Preferred	Muni National Long	-6.40%
488	PowerShares 1-30 Laddered Treasury	PLW	ETF	PowerShares	Fixed Income	Long Government	-8.17%
530	Market Vectors Long Municipal Index ETF	MLN	ETF	Van Eck	Tax Preferred	Muni National Long	-8.19%
533	iShares 10-20 Year Treasury Bond	TLH	ETF	iShares	Fixed Income	Long Government	-8.48%
649	iShares Core Long-Term US Bond	ILTB	ETF	iShares	Fixed Income	Long-Term Bond	-8.72%
650	Vanguard Long-Term Bond Index ETF	BLV	ETF	Vanguard	Fixed Income	Long-Term Bond	-9.03%

Source: Based on data from Morningstar Direct

Note that this filter seems as though it only applies to the already filtered data, but it is actually filtering the entire table. The filters on the Morningstar Category field still ensure that we only see long-term bond funds. Exhibit 15-3 shows the result of our filters. Clear the filters before continuing.

You may have noticed that the drop-down buttons change to indicate when a filter or sort has been applied to the field. Figure 15-4 shows the different buttons and the conditions that they represent.

FIGURE 15-4
POSSIBLE COLUMN HEADER BUTTONS

▾ No Filter or Sort

↓ Sort Applied

▼ Filter Applied

▼ Sort and Filter Applied

There are many other filters available, but be aware that if you filter on more than one field then the results may not be what you expect. For example, you might want to see the top-performing ETFs based on 2013 returns sorted from largest to smallest. Further, you want to restrict the list to the ProShares Advisors funds.

First, sort the table from largest to smallest by Return 2013. Now, filter the Branding Name field by selecting only ProShares from the list of brands. Next, click the arrow button for the Return 2013 field and choose the Top 10 filter from Number **F**ilters.

---

1. Several columns have been hidden for purposes of the illustration. Because of the size of the dataset, we will continue to hide columns and rows in other exhibits when necessary.

EXHIBIT 15-4
PROSHARES ADVISORS ETFS IN TOP 10 PERFORMERS FOR 2013

	A	B	C	D	F	G	M
1	**Fund Name**	**Ticker**	**Structure**	**Branding Name**	**Broad Category**	**Morningstar Category**	**Return 2013**
6	ProShares UltraPro S&P500	UPRO	ETF	ProShares	Alternative	Trading-Leveraged Equity	118.56%
9	ProShares Ultra Russell2000 Growth	UKK	ETF	ProShares	Alternative	Trading-Leveraged Equity	98.45%
10	ProShares Ultra Consumer Services	UCC	ETF	ProShares	Alternative	Trading-Leveraged Equity	96.22%
11	ProShares Ultra Health Care	RXL	ETF	ProShares	Alternative	Trading-Leveraged Equity	94.55%

Source: Based on data from Morningstar Direct

(You can choose a different number in the dialog box, but 10 is the default.) This operation results in only four funds being displayed, as seen in Exhibit 15-4. The reason that you don't see the top 10 ProShares funds is because multiple filters do not build upon each other. As we will soon see, pivot tables can do this and much more.

Using Formulas in Tables

Unlike in an ordinary range, when you add a formula to a cell in a table it is automatically extended to all other cells in the column. This is a great time saver, and it helps to ensure consistency and avoid errors. If necessary you can override this default behavior, but most of the time this is what you want.

Table formulas use a different style of cell referencing than the usual A1 style. Tables typically use a *structured reference*, though you can still force the A1 style by typing cell addresses directly. The advantage of structured referencing is primarily that it allows you to easily refer to entire columns of data, to special items such as column headers, or to the totals row. These formulas are also easier to understand as they use column header names in a way that is similar to defined names (see page 9).

Creating a structured reference can be complex, but Excel helps by automatically creating the references when you click on cells in the table while entering the formula. For example, we might want to calculate the average of the expense ratios for all of the funds. Select a blank cell outside of the table and enter: =AVERAGE(Table1[Expense Ratio %]). Note that we use the **AVERAGE** function as usual, but the range is specified using a structured reference. The first part of the reference, Table1, specifies the name of the table from which the data is to be obtained.[2] The second part, [Expense Ratio %], specifies the column to use. By using structured references, the formula is easy to understand, and the reference will automatically include new data as it gets added to the bottom of the table.

Let's now create a *calculated column* in our table. A calculated column is a data field that wasn't included in the original data, but is calculated using data in the table (or elsewhere).

---

2. Tables are automatically named Table1, Table2, and so on. You can rename the table on the Design tab.

Our formula will calculate the average return in 2013 for all funds in the same category as the one in the current row. To do this, we need a function that will average only those items that meet certain criteria. The **AVERAGEIF** function does exactly this, and is defined as:

AVERAGEIF(*RANGE*, *CRITERIA*, *AVERAGE_RANGE*)

where *RANGE* is the range of cells to check against the *CRITERIA*, and *AVERAGE_RANGE* is the range of cells to use in the calculation. If Average_Range is omitted then the cells in Range will be averaged. So, Range will refer to the entire column of fund categories, Criteria will be the category of the fund in the current row, and Average_Range will be the Return 2013 values. Using the traditional A1 referencing, the formula would be: `=AVERAGEIF($G$2:$G$764,G2,$M$2:$M$764)`. Since it uses absolute references, this formula will only work until we add new data at the bottom of the table. However, if we use structured referencing the ranges will automatically expand if we add new data.

To create the formula using structured references, first insert a new column to the left of column N. In N1 overwrite the default column header with `Cat 2013 Return`. In N2 type: `=AVERAGEIF([Morningstar Category],[@[Morningstar Category]],[Return 2013])`. Again, you don't need to actually type the parts in square brackets, you can select the ranges or click the cells and Excel will automatically enter the column names.

In this formula [Morningstar Category] tells Excel to use the entire range of categories (column G), while [@[Morningstar Category]] tells it to use just the single value in the current row. The @ sign is interpreted to mean "this row." Similarly, [Return 2013] refers to the entire column because it lacks the @ sign. Note also that you don't need to use the table name in the reference because it is implicitly assumed to be in the same table as the formula. If you were referencing data from a different table, then you would have to explicitly reference the table name as we did in our first formula.

Structured referencing is a powerful tool, and we have just scratched the surface. You can also use structured references to refer to special items such as the column headers, grand totals, and more. Check Excel's help for more information.

Using Pivot Tables

In the previous section, we have seen how tables can make it easy to manage, sort, and filter a dataset. As useful as that is, it doesn't do much to help us to gain valuable insight into the data. A pivot table is another type of table that allows us to easily summarize, filter, and rearrange a dataset in useful ways that increase our understanding. For example, we might be interested in knowing the average expense ratio by fund family. Or, we might want to know the average return of the funds by category, as we just did with a calculated column in the table. It is much easier, though, with a pivot table.

The data for a pivot table can come from a table or range in a worksheet, from an external source such as a table or query from a database file, or even from a text file. It is important to note that the pivot table stores a snapshot of the data in the pivot table cache. Once created, the cache is separate from the original data. Therefore, if the underlying data changes you must refresh the pivot table. Otherwise it will be using outdated data.

Creating a Pivot Table

Before creating the first pivot table, we should make sure that an option is turned off to avoid potential problems. Go to the File tab and choose Options. Select the Advanced tab on the left side and scroll down to the Data section. Be sure that the check box for Prefer the Excel Data Model when creating Pivot Tables, Query Tables and Data Connections is turned off.

PivotTable

For this example we will be using the ETF/ETN data from the ETF Data worksheet as the source for our pivot table. Make sure that the active cell is within the table and then go to the Insert tab and click the PivotTable button. You will see the dialog box shown in Figure 15-5. Here, as is typical, we will click OK to accept the defaults.

FIGURE 15-5
THE CREATE PIVOTTABLE DIALOG BOX

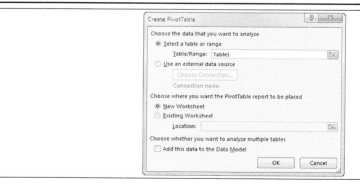

This will create a new worksheet as shown in Exhibit 15-5. If you have never created a pivot table before, it will look quite confusing. On the right-hand side you will see a list of the fields that were in the table. Below that are four "drop zones" where you can drag fields to add them to the pivot table. It may take having a few pivot tables under your belt for the drop zones to make sense, but here is a quick description of each of them:

- **Filters** – Any field in this area will appear above the pivot table and will be used to filter the report. For example, if you want to filter by fund family then you could drag the Branding Name field into this area.

EXHIBIT 15-5
A BLANK PIVOT TABLE

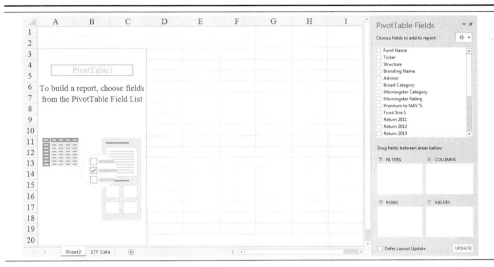

- **Columns** – Drag a field to this area to create a column in the pivot table for each value of the field. For example, dragging the Structure field to this area will create three columns: ETF, ETN, and UIT. Often, you will leave this area empty.

- **Rows** – This area is where the fields that you want to use as labels will go. For example, we might want to use the ticker symbol as the label for each row. You can have more than one row label by dragging more fields to this area. You can change their order by simply rearranging them within the area.

- **Values** – This area holds the fields that you want to summarize. Fields can be summarized by a number of functions, including Sum, Count, Average, and several others. By default, numeric fields will be summed, and text fields will be counted.

You can drag as many fields as necessary into any of the areas. In fact, you can drag a field into more than one of the areas, or even into the same area, so that it appears twice or more. To remove a field from the pivot table, just drag it back to the Pivot Table Field area. The ability to move fields in this way and instantly get an updated report is referred to as "pivoting" and is what gives pivot tables their name.

Recall that for Exhibit 15-4 we tried to show the top 10 ProShares funds by year-to-date returns. However, because the table filters don't build upon each other, we were unsuccessful and ended up with only four funds displayed. We can easily organize our pivot table to show this data.

EXHIBIT 15-6
UNFORMATTED PIVOT TABLE SHOWING 2013 RETURNS FOR EACH ETF

	A	B	C
1	Branding Name	(All)	
2			
3	Row Labels	Sum of Return 2013	
4	⊟ALPS Equal Sector Weight ETF	0.3017633	
5	EQL	0.3017633	
6	⊟Barclays Long B Leveraged S&P 500 TR ETN	0.638143	
7	BXUB	0.638143	
8	⊟BLDRS Asia 50 ADR Index	0.1401346	
9	ADRA	0.1401346	
10	⊟BLDRS Developed Markets 100 ADR Index	0.2191742	
11	ADRD	0.2191742	
12	⊟BLDRS Emerging Markets 50 ADR Index	-0.0496047	
13	ADRE	-0.0496047	
14	⊟BLDRS Europe 100 ADR Index	0.223735	
15	ADRU	0.223735	
16	⊟Claymore CEF GS Connect ETN	0.1295916	
17	GCE	0.1295916	
18	⊟Cohen & Steers Global Realty Majors ETF	0.0135243	
19	GRI	0.0135243	
20	⊟Columbia Large Cap Growth ETF	0.3308195	

PivotTable Fields

Choose fields to add to report:

- ☑ Fund Name
- ☑ Ticker
- ☐ Structure
- ☑ Branding Name
- ☐ Advisor
- ☐ Broad Category
- ☐ Morningstar Category
- ☐ Morningstar Rating
- ☐ Premium to NAV %
- ☐ Fund Size $
- ☐ Return 2011
- ☐ Return 2012
- ☑ Return 2013

Drag fields between areas below:

▼ FILTERS	⊞ COLUMNS
Branding Name ▼	

⊞ ROWS	Σ VALUES
Fund Name ▼	Sum of Return 2013 ▼
Ticker ▼	

☐ Defer Layout Update   UPDATE

Sheet2 ETF Data ⊕

Source: Based on data from Morningstar Direct

To begin, drag the Branding Name field into the Filters area. This will allow us to display one fund family at a time in the pivot table. Next, drag both the Fund Name and Ticker fields into the Rows area. Finally, drag the Return 2013 field into the Values area. Your pivot table should now look like the one in Exhibit 15-6.

Formatting the Pivot Table

Report Layout ▼

We now have the basic structure of the pivot table, but it needs to be cleaned up a bit in order to be useful. First notice that the ticker symbol for each fund appears on the row below its name. This layout, known as the Compact Form, would be useful if we had multiple ticker symbols for each name, but that isn't the case. We can make the ticker symbol appear next to the name by changing to Tabular Form. On the Design tab click the Report Layout button and choose Show in Tabular Form.

Subtotals ▼

Notice that the return for each fund is now shown twice. The first is the return for the Symbol, and the second is a subtotal of the Fund Name field. Again, since there is only one fund per name, this makes no sense and is confusing. To remove the subtotals click the Subtotals button on the Design tab and choose Do Not Show Subtotals.

The next step in formatting the pivot table is to display the 2013 returns as percentages. Right-click on any row in the Sum of Return 2013 field and choose Number Format. Select a number format from the Percentage category with two decimal places.

We will now change the way that the Return 2013 field is summarized. As mentioned above, the default is to sum numeric fields. Because there is only one year-to-date return for each fund, it doesn't much matter which function we choose. However, the summary function will affect any subtotals and grand totals. Summing returns from different funds doesn't make much sense, so we will change the summary function to the average instead. Right-click any cell in the field, select Su**m**marize Values By and then choose **A**verage. Scroll all the way to the bottom of the pivot table and notice that the average 2013 return for all 763 funds is 16.29%.

Now, let's change the text at the top of the column by typing `2013 Return` into C3. You can change the label to any text as long as it doesn't replicate an existing field name. By replacing the text, we can remove the summary method from the name. You can also apply any other formatting to the column header, so center the text and set the column width to an appropriate value.

We now have a pivot table report that shows all of our funds (sorted by name), their ticker symbols, and their 2013 returns. However, recall that we want to see only the top performing ProShares funds. From the Report Filter choose ProShares to limit the report to these funds.

To show only the top 10 ProShares funds, we need to apply a filter to the 2013 Return field. Click the drop-down for Fund Name and choose **V**alue Filters. Select the **T**op 10 filter, make sure that it is selecting items by 2013 Return, and click OK. Lastly, we want to sort the list from the highest return to the lowest. Click the drop-down for the Fund Name again and choose **M**ore Sort Options. In the dialog box select **D**escending and 2013 Return for the field. The pivot table should now look like the one in Exhibit 15-7.

You can see that these ETFs did very well in 2013, with an average return of 91.76%. However, go back to the **T**op 10 value filter for the Fund Name. This time change it from a Top 10 to a Bottom 10 filter. You will see that the 10 worst ProShares ETFs had an average return in 2013 of –53.12%. The reason for the dramatic results is that these are leveraged funds.

Now that the pivot table report has been created, it can be copied into a new worksheet or a word processing document for presentation to a client. Note that if you copy only a portion of the pivot table, say A3:C14, and then paste into another worksheet you will end up with a normal range of data. However, if you were to select the entire pivot table (A1:C14) then you would create a new pivot table that uses the same pivot cache. Having two or more pivot tables based on the same data can be useful at times. On the other hand, if all that you want is a copy of the report, then copy the pivot table and use Paste **S**pecial Values.

EXHIBIT 15-7
TOP 10 PROSHARES ETFS BY 2013 RETURN

	A	B	C
1	Branding Name	ProShares	
2			
3	**Fund Name**	**Ticker**	**2013 Return**
4	ProShares UltraPro S&P500	UPRO	118.56%
5	ProShares Ultra Russell2000 Growth	UKK	98.45%
6	ProShares Ultra Consumer Services	UCC	96.22%
7	ProShares Ultra Health Care	RXL	94.55%
8	ProShares Ultra SmallCap600	SAA	93.40%
9	ProShares Ultra Industrials	UXI	91.12%
10	ProShares Ultra Russell2000	UWM	87.02%
11	ProShares Ultra QQQ	QLD	81.83%
12	ProShares Ultra Russell MidCap Growth	UKW	78.56%
13	ProShares Ultra Semiconductors	USD	77.92%
14	**Grand Total**		**91.76%**

Source: Based on data from Morningstar Direct

Rearranging the Pivot Table and Adding Fields

Imagine that you now wish to look at average 2013 returns by brand name. Because we now only care about the brand, and not the individual funds, drag the Fund Name and Ticker fields back to the Pivot Table Field List to remove them from the pivot table. Next drag the Branding Name field from the Report Filter area into the Row Labels area. Finally, click the drop-down next to Branding Name, choose **M**ore Sort Options, and sort in descending order based on the 2013 Return field.

Fidelity has the best performance of all of the providers. However, this may be misleading due to the number of funds offered and the diversity of categories. So, to begin investigating, you want to know how many ETFs each provider offers. Drag the Ticker field into the Values area to get this count. Because this is a text item, the only summary method that will provide useful data is count, which is the default. You can now see that Fidelity only has one ETF in our list, and it performed well, which explains why it has the highest average return.

To investigate further, drag the Ticker field from the Values area into the Rows area. This will allow us to see the return of each fund in each family as shown in Exhibit 15-8. Note that the new Ticker column (B) will not show any symbols if the Branding Name field is collapsed. To view the funds for a single brand expand the list by clicking the outline button to the left of the provider name. To view all of the funds, right-click any cell in the Branding Name column, select **E**xpand/Collapse, and then choose **E**xpand Entire Field. Finally, click the Subtotals button on the Design tab to add subtotals at the bottom of each group.

EXHIBIT 15-8
2013 RETURNS BY FUND WITH SUBTOTALS BY BRANDING NAME

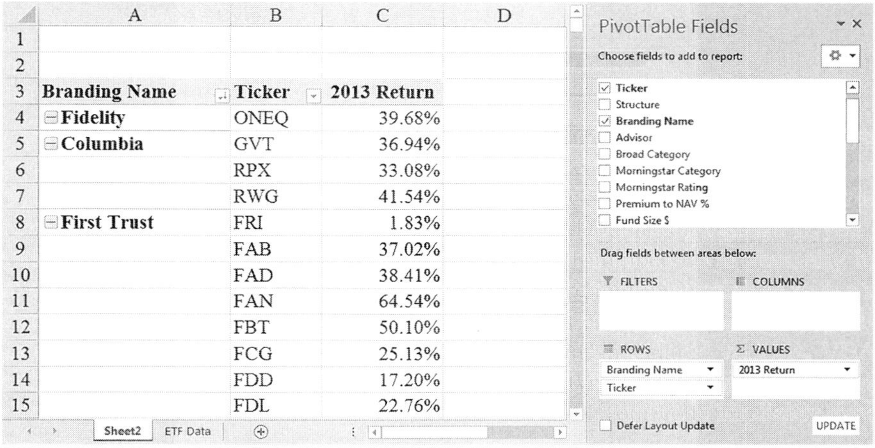

	A	B	C	D
1				
2				
3	**Branding Name**	**Ticker**	**2013 Return**	
4	**Fidelity**	ONEQ	39.68%	
5	**Columbia**	GVT	36.94%	
6		RPX	33.08%	
7		RWG	41.54%	
8	**First Trust**	FRI	1.83%	
9		FAB	37.02%	
10		FAD	38.41%	
11		FAN	64.54%	
12		FBT	50.10%	
13		FCG	25.13%	
14		FDD	17.20%	
15		FDL	22.76%	

Source: Based on data from Morningstar Direct

We can now see that average returns by provider can be misleading because some firms offer more ETFs than others. To mitigate the problem somewhat, you might decide that you only want to see those brands that offer at least 30 funds. To filter the pivot table for this criteria, we need to know how many funds are offered by each provider. Drag another copy of the Ticker field into the Values area. Note that this field is now shown in two different areas of the pivot table. Since Ticker is a text field, it will be summarized by count. Now click the drop-down next to Branding Name and choose Value Filters. Select the Greater Than Or Equal To filter and choose Count of Ticker as the field and 30 for the value. Finally, collapse the pivot table to the Branding Name level and the result is shown in Exhibit 15-9.

Transforming the Data Field Presentation

Suppose that we aren't interested in the number of funds per family, and instead we would like to know the percentage of funds in our list that are offered by each provider. First, clear the filter that we applied in the previous section so that all providers are shown. Now right-click on any of the values in column D and select Show Values As. This allows us to transform the data in the column in a number of useful ways.

For example, to see the percentage of the total number of funds by provider, simply choose % of Grand Total. By looking at the percentages, you can easily see that Fidelity has the smallest number of funds in our list, and iShares has the largest number.

EXHIBIT 15-9
AVERAGE 2013 RETURNS FOR BRANDING NAMES WITH 30 OR MORE FUNDS

	A	B	C	D	E
1					
2					
3	**Branding Name**	⟂ Ticker	⟂ 2013 Return	Count of Ticker	
4	⊞ **First Trust**		36.10%	40	
5	⊞ **Guggenheim**		30.90%	37	
6	⊞ **PowerShares**		21.27%	96	
7	⊞ **Vanguard**		19.84%	46	
8	⊞ **State Street**		18.80%	88	
9	⊞ **iShares**		18.48%	186	
10	⊞ **WisdomTree**		16.42%	39	
11	⊞ **ProShares**		6.29%	77	
12	⊞ **Barclays**		-9.05%	34	
13	**Grand Total**		**17.81%**	643	
14					
15					

PivotTable Fields

Choose fields to add to report:

- ☐ Fund Name
- ☑ Ticker
- ☐ Structure
- ☑ Branding Name
- ☐ Advisor
- ☐ Broad Category
- ☐ Morningstar Category
- ☐ Morningstar Rating
- ☐ Premium to NAV %

Drag fields between areas below:

▼ FILTERS

▦ COLUMNS
Σ Values

▤ ROWS
Branding Name
Ticker

Σ VALUES
2013 Return
Count of Ticker

☐ Defer Layout Update   UPDATE

Sheet2   ETF Data

Source: Based on data from Morningstar Direct

Another way to accomplish a similar result is to rank the providers by the number of funds. Again, right-click in column D and choose Show Values As. Now select Rank Largest to Smallest. You can see that iShares is ranked number 1, and Fidelity and JP Morgan are ranked 19. Note that ties are given the same rank.

If you now perform the same ranking based on the 2013 Return field, you can see that Fidelity is the best performing provider, as we saw earlier. To change the ranking so that it is done at the fund level go back to Rank Largest to Smallest, but choose Ticker as the Base Field. Now, right-click any Branding Name and choose Expand/Collapse and then Expand Entire Field.

Before continuing, reset the 2013 Return field to No Calculation, and drag the Ticker field from the Values area back to the PivotTable field list.

Calculations in Pivot Tables

We can create completely new fields that are calculated from existing fields. This type of field is known as a *calculated field*, and it is analogous to the calculated column that we created in our original table.

Recall that on page 485 we added a calculated column, Cat 2013 Return, to our original table. That field is available in the pivot table, so we will use it as a part of our calculated field. Specifically, we will create a field that calculates the difference between each fund's

2013 return and the same for the category. The result will allow us to easily see which funds are outperforming (or underperforming) their peers.

Fields, Items, & Sets ▾

To create a calculated field, start by clicking the Fields, Items, & Sets button on the Analyze tab and choose Calculated Field. This will launch the dialog box shown in Figure 15-6. Give the field a name by typing `Relative to Cat` into the Name box. To define the formula select the Return 2013 field from the Fields list and then click the Insert Field button. Now type a minus sign and then select and insert the Cat YTD Return field. Click the OK button to add the calculated field to the bottom of the PivotTable Field List. You can now use the calculated field just like any other field.

FIGURE 15-6
THE INSERT CALCULATED FIELD DIALOG BOX

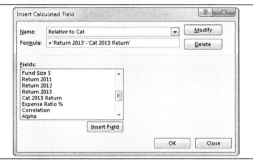

Drag the Cat 2013 Return and Relative to Cat fields into the Values area, summarize both by the Average, and format them as a percentages with two decimal places. Next, replace the Branding Name field in the Row Labels area with the Fund Name field. You should now see each fund name, ticker, 2013 return, category 2013 return, and the return relative to the category.

Remember that we want to see only those funds that have outperformed their peers. You might think that you could filter the pivot table with a Greater Than filter that specifies that the 2013 Return field is greater than the Cat YTD Return. However, that filter only allows you to specify a number, not another field. That is why we need the calculated field. So, click the drop-down next to Fund Name and select the Greater Than filter. Choose the Average of Relative to Cat field in the list, and enter 0 into the appropriate edit box. Your pivot table should now look like the one in Exhibit 15-10.

Another useful way to look at this same data is by category. Drag the Fund Name field back to the Pivot Table Field List, and replace it with the Broad Category field. This will make it easy to see which funds in each category are outperforming. You can also rank funds within the categories by right-clicking the Relative to Cat field and selecting Show Values As. Choose to Rank Largest to Smallest with Ticker as the Base Field.

EXHIBIT 15-10
FUNDS THAT ARE OUTPERFORMING THEIR PEERS

	A	B	C	D	E
1					
2					
3	**Fund Name**	**Ticker**	**2013 Return**	**Average of Cat 2013 Return**	**Average of Relative to Cat**
4	**Direxion Daily Small Cap Bull 3X Shares**	TNA	146.87%	65.23%	81.64%
5	**Guggenheim Solar**	TAN	129.94%	43.81%	86.13%
6	**Direxion Daily Financial Bull 3X Shares**	FAS	125.94%	65.23%	60.71%
7	**Direxion Daily Mid Cap Bull 3X Shares**	MIDU	119.97%	65.23%	54.74%
8	**ProShares UltraPro S&P500**	UPRO	118.56%	65.23%	53.33%
9	**Direxion Daily S&P500 Bull 3X Shares**	SPXL	117.94%	65.23%	52.71%
10	**Market Vectors Solar Energy ETF**	KWT	101.73%	43.81%	57.92%
11	**ProShares Ultra Russell2000 Growth**	UKK	98.45%	65.23%	33.22%
12	**ProShares Ultra Consumer Services**	UCC	96.22%	65.23%	30.99%
13	**ProShares Ultra Health Care**	RXL	94.55%	65.23%	29.32%
14	**ProShares Ultra SmallCap600**	SAA	93.40%	65.23%	28.17%

Sheet2 | ETF Data

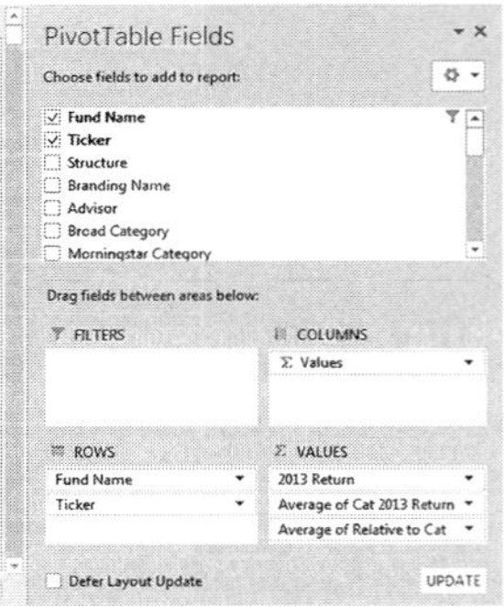

Source: Based on data from Morningstar Direct

Pivot Tables for Financial Statements

We can also use pivot tables to analyze a company's financial statements over time. For this section we will be using the GOOG Financials.xlsx workbook, which is available on the official Web site of this book. This workbook contains quarterly financial statements for Google from March 2009 to December 2013 (five years). We will only use the income statements in this chapter, but the end-of-chapter problems will also make use of the balance sheets.

As we've seen in previous chapters, financial statements are typically organized with time periods in the first row and items in the first column. However, since the items are the data fields we will need to transpose the financial statements for use in a pivot table. Exhibit 15-11 shows the result that we want to achieve. To do so, select A5:U21 on the GOOG Quarterly IS worksheet and copy it. Next right-click A24, choose Paste Special, and then select the checkbox next to Transpose.

Once the data is transformed, type `Date` into A24. This will provide a field name for the dates. To create the pivot table, click anywhere within the transformed data area and click the PivotTable button on the Insert tab. Rename the pivot table worksheet to `IS Pivot Table`.

EXHIBIT 15-11
TRANSPOSING THE INCOME STATEMENT

	A	B	C	D	E
1	GOOGLE, INC. CLASS A (GOOG) INCOME STATEMENT				
2	Fiscal year ends in December. USD in millions except per share data.				
3	Source: Morningstar Direct (Retrieved 2/14/2014)				
4					
5		Mar 2009	Jun 2009	Sep 2009	Dec 2009
6	Revenue	5,508,990,000	5,522,897,000	5,944,851,000	6,673,825,000
7	Cost of revenue	2,101,504,000	2,107,971,000	2,226,240,000	2,408,400,000
8	Gross profit	3,407,486,000	3,414,926,000	3,718,611,000	4,265,425,000
9	Research and development	641,643,000	707,626,000	757,524,000	736,234,000
10	Sales, General and administrative	882,252,000	833,406,000	887,369,000	1,048,208,000
11	Total operating expenses	1,523,895,000	1,541,032,000	1,644,893,000	1,784,442,000
12	Operating income	1,883,591,000	1,873,894,000	2,073,718,000	2,480,983,000
13	Interest Expense	-	-	-	-
14	Other income (expense)	6,210,000	(17,718,000)	(7,177,000)	87,688,000
15	Income before taxes	1,889,801,000	1,856,176,000	2,066,541,000	2,568,671,000
16	Provision for income taxes	466,973,000	371,631,000	427,566,000	594,571,000
17	Net income (continuing operations)	1,422,828,000	1,484,545,000	1,638,975,000	1,974,100,000
18	Net income (discontinued operations)	-	-	-	-
19	Net income	1,422,828,000	1,484,545,000	1,638,975,000	1,974,100,000
20	Basic EPS	4.51	4.70	5.18	6.22
21	Shares Outstanding	316,422,000	316,935,000	317,772,000	318,274,000

	A	B	C	D	E
1	GOOGLE, INC. CLASS A (GOOG) INCOME STATEMENT				
2	Fiscal year ends in December. USD in millions except per share data.				
3	Source: Morningstar Direct (Retrieved 2/14/2014)				
4					
24	Date	Revenue	Cost of revenue	Gross profit	Research and development
25	Mar 2009	5,508,990,000	2,101,504,000	3,407,486,000	641,643,000
26	Jun 2009	5,522,897,000	2,107,971,000	3,414,926,000	707,626,000
27	Sep 2009	5,944,851,000	2,226,240,000	3,718,611,000	757,524,000
28	Dec 2009	6,673,825,000	2,408,400,000	4,265,425,000	736,234,000
29	Mar 2010	6,775,000,000	2,452,000,000	4,323,000,000	818,000,000
30	Jun 2010	6,820,000,000	2,467,000,000	4,353,000,000	898,000,000
31	Sep 2010	7,286,000,000	2,552,000,000	4,734,000,000	994,000,000
32	Dec 2010	8,440,000,000	2,946,000,000	5,494,000,000	1,051,000,000
33	Mar 2011	8,575,000,000	2,936,000,000	5,639,000,000	1,226,000,000
34	Jun 2011	9,026,000,000	3,172,000,000	5,854,000,000	1,234,000,000
35	Sep 2011	9,720,000,000	3,378,000,000	6,342,000,000	1,404,000,000
36	Dec 2011	10,583,000,000	3,703,000,000	6,880,000,000	1,301,000,000
37	Mar 2012	10,645,000,000	3,789,000,000	6,856,000,000	1,441,000,000
38	Jun 2012	12,214,000,000	5,013,000,000	7,201,000,000	1,585,000,000
39	Sep 2012	14,101,000,000	6,554,000,000	7,547,000,000	2,009,000,000
40	Dec 2012	13,215,000,000	5,278,000,000	7,937,000,000	1,758,000,000

Source: Based on data from Morningstar Direct

Grouping Data by Date

→ Group Selection

Pivot tables allow you to group records together by selecting some values (they don't need to be in a contiguous range) in the Row Labels area and clicking the Group Selection button on the Analyze tab. This is useful because it allows you to calculate subtotals by any groups that you choose to define.

When the data in the pivot table are date related, as in a financial statement, you can easily create groups by date. You can choose to group by time (hours, minutes, seconds) and by date (days, months, quarters, years). In order to use this functionality, Excel must be able to recognize the dates and this is not always the case. Often when you retrieve financial statements from Web sites or databases the dates will be in an unusual format that Excel will see as text or a number, instead of a date. For example, if you download a balance sheet from the SEC's Edgar Web site, a date may appear as "March 31, 2015" and Excel will see it as text. You must either retype the date in a format that Excel will recognize (e.g., 3/31/2015) or use the various text functions (e.g., **LEFT**, **RIGHT**, and **MID**) to process the text into a date. This has already been done in the GOOG Financials.xlsx workbook.

Because our income statement data are provided quarterly, we will choose to group this data into months, quarters, and years. Drag the Date field into the Row Labels area and Revenue into the Values area. Now right-click in A4 and select **G**roup. The dialog box shown in Figure 15-7 will appear, and you should select Months, Quarters, and Years as shown. Format the Revenue field as a number with no decimal places.

FIGURE 15-7
THE GROUPING DIALOG BOX FOR DATES

Two additional fields have been added to the pivot table: Quarters and Years. These fields can be used in any of the pivot table areas, though they are most useful as either report filters or row labels. Change the Report Layout to Show in **T**abular Form. This allows us to see quarterly Revenue (or any other field) by Year. Turn on subtotals by clicking the SubTotals button and selecting Show all Subtotals at **B**ottom of Group. By adding subtotals, we can also see full-year sales for each year, as shown in Exhibit 15-12.

EXHIBIT 15-12
QUARTERLY REVENUE BY YEAR FOR GOOGLE

Years	Quarters	Sum of Revenue
⊟2009	Qtr1	5,508,990,000
	Qtr2	5,522,897,000
	Qtr3	5,944,851,000
	Qtr4	6,673,825,000
2009 Total		23,650,563,000
⊟2010	Qtr1	6,775,000,000
	Qtr2	6,820,000,000
	Qtr3	7,286,000,000
	Qtr4	8,440,000,000
2010 Total		29,321,000,000
⊟2011	Qtr1	8,575,000,000
	Qtr2	9,026,000,000
	Qtr3	9,720,000,000
	Qtr4	10,583,000,000
2011 Total		37,904,000,000

Source: Based on data from Morningstar Direct

Typically, analysts are more interested in growth rates than in actual revenue. So, we might want to look at year-over-year growth in quarterly revenue. To change our pivot table so that it displays these growth rates, right-click in C4 and select Show Values As and then % Difference From. In the dialog box choose Years as the base field and (Previous) as the base item. Your pivot table should now look like the one in Exhibit 15-13.

EXHIBIT 15-13
YEAR-OVER-YEAR QUARTERLY REVENUE GROWTH FOR GOOGLE

	A	B	C	D	E
1					
2					
3	Years	Quarters	Sum of Revenue		
4	⊟2009	Qtr1			
5		Qtr2			
6		Qtr3			
7		Qtr4			
8	2009 Total				
9	⊟2010	Qtr1	22.98%		
10		Qtr2	23.49%		
11		Qtr3	22.56%		
12		Qtr4	26.46%		
13	2010 Total		**23.98%**		
14	⊟2011	Qtr1	26.57%		
15		Qtr2	32.35%		
16		Qtr3	33.41%		
17		Qtr4	25.39%		
18	2011 Total		**29.27%**		

PivotTable Fields — Choose fields to add to report: Date, ☑ Revenue, Cost of revenue, Gross profit. Drag fields between areas below: FILTERS, COLUMNS, ROWS (Years, Quarters), Σ VALUES (Sum of Revenue). Defer Layout Update — UPDATE. Sheet tab: IS Pivot Table.

Source: Based on data from Morningstar Direct

You can now see, for example, that Qtr1 Revenue in 2010 was 22.98% higher than in the Qtr1 of 2009. Note that the subtotal for each year shows the full year percentage change in revenue. So, 2010 sales were 23.98% higher than in 2009. There are no growth rates for 2009 because we don't have data from 2008.

Using Pivot Charts to Show Trends Over Time

In the previous section, we created a pivot table that shows sales growth over time. You may have noticed that while Google's sales have been growing rapidly, the rate of growth may be slowing a bit. We can show this trend in a *pivot chart*, which is simply a chart created directly from pivot table data.

PivotChart

A pivot chart will include each of the fields that is in the Values area, so they are best used when you have only a few fields. Otherwise, the chart can quickly become crowded and difficult to understand. To create the pivot chart, click the PivotChart button on the Analyze tab, and it will automatically appear. Figure 15-8 shows the pivot chart after a small amount of formatting. You can see that sales growth has been quite volatile, and may be slowing.

FIGURE 15-8
A PIVOT CHART SHOWING REVENUE GROWTH RATES YEAR-OVER-YEAR

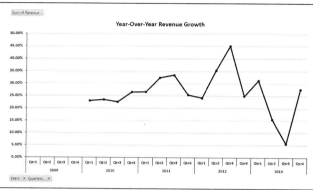

Source: Based on data from Morningstar Direct

Take note of the field buttons in the pivot chart. These can be used to filter or sort the data, and you can rearrange the chart. For example, right-click on the Quarters button and choose Move <u>U</u>p. This will display four charts that show growth rates by quarter for each year. In this case, you can easily see that over this period, first quarter revenue growth has trended up, second and third quarter revenue growth has been very volatile, and fourth quarter growth has been relatively flat.

Field
Buttons ▾

Changes made to the pivot chart are also made to the pivot table, and vice versa. The field buttons can be turned on or off with the Field Buttons button on the Analyze tab.

Displaying Multiple Subtotals

The pivot tables that we have created so far either don't show subtotals, or show only one. For example, the pivot table in Exhibit 15-13 shows the total sales for each year. Suppose that you are also interested in seeing the average level of quarterly sales for each year.

First, right-click in the Revenue field, select Show V<u>a</u>lues As, and choose <u>N</u>o Calculation. This will return the Revenue field to the actual dollar amount of sales for each quarter. Now right-click in any of the subtotals in column A (say, A8) and then select Field Setti<u>n</u>gs from the menu. Click the Custom radio button and then choose both the Sum and Average functions as shown in Figure 15-9.

You will now see, for example, that total revenue in 2009 was $23.65 million, while average quarterly sales were $5.91 million. You can use this same technique to change the subtotal calculation. For example, the values in the Revenue field are summed and the default subtotal is also the sum. You could change that to the average by following the steps above. Before continuing, drag the Revenue field out of the pivot table. Leave the Years and Quarters fields in the Row area as we will be using them in the next section.

FIGURE 15-9
THE FIELD SETTINGS DIALOG BOX FOR SUBTOTALS

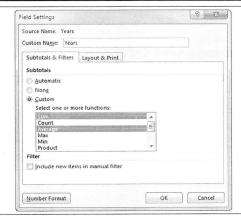

Using Calculated Fields for Financial Ratios

In Chapter 4 we saw how financial ratios can provide valuable analytical information. Now that we have the income statement in a pivot table we might want to closely examine some of the ratios over time. We can use calculated fields (see page 492) to add ratios to the pivot table. If we need to have all of the ratios in the pivot table, it would be easier to use calculated columns in the original table. In this case we will use a calculated field because we only need to examine one ratio.

Suppose that we are interested in seeing if there is any significant seasonality in Google's net operating profit margin. We know that some companies earn most of their profits in certain quarters of the year, but we don't know if Google follows a similar pattern. Because revenues have been growing, it would be difficult to see the seasonality, if it exists, in either sales or net operating profits.

To eliminate the problems inherent in using dollar values, we will create a calculated field for the operating profit margin. On the Analyze tab click the Fields, Items, & Sets button and choose to create a calculated field. Give the field a name of NOPM, and set the formula to: ='Operating income'/Revenue. This will immediately add the NOPM field into the Values area of the pivot table (if not, then drag it there).

Format the numbers to a percentage format with two decimal places, and drag the Quarters field above the Years field in the Rows area. If there are no subtotals displayed, click the Subtotals button and select Show all Subtotals at **B**ottom of Group.

EXHIBIT 15-14
QUARTERLY OPERATING PROFIT MARGINS

	A	B	C	D	E	F	G	H	I
3	Quarters	Years	Sum of NOPM						
4	Qtr1	2009	34.19%						
5		2010	36.72%						
6		2011	32.61%						
7		2012	31.84%						
8		2013	24.89%						
9	Qtr1 Total		30.86%						
10	Qtr2	2009	33.93%						
11		2010	34.68%						
12		2011	31.92%						
13		2012	26.22%						
14		2013	22.14%						
15	Qtr2 Total		28.20%						
16	Qtr3	2009	34.88%						
17		2010	34.96%						
18		2011	31.46%						
19		2012	19.40%						
20		2013	23.12%						
21	Qtr3 Total		26.68%						
22	Qtr4	2009	37.17%						
23		2010	35.33%						
24		2011	33.14%						
25		2012	25.97%						
26		2013	23.26%						
27	Qtr4 Total		29.27%						

Source: Based on data from Morningstar Direct

Exhibit 15-14 shows the resulting pivot table along with a pivot chart of the data. Note that while there is some year-to-year variability, there doesn't seem to be any obvious seasonality in Google's net operating profit margin. We can see, however, that year-over-year operating profitability appears to be declining over time. This may be more obvious if you change the chart type to a Line chart.

It is important to understand how the subtotals are calculated. In C9 the Qtr1 Total is 30.86%, but that is not the sum of the first quarter operating profit margins, nor is it the average of them. Instead, Excel calculates these totals using the sum of all first quarter operating profits divided by the sum of all first quarter sales. In effect, this creates a weighted average of NOPM. You can confirm this by dragging the Revenues and Operating Income fields into the Values area and doing the calculation by hand.

To get a clearer view of the data we will pivot the table. Drag the Years field from the Row Labels area to the Column Labels area. Next, enable grand totals by clicking the Grand Totals button on the Design tab and choosing O**n** for Rows and Columns. By comparing the values in column G (the row grand totals), you can see that the operating profit margin is quite similar regardless of the quarter of the year. Exhibit 15-15 shows the result.

EXHIBIT 15-15
QUARTERLY OPERATING PROFIT MARGIN BY YEAR

	A	B	C	D	E	F	G
3	**Sum of NOPM**	**Years**					
4	**Quarters**	**2009**	**2010**	**2011**	**2012**	**2013**	**Grand Total**
5	Qtr1	34.19%	36.72%	32.61%	31.84%	24.89%	30.86%
6	Qtr2	33.93%	34.68%	31.92%	26.22%	22.14%	28.20%
7	Qtr3	34.88%	34.96%	31.46%	19.40%	23.12%	26.68%
8	Qtr4	37.17%	35.33%	33.14%	25.97%	23.26%	29.27%
9	**Grand Total**	**35.15%**	**35.41%**	**32.30%**	**25.43%**	**23.34%**	**28.71%**

PivotTable Fields

Choose fields to add to report:

- ☐ Research and development
- ☐ Sales, General and administrative
- ☐ Total operating expenses
- ☐ Operating income
- ☐ Interest Expense
- ☐ Other income (expense)
- ☐ Income before taxes
- ☐ Provision for income taxes
- ☐ Net income from continuing opera...
- ☐ Net income from discontinued op...
- ☐ Net income
- ☐ Basic EPS
- ☐ Shares Outstanding
- ☑ Quarters
- ☑ Years
- ☑ NOPM

Drag fields between areas below:

▼ FILTERS	‖ COLUMNS
	Years ▼

≡ ROWS	Σ VALUES
Quarters ▼	Sum of NOPM ▼

☐ Defer Layout Update   UPDATE

Operating Profit Margin by Quarter

(Chart: Sum of NOPM — Quarters — bar chart showing Qtr1, Qtr2, Qtr3, Qtr4 with y-axis 0% to 40%)

IS Pivot Table ⊕

Source: Based on data from Morningstar Direct

Filtering Data with Slicers and Timelines

In our original ETF pivot table (see Exhibit 15-7 on page 490), we saw that you can filter the data in a pivot table by dragging a field to the Filters area. Although that works well in most cases, there are some drawbacks. First, when multiple items are selected, the report filter drop-down displays "(Multiple Items)." That doesn't make it easy to see which items are being used in the filter. Second, the filter only works with one pivot table at a time.

In Excel 2010 slicers were introduced as a way to mitigate these problems and to make filtering less cumbersome. A *slicer* is a visual control that allows you to more easily filter one or more pivot tables. Furthermore, a slicer can be on a different worksheet than the pivot table, making interactive dashboards much easier to create.

Insert
Slicer

To add a slicer, simply click the Insert Slicer button on the Analyze tab, and select one or more fields. A separate slicer will be created for each field selected, and they will automatically be connected to the active pivot table. In this case, select only the Quarters field. The new slicer is shown in Figure 15-10.

FIGURE 15-10
THE QUARTERS FIELD SLICER FILTERING FOR QTR1 AND QTR4

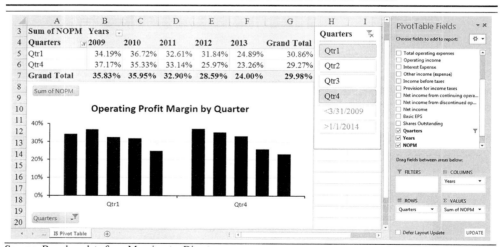

To filter the pivot table by Quarter, simply select one or more items in the slicer. You can select an item by clicking one of them, Ctrl+clicking more than one, or by clicking and dragging to select a range of items. In Figure 15-10 both Qtr1 and Qtr4 are selected.

EXHIBIT 15-16
THE PIVOT TABLE WITH SLICER AND PIVOT CHART

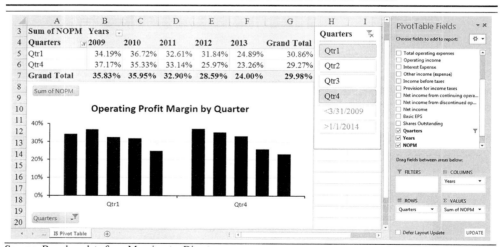

Source: Based on data from Morningstar Direct

To clear the filter from the slicer, simply click the filter icon in the upper-right corner. The slicer can be deleted by selecting it and pressing the Delete button on your keyboard, or right-clicking the slicer and selecting Remove "Quarters" from the menu. Note that deleting a slicer does not clear the filters. You can change some of the slicer's settings by right-clicking and choosing Slicer Settings. For example, you may want to hide the last two items because they have no data. Go into the settings dialog box and check **H**ide items with no data. In addition, you can change the formatting of the slicer on the Options tab that appears when a slicer is selected.

Insert
Timeline

Another filtering tool, the timeline, was made available in Excel 2013. A *timeline* allows you to filter based on dates, and is very useful for dashboard creation. To insert a timeline, click the Insert Timeline button. The result will look similar to that in Figure 15-11.

FIGURE 15-11
A TIMELINE FILTERING FOR 2012 AND 2013 DATA

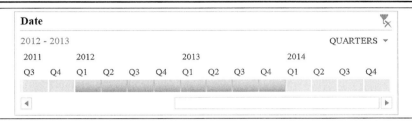

To use the timeline, simply click on the line and drag to select the time periods of interest. You can change the time level of detail by clicking the drop-down list (it says quarters in Figure 15-11) and selecting Years, Quarters, Months, or Days. You can also do some simple formatting in the Options tab that appears when a timeline is selected. To delete a timeline, right-click it and select Remove Timeline from the menu.

Extracting Data from a Pivot Table

It is common to use a pivot table as a source of data for formulas outside of the pivot table. That is, a formula that you create will refer to data in the pivot table. One way to do this is to simply type a cell reference as usual. For example, using the same pivot table as in Exhibit 15-15 select I5 and type: =F5. The result should be the operating profit margin for 2013 (24.89%). Now, rearrange the pivot table by dragging the Years field to the Rows area. Notice that the formula in I5 now returns 0% because cell F5 is no longer in the pivot table and is blank. Drag Years back to the Column Labels area and the value will return.

Directly referencing cells in a pivot table works fine as long as you know that the pivot table will never be changed. But that is an unrealistic expectation in many cases. Therefore, we need a way to consistently refer to data in the pivot table even if it is changed. Excel provides the **GETPIVOTDATA** function for exactly this purpose. It is defined as:

GETPIVOTDATA(*DATA_FIELD*, *PIVOT_TABLE*, *FIELD1*, *ITEM1*, ...)

where ***DATA_FIELD*** is the name of the field (must be in quotes), ***PIVOT_TABLE*** is a cell address anywhere in the pivot table, *FIELD1* and *ITEM1* are a field/item pair. You can specify up to 126 field/item pairs. This function can be used on any worksheet, not just the one that contains the pivot table.

The **GETPIVOTDATA** function has some flaws, for example it will return a #REF! error if the field is removed from the pivot table. Still, it is better than directly referencing data by cell address. The function is also complicated to type, but Excel can helpfully generate it for you. To tell Excel to generate the function, click in the pivot table and go to the Analyze tab. At the far left drop the Options menu and make sure that <u>G</u>enerate GetPivotData is checked.

As an example of using this function, delete the formula in I5 and then type = and click on cell F5. Excel should generate the formula: =GETPIVOTDATA("NOPM",$A$3, "Quarters",1,"Years",2013). Now try rearranging the pivot table by dragging the Years field to the Rows area and notice that the value in I5 doesn't change. That is because the GetPivotData function isn't referencing a particular cell. Instead, it is referencing a particular value. In this case the NOPM for the first quarter of the year 2013.

Another way to get data from a pivot table is to simply copy and paste. If you do this, Excel will only paste the data from the visible cells. The result will not be in a pivot table, unless you copy and paste the entire pivot table.

Summary

In this chapter we have demonstrated how to use Excel tables and pivot tables to sort, filter, and analyze large datasets. Tables allow us to easily manage a dataset by adding and deleting data, sorting it, or filtering it to show only those data that meet certain criteria. Pivot tables are much more powerful, allowing us to summarize and rearrange the data in useful ways. Furthermore, pivot tables enable us to create custom fields that don't exist in the original dataset, create pivot charts that show the data graphically, and display data fields differently (e.g., as a percentage of the grand total, or as a rank).

TABLE 15-1
FUNCTIONS INTRODUCED IN THIS CHAPTER

Purpose	Function	Page
Calculate an average of the data that meet the criteria	**AVERAGEIF**(*RANGE*, *CRITERIA*, *AVERAGE_RANGE*)	485
Return values from a pivot table	**GETPIVOTDATA**(*DATA_FIELD*, *PIVOT_TABLE*, *FIELD1*, *ITEM1*, …)	503

☑ Check Box after Copying highlighted Notes

Problems

1. Using the data in the GOOG Financials.xlsx workbook that was used in the chapter:

   a. Convert the balance sheet into a format that is suitable for a pivot table by transposing the data. Don't forget to enter the word "Date" above the dates.

   b. Build a pivot table from the data and group the dates by months, quarters, and years.

   c. Create a calculated field that shows the current ratio in the pivot table, and format the numbers with two decimal places.

   d. Create a pivot chart that shows the current ratio over time. Has Google's short-term liquidity position deteriorated or improved over this five-year period?

   e. Now, use a Timeline to filter the pivot table so that it only shows 2009 to 2010. Now show only 2012 to 2013. Is there a difference in the trend of the current ratio in the two time periods?

2. Using the same workbook, copy both datasets into one worksheet so that they can be used together in a pivot table.

   a. Create a pivot table that shows the quarter over quarter change in both Revenue and Total Assets.

   b. Create a pivot line chart that shows the data from part a. Does there appear to be a strong correlation between the two data series? Now put Revenue on a secondary y-axis so that the scales are comparable. Does that change your original answer?

   c. Create a calculated field that shows Google's return on equity for each quarter.

   d. Create a pivot line chart that shows the ROE over time. Does it appear that there is any trend in the ROE? If so, is it up or down?

   e. Add a linear trend line to the pivot chart from part d, and show the equation on the chart. Does this change or confirm your previous answer?

3. Using the ETF Data.xlsx workbook from the chapter:

    a. Create a calculated column in the original data that calculates the three-year total return for each ETF and for each Morningstar Category. Be sure to properly account for compounding of returns.

    b. Create a pivot table to show the average three-year total return for each category, and sort the pivot table from the highest return category to the lowest. Which category did the best? The worst?

    c. Create a pivot bar chart that shows the returns of the top 10 best performing fund categories over the last three years.

    d. Create another pivot table from this dataset, and then a calculated field that shows each ETF's three-year return less the category three-year return. Which fund did best compared to its category over the three-year period? Which did the worst?

4. Financial researchers have found various violations of market efficiency that are referred to as "calendar effects." Using the S&P 500 1950 to 2013 Daily.xlsx file from the official website:

    a. Create a pivot table and pivot chart that shows the average percentage change by day of the week for the entire period. Are the average returns different for each day? If so, which are the best and worst days of the week?

    b. Now add the Decade field to the Row area of your pivot table. Are there any decades in which Mondays had a positive average return?

    c. Change your pivot table to show the average daily return by month for the entire period. What is the best month on average? Which is the worst? Does this vary by decade?

    d. What was the best decade in which to invest based on average daily return? What was the sum of the daily returns in each decade (ignore compounding of returns)?

5. Using the S&P 500 Company Data.xlsx workbook from the official website:

    a. Create a calculated column that calculates the total return for the last three years. Name it "Total Return 3 Yr." Make a pivot table that shows the average three-year total return by S&P Sector.

b. Now add the S&P Industry field to the pivot table. Which industry was the best performer in the worst sector over the past three years? Sort the fields in your pivot table so that this sector and industry is at the very top of the table.

c. Create a new pivot table from the data that shows the top 20 S&P Sub-Industries by market capitalization. Also include a count of the number of companies in each sub-industry.

d. Use the GetPivotData function to calculate the average market capitalization of each Sub-Industry in a column that is outside of the pivot table created for part c.

e. Create a new pivot table that shows the average net profit margin by S&P Industry. Which is the most profitable industry? Which is the least profitable industry?

f. Create a pivot table that shows beta and the Total Return 3 Yr for each company. Now, copy and paste the data to another location in the worksheet. Create a regular XY Scatter chart of the data. What relationship do you see between beta and historical three-year returns?

6. In footnote 1. on page 76 some claims were made about the average level of fourth quarter sales for Target Corp. Using the Target Quarterly Sales.xlsx workbook from the official website verify those claims.

a. Create a line chart of Target's quarterly revenue and net income, with net income on a secondary y-axis. Does there appear to be any seasonality in its revenue? Net income?

b. Create a pivot table that has Fiscal Year and Fiscal Quarter in the Rows field, and Revenue in the Values field. Be sure to show subtotals for each year at the bottom of each group.

c. Add Revenue to the Values field a second time. Use Show Values As % of Parent Total to show quarterly sales as a percentage of full year sales. What is the average for the fourth quarter? First quarter?

d. Add Revenue to the Values field a third time. Use Show Values As % Difference From to show the year-over-year percentage change in quarterly sales.

Internet Exercise

1. Go to http://www.microsoft.com/Investor/EarningsAndFinancials/ TrendedHistory/AnnualStatements.aspx and download Microsoft's annual income statements from 1994 to the most recent year available. There is a direct link to the Excel file on that page.

   a. Reformat the worksheet so that it is suitable for a pivot table. This will require changing the year headings to actual dates, deleting any blank rows or columns, and then transposing the data.

   b. Create a pivot table that shows the net profit margin for each year and format it appropriately. This will require you to create a calculated field.

   c. Add a pivot chart that displays the results from part b over time.

   d. Filter the dates so that only the last five years are displayed in the pivot table and pivot chart. This will require a custom date filter using the "is after or equal to" option.

   e. How does Microsoft's net profit margin compare to the average of the company's in the S&P 500 index? (Hint: Use the data file from problem 5 to calculate this answer.)

Directory of User-Defined Functions in Famefncs.xlam

Famefncs.xlam is an Excel 2007 to 2013 add-in that contains user-defined functions that are useful but not available in Excel. The add-in may be obtained as a download from the official Web site for this book (http://www.cengagebrain.com/). Once installed and activated on your computer, Excel will automatically open the add-in every time you start Excel and the functions will be available via the User Defined category in the Insert Function dialog box.

Once downloaded, the add-in is easy to install. Click the File tab and then choose Options. Choose the Add-Ins category and then click the Go button. Use the Add-Ins dialog box to browse to the directory where you saved the add-in file. Click on the file name and then press the OK button. You should now see "Functions for Financial Analysis" appear in the list of add-ins. It is now installed, activated, and ready to use. If you ever wish to disable the add-in, simply remove the check mark in the Add-Ins dialog box.

The following functions are included in the add-in:

FAME_CAPM(*RISKFREERATE, MARKETRETURN, BETA*)
Calculates the expected return of a security or portfolio using the CAPM (Capital Asset Pricing Model).

FAME_CONVEXITY(*SETTLEMENT, MATURITY, FACEVALUE, COUPON, YLD, FREQUENCY*)
Calculates the convexity of a bond on a coupon date. It is important to note that this only works on a coupon date, not between coupon dates. This function was created because, although Excel has functions for duration and modified duration, it does not have one for convexity.

FAME_CORR(*VALUES1*, *VALUES2*, *PROBABILITIES*)

Calculates the correlation coefficient between two variables using the probabilities of occurrence for each value. Excel's **CORREL** function does not handle the probabilities of occurrence.

FAME_COVAR(*VALUES1*, *VALUES2*, *PROBABILITIES*)

Calculates the covariance between two variables using the probabilities of occurrence for each value. Excel's **COVAR** function does not handle the probabilities of occurrence.

FAME_CV(*VALUES*, *PROBABILITIES*)

Calculates the coefficient of variation using the probabilities of occurrence. Excel does not have a similar function. This is a measure of risk per unit of return and is calculated by dividing the standard deviation by the expected value.

FAME_EAR(*PERIODIC_RATE*, *NPERYEAR*)

Calculates the effective annual rate of a periodic rate. For example, if you know that a quarterly rate is 2%, this function will tell you that it is 8.24% annualized. This does the same thing as Excel's **EFFECT** function.

FAME_EXPVALUE(*VALUES*, *PROBABILITIES*)

Calculates the expected value of a random variable using the probabilities of occurrence for each potential value.

FAME_GEOMEAN(*DOLLARVALUES*)

Calculates the geometric mean rate of growth from a range of dollar values. Note that Excel's **GEOMEAN** function does not (necessarily) calculate the geometric mean rate of growth (unless you feed in a range of growth rates). Instead it will calculate the geometric mean in the same units as the original data. This function should only be used for the data in Chapter 1.

FAME_GGMCOSTEQUITY(*DIV1*, *VALUE*, *GROWTHRATE*)

Calculates the cost of equity, or required return, of a stock using the constant-growth dividend discount model (also known as the Gordon Growth Model).

FAME_GGMVALUE(*DIV1*, *REQRET*, *GROWTHRATE*)

Calculates the intrinsic value of a stock using the constant-growth dividend discount model (also known as the Gordon Growth Model).

FAME_HMODELVALUE(*DIV1*, *REQRATE*, *GROWTHRATE1*, *GROWTHRATE2*, *G1PERIODS*, *TRANSPERIODS*)

Calculates the intrinsic value of a stock using the H-model. Note that *G1PERIODS* is the length of the first period of growth, and *TRANSPERIODS* is the length of the transition period between fast growth and constant-growth.

FAME_MACRS(*Cost, MacrsClass, Year, Table*)

Calculates the MACRS depreciation for an asset with a MACRS class of 3, 5, 7, 10, 15, or 20 years. This function returns the depreciation expense for a selected *Year*. *Table* is an optional argument (True or False) that specifies whether the function uses a table lookup or an exact calculation. It will return a #VALUE! error if either *MacrsClass* or *Year* are incorrect.

FAME_Mirr(*CashFlows, ReinvestRate*)

Calculates the Modified Internal Rate of Return for a series of cash flows. This is different than Excel's built-in function in the way it handles negative cash flows after period 0. This function calculates the total future value of all cash flows after period 0 (using the specified reinvestment rate). Excel's **Mirr** function first calculates the present value of all negative cash flows and then calculates the future value of all positive cash flows. Normally, both functions will return the same answer. However, when there are negative cash flows after period 0, there will be a difference (sometimes significant).

FAME_Payback(*CashFlows, Rate*)

Calculates the Payback Period of a series of cash flows, assuming that the first cash flow (period 0) is negative. *Rate* is an optional argument. If you include a discount rate, the function will calculate the discounted payback period. For the regular Payback Period, either don't supply a rate or make it equal to 0%.

FAME_PortRet(*Values, Weights*)

Calculates the expected return for a portfolio of securities given the expected returns of each security and their weight in the portfolio.

FAME_PortVar1(*VarCovMat, Weights*)

Calculates the variance of a portfolio of securities given a variance/covariance matrix and the weights of the individual securities. Note that you must supply a complete variance/covariance matrix, not just the upper or lower diagonal.

FAME_PortVar2(*CorrMat, StdDevs, Weights*)

Calculates the variance of a portfolio of securities given a correlation matrix, the standard deviations, and weights of the individual securities. Note that you must supply a complete variance/covariance matrix, not just the upper or lower diagonal.

FAME_PVGA(*Pmt, Nper, GrowthRate, DiscRate, BegEnd*)

Calculates the present value of a graduated (growing) annuity. Note that *BegEnd* is an optional argument that tells the function whether the first cash flow is at the end of the period (0) or the beginning (1) of the period. End of period (0) is the default if no *BegEnd* argument is supplied.

FAME_STDDEV(*VALUES*, *PROBABILITIES*)

Calculates the standard deviation of a random variable given the probabilities of each potential outcome (it is a population standard deviation). Note that this function is different from Excel's built-in **STDEV.P** function in that it allows the probabilities to differ. Excel's function assumes that all probabilities are equal.

FAME_THREESTAGEVALUE(*DIV1*, *REQRATE*, *GROWTHRATE1*, *GROWTHRATE2*, *G1PERIODS*, *TRANSPERIODS*)

Calculates the intrinsic value of a stock using the three-stage dividend discount model. Note that *G1PERIODS* is the length of the first period of growth, and *TRANSPERIODS* is the length of the transition period between fast growth and constant-growth.

FAME_THREESTEPVALUE(*DIV1*, *REQRATE*, *GROWTHRATE1*, *GROWTHRATE2*, *GROWTHRATE3*, *G1PERIODS*, *TRANSPERIODS*)

Calculates the intrinsic value of a stock using the three-step dividend discount model (three constant-growth periods). Note that *G1PERIODS* is the length of the first period of growth, and *TRANSPERIODS* is the length of the transition period between fast growth and constant-growth.

FAME_TWOSTAGEVALUE(*DIV1*, *REQRATE*, *GROWTHRATE1*, *GROWTHRATE2*, *G1PERIODS*)

Calculates the intrinsic value of a stock using the two-stage dividend discount model. Note that *G1PERIODS* is the length of the first period of growth.

FAME_VAR(*VALUES*, *PROBABILITIES*)

Calculates the variance of a random variable given the probabilities of each potential outcome. Note that this function is different from Excel's built-in **VAR** and **VARP** functions in that it allows the probabilities to differ. Excel's functions assume that all probabilities are equal.

Index